Conference of the North American Chapter of the Association for Computational Linguistics: Human Language Technologies (NAACL HLT 2021)

Industry Papers

Online
6 – 11 June 2021

ISBN: 978-1-7138-3010-8

Printed from e-media with permission by:

Curran Associates, Inc.
57 Morehouse Lane
Red Hook, NY 12571

proceedings.com

Some format issues inherent in the e-media version may also appear in this print version.

Association for Computational Linguistics
209 N. Eighth Street
Stroudsburg, Pennsylvania 18360

Phone: 1-570-476-8006
Fax: 1-570-476-0860

acl@aclweb.org

Additional copies of this publication are available from:

Curran Associates, Inc.
57 Morehouse Lane
Red Hook, NY 12571 USA
Phone: 845-758-0400
Fax: 845-758-2633
Email: curran@proceedings.com
Web: www.proceedings.com

NAACL-HLT 2021

The 2021 Conference of the North American Chapter of the Association for Computational Linguistics: Human Language Technologies

Industry Papers

June 6 - 11, 2021

Message from the Industry Track Chairs

Language technologies and their applications are an integral and critical part of our daily lives. The development of many of these technologies trace their roots to academic and industrial research laboratories where researchers invented a plethora of algorithms, benchmarked them against shared datasets and perfected the performance of these algorithms to provide plausible solutions to real-world applications. While a controlled laboratory setting is vital for a deeper scientific understanding of the language problem and the impact of algorithmic design choices on the performance of a technology, transitioning the technology to real-world industrial strength applications raises a different, yet challenging, set of technical issues.

The Industry Track at NAACL HLT 2021 represents innovations and implementations in speech and natural language processing technologies and systems that are relevant to industrial applications. The primary focus of this track is on papers that advance the understanding of, and demonstrate the effective handling of, practical issues related to the deployment of language processing technologies in non-trivial real-world systems. By "non-trivial real-world system" we mean an application that is deployed for real-world use, i.e. outside controlled environments such as a laboratories, classrooms or experimental crowd-sourced setups, and that uses natural language processing (including speech technology), even if not state of the art in terms of research. There is no requirement that the system be made by a for-profit company, but the users of the system must be outside of the NLP research community.

We received 132 papers, and accepted 39, or 29.5%. This year, nearly half the papers in the Industry Track are about dialog processing, reflecting the importance of interactive systems in industrial applications today. Additional topics include semantics, machine translation, information retrieval, and sentiment analysis.

We hope that these papers will provide an interesting complement to the Main Track papers.

Young-bum Kim, Yunyao Li, Owen Rambow

Organizing Committee

Young-bum Kim, Amazon, Inc. (youngbum@amazon.com)
Yunyao Li, IBM, Inc. (yunyaoli@us.ibm.com)
Owen Rambow, Stony Brook University (owen.rambow@stonybrook.edu)

Reviewers

We thank our reviewers, without whom the Industry Track would not be possible. This list also includes reviewers for the secondary ethics review.

Jade Abbott, Mohamed Abdelhady, George Acquaah-Mensah, Gilles Adda, Shazia Afzal, Sachin Agarwal, Hua Ai, Alan Akbik, Mohamed AlTantawy, Shankar Ananthakrishnan, Ankit Arun, Venkatesh Baglodi, Srinivas Bangalore, Nikoletta Basiou, Daniel Bauer, Frederic Bechet, Tilman Becker, Emily M. Bender, Luciana Benotti, Dan Bikel, Claudia Borg, Trung Bui, Greg Burnham, Donna Byron, Aoife Cahill, Vitor Carvalho, Thiago Castro Ferreira, Sourish Chaudhuri, Ciprian Chelba, John Chen, Minhua Chen, Laura Chiticariu, Justin Chiu, Eunah Cho, Jaesik Choi, Jaegul Choo, Jennifer Chu-Carroll, Hyung Won Chung, Rylan Conway, Deborah Dahl, Marina Danilevsky, Budhaditya Deb, Lingjia Deng, Giuseppe Di Fabbrizio, Christine Doran, Dejing Dou, Pablo Duboue, Matthew Dunn, David Elson, Ramy Eskander, Xing Fan, Song Feng, Oliver Ferschke, Michael Flor, Karën Fort, Annemarie Friedrich, Ankur Gandhe, Rashmi Gangadharaiah, Judith Gaspers, Anna Lisa Gentile, Ryan Georgi, Debanjan Ghosh, Honglei Guo, Yufan Guo, Daniel Hardt, Hua He, Enrique Henestroza Anguiano, Sanjika Hewavitharana, Christopher Hidey, Derrick Higgins, Lynette Hirschman, Yufang Hou, Samar Husain, Javid Huseynov, Hyesung Ji, Hongxia Jin, Mahesh Joshi, Mohammad Kachuee, Jun Seok Kang, Yoav Katz, Saurabh Khanwalkar, Sun Kim, Dongchan Kim, Yoon Kim, Joo-Kyung Kim, Yu-Seop Kim, Jin-Dong Kim, Jared Kramer, Sanjeev Kumar, Anjishnu Kumar, Rohit Kumar, Gakuto Kurata, Sarasi Lalithsena, Anastassia Lastname, Young-Suk Lee, Han Li, Constantine Lignos, Heuiseok Lim, Chin-Yew Lin, Xiaohu Liu, Anastassia Loukina, Alex Marin, Yuval Marton, Yuji Matsumoto, David McDonald, Angeliki Metallinou, Lisa Michaud, Margot Mieskes, Nyalleng Moorosi, Michelle Morales, Isabelle Moulinier, Matthew Mulholland, Udhyakumar Nallasamy, Jinseok Nam, Nobal B. Niraula, Elnaz Nouri, Mari Olsen, Cecile Paris, Youngja Park, Taiwoo Park, Dookun Park, Patrick Paroubek, Ioannis Partalas, Siddharth Patwardhan, Karl Pichotta, Vassilis Plachouras, Alexandros Potamianos, Saloni Potdar, Rashmi Prasad, Long Qin, Elio Querze, Sravana Reddy, Ehud Reiter, Nicholas Ruiz, Alicia Sagae, Avneesh Saluja, Mark Sammons, Ruhi Sarikaya, Hassan Sawaf, Frank Schilder, Ethan Selfridge, Igor Shalyminov, Michal Shmueli-Scheuer, Lei Shu, Sunayana Sitaram, AJ Stent, Svetlana Stoyanchev, Chengwei Su, Tara Taghavi, Joel Tetreault, Sudarshan R. Thitte, Isabel Trancoso, Keith Trnka, Ling Tsou, Morgan Ulinski, Ngoc Phuoc An Vo, Yi-Chia Wang, Lucy Lu Wang, Guoyin Wang, Kyle Williams, Puyang Xu, Yeongyook Yang, Kai Yu, Seunghak Yu, Liyuan Zhang, Yefeng Zheng

Table of Contents

This page intentionally left blank.

Industry Track Program

Mon 07 Jun 2021 (all times PDT, UTC-7)

09:00–10:20 IND1-Oral: Dialogue (Industry Track)

When does text prediction benefit from additional context? An exploration of contextual signals for chat and email messages
Stojan Trajanovski, Chad Atalla, Kunho Kim, Vipul Agarwal, Milad Shokouhi and Chris Quirk

Identifying and Resolving Annotation Changes for Natural Language Understanding
Jose Garrido Ramas, Giorgio Pessot, Abdalghani Abujabal and Martin Rajman

Optimizing NLU Reranking Using Entity Resolution Signals in Multi-domain Dialog Systems
Tong Wang, Jiangning Chen, Mohsen Malmir, Shuyan Dong, Xin He, Han Wang, Chengwei Su, Yue Liu and Yang Liu

Entity Resolution in Open-domain Conversations
Mingyue Shang, Tong Wang, Mihail Eric, Jiangning Chen, Jiyang Wang, Matthew Welch, Tiantong Deng, Akshay Grewal, Han Wang, Yue Liu, Yang Liu and Dilek Hakkani-Tur

Pretrain-Finetune Based Training of Task-Oriented Dialogue Systems in a Real-World Setting
Manisha Srivastava, Yichao Lu, Riley Peschon and Chenyang Li

Contextual Domain Classification with Temporal Representations
Tzu-Hsiang Lin, Yipeng Shi, Chentao Ye, Yang Fan, Weitong Ruan, Emre Barut, Wael Hamza and Chengwei Su

10:20–11:40 IND2-Oral: Spoken Dialogue (Industry Track)

Bootstrapping a Music Voice Assistant with Weak Supervision
Sergio Oramas, Massimo Quadrana and Fabien Gouyon

Continuous Model Improvement for Language Understanding with Machine Translation
Abdalghani Abujabal, Claudio Delli Bovi, Sungho Ryu, Turan Gojayev, Fabian Triefenbach and Yannick Versley

A HYBRID APPROACH TO SCALABLE AND ROBUST SPOKEN LANGUAGE UNDERSTANDING IN ENTERPRISE VIRTUAL AGENTS
Ryan Price, Mahnoosh Mehrabani, Narendra Gupta, Yeon-Jun Kim, Shahab Jalalvand, Minhua Chen, Yanjie Zhao and Srinivas Bangalore

Proteno: Text Normalization with Limited Data for Fast Deployment in Text to Speech Systems
Shubhi Tyagi, Antonio Bonafonte, Jaime Lorenzo-Trueba and Javier Latorre

Mon 07 Jun 2021 (continued; all times PDT, UTC-7))

18:20–19:40 IND3-Oral: Machine Translation (Industry Track)

Addressing the Vulnerability of NMT in Input Perturbations
Weiwen Xu, AiTi Aw, Yang Ding, Kui Wu and Shafiq Joty

Cross-lingual Supervision Improves Unsupervised Neural Machine Translation
Mingxuan Wang, Hongxiao Bai, Lei Li and Hai Zhao

Should we find another model?: Improving Neural Machine Translation Performance with ONE-Piece Tokenization Method without Model Modification
chanjun park, Sugyeong Eo, Hyeonseok Moon and Heuiseok Lim

Autocorrect in the Process of Translation — Multi-task Learning Improves Dialogue Machine Translation
Tao Wang, Chengqi Zhao, Mingxuan Wang, Lei Li and Deyi Xiong

LightSeq: A High Performance Inference Library for Transformers
Xiaohui Wang, Ying Xiong, Yang Wei, Mingxuan Wang and Lei Li

Practical Transformer-based Multilingual Text Classification
Cindy Wang and Michele Banko

19:40–21:00 IND4-Oral: Sentiment Analysis and Information Retrieval (Industry Track)

An Emotional Comfort Framework for Improving User Satisfaction in E-Commerce Customer Service Chatbots
Shuangyong Song, Chao Wang, Haiqing Chen and Huan Chen

Language Scaling for Universal Suggested Replies Model
Qianlan Ying, Payal Bajaj, Budhaditya Deb, Yu Yang, Wei Wang, Bojia Lin, Milad Shokouhi, Xia Song, Yang Yang and Daxin Jiang

Graph-based Multilingual Product Retrieval in E-Commerce Search
Hanqing Lu, Youna Hu, Tong Zhao, Tony Wu, Yiwei Song and Bing Yin

Query2Prod2Vec: Grounded Word Embeddings for eCommerce
Federico Bianchi, Jacopo Tagliabue and Bingqing Yu

Mon 07 Jun 2021 (continued; all times PDT, UTC-7))

An Architecture for Accelerated Large-Scale Inference of Transformer-Based Language Models
Amir Ganiev, Colton Chapin, Anderson De Andrade and Chen Liu

When and Why a Model Fails? A Human-in-the-loop Error Detection Framework for Sentiment Analysis
Zhe Liu, Yufan Guo and Jalal Mahmud

Tue 08 Jun 2021 (all times PDT, UTC-7)

09:00–10:20 IND5-Oral: Semantics (Industry Track)

Technical Question Answering across Tasks and Domains
Wenhao Yu, Lingfei Wu, Yu Deng, Qingkai Zeng, Ruchi Mahindru, Sinem Guven and Meng Jiang

Cost-effective Deployment of BERT Models in Serverless Environment
Marek Suppa, Katarína Benešová and Andrej Švec

Noise Robust Named Entity Understanding for Voice Assistants
Deepak Muralidharan, Joel Ruben Antony Moniz, Sida Gao, Xiao Yang, Justine Kao, Stephen Pulman, Atish Kothari, Ray Shen, Yinying Pan, Vivek Kaul, Mubarak Seyed Ibrahim, Gang Xiang, Nan Dun, Yidan Zhou, Andy O, Yuan Zhang, Pooja Chitkara, Xuan Wang, Alkesh Patel, Kushal Tayal, Roger Zheng, Peter Grasch, Jason D Williams and Lin Li

Goodwill Hunting: Analyzing and Repurposing Off-the-Shelf Named Entity Linking Systems
Karan Goel, Laurel Orr, Nazneen Fatema Rajani, Jesse Vig and Christopher Ré

Intent Features for Rich Natural Language Understanding
Brian Lester, Sagnik Ray Choudhury, Rashmi Prasad and Srinivas Bangalore

Development of an Enterprise-Grade Contract Understanding System
Arvind Agarwal, Laura Chiticariu, Poornima Chozhiyath Raman, Marina Danilevsky, Diman Ghazi, Ankush Gupta, Shanmukha Guttula, Yannis Katsis, Rajasekar Krishnamurthy, Yunyao Li, Shubham Mudgal, Vitobha Munigala, Nicholas Phan, Dhaval Sonawane, Sneha Srinivasan, Sudarshan R. Thitte, Mitesh Vasa, Ramiya Venkatachalam, Vinitha Yaski and Huaiyu Zhu

Wed 09 Jun 2021 (all times PDT, UTC-7)

18:20–19:40 IND6-Oral: Natural Language Generation and Dialogue (Industry Track)

Discovering Better Model Architectures for Medical Query Understanding
Wei Zhu, Yuan Ni, Xiaoling Wang and Guotong Xie

OodGAN: Generative Adversarial Network for Out-of-Domain Data Generation
Petr Marek, Vishal Ishwar Naik, Anuj Goyal and Vincent Auvray

Coherent and Concise Radiology Report Generation via Context Specific Image Representations and Orthogonal Sentence States
Litton J Kurisinkel, Ai Ti Aw and Nancy F Chen

An Empirical Study of Generating Texts for Search Engine Advertising
Hidetaka Kamigaito, Peinan Zhang, Hiroya Takamura and Manabu Okumura

Ad Headline Generation using Self-Critical Masked Language Model
Yashal Shakti Kanungo, Sumit Negi and Aruna Rajan

19:40–21:00 IND7-Oral: Machine Learning (Industry Track)

LATEX-Numeric: Language Agnostic Text Attribute Extraction for Numeric Attributes
Kartik Mehta, Ioana Oprea and Nikhil Rasiwasia

Training Language Models under Resource Constraints for Adversarial Advertisement Detection
Eshwar Shamanna Girishekar, Shiv Surya, Nishant Nikhil, Dyut Kumar Sil, Sumit Negi and Aruna Rajan

Combining Weakly Supervised ML Techniques for Low-Resource NLU
Victor Soto and Konstantine Arkoudas

Label-Guided Learning for Item Categorization in e-Commerce
Lei Chen and Hirokazu Miyake

Benchmarking Commercial Intent Detection Services with Practice-Driven Evaluations
Haode Qi, Lin Pan, Atin Sood, Abhishek Shah, Ladislav Kunc, Mo Yu and Saloni Potdar

Wed 09 Jun 2021 (continued; all times PDT, UTC-7))

When does text prediction benefit from additional context? An exploration of contextual signals for chat and email messages

Stojan Trajanovski
Microsoft

Chad Atalla
Microsoft

Kunho Kim
Microsoft

Vipul Agarwal
Microsoft

Milad Shokouhi
Microsoft

Chris Quirk
Microsoft

{sttrajan,chatalla,kuki,vipulag,milads,chrisq}@microsoft.com

Abstract

Email and chat communication tools are increasingly important for completing daily tasks. Accurate real-time phrase completion can save time and bolster productivity. Modern text prediction algorithms are based on large language models which typically rely on the prior words in a message to predict a completion. We examine how additional contextual signals (from previous messages, time, and subject) affect the performance of a commercial text prediction model. We compare contextual text prediction in chat and email messages from two of the largest commercial platforms Microsoft Teams and Outlook, finding that contextual signals contribute to performance differently between these scenarios. On emails, time context is most beneficial with small relative gains of 2% over baseline. Whereas, in chat scenarios, using a tailored set of previous messages as context yields relative improvements over the baseline between 9.3% and 18.6% across various critical service-oriented text prediction metrics.

1 Introduction

Email and chat communication tools are increasingly important for completing daily professional and personal tasks. Given the recent pandemic and shift to remote work, this usage has surged. The number of daily active users in Microsoft Teams, the largest business communication and chat platform, has increased from 20 million (2019, pre-pandemic) to more than 115 million in October (2020). On the other hand, email continues to be the crucial driver for formal communication showing ever increasing usage. Providing real-time suggestions for word or phrase auto-completions is known as text prediction. The efficiency of these communications is enhanced by suggesting highly accurate text predictions with low latency. Text prediction services have been deployed across popular communication tools and platforms such as (Microsoft Text Predictions, 2020) or GMail Smart Compose (Chen et al., 2019).

Modern text prediction algorithms are based on large language models and generally rely on the prefix of a message (characters typed until cursor position) to create predictions. We study to what extent *additional contextual signals* improve text predictions in chat and email messages in two of the largest commercial communication platforms: Microsoft Teams and Outlook. Our contributions are summarized as:

- We demonstrate that prior-message context provides the greatest lift in the Teams (chat) scenario. A 5 minute window of prior messages from both senders works the best, with relative gains from 9.3% up to 18.6% across key metrics (total match and estimated characters accepted). This 5 minute window of prior messages from both senders outperforms the corresponding 2 and 10 minute scenarios.
- We find that context about message composition time provides the largest gains for the Outlook (email) scenario, while adding the subject as context only marginally helps. These relative gains are moderate (2-3% across various metrics).
- We conclude that the different characteristics of chat and email messages impede domain transfer. The best contextual text prediction models are custom trained for each scenario, using the most impactful subset of contextual signals.

The remainder of the paper is organized as follows. We give an overview of state-of-the-art related research in Section 2. More details on the signals used for contextualization are provided in Section 3. Section 4 provides information on the language model, performance metrics, and statistical details

Proceedings of NAACL HLT 2021: IndustryTrack Papers, pages 1–9
June 6–11, 2021. ©2021 Association for Computational Linguistics

about the data. Experiment results and comparisons are presented in Section 5. We conclude in Section 6. Ethical considerations on the data and processes are discussed in Section 7.

2 Related work

Text prediction services have been applied for various applications, including text editor (Darragh et al., 1990), query autocompletion on search engine (Bast and Weber, 2006; Bar-Yossef and Kraus, 2011), mobile virtual keyboard (Hard et al., 2018). Recently prediction service is applied on communication tools for composing email and chat messages to improve user writing productivity (Kannan et al., 2016; Deb et al., 2019; Chen et al., 2019; Microsoft Text Predictions, 2020).

To predict correct text continuation, such applications leverage efficient lookups with pre-generated candidates, using most popular candidates (MPC) (Bar-Yossef and Kraus, 2011), or using large-scale language models (Bengio et al., 2003). State-of-the-art language models (Jozefowicz et al., 2016; Mnih and Hinton, 2009; Melis et al., 2018) rely on the most recent deep learning architectures, including large LSTMs (Hochreiter and Schmidhuber, 1997) or transformers (Vaswani et al., 2017), while prior approaches involve n-gram modeling (Kneser and Ney, 1995; James, 2000; Bickel et al., 2005).

In this work, we focus on the application of text prediction on production-level online communication tools, to help users compose emails (Chen et al., 2019; Microsoft Text Predictions, 2020), and in addition chat messages. In particular, we focus on examining useful contextual signals to give more accurate predicted text, using time, subject, and prior messages. Various contextualization techniques (e.g., hierarchical RNNs) have been applied to add useful additional signals such as preceding web interaction, linking pages, similar search queries or visitor interests of a page (White et al., 2009); previous sequence of utterances (Park et al., 2018; Zhang et al., 2018; Yoo et al., 2020) or related text snippets (Ke et al., 2018).

3 Contextualization concepts

We examine several signals accompanying the main message text: **message compose time**, **subject**, and **previous messages**. We combine these signals with the message body into a single "contextualized" string, using *special tokens* to separate signals, as shown in Figure 1a. This approach is inspired by (Chen et al., 2019), as they showed that concatenating contextual signals into a single input string gave a comparable result to more complex methods encoding these signals separately[1]. The remainder of this section explains details about each contextual signal we use.

Time Composition time is a contextual signal which can provide added value for text prediction, enabling suggestions with relevant date-time words, like "weekend", "tonight". We encode local date and time, as shown in Figure 1a, and use `<BOT>` and `<EOT>` to separate from other signals.

Subject Message subjects often contain the purpose or summarized information of a message. In the email scenario, we use *subject* as context. In the chat scenario, subject is not available, so we use the *chat window name* as a proxy for subject (can be auto-generated or manually set by users). In both cases, the subject context is wrapped with `<BOU>` and `<EOU>` special tokens.

Previous email messages Previous messages can provide valuable background information which influences the text of the current message being composed. In the email case, we create pairs of messages and replies. These pairs are concatenated with a `<COT>` special token to create a single contextual string. In cases where the email was the first in a thread, the prior email context is left blank.

Previous chat messages Prior message contextualization for chat scenario is much more complex. Chat conversations typically consist of many small messages sent in quick succession. Given the email and chat message length statistics in Section 4, we expect chat messages to be about $10\times$ smaller than emails. So, we limit chat histories to 20 messages, which is roughly equivalent to an email-reply pair in length. Among these prior messages, any number and any order could be from the current sender, or the other participant.

We segment chat histories by *message blocks* and *time windows*. A series of uninterrupted messages sent by one sender is considered as a single *message block*. Messages sent within the past N minutes are within a *time window*, which enforces recency as a proxy for relevance.

We define three prior message context aggregation modes in the chat scenario (visualized in

[1]They also use subject and previous email as contexts.

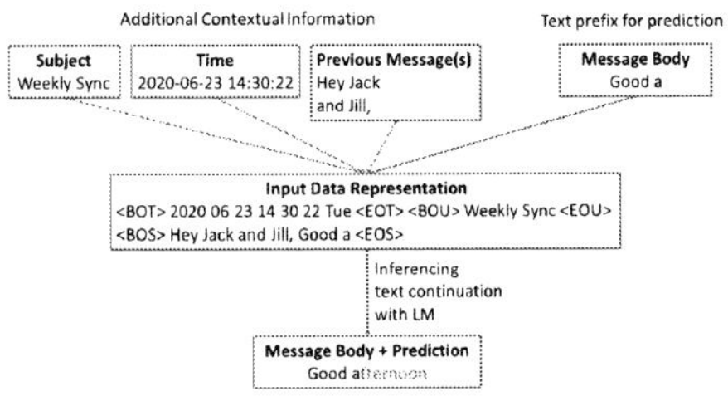

(a) Context extraction and encoding.

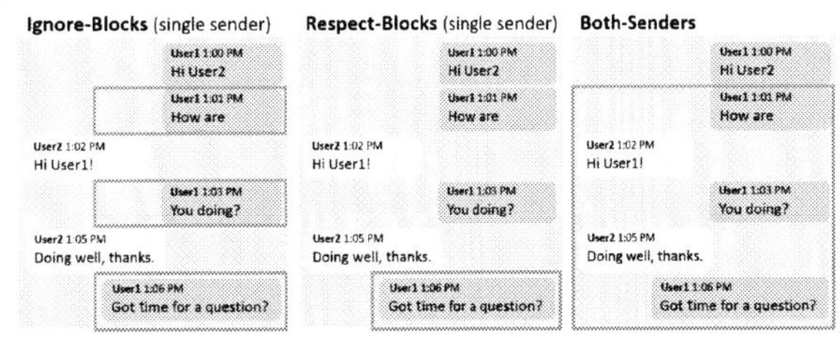

(b) Aggregating a 5 min prior chat window in various context modes.

Figure 1: Examples of (a) context encoding pipeline and (b) chat prior message aggregation modes.

Figure 1b), mimicking prior email context:

(i) *Ignore-Blocks*: chat messages from the *current sender*, in the past N minutes, ignoring any message block boundaries.

(ii) *Respect-Blocks*: chat messages from the *current sender*, in the past N minutes, confined to the *most recent message block.*

(iii) *Both-Senders*: chat messages from *both senders*, in the past N minutes. When the sender turn changes, strings are separated by a space or a special token <COT>.

For each mode, we consider time windows of $N = \{2, 5, 10\}$ minutes.

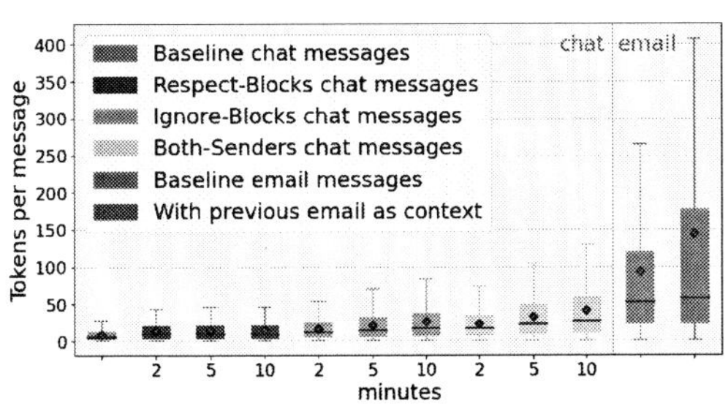

Figure 2: Box-plot statistics: number of tokens in a context-aggregated message from Microsoft Teams and Outlook. Green diamond markers represent the mean, bold red lines are the medians, margins of the boxes are lower and upper quartiles while whiskers end-points are the minimums and maximums.

4 Data and Language Model

4.1 Data

Our model training depends on real messages from two of the largest commercial communication platforms Microsoft Teams and Outlook; this involves a multi-pronged system for ensuring our customers' privacy. We work within rigorous privacy rules, using tools with privacy features built in, and preprocessing all data through multiple privacy precautions before it is digested by our models. User data from our communication platforms is never visible to humans for analysis, in any raw or preprocessed format. We run this data through our pipelines and are only able to view resulting text prediction metrics. Section 7 contains more details about these privacy precautions.

Chat messages We sample Teams data from more than 3.8 billion curated one-on-one chat messages that span 6 months (say May - October 2020), followed by privacy precautions and noise filters. The data is sorted by time and split into train, validation, and test sets in non-overlapping time periods. We use over 90% of the data for training, holding out 75,000 samples for validation and 25,000 samples for testing. Each message is recorded in its respective dataset along with all associated context. In a statistical analysis of the chat message lengths (see Figure 2, blue box) we find that mean tokens number is 9.15 (length in characters is 48), while median tokens number is 6 (with character length 31). Therefore, when iterating character-by-character through the messages, as done in inference for text predictions, the test set has over 1M evaluation points (resampled periodically, see Section 7.1).

Email messages In email experiments, we use approximately 150 million Outlook commercial emails from a period of 6 months, which go through the same privacy precautions mentioned above and in Section 7. The emails are then sorted, filtered for noise, and cut into train, validation, and test sets by their date ranges. A statistical analysis of email lengths (see Figure 2, green box) reveals that mean number of tokens is 94 (with length in characters being 561), while the median is 53 tokens (and 316 characters). This is roughly 10× larger than chat messages. When splitting train, test, and validation sets, over 90% of the data is allocated to the training set. The test set is subsampled to 3,000 emails (unlike the 25,000 messages for the chat test set) since this roughly leads to final contextualized datasets of the same size. Each resulting test set contains just over 1 million evaluation points, as in the chat setting.

Additionally, we use the Avocado dataset as a publicly available dataset, which consists of emails from 279 accounts of a defunct IT company referred to as "Avocado" see details in (Oard et al., 2015), for debugging and validation, allowing us to directly view data and outputs. This dataset is split into validation and test sets, each with roughly 3,000 emails for evaluation.

4.2 Prior-message aggregation statistics

When applying the chat-specific prior-message grouping modes defined in Section 3, the number of prior messages fetched as context varies. Table 1 presents details on how many messages the different aggregation modes end up grouping. Both single-sender modes introduce smaller volumes of context than the *Both-Senders* mode. For example, the amount of prior messages grouped in the 5 minutes *Ignore-Blocks* mode is similar to the 2 minutes *Both-Senders* mode; where 2.5 chat messages are combined on average, and 56-59% of chat messages have at least one message as context. For emails, only around 50% have prior email context.

The number of tokens per contextualized message (including current and aggregated prior messages) varies between the email scenario and various aggregation modes in the chat scenario. Figure 2 provides statistics on these aggregated message lengths. In the chat case, the *Both-Senders* mode with a 10 minute time window results in the largest aggregate length, with a median around 27 tokens, and mean above 40 tokens. The *Respect-Blocks* mode does not show significant length increases as the time window grows, due to the message block boundary limits. For emails, the median total tokens remains similar regardless of including the previous message. This is because half of emails are not part of an email-reply pair.

4.3 Language model

Once the message data is preprocessed and jointly encoded with contextual signals, it is passed as an input to the Language Model. The production system uses a two-layer (550, 550) LSTM (with 6000 sampled softmax size loss) which is optimized to maximize the Estimated Characters Accepted metric (described in Section 5.1). All contextualization experiments use the production model architecture as the baseline. Both baseline and contextual models are trained on 16 GPUs.

Configuration	**% msgs with context**	**mean msgs as context**
2 min Respect-Blocks	30.76%	1.44
5 min Respect-Blocks	34.19%	1.54
10 min Respect-Blocks	35.54%	1.59
2 min Ignore-Blocks	43.31%	1.76
5 min Ignore-Blocks	55.94%	2.51
10 min Ignore-Blocks	63.24%	3.23
2 min Both-Senders	58.90%	2.51
5 min Both-Senders	70.20%	3.99
10 min Both-Senders	76.10%	5.40

Table 1: Microsoft Teams chat message statistics - amount of aggregated context per message.

We have conducted experiments with more complex language models (e.g., transformers, deeper LSTMs), but we use the production model in this paper as (i) its simpler architecture enables large-scale low-latency text prediction serving and (ii) the goal of this work is to explore how different contextual signals add to the baseline performance.

5 Experiments and results

We conduct experiments for both email and chat messages with individual contextual signals (time, subject, prior messages) and combinations of those.

5.1 Performance Metrics

In all experiments, we level the **S**uggestion **R**ate (SR) (number of suggestions per message), then evaluate model variant performance against the following text prediction metrics:

- **MR**: **M**atch **R**ate is the ratio of the number of matched suggestions and the total number of generated suggestions.
- **ChM / sugg**: **Ch**aracters **M**atched per **sugg**estion is the average number of matched characters per given suggestion
- **Est. ChS / sugg**: **Est**imated **Ch**aracters **S**aved per **sugg**estion is the estimated number of characters that the user is saved from typing, per suggestion. (Based on observed acceptance probabilities from real users.)

Configuration / context mode	MR	ChM / sugg	Est. ChS / sugg	TM	ChM	Est. ChA
Chat name	+5.38%↑	+6.05%↑	+7.83%↑	+5.22%↑	+5.99%↑	+7.86%↑
Time	-3.49%↓	-4.28%↓	-6.33%↓	-3.48%↓	-4.25%↓	-6.36%↓
Time+Chat name	-13.98%↓	-14.72%↓	-16.57%↓	-13.96%↓	-14.67%↓	-16.57%↓
2 min Respect-Blocks	+5.91%↑	+7.65%↑	+12.65%↑	+5.95%↑	+7.72%↑	+12.62%↑
2 min Ignore-Blocks	+5.91%↑	+7.68%↑	+12.95%↑	+5.78%↑	+7.62%↑	+12.84%↑
2 min Both-Senders	+5.91%↑	+8.77%↑	+16.87%↑	+6.01%↑	+8.77%↑	+17.01%↑
5 min Respect-Blocks	+5.65%↑	+7.79%↑	+13.86%↑	+5.56%↑	+7.74%↑	+13.72%↑
5 min Ignore-Blocks	+6.72%↑	+9.01%↑	+15.66%↑	+6.59%↑	+8.96%↑	+15.48%↑
5 min Both-Senders	**+9.41%↑**	**+11.76%↑**	**+18.67%↑**	**+9.30%↑**	**+11.72%↑**	**+18.67%↑**
10 min Respect-Blocks	+5.65%↑	+7.79%↑	+13.55%↑	+5.63%↑	+7.67%↑	+13.53%↑
10 min Ignore-Blocks	+6.99%↑	+9.32%↑	+15.66%↑	+6.92%↑	+9.24%↑	+15.56%↑
10 min Both-Senders	+8.06%↑	+10.57%↑	+17.77%↑	+7.86%↑	+10.51%↑	+17.55%↑
Time+ 5 min Respect-Blocks	+3.76%↑	+5.51%↑	+10.24%↑	+3.84%↑	+5.51%↑	+10.22%↑
Chat name+5 min Respect-Blocks	+5.11%↑	+6.36%↑	+9.34%↑	+5.13%↑	+6.35%↑	+9.40%↑
Time+Chat name+5 min Respect-Blocks	+5.38%↑	+7.79%↑	+14.16%↑	+5.43%↑	+7.82%↑	+14.26%↑
Time+Chat name+5 min Ignore-Blocks	+5.11%↑	+6.97%↑	+12.05%↑	+5.15%↑	+6.99%↑	+12.00%↑
Time+Chat name+5 min Both-Senders	+8.87%↑	+11.53%↑	+18.37%↑	+8.91%↑	+11.52%↑	+18.36%↑

Table 2: Microsoft Teams chat messages experiment results with various contextualization modes. First column is the experiment configuration, other columns are **relative gains**, over the noncontextual baseline, of the performance metrics (Section 5.1) with a leveled suggestion rate of 0.5.

- **TM**: **T**otal **M**atches is the number of suggestions which match the upcoming text.
- **ChM**: **Ch**aracters **M**atched is the number of matched characters from all suggestions.
- **Est. ChA**: **Est**imated **Ch**aracters **A**ccepted is the estimated[2] total number of suggested characters accepted by users.

5.2 Experiments with chat messages

The performance results for chat messages from Microsoft Teams compared to the non-contextual baseline model are shown in Table 2. For comparability, we train the model's confidence threshold to level each model's suggestion rate (SR) at 0.5 suggestions / message.

Contextualization with just the chat window name (subject) yields moderate gains, possibly because the typically short chat messages are so sparse on context that a chat topic name, or participant names from a chat header, provides a starting foothold for relevance. In contrast, from the last table rows, we see that the benefits from subject context diminish once prior messages are used as a context, suggesting that the subject proxy is much weaker than prior message context. Table 2 also shows that compose-time can act as a confounding context signal for chat messages, especially in experiments with no prior messages as a context. This is possibly due to the numerically-heavy time encoding confusing the model in contrast to the short text of chat messages. The experiments also show that the benefits of these contextual signals are not additive.

All three prior message aggregation modes (*Ignore-Blocks*, *Respect-Blocks*, and *Both-Senders*) show gains across all performance metrics, with all time window sizes. *Both-Senders* mode achieves the most significant relative gains: above 9.3% for Match Rate and the Total Matches; more than 11.7% for the character match and character match per suggestion; and more than 18.6% for the characters saved per suggestion and character acceptance. This indicates that messages from the other sender provide significant value, when used with a well-tuned time window. It provides relevant conversation context from all senders, eliminating confusing gaps between messages, and enables suggestions in response to questions posed by the other sender. In particular, the *Ignore-Blocks* mode does worse than *Both-Senders*, since *Ignore-Blocks* can violate conversation continuity, including messages $[k, k+2]$ from the current sender, and skipping message $k+1$ from the other sender.

For the single-sender modes, *Respect-Blocks* generally performs slightly worse as it utilizes only part of the messages taken by the *Ignore-Blocks* mode. This indicates that seeing a longer prefix of the current message block (more similar to writing a long email) makes an impact on text prediction in chat messages. Lastly, we observe that a 5 minute time window works better than 2 and 10 minute time windows. Shorter time windows seem to miss important prior context while a larger windows lead

[2]Based on observed acceptance probabilities on large-scale production traffic, users tend to accept longer suggestions.

Configuration / context mode	MR	ChM / sugg	Est. ChS / sugg	TM	ChM	Est. ChA
Subject	-0.81%↓	-0.36%↓	+0.76%↑	-0.74%↓	-0.35%↓	+0.76%↑
Time	**+2.02%↑**	**+2.25%↑**	**+2.88%↑**	**+2.01%↑**	**+2.22%↑**	**+2.83%↑**
Previous Email	-9.72%↓	-10.56%↓	-13.05%↓	-9.65%↓	-10.56%↓	-13.12%↓
Time+Subject	+0.20%↑	+0.47%↑	+1.06%↑	+0.23%↑	+0.49%↑	+1.11%↑

Table 3: Microsoft Outlook email messages experiment results with various contextualization modes. First column is experiment configuration, other columns are **relative gains**, over the noncontextual baseline, of the performance metrics (Section 5.1) with a leveled suggestion rate of 3.8.

Configuration / context mode	MR	ChM / sugg	Est. ChS / sugg	TM	ChM	Est. ChA
Subject	-1.46%↓	-0.21%↓	+1.77%↑	-1.58%↓	-0.22%↓	+1.80%↑
Time	+0.24%↑	+1.59%↑	**+4.87%↑**	+0.20%↑	+1.55%↑	**+4.75%↑**
Previous Email	-3.89%↓	-3.50%↓	-2.43%↓	-3.85%↓	-3.42%↓	-2.43%↓
Time+Subject	**+1.70%↑**	**+2.32%↑**	+3.32%↑	**+1.75%↑**	**+2.34%↑**	+3.41%↑

Table 4: Avocado test set (Oard et al., 2015) messages experiment results for various contextualization modes. First column is experiment configuration, other columns are **relative gains**, over the noncontextual baseline, of performance metrics (Section 5.1) with a leveled suggestion rate of 2.5.

to over-saturation of irrelevant information.

5.3 Experiments with email messages

The gains from the contextualization in email messages are more moderate compared to those from chat messages. The comparison of the contextualized models with the baseline on commercial Microsoft Outlook emails and Avocado dataset are given in Table 3 and 4 respectively. For emails, the results suggest that time as a context (or time+subject in the Avocado dataset) offers most promising relative gains of 2-3%. This contrasts the observed trend from chat messages. Time is more important for emails since emails are often longer, contain greetings, farewells, and meeting requests with time-related keywords (e.g., "tomorrow", "last night", "after the weekend"). Additionally, numerical tokens from the time context are less likely to outnumber the message content tokens, since emails are about 10×longer than chat messages.

With the chosen architecture, neither subject nor prior message context signals provide value in the email scenario. Subjects may introduce keywords, but the implemented method of encoding context and body into a single string did not demonstrate an ability to pull out those key words for suggestions. Likewise, prior message context did not benefit the email scenario. As Figure 2 shows, emails with prior messages are significantly longer than any of the chat context aggregations. Prior emails may have critical information steering the direction of an email thread, but our production-oriented metric are not significantly affected. The implemented architecture may not be strong enough to isolate and make use of those cues, instead becoming confounded by the vast influx of tokens from another sender. This emphasizes that the email and chat scenarios require different context signals, and may benefit from different underlying architectures.

Qualitative analysis with the Avocado set Given our commercial data-visibility constraints due to the privacy considerations, we perform a qualitative analysis on the public Avocado dataset (Oard et al., 2015). Using this public data, we evaluate text predictions from one of the promising email context modes: time context. As shown in Table 5, we use diff tools to identify when the time context model and baseline model create (i) correct suggestions, (ii) wrong suggestions, and (iii) no suggestions. We see that the time context model improves on all three columns. When directly examining cases where the time-context model renders a new correct suggestion, compared to the baseline, we observe a trend of time-related n-grams. Words like "tomorrow", "available", "September" are seen more frequently in correct suggestions (see Figure 3). The same trend is also observed in the Time+Subject model.

	Time as context / Baseline in Avocado test set		
cases	correct / wrong	correct / no sugg	no sugg / wrong
context win	**256**	**1494**	**2825**
context loss	239	1400	2553

Table 5: Comparing text predictions of time-context model vs baselines. "Context win" row holds counts of cases where contextual model suggestions beat baseline suggestions.

6 Conclusions

We study the role of context in text prediction for chat and email platforms. Testing with previous messages, subject, time as additional contextual

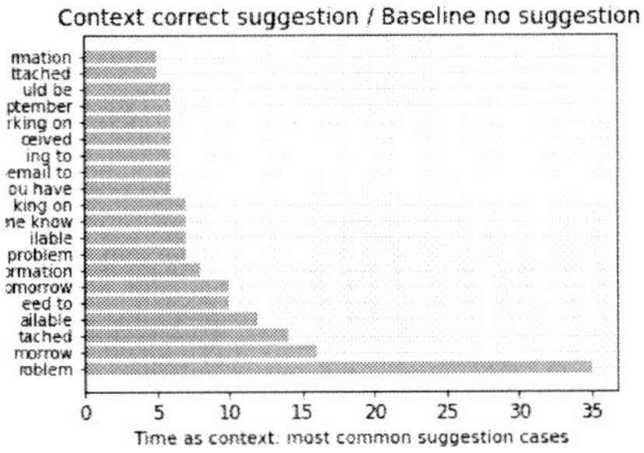

Figure 3: The 20 most common new suggestions triggered by the time-context model, on data points from the Avocado test set (Oard et al., 2015) where the baseline renders zero suggestions.

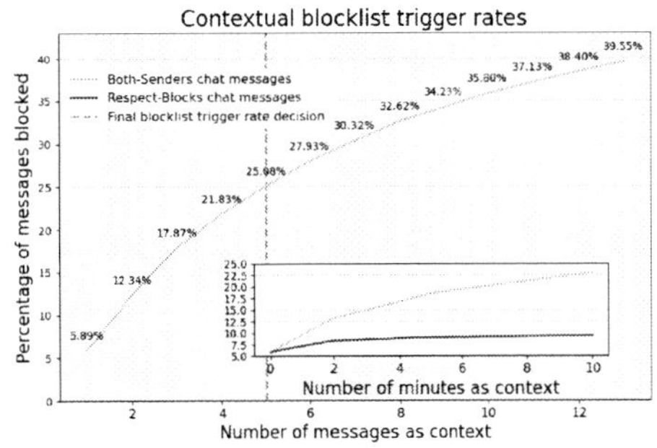

Figure 4: Initial blocklist trigger rates for various contextualization merging modes in Microsoft Teams chat messages.

signals, we find that the different characteristics of emails and chat messages influence the selection of contextual signals to use. Previous message contextualization leads to significant gains for chat messages from Microsoft Teams, when using an appropriate message aggregation strategy. By using a 5 minute time window and messages from both senders, we see a 9.4% relative increase in the match rate, and an 18.6% relative gain on estimated characters accepted. Chat messages are often short and can lack context about a train of thought; previous messages can bring necessary semantics to the model to provide a correct prediction. Benefits are comparatively insignificant for subject and compose time as contextual signals in chat messages.

In the email scenario based on Microsoft Outlook, we find that time as a contextual signal yields the largest boost with a 2.02% relative increase on the match rate, while subject only helps in conjunction with time, and prior messages yields no improvement. More complex models may be needed to reap subject and prior message gains for emails, but the current architecture was chosen for large-scale serving latency.

Future work involves exploring different encodings for contextual signals, such as utilizing hierarchical RNNs (Park et al., 2018; Yoo et al., 2020) to better capture context, or using more advanced architectures such as transformers or GPT-3.

7 Ethical Considerations

When working with sensitive data and running a service which generates text predictions for the general public, we are responsible for preserving user privacy and serving fair and inclusive suggestions.

7.1 Privacy considerations on user data

Our service framework follows the regulatory requirements of internal company-wise standards and General Data Protection Regulation (GDPR) (2018) to meet the user privacy regulations and customer premises. All customer chat and email data, from Teams and Outlook, used in this work are classified as customer content, which is not visible to humans for any purpose. Only system byproduct data, which is not linkable to specific users or groups, is obtained and viewed for quantitative evaluation. This includes internal service logs or numerical metrics (shown in Section 5.1). We also regularly re-sample training and test data due to our privacy and data retention policies, preserving similar data set sizes. We strictly use only publicly available data, such as the Avocado dataset (Oard et al., 2015), for debugging and visible qualitative evaluation.

7.2 Blocklisting

In pursuit of fair, respectful, and responsible suggestions, we employ a blocklist. This blocklist step in our text prediction system consists of a large dictionary containing denigrative, offensive, controversial, sensitive, and stereotype-prone words and phrases. Text from the message body and contextual signals serves as input to the blocklist. Then, if any word or phrase from the blocklist is found in the input, all further suggestions are suppressed for the message.

In the email scenario, the full body and context is used for blocklist checks, resulting in a blocklist trigger rate of 47.42%. This means that 47.42% of our data points contain a blocklisted term in their input text, and we avoid triggering suggestions on those points. Naturally, this rate of blocklist triggering increases as more context is added to the pool of text being checked.

This phenomenon introduces an added complexity to the chat scenario. A noncontextual baseline chat model would fail to trigger the blocklist on a response to an offensive statement from two messages ago. Figure 4 shows how the blocklist trigger rate varies as larger windows of chat history are used as context. We ensure that all chat models check the past 5 messages against the blocklist, no matter how many prior messages are used for text prediction inference. With 5 prior messages fed to the blocklist in chat conversations, the blocklist trigger rate is 25.08%, instead of 5.89% with no added prior messages.

Acknowledgements

We would like to thank the members of Microsoft Search, Assistant and Intelligence (MSAI) group for their useful comments and suggestions.

References

Ziv Bar-Yossef and Naama Kraus. 2011. Context-sensitive query auto-completion. In *Proc. of the 20th Intl. Conf. on World Wide Web (WWW)*, pages 107–116.

Holger Bast and Ingmar Weber. 2006. Type less, find more: fast autocompletion search with a succinct index. In *Proc. of the 29th Annual Intl. ACM Conf. on Research and Development in Information Retrieval (SIGIR)*, pages 364–371.

Yoshua Bengio, Réjean Ducharme, Pascal Vincent, and Christian Janvin. 2003. A neural probabilistic language model. *Jour. of Machine Learning Research*, 3:1137–1155.

Steffen Bickel, Peter Haider, and Tobias Scheffer. 2005. Learning to complete sentences. In *European Conf. on Machine Learning (ECML)*, pages 497–504. Springer.

Mia Xu Chen, Benjamin N Lee, Gagan Bansal, Yuan Cao, Shuyuan Zhang, Justin Lu, Jackie Tsay, Yinan Wang, Andrew M Dai, Zhifeng Chen, et al. 2019. Gmail Smart Compose: Real-time Assisted Writing. In *Proc. of the 25th ACM SIGKDD Intl. Conf. on Knowledge Discovery & Data Mining*, pages 2287–2295.

John J. Darragh, Ian H. Witten, and Mark L. James. 1990. The reactive keyboard: A predictive typing aid. *Computer*, 23(11):41–49.

Budhaditya Deb, Peter Bailey, and Milad Shokouhi. 2019. Diversifying reply suggestions using a matching-conditional variational autoencoder. In *Proc. of Conf. of the North American Chapter of the Association for Computational Linguistics: Human Language Technologies (NAACL-HLT)*, pages 40–47. Association for Computational Linguistics.

European Commission. 2018. EU data protection rules. `https://ec.europa.eu/info/law/law-topic/data-protection/eu-data-protection-rules_en`. Online; accessed 6 January 2021.

Andrew Hard, Kanishka Rao, Rajiv Mathews, Swaroop Ramaswamy, Françoise Beaufays, Sean Augenstein, Hubert Eichner, Chloé Kiddon, and Daniel Ramage. 2018. Federated learning for mobile keyboard prediction. *arXiv:1811.03604*.

Sepp Hochreiter and Jürgen Schmidhuber. 1997. Long short-term memory. *Neural Computation*, 9(8):1735–1780.

Frankie James. 2000. Modified kneser-ney smoothing of n-gram models. Technical report, RIACS.

Jared Spataro. 2019. 5 attributes of successful teams. `https://www.microsoft.com/en-us/microsoft-365/blog/2019/11/19/5-attributes-successful-teams/`. Online; accessed 6 January 2021.

Jared Spataro. 2020. Microsoft Teams reaches 115 million DAU—plus, a new daily collaboration minutes metric for Microsoft 365. `https://www.microsoft.com/en-us/microsoft-365/blog/2020/10/28/microsoft-teams-reaches-115-million-dau-plus-a-new-daily-collaboration-minutes-metric-for-microsoft-365/`. Online; accessed 6 January 2021.

Rafal Jozefowicz, Oriol Vinyals, Mike Schuster, Noam Shazeer, and Yonghui Wu. 2016. Exploring the limits of language modeling. *arXiv:1602.02410*.

Anjuli Kannan, Karol Kurach, Sujith Ravi, Tobias Kaufman, Balint Miklos, Greg Corrado, Andrew Tomkins, Laszlo Lukacs, Marina Ganea, Peter Young, and Vivek Ramavajjala. 2016. Smart reply: Automated response suggestion for email. In *Proc. of the ACM SIGKDD Conf. on Knowledge Discovery and Data Mining (KDD)*, page 955–964.

Nan Rosemary Ke, Konrad Żołna, Alessandro Sordoni, Zhouhan Lin, Adam Trischler, Yoshua Bengio, Joelle Pineau, Laurent Charlin, and Christopher Pal. 2018. Focused hierarchical RNNs for conditional sequence processing. In *Proc. of the 35th Intl. Conf. on Machine Learning (ICML)*, volume 80, pages 2554–2563, Stockholm, Sweden.

Reinhard Kneser and Hermann Ney. 1995. Improved backing-off for m-gram language modeling. In *Intl. Conf. on Acoustics, Speech, and Signal Processing (ICASSP)*, volume 1, pages 181–184.

Gábor Melis, Chris Dyer, and Phil Blunsom. 2018. On the state of the art of evaluation in neural language models. In *6th Intl. Conf. on Learning Representations (ICLR)*, Vancouver, BC, Canada.

Microsoft Text Predictions. 2020. Write faster using text predictions in Word, Outlook. https://insider.office.com/en-us/blog/text-predictions-in-word-outlook. Online; accessed 7 April 2021.

Andriy Mnih and Geoffrey E Hinton. 2009. A scalable hierarchical distributed language model. In *Advances in Neural Information Processing Systems (NeurIPS)*, pages 1081–1088.

Douglas Oard, William Webber, David A. Kirsch, and Sergey Golitsynskiy. 2015. Avocado research email collection LDC2015T03. Philadelphia: Linguistic Data Consortium.

Yookoon Park, Jaemin Cho, and Gunhee Kim. 2018. A hierarchical latent structure for variational conversation modeling. In *Proc. of the Conf. of the North American Chapter of the Association for Computational Linguistics: Human Language Technologies (NAACL-HLT)*, pages 1792–1801, New Orleans, LA, USA. Association for Computational Linguistics.

Ashish Vaswani, Noam Shazeer, Niki Parmar, Jakob Uszkoreit, Llion Jones, Aidan N Gomez, Łukasz Kaiser, and Illia Polosukhin. 2017. Attention is all you need. In *Advances in Neural Information Processing Systems (NeurIPS)*, pages 5998–6008.

Ryen W. White, P. Bailey, and Liwei Chen. 2009. Predicting user interests from contextual information. In *Proc. of the 32nd Intl. ACM Conf. on Research and development in information retrieval (SIGIR)*.

Kang Min Yoo, Hanbit Lee, Franck Dernoncourt, Trung Bui, W. Chang, and Sang-goo Lee. 2020. Variational hierarchical dialog autoencoder for dialogue state tracking data augmentation. In *Proc. of the Conf. on Empirical Methods in Natural Language Processing (EMNLP)*.

Zhuosheng Zhang, Jiangtong Li, Pengfei Zhu, Hai Zhao, and Gongshen Liu. 2018. Modeling multi-turn conversation with deep utterance aggregation. In *Proc. of the 27th Intl. Conf. on Computational Linguistics (COLING)*, pages 3740–3752, Santa Fe, New Mexico, USA. Association for Computational Linguistics.

Identifying and Resolving Annotation Changes for Natural Language Understanding

Jose Garrido Ramas
Amazon Alexa AI, Germany
jrramas@amazon.de

Giorgio Pessot
Amazon Alexa AI, Germany
pessot@amazon.de

Abdalghani Abujabal
Amazon Alexa AI, Germany
abujabaa@amazon.de

Martin Rajman
EPFL, Lausanne, Switzerland
martin.rajman@epfl.ch

Abstract

Annotation conflict resolution is crucial towards building machine learning models with acceptable performance. Past work on annotation conflict resolution had assumed that data is collected at once, with a fixed set of annotators and fixed annotation guidelines. Moreover, previous work dealt with atomic labeling tasks. In this paper, we address annotation conflict resolution for Natural Language Understanding (NLU), a structured prediction task, in a real-world setting of commercial voice-controlled personal assistants, where (1) regular data collections are needed to support new and existing functionalities, (2) annotation guidelines evolve over time, and (3) the pool of annotators changes across data collections. We devise an approach combining information-theoretic measures and a supervised neural model to resolve conflicts in data annotation. We evaluate our approach both intrinsically and extrinsically on a real-world dataset with 3.5M utterances of a commercial dialog system in German. Our approach leads to dramatic improvements over a majority baseline especially in contentious cases. On the NLU task, our approach achieves 2.75% error reduction over a no-resolution baseline.

1 Introduction

Supervised learning is ubiquitous as a form of learning in NLP (Abujabal et al., 2019; Finkel et al., 2005; Rajpurkar et al., 2016), but supervised models require access to high-quality and manually annotated data so that they perform reasonably. It is often assumed that (1) such annotated data is collected once and then used to train and test various models, (2) the pool of annotators is fixed, and (3) annotation guidelines are fixed (Benikova et al., 2014; Manning, 2011; Poesio and Artstein, 2005; Versley, 2006). In real-world NLP applications e.g., voice-controlled assistants such as Google Home or Amazon Alexa, such assumptions are unrealistic. The assistant is continuously evolving and extended with new functionalities, and hence, changes to annotation guidelines are frequent. The assistant also needs to adapt to language variations over time, both lexical and semantic. Therefore, annotated data needs to be collected regularly i.e., new collections of data at different time points, where the same utterance text can be re-annotated over time. Additionally, the set of annotators might change across collections. In this work, we tackle the problem of resolving annotation conflicts in a real-world scenario of a commercial personal assistant.

To minimize annotation conflicts, the same data point is often labeled by multiple annotators and the annotation with unanimous agreement, or the one with majority votes is deemed correct (Benikova et al., 2014; Bobicev and Sokolova, 2017; Brants, 2000). While such measures ensure the quality of annotations within the same batch, they cannot ensure it across batches at different time points, particularly when the same data point is present in different batches with inevitable changes to annotation guidelines. For detecting and resolving conflicts, two main methodologies have been explored; Bayesian modeling and training a supervised classification model (Hovy et al., 2013; Plank et al., 2014; Snow et al., 2008; Versley and Steen, 2016; Volokh and Neumann, 2011). Both methodologies make certain assumptions about the setting, for example, annotation guidelines and the pool of annotators are fixed, which is not the case for our use case. Additionally, while Bayesian modeling is reasonably efficient for small datasets, it is prohibitively expensive for large-scale datasets with millions of utterances. We adopt a combination of information-theoretic measures and a classification neural model to detect and resolve conflicts.

NLU is a key component in language-based applications, and is defined as the combination of: (1) An Intent Classifier (IC), which classifies an utterance into one of N intent labels (e.g. `PlayMusic`), and (2) A slot labeling (SL) model, which classifies

Proceedings of NAACL HLT 2021: IndustryTrack Papers, pages 10–18

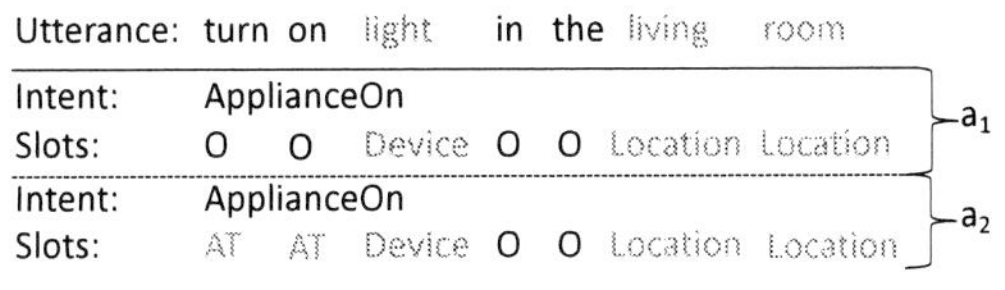

Figure 1: An example utterance with two conflicting annotations, a_1 and a_2. The phrase *turn on* has two conflicting slot labels. AT stands for `ActionTrigger`. Non-entities are labeled with O (i.e., Other).

tokens into slot types, out of a predefined set (e.g. `SongName`) (Goo et al., 2018; Jolly et al., 2020). An example utterance is shown in Figure 1, with two conflicting annotations. In this paper, we consider the task of NLU for personal assistants and assume that utterances arrive at different points in time, and that the annotation guideline evolves over time. The same utterance text, e.g., the one shown in Figure 1, often occurs multiple times across collections, which gives the opportunity to conflicting annotations. Moreover, changes to the annotation guidelines over time lead to more conflicts.

Given an NLU dataset with utterances having multiple, possibly conflicting annotations (IC and SL), our goal is to find the right annotation for each such utterance. To this end, we first detect guideline changes using a maximum information gain cut (Section 3.3). Then we compute the normalized entropy of the remaining annotations after dropping the ones before a guideline change. In case this entropy is low, we simply use majority voting, otherwise, we rely on a classifier neural-based model to resolve the conflict (Section 3.4). Our approach is depicted in Figure 2.

We evaluate our approach both intrinsically and extrinsically, and show improved performance over baselines including random resolution or no resolution in six domains, as detailed in Section 4.

2 Related Work

Annotation conflicts could emerge due to different reasons, be it imprecision in the annotation guideline (Manning, 2011; van Deemter and Kibble, 2000), vagueness in the meaning of the underlying text (Poesio and Artstein, 2005; Recasens et al., 2011, 2010; Versley, 2006), or annotators being careless or inexperienced (Manning, 2011; Hovy et al., 2013). Manning et al. (2011) report, on the WSJ Part-of-Speech (POS) corpus, that 28.0% of POS tagging errors stem from imprecise annotation guideline that caused inconsistent annotations, while 15.5% of the errors are due to wrong gold standard, which could be attributed to careless or inexperienced annotators. In our case, conflicts could occur due to changes to the annotation guidelines and having different, possibly inexperienced, annotators within and across data collections.

Past work on conflict resolution has assumed that data is collected once and then used for model training and testing. Consequently, the proposed methods to detect and resolve conflicts are geared towards this setting (Benikova et al., 2014; Manning, 2011; Poesio and Artstein, 2005; Recasens et al., 2011, 2010; van Deemter and Kibble, 2000; Versley, 2006). In our scenario, we deal with an ever-growing data which is collected across different data collections at different time points. This increases the likelihood of conflicts especially with frequent changes to the annotation guideline. In Dickinson and Meurers (2003), an approach is proposed to automatically detect annotation errors in gold standard annotations for POS tagging using n-gram tag variation i.e., looking at n-grams occurring in the corpus with multiple tagging.

Bayesian modeling is often used to model how reliable each annotator is and to correct/resolve wrong annotations (Hovy et al., 2013; Snow et al., 2008). In Hovy et al. (2013), they propose MACE, an item-response based model, to identify *spammer* annotators and to predict the correct underlying labels. Applying such models is prohibitively expensive in our case due to the large amount of utterances we deal with. Additionally, our annotator pool changes over time. A different line of work has explored resolving conflicts in a supervised classification setting, similar to our approach for resolving high normalized entropy conflicts. Volokh and Neumann (2011) use an ensemble of two off-the-shelf parsers that re-annotate the training set to detect and resolve conflicts in dependency treebanks. Versley et al. (2016) use a similar approach on out-of-domain treebanks. Finally, Plank et al. (2014) introduce the inter-annotator agreement loss to ensure consistent annotations for POS tagging.

Intent classification and slot labeling are two fundamental tasks in spoken language understanding, dating back to early 90's (Price, 1990). With the rise of task-oriented personal assistants, the two tasks got more attention and progress has been made by applying various deep learning techniques (Abujabal and Gaspers, 2019; Goo et al., 2018;

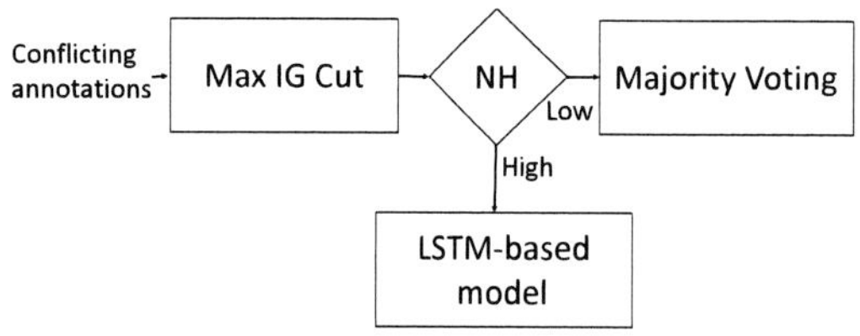

Figure 2: Our approach for conflict resolution. Given conflicting annotations, we first use the Max Information Gain (*IG*) Cut to detect changes in annotation guidelines. Then, low entropy conflicts are resolved using majority voting. High entropy conflicts are resolved using a classifier LSTM-based model.

Jolly et al., 2020; Mesnil et al., 2013; Zhang and Wang, 2016). While we focus on resolving annotation conflicts for NLU with linear labeling i.e., intent and slot labels, our approach can be still used for other more complex tree-based labeling e.g., labeling dependency parses or ontology trees (Chen and Manning, 2014), with the minor change of replacing the task-specific neural LSTM-based classification model. We plan to investigate this in the future.

3 Annotation Conflict Resolution

3.1 Overview

Given multiple conflicting annotations of an utterance, our goal is to find the right annotation. We assume that annotations arrive at different points in time and that the same utterance can be re-annotated over time. Moreover, we assume that annotators might differ both within and across data collections, that each annotation is time stamped, and that there is always one correct annotation. Our pipeline for conflict resolution is depicted in Figure 2. Given an utterance with conflicting annotations, we first detect guideline changes using a maximum information gain cut. Then we compute the normalized entropy of the remaining annotations i.e., without the annotations before a guideline change. In case this entropy is low, we simply use majority voting, otherwise, we rely on a classifier model to resolve the conflict.

A natural choice to easily resolving annotation conflicts is to use majority voting. However, we argue that this is not sufficient for our use case, where (1) regular data collection and annotation are required at different time points, and (2) changes to annotation guideline are frequent. We use the normalized entropy to *detect* whether there is high or low disagreement among annotations. In the extreme case where the normalized entropy is 1, majority voting gives a random output and any model that performs better than random will be better than majority voting in resolving conflicts. In our experiments we show that, for high normalized entropy values, the classifier model significantly outperforms majority voting.

Note that our conflict resolution pipeline does not drop utterances with wrong annotations, but rather replaces the wrong annotations with the correct ones. We do so to avoid changing the data distribution.

We apply our pipeline to training data only. The test set is of higher quality compared to the train set as each collection of test set data is annotated multiple times and we use the most recent test set collection.

3.2 Normalized Entropy

Entropy measures the uncertainty of a probability distribution (Yang and Qiu, 2014). Given an utterance present N times in the dataset and annotated in K distinct ways, each occurring n_i times such that $\sum_{i=1}^{K} n_i = N$, we define the *normalized empirical entropy* of the list of conflicting annotations A, $NH(A)$ as:

$$NH(A) = \frac{-\sum_{i=1}^{K} \frac{n_i}{N} * \log\left(\frac{n_i}{N}\right)}{\log K}, \; for \; K > 1$$

For example, assume an utterance u with three distinct annotations; a_1, a_2 and a_3. Then, the list A corresponds to $\{a_1, a_2, a_3\}$, $K = 3$, and p_i of each annotation corresponds to its relative frequency in the dataset ($\frac{n_i}{N}$) (Mahendra et al., 2014).

In this work, we harness normalized entropy (NH) to determine whether majority voting should be used. NH is a value between 0 and 1, where the higher it is, the harder the conflict. In the edge case of a uniform distribution, where NH is 1, majority voting gives a random output. Therefore, in such cases, we do not rely on majority voting for conflict resolution but rather on a classification model. We use the normalized entropy over entropy as the latter increases as K increases when the distribution is uniform. For example, assume $K = 3$ and distribution is uniform, then entropy is $H = \log 3$, and $NH = 1$. If $K = 2$ and distribution is uniform, then $H = \log 2$ and $NH = 1$, and so on. When the distribution is uniform (and thus majority voting will be outperformed by a model regardless of K), NH takes its maximum value of 1, while H increases as K increases (Kvålseth, 2017).

3.3 Changes in Annotation Guideline: Max Information Gain Cut

We rely on max information gain cut to find out if there was a change in the annotation scheme that caused a conflict, and to identify the exact date d of the change. Let us assume the relatively common case that there is exactly one relevant change in the guideline. Then, we aim to split the annotations of an utterance to two lists; one list containing annotations prior to the change, and the other one containing annotations after the change.

Inspired by methods used for splitting on a feature in decision trees (Mahendra et al., 2014), we harness *information gain* (IG) to determine the date to split at. Concretely, given a list B of chronologically ordered annotations for the same utterance, and their corresponding annotation dates, we choose the date d that maximizes IG. If the value of IG is larger than a threshold IG_0, we deem the annotations prior to d incorrect. The higher the IG is, the more probable the annotations prior to d to be incorrect. We define a boolean variable D which is true if the date of an annotation comes after d, and false otherwise. It divides the list of annotations B to two sublists, B_b of size N_b of annotations before date d, and B_a of size N_a of annotations after date d. We compute IG as follows:

$$IG(B, D) = NH(B) - NH(B|D), where$$

$$NH(B|D) = \frac{N_b * NH(B_b) + N_a * NH(B_a)}{N}$$

We use the normalized entropy (NH) for IG computation, as shown in the equation above. As a result, IG is no longer strictly positive.

In the case of changes in the annotation guideline, there will be high disagreement among annotations before and after the change, and thus, $NH(B)$ will be high. Moreover, annotations before the change will agree among each other, and similarly, for annotations after the change. Therefore, $NH(B|D)$ will be low. Then $IG(B, D)$ takes its maximum value at the date of the guideline change, and annotations after this date, which belong to the latest guideline, are correct. For example, for the following date-ordered annotations; $\{a_1$(03-2019), a_1(07-2019), a_1(08-2019), a_2(10-2019), a_2(11-2019), a_3(12-2019), a_2(01-2020), a_2(02-2020)$\}$, spliting at d =

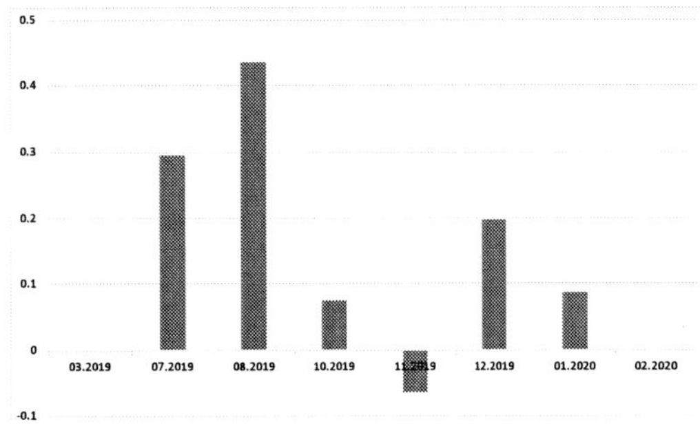

Figure 3: IG values at each date. The split at d =08-2019 has the highest IG value. We cannot split at the first and last dates.

(08-2019) yields the highest IG value, as shown in Figure 3. This indicates that there was a change in the annotation of this utterance on 08-2019. Hence, a_1 annotation is deemed wrong. In Section 4.2, we empirically prove that for high IG values, a large percentage of annotations occurring in the first half of the Max IG Cut split is incorrect, whereas a large percentage of annotations in the second half is correct.

After the split, NH is computed for the remaining annotations i.e., annotations after d. If NH is less than a threshold NH_0, we assign the utterance the annotation with maximum frequency (i.e., *majority voting*). In the example above, NH is low after the split, and the conflict is resolved by changing all annotations (i.e., a_1 and a_3) to a_2. Our reasoning is that, when NH is high, majority voting will likely be outperformed by an alternative model (LSTM-based method, explained next) as there is high disagreement between the annotators. Note that we do not drop any utterances, we replace wrong annotations with the correct ones.

3.4 High Entropy Conflicts: LSTM

To make classification in the ambiguous high NH cases, we use a supervised classifier trained on the unambiguous examples from our data, in this case an LSTM-based neural model (Hochreiter and Schmidhuber, 1997). For the following list of annotations, $\{a_1, a_2, a_3, a_2, a_1, a_3\}$, no split with IG greater than a threshold can be found, and $NH = 1$. For such utterances, we rely on a neural model to estimate the probability of each annotation i.e., a_1, a_2, and a_3. Then we assign the annotation with highest probability to the utterance. Concretely, we use the model of Chiu et al. (2016), a bidirectional word-level LSTM model with a character-based

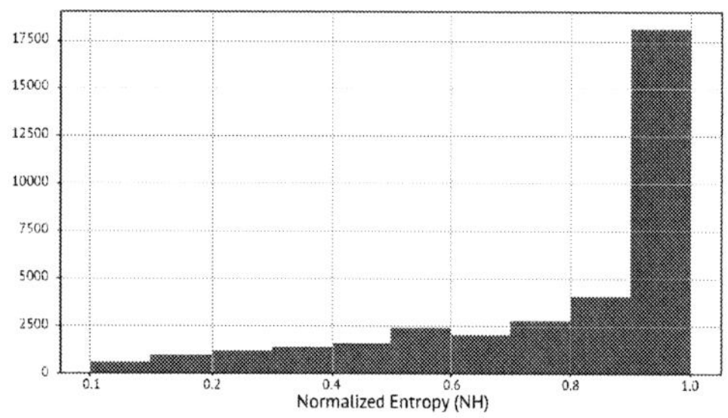

Figure 4: Histogram of conflicts in the training data. Most conflicts have high entropy.

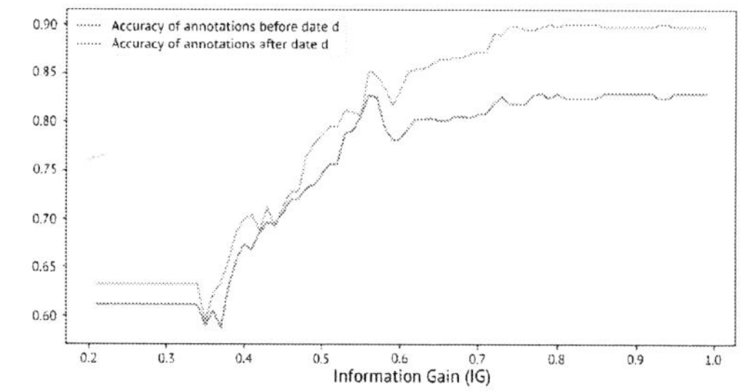

Figure 5: Accuracy of the rule change detection method described in Section 3.3. For high IG values, the accuracy of annotations after a date d, at which there is a guideline change, is 90%, while the accuracy of annotations before d is over 80%.

CNN layer. A softmax layer is used on top of the output of the bidirectional LSTM, which computes a probability distribution over the output slot labels for a given input token. We extend the model to a multi-task setting to support IC by concatenating the last hidden states of the Bi-LSTM, and passing them to a softmax layer, similar to Yang et al. (2016). We harness the probabilities of the output of the softmax layer and compute the final probability of the annotation by multiplying the probability of each of its slots and of the intent.

4 Experiments

In this section we evaluate our method both intrinsically and extrinsically.

4.1 Setup

Data. We use a real-world dataset of a commercial dialog system in German, belonging to six different domains covering different, macro-purposes like, for instance, musical or movies requests. For the purpose of IC and SL, domains are treated as separate datasets. Utterances were manually transcribed and annotated with domain, intent and slot labels across many different batches at different points of time. In total we have 3.5M and 560K training and testing utterances, respectively. The percentage of conflicts in the training data varies across domains, ranging from 4.9% to 10.9%. Most conflicts are of high entropy, as shown in Figure 4. The test set is of higher quality compared to the train set as each collection of test set data is annotated twice. Generally, the test set has lower number of conflicts compared to the train set. We do not resolve the conflicts in the test data to avoid artificial inflation of results.

LSTM model. For high entropy conflicts, we use a single layer network for the forward and the backward LSTMs whose dimensions are set to 256. We use Glove pretrained German word embeddings (Pennington et al., 2014) with 300 dimensions. For the CNN layer, character embeddings were initialized randomly with 25 dimensions. We used a mini-batch Adam optimizer (Kingma and Ba, 2015) with a learning rate of 0.001. We tried different optimizers with different learning rates (e.g., stochastic gradient descent), however, they performed worse than Adam. We also applied Dropout of 0.5 to each LSTM output (Hinton et al., 2012). For training, we use the data described above (i.e., 3.5M utterances) after applying the Max IG Cut and majority voting to resolve low entropy conflicts, as described in Section 3.3. High-entropy conflicts are left unresolved. After 10 epochs, training is terminated. After training is done, the model is used for conflict resolution for high entropy cases.

4.2 Intrinsic Evaluation

To asses the quality of our method, an expert linguist is asked to resolve 490 conflicts in two different domains e.g., Music. The linguist is asked to use the latest annotation guideline. On average, we have 12.6 utterances per conflict, with a total number of 6173 utterances for the 490 conflicts. The maximum number of utterances of a conflict is 181. On the annotation side, the maximum number of unique annotations of a conflict is 8, while the average number is 2.35 (Table 1).

We used our pipeline to resolve the 490 conflicts that were resolved by the linguist, where 229 conflicts out of the 490 were resolved with the LSTM model, which means that 46.7% of the conflicts were of high normalized entropy ($\geq NH_0 = 0.75$).

	#Utterances per Conflict	#Unique Annotations per Conflict
Min	2	2
Average	12.6	2.35
Max	181	8
Total	6173	1151

Table 1: Statistics on the 490 conflicts used for our evaluation.

Guideline change detected	120
Resolved with LSTM model	229
Resolved with majority voting	261

Table 2: Out of the 490 conflicts, 229 were resolved with the LSTM model, while 261 conflicts were resolved with majority voting.

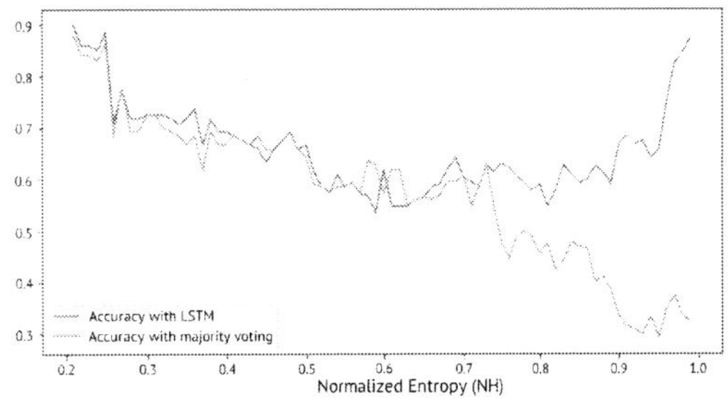

Figure 6: Accuracy with majority voting (orange) and with the LSTM-based method (blue) on the 490 conflicts with respect to ground-truth resolution provided by the linguist. For high values of NH, the LSTM-based model performs better than majority voting.

The remaining 261 conflicts were resolved with majority voting. 120 out of the 490 conflicts had at least one guideline change (Table 2).

Max IG cut. For those conflicts with guideline changes we evaluate, after splitting the list of annotations at date d, whether the annotations after d are correct (a^i_{after}), and whether the annotations before d are incorrect (a^i_{before}). To this end, for each conflict with $IG \geq 0.2$, we compare each annotation after and before d with the ground-truth annotation (a_{gt}) provided by the linguist. a^i_{after} annotations should be correct, therefore, accuracy is 1 if a^i_{after} agrees with a_{gt}, and 0 otherwise. On the other hand, a^i_{before} annotations should be incorrect, and hence, accuracy is 1 if a^i_{before} does not agree with a_{gt}, and 0 otherwise. We compute the average accuracy over a^i_{after} annotations and the average accuracy over a^i_{before} annotations for each conflict. We also compute the average across those conflicts with the same IG value.

We depicted the results in Figure 5. For high IG values, high accuracies are achieved for annotations after and before a split at a date d. For example, at IG = 0.9, the accuracy of annotations before d is almost 0.83, while the accuracy of annotations after d is 0.90. This shows that our max IG cut method was able to identify the right date d to split the list of annotations at for the majority of conflicts with guideline changes. We set IG_0 to 0.4.

Majority Voting vs. LSTM. We evaluate the resolution of the 490 conflicts with the LSTM-based model and majority voting at different levels of NH. For each conflict, we apply the max IG cut and then resolve it using both methods of majority voting and LSTM. We then compare the final annotation each method delivers as correct with that delivered by the linguist. If both agree, then accuracy is 1, and 0 otherwise. For each NH value, we compute the average accuracy of the set of 50 conflicts with closest NH.

As expected, the accuracy with majority voting significantly drops with high entropy conflicts, as shown in Figure 6. The LSTM-based model becomes more accurate as NH increases, reaching the highest accuracy in the case where $NH = 1$. In the training data, 29.3% of conflicts have $NH = 1$. As seen in the figure, accuracy diverges at $NH = 0.75$, which we use as NH_0. That is, if $NH \geq 0.75$, we use the LSTM-based model, and majority voting otherwise. For NH below 0.75, both majority voting and the LSTM-based model behave similarly, however, we use majority voting for low entropies as it is more intuitive.

4.3 Effect on NLU

To evaluate our method extrinsically on the downstream task of NLU, we trained a multi-task LSTM-based neural model for intent classification and slot labeling on the 3.5M utterances after resolving annotation conflicts using our proposed method (Figure 2). Architecture-wise, the model is similar to the one we use for conflict resolution, described in Section 3.4. We compared this model with two baseline models trained as follows:

1. **NoResolution**: this model was trained on the full training data without conflict resolution (i.e., 3.5M utterances).

Method	Error Rate (Rel. Change)
Random Resolution	0.55%
Our Pipeline	**2.75%**

Table 3: Results on the NLU task. Our pipeline achieved 2.75% relative change in error rate with respect to the NoResolution baseline.

2. **Rand**: We trained this model with conflicts resolved by choosing one annotation randomly.

The three models were tested on the same test set described above (560K utterances). We report the relative change in error rate with respect to the NoResolution model. The error rate is defined as the fraction of utterances in which there is at least an error either in IC or in SL.

Results are shown in Table 3. Overall, random conflict resolution slightly reduced the error rate with 0.55% relative change on average across domains, while our method achieved 2.75% error reduction. For each of the six domains, resolving conflicts with our method improves performance over random resolution and over no resolution. In one domain, a reduction in error rate of 4.7% is observed. For five domains, the difference in performance passes a two-sided paired t-test for statistical significance at 95% confidence level.

5 Conclusion

In this paper, we tackled the problem of annotation conflicts for the task of NLU for voice-controlled personal assistants. We presented a novel approach that combines information-theoretic measures and an LSTM-based neural model. We evaluated our method on a real-world large-scale dataset, both intrinsically and extrinsically.

Although we focused on the task of NLU, our conflict resolution pipeline could be applied to any manual annotation task. In the future, we plan on investigating how the choice of the task-specific classification model affects performance. Moreover, we plan to study annotation conflict resolution for other NLP tasks e.g., PoS tagging and dependency parsing.

Acknowledgements

We thank Melanie Bradford and our anonymous reviewers for their thoughtful comments and useful discussions.

References

Abdalghani Abujabal and Judith Gaspers. 2019. Neural Named Entity Recognition from Subword Units. In *Proc. Interspeech 2019*, pages 2663–2667.

Abdalghani Abujabal, Rishiraj Saha Roy, Mohamed Yahya, and Gerhard Weikum. 2019. Comqa: A community-sourced dataset for complex factoid question answering with paraphrase clusters. In *Proceedings of the 2019 Conference of the North American Chapter of the Association for Computational Linguistics: Human Language Technologies, NAACL-HLT 2019, Minneapolis, MN, USA, June 2-7, 2019, Volume 1 (Long and Short Papers)*, pages 307–317. Association for Computational Linguistics.

Darina Benikova, Chris Biemann, and Marc Reznicek. 2014. NoSta-d named entity annotation for German: Guidelines and dataset. In *Proceedings of the Ninth International Conference on Language Resources and Evaluation (LREC'14)*, pages 2524–2531, Reykjavik, Iceland. European Language Resources Association (ELRA).

Victoria Bobicev and Marina Sokolova. 2017. Inter-annotator agreement in sentiment analysis: Machine learning perspective. In *Proceedings of the International Conference Recent Advances in Natural Language Processing, RANLP 2017*, pages 97–102, Varna, Bulgaria. INCOMA Ltd.

Thorsten Brants. 2000. Inter-annotator agreement for a German newspaper corpus. In *Proceedings of the Second International Conference on Language Resources and Evaluation (LREC'00)*, Athens, Greece. European Language Resources Association (ELRA).

Danqi Chen and Christopher D. Manning. 2014. A fast and accurate dependency parser using neural networks. In *Proceedings of the 2014 Conference on Empirical Methods in Natural Language Processing, EMNLP 2014, October 25-29, 2014, Doha, Qatar, A meeting of SIGDAT, a Special Interest Group of the ACL*, pages 740–750. ACL.

Jason P. C. Chiu and Eric Nichols. 2016. Named entity recognition with bidirectional lstm-cnns. *TACL*, 4:357–370.

Markus Dickinson and W. Detmar Meurers. 2003. Detecting errors in part-of-speech annotation. In *10th Conference of the European Chapter of the Association for Computational Linguistics*, Budapest, Hungary. Association for Computational Linguistics.

Jenny Rose Finkel, Trond Grenager, and Christopher D. Manning. 2005. Incorporating non-local information into information extraction systems by gibbs sampling. In *ACL 2005, 43rd Annual Meeting of the Association for Computational Linguistics, Proceedings of the Conference, 25-30 June 2005, University of Michigan, USA*, pages 363–370. The Association for Computer Linguistics.

Chih-Wen Goo, Guang Gao, Yun-Kai Hsu, Chih-Li Huo, Tsung-Chieh Chen, Keng-Wei Hsu, and Yun-Nung Chen. 2018. Slot-gated modeling for joint slot filling and intent prediction. In *Proceedings of the 2018 Conference of the North American Chapter of the Association for Computational Linguistics: Human Language Technologies, NAACL-HLT, New Orleans, Louisiana, USA, June 1-6, 2018, Volume 2 (Short Papers)*, pages 753–757. Association for Computational Linguistics.

Geoffrey E. Hinton, Nitish Srivastava, Alex Krizhevsky, Ilya Sutskever, and Ruslan Salakhutdinov. 2012. Improving neural networks by preventing co-adaptation of feature detectors. *CoRR*, abs/1207.0580.

Sepp Hochreiter and Jürgen Schmidhuber. 1997. Long short-term memory. *Neural Comput.*, 9(8):1735–1780.

Dirk Hovy, Taylor Berg-Kirkpatrick, Ashish Vaswani, and Eduard H. Hovy. 2013. Learning whom to trust with MACE. In *Human Language Technologies: Conference of the North American Chapter of the Association of Computational Linguistics, Proceedings, June 9-14, 2013, Westin Peachtree Plaza Hotel, Atlanta, Georgia, USA*, pages 1120–1130. The Association for Computational Linguistics.

Shailza Jolly, Tobias Falke, Caglar Tirkaz, and Daniil Sorokin. 2020. Data-efficient paraphrase generation to bootstrap intent classification and slot labeling for new features in task-oriented dialog systems. In *Proceedings of the 28th International Conference on Computational Linguistics: Industry Track*, pages 10–20, Online. International Committee on Computational Linguistics.

Diederik P. Kingma and Jimmy Ba. 2015. Adam: A method for stochastic optimization. In *3rd International Conference on Learning Representations, ICLR 2015, San Diego, CA, USA, May 7-9, 2015, Conference Track Proceedings*.

Tarald O. Kvålseth. 2017. On normalized mutual information: Measure derivations and properties. *Entropy*, 19(11).

M.S. Mahendra, E.J. Neuhold, A.M. Tjoa, and I. You. 2014. *Information and Communication Technology: Second IFIP TC 5/8 International Conference, ICT-EurAsia 2014, Bali, Indonesia, April 14-17, 2014, Proceedings*. Lecture Notes in Computer Science. Springer Berlin Heidelberg.

Christopher D. Manning. 2011. Part-of-speech tagging from 97% to 100%: Is it time for some linguistics? In *Computational Linguistics and Intelligent Text Processing - 12th International Conference, CICLing 2011, Tokyo, Japan, February 20-26, 2011. Proceedings, Part I*, volume 6608 of *Lecture Notes in Computer Science*, pages 171–189. Springer.

Grégoire Mesnil, Xiaodong He, Li Deng, and Yoshua Bengio. 2013. Investigation of recurrent-neural-network architectures and learning methods for spoken language understanding. In *INTERSPEECH 2013, 14th Annual Conference of the International Speech Communication Association, Lyon, France, August 25-29, 2013*, pages 3771–3775. ISCA.

Jeffrey Pennington, Richard Socher, and Christopher D. Manning. 2014. Glove: Global vectors for word representation. In *Proceedings of the 2014 Conference on Empirical Methods in Natural Language Processing, EMNLP 2014, October 25-29, 2014, Doha, Qatar, A meeting of SIGDAT, a Special Interest Group of the ACL*, pages 1532–1543. ACL.

Barbara Plank, Dirk Hovy, and Anders Søgaard. 2014. Learning part-of-speech taggers with inter-annotator agreement loss. In *Proceedings of the 14th Conference of the European Chapter of the Association for Computational Linguistics, EACL 2014, April 26-30, 2014, Gothenburg, Sweden*, pages 742–751. The Association for Computer Linguistics.

Massimo Poesio and Ron Artstein. 2005. The reliability of anaphoric annotation, reconsidered: Taking ambiguity into account. In *Proceedings of the Workshop on Frontiers in Corpus Annotations II: Pie in the Sky@ACL 2005, Ann Arbor, MI, USA, June 29, 2005*, pages 76–83. Association for Computational Linguistics.

P. J. Price. 1990. Evaluation of spoken language systems: the ATIS domain. In *Speech and Natural Language: Proceedings of a Workshop Held at Hidden Valley, Pennsylvania, USA, June 24-27, 1990*. Morgan Kaufmann.

Pranav Rajpurkar, Jian Zhang, Konstantin Lopyrev, and Percy Liang. 2016. Squad: 100, 000+ questions for machine comprehension of text. In *Proceedings of the 2016 Conference on Empirical Methods in Natural Language Processing, EMNLP 2016, Austin, Texas, USA, November 1-4, 2016*, pages 2383–2392. The Association for Computational Linguistics.

Marta Recasens, Eduard Hovy, and M. Antònia Martí. 2010. A typology of near-identity relations for coreference (NIDENT). In *Proceedings of the Seventh International Conference on Language Resources and Evaluation (LREC'10)*, Valletta, Malta. European Language Resources Association (ELRA).

Marta Recasens, Eduard Hovy, and M Antònia Martí. 2011. Identity, non-identity, and near-identity: Addressing the complexity of coreference. *Lingua*, 121(6):1138–1152.

Rion Snow, Brendan O'Connor, Daniel Jurafsky, and Andrew Y. Ng. 2008. Cheap and fast - but is it good? evaluating non-expert annotations for natural language tasks. In *2008 Conference on Empirical Methods in Natural Language Processing, EMNLP 2008, Proceedings of the Conference, 25-27 October*

2008, Honolulu, Hawaii, USA, A meeting of SIGDAT, a Special Interest Group of the ACL, pages 254–263. ACL.

Kees van Deemter and Rodger Kibble. 2000. On coreferring: Coreference in MUC and related annotation schemes. *Comput. Linguistics*, 26(4):629–637.

Yannick Versley. 2006. Disagreement dissected: Vagueness as a source of ambiguity in nominal (co-) reference. In *Ambiguity in Anaphora Workshop Proceedings*, pages 83–89.

Yannick Versley and Julius Steen. 2016. Detecting annotation scheme variation in out-of-domain treebanks. In *Proceedings of the Tenth International Conference on Language Resources and Evaluation LREC 2016, Portorož, Slovenia, May 23-28, 2016*. European Language Resources Association (ELRA).

Alexander Volokh and Günter Neumann. 2011. Automatic detection and correction of errors in dependency treebanks. In *The 49th Annual Meeting of the Association for Computational Linguistics: Human Language Technologies, Proceedings of the Conference, 19-24 June, 2011, Portland, Oregon, USA - Short Papers*, pages 346–350. The Association for Computer Linguistics.

Jiping Yang and Wanhua Qiu. 2014. Normalized expected utility-entropy measure of risk. *Entropy*, 16:3590–3604.

Zhilin Yang, Ruslan Salakhutdinov, and William W. Cohen. 2016. Multi-task cross-lingual sequence tagging from scratch. *CoRR*, abs/1603.06270.

Xiaodong Zhang and Houfeng Wang. 2016. A joint model of intent determination and slot filling for spoken language understanding. In *Proceedings of the Twenty-Fifth International Joint Conference on Artificial Intelligence, IJCAI 2016, New York, NY, USA, 9-15 July 2016*, pages 2993–2999. IJCAI/AAAI Press.

Optimizing NLU Reranking Using Entity Resolution Signals in Multi-domain Dialog Systems

Tong Wang*, Jiangning Chen*, Mohsen Malmir, Shuyan Dong, Xin He, Han Wang, Chengwei Su, Yue Liu, Yang Liu
Amazon Alexa
{tonwng, cjiangni, malmim, shuyand, xih, wnghn, chengwes, lyu, yangliud}@amazon.com

Abstract

In dialog systems, the Natural Language Understanding (NLU) component typically makes the interpretation decision (including domain, intent and slots) for an utterance before the mentioned entities are resolved. This may result in intent classification and slot tagging errors. In this work, we propose to leverage Entity Resolution (ER) features in NLU reranking and introduce a novel loss term based on ER signals to better learn model weights in the reranking framework. In addition, for a multi-domain dialog scenario, we propose a score distribution matching method to ensure scores generated by the NLU reranking models for different domains are properly calibrated. In offline experiments, we demonstrate our proposed approach significantly outperforms the baseline model on both single-domain and cross-domain evaluations.

1 Introduction

In spoken dialog systems, natural language understanding (NLU) typically includes domain classification (DC), intent classification (IC), and named entity recognition (NER) models. After NER extracts entity mentions, an Entity Resolution (ER) component is used to resolve the ambiguous entities. For example, NLU interprets an utterance to Alexa (or Siri) "play hello by adele" as in the 'Music' domain, 'play music' intent, and labels "hello" as a song name, "adele" as an artist name. ER queries are then formulated based on such a hypothesis to retrieve entities in music catalogs. Often times NLU can generate a list of hypotheses for DC, IC, and NER, and then a reranking model uses various confidence scores to rerank these candidates (Su et al., 2018).

Since ER is performed after NLU models, the current NLU interpretation of the utterance is limited to the raw text rather than its underlying entities. Even in NLU reranking (Su et al., 2018), only DC, IC, and NER confidence scores were used, and as a result, the top hypothesis picked by NLU reranking might not be the best interpretation of the utterance. For example, in the absence of entity information, "the beatles" in the utterance "play with the beatles" is interpreted as an artist name. If the reranker could search the ER catalog, it would promote the hypothesis that has "with the beatles" as an album name. Such NLU errors may propagate to ER and downstream components and potentially lead to end-customer friction.

In this work, we thus propose to incorporate ER features in the NLU reranking model, called NLU-ER reranking. For a domain, we use its corresponding catalogs to extract entity related features for NLU reranking for this domain. To enhance ER feature learning, we add a novel loss term when an NER hypothesis cannot be found in the catalog. One additional challenge arises in the multi-domain systems. In large-scale NLU systems, one design approach is to modularize the system as per the concept of domains (such as Music, Video, Smart Home), and each domain has its own NLU (DC, IC, NER) and reranking models that are trained independently. Under this scheme, each domain's NLU reranking plays an important role in both in-domain and cross-domain reranking, since it not only ranks hypotheses within a domain to promote the correct hypothesis, but also produces ranking scores that need to be comparable across all different domains. In (Su et al., 2018), the scores for the hypotheses from different domains are calibrated through training on the same utterance data with similar models . However, we may only use NLU-ER reranking for some domains (due to reasons such as lack of entity catalog, different production launch schedule, etc.), and the scores from such rerankers may no longer be comparable with other domains using the original reranker model. To mitigate this issue, we introduce a score distribution matching method to adjust the score distributions.

*The first two authors have equal contribution

Proceedings of NAACL HLT 2021: IndustryTrack Papers, pages 19–25
June 6–11, 2021. ©2021 Association for Computational Linguistics

We evaluate our NLU-ER reranking model on multiple data sets, including synthetic and real dialog data, and for both single domain and cross-domain setups. Our results show improved NLU performance compared to the baseline, and the improvement is contributed to our proposed ER features, loss term, and score matching method.

2 Related Work

Early reranking approaches in NLU systems use a single reranker for all the domains. Robichaud et al. (Robichaud et al., 2014) proposed a system for multi-domain hypothesis ranking (HR) that uses LambdaMART algorithm (Burges et al., 2007) to train a ranking system. The features in the ranking system include confidence scores for intents and slots, relevant database hits and contextual features that embed relationship to previous utterances. The authors showed improved accuracy in top domains using both non-contextual and contextual features. Crook et al. adapted a similar reranking scheme for multi-language hypothesis ranking (Crook et al., 2015). The set of features in the reranker include binary presence variables, for example presence of an intent, coverage of tagged entities and contextual features. They adapted the LambdaMART algorithm to train a Gradient Boosted Decision Trees model (Friedman, 2001) for cross language hypothesis ranking, and demonstrated comparable performance of the cross language reranker to the language-specific reranker. These models did not explicitly use ER signals for reranking. In addition, reranking is done across domains. Such single reranker approach is not practical in NLU systems with a large set of independent domains. In contrast, our approach emphasizes domain independence, allowing reranking to be performed for each domain independently. Furthermore, we rely on ER signal as a means to improve reranking.

To the best of our knowledge, the most related work to ours is Su et al. (Su et al., 2018), which proposed a re-ranking scheme to maximize the accuracy of the top hypothesis while maintaining the independence of different domains through implicit calibration. Each domain has its NLU reranker, and the scores for the hypotheses from reranking are compared across all the domains to pick the best hypothesis. The feature vector for each reranker is composed of intent, domain and slot tagging scores from the corresponding domain. Additionally, a cross entropy loss term is used to ensure calibration across domains. In a series of experiments, they demonstrated improvement of semantic understanding. Our work is an extension of that work as we utilize ER signals, in addition to the DC, IC, and NER scores, and introduce a new loss term to improve the reranking accuracy.

To resolve the score non-comparable problem in a multi-domain system, traditional calibration methods utilize Platt Scaling or Isotonic Regression to calibrate the prediction distribution into a uniform distribution (Zadrozny and Elkan, 2001, 2002; Platt et al., 1999; Niculescu-Mizil and Caruana, 2005; Wilks, 1990). However, this does not work in our scenario since the data in different domains are imbalanced, which causes domains with big traffic to have lower confidence scores. Instead of using probability calibration methods, we propose a solution based on power transformation to match the prediction score distribution back to the original score distribution, thus making the scores comparable even after ER information is added to NLU reranking.

3 Reranking Model

The baseline NLU reranking model is implemented as a linear function that predicts the ranking score from DC, IC, and NER confidence scores. We augment its feature vector using ER signals and introduce a novel loss term that penalizes the hypotheses that do not have a matched entity in the catalog. Similar to (Su et al., 2018), we tested using a neural network model for reranking, but observed no improvements, therefore we focus on the linear model.

3.1 ER Features in Reranking

The features used in the baseline NLU reranker include scores for DC (d), IC (i), NER (n) hypotheses, and ASR scores that are obtained from upstream components and used for all the domains. The additional ER features used in NLU-ER reranker are extracted and computed from the ER system, and can be designed differently for individual domains. For example, in this work, for the Music domain, ER features we use are aggregated from NER slot types such as: *SongName, ArtistName*, and the ER features are defined as:

ER success e_{s_i}: if a hypothesis contains a slot s_i that is successfully matched by any of the ER catalogs, this feature is set to 1, otherwise 0. ER success feature serves as a positive signal to promote the corresponding hypothesis score.

ER no match m_{s_i}: if a slot s_i in a hypothesis does not have any matched entities in the ER catalogs, this feature value is 1, otherwise 0. ER no match feature serves as a negative signal to penalize the hypothesis score. We find 'ER no match' is a stronger signal than 'ER success' because over 90% of the time, ER no match implies the corresponding hypothesis does not agree with the ground truth.

Similarity feature l_{s_i}: this feature is nonzero only if the ER success feature e_{s_i} is 1. In each catalog, a lexical or semantic similarity score between the slot value and every resolved entity is computed, and the maximum score among them is selected as the feature value. This indicates the confidence of the ER success signal.

Not in Gazetteer: this feature is set to 1 when ER features are not in the gazetteer (neither ER success nor no match), otherwise 0. We will discuss the gazetteer in the next section.

3.2 ER Gazetteer Selection

Since NLU and reranking happen before ER, in runtime retrieving ER features from large catalogs for NLU reranking is not trivial. Therefore we propose to cache the ER signals offline and make it accessible in NLU reranking in the form of a gazetteer. To make the best use of the allocated amount of runtime memory, we design a gazetteer selection algorithm to include the most relevant and effective ER features in the gazetteer.

We define Frequent Utterance Database (FUD) as the live traffic data where the same utterance has been spoken by more than 10 unique customers. To formalize the selection procedure, we define outperforming and underperforming utterances by friction (e.g., request cannot be handled) rate fr and 30s playback queue (playback $\geq$ 30s) rate qr. For all FUD utterances in a given period, an utterance u is defined as outperforming if $fr(u) \leq \mu_{fr} - \lambda_1 * \sigma_{fr}$ and $qr(u) \geq \mu_{qr} + \lambda_2 * \sigma_{qr}$, where μ and σ are the mean and standard deviation, λ_1 and λ_2 are hyperparameters. Underperforming utterances are defined likewise.

The detailed gazetteer selection algorithm is described in Algorithm 1. u_{h_1}, ..., u_{h_n} denote n-best NLU hypotheses of the utterance u. The idea is to encourage the successful hypotheses and avoid the friction hypotheses based on the historical data. For instance, if u is an underperforming utterance and u_{h_1} is *ER_NO_MATCH*, we want to penalize u_{h_1} to down-rank it, and promote other hypotheses u_{h_i} ($i \neq 1$) that receive the *ER_SUCCESS* signal. For the utterance hypotheses that are not selected in the gazetteer, we will use the Not_in_gazetteer (NG) feature.

Algorithm 1: Gazetteer Data Selection

```
Obtain outperforming and underperforming
  utterances from FUD;
for u ∈ outperforming utterances do
    if u_h1 is ER_SUCCESS then
        select ER features in u_h1 to the
          gazetteer;
    end
end
for u ∈ underperforming utterances do
    if u_h1 is ER_NO_MATCH then
        select ER features in u_h1 to the
          gazetteer;
    end
    if u_hi is ER_SUCCESS, and h_i ≠ h_1
      then
        select ER features in u_hi to the
          gazetteer;
    end
end
```

3.3 NLU-ER Reranker

For an utterance, the hypothesis score y is defined as the following:

$$y = W_G G + \sum_{s_i \in S} \mathbb{1}_{slot=s_i}(W_{s_i} ER_{s_i}) + \mathbb{1}_{NG} w_d \quad (1)$$

The first part in (1) is the baseline NLU reranker model:

$$y = W_G G \quad (2)$$

where $G = [g_1, g_2, \ldots, g_p]^T$ is the NLU general feature vector, $W_G = [w_1, w_2, \ldots, w_p]$ is the corresponding weight vector. The rest of the features are ER related. $\mathbb{1}$ is the indicator function. S is the set of all slot types, $ER_{s_i} = [er_1, er_2, \ldots, er_q]^T$ is the ER feature vector and $W_{s_i} = [w_{s_i 1}, w_{s_i 2}, \ldots, w_{s_i p}]$ is the corresponding weight vector. If an utterance in Music only contains SongName slot s_1, then $y = W_G G + W_{s_1} ER_{s_1}$, the rest of the terms are all 0s. If an utterance does not have any ER features from all the defined slot types, $y = W_G G + w_d$. w_d serves as the default ER feature value to the reranker when no corresponding ER features are found in the gazetteer described above. Its value is also learned during the model training.

3.4 Loss Function

We use SemER (Semantic Error Rate) (Su et al., 2018) to evaluate NLU performance. For a hypothesis, SemER is defined as E/T, where E is the total number of substitution, insertion, deletion errors of the slots, T is the total number of slots.

One choice of the loss function is the combination of expected SemER loss and expected cross entropy loss (Su et al., 2018). The loss function L_u of an utterance is defined as:

$$L_u = k_1 S_u + k_2 C_u \tag{3}$$

where S_u is the expected SemER loss: $S_u = \sum_i^N p_i \times SemER_i$, and C_u is the expected cross entropy loss: $C_u = \sum_i^N p_i \times [-t_i \log r_i - (1 - t_i)\log(1 - r_i)]$, where $r_i = \frac{1}{1+e^{-y_i}}$, $p_i = \frac{e^{y_i}}{\sum_j^5 e^{y_j}}$, $t_i = (SemER_i == 0)$, N is the number of hypotheses in utterance u.

Since our analysis showed that *ER_NO_MATCH* is a stronger signal and we expect the top hypothesis to get ER hits, we add a penalty term N_u to the loss function to penalize the loss when the 1-best hypothesis gets *ER_NO_MATCH*.

Let $r_j = max_i(r_i)$ be the best score in the current training step, and j the index for the current best hypothesis. Then no match loss term is defined as:

$$N_u = -e_j \times \log(1 - r_j) \tag{4}$$

where $e_i = \frac{\#(slot_{er\_no\_match})}{\#(slot)}$. It is the ratio of the slots with *ER_NO_MATCH* to all the slots in the ith hypothesis, and if no slot gets *ER_NO_MATCH*, the loss term is zero. Then the overall loss function is updated as:

$$L_u = k_1 S_u + k_2 C_u + k_3 N_u \tag{5}$$

N_u will penalize more the hypothesis that has a high score but gets no ER hits. $k_{1,2,3}$ are the hyperparameters, L_u is the final loss term for NLU-ER Reranker.

In our experiments, we observed that the weights are higher for the ER no match feature, and the model with the new loss term had a better performance under in-domain setup, which is as expected. Also, giving higher weight to 'ER no match' decreases the confidence scores generated by a domain NLU-ER reranker, which can help with the cross domain calibration problem. We will discuss how to ensure comparable scores in the next section.

4 Score Distribution Matching

Before adding the ER features, the reranking scores are calibrated through training on the same utterance data with similar models. However, adding the ER features in NLU reranking for a single domain may lead to incomparable scores with other domains. Using the loss function in Eq (3), we have the following theorem:

Theorem 4.1. *Under the loss function in Eq* (3)*, assuming hypothesis 1 is the ground truth, and* $0 = SemER_1 < SemER_2 < SemER_3 < SemER_4 < SemER_5$*, with a uniform score assumption* $\sum_j^5 e^{y_j} = c$*; Eq* (1) *will obtain a higher positive label hypothesis score and a lower negative label score than Eq* (2).

Proof. For the expected SemER loss S_u, since it is the linear combination of $SemER_i$, the solution of the minimization problem will be: $p_1 \to 1, p_2 = p_3 = p_4 = p_5 \to 0$. This leads to:$y_1 \to \infty, y_2 = y_3 = y_4 = y_5 \to -\infty$. Then for the expected cross entropy loss C_u, let $x_i = e^{y_i}$, the minimization of C_u becomes:

$$\min -x_1 \log \frac{x_1}{1+x_1} - \sum_{j \neq 1} x_j \log \frac{1}{1+x_j} = \min -I_1 - I_2.$$

The first part (I_1) is monotonically increasing, while the second part (I_2) is monotonically decreasing when $x_j > 0$. This also leads to: $y_1 \to \infty, y_2 = y_3 = y_4 = y_5 \to -\infty$. Thus, solving the minimization problem $minL_u$ is equivalent to solving the linear system:

$$\begin{cases} F_+\vec{w} = y\mathbf{1}_+ \\ F_-\vec{w} = -y\mathbf{1}_- \end{cases} \tag{6}$$

when $y \to \infty$ associated with the given loss in Eq (3), where F_+ is the feature matrix for the positive labels, F_- is the feature vector for the negative labels, $\vec{w}$ is the weight vector we need to solve, and $\mathbf{1}_+, \mathbf{1}_-$ are the unit vectors with the same dimension as the number of positive samples and negative samples respectively.

We can rewrite Eq (6) into: $F\vec{w} = \vec{y}$, and its solution will be the projection associated with the loss in Eq (3) of $\vec{y}$ onto the solution space spanned by the column vectors of matrix F. Now define this projection as $P_F(\vec{y})$. For the feature matrix of the NLU model in Eq (2), we have $F_N = G$, and for the feature matrix of NLU-ER model in Eq (1) we have $F_{ER} = [G, ER_{s_1}, ER_{s_2}, \ldots, ER_{s_q}, \mathbb{1}_{default}]$. Since F_N is the submatrix of F_{ER}, we have $spanF_N \subset spanF_{ER}$, thus:

$$P_{F_N}(\vec{y}) \leq P_{F_{ER}}(\vec{y})$$

□

In Theorem 4.1, we show that the candidate hypothesis from a more complicated model will be more likely to have a higher score than the domains using the original reranker model. Thus the domains using the NLU-ER reranker are no longer comparable to the domains using the original model. We observed this scenario in our experiments empirically. When we only experiment with Music domain, it will generate higher confidence scores and have more false positives.

To solve this problem, since we would like the confidence scores for each domain to have stabilized variance and minimized skewness, we propose to use power transformation, which is able to map data from any distribution to an approximately standard Gaussian distribution. In our case, the confidence scores from Eq (1) might be zero or negative, thus we consider the Yeo-Johnson transformation with $\lambda \neq 0$ and $\lambda \neq 2$:

$$x_i^{(\lambda)} = \begin{cases} [(x_i+1)^\lambda - 1]/\lambda & \text{if } x_i \geq 0, \\ \frac{-[(-x_i+1)^{2-\lambda}-1]}{2-\lambda} & \text{if } x_i < 0, \end{cases} \quad (7)$$

We have the inverse function:

$$x_i^{(\lambda)} = \begin{cases} (\lambda x_i + 1)^{\frac{1}{\lambda}} - 1 & \text{if } x_i \geq 0, \\ 1 - [1 - (2-\lambda)x_i]^{\frac{1}{2-\lambda}} & \text{if } x_i < 0, \end{cases} \quad (8)$$

where parameter λ is determined through maximum likelihood estimation. The idea is to first map both the NLU reranker model scores and the NLU-ER reranker scores to a standard Gaussian distribution and obtain λ_{NLU} and λ_{NLU-ER}. Then to calculate a new score from the NLU-ER reranker, we first use Eq (7) to transform the score into a standard Gaussian score with $\lambda = \lambda_{NLU-ER}$, followed by Eq (8) to transform the standard Gaussian score back into the original NLU reranker scores with $\lambda = \lambda_{NLU}$. Notice that when $\lambda > 0$, both Eq (7) and (8) are monotonic functions, thus the mapping method can only change the score distribution while maintaining the in-domain ranking order.

5 Experiment

5.1 Experimental Setup

We use the following data sets for training and evaluation:

Annotation Data (AD): It contains around 1 million annotated utterances from internal traffic. Training and testing split is 50:50. For testing, we further evaluate two different conditions: (i) 'AD All' using utterances from all domains for cross-domain evaluation. (ii) 'AD Music', 'AD Video', 'AD LS' using utterances from the Music domain, Video Domain and Local Search domain, respectively, for in-domain evaluation.

Synthetic Data (SD): These are synthetically generated ambiguous utterances used for in-domain evaluation. For Music and Video domains, utterances are in the form of "play X". Slot type of X could be ArtistName, SongName, AlbumName, VideoName, etc. X is an actual entity sampled from the corresponding ER song, video, artist, or album catalogs, and it is not in the training data, such that the model cannot infer the slot by simply "memorizing" it from the training data. We only report SongName (10K data) results in Music domain, and VideoName results in Video domain, due to the space limitation. For Local Search domain, utterances are in the form of "give me the direction to X", slot type of X could be PlaceName, DestinationName, etc. Note this data set is more ambiguous than the above one from real traffic in that "X" has multiple interpretations, whereas in real traffic users often add other words to help disambiguate, for example 'play music ...'.

We initialize the general feature weights to the same weights used in the baseline model. ER feature weights are set to smaller values (3 times less than the general feature weights). We find the expected SemER loss is less effective, so we set k_1 = 0.01, k_2 = 0.9, k_3 = 0.1. Besides, we use Adam optimizer (Kingma and Ba, 2014) with a learning rate of 0.0001 and train the model for 10 epochs.

5.2 Results

Table 1 presents the NLU-ER reranker results for cross-domain (AD All) and in-domain (AD Music, SD) settings. All the results are the SemER metric relative improvements compared to the baseline reranker. We have DC, IC, NER scores as the general NLU features. NLU-ER reranker uses additional ER features: ER success, no match, and lexical similarity of different slot types, and the

Table 1: NLU-ER reranking results on different data sets. The reported numbers show relative improvements compared with the baseline model using SemER evaluation metric. Baseline: NLU reranker with general features; ER: NLU-ER reranker with gazetteer selection; +N: with loss term for No Match feature; +R: with regression score matching; +P: with power transformation score matching. All the results in the table are statistically significant with p-value < 0.01.

	ER	ER+N	ER+N+R	ER+N+P
AD All	-0.22%	+0.19%	+0.26%	+0.32%
AD Music	+0.87%	+0.99%	+0.99%	+0.99%
AD Video	+0.95%	+1.01%	+1.01%	+1.01%
AD LS	+0.08%	+0.09%	+0.09%	+0.09%
SD Music	+20.74%	+28.58%	+28.58%	+28.58%
SD Video	+14.21%	+18.69%	+18.69%	+18.69%
SD LS	+12.53%	+17.37%	+17.37%	+17.37%

gazetteer selection algorithm is applied to retrieve the ER features. For the in-domain results, NLU-ER reranker has statistically significant improvement on both AD and SD. The improvement is more substantial on SD data, over 20%, which indicates ER features are more helpful when the utterances have ambiguity. Note there is some degradation in cross domain results on AD All when NLU-ER is used, due to the non-comparable score issue. After adding the loss term for ER no match feature, we observed additional improvements on both the in-domain and cross-domain settings.

As discussed earlier, because the scores from the baseline model are already well calibrated across domains, we use Yeo-Johnson transformation to match the domain score distribution back into the baseline score distribution. For Music domain, we use maximum likelihood estimation to get $\lambda_{NLU} = 1.088$ and $\lambda_{NLUER} = 1.104$. With these two estimations, we map NLU-ER reranker scores back to obtain a score in the baseline reranker score distribution. Using this updated score, we can see the cross-domain SemER score is improved by 0.32% relatively. Among the improved cases, we found that the number of False Positive utterances is decreased by 7.37% relatively. For comparison, we also trained a univariate neural network regression model to predict the original reranker score given the NLU-ER reranker score. Although this method also yields improvements, we can see that power transformation has a better performance and is also easy to implement. Note again that the in-domain performance remains the same since these score mapping approaches do not affect the in-domain ranking order. We perform the same experiments for Video domain and Local Search domain as well, and have the similar observations.

To illustrate the effectiveness of our proposed NLU-ER reranker and analyze the reasons for performance improvement, we compare the generated 1-best hypothesis from the baseline model with our new reranker. For utterance "play hot chocolate by polar express", the correct type for "polar express" is album. The baseline model predicts "polar express" as an artist because it is not in the training set, and "Song by Artist" appears more frequently than "Song by Album". However, our model successfully selected this hypothesis ("polar express" is an album), since *ER_SUCCESS* signal is found from the ER album catalog but *ER_NO_MATCH* is found from ER artist catalog. Similarly, in another example "play a sixteen z" where "a sixteen z" is ambiguous and not in the training set, the baseline model predicts it as a song since utterances with SongName slot have higher frequency in the training data, whereas our model can correctly select ProgramName as the 1-best hypothesis using ER signals.

6 Conclusion

In this work, we proposed a framework to incorporate ER information in NLU reranking. We developed a new feature vector for the domain reranker by utilizing entity resolution features such as hits or no hits. To provide the ER features to the NLU reranker, we proposed an offline solution that distills the ER signals into a gazetteer. We also introduced a novel loss term based on ER signals to discourage the domain reranker from promoting hypotheses with ER no match and showed that it leads to better model performance. Finally, since domain rerankers predict the ranking scores independently, we introduced a score matching method to transform the NLU-ER model score distribution to make the final scores comparable across domains. Our experiments demonstrated that the Music domain reranker performance is significantly improved when ER information is incorporated in the feature vector. Also with score calibration, we achieve moderate gain for the cross-domain scenario.

7 Acknowledgement

We acknowledge Kyle Saggar, Grace Deng, Ian Gardiner, Mark Cusick, Justin Flammia, Apoorva

Balevalachilu, Huitian Lei, Tan Xiao, Tian Zhu, Prajit Reddy Muppidi, Priya Khokher, Adi Gollapudi, Bo Xiao for their contributions to this effort.

References

Christopher J. Burges, Robert Ragno, and Quoc V. Le. 2007. Learning to rank with nonsmooth cost functions. In B. Schölkopf, J. C. Platt, and T. Hoffman, editors, *Advances in Neural Information Processing Systems 19*, pages 193–200. MIT Press.

Paul A Crook, Jean-Philippe Robichaud, and Ruhi Sarikaya. 2015. Multi-language hypotheses ranking and domain tracking for open domain dialogue systems. In *Sixteenth Annual Conference of the International Speech Communication Association*.

Jerome H Friedman. 2001. Greedy function approximation: a gradient boosting machine. *Annals of statistics*, pages 1189–1232.

Diederik P Kingma and Jimmy Ba. 2014. Adam: A method for stochastic optimization. *arXiv preprint arXiv:1412.6980*.

Alexandru Niculescu-Mizil and Rich Caruana. 2005. Predicting good probabilities with supervised learning. In *Proceedings of the 22nd international conference on Machine learning*, pages 625–632.

John Platt et al. 1999. Probabilistic outputs for support vector machines and comparisons to regularized likelihood methods. *Advances in large margin classifiers*, 10(3):61–74.

Jean-Philippe Robichaud, Paul A Crook, Puyang Xu, Omar Zia Khan, and Ruhi Sarikaya. 2014. Hypotheses ranking for robust domain classification and tracking in dialogue systems. In *Fifteenth Annual Conference of the International Speech Communication Association*.

Chengwei Su, Rahul Gupta, Shankar Ananthakrishnan, and Spyros Matsoukas. 2018. A re-ranker scheme for integrating large scale nlu models. In *2018 IEEE Spoken Language Technology Workshop (SLT)*, pages 670–676. IEEE.

Daniel S Wilks. 1990. On the combination of forecast probabilities for consecutive precipitation periods. *Weather and forecasting*, 5(4):640–650.

Bianca Zadrozny and Charles Elkan. 2001. Obtaining calibrated probability estimates from decision trees and naive bayesian classifiers. In *Icml*, volume 1, pages 609–616. Citeseer.

Bianca Zadrozny and Charles Elkan. 2002. Transforming classifier scores into accurate multiclass probability estimates. In *Proceedings of the eighth ACM SIGKDD international conference on Knowledge discovery and data mining*, pages 694–699.

Entity Resolution in Open-domain Conversations

Mingyue Shang*, Tong Wang*, Mihail Eric, Jiangning Chen, Jiyang Wang
Matthew Welch, Tiantong Deng, Akshay Grewal, Han Wang, Yue Liu
Imre Kiss, Yang Liu, Dilek Hakkani-Tur
Amazon Alexa
{myshang, tonwng, mihaeric, cjiangni, welcmtt, jiyangw, gracdeng, aksgrewa, wnghn, lyu, ikiss, yangliud, hakkanit}@amazon.com

Abstract

In recent years, incorporating external knowledge for response generation in open-domain conversation systems has attracted great interest. To improve the relevance of retrieved knowledge, we propose a neural entity linking (NEL) approach. Different from formal documents such as news, conversational utterances are informal and multi-turn, which makes it more challenging to disambiguate the entities. Therefore, we present a context-aware named entity recognition model (NER) and entity resolution (ER) model to utilize dialogue context information. We conduct NEL experiments on three open-domain conversation datasets and validate that incorporating context information improves the performance of NER and ER models. Furthermore, we verify that using knowledge sentences identified based on NEL benefits the neural response generation model.

1 Introduction

Building an informative open-domain conversational agent that can naturally interact with humans has been one of recent scientific research topics. Inspired by the development of neural networks, neural generation based conversation systems have made great progress (Sutskever et al., 2014; Vinyals and Le, 2015; Li et al., 2017; Wolf et al., 2019a; Zhou et al., 2020). However, one issue in such approaches is that the neural models often produce universal and less informative responses (Huang et al., 2020). To address this issue, previous work proposed to incorporate external information into the response generation models, such as topics (Xing et al., 2017) and emotions (Zhou et al., 2018a). One line of research investigates the use of external knowledge to enrich the information of the responses (Ghazvininejad et al., 2018; Young et al., 2018; Dinan et al., 2018; Gopalakrishnan et al., 2019; Meng et al., 2020).

*The first two authors have equal contribution

Most existing studies retrieve relevant knowledge from a knowledge base using the entities and noun phrases in the input text. Thus, correctly identifying these entities is crucial to find the relevant knowledge for a given dialog context. This typically involves two subtasks: given a user utterance, the system first identifies any named entities it contains (NER task) and then performs entity resolution (ER) to disambiguate the mentioned entities using a knowledge base. Both NER and ER (or NEL) have been well explored in previous studies and demonstrated to perform highly for news or well written text. However, for open domain spoken conversations and human-bot dialog, performance suffers due to ASR errors, incomplete or ungrammatical sentences from users, difference of spoken and written style, and less training data for such tasks.

In this paper, we propose to use neural entity linking (NEL) technologies that leverage both utterance-level and dialog-level context to retrieve relevant knowledge. As shown in the example in Figure 1, dialogues often contain multiple turns and information is dispersed throughout each turn. Thus, a single turn of interaction may be insufficient for entity disambiguation. Therefore, we leverage previous utterances in the dialogue as the context information and propose context-aware models to better solve the NER and ER tasks in open-domain conversation systems. When recognizing and disambiguating entities in a given utterance, we encode dialog context, and adopt the attention mechanism to extract the information related to the current utterance. To verify the effectiveness of context-aware models, in addition to the intrinsic evaluations, i.e., NER and ER standalone performance, we conduct an extrinsic evaluation where NER and ER results are integrated in a knowledge grounded neural response generation model in an open domain conversation system and response quality is evaluated. Our major contributions can

Proceedings of NAACL HLT 2021: IndustryTrack Papers, pages 26–33
June 6–11, 2021. ©2021 Association for Computational Linguistics

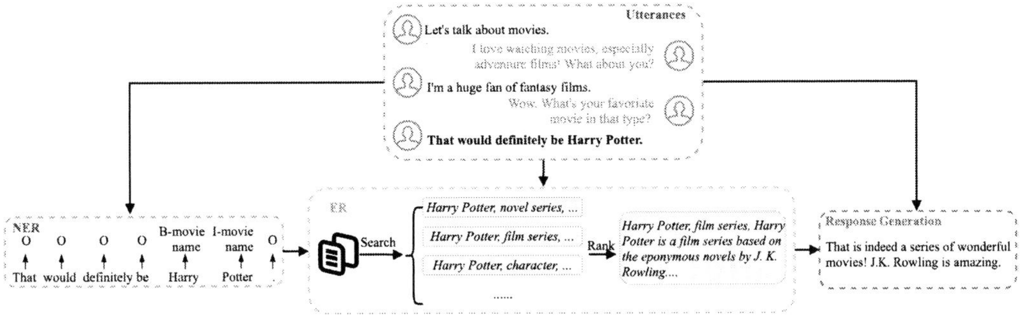

Figure 1: An example dialog illustrating the pipeline of NER, ER, and response generation. The bold sentence in the utterances is the current utterance and the previous utterances are the context. The current utterance and its context are fed to the NER module to identify the entity mentions. Then the ER module takes the entity mentions and all the sentences as input to resolve the entity. The response generation module produces an output based on the knowledge entity information and the dialog input.

be summarized as follows:

- We propose neural network based context-aware models for NER and ER respectively in open domain conversations.
- Experimental results on different conversation datasets show that our proposed context-aware NER and ER models outperform other state-of-the-art models that do not use context information.
- In an end2end evaluation, we demonstrate that incorporating ER information improves quality of neural response generation models in open domain conversations.

2 Related Work

2.1 Open-domain Conversation System

Inspired by the availability of conversational data and the prosperity of neural networks, building open-domain conversation systems by data-driven approaches has achieved great progress. Previous methods can be roughly divided into two categories, retrieval-based (Zhang et al., 2018; Wu et al., 2019; Tao et al., 2019) and generation-based (Vinyals and Le, 2015; Li et al., 2017; Asghar et al., 2018; Tao et al., 2018). Chen et al. (2017) point out that conventional sequence-to-sequence methods tend to generate trivial responses that lack information and diversity. To address this issue, a line of research proposes to incorporate external knowledge into the generation process. Most of the work in this line retrieves knowledge based on a search or retrieval step first, and followed by further reranking of retrieved relevant knowledge snippets (Ghazvininejad et al., 2018; Young et al., 2018; Zhou et al., 2018b; Gopalakrishnan et al., 2019; Zhao et al., 2020). In our work, we propose neural entity recognition and linking to identify and resolve entities more accurately in order to obtain more relevant knowledge for knowledge grounded response generation.

2.2 Neural Entity Linking

NEL typically involves two tasks: recognizing named entities in a given text and then disamgibuating the entity mentions according to the knowledge base (KB). Researchers have shown great success in NER with the help of Convolutional Neural Networks (CNNs), Bidirectional Recurrent Neural Networks (Bi-RNNs), and attention mechanisms along with a CRF decoder (Chiu and Nichols, 2016; Akbik et al., 2018; Ghaddar and Langlais, 2018; Jiang et al., 2019; Baevski et al., 2019; Yamada et al., 2020). Deep neural networks (DNNs) are also dominant in entity resolution tasks. They are used to calculate the semantic similarity between the recognized entity mentions and the entities in the KB (Yamada et al., 2016; Ganea and Hofmann, 2017; Sil et al., 2018; Raiman and Raiman, 2018). However, previous NEL work has mainly focused on news or formal documents, which is different from open-domain dialogues in many aspects. Sentences in open-domain dialogues are more informal, making it more difficult to recognize and disambiguate entities. In addition, since conversations are multi-turn, the semantic information in the current utterance is ambiguous and context needs to be considered. In this paper, we investigate NEL in open-domain conversational data and propose context-aware NER and ER models.

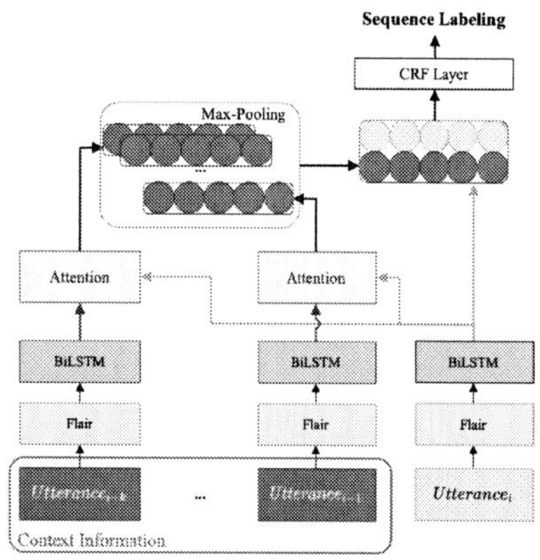

Figure 2: Context-aware NER model: information from previous k utterances is used while performing NER on utterance i.

3 Methodology

3.1 Problem Formulation

Our problem can be formulated as follows. Given an open-domain dialogue until a time point $D = c_i, x_i$, where x_i is the current utterance, we define the utterance context $c_i = \{u_1, \ldots, u_k\}$ as the list of utterances prior to x_i, and k is the size of the context. For each x_i given c_i, an NER model is applied to detect entity mentions in the form of BIO labels.[1] Then for each predicted entity mention, y_j, a query is formulated to search a knowledge base to get a list of candidate entities, $\{e_1, \ldots, e_m\}$, where m is the size of the returned entities from the search. An ER model is then used to rank the entities and identify the most relevant entity, e_t. Finally, a response, r_i, is generated based on c_i, x_i, and knowledge sentences obtained from the linked entities e_t. Note a knowledge ranking algorithm is applied when there are multiple knowledge sentences corresponding to e_t or there are multiple entity mentions in x_i. Figure 1 overviews the pipeline of generating responses with NER and ER modules.

3.2 Context-Aware Named Entity Recognition Model

Figure 2 gives the overall architecture of the context-aware NER model. Following the framework presented by Chiu and Nichols (2016), we employ a bi-directional, long short-term memory (Bi-LSTM) model to extract word features and a conditional random field (CRF) to predict the NER labels.

[1]These labels are widely used for NER and indicate a token is *Begin*, *Inside*, or *Outside* an entity mention, respectively.

Suppose we have an utterance $x_i = \{w_1^i, \ldots, w_T^i\}$, where T is the length of x_i and w_t is the t-th token. After converting each token in x_i to its vector representation through a word embedding table[2], the Bi-LSTM layer encodes the sentence into hidden states h_t^i, which are the concatenation of $\overrightarrow{h}_t^i$ from the forward LSTM and $\overleftarrow{h}_t^i$ from the backward LSTM. The CRF layer then takes the hidden states as input to predict the label probability.

As discussed earlier, as opposed to news or documents, recognizing and disambiguating the named entities in conversational utterances requires consideration of the context information. Therefore, we employ another Bi-LSTM layer to encode the context utterances from the previous turns,

$$s_t^j = [\overrightarrow{s}_t^j; \overleftarrow{s}_t^j] \tag{1}$$

where $\overrightarrow{s}_t^j$ is the forward hidden state of the t-th token in the context utterance u_j and $\overleftarrow{s}_t^j$ is the backward hidden state.

We use an attention mechanism to model the different impact of the previous utterances in the context:

$$\text{Attention} = \text{softmax}\left(\frac{QK^T}{\sqrt{d_k}}\right) V \tag{2}$$

where Q, K, V refer to the query, key, and value, respectively. Here, the key and value are the context sentences, and the query is the current utterance. To aggregate the context information, a max-pooling operation is performed on the dimension of sentences. Then, the context vector is concatenated with the sentence vector, and then is supplied as the input of the CRF layer.

3.3 Context-aware Entity Resolution Model

Our entity resolution model contains two steps: coarse-grained candidate selection and fine-grained candidate ranking.

Candidate selection At this stage we retrieve relevant entities from the KB. We create an Elasticsearch (Gormley and Tong, 2015) index with the entity labels and apply both an exact and a Levenshtein distance based fuzzy match to obtain candidate entities. For each entity mention, we take the top 10 search results, ranked by Elasticsearch, as the candidates for the subsequent reranking step.

[2]Here we adopt the stacked embedding released by Flair (Akbik et al., 2018).

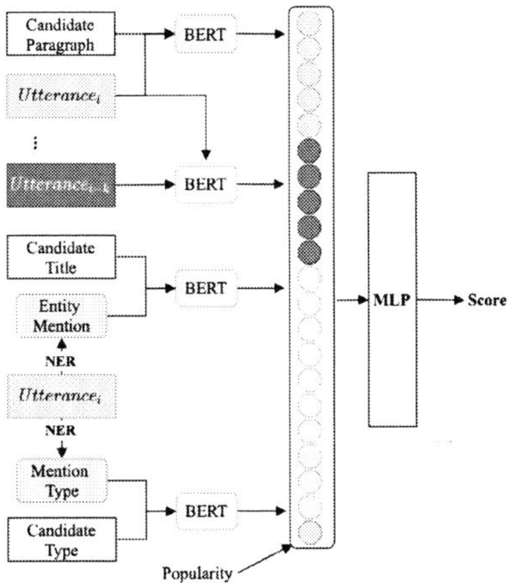

Figure 3: Context-aware ER reranking.

Reranking At this stage the candidate entities are re-ranked based on the match scores from our context-aware model. We propose to compute the relevance score from the entity, utterance and session levels. The structure of the multi-level reranking model is shown in Figure 3.

Entity-Level Matching: This considers the candidate entity's label and type attributes, and matches with the entity mention and the predicted type, respectively.

Utterance-Level Matching: This measures the matching degree between the candidate entity's description and the current utterance based on sentence-level semantic information.

Session-Level Matching: This treats the context and current utterance as a conversation session, and computes its match score with the candidate entity's description.

For each matching level, we first concatenate the representations from the entity candidate in the KB and the dialog side, and then employ BERT (Devlin et al., 2018) to get their representations. v_{label}, v_{type}, $v_{utterance}$, $v_{session}$ represent the output of BERT corresponding to the mention label and type (entity-level), utterance-level, and session-level, respectively. We also define the popularity of an entity based on the number of views in the last 60 days, represented as v_p. All these features are concatenated and then fed into an MLP layer to predict the ranking score:

$$\begin{aligned} v &= [v_{label}; v_{type}; v_{utterance}; v_{session}; v_p] \\ s &= \text{MLP}(v) \end{aligned} \tag{3}$$

To train this model, we minimize the pair-wise hinge-loss, defined as:

$$l_r = max(0, \sigma + s^- - s^+) \tag{4}$$

where s^+ is the ranking score of the ground-truth entity and s^- is the ranking score of a negative entity sampled from candidates other than the ground-truth. σ is a constant margin and is set to 0.5.

3.4 Response Generation Model

Given the linked entities, we employ a transformer-based response generation model that is trained to leverage the context of a dialogue along with the knowledge relevant at a given turn. More specifically, we first fine-tune a GPT2-medium model using the Wizard of Wikipedia (WOW) dataset (Dinan et al., 2018). WOW is a suitable dataset for fine-tuning as it involves knowledge-grounded conversations dealing with Wikipedia articles, a data source we are using for entity linking in this work.

The GPT2 generation model is fine-tuned in a matter consistent with (Wolf et al., 2019b; Gopalakrishnan et al., 2020). During generation, we are provided a dialogue context, $C = \{c_1, c_2, ..., c_{i-1}\}$ containing utterances before c_i. We use our linked entities to query the relevant Wikipedia articles, and use the first paragraph of the returned articles, giving us a collection of knowledge sentences, $K = \{k_1, k_2, ..., k_n\}$.

Next, we truncate each knowledge sentence with more than 64 tokens and provide a concatenated input consisting of the dialogue context and the knowledge sentences. We then sample from the language model, one token at a time, using nucleus sampling to form our generated system response.

4 Experiment Setup

4.1 Datasets

We rely on Wikipedia and Wiki data[3] to build the knowledge base for this task. We built a Knowledge Graph (KG) containing over 6M entities including attributes such as Wiki ID, title, type, and introduction. To perform NEL on conversational data, we collect a **M**ulti-turn **O**pen-domain **C**onversation Dataset (MOC) and ask crowd worker annotators to first annotate NER labels (entity mention and type), and then give ER labels – the ground truth Wikidata ID. Different from the entity labels in regular NER tasks, we define 50 entity types across 8 popular domains in open-domain conversations

[3]https://www.wikidata.org/wiki/,https://www.wikipedia.org/

including Fashion, Politics, Books, Sports, Music, Science/Technology, Game, Video/Movies. In addition, we created a synthetic dataset that contains ambiguous entities that can only be understood through dialog context. For example, in the utterance "I like Harry Potter", the model needs to understand the context of the utterance to figure out if the user is referring to the movie or the book. We also randomly selected some conversations from Wizard of Wikipedia (WoW), which is a collection of open-domain dialogues grounded on Wikipedia knowledge (Dinan et al., 2018). The statistics of the datasets we used are shown in Table 1.

Dataset	Train	Validation	Test
MOC	5,962	662	1,111
Synthetic	8,150	905	2,896
WoW	1,948	216	540

Table 1: Number of utterances of the open-domain conversation data sets used in this study.

4.2 Model Setup

All models are implemented in Pytorch (Paszke et al., 2017). For the NER model, we initialize the word embedding with stacked embeddings, including Flair embeddings (Akbik et al., 2018) and FastText embeddings (Bojanowski et al., 2017). The sizes of the word embeddings and hidden state are 300 and 256, respectively. We adopt the SGD optimizer with an initial learning rate of 0.1 and decay rate of 0.5. The batch size is set to 16 and the maximum training epoch is set to 15 with an early stopping strategy. For the ER model, we use Adam as the optimizer and set the learning rate to 0.0005. The hidden size is 762 and the batch size is 8. The maximum sentence length in all the experiments is set to 128.

5 Results and Analysis

5.1 NER Results

The performance of the NER models is evaluated using precision, recall and F-1. We consider both the span of an entity and its type. Table 2 shows the results of NER models on three datasets. To compare with our context-aware NER model, we use Flair as the baseline, which is a state-of-the-art NER model on benchmarks in several domains (Akbik et al., 2018). It shows that our context-aware model achieves the best performance on most metrics. In particular, we observe the largest gain of our model using contextual information on the synthetic dataset. This is because that data was created to contain more ambiguous entities and thus requires dialog context to determine entity types.

Model	Dataset	P	R	F-1
Flair	MOC	-	-	-
Flair w/ context		- 0.1	2.7	1.2
Flair	Synthetic	-	-	-
Flair w/ context		16.0	17.7	16.9
Flair	WoW	-	-	-
Flair w/ context		0.7	1.8	1.2

Table 2: Results of NER models (relative gains compared to Flair in %).

5.2 ER Results

For the ER task, we evaluate the recall@n values (n = 1, 3, 5), which measures the ranking ability of the models. We compare our model with the following two baselines:

Search. After performing entity retrieval through Elasticsearch, we rank the candidate entities based on their popularity, i.e., the number of views in last 60 days.

Ranking. Similar to our method, here we only use entity and utterance-level matching scores, without dialog context in the ranking model.

Table 3 shows the ER results when ground-truth NER is provided as input. We can see that a ranking model can significantly improve the top entity relevance over the search baseline on all the three datasets. Compared to the non-context ranking model, our proposed context-aware model could further improve the results, especially for R@1.

Model	Dataset	R@1	R@3	R@5
Search		-	-	-
Rank	MOC	64.5	29.4	2.8
Rank w/ context		**65.0**	**29.7**	**2.9**
Search		-	-	-
Rank	Synthetic	82.9	**22.2**	9.4
Rank w/ context		**91.0**	21.9	**10.0**
Search		-	-	-
Rank	WoW	82.1	28.8	**11.2**
Rank w/ context		**89.1**	**29.2**	**11.2**

Table 3: Results of ER models (relative gains compared to baseline search in %) using ground-truth NER information.

5.3 End-to-end NEL Results

In Section 5.2, the input of the ER task is the ground-truth NER results. In the practical scenario, the input is the prediction of the NER models.

Context	Utterance	Model	NER	ER	Entity Description
In the 1968 three of the genre most famous acts Led Zeppelin, Black Sabbath	I love led Zeppelin! they have really influenced many bands.	w/o context Search	led Zeppelin, person	led Zeppelin, band	English rock band
		w/o context Rank	led Zeppelin, person	Jason Bonham, human	English hard rock drummer (born 1966)
		w/ context Rank	led Zeppelin, person	led Zeppelin, band	English rock band
		Groundtruth	led Zeppelin, person	led Zeppelin, band	English rock band
Well, So what gaming platform do you prefer console or computer?	Uh I don't know what a Nintendo WII is	w/o context Search	Nintendo, device	Nintendo Switch, hybrid video game console	hybrid video game console developed by Nintendo
		w/o context Rank	Nintendo, device	Nintendo, business	Japanese multinational video game and consumer electronics company
		w/ context Rank	Nintendo WII, device	Wii, home video game console	seventh-generation home video game console by Nintendo
		Groundtruth	Nintendo WII, device	Wii, home video game console	seventh-generation home video game console by Nintendo

Table 4: Examples of NEL in open-domain conversations.

Therefore, we also evaluate the performance of end-to-end NEL, where the predictions of NER models are used for ER. For performance metrics, we compare the predicted entity with the ground-truth one, and compute precision, recall and F-1. The results are shown in Table 5. Here we observe again that a ranking model can significantly improve results, and the context model yields further gain.

NER	ER	Dataset	P	R	F-1
Flair	Search	MOC	-	-	-
Flair	Rank		62.1	59.7	60.6
w/ context	w/ context		**62.9**	**63.4**	**62.8**
Flair	Search	Synthetic	-	-	-
Flair	Rank		68.2	68.9	68.4
w/ context	w/ context		**71.0**	**71.0**	**71.0**
Flair	Search	WoW	-	-	-
Flair	Rank		62.0	62.0	62.1
w/ context	w/ context		**75.4**	**72.8**	**73.9**

Table 5: End-to-end experimental results (relative gains in % compared to the end-to-end model of Flair NER and baseline ER search).

5.4 Case Study

Table 4 shows NER and ER results for two example utterances along with their context. We can see when there is an ambiguity in the current utterance, our context-aware model can use context information to correctly recognize the entities and link them to the right entities in KB. In the first example, the named entity is correctly recognized by all the models, however, the model without context failed in the ER task because of insufficient information. In the second case, models without using context information recognize a wrong entity and then link it to a seemingly reasonable but not the most appropriate entity.

5.5 Response Generation Results

We generate outputs for 100 distinct conversational contexts in the WoW data set using using configurations: Baseline GPT2 and GPT2 with NEL. Here, we provide crowd-worker annotators the conversational context along with the generated response, without the associated knowledge extracted through linking. We then ask the workers to evaluate according to two metrics, appropriateness and informativeness, on an ordinal scale from 0-2.

Our results show that in the generated responses, GPT2 with NEL module is superior over baseline GPT2 on both the appropriateness and informativeness metrics, suggesting that our solution can better understand conversation context and is able to generate informative and appropriate responses.

Model	Appropr.	Inform.
GPT2	-	-
GPT2 w/ NEL	25.5	53.8

Table 6: Human evaluation of generated responses. (%, relative gains compared to GPT2)

6 Conclusion

In this paper, we investigate NEL in multi-turn open-domain conversations. Considering the characteristic of dialogs, where the meaning of the current utterance often varies depending on the context, we design a context-aware NER model and an ER model. Experimental results on three datasets prove that using context information improves the entity recognition and resolution performance. Extrinsic evaluation on response generation also validates the effectiveness of the entity information.

References

Alan Akbik, Duncan Blythe, and Roland Vollgraf. 2018. Contextual string embeddings for sequence labeling. In *COLING 2018, 27th International Conference on Computational Linguistics*, pages 1638–1649.

Nabiha Asghar, Pascal Poupart, Jesse Hoey, Xin Jiang, and Lili Mou. 2018. Affective neural response generation. In *European Conference on Information Retrieval*, pages 154–166. Springer.

Alexei Baevski, Sergey Edunov, Yinhan Liu, Luke Zettlemoyer, and Michael Auli. 2019. Cloze-driven pretraining of self-attention networks. *arXiv preprint arXiv:1903.07785*.

Piotr Bojanowski, Edouard Grave, Armand Joulin, and Tomas Mikolov. 2017. Enriching word vectors with subword information. *Transactions of the Association for Computational Linguistics*, 5:135–146.

Hongshen Chen, Xiaorui Liu, Dawei Yin, and Jiliang Tang. 2017. A survey on dialogue systems: Recent advances and new frontiers. *Acm Sigkdd Explorations Newsletter*, 19(2):25–35.

Jason PC Chiu and Eric Nichols. 2016. Named entity recognition with bidirectional lstm-cnns. *Transactions of the Association for Computational Linguistics*, 4:357–370.

Jacob Devlin, Ming-Wei Chang, Kenton Lee, and Kristina Toutanova. 2018. Bert: Pre-training of deep bidirectional transformers for language understanding. *arXiv preprint arXiv:1810.04805*.

Emily Dinan, Stephen Roller, Kurt Shuster, Angela Fan, Michael Auli, and Jason Weston. 2018. Wizard of wikipedia: Knowledge-powered conversational agents. *arXiv preprint arXiv:1811.01241*.

Octavian-Eugen Ganea and Thomas Hofmann. 2017. Deep joint entity disambiguation with local neural attention. *arXiv preprint arXiv:1704.04920*.

Abbas Ghaddar and Philippe Langlais. 2018. Robust lexical features for improved neural network named-entity recognition. *arXiv preprint arXiv:1806.03489*.

Marjan Ghazvininejad, Chris Brockett, Ming-Wei Chang, Bill Dolan, Jianfeng Gao, Wen-tau Yih, and Michel Galley. 2018. A knowledge-grounded neural conversation model. In *Proceedings of the AAAI Conference on Artificial Intelligence*, volume 32.

Karthik Gopalakrishnan, Behnam Hedayatnia, Qinlang Chen, Anna Gottardi, Sanjeev Kwatra, Anu Venkatesh, Raefer Gabriel, and Dilek Hakkani-Tür. 2019. Topical-Chat: Towards Knowledge-Grounded Open-Domain Conversations. In *Proc. Interspeech 2019*, pages 1891–1895.

Karthik Gopalakrishnan, Behnam Hedayatnia, Longshaokan Wang, Yang Liu, and Dilek Hakkani-Tür. 2020. Are Neural Open-Domain Dialog Systems Robust to Speech Recognition Errors in the Dialog History? An Empirical Study. In *INTERSPEECH*.

Clinton Gormley and Zachary Tong. 2015. *Elasticsearch: the definitive guide: a distributed real-time search and analytics engine.* " O'Reilly Media, Inc.".

Minlie Huang, Xiaoyan Zhu, and Jianfeng Gao. 2020. Challenges in building intelligent open-domain dialog systems. *ACM Transactions on Information Systems (TOIS)*, 38(3):1–32.

Yufan Jiang, Chi Hu, Tong Xiao, Chunliang Zhang, and Jingbo Zhu. 2019. Improved differentiable architecture search for language modeling and named entity recognition. In *Proceedings of the 2019 Conference on Empirical Methods in Natural Language Processing and the 9th International Joint Conference on Natural Language Processing (EMNLP-IJCNLP)*, pages 3576–3581.

Jiwei Li, Will Monroe, Tianlin Shi, Sébastien Jean, Alan Ritter, and Dan Jurafsky. 2017. Adversarial learning for neural dialogue generation. *arXiv preprint arXiv:1701.06547*.

Chuan Meng, Pengjie Ren, Zhumin Chen, Christof Monz, Jun Ma, and Maarten de Rijke. 2020. Refnet: A reference-aware network for background based conversation. In *Proceedings of the AAAI Conference on Artificial Intelligence*, volume 34, pages 8496–8503.

Adam Paszke, Sam Gross, Soumith Chintala, Gregory Chanan, Edward Yang, Zachary DeVito, Zeming Lin, Alban Desmaison, Luca Antiga, and Adam Lerer. 2017. Automatic differentiation in pytorch.

Jonathan Raiman and Olivier Raiman. 2018. Deeptype: multilingual entity linking by neural type system evolution. In *Proceedings of the AAAI Conference on Artificial Intelligence*, volume 32.

Avirup Sil, Gourab Kundu, Radu Florian, and Wael Hamza. 2018. Neural cross-lingual entity linking. In *Proceedings of the AAAI Conference on Artificial Intelligence*, volume 32.

Ilya Sutskever, Oriol Vinyals, and Quoc V Le. 2014. Sequence to sequence learning with neural networks. *Advances in neural information processing systems*, 27:3104–3112.

Chongyang Tao, Shen Gao, Mingyue Shang, Wei Wu, Dongyan Zhao, and Rui Yan. 2018. Get the point of my utterance! learning towards effective responses with multi-head attention mechanism. In *IJCAI*, pages 4418–4424.

Chongyang Tao, Wei Wu, Can Xu, Wenpeng Hu, Dongyan Zhao, and Rui Yan. 2019. One time of interaction may not be enough: Go deep with an interaction-over-interaction network for response selection in dialogues. In *Proceedings of the 57th Annual Meeting of the Association for Computational Linguistics*, pages 1–11.

Oriol Vinyals and Quoc Le. 2015. A neural conversational model. *arXiv preprint arXiv:1506.05869*.

Thomas Wolf, Victor Sanh, Julien Chaumond, and Clement Delangue. 2019a. Transfertransfo: A transfer learning approach for neural network based conversational agents. *arXiv preprint arXiv:1901.08149*.

Thomas Wolf, Victor Sanh, Julien Chaumond, and Clement Delangue. 2019b. Transfertransfo: A transfer learning approach for neural network based conversational agents. *ArXiv*, abs/1901.08149.

Yu Wu, Wei Wu, Chen Xing, Can Xu, Zhoujun Li, and Ming Zhou. 2019. A sequential matching framework for multi-turn response selection in retrieval-based chatbots. *Computational Linguistics*, 45(1):163–197.

Chen Xing, Wei Wu, Yu Wu, Jie Liu, Yalou Huang, Ming Zhou, and Wei-Ying Ma. 2017. Topic aware neural response generation. In *Proceedings of the AAAI Conference on Artificial Intelligence*, volume 31.

Ikuya Yamada, Akari Asai, Hiroyuki Shindo, Hideaki Takeda, and Yuji Matsumoto. 2020. Luke: deep contextualized entity representations with entity-aware self-attention. *arXiv preprint arXiv:2010.01057*.

Ikuya Yamada, Hiroyuki Shindo, Hideaki Takeda, and Yoshiyasu Takefuji. 2016. Joint learning of the embedding of words and entities for named entity disambiguation. *arXiv preprint arXiv:1601.01343*.

Tom Young, Erik Cambria, Iti Chaturvedi, Hao Zhou, Subham Biswas, and Minlie Huang. 2018. Augmenting end-to-end dialogue systems with commonsense knowledge. In *Proceedings of the AAAI Conference on Artificial Intelligence*, volume 32.

Zhuosheng Zhang, Jiangtong Li, Pengfei Zhu, Hai Zhao, and Gongshen Liu. 2018. Modeling multi-turn conversation with deep utterance aggregation. *arXiv preprint arXiv:1806.09102*.

Xueliang Zhao, Wei Wu, Can Xu, Chongyang Tao, Dongyan Zhao, and Rui Yan. 2020. Knowledge-grounded dialogue generation with pre-trained language models. *arXiv preprint arXiv:2010.08824*.

Hao Zhou, Minlie Huang, Tianyang Zhang, Xiaoyan Zhu, and Bing Liu. 2018a. Emotional chatting machine: Emotional conversation generation with internal and external memory. In *Proceedings of the AAAI Conference on Artificial Intelligence*, volume 32.

Hao Zhou, Tom Young, Minlie Huang, Haizhou Zhao, Jingfang Xu, and Xiaoyan Zhu. 2018b. Commonsense knowledge aware conversation generation with graph attention. In *IJCAI*, pages 4623–4629.

Li Zhou, Jianfeng Gao, Di Li, and Heung-Yeung Shum. 2020. The design and implementation of xiaoice, an empathetic social chatbot. *Computational Linguistics*, 46(1):53–93.

Pretrain-Finetune Based Training of Task-Oriented Dialogue Systems in a Real-World Setting

Manisha Srivastava
Amazon Inc.
Seattle, USA
mansri@amazon

Yichao Lu
Amazon Inc.
Seattle, USA
yichaolu@amazon

Riley Peschon
Amazon Inc.
Seattle, USA
peschon@amazon

Chenyang Li
Amazon Inc.
Seattle, USA
cli@amazon

Abstract

One main challenge in building task-oriented dialogue systems is the limited amount of supervised training data available. In this work, we present a method for training retrieval-based dialogue systems using a small amount of high-quality, annotated data and a larger, unlabeled dataset. We show that pretraining using unlabeled data can bring better model performance with a 31% boost in Recall@1 compared with no pretraining. The proposed finetuning technique based on a small amount of high-quality, annotated data resulted in 26% offline and 33% online performance improvement in Recall@1 over the pretrained model. The model is deployed in an agent-support application and evaluated on live customer service contacts, providing additional insights into the real-world implications compared with most other publications in the domain often using asynchronous transcripts (e.g. Reddit data). The high performance of 74% Recall@1 shown in the customer service example demonstrates the effectiveness of this pretrain-finetune approach in dealing with the limited supervised data challenge.

1 Introduction

Retrieval-based dialogue systems are popular in task-oriented domains. A typical retrieval-based system encodes the dialogue context and a large set of candidate responses (templates) in a joint semantic space, and then scores how appropriate each candidate is given the dialogue context; the template with the highest score is selected as the response. These systems can use a sequence-to-sequence model (Kannan et al., 2016) or a dual-encoder style architecture (Lu et al., 2017; Lowe et al., 2015) to encode and score the context-response pair.

One major challenge for any task-oriented dialogue system is the scarcity of training data. High-quality data with all the required annotations are needed to train an accurate model. Such datasets are not readily available, and collecting them is a costly and labor-intensive process. A few synthetic datasets (Weston et al., 2015; Asri et al., 2017; Budzianowski et al., 2018) have been proposed but they do not capture the real-world variations and subtleties of the task-oriented dialogues. The limited amount of supervised training data available makes it difficult to train these models from scratch.

To overcome the issue of limited training data, the idea of finetuning a pretrained model has become a popular approach in other domains like computer vision and is recently gaining popularity in the natural language processing (NLP) domain. Pretrained models in NLP such as ELMo (Peters et al., 2018), OpenAI GPT (Radford et al., 2018), and BERT (Devlin et al., 2018) have attracted a lot of attention and achieved state-of-the-art accuracy in multiple natural language understanding tasks. In this paper, we present a methodology for training retrieval-based dialogue systems using a small amount of supervised data and a large, low-quality, unannotated dataset.

1. We demonstrate that finetuning a model (Lu et al., 2019) pretrained using the unannotated dataset performs better than directly finetuning on the clean, annotated data.
2. We experiment with different finetuning loss functions and show that a ranking based loss function performs better than classification loss for template-retrieval based dialogue systems.
3. We deploy the finetuned model in an agent assistance application for customer service, and present real-world results on live customer contacts.

In the sections that follow, we describe the data from the customer service domain that is used for pretraining and finetuning the model in section 2. In section 3, we explain how we pretrain the model

Proceedings of NAACL HLT 2021: IndustryTrack Papers, pages 34–40
June 6–11, 2021.

Raw text:
Customer: I want to cancel the shoes I ordered yesterday.
Agent: Welcome to Customer Service.
Agent: I am here to help you.
Agent: Give me a moment to look into this.

Training Sample:
Context: **CUSTOMERSTART** I want to cancel the shoes I ordered yesterday. **AGENTSTART** Welcome to Customer Service. **AGENTSTART** I am here to help you. **PROFILESTART** cancellable, carrier, membership-status. **Response**: Give me a moment to look into this.
Label: Positive

Figure 1: Training sample creation process. Given a chat transcript and profile features, a training sample is created by appending the dialogue turns and profile features. True agent response is used to create positive samples and random agent responses are used to create negative samples.

using the next-turn prediction task along with the results. Next, we present the proposed finetuning strategy, and the associated experimental setup and the results. In section 5, we present the real-world results of the deployed model. Section 6 describes the conclusion and direction for future work.

2 Data

In this work, we use data from the customer service domain —customer service chats handled in English. When customers contact customer service regarding their issue (e.g., order tracking, payment questions), the routing system connects the customer to an agent based on the specific issue type. Agents resolving customer issues have access to a wide variety of profile information (e.g. customer details, order status, and internal APIs) to execute actions such as canceling or refunding an order. For our experiments, we select a delivery-related customer issue. In the following subsection, we explain how we collect the pretraining and finetuning data.

2.1 Pretraining Data

The pretraining data include historical customer service chat transcripts for a delivery-related issue. It is important to note these transcripts only contain the dialogue turns. Contextual information (e.g. customer profile, order details, actions executed by the agents) is either missing or inaccurate. The pretraining dataset consists of a few hundred thousand chats (see Table 1). The conversation in these chat transcripts can exhibit high variability, despite following the same customer issue, due to policy changes, unconstrained conversations like side talks, and agent locale variability.

Table 1: Training data statistics.

DATASETS	PRETRAIN TRAINING	PRETRAIN TEST	FINETUNE TRAINING	FINETUNE TEST
NUMBER OF CHATS	382,688	2000	6366	400
NUMBER OF AGENTS TURNS	8045059	4498	65908	3188

Figure 1 shows part of a chat transcript and how it is processed to create the training data. Each agent turn in the transcript is converted into a training sample. To create the dialogue context, previous turns in the conversation history, prior to the current agent turn, are prepended by a special token to indicate whether it is an agent or customer turn. A separate token is used to distinguish profile features (e.g. customer's profile, order details) from the dialogue turns. As explained in section 3, pretraining is done using next sentence prediction task and so it requires positive and negative context response pairs. To create the pretraining dataset, true agent responses create a positive pair, while random agent responses create negative pairs. We also use the incomplete and noisy profile information that is available without any human annotation. We call this **pretrain training dataset**.

2.2 Finetuning Data

The large pretraining dataset is not collected in a standardized manner. As a result, said dataset is noisy —there are inconsistencies in chat dialogues and profile information (e.g. order details, customer profile, and actions) is missing and inaccurate. The finetuning dataset, in contrast, is collected in a controlled manner using specialist agents to ensure accurate and complete annotations.

The finetuning data consists of a few thousand chats for the selected delivery issue, collected over a period of 2 months, handled by a group of 20 specialist agents. These chats have all relevant annotations (customer profile and order details) for each dialogue turn. Agents are instructed to choose the response from a template pool as much as possible, free-typing only if the response does not exist in the template pool. The pool consists of 85 template responses. These responses are extracted from historical chat transcripts and cover the most common delivery-related use cases. The specialist agents are trained to handle contacts in a constrained and consistent manner without sacrificing the customer experience. For example, they are trained to drive

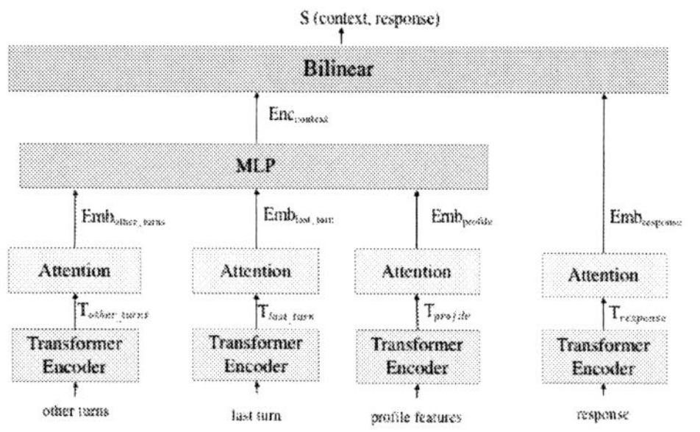

Figure 2: Pretraining model architecture. Separate transformer encoders are used to encode the dialogue history (last turn, other turns), profile features, and response. The encoded dialogue turns and profile are passed through MLP to get the encoded context. The encoded response and context are passed through bilinear layer to get the final score of the pair.

the conversation towards the solution and avoid side conversations. To ensure consistency, we instituted general rules to the agents on how and when to greet, apologize, make policy exceptions, provide reassurance, etc. The agent training ensured customers are not adversely affected in the process of this constrained data collection.

The collected chats are processed in the same way as shown in Figure 1 and explained in the last section. The dataset, referred to as **finetune training dataset**, is generated in the same way as pretraining data with one caveat: for each conversation context, negative samples are generated using templates scored high by the pretrained model, as opposed to random sampling unrelated agent responses. The number of negative samples is selected using cross-validation.

2.3 Evaluation Data

We have two evaluation datasets – **pretrain test** and **finetune test**. To create the pretrain test dataset, we use historical chat transcripts from a period that does not overlap with the pretrain training dataset. Each test sample includes conversation context (previous turns and extracted profile features) and random responses (including the true agent's response). During evaluation, the trained model is used to rank the responses for each dialogue context. Similarly, to create the finetune test dataset, we use the dataset collected from the specialized agents. For each dialogue context, we store the template response selected by the agent as positive and all other template responses as negative.

Table 1 shows the statistics for each of the pretrain and finetune datasets. During the evaluation, the model ranks all responses for a given dialogue context. We use Recall@1 as our evaluation metric, which measures how many times the correct response was ranked at the top by the model. We also report MRR (mean reciprocal rank), which is the harmonic mean of the rank of the correct response.

3 Pretraining

In this section, we introduce the next sentence prediction based pretraining used to pretrain the model.

3.1 Model

Our binarized next sentence prediction pretraining is effectively a classification task, classifying a pair of conversation context and agent response as positive (appropriate) or negative (not appropriate). The input to the pretraining model is the context (C) response (R) pair where the conversation context includes dialogue turns (last turn, other turns) and profile features. The pretraining model is similar to (Lu et al., 2019) as the response ranking model uses multiple transformer-based (Vaswani et al., 2017) encoders to encode different parts of the context and the response.

The context is encoded using three transformer encoders (Figure 2) that separately encode the profile features, last-turn, and all other turns in the context; see equation 1, 2, 3. Dot Product Attention (Luong et al., 2015) is applied to the transformer outputs. The transformer outputs are the key and value, while separate query vectors are learned for each output. Each query vector is randomly initialized and trained like other model parameters. The encoded last turn, profile features, and other turns are passed through a Multi-Layer Perceptron to get the encoded context (Enc_C). The response encoding (Emb_R) is also obtained using equation 2 and 3.

$$\begin{aligned} Enc_C =& MLP(Emb_{other\_turns} \\ &|Emb_{last\_turn}|Emb_{profile}) \end{aligned} \tag{1}$$

$$Emb_x = Attention(T_x, q_x) \tag{2}$$

$$T_x = Transformer(emb_x) \tag{3}$$

where | is the concatenation, emb_x is a vector of size $e \times n$: e is the embedding dimension, n is the number of words; T_x is a vector of size $h \times n$: h is

Table 2: We present MRR and Recall@1 of the finetuned models on the finetune test dataset. The baseline 'No pretraining'is a model without any pretraining, 'Pretrained mode'is pretrained on pretrain training dataset.

MODELS	MRR (%)	RECALL@1(%)
NO PRETRAINING($M_{baseline}$)	32.8	23.2
PRETRAINED MODEL(M_{tuned})	60.6	54.6

the hidden size; q_x is a query vector of dimension h which is initialized randomly and trained along with other parameters. Emb_x and Enc_C are both vectors of dimension h. Enc_C and Emb_R are then passed through a bilinear layer that outputs a probability score grading how appropriate the candidate response is given the context; see 4 and 5.

$$P[(y_t = +1)|(C, R)] = Sigmoid(S) \quad (4)$$

$$S = Enc_C \cdot Emb_R \quad (5)$$

where $y_t \in \{0, 1\}$ is the label of context response pair; $P[(y_t = +1)|(C, R)]$ is the probability that the context response pair is positive; $\cdot$ is the dot product operator. Since we treat this as a classification problem, we use binary cross-entropy loss for training.

3.2 Training Setup

We train the pretrained model (M) using the pretrain training dataset as described in Section 2. We use the transformer implementation provided by MXNet Gluon NLP [1]. We use 4 encoder layers, 4 heads in multi-head attention, hidden size of 512 and vocabulary size of 10K. The maximum sequence length of the context is 180 tokens, last turn is 35 tokens, profile feature is 6 tokens, and response is 35 tokens. We train the model using binary cross-entropy loss and stop when the validation MRR and Recall@1 start dropping.

We finetune the pretrained model on the finetune training dataset and evaluate it on the finetune test dataset. To finetune the model, we initialize the model M with the pretrained model parameters and run a few epochs on the finetune training dataset, stopping when the validation performance begins dropping. Let's call this finetuned model M_{tuned}. We also train a baseline model ($M_{baseline}$) that is another model like M but trained directly on the small finetune training dataset.

[1] https://gluon-nlp.mxnet.io/

3.3 Results

Table 2 shows the MRR and Recall@1 on the finetune test dataset. M_{tuned} demonstrates an average improvement of 31.4% on Recall@1 and 28% on MRR compared to $M_{baseline}$. These results show that pretraining on a large, unannotated dataset can give significant performance boost over a model with no pretraining.

4 Finetuning

Simple finetuning using the small finetune training dataset can lead to overfitting. In this section, we describe our finetuning approach, which incorporates regularization to avoid overfitting and the loss function that better caters to the task of template ranking.

4.1 Model

Due to the limited amount of finetune training data available, simple finetuning M can lead to overfitting —forgetting knowledge acquired during pretraining. As shown in Table 3, simple finetuning M on the finetune training dataset degrades the performance of the model on the pretrain test data significantly. In order to prevent the model from forgetting, both M and M_{tuned} should have similar performance on the pretrain test data.

4.1.1 Regularization

To prevent the forgetting issue, a fraction of the pretrain training dataset is mixed with every batch of the finetuning training dataset (He et al., 2019). During each gradient descent step of finetuning, one gradient step is taken on the finetune data batch, with another gradient step on the pretrain data batch.

4.1.2 Training loss

During pretraining, we use binary cross-entropy loss (L_{BCE}), classifying each context response pair as positive or negative. Given context response pairs and the corresponding labels, cross-entropy loss can be calculated as follows:

$$\begin{aligned} L_{BCE} = -\sum_{t=1}^{n} y_t * log(S(C, R)) \\ + (1 - y_t) * log(1 - S(C, R)) \end{aligned} \quad (6)$$

where $y_t \in 0, 1$ is the label of the context response pair (C, R); $S(C, R)$ is calculated using equation 5. L_{BCE} is limited by its inability to capture the relative score of the templates —essentially the

Table 3: The performance of model M finetuned on the finetune training dataset with and without regularization. We show that data-mix regularization is effective in maintaining the performance of the model on the pretrain test dataset.

DATASETS	PRETRAIN TEST DATASET		FINETUNE TEST DATASET	
	MRR(%)	RECALL@1(%)	MRR (%)	RECALL@1 (%)
M(NO FINETUNING)	80.3	76.9	41.3	32.8
M_{tuned} WITH NO REGULARIZATION	33.7	22.5	60.6	54.6
M_{tuned} USING DATA-MIXING REGULARIZATION	78.7	75.1	60.7	54.5

base logic for ranking of templates. This is critical for retrieval-based dialogue systems because, for each context, all templates receive a ranking and the top-ranked template from the pool is selected.

Hence, for finetuning, we chose a new loss function to incorporate relative scores of templates similar to (Henderson et al., 2017). We directly minimize the negative log probability of the true response given the context as shown below:

$$L_{ranking} = -log(P(R/C)) \propto \frac{e^{S(C,R)}}{\sum_{i=1}^{n} e^{S(C,R_i}} \tag{7}$$

where C is the context; R is the true agent response; $P(R|C)$ is the probability of the true response given the context; R_i is i^th response; n is all possible responses; $S(C,R)$ is the score of a pair of context and response calculated using equation 5. Instead of normalizing over all R_i, we sample 10 responses from the template pool (including the correct response). This new loss function better represents the ranking problem.

4.2 Experimental Setup

For finetuning the model, we initialize the model with the pretrained model parameters and finetune all layers using the finetune training dataset.

4.3 Results

In this section, we study the effect of regularization and the different loss functions on finetuning.

4.3.1 Regularization

The effect of regularization during finetuning is summarized in Table 3. We show the MRR and Recall@1 metrics on both the pretrain test and finetune test datasets. As a baseline, we don't finetune the model (M) at all, but directly evaluate the pretrained model on both the test datasets. From the results, we see that data-mix regularization maintains the performance of the model on the pretrain test dataset.

Table 4: The performance of the finetuned model on the finetune test dataset, the model trained using ranking loss outperforms the cross-entropy loss based finetuned model.

	MRR (%)	RECALL@1(%)
CROSS-ENTROPY LOSS	60.7	54.5
RANKING LOSS	63.9	58.3

4.3.2 Ranking Loss

Table 4 shows the result of changing the loss function from L_{BCE} to $L_{ranking}$. The result shows the effect of different loss functions on M finetuned using mix data regularization; the same effect is seen with other regularization strategies. Changing the loss function to $L_{ranking}$ improves the performance of the model by 3% on MRR and 4% on Recall@1 on the finetune test dataset.

5 Online Evaluation

5.1 Setup

We deployed the proposed model in a customer service agent-support application that agents use to resolve live customer contacts. The model is deployed as a service using Amazon Sagemaker [2]. The agent-support application calls the Sagemaker endpoint with the current context (previous dialogue turns and profile information), and the model returns the highest scored response from the template pool. The proposed model is able to recommend responses without any significant latency impact on the overall application.

The agent-support application presents the agents with the standard chat interface, except it replaces the text box with the top-suggested response from the model. Every time the customer or the agent enters text into their chat window, the model refreshes the response recommendations for the next agent utterance. The agents can accept or reject the model's response recommendation. If they reject the model's recommendation, they can type on their own. Since the model is deployed in a human-in-the-loop setup, we use it to evaluate the performance of the pretrained and finetuned

[2] https://docs.aws.amazon.com/sagemaker/

Table 5: The Recall@1 and % contacts resolved of pretrained and two finetuned models using cross-entropy and ranking loss respectively on live customers. M is the pretrained model; M_{tuned} is finetuned model.

	M	M_{tuned} WITH L_{BCE}	M_{tuned} WITH $L_{ranking}$
NUMBER OF CONTACTS	3094	3636	2212
RECALL@1 (%)	40.8	62.7	74.0
PERCENTAGE OF CONTACTS RESOLVED (%)	0.9	5.3	13.6

models on live customer contacts. We present the results of the model on delivery related issue.

5.2 Results

Table 5 shows the online results for the three models on live customer contacts: pretrained model (M) as explained in section 3, finetuned model (M_{BCE}) with BCE loss and data regularization; and finetuned model ($M_{ranking}$) with ranking loss and data regularization. For each model, we calculate Recall@1 as the fraction of total responses that were accepted by the agents. We also report the percentage of contacts resolved, which represents the percentage of contacts when the model's recommendations were accepted at every turn.

After finetuning using BCE, the Recall@1 of the model showed an absolute increase of 22% over the pretrained model. Finetuning using the ranking loss outperformed the pretrained model by 33%, and BCE finetuned model by 11%. For the ranking loss based finetuning, the percentage of contacts resolved completely using the model's recommendations went up by 13% compared to the pretrained model.

5.3 Error Analysis

To better understand the model's failure cases, we manually read 100 turns where the agents rejected the model's recommended response and typed on their own. For this study, we focus on the best model - finetuned using ranking loss and data regularization.

We found that 17% of the model's errors were caused because the conversation had gone off the common path. The model is not able to recommend the correct response in these cases because it has not seen these types of conversations during the training, leading to the template pool being unable to cover many of said cases. Examples of why conversations may go long or off-track include, but are not limited to, a customer being unhappy with the solution, experiencing multiple issues within the same chat, and/or participating in side conversations.

Another major reason for rejection was due to missing and/or incomplete context data available to the model. To contrast, this means agents had access to a richer profile information than what was available to the model. As a result, the model did not have the relevant context to recommend the right response. In 28% of the cases, there were extra profile features available to the agents, such as being able to check the carrier's website, that were not available to the model.

In dialogues, usually there is more than one correct response, giving room to agent's subjectivity in accepting/rejecting a model's response. We found that 15% of rejected turns occurred because the agent decided to reject the model's suggestion in favor of a stylistically different but semantically similar message. For example, some agents preferred closing the contact with 'Thank you for contacting 'while others preferred to directly say 'Take care and have a nice day '.

6 Conclusion and Future Work

In this paper, we study a less explored approach of finetuning a retrieval-based dialogue system based on a small amount of high-quality, annotated data that resulted in 26% offline and 33% online performance improvement in Recall@1 over a pretrained model.We deployed the model in an agent-support application, and demonstarte that the proposed model achieves 74% Recall@1, suggesting these models are effective in assisting agents by recommending text responses. The results demonstrate the effectiveness of pretrain-finetune approach in dealing with the limited supervised data challenge. In this paper, we focus on a customer service delivery issue, but since this technique can scale to other task-oriented dialog systems with a wide range of applications.

We believe that additional investment in contextual and profile features would help improve the model performance. As discussed in the error analysis section, 28% of the model's error is caused due to missing context information. In addition, manual study of the rejection reasons highlights the issue of subjective evaluation. More investment is needed in agent training and standardization of annotation. We believe the model can significantly benefit from better annotation and evaluation.

References

Layla El Asri, Hannes Schulz, Shikhar Sharma, Jeremie Zumer, Justin Harris, Emery Fine, Rahul Mehrotra, and Kaheer Suleman. 2017. Frames: A corpus for adding memory to goal-oriented dialogue systems. *arXiv preprint arXiv:1704.00057*.

Paweł Budzianowski, Tsung-Hsien Wen, Bo-Hsiang Tseng, Inigo Casanueva, Stefan Ultes, Osman Ramadan, and Milica Gašić. 2018. Multiwoz-a large-scale multi-domain wizard-of-oz dataset for task-oriented dialogue modelling. *arXiv preprint arXiv:1810.00278*.

Jacob Devlin, Ming-Wei Chang, Kenton Lee, and Kristina Toutanova. 2018. Bert: Pre-training of deep bidirectional transformers for language understanding. *arXiv preprint arXiv:1810.04805*.

Tianxing He, Jun Liu, Kyunghyun Cho, Myle Ott, Bing Liu, James Glass, and Fuchun Peng. 2019. Mix-review: Alleviate forgetting in the pretrain-finetune framework for neural language generation models. *arXiv preprint arXiv:1910.07117*.

Matthew Henderson, Rami Al-Rfou, Brian Strope, Yun-Hsuan Sung, László Lukács, Ruiqi Guo, Sanjiv Kumar, Balint Miklos, and Ray Kurzweil. 2017. Efficient natural language response suggestion for smart reply. *arXiv preprint arXiv:1705.00652*.

Anjuli Kannan, Karol Kurach, Sujith Ravi, Tobias Kaufmann, Andrew Tomkins, Balint Miklos, Greg Corrado, Laszlo Lukacs, Marina Ganea, Peter Young, et al. 2016. Smart reply: Automated response suggestion for email. In *Proceedings of the 22nd ACM SIGKDD International Conference on Knowledge Discovery and Data Mining*, pages 955–964.

Ryan Lowe, Nissan Pow, Iulian Serban, and Joelle Pineau. 2015. The ubuntu dialogue corpus: A large dataset for research in unstructured multi-turn dialogue systems. *arXiv preprint arXiv:1506.08909*.

Yichao Lu, Phillip Keung, Shaonan Zhang, Jason Sun, and Vikas Bhardwaj. 2017. A practical approach to dialogue response generation in closed domains. *arXiv preprint arXiv:1703.09439*.

Yichao Lu, Manisha Srivastava, Jared Kramer, Heba Elfardy, Andrea Kahn, Song Wang, and Vikas Bhardwaj. 2019. Goal-oriented end-to-end conversational models with profile features in a real-world setting. In *Proceedings of the 2019 Conference of the North American Chapter of the Association for Computational Linguistics: Human Language Technologies, Volume 2 (Industry Papers)*, pages 48–55.

Minh-Thang Luong, Hieu Pham, and Christopher D Manning. 2015. Effective approaches to attention-based neural machine translation. *arXiv preprint arXiv:1508.04025*.

Matthew E Peters, Mark Neumann, Mohit Iyyer, Matt Gardner, Christopher Clark, Kenton Lee, and Luke Zettlemoyer. 2018. Deep contextualized word representations. *arXiv preprint arXiv:1802.05365*.

Alec Radford, Karthik Narasimhan, Tim Salimans, and Ilya Sutskever. 2018. Improving language understanding by generative pre-training. *URL https://s3-us-west-2. amazonaws. com/openai-assets/researchcovers/languageunsupervised/language understanding paper. pdf*.

Ashish Vaswani, Noam Shazeer, Niki Parmar, Jakob Uszkoreit, Llion Jones, Aidan N Gomez, Łukasz Kaiser, and Illia Polosukhin. 2017. Attention is all you need. In *Advances in neural information processing systems*, pages 5998–6008.

Jason Weston, Antoine Bordes, Sumit Chopra, Alexander M Rush, Bart van Merriënboer, Armand Joulin, and Tomas Mikolov. 2015. Towards ai-complete question answering: A set of prerequisite toy tasks. *arXiv preprint arXiv:1502.05698*.

Contextual Domain Classification with Temporal Representations

Tzu-Hsiang Lin, **Yipeng Shi**, **Chentao Ye**, **Fan Yang**, **Weitong Ruan**, **Emre Barut**, **Wael Hamza**, and **Chengwei Su**

Amazon Alexa AI

{tzuhsial,syipeng,ychentao,fyaamz,weiton,ebarut,waelhamz,chengwes}@amazon.com

Abstract

In commercial dialogue systems, the Spoken Language Understanding (SLU) component tends to have numerous domains thus context is needed to help resolve ambiguities. Previous works that incorporate context for SLU have mostly focused on domains where context is limited to a few minutes. However, there are domains that have related context that could span up to hours and days. In this paper, we propose temporal representations that combine wall-clock second difference and turn order offset information to utilize both recent and distant context in a novel large-scale setup. Experiments on the Contextual Domain Classification (CDC) task with various encoder architectures show that temporal representations combining both information outperforms only one of the two. We further demonstrate that our contextual Transformer is able to reduce 13.04% of classification errors compared to a non-contextual baseline. We also conduct empirical analyses to study recent versus distant context and opportunities to lower deployment costs.

1 Introduction

Voice assistants such as Amazon Alexa, Apple Siri, Google Assistant and Microsoft Cortana provide a wide range of functionalities, including listening to music, inquiring about the weather, controlling home appliances and question answering. To understand user requests, the Spoken Language Understanding (SLU) component needs to first classify an utterance into a domain, followed by identifying the domain-specific intent and entities (Tur, 2011; Su et al., 2018a), where each domain is defined for a specific application such as music or weather. In commercial systems, the number of domains tend to be large, resulting in multiple possible domain interpretations for user requests (Kim et al., 2018; Li et al., 2019). For example, *"play american pie"* can be interpreted as either playing a song or a movie. Also, *"what does your light color mean?"* can be classified as *Question Answering*, or as a complaint which does not necessarily require a meaningful response.

Multiple prior works have attempted to incorporate context in SLU to help resolve such ambiguities. However, these works often report results on datasets with limited amount of training data (Bhargava et al., 2013; Xu and Sarikaya, 2014; Shi et al., 2015; Liu et al., 2015), or resort to synthesize contextual datasets (Gupta et al., 2018, 2019) that may not reflect natural human interaction. Furthermore, the majority of these works focus on domains where session context is recent and collected within a few minutes. Though this setup works well for domains that bias towards immediate preceding context such as *Communication* (Chen et al., 2016) and *Restaurant Booking* (Henderson et al., 2014; Bapna et al., 2017), there are also domains that have useful context spanning over hours or even up to days. In the *SmartHome* domain, it is natural for users to turn on T.V., watch for a couple of hours and then ask to turn it off. In the *Notifications* domain, users setup alarms or timers which occur hours and days away. We hypothesize that distant context, if properly utilized, can improve performance in instances where recent context cannot.

In this paper, we propose temporal representations to effectively leverage both recent and distant context on the Contextual Domain Classification (CDC) task. We introduce a novel setup that contains both recent and distant context by including previous 9 turns of context within a few days, so that context not just come from minutes but can also come from hours or days ago. We then propose temporal representations to indicate the closeness of each previous turn. The key idea of our approach is to combine both wall-clock second difference (Conway and Mathias, 2019) and turn order offset (Su et al., 2018b) so that a distant previous turn can still be considered as important.

Proceedings of NAACL HLT 2021: IndustryTrack Papers, pages 41–48
June 6–11, 2021.

We conduct experiments on a large-scale dataset with utterances spoken by users to a commercial voice assistant. Results with various encoder architectures show that combining both wall-clock second difference and turn order offset outperforms using only one of them. Our best result is achieved with Transformer of 13.04% error reduction, which is a 0.35% improvement over using only wall-clock second difference and 2.26% over using only turn order offset. To understand the role of context in CDC, we conduct multiple empirical analyses that reveal the improvements from context and discuss trade-offs between efficiency and accuracy.

To summarize, this paper makes the following contributions:

- A novel large-scale setup for CDC that showcases the usefulness of distant context, comparing to previous works whose datasets are limited to thousands and context within minutes.
- Temporal representations combining wall-clock second and turn-order offset information that can be extended and applied to other tasks.
- Empirical analyses that study context from 4 different aspects to guide future development of commercial SLU.

2 Related Work

2.1 Contextual SLU

Context in commercial voice assistants may belong to widely different domains, as users expect them to understand their requests in a single utterance, which is different from the conventional dialogue state tracking task (Williams et al., 2016). Earlier works seek better representations of context, such as using recurrent neural networks (Xu and Sarikaya, 2014; Liu et al., 2015), or memory networks to store past utterances, intents, and slot values (Chen et al., 2016). Recently, Gupta et al. (2019) proposes a self-attention architecture that fuses multiple signals including intents and dialog act with a variable context window. On other aspects of contextual SLU, Naik et al. (2018) proposes a scalable slot carry over paradigm where the model decides whether a previous slot value is referred in the current utterance. For rephrased user requests, Rastogi et al. (2019) formulates rephrasing as the Query Rewriting (QR) task and uses sequence-to-sequence pointer generator networks to perform both anaphora resolution and DST. In contrast, our work proposes temporal representations to utilize both recent and distant context for domain classification.

2.2 Temporal Information

Most previous works use recurrent neural networks to model natural turn order (Shi et al., 2015; Gupta et al., 2018). Assuming context follows a decaying relationship, Su et al. (2018b) presents several hand-crafted turn-decaying functions to help the model focus on the most recent context. Kim and Lee (2019) further expands upon this idea by learning latent turn-decaying functions with deep neural networks. On the other hand, wall-clock information has not been exploited until the recent *Time Mask* module proposed in Conway and Mathias (2019). From the lens of wall-clock, they show that context importance does not strictly follow a decaying relationship, but rather occurs in certain time spans. Our work combines both wall-clock and turn order information and models their relationship.

3 Methodology

In this section, we describe our model architecture in Section 3.1 and our proposed temporal representations in Section 3.2.

3.1 Model Architecture

Our model is depicted in Figure 1 and consists of 3 components: (1) utterance encoder, (2) context encoder, and (3) output network. We next describe each component in detail.

Utterance Encoder We use a bi-directional LSTM (Hochreiter and Schmidhuber, 1997) and pre-trained word embeddings to encode the current utterance into an utterance embedding. For pre-trained word embeddings, we use FastText (Bojanowski et al., 2017) concatenated with Elmo (Peters et al., 2018) trained on an internal SLU dataset.

Context Encoder Context encoder is a hierarchical model that consists of a turn encoder and a sequence encoder. For each previous turn, turn encoder encodes 3 types of features: (1) utterance text, (2) hypothesized domain, and (3) hypothesized domain-specific intent, which are also used in Naik et al. (2018). Utterance text is encoded using the same model architecture as in utterance

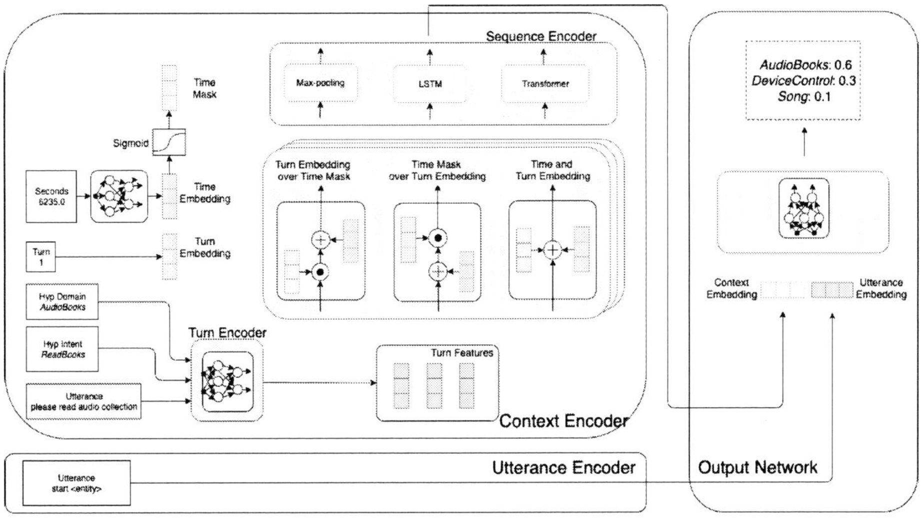

Figure 1: Overview of our model and proposed temporal representations.

encoder. Hypothesized domain and intent are first represented using one-hot encoding then projected into embeddings. We stack the 3 representations, perform max-pooling then feed into a 2 layer fully connected neural network to produce a turn representation. Temporal representations (Section 3.2) are then applied to indicate their closeness. Finally, sequence encoder encodes the sequence of temporal encoded turn representations into a single context embedding that is fed to the output network.

Output Network Output network concatenates utterance embedding and context embedding as input and feeds into a 2 layer fully-connected network to produce classification logits.

Response Time Considerations State-of-the-art contextual models encode the entire context and utterance to learn coarse and fine relationships with attention mechanisms (Gupta et al., 2019; Heck et al., 2020). Since commercial voice assistants need to provide immediate responses to users, encoding context and utterance is computationally expensive such that the system would not respond in-time at industrial-scale (Kleppmann, 2017). We separate context encoder from utterance encoder so that we can encode context when user is idle or when the voice assistant is responding. Moreover, the hierarchical design allows us to cache previously encoded turn representations to avoid re-computation.

3.2 Temporal Representations

In this section, we present the temporal representations used in our experiments. For the following, given previous turn t and its turn features $h^t(c)$ from turn encoder, we denote its wall-clock second difference and turn order offset as $d_{\Delta sec}$, $d_{\Delta turn}$. For operators, we denote $\odot$ and $\oplus$ as element-wise multiplication and summation.

Time Mask (TM) (Conway and Mathias, 2019) feeds $d_{\Delta sec}$ into a 2 layer network and sigmoid function to produce a masking vector $m_{\Delta sec}$ that is multiplied with the context feature h_c^T, and show that important features occur in certain time spans. The equations are given as follows.

$$e_{\Delta sec} = W_{s2} \cdot \phi(W_{s1} \cdot d_{\Delta sec} + b_{s1}) + b_{s2}, \tag{1}$$

$$m_{\Delta sec} = \sigma(e_{\Delta sec}), \tag{2}$$

$$h^t_{TM}(c) = m_{\Delta sec} \odot h^t(c), \tag{3}$$

Here $W_{s1}, W_{s2}, b_{s1}, b_{s2}$ are weight matrices and bias vectors, ϕ and σ are ReLU activation and sigmoid functions, and $h^t_{TM}(c)$ denotes the time masked features. We also considered binning second differences instead of working with $d_{\Delta sec}$. However, we find that binning significantly underperforms compared to the latter.

Turn Embedding (TE) We first represent $d_{\Delta turn}$ as a one-hot encoding then project it into a fixed-size embedding $e_{\Delta turn}$. We then sum the turn embedding with context features as in positional

Temporal Representations	Max-pooling	LSTM	Transformer
–	4.41	11.02	10.18
Time Mask	7.62	11.91	12.69
Turn Embedding	7.09	11.44	10.78
Turn Embedding over Time Mask	4.59	**12.51**	**13.04**
Time Mask over Turn Embedding	7.56	12.21	12.75
Time and Turn Embedding	**10.13**	11.31	11.79

Table 1: ARER % (↑) results computed against an utterance-only baseline with different temporal representations and sequence encoders. "–" indicates that no temporal representation is applied. Best results are boldfaced.

encoding in Transformer (Vaswani et al., 2017).

$$h^t_{TE}(c) = e_{\Delta turn} \oplus h^t(c), \quad (4)$$

It is natural and intuitive to assume that a closer context is more likely to correlate with the current user request. Assuming we are given user requests *"Where is Cambridge?"* and *"How is the weather there?"*. It is more likely that the user is inquiring about weather in Cambridge if the second request immediately follows the first, compared to the case where these two requests are hours or multiple turns apart. For a proper comprehension of closeness, both wall-clock and turn order information are needed, as having the same wall-clock difference would require us to know the turn order difference, and vice versa. Here we propose 3 representations that combines the two information based on different hypotheses.

Turn Embedding over Time Mask (TEoTM) provides turn order information on top of seconds. We do so by first masking the context features using *Time Mask* then mark the relative order with *Turn Embedding*. This variant assumes that the past context is important despite the fact that they might be distant in seconds.

$$h^t_{TEoTM}(c) = e_{\Delta turn} \oplus (m_{\Delta sec} \odot h^t(c)), \quad (5)$$

Time Mask over Turn Embedding (TMoTE) applies wall-clock second and turn offset information in reverse order of *TEoTM* by first summing *Turn Embedding* and then multiplying it with *Time Mask*. This assumes that second is more important than turn order as it can overrule by masking when needed.

$$h^t_{TMoTE}(c) = m_{\Delta sec} \odot (e_{\Delta turn} \oplus h^t(c)), \quad (6)$$

Time and Turn Embedding (TaTE) Our third variant assumes wall-clock second and turn offset have equal importance by removing the masking sigmoid of *Time Mask* in Equation (1) and sum with *Turn Embedding*.

$$h^t_{TaTE}(c) = e_{\Delta sec} \oplus e_{\Delta turn} \oplus h^t(c), \quad (7)$$

4 Results

In this section, we first describe our experimental setup in Section 4.1, present our main results in Section 4.2, followed by our analyses in Section 4.3.

4.1 Experimental Setup

Dataset We use an internal SLU dataset that is privatized so that users are not identifiable. Our training, validation and test set contains on the order of several million, several hundred thousand, and one million utterances, respectively. For each utterance, we collect the previous 9 turns within a few days as context. Our dataset has a total of 24 domains that includes common voice assistant use cases (Liu et al., 2019).

Metric For evaluation, we report Accuracy Relative Error Reduction Percentage (ARER %). ARER % is computed with the following equation.

$$ARER_{ctx} = \frac{(1 - ACC_{utt}) - (1 - ACC_{ctx})}{1 - ACC_{utt}}, \quad (8)$$

Here ACC_{utt} is the accuracy of an utterance-only baseline that masks context information, and ACC_{ctx} is the accuracy of a contextual model.

Implementation Details We set both FastText and Elmo embedding dimensions to 300 and hidden dimension to 256 for all neural network layers, hypothesized domain and intent, time and turn embeddings. We used a bi-directional LSTM for turn encoder, uni-directional LSTM for sequence encoder and set both to 2 layers. For Transformer,

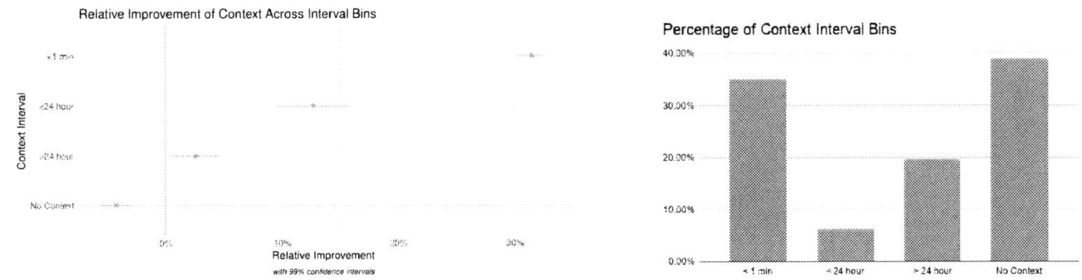

(a) (b)

Figure 2: (a) Left figure plots the ARER % (↑) with confidence intervals of our best model on different time interval bins. (b) Right figure depicts the percentage of each bin within our dataset.

we used 1 layer with 4 heads. Dropout rate is set to 0.2 for all fully-connected layers, and we used Adam (Kingma and Ba, 2015) as optimizer with learning rate set to 0.001. For utterances that do not have context, we use a special <PAD> token to pad the turn features. For consistency, we report results averaging 3 random seeds. We use the MXNet (Chen et al., 2015) framework to develop our models.

4.2 Main Results

In Table 1, we report performance of temporal representations with sequence encoders (1) Max-pooling, (2) LSTM, and (3) Transformer, computed with respect to an utterance-only baseline. For all sequence encoders, temporal representations combining both wall-clock second difference and turn order offset achieved best results. Specifically, *Time and Turn Embedding* works best for Max-pooling, and *Turn Embedding over Time Mask* works best for LSTM and Transformer. Transformer achieved the best results of 13.04%, improving 0.35% over using wall-clock and 2.26% using turn offset. Similar trends are observed with LSTM and Max-pooling, with both information outperforming using only one. In general, having *Time Mask* performs better than *Turn Embedding*, suggesting that wall-clock is more important than turn offset in CDC. Also, despite being a natural time series encoder, temporal representations further improve LSTM performance by up to an additional 1.49%.

4.3 Analysis

In this section, we conduct analyses to better understand the role of context in CDC.

Utt	Hyp-Domain	Hyp-Intent	ARER % (↑)
✓	✓	✓	13.04
✗	✓	✓	12.70
✓	✗	✓	10.20
✓	✓	✗	12.70
✓	✗	✗	5.37
✗	✓	✗	11.27
✗	✗	✓	10.73
✗	✗	✗	0.00

Table 2: Analysis on turn features used in Context Encoder. ✓ indicates the feature is used. ✗ indicates the feature is masked.

Recent & Distant Context To understand whether distant context actually improves SLU, we use the second difference of the first previous turn $d^1_{\Delta sec}$ to indicate absolute closeness and divide the test set into 3 non-overlapping interval bins: (1) < *1 min*, (2) < *24 hr*, (3) > *24 hour*, where (1) represents recent context and (2), (3) are the more distant context. We also include a fourth bin (4) *No Context* for utterances that do not have context. Figure 2 depicts performance of our best model from Section 4.2 on each bin. While improvements are largest for (1), there are still statistically significant improvements for the more distant (2) and (3), suggesting that distant context is indeed helpful, albeit decreases with distance and at a smaller scale. Interestingly, our best model performed worse on (4), suggesting that models trained with context exhibit certain biases when evaluating without context.

Amount of Context Next, we analyze the number of previous turns needed for CDC. We trained and evaluated our best model from Section 4.2

Previous Turn		Current Turn		
Utterance	buy stuff	Utterance	t.v.	
Hyp-Domain	*Shopping*	Baseline	*SmartHome*	✗
Seconds	6.0	Best Model	*Shopping*	✓
Utterance	play <entity1>	Utterance	<entity1> by <entity2>	
Hyp-Domain	*Song*	Baseline	*AudioBooks*	✗
Seconds	54.0	Best Model	*Song*	✓
Utterance	please read audio collection	Utterance	start <entity>	
Hyp-Domain	*AudioBooks*	Baseline	*DeviceControl*	✗
Seconds	6235.0 (1 hr, 43 mins)	Best Model	*AudioBooks*	✓
Utterance	turn on <entity>	Utterance	turn off <entity>	
Hyp-Domain	*SmartHome*	Baseline	*DeviceControl*	✗
Seconds	212421.0 (2 days, 11hrs)	Best Model	*SmartHome*	✓

Table 3: Examples showing predictions of an utterance-only baseline and our best model from Section 4.2 with context from the first previous turn. Our best model is able to make correct predictions by utilizing context from recent and distant time ranges when the current turn utterance is ambiguous. We anonymize entities and modify certain utterances for user privacy. Hypothesized domain-specific intents and additional previous turns are not included for clarity.

using 1 and 5 previous turns, which resulted in ARER% of 10.00%, and 12.86%, respectively. Compared to 13.04% of using 9 previous turns, this suggests that while more than 1 previous turn is needed for performance, using 5 turns is comparable as using 9 turns and can potentially save caching costs.

Where Does Context Improve SLU Most CSLU works are motivated by rephrases and reference resolution (Chen et al., 2016; Rastogi et al., 2019). Noticing that in both phenomena users follow up their requests within the same domain, we split our test set based on whether the previous turn's hypothesized domain (PTHD) is same as or different from the target domain. Our model largely improved ARER % by 22.82% on the *PTHD Same* set, and has comparable performance of −0.03% on the *PTHD Different* set. This suggests that our model learns to carryover previous domain prediction when the current utterance is ambiguous and not over rely on them. We also include several examples with recent and distant context in Table 3 that exhibits this behavior.

Types of Context Information Last, we conducted an ablation study of turn features used in the context encoder. We mask 1 or retain 1 of the 3 features and show results in Table 2. The most effective feature we observed is the previously hypothesized domain, as masking domain yielded the worst results, and keeping domain yielded the best results. Since domain is a crude label, we hypothesize that previous domain predictions are sufficient for CDC, and utterance text will be more useful for more fine-grained tasks such as intent classification or slot labeling.

The upside of this analysis comes from deployment costs. Since pre-trained Elmo embeddings are computation heavy and may require GPU machines, using only hypothesized domain as turn features can largely lower the costs as we can inference using CPUs while sacrificing little accuracy.

5 Conclusions

We presented a novel large-scale industrial CDC setup and show that distant context also improves SLU. Our proposed temporal representations combining both wall-clock and turn order information achieved best results for various encoder architectures in a hierarchical model and outperforms using only one of the two. Our empirical analyses revealed how previous turn helps disambiguation and showed opportunities on reducing deployment costs.

For future work, we plan to explore more turn features such as responses, speaker and device information. We also plan to apply temporal representations on other tasks, such as intent classification, slot labeling, and dialogue response generation.

6 Ethics Statement

Our dataset is annotated by in-house workers who are compensated with above minimum wages. Annotations were acquired for individual utterances and not for aggregated sets of utterances. To protect user privacy, user requests that leak personally-identifiable information (e.g., *address*, *credit card number*) were removed during dataset collection. As our model is a classification based which output is within a finite label set, incorrect predictions will not cause harm to the user besides an unsatisfactory experience.

Acknowledgements

We would like to thank the anonymous reviewer's for their useful suggestions, Yuval Merhav and Bo Xiao for their helpful feedback on the early versions of this paper, and Alan Packer for proofreading during internal review process.

References

Ankur Bapna, G. Tür, Dilek Z. Hakkani-Tür, and Larry Heck. 2017. Sequential dialogue context modeling for spoken language understanding. In *SIGDIAL Conference*.

A. Bhargava, A. Çelikyilmaz, Dilek Z. Hakkani-Tür, and R. Sarikaya. 2013. Easy contextual intent prediction and slot detection. *2013 IEEE International Conference on Acoustics, Speech and Signal Processing*, pages 8337–8341.

P. Bojanowski, E. Grave, Armand Joulin, and Tomas Mikolov. 2017. Enriching word vectors with subword information. *Transactions of the Association for Computational Linguistics*, 5:135–146.

Tianqi Chen, Mu Li, Yutian Li, Min Lin, Naiyan Wang, Minjie Wang, Tianjun Xiao, Bing Xu, Chiyuan Zhang, and Zheng Zhang. 2015. Mxnet: A flexible and efficient machine learning library for heterogeneous distributed systems. *arXiv preprint arXiv:1512.01274*.

Yun-Nung Chen, Dilek Hakkani-Tur, Gokhan Tur, Jianfeng Gao, and Li Deng. 2016. End-to-end memory networks with knowledge carryover for multi-turn spoken language understanding. In *Proceedings of Interspeech*.

Rylan T. Conway and Lambert Mathias. 2019. Time masking: Leveraging temporal information in spoken dialogue systems. In *SIGdial*.

Arshit Gupta, Peng Zhang, Garima Lalwani, and Mona Diab. 2019. CASA-NLU: Context aware self attentive natural language understanding for task-oriented chatbots. In *Proceedings of the 2019 Conference on Empirical Methods in Natural Language Processing and the 9th International Joint Conference on Natural Language Processing (EMNLP-IJCNLP)*, pages 1285–1290, Hong Kong, China. Association for Computational Linguistics.

Raghav Gupta, Abhinav Rastogi, and Dilek Hakkani-Tür. 2018. An efficient approach to encoding context for spoken language understanding. *Proc. Interspeech 2018*, pages 3469–3473.

Michael Heck, Carel van Niekerk, Nurul Lubis, Christian Geishauser, Hsien-Chin Lin, Marco Moresi, and Milica Gasic. 2020. TripPy: A triple copy strategy for value independent neural dialog state tracking. In *Proceedings of the 21th Annual Meeting of the Special Interest Group on Discourse and Dialogue*, pages 35–44, 1st virtual meeting. Association for Computational Linguistics.

Matthew Henderson, Blaise Thomson, and Jason Williams. 2014. The second dialog state tracking challenge. In *15th Annual Meeting of the Special Interest Group on Discourse and Dialogue*, page 263. Citeseer.

Sepp Hochreiter and Jürgen Schmidhuber. 1997. Long short-term memory. *Neural Computation*, 9:1735–1780.

Jonggu Kim and Jong-Hyeok Lee. 2019. Decay-function-free time-aware attention to context and speaker indicator for spoken language understanding. In *Proceedings of the 2019 Conference of the North American Chapter of the Association for Computational Linguistics: Human Language Technologies, Volume 1 (Long and Short Papers)*, pages 3718–3726, Minneapolis, Minnesota. Association for Computational Linguistics.

Young-Bum Kim, Dongchan Kim, Joo-Kyung Kim, and Ruhi Sarikaya. 2018. A scalable neural shortlisting-reranking approach for large-scale domain classification in natural language understanding. In *Proceedings of the 2018 Conference of the North American Chapter of the Association for Computational Linguistics: Human Language Technologies, Volume 3 (Industry Papers)*, pages 16–24.

Diederik P. Kingma and Jimmy Ba. 2015. Adam: A method for stochastic optimization. In *3rd International Conference on Learning Representations, ICLR 2015, San Diego, CA, USA, May 7-9, 2015, Conference Track Proceedings*.

Martin Kleppmann. 2017. *Designing Data-Intensive Applications*. O'Reilly, Beijing.

Han Li, Jihwan Lee, Sidharth Mudgal, Ruhi Sarikaya, and Young-Bum Kim. 2019. Continuous learning for large-scale personalized domain classification. In *Proceedings of the 2019 Conference of the North American Chapter of the Association for Computational Linguistics: Human Language Technologies, Volume 1 (Long and Short Papers)*, pages 3784–3794, Minneapolis, Minnesota. Association for Computational Linguistics.

Chunxi Liu, Puyang Xu, and Ruhi Sarikaya. 2015. Deep contextual language understanding in spoken dialogue systems. In *INTERSPEECH*.

Xingkun Liu, Arash Eshghi, Pawel Swietojanski, and Verena Rieser. 2019. Benchmarking natural language understanding services for building conversational agents. In *10th International Workshop on Spoken Dialogue Systems Technology 2019*.

Chetan Naik, Arpit Gupta, Hancheng Ge, Lambert Mathias, and Ruhi Sarikaya. 2018. Contextual slot carryover for disparate schemas. In *INTERSPEECH*.

Matthew Peters, Mark Neumann, Mohit Iyyer, Matt Gardner, Christopher Clark, Kenton Lee, and Luke Zettlemoyer. 2018. Deep contextualized word representations. In *Proceedings of the 2018 Conference of the North American Chapter of the Association for Computational Linguistics: Human Language Technologies, Volume 1 (Long Papers)*, pages 2227–2237, New Orleans, Louisiana. Association for Computational Linguistics.

Pushpendre Rastogi, Arpit Gupta, Tongfei Chen, and Lambert Mathias. 2019. Scaling multi-domain dialogue state tracking via query reformulation. In *Proceedings of the 2019 Conference of the North American Chapter of the Association for Computational Linguistics*. Association for Computational Linguistics.

Yangyang Shi, Kaisheng Yao, Hu Chen, Yi-Cheng Pan, Mei-Yuh Hwang, and Baolin Peng. 2015. Contextual spoken language understanding using recurrent neural networks. *2015 IEEE International Conference on Acoustics, Speech and Signal Processing (ICASSP)*, pages 5271–5275.

Chengwei Su, Rahul Gupta, Shankar Ananthakrishnan, and Spyridon Matsoukas. 2018a. A reranker scheme for integrating large scale nlu models. *2018 IEEE Spoken Language Technology Workshop (SLT)*, pages 670–676.

Shang-Yu Su, Pei-Chieh Yuan, and Yun-Nung Chen. 2018b. How time matters: Learning time-decay attention for contextual spoken language understanding in dialogues. In *Proceedings of the 2018 Conference of the North American Chapter of the Association for Computational Linguistics: Human Language Technologies, Volume 1 (Long Papers)*, pages 2133–2142, New Orleans, Louisiana. Association for Computational Linguistics.

Gokhan Tur. 2011. *Spoken Language Understanding: Systems for Extracting Semantic Information from Speech*.

Ashish Vaswani, Noam Shazeer, Niki Parmar, Jakob Uszkoreit, Llion Jones, Aidan N. Gomez, undefinedukasz Kaiser, and Illia Polosukhin. 2017. Attention is all you need. In *Proceedings of the 31st International Conference on Neural Information Processing Systems*, NIPS'17, page 6000–6010, Red Hook, NY, USA. Curran Associates Inc.

Jason D. Williams, Antoine Raux, and Matthew Henderson. 2016. The dialog state tracking challenge series: A review. *Dialogue Discourse*, 7:4–33.

Puyang Xu and Ruhi Sarikaya. 2014. Contextual domain classification in spoken language understanding systems using recurrent neural network. *2014 IEEE International Conference on Acoustics, Speech and Signal Processing (ICASSP)*, pages 136–140.

Bootstrapping a Music Voice Assistant with Weak Supervision

Sergio Oramas* and **Massimo Quadrana*** and **Fabien Gouyon**
Pandora Media LLC.
Oakland, USA
{soramas, mquadrana, fgouyon}@pandora.com

Abstract

One of the first building blocks to create a voice assistant is the task of tagging entities or attributes in user queries. This can be particularly challenging when the number of entities are in the tenth of millions, as is the case of music catalogs. Training slot tagging models at an industrial scale requires large quantities of accurately labeled user queries, which are often hard and costly to gather. On the other hand, voice assistants typically collect plenty of unlabeled queries that often remain unexploited. This paper presents a weakly-supervised methodology to label large amounts of voice query logs, enhanced with a manual filtering step. Our experimental evaluations show that slot tagging models trained on weakly-supervised data outperform models trained on hand-annotated or synthetic data, at a lower cost. Further, manual filtering of weakly-supervised data leads to a very significant reduction in Sentence Error Rate, while allowing us to drastically reduce human curation efforts from weeks to hours, with respect to hand-annotation of queries. The method is applied to successfully bootstrap a slot tagging system for a major music streaming service that currently serves several tens of thousands of daily voice queries.

1 Introduction

Music listening is among the top-5 reasons of daily usage of voice assistants in the US.[1] Users can have different goals when formulating a music-related query to their home voice assistant or mobile phones. For instance, users may look for a specific entity, which can be either explicit (e.g., "play Led Zeppelin") or implicit (e.g., "play the latest album by Foo Fighters"). They may also ask queries without having a specific entity in mind (e.g., "play some reggae music"), or make open-ended requests like "play something that I like" (Ostuni, 2019; Volokhin and Agichtein, 2018).

Given a transcribed voice query, a fundamental task towards its understanding is to identify entities and musical attributes in it. However, this can be a non-trivial task, especially when the catalog is composed of possibly millions of different entities. In such situations, the chances that the name of one entity will overlap even partially with another entity are non-negligible. It is even more likely to find overlaps between entities and musical attributes, or between entities and other commonly-used natural language phrases in the query (Guy, 2018). For example, the word "happy" is at the same time a song by Pharrell Williams and an attribute belonging to the "Mood" category in our taxonomy of musical attributes. Mislabeling entities in a user query can potentially lead to awkward user experiences.

Slot tagging, or slot filling, is traditionally tackled as a supervised sequence labeling problem and it is often based on methods such as Recurrent Neural Networks (Goyal et al., 2018), Conditional Random Fields (Reimers and Gurevych, 2017) or pre-trained language models like BERT (Chen et al., 2019). In real-world industrial applications, however, the choice and optimization of the Machine Learning architecture is just the tip of the iceberg. Most of the time and cost are actually spent in gathering sufficient accurately-labeled training data. This process generally requires the manual annotation of up to millions of user queries, a process that should be routinely repeated to keep up with natural drifts in user queries due to, e.g., new interests from users or items that are added or removed from the catalog of searchable products. Manual annotation can be complemented, or even replaced, with synthetically generated training data based on patterns curated by experts (Goyal et al., 2018). While synthetic generation unlocks the possibility of gathering nearly infinite labeled training sam-

*Equal contribution.

[1]Source: https://www.pwc.com/us/en/advisory-services/publications/consumer-intelligence-series/voice-assistants.pdf

Proceedings of NAACL HLT 2021: IndustryTrack Papers, pages 49–55
June 6–11, 2021.

ples, it still requires solid domain expertise to create a sufficiently rich set of patterns to cover as many query variations as possible.

Both manual annotation and generation of training data requiring a significant financial and human resources; another line of thoughts is to exploit unlabeled query data, which is generally cheap and abundant, and to label it via weak supervision.

Weak supervision –or distant supervision– has demonstrated its suitability to a number of natural language processing tasks such as relation extraction (Mintz et al., 2009) or entity recognition (Lison et al., 2020). Moreover, it has been shown as a useful method to bootstrap conversational systems, being applied to intent detection (Mallinar et al., 2019) or slot tagging (Surdeanu et al., 2011) tasks. Given this success, flexible frameworks like Snorkel (Ratner et al., 2017) have been created to help on building weak supervision pipelines at scale. However, these frameworks are not easily adaptable to sequence labeling tasks (Lison et al., 2020).

In this paper, we present our own methodology inspired by weak supervision to label large sets of transcribed voice queries with entities and attributes from a catalog with millions of entries. The resulting labels are, albeit noisy, sufficiently accurate to be used for training slot tagging models. We show how our methodology allows us to control the amount of noisy labels injected in the training dataset by combining weak supervision and human filtering, and provide experimental evidence of how it was exploited to successfully bootstrap a slot tagging system that now serves tens of thousands of voice queries every day in a major music streaming platform. It is worth noticing that the proposed methodology, while defined and tested specifically for the music domain, is generic enough to be applied to other voice search applications that face similar challenges, like e.g. Video On-Demand (Rao et al., 2018) or online shopping.

2 Training Data Creation Methodology

Starting with large amounts of unlabeled voice query transcripts,[2] we automatically label selected terms with respect to both a set of music entities (i.e., artists, albums and tracks) and to attributes from an in-house taxonomy of musical attributes (e.g., genres, instruments, moods, etc.). Some of these annotated queries are then discarded, while the remainder are selected for training purposes (see Section 3). This methodology requires the following basic components:

- A large set of unlabeled queries (in the scale of 100k+).
- A large catalog of entities (10M+).
- A taxonomy of attributes (1k+) classified into semantic categories.

There are two main steps to our methodology. First, a heuristic labeling function makes use of corpus statistics and string matching rules to fully-automatically label queries, while discarding some queries whose annotations cannot be established with sufficient confidence. Then, query patterns are extracted from this first set of labeled queries, and leveraged in a human filtering task where erroneously-labeled queries are discarded.

2.1 Heuristic labeling

2.1.1 Categorizing Entities

A pre-processing step of the catalog of entities is necessary before processing the queries. Indeed, working with very large catalogs of entities implies potential ambiguities between entity surface forms and common natural language phrases or even attributes from the taxonomy. For example, in tens of millions of tracks, as those in our catalog, we can find almost any word or expression as a track name (see Table 1). Simple string matching cannot disambiguate whether a user is asking for a specific track, or saying anything else.

Our approach to tackle this issue is to separate entities into three distinct subsets: the *safe-set*, *ignore-set* and *unsure-set*, illustrated in Table 1. The first subset is for entities for which we have high confidence that, when appearing in a query, the user is in fact referring to the entity, regardless of the context (i.e, the other words present in the query). In opposition, the second subset is for entities for which we have high confidence that the user is in fact not asking for that specific entity, but saying something else. Finally, the third subset is for entities where our confidence to assess any of the two previous statements is low.

To decide on the subset of a given entity, we define the concepts of *corpus frequency* of an entity e as the number of times its surface form appears in the corpus of unlabeled queries, and *intrinsic*

[2]In this paper we do not deal with the aspect of Automatic Speech Recognition (ASR), i.e. transcribing voice audio signals to text. The terms "query" and "query transcript" are used interchangeably.

popularity of an entity as the number of times this entity has been interacted with in our product (e.g., by considering number of streams, their Click Through Rates, or through any other notion of popularity relevant to the product at hand). We empirically observed that whenever an entity has a very high corpus frequency but very low intrinsic popularity, it is highly likely that the user is not referring to the entity in their query, even if there is a perfect string matching between the surface form of the entity and a text span in the query. This observation led to the definition of simple rules for entity categorization, making use of the following concepts:

- *Frequency-popularity ratio*: is computed as follows:

$$r(e) = \frac{popularityRank(e)}{frequencyRank(e)} \quad (1)$$

  where $frequencyRank(e)$ is the ranking of entity e with respect to its corpus frequency,[3] and $popularityRank(e)$ is instead its rank with respect to its intrinsic popularity. We compute $r(e)$ for all entities in the catalog, and then normalize to the $[0, 1]$ range. Values close to 1 will reflect cases where the entity is very frequent in queries but not interacted very much with in our product.
- *Attribute overlap*: Given T the set of all attributes in the taxonomy we say that an entity e has an overlap with T if *every token* in the surface form of e pertains to T. For example, the entity "Spanish House" has attribute overlap, because "Spanish" and "House" are both attributes in our taxonomy.

We then use simple rules based on two thresholds τ and ϵ, with $\tau > \epsilon$, to assign entities to either the safe-set, ignore-set or unsure-set. Given the ratio $r(e)$ of an entity e:

- If $r(e) \geq \tau$, e is added to the ignore-set. This is likely a mismatch with a natural language phrase or an attribute.
- If $\tau > r(e) \geq \epsilon$, e is added to the ignore-set or to the unsure-set, depending on their attribute overlap: If there is attribute overlap, it is added to the ignore-set, as this is likely a mismatch with an attribute; otherwise they go to the unsure-set.

[3]Higher frequency means higher rank.

Entity	$r(e)$	T overlap	Category
Could You	0.99	no	ignore-set
Play Music	0.99	no	ignore-set
Xmas	0.99	yes	ignore-set
You Did Something	0.94	no	unsure-set
Country Joe	0.94	no	unsure-set
Acoustic Piano	0.92	yes	ignore-set
Little Snowflake	0.84	no	safe-set
Spanish House	0.47	yes	unsure-set
I am a Human	0.37	no	safe-list

Table 1: Illustration of ambiguities between entities, natural language sentences and taxonomy attributes: Examples of actual entities (music tracks, albums or artists) as found in our catalog, their $r(e)$ ratio, whether they overlap with our taxonomy C, and their corresponding category. The categorization was performed using $\tau = 0.99$, $\epsilon = 0.90$.

- If $r(e) < \epsilon$, e is added to the unsure-set or to the safe-set, depending also on their attribute overlap: If there is attribute overlap they go to the unsure-set; otherwise they go to the safe-set.

Table 1 shows some actual examples of entities from our catalog, with the corresponding ratio, attribute overlap and the resulting category. For instance, *Acoustic Piano* is the name of a rather unpopular album in our catalog which frequently appears in user queries. Since it completely overlaps with the attributes "acoustic" and "piano" of our taxonomy and its frequency-popularity ratio is between τ and ϵ, it is added the ignore-set.

2.1.2 Labeling Function

Once we have categorized all entities in the catalog into the aforementioned three sets, we use this information for disambiguation purposes in the heuristic labeling process. Given a query, we extract all n-grams and look for all the possible matches with the entities within the union of the safe and the unsure sets, and select the longest non-overlapping matches. Then, we apply the following rules:

- If *any* of the matched entities was categorized in the unsure-set, we discard the whole query;
- Otherwise, the matched n-grams in the query are labeled as the corresponding entity types of the matched entities from the safe-set (e.g., artist, album, track). In case of multiple matches (e.g., an artist and a song having the same name) we pick the entity type with the highest intrinsic popularity.

All entities classified in the ignore-set are simply ignored in this process. After the labeling of entities in the query, we look for matches in the list of attributes from the taxonomy among the words that were left unlabeled. The number of musical attributes in the taxonomy is orders of magnitude smaller than the number of entities, and the probability of a confusion between an attribute and a natural language phrase is very low, so we choose to rely on simple string matching to label the attributes, once the entities are labeled in the query.

To illustrate this process, consider the query "could you play the xmas song little snowflake". Our method finds three matches with the catalog of entities: "could you", "xmas" and "little snowflake". The first two matches belong to the ignore-set and the third one belongs to the safe-set (see Table 1). Since no matched entity is classified in the unsure-set, the query is not discarded. The words in the query corresponding to the entity in the safe-set "little snowflake" are labeled as an entity (specifically a music track); the word "xmas" belongs to our taxonomy (under the "theme" category) and, since it does not overlap with any entity annotation, is labeled as an attribute (specifically a theme), see the final annotation in Figure 1.

2.2 Pattern Filtering via Human Curation

2.2.1 Pattern Extraction

For each heuristically labeled query, we extract the corresponding pattern by substituting all the attributes and entities in the query with a placeholder that is assigned to its corresponding class. For example, the pattern corresponding to the query in Figure 1 is "could you play the [theme] song [track]", being [theme] and [track] the placeholders of any theme attribute and any track name. Following this process, we first extract the patterns of all queries annotated by the heuristic labeling stage, and then group queries belonging to the same pattern. For example, the query "could you play the Halloween song I want candy" belongs to the same pattern of the query in Figure 1.

2.2.2 Human Filtering

After pattern extraction, a filtering process is applied, as follows. Given the set of extracted patterns, we identify the vocabulary of words present in those patterns, and compute their respective frequency in the pattern corpus. This list of words is presented to a human curator who –starting from the most frequent words to the less frequent ones–

could you play the xmas song little snowflake

attribute::theme   entity::track

Figure 1: Example query

must identify words that should *not* be part of a pattern, and discard them from the vocabulary. Optionally, if the vocabulary of words is very large, the curator can also select a frequency threshold below which all words are discarded.

From the full set of extracted patterns, we then keep only those patterns for which *all* words are included in the cleaned-up vocabulary, and discard the remaining patterns. Finally, all queries from the remaining patterns will form the final set of filtered queries.

This process helps us to avoid labeling errors made by the heuristic labeling step, which can be caused either by limitations of the method itself, inconsistent queries made by users, ASR errors, multilingual queries or entities not present in our catalog. Removing queries with wrong labels is fundamental to avoid noisy patterns and have a clean training dataset. Take for example the query "can you play la modelo by osona." The extracted pattern is "can you play [track] by osona". The word "osona" is not in our catalog of entities (therefore not labeled as an artist). It also very rarely appears in the patterns. This word, and respective pattern, are therefore discarded. Note that artist "Ozuna" is in our catalog of entities. In this particular example, an error was probably introduced by the ASR system.

3 Experimental Setup

We evaluate different quantities of weakly-supervised labeled queries as training data for slot tagging models, from a few thousands up to millions, on a sample of actual voice traffic collected from our application. With the goal of showing the potential of weakly-annotated training data, we compare it to models trained on a dataset of human-annotated queries and different synthetically generated datasets. All datasets are described in Table 2.

3.1 Manual and Synthetic Baselines

We asked two expert human annotators to annotate a set of 7000 randomly selected queries from our logs. They also had to discard all nonsense queries from the original set (e.g., incomplete queries, unrelated queries, incomprehensible ASR transcriptions). We kept only the non-discarded queries having complete agreement between annotators.

Eventually, we obtained a set of 5000 manually annotated queries. We used 70% of those for the training of a slot tagging model which serves as our first baseline (MAN). Then, we used 10% as our validation set in all the approaches and baselines. The remaining 20% (i.e., the test set) was used to evaluate the performance of all trained models. We used Sentence Error Rate (SER), i.e. the ratio of queries with at least one slot classification error over all queries, as our evaluation metric. For space reasons we do not report slot-level metrics such F1 score, which showed strong correlation with SER in our experiments.

We generated 4 additional baselines using synthetic query generation to enhance the training set (SYN). Synthetic queries have shown useful for training slot tagging models in low resources scenarios (Goyal et al., 2018), providing the possibility of introducing novel patterns, attributes or entities in the training data. For our experiments, we started from the patterns extracted using the procedure described in Section 2.2.1 over the manual annotated queries from the training set. Every pattern is filled several times using the entities and attributes available in our catalog and in the taxonomy.[4] We generated 4 different synthetic datasets of different sizes, called respectively SYN_S, SYN_M, SYN_L and SYN_{XL} in Table 2.

3.2 Weakly-Supervised Datasets

We compared the baseline annotations against four different weakly-supervised training sets generated using our methodology. We applied the heuristic labeling function (Section 2.1.2) on four random samples from our query logs, respectively containing 100k, 1M, 10M and 100M unlabeled queries. The threshold hyper-parameters τ and ϵ were tuned on the validation set. These datasets are respectively called WS_S, WS_M, WS_L and WS_{XL} in Table 2 and have the same size of the synthetic datasets described in the previous section.

Finally, we generated the WS(F) dataset with human filtering (see Section 2.2) on the same dataset with 100M unlabeled queries used to generate WS_{XL}. Notice that, because of human filtering, the resulting dataset WS(F) has a smaller number of queries than WS_L.

[4]Entities and attributes were sampled proportionally to their intrinsic popularity.

3.3 Model architecture

In order to provide a fair comparison between the several procedures to generate training data, we trained the *same* architecture using the *same* procedure for all datasets.

We used a single layer BiLSTM-CRF network with 100 hidden units and pre-trained word embeddings of size 250 (Reimers and Gurevych, 2017). We used a concatenation of FastText (Mikolov et al., 2018) and Word2Vec (Mikolov et al., 2013) word embeddings trained on an internal corpus of artist biographies. The word embeddings were kept fixed during training to reduce the risk of undesired semantic shifts.

Each instance of the model was trained using ADAM (Kingma and Ba, 2015) with batch size 100 and dropout 0.2 for a maximum of 100k iterations. The initial learning rate was set to 0.001 and damped by factor 0.5 every 7.5k iterations. We used early-stopping to terminate the training whenever the SER on the validation set did not improve for at least 2.5k consecutive iterations. The experimentation was run using TensorFlow (Abadi et al., 2016) and follows closely that of (Reimers and Gurevych, 2017).

4 Results and Discussion

The test set presents a representative sample of the queries that are effectively asked by users using our voice assistant and hence provide valuable insights of how the system will likely perform online. The SER obtained by the BiLSTM-CRF model trained on each of the training datasets is shown in Table 2.

We can immediately notice that the MAN baseline is outperformed by all the SYN, WS and WS(F) variants that we tested. The improvement brought by weak supervision over the baseline grows noticeably with size. When training using small datasets, SYN_S outperforms MAN and WS_S. However, the SER of models trained on SYN data *increases* with training set size. We hypothesize this behavior to be due to an amplification of the bias coming from the relatively small amount of patterns used in data generation. Indeed, in our experimentation setup, we are focusing on a relatively small amount of human-labeled queries. One way of overcoming this issue would be to add more hand-curated queries or patterns –with the corresponding implications in terms of cost and time. Further, research should be also be dedicated to evaluate different ways to generate synthetic data.

Training Dataset	Description	Label	# patterns	# words	# queries	Test SER
MAN	*manually annotated queries*	*MAN*	-	-	*5k*	*31.64*
SYN	*synthetically generated queries*	*SYN_S*	*1k*	*630*	*33k*	*25.11*
		SYN_M	*1k*	*630*	*180k*	*26.75*
		SYN_L	*1k*	*630*	*875k*	*29.65*
		SYN_{XL}	*1k*	*630*	*3.5M*	*29.19*
WS	weakly-supervised annotation	WS_S	8k	732	33k	29.83
		WS_M	38k	2,105	180k	24.93
		WS_L	180k	8,785	875k	23.03
		WS_{XL}	805k	33,984	3.5M	21.94
WS(F)	weakly-supervised annotation + human filtering	WS(F)	101k	468	2.5M	**13.58**

Table 2: Different configurations of training datasets used in the experiments and respective performances as evaluated by SER on the test set (smaller is better). We report the numbers of distinct patterns and words in the patterns for the synthetic and weakly-supervised datasets, and the total number of training queries for every dataset. Baselines are in *italic*. The best test SER overall is highlighted in **bold**.

In opposition, the weakly-supervised WS datasets are able to feed the network with a set of query patterns and annotations whose variety naturally grows with size. This characteristic turns out to be extremely beneficial, as evidenced by the incremental reduction in SER with dataset size. When considering the largest datasets, the models trained on the WS_{XL} dataset show a reduction in SER of 9.7 w.r.t. the MAN baseline, 7.25 w.r.t. the SYN_{XL} dataset of the same size and of 3.17 w.r.t. the best SYN dataset (SYN_S).

We can however notice that the reduction in SER slows down as size grows. One possible explanation can be that the inherent noise in the data. As shown in Table 2, the size of the vocabulary of pattern words drastically increases with the query sample size, implying more possibilities of having wrongly annotated training queries. Once convergence level is reached, manual curation is needed to further improve the peformance of the model. The WS(F) dataset showcases the improvements that can be achieved enhancing the WS_{XL} dataset with a reasonable manual curation effort, removing noise from the vocabulary of pattern words, and therefore, from the training data. This simple but effective curation step results in a reduction of 8.36 in SER w.r.t. the model trained on WS_{XL} dataset and a reduction of 18.06 w.r.t. the MAN baseline.

Moreover, the curation task followed to create WS(F) is much faster than query annotation, not only because the number of words to review is smaller than the number of raw queries, but also because the task itself is easier. We measured that an expert trained annotator is able to manually annotate approximately 100 queries per hour, whereas the pattern vocabulary can be curated following our methodology in less than 4 hours. Therefore, annotating 7000 queries by two annotators took approximately 140 hours, which is orders of magnitude more than the time needed for the vocabulary curation proposed here.

5 Summary and Future Work

This paper presents a methodology to create training data for training slot tagging models inspired by weak supervision. The methodology consists of two steps. First, a simple heuristic query labeling process is applied, that leverages corpus statistics obtained from query logs and comparing them with entity popularity metrics. Second, a pattern extraction and filtering process is applied to the labeled queries, that makes use of human curation.

Our experimental evaluation clearly shows the value of weak supervision for building training datasets to bootstrap slot tagging models. We show that training with large amounts of weakly-supervised data generated from unlabeled voice queries using the proposed methodology outperforms smaller yet reasonable amounts of hand-annotated data. It also outperforms training with large amounts of synthetic data generated from the same hand-annotated data. We showed that the proposed methodology can be combined with a much less time-consuming word vocabulary curation task with very significant reduction in the end model Sentence Error Rate.

Future work should include experimenting with other manual curation tasks, such as manual cleaning of remaining patterns after vocabulary curation, which could help to increase even more model accuracy with a task still much faster than manual annotation of queries. In addition, further study should focus on how synthetic generated queries can complement weakly-supervised datasets, which may help not only in terms of accuracy, but also to assess the quality of labeling of less frequently queried entities or attributes. Moreover, other model architectures could be experimented with, such as pre-trained language models. Finally, experiments could evaluate the applicability of our weakly-supervised methodology to other domains with very large catalogs of entities.

References

Martín Abadi, Paul Barham, Jianmin Chen, Zhifeng Chen, Andy Davis, Jeffrey Dean, Matthieu Devin, Sanjay Ghemawat, Geoffrey Irving, Michael Isard, et al. 2016. Tensorflow: A system for large-scale machine learning. In *12th USENIX Symposium on Operating Systems Design and Implementation (OSDI 16)*, pages 265–283.

Qian Chen, Zhu Zhuo, and Wen Wang. 2019. BERT for joint intent classification and slot filling. *arXiv preprint arXiv:1902.10909*.

Anuj Kumar Goyal, Angeliki Metallinou, and Spyros Matsoukas. 2018. Fast and scalable expansion of natural language understanding functionality for intelligent agents. In *Proceedings of the 2018 Conference of the North American Chapter of the Association for Computational Linguistics: Human Language Technologies, Volume 3 (Industry Papers)*, pages 145–152, New Orleans - Louisiana. Association for Computational Linguistics.

Ido Guy. 2018. The characteristics of voice search: Comparing spoken with typed-in mobile web search queries. *ACM Trans. Inf. Syst.*, 36(3):30:1–30:28.

Diederik P. Kingma and Jimmy Ba. 2015. Adam: A method for stochastic optimization. In *3rd International Conference on Learning Representations, ICLR 2015, San Diego, CA, USA, May 7-9, 2015, Conference Track Proceedings*.

Pierre Lison, Aliaksandr Hubin, Jeremy Barnes, and Samia Touileb. 2020. Named entity recognition without labelled data: A weak supervision approach. *arXiv preprint arXiv:2004.14723*.

Neil Mallinar, Abhishek Shah, Rajendra Ugrani, Ayush Gupta, Manikandan Gurusankar, Tin Kam Ho, Q Vera Liao, Yunfeng Zhang, Rachel KE Bellamy, Robert Yates, et al. 2019. Bootstrapping conversational agents with weak supervision. In *Proceedings of the AAAI Conference on Artificial Intelligence*, volume 33, pages 9528–9533.

Tomas Mikolov, Kai Chen, Greg Corrado, and Jeffrey Dean. 2013. Efficient estimation of word representations in vector space. In *1st International Conference on Learning Representations, ICLR 2013, Scottsdale, Arizona, USA, May 2-4, 2013, Workshop Track Proceedings*.

Tomas Mikolov, Edouard Grave, Piotr Bojanowski, Christian Puhrsch, and Armand Joulin. 2018. Advances in pre-training distributed word representations. In *Proceedings of the International Conference on Language Resources and Evaluation (LREC 2018)*.

Mike Mintz, Steven Bills, Rion Snow, and Dan Jurafsky. 2009. Distant supervision for relation extraction without labeled data. In *Proceedings of the Joint Conference of the 47th Annual Meeting of the ACL and the 4th International Joint Conference on Natural Language Processing of the AFNLP*, pages 1003–1011.

Vito Claudio Ostuni. 2019. "Just Play Something Awesome": The personalization powering voice interactions at Pandora. In *Proceedings of the 13th ACM Conference on Recommender Systems*, RecSys '19, page 523, New York, NY, USA. Association for Computing Machinery.

Jinfeng Rao, Ferhan Ture, and Jimmy Lin. 2018. Multitask learning with neural networks for voice query understanding on an entertainment platform. In *Proceedings of the 24th ACM SIGKDD International Conference on Knowledge Discovery Data Mining*, KDD '18, page 636–645, New York, NY, USA. Association for Computing Machinery.

Alexander Ratner, Stephen H. Bach, Henry Ehrenberg, Jason Fries, Sen Wu, and Christopher Ré. 2017. Snorkel: Rapid training data creation with weak supervision. *Proc. VLDB Endow.*, 11(3):269–282.

Nils Reimers and Iryna Gurevych. 2017. Optimal hyperparameters for deep lstm-networks for sequence labeling tasks. *CoRR*, abs/1707.06799.

Mihai Surdeanu, Sonal Gupta, John Bauer, David McClosky, Angel X Chang, Valentin I Spitkovsky, and Christopher D Manning. 2011. Stanford's distantly-supervised slot-filling system.

Sergey Volokhin and Eugene Agichtein. 2018. Towards intent-aware contextual music recommendation: Initial experiments. In *The 41st International ACM SIGIR Conference on Research & Development in Information Retrieval*, pages 1045–1048.

Continuous Model Improvement for Language Understanding with Machine Translation

Abdalghani Abujabal
Amazon Alexa AI, Germany
abujabaa@amazon.de

Claudio Delli Bovi
Amazon Alexa AI, Germany
boviclau@amazon.de

Sungho Ryu
Amazon Alexa AI, Germany
shryu@amazon.de

Turan Gojayev
Amazon Alexa AI, Germany
tgojayev@amazon.de

Yannick Versley
Amazon Alexa AI, Germany
yversley@amazon.de

Fabian Triefenbach
Amazon Alexa AI, Germany
triefen@amazon.de

Abstract

Scaling conversational personal assistants to a multitude of languages puts high demands on collecting and labelling data, a setting in which cross-lingual learning techniques can help to reconcile the need for well-performing natural language understanding (NLU) with a desideratum to support many languages without incurring unacceptable cost. In this paper, we show that automatically annotating unlabeled utterances using machine translation in an offline fashion and adding them to the training data can improve performance for existing NLU features for low-resource languages, where a straightforward *translate-test* approach as considered in existing literature would fail the latency requirements of a live environment. We demonstrate the effectiveness of our method with intrinsic and extrinsic evaluation using a real-world commercial dialog system in German. We show that 56% of the resulting automatically labeled utterances had a perfect match with ground-truth labels. Moreover, we see significant performance improvements in an extrinsic evaluation settings when manually labeled data is available in small quantities.

Utterance:	Turn	off	the	light	in	the	hallway
Intent:	ApplianceOff						
Slots:	ActionTrigger	O	Device	O	O	Location	

Figure 1: An example NLU annotated utterance. Non-slots are labeled with O (Other).

1 Introduction

1.1 Motivation and Background

Voice-controlled personal assistants such as Amazon Alexa or Google Assistant have scaled to a large number of languages and see a constant influx of new functionalities that are exposed via the natural language interface. As a result, they have seen much interest around the development of multi-lingual and cross-lingual learning techniques that take this setting into consideration.

Beyond a setting where no target language data is available (*language expansion*, or *cross-lingual bootstrapping*), ongoing development also involves use cases where new functionalities from a resource-rich language (typically English) as the source language have to be integrated into existing training sets in the target language (*feature expansion*), or even settings where target language training data of current functionalities exists in small quantities, but accuracy falls short of its aim and an influx of unlabeled data in the target language exists and could be used for continuous model improvement (*feature improvement*). In this work, we consider feature improvement use case for natural language understanding (NLU) in low-resource languages. We define the task of NLU as the combination of: (1) Intent Classification (IC), which classifies an utterance into a fixed set of intent labels (e.g. `ApplianceOff`), and (2) Slot Labeling, which classifies slot values into a predefined set of slot types (e.g. `SongName`) (Weld et al., 2021). For example, as shown in Figure 1, a valid NLU annotation for the English utterance *"turn off the light in the hallway"* would be: `ApplianceOff`: (*turn*, `ActionTrigger`), (*off*, `ActionTrigger`), (*light*, `Device`), (*hallway*, `Location`), where `ApplianceOff` is the intent label, and `ActionTrigger`, `Device` and `Location` are the slot types. We leverage machine translation to automatically annotate unlabeled utterances with intent and slot labels. Collecting and labeling data for NLU is an expensive and time-consuming process, hardly scalable to an increasing number of languages without automation.

1.2 State of the Art and its Limitations

Many works on academic datasets naturally address the language expansion setting, including zero-shot

Proceedings of NAACL HLT 2021: IndustryTrack Papers, pages 56–62
June 6–11, 2021.

learning results, or involve a multilingual learning approach where similar amounts of training data for each of the languages are available from the start. However, we want to argue that the setting where target-language data is available but considerably smaller is particularly relevant in practice. Such an imbalance is often due cost considerations (manual annotation is expensive).

A first line of work on cross-lingual bootstrapping has combined annotation transfer with (to varying extent) either machine translation (MT) or parallel corpora. Generally, MT has been harnessed either in *translate-train* or *translate-test* settings. While in *translate-train*, source training data e.g., in English is translated into the target language (Gaspers et al., 2018), in *translate-test*, incoming unlabeled utterances in the target language are translated into the source language and then source NLU model is used to collect labels. For the feature improvement use case, on one hand, *translate-train* ignores the influx of unlabeled utterances in the target language. On the other hand, a *translate-test* approach is not directly applicable to production use in a conversational agent because a system with MT in the loop would fail the latency requirements for live use. As a consequence, we propose to use the label projection from the source language as a way to get more reliable labels than the existing target language model on less confident-cases, and augmenting the target language training data with these automatically labeled examples.

In sentiment classification, Mihalcea et al. (2007) compare translation of a lexicon with translating the training data (*translate-train*) or translating the data to be annotated (*translate-test*) for cross-lingual bootstrapping of sentiment classification. Akbik et al. (2015) investigate cross-lingual bootstrapping in the context of Semantic Role Labeling, where a parallel corpus is first annotated with English labels which are then projected and filtered to gain a target language training corpus. In dialogue systems and conversational agent training, He et al. (2013) show that adding some MT distortion to the source-language training data in a translate-test setting can be beneficial. Gaspers et al. (2018) show that a translate-train approach that uses machine translation in conjunction with filtering based on MT confidence can be successful in achieving a smaller error rate, with a combination of translated and target-language manually annotated data achieving the best possible error rate.

A second line of work concerns the use of shared representations across languages to cross-lingual transfer learning or learning of multilingual representations, as demonstrated by Upadhyay et al. (2018) who compare translate-train and translate-test approaches with zero-shot and minimally supervised multilingual approaches. It shows that the helpful bias from shared representations gives a boost in the minimally supervised setting but is especially helpful when very few target-language examples are available. Johnson et al. (2019) and Do et al. (2019) show that these effects generally also hold at a larger scale, and that training data selection also helps when transfer learning is used instead of machine translation in a translate-train setting.

Finally, and partially relevant for feature improvement when a smaller-than-source amount of target data is available, we have approaches that perform data augmentation on the smaller target-language training data: Malandrakis et al. (2019), and Jolly et al. (2020) explore the use of sentence-to-sentence paraphrasing and interpretation-to-sentence generation approaches to generate labeled paraphrases of conversational NLU training data.

1.3 Approach and Contribution

In this paper we investigate whether a *translate-test* approach of doing machine translation and annotation projection of target-language utterances with labels from the more resource-rich source language can be used in a *feature improvement* setting, where target-language training data is available but in smaller quantities than in the source language.

Our approach, depicted in Figure 2, makes use of MT in conjunction with an NLU model already trained for the source language to annotate unlabeled utterances. We assume that this reference NLU model was previously trained on the features of interest for the target language. Similar to Gaspers et al. (2018), we also assume access to an MT system trained on general-purpose parallel data, but instead of relying on MT from reference to target language, (*forward MT*), we consider MT in the opposite direction i.e. from target to reference language (*backward MT*). Our goal is to cheaply improve NLU features using readily available MT and NLU models. For example, we do not require in-domain MT model.

Experimentally, we considered a scenario with

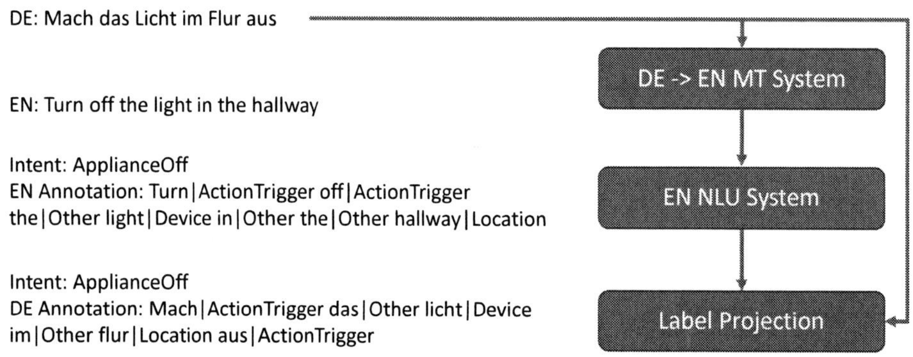

Figure 2: Given an unlabeled utterance in some target language e.g., German, our method translates it into a reference language e.g., English using MT, labels it with intent and slot types using an (EN) NLU model, and projects the labels back onto the unlabeled utterance.

English (EN) as reference language and German (DE) as target language, and carried out both an intrinsic and an extrinsic evaluation, where we selected a set of five diverse NLU features to improve. We compared against a baseline approach that generates synthetic training examples directly in the target language.

We demonstrate the effectiveness of our method using a real-world commercial dialog system in German. We show that 56% of the resulting automatically labeled utterances had a perfect match with ground-truth labels. We also show that using our method leads to 90% reduction in manually labeled data, while achieving better performance. In the remainder of the paper, Section 2 contains details on the methods used, whereas Section 3 describes our experimental setup. Section 4 discusses the results of our experiments.

2 Method

Given unlabeled utterances in a target language e.g. German (DE), for example *"mach das licht im flur aus"*, our goal is to automatically annotate them with an intent label, and slot types for every token, as shown in the example in Figure 1. To this end, we consider the pipeline shown in Figure 2, which consists of three components: (1) Machine translation system, (2) NLU model, and (3) Label projection model. First, the MT system translates the unlabeled utterances into a reference language e.g. English. For the German utterance above, a valid English translation would be *"turn off the light in the hallway"*. Note that we do not make any assumption on the architecture of the MT system, be it statistical or neural, or on the way it is trained. We assume, however, a label projection model trained on the same data as the MT system. In a standard MT bootstrapping setting (Gaspers et al., 2018) this is usually a word alignment model, either embedded in the MT system itself (as in phrase-based MT we used in Section 3) or trained as a stand-alone component. After translation, we use an English NLU model on the translated utterances in order to get predictions for the intent label and the slot types.[1] For the example above, the result of this step would be the following annotated utterance: [`ApplianceOff` *turn*/`ActionTrigger` *off*/`ActionTrigger` *the*/`Other` *light*/`Device` *in*/`Other` *the*/`Other` *hallway*/`Location`]. Finally, we use the word alignment model to project the slot types from the (EN) labeled utterances onto the unlabeled (DE) utterances. For example, if the two words *'light'* and *'licht'* are aligned, the slot label of *'light'* is copied over onto *'licht'*. In our experiments (Section 3), we make use of alignment models trained for the MT system to avoid building standalone alignment models. For the intent label, we simply copy it over from the English labeled utterance to the German unlabeled one.

For reasons of simplicity and better interpretability, we used statistical machine translation (SMT) as well as linear models (CRF and maximum entropy) for the NLU component, however we believe that the improvements gained with this method would carry over to a case where neural MT and transformer-based NLU components are used.

[1]Note that this NLU model is pre-trained independently and it is completely decoupled from our pipeline.

3 Experimental Setup

In our experiments, we translate target-language (German) utterances from live conversational agent usage using an existing MT system (§3.1), tag these using the English NLU system (§3.2) and project the labels back onto the target language using word alignments. We report results using first intrinsic evaluation (How well does the *translate-test* approach perform in labeling the utterances?) and then a full evaluation in a *feature improvement* setting, and we evaluate these using a Semantic Error Rate metric (SemER, §3.3).

3.1 MT System

We used an internal phrase-based MT system trained with Moses (Koehn et al., 2007). The system comprises a general-purpose MT model trained on DE-EN parallel data. We plan to investigate the usage of neural machine translation (NMT) models in the future. To better match the spoken user utterances of an NLU system, training data of the MT system is converted into *spoken form* using an internal written-to-spoken converter. For example, *"1994"* is converted to *"nineteen ninety four"*. The MT model was fine-tuned on 4K in-domain parallel utterances. To project slot type labels from the machine-translated English utterance (labeled by the English NLU model) to the unlabeled German utterance, we make use of the word alignment model trained for the MT system (Dyer et al., 2013). We opted for using a general-purpose MT model since it is readily available, and hence cheaper (as opposed to building in-domain MT model). Also, using phrase-based MT enabled us to leverage the word alignment model trained for MT for our label projection step.

3.2 NLU System

We used Conditional Random Fields (Lafferty et al., 2001) for slot labeling, and a Maximum Entropy classifier for the IC task (Berger et al., 1996). The English NLU system was trained on a large dataset of NLU-annotated utterances. The training data covers multiple domains e.g., `HomeAutomation`, with a diverse set of intents and slot types, with more than 200 intents and several hundreds of slot types. For example, intents like `PlayMusic` and slot types like `City` and `SongName`. The quality of the reference NLU model (e.g., English) is important for our pipeline to work. Our assumption is that English NLU models perform well, while NLU models for other languages still suffer (most industrial NLP applications support English pretty well).

Feature	#Auto labeled utterances	#Test utterances
DailyBriefing	21, 894	3, 530
PlayMusic	194, 180	66, 959
SendMessage	1, 690	1, 783
SmartHome	108, 210	29, 056
SetNotification	26, 074	9, 616

Table 1: The size of automatically labeled and test data for each feature.

3.3 SemER Evaluation Metric

Following Gaspers et al. (2018) we report the Semantic Error Rate (SemER), which is computed as follows:

$$SemER = \frac{\#(slots + intent\ errors)}{\#slots\ in\ reference + 1}$$

Errors correspond to the number of insertions, deletions and substitutions for slots and the intent in a recognized utterance.

Note that as the task of NLU is our main focus, we report evaluation metrics on the NLU rather intrinsically evaluating each component of our approach e.g., the MT model. We plan to invest in this direction in the future. Moreover, while intrinsic evaluation measures of individual components would assess their quality e.g., BLEU for MT, there is no correlation between these measures and NLU metrics. In other words, having higher BLEU scores does not necessarily mean lower SemER.

3.4 Utterance Dataset

To simulate a continuous model improvement scenario for DE, we selected a diverse set of features that belong to different domains:

1. *DailyBriefing*, which enables users to play daily briefing e.g., news,
2. *PlayMusic*, which enables playing music,
3. *SendMessage*, which allows users to exchange messages,
4. *SmartHome*, which enables users to control home appliances,
5. *SetNotification*, which enables users to set notifications and reminders.

Model	Size of training data	SemER (%)
DE	$6.4M$	41.4
DE_0.5	$3.7M$	**37.4**
DE_0.7	$3.2M$	37.8
DE_grammars	$1.0M$	57.0

Table 2: The effect of filtering the data based on NLU confidence. Using 0.5 achieved best results.

Features span across multiple intents with different slot labels. For example, *SmartHome* supports the intents of turning an appliance on and off, and supports the slot lables of appliance names and their locations. We assume that the five features have been just launched either using grammars, very little labeled data or using the approach of Gaspers et al. (2018). Our goal is to continuously improve performance on the five features using our method.

For each feature, we randomly selected 10,000 manually labeled utterances from its training data. Next, we generated five splits out of the 10,000 utterances: 100, 500, 1000, 5000 and 10,000. Each split corresponds to the size of data, for example, the split of 100 indicates that 100 manually labeled utterances are used. For each split, we trained two DE NLU models:

- **Baseline model**, which contains only manually labeled feature data, and
- **Combined model**, which contains both manually and automatically labeled feature data.

Note that the training data of the NLU models contain data for other features that were launched already. We report absolute SemER difference between the two models.

We collected 3,651,039 unlabeled DE utterances in order to run the MT-based automatic annotation. Table 1 shows the size of the automatically labeled data for each feature. We also collected test data for each feature (Table 1).

4 Results

4.1 Accuracy of Automatic Labeling

To intrinsically measure the accuracy of our method, we collected 1.2 million labeled utterances from features already launched in a real-world commercial dialog system in German, and simulated a scenario where the corresponding labels were not available. We then used our method to label them: we translated them into English, ran the English NLU model on them, and projected back all the predicted labels. We observed that 56.35% of the resulting automatically labeled utterances had a perfect match with ground-truth labels (i.e., they agreed on both the intent label and all the slot types), while 81.87% of them agreed on the intent only, with at least one unmatched slot type.

4.2 Effect of English NLU Confidence

We studied the effect of the English NLU model's prediction confidence. We collected 6.4M unlabeled German utterances and then used our method to annotate them. Each prediction (intent and slot labels) is associated with a score $\in [0, 1]$ that reflects the confidence of the English NLU model about the prediction. We then trained three DE NLU models: (1) DE, where confidence equals 0.0 i.e., 6.4M utterances are kept, (2) $DE\_0.5$, and (3) $DE\_0.7$, where utterances whose confidence score is greater than 0.5 and 0.7 are kept, respectively. The three models were tested on the same test set with 120K German utterances that were manually transcribed and annotated with intents and slot types. The test set spans multiple domains with different intents and slot types. As shown in Table 2, $DE\_0.5$ outperformed other baselines, indicating the importance of using NLU confidence scores. We attribute this to the fact that some translations are malformed, and hence incorrectly labeled by the English NLU model. When incorrect labels are propagated to the DE NLU model, they negatively impact performance. We set the EN NLU model's confidence score to 0.5 for the subsequent experiments.

We also trained an NLU model using randomly sampled utterances from manually curated grammars ($DE\_grammars$), which achieved 57.0 SemER and was outperformed by $DE\_0.5$, with 19.6 absolute SemER difference.

4.3 Feature Improvement

Table 3 shows the results on the five features, showing the SemER difference between a baseline (trained with the given number of hand-annotated utterances) and a version with our proposed method, combining the hand-annotated utterances with additional data which has been automatically labeled.

Combining manually and automatically labeled data improves performance across features and splits. The greatest gains are achieved for smaller splits i.e., 100 and 500, which suggest that our

Split	DailyBriefing	PlayMusic	SendMessage	SmartHome	SetNotification
100	**−38.65**	**−26.98**	**−13.25**	**−74.34**	**−19.42**
500	−10.72	−20.17	−1.47	−19.22	-9.97
1000	−7.24	−14.96	−0.88	−8.11	−7.5
5000	−1.69	−0.97	−0.21	+3.71	−0.18
10,000	−0.63	+2.72	−0.37	+3.12	−0.06

Table 3: SemER difference between the baseline and the combined model on the five features (lower is better). Across features, using automatically labeled data improved performance.

method is especially effective for an early feature improvement. For example, the difference in SemER between the baseline and the combined model is −38.65 on DailyBriefing at 100 split. For PlayMusic, SmartHome and SetNotification, the SemER value of the Combined model at 100 split is better than the one achieved by the baseline at 1000 split i.e., a reduction in labeled data of 90%.

As the size of manually labeled data increases (i.e., larger splits), the positive effect of the automatically labeled data decreases. For example, on DailyBriefing, the SemER difference between the baseline and Combined models is −0.63 absolute at 10,000 split. For the largest split at 10,000, the automatically labeled data hurts the performance for PlayMusic and SmartHome, with SemER difference of +2.72 and +3.12, respectively. This is largely due to cumulated errors in both the MT system and the label projection module, which inject noise in the downstream NLU task. To mitigate this, we are currently investigating ways to automatically combine training data with varying quality for NLU. We also carried out similar experiments to improve the same features in French and so far observed the same trends. We are planning to expand our evaluation to other languages.

5 Conclusion

This paper presents a new method to automatically annotate utterances with intents and slot types, leading to faster and cheaper early improvement of features. Our method harnesses existing MT, English NLU and word alignment models which have been trained on general-domain data but adapted to our specific use case through preprocessing and fine-tuning. Intrinsic evaluation results show that a *translate-test* approach is a viable way to get data labels in a way that is independent from the target language production system, whereas our extrinsic evaluation results suggest that the approach is especially useful when a given feature has not seen extensive use yet.

We plan to address in future work whether certain properties of a given feature can predict the viability of a *translate-test* approach in general and data augmentation with translated examples in particular, and whether the use of neural machine translation models would suggest modifications to this approach, as translations are often better but alignment results can be less clear-cut.

References

Alan Akbik, Laura Chiticariu, Marina Danilevsky, Yunyao Li, Shivakumar Vaithyanathan, and Huaiyu Zhu. 2015. Generating high quality proposition Banks for multilingual semantic role labeling. In *Proceedings of the 53rd Annual Meeting of the Association for Computational Linguistics and the 7th International Joint Conference on Natural Language Processing (Volume 1: Long Papers)*, pages 397–407, Beijing, China. Association for Computational Linguistics.

Adam L. Berger, Stephen Della Pietra, and Vincent J. Della Pietra. 1996. A maximum entropy approach to natural language processing. *Computational Linguistics*, 22(1):39–71.

Quynh Ngoc Thi Do and Judith Gaspers. 2019. Cross-lingual transfer learning with data selection for large-scale spoken language understanding. In *Proceedings of the 2019 Conference on Empirical Methods in Natural Language Processing and the 9th International Joint Conference on Natural Language Processing, EMNLP-IJCNLP 2019, Hong Kong, China, November 3-7, 2019*, pages 1455–1460. Association for Computational Linguistics.

Chris Dyer, Victor Chahuneau, and Noah A. Smith. 2013. A simple, fast, and effective reparameterization of IBM model 2. In *Human Language Technologies: Conference of the North American Chapter of the Association of Computational Linguistics, Pro ceedings, June 9-14, 2013, Westin Peachtree Plaza Hotel, Atlanta, Georgia, USA*, pages 644–648. The Association for Computational Linguistics.

Judith Gaspers, Penny Karanasou, and Rajen Chatterjee. 2018. Selecting machine-translated data for quick bootstrapping of a natural language understanding system. In *Proceedings of the 2018 Conference of the North American Chapter of the 2018 of the Association for Computational Linguistics: Human Language Technologies, NAACL-HLT 2018, New Orleans, Louisiana, USA, June 1-6, 2018, Volume 3 (Industry Papers)*, pages 137–144. Association for Computational Linguistics.

X. He, L. Deng, D. Hakkani-Tur, and G. Tur. 2013. Multi-style adaptive training for robust cross-lingual spoken language understanding. In *2013 IEEE International Conference on Acoustics, Speech and Signal Processing*, pages 8342–8346.

Andrew Johnson, Penny Karanasou, Judith Gaspers, and Dietrich Klakow. 2019. Cross-lingual transfer learning for japanese named entity recognition. In *Proceedings of the 2019 Conference of the North American Chapter of the Association for Computational Linguistics: Human Language Technologies, NAACL-HLT 2019, Minneapolis, MN, USA, June 2-7, 2019, Volume 2 (Industry Papers)*, pages 182–189. Association for Computational Linguistics.

Shailza Jolly, Tobias Falke, Caglar Tirkaz, and Daniil Sorokin. 2020. Data-efficient paraphrase generation to bootstrap intent classification and slot labeling for new features in task-oriented dialog systems. In *Proceedings of the 28th International Conference on Computational Linguistics: Industry Track*.

Philipp Koehn, Hieu Hoang, Alexandra Birch, Chris Callison-Burch, Marcello Federico, Nicola Bertoldi, Brooke Cowan, Wade Shen, Christine Moran, Richard Zens, Chris Dyer, Ondrej Bojar, Alexandra Constantin, and Evan Herbst. 2007. Moses: Open source toolkit for statistical machine translation. In *ACL 2007, Proceedings of the 45th Annual Meeting of the Association for Computational Linguistics, June 23-30, 2007, Prague, Czech Republic*. The Association for Computational Linguistics.

John D. Lafferty, Andrew McCallum, and Fernando C. N. Pereira. 2001. Conditional random fields: Probabilistic models for segmenting and labeling sequence data. In *Proceedings of the Eighteenth International Conference on Machine Learning (ICML 2001), Williams College, Williamstown, MA, USA, June 28 - July 1, 2001*, pages 282–289. Morgan Kaufmann.

Nikolaos Malandrakis, Minmin Shen, Anuj Kumar Goyal, Shuyang Gao, Abhishek Sethi, and Angeliki Metallinou. 2019. Controlled text generation for data augmentation in intelligent artificial agents. In *Proceedings of the 3rd Workshop on Neural Generation and Translation@EMNLP-IJCNLP 2019, Hong Kong, November 4, 2019*, pages 90–98. Association for Computational Linguistics.

Rada Mihalcea, Carmen Banea, and Janyce Wiebe. 2007. Learning multilingual subjective language via cross-lingual projections. In *Proceedings of the 45th Annual Meeting of the Association of Computational Linguistics*, pages 976–983, Prague, Czech Republic. Association for Computational Linguistics.

Shyam Upadhyay, Manaal Faruqui, Gökhan Tür, Dilek Hakkani-Tür, and Larry P. Heck. 2018. (almost) zero-shot cross-lingual spoken language understanding. In *2018 IEEE International Conference on Acoustics, Speech and Signal Processing, ICASSP 2018, Calgary, AB, Canada, April 15-20, 2018*, pages 6034–6038. IEEE.

Henry Weld, Xiaoqi Huang, Siqi Long, Josiah Poon, and Soyeon Caren Han. 2021. A survey of joint intent detection and slot-filling models in natural language understanding. *CoRR*, abs/2101.08091.

A hybrid approach to scalable and robust spoken language understanding in enterprise virtual agents

Ryan Price, Mahnoosh Mehrabani, Narendra Gupta, Yeon-Jun Kim
Shahab Jalalvand, Minhua Chen, Yanjie Zhao, Srinivas Bangalore
Interactions, LLC

Abstract

Spoken language understanding (SLU) extracts the intended meaning from a user utterance and is a critical component of conversational virtual agents. In enterprise virtual agents (EVAs), language understanding is substantially challenging. First, the users are infrequent callers who are unfamiliar with the expectations of a pre-designed conversation flow. Second, the users are paying customers of an enterprise who demand a reliable, consistent and efficient user experience when resolving their issues. In this work, we describe a general and robust framework for intent and entity extraction utilizing a hybrid of statistical and rule-based approaches. Our framework includes confidence modeling that incorporates information from all components in the SLU pipeline, a critical addition for EVAs to ensure accuracy. Our focus is on creating accurate and scalable SLU that can be deployed rapidly for a large class of EVA applications with little need for human intervention.

1 Introduction

Advances in speech recognition in recent years have enabled a variety of virtual agents that answer questions, execute commands and engage in task-oriented dialogs in customer care applications. Beyond the accurate transcription of the user's speech, these virtual agents critically rely on interpreting the user's utterance accurately. Interpretation of a user's utterance – spoken language understanding (SLU) is broadly characterized as extracting intents – expressions that refer to actions, and entities – expressions that refer to objects. The entity expressions are further grounded to specific objects in the domain of the dialog (eg. `latest iphone` → `iphone 11`) or through world knowledge (eg. `Christmas` → `12/25`).

SLU has been a topic of research for the past three decades. Public data sets like ATIS (Price, 1990), SNIPS (Coucke et al., 2018), and recently FSC (Lugosch et al., 2019) have allowed for comparing various methodologies, including many recent developments driven by deep learning (Mesnil et al., 2014; Xu and Sarikaya, 2013; Liu and Lane, 2016; Price, 2020; Tomashenko et al., 2019). Such data sets are also a reasonable proxy for the intent classification and entity extraction handled by many consumer virtual agents (CVAs), applications that provide single shot question-answering and command-control services through smart-speakers or smart-home appliances. However, in contrast to the CVAs and the aforementioned data sets, enterprise virtual agents (EVAs) provide customer care services that rely on SLU in a dialog context to extract a diverse range of intents and entities that are specific to that business. SLU for EVAs encompasses a wide-ranging set of challenges. Speech recognition needs to be robust to varying microphone characteristics, diverse background noises, and accents. For EVAs, the robustness is further underscored as they are expected to deliver a better user experience to paying customers. Furthermore, SLU in EVAs needs to extract entities and intents that are specific to the domain of the enterprise. Matching expectations of novice users with the capabilities of SLU systems is challenging (Glass, 1999). Unlike users of CVAs, the users of EVAs are typically non-repeat users, who are not familiar with a particular EVA's conversational flow, leading them to provide unexpected and uncooperative responses to system prompts. Accordingly, EVAs need to contend with a larger space of alternative intents in a given dialog state. Other factors, like changes to the system that are dictated by business needs and continuous development of applications for new customers for which there is no labeled data yet, create a strong need for an SLU framework that can scale. Finally, while deep learning models with large modeling capacity can offer excellent results, latency at runtime is of great concern in paid for services like EVAs so designing towards lower computational complexity may be necessary (Tyagi et al., 2020).

To address the several challenges that relate to SLU in EVAs, we describe a general and robust framework for intent and entity extraction. Our primary goal is to create accurate and scalable SLU that can be widely deployed for a large class of EVA applications with little need for human intervention. We focus on techniques for the extraction and grounding of general entities (eg. dates, names, digit sequences) that are broadly used in SLU for EVAs, and also address the critical need for the extracted entities and intents to be associated with confidence scores that could be used by the dialog manager to

Proceedings of NAACL HLT 2021: IndustryTrack Papers, pages 63–71
June 6–11, 2021.

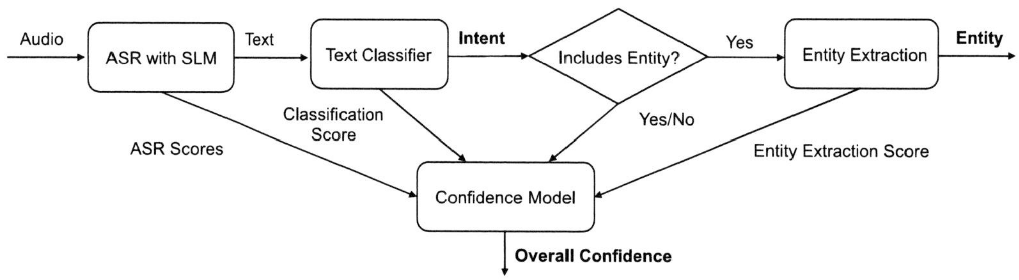

Figure 1: Flow diagram of the proposed pipeline. The outputs of interest for our human-in-the-loop SLU system are intents, entities, and overall confidence score.

either reprompt or to request human assistance. A variety of design considerations are discussed with insights drawn from real world EVA applications. We know of few previous studies having similar aim and scope of work as ours. Early work on industrial SLU systems sharing the aim of scalable SLU without human intervention was described in (Gupta et al., 2005), though without confidence modeling. An SLU pipeline is also addressed in (Coucke et al., 2018), but with design considerations made for CVA-like applications running on a device. While Gupta *et al.* (Gupta et al., 2019) does recognize that the needs of EVAs are different, their work primarily focuses on a framework for joint intent classification and slot filling that is modularized into different components.

This paper presents a complete study of a deployed SLU pipeline for handling intents and entities. The models described have been deployed in applications for Fortune 500 companies and a variety of design considerations are discussed with insights drawn from these real world EVA applications. In particular, we focus on improving performance on entities and intents for several core subtasks in a goal directed conversational system, namely date capture, number capture and name capture. Our contributions in this paper include (a) a unified framework for intent and entity identification (b) a synergistic combination of the robustness of statistical entity extraction models with rule-based value grounding (c) uncertainty modeling through confidence scoring and rejection criteria to maximize user experience (d) application of the framework for intent and entity extraction to new applications without the need for annotated data.

The outline of the paper is as follows. Section 2 provides an overview of the SLU framework for intent classification and entity extraction. Our experiments are presented in Sections 3, 4, and 5. Finally, conclusions and future work are given in Section 6.

2 Framework for Intent and Entity Extraction

In this section we describe the framework for simultaneous intent and entity extraction with confidence modeling. An illustration of the overall pipeline is show in Figure 1. We introduce the main components consisting of ASR, Text Classification, Entity Extraction, and Confidence Modeling depicted in Figure 1 in Sections 2.1, 2.2, 2.3, and 2.4, respectively. More details on the specific manifestations these components take on for a given task are described in Sections 3, 4, and 5.

2.1 ASR

The ASR systems used in our experiments consist of hybrid DNN acoustic models trained to predict tied context-dependent triphone HMM states with cross-entropy and sequential loss functions using 81-dimensional log-spectrum features. The pronunciation dictionaries consist of hand-crafted pronunciations for common words and grapheme-to-phoneme generated pronunciations for the rest.

Grammar-based language models (GLMs) can be very accurate in scenarios where the domain is constrained and the structure of likely utterances is predictable. Furthermore, GLMs have the advantage of not requiring much training data and provide recognition and semantic interpretation together, eliminating the need for an intent classifier and entity extractor. While there can be some overlap in GLMs used across similar dialog states making them attractive for immediate deployment, to really achieve peak accuracy in a non-trivial dialog state requires manual tuning by an expert, which is an obstacle to deploying GLMs rapidly at scale. Although it may seem that entity capture states in a well-designed dialog would elicit predictable user responses making them suitable for recognition with GLMs, in our goal-oriented dialogs deployed in EVAs we have observed that is not always the case. Statistical language models (SLMs) paired with intent classifiers and entity extraction methods can outperform GLMs. Therefore, we use SLMs built from n-grams or a hybrid LM combining SLMs and GLMs.

2.2 Intent Classification

We employ a linear Support Vector Machine (SVM) for intent classification, using n-gram based TF-IDF features. Although classifiers based on deep neural networks have gained popularity in recent years (Kim, 2014), linear classifiers remain as strong baselines (Wang and Manning, 2012), particularly on short text, with their ability to efficiently handle high-dimensional sparse features, and their training stability through convex optimization.

In SLU, the outputs from ASR are inherently uncertain and erroneous. For example, an utterance corresponding to "I want to buy a phone" may result in multiple recognition hypotheses: ("I want to buy phone", "Want to buy phone", "I want a phone"), which we call ASR n-best. Instead of relying only on the first best ASR hypothesis, for intent extraction we use ASR n-best for better robustness and accuracy. There is a long history of leveraging information beyond the ASR 1-best for SLU in the literature (Hakkani-Tür et al., 2006; Li et al., 2020; Henderson et al., 2012).

To incorporate the ASR n-best information we take a sample-based approach. In this approach, we treat the hypotheses of an utterance as independent samples (with equal sample weights that sum to one), hence the number of samples will be larger than the number of original utterances. We apply this sample-augmentation process in the training phase, to account for the uncertainties in the ASR hypotheses. While in the testing phase, we first obtain the model scores for those independent samples, and then aggregate scores from the same utterance to yield the final scores for decision making. We use equal sample weights for hypotheses in the n-best because the weighting schemes we have tried based on ASR confidence for the entries in the n-best was not found to improve classification accuracy. Additionally, we found that an n-best list of three was sufficient for the tasks studied in this paper and increasing the number further just adds additional training time. The number of intents modeled by the text classifiers for the date, number, and name capture tasks we study ranges from approximately 20 to 40 different intents.

2.3 Entity Extraction

While increasingly accurate sequence tagging models for named entity recognition (NER) have been developed over the years, NER on speech input adds another complexity which cannot be mitigated by advanced algorithms developed for text alone. For speech input, recognition errors have to be accounted for at least in the form of a confidence value on the extracted values. EVAs must handle different types of spoken entities. Some appear with minor variations in surface forms (lexical strings) and appear in contexts where they are mostly unambiguous. For example, account numbers and phone numbers appear in the form of digit sequences of a predetermined length. Although ASR errors present some difficulties, such entities can be directly captured by a rule-based system and require little or no normalization. On the other hand, entities such as dates can appear in many surface forms like "this Monday", "New Year's day", "on the 7th", for example, and their context can cause ambiguities which require sequence tagging algorithms. In addition to sequence tagging, normalization is needed to convert the entity to the desired format. In any case, additional confidence models to account for ASR errors are required.

We also address entity capture tasks such as last name capture, that provide unique challenges in the context of speech input, but also have structure that can be leveraged to improve capture accuracy. EVAs for customer care dialogs must contend with a large number of unique names. Furthermore, many names may occur rarely and have unreliable pronunciations in the ASR lexicon. As a result, the main challenge is accurately recognizing the spoken name, rather than tagging and normalization. To accurately capture last names we leverage the spelling of the last name and utilize a hierarchical language model which combines SLMs and grammars.

2.4 Confidence Modeling

In order to maintain the high standard of customer experience demanded of EVAs, our SLU system utilizes a human-in-the-loop approach to ensure a sufficiently low error rate of the SLU system. Only high-confidence results from the SLU system are accepted, and utterances with low SLU confidence are handed-off to human agents who label them in real-time instead of being automated using the SLU output. The rejection of an SLU output is based on comparing the overall confidence measure for each utterance to a threshold. This utterance-level semantic confidence score quantifies the reliability of the information extracted from a spoken utterance, including entities and intents. It has been shown that combining speech recognition scores with semantic features to train a confidence model is an effective approach for semantic confidence estimation (Sarikaya et al., 2005; Mehrabani et al., 2018; San-Segundo et al., 2001). We use a logistic regression confidence model that is trained by passing each utterance through the SLU pipeline and the predicted result (intents and entities) is compared with the reference label containing the spoken intents and entities. After this binary model is trained, the following is used as the confidence measure:

$$p(\hat{y} = y|\vec{x}) = \frac{1}{1 + exp\big(- \sum_j \lambda_j x_j \big)} \quad (1)$$

where $\vec{x}$ is the confidence predictor feature vector, $\hat{y}$ is the predicted label (including all entities and intents) and y is the reference label. Confidence predictors x_j depend on the inputs and outputs of the SLU system and the feature weights that are estimated during confidence model training are denoted by λ_j.

We used a number of ASR confidence scores, based on posterior probabilities, as well as comparing the ASR best path to alternative paths (Williams and Balakrishnan, 2009). Basic statistics of word-level scores were computed to create utterance-level features. The number of ASR n-best was used as another feature as an indication of ASR uncertainty (larger number of n-best shows uncertainty). We also used the text classification scores as semantic features. Another semantic feature that we used was the predicted intent category encoded as a 1-hot vector over the intent classes. ASR confidence for digits or the number of digits in the ASR n-best text were also added as features. Finally, since for number and date capture dialog states we utilized a text classifier that in addition to intent, showed if the utterance included the relevant entity or not, we used this as a binary feature which was an effective indicator of semantic confidence.

3 Date Capture

In this section, we apply the described framework to the task of date capture and we also describe our approach to creating a generic date capture model in Section 3.1. Typically, dialog-state specific models are built using labeled data from a single dialog state to train an intent classifier and entity extraction pipeline for the target state. However, the generic date capture model enables rapid deployment of models for date capture states in new applications before any data can be collected.

At least four different components are essential for capturing dates in speech input. 1) A language model for ASR to reliably transcribe the input speech. 2) A sequence tagger for identifying the span of transcribed speech containing the date specifications. 3) A function that takes into account chances of errors and computes a confidence value in the extracted entity. Finally, 4) a normalizer that converts the identified span into the desired date format. In a fully rule-based approach, the grammar-based LM performs the functions of all four components. For ASR, we use an SLM trained on a large corpus of utterances containing dates as well as utterances containing different intents instead of date entities. For span identification we use a statistical sequence tagger (MEMM (McCallum et al., 2000) or BLSTM-CRF (Huang et al., 2015)) trained on date tagged data. For entity extraction confidence, we use logistic regression models trained with scores from the tagger and from text-based binary `Date` or `No-Date` classifiers. For normalization, we use a rule-based approach applying a grammar to the tagged sequence of text.

While a large majority of users do provide a response with a date to a system prompt requesting a date, a significant number of users do not, and instead respond with utterances expressing different intents that must be robustly identified for the dialog to progress gracefully. We trained a text classifier as described in Section 2.2, which in addition to many non-date related intents such as `Cancel Reservation`, `Billing and Charges`, and `Live Agent`, includes a `Date` label, as well as `Vague Date`, for when the user responds with a partial date, such as only the month, rather than an utterance with a date expression that could be grounded to a specific date. A `Vague Date` intent can be used to trigger a reprompting of the user to disambiguate. In the case that the sequence tagger detects a date but the intent classifier does not return a `Date` intent, the detected date entity is still returned by the system. Including the `DATE` intent, there are a total of 41 intents in this date capture task.

The training, development and test sets consist of approximately 53K, 5K, and 10K utterances labeled by humans-in-the-loop, respectively. We compare the proposed framework with an SLM and a MEMM sequence tagger against a grammar-based LM that has been hand-tuned for accuracy on the target dialog state. Confidence-based rejection is typically employed to ensure a sufficiently low error rate of EVAs at run-time. Therefore, it is more informative to analyze the performance of SLU systems by examining the error rate as a function of the utterance rejection rate at different thresholds, rather than just reporting the average error rate at 100% automation. In this way, a suitable operating point at a low error rate can be selected to evaluate the performance of an SLU system.

We plotted the error rate of accepted utterances versus the percentage of utterances rejected using a confidence-based threshold (FA-Rej curve) for each system in Figure 2. Both intent classification and entity extraction performance are reflected in these plots because both the intent and entity, if present, must be correct. We observe superior performance with the proposed approach, noting that the proposed approach starts with a slightly lower error rate but due to the effectiveness of the designed confidence modeling, the gap in performance between the two approaches grows considerably wider as low-confidence utterances are rejected. At an operating point of 5% error, the proposed approach offers about 10% more automation compared to the grammar-based approach, a significant gain.

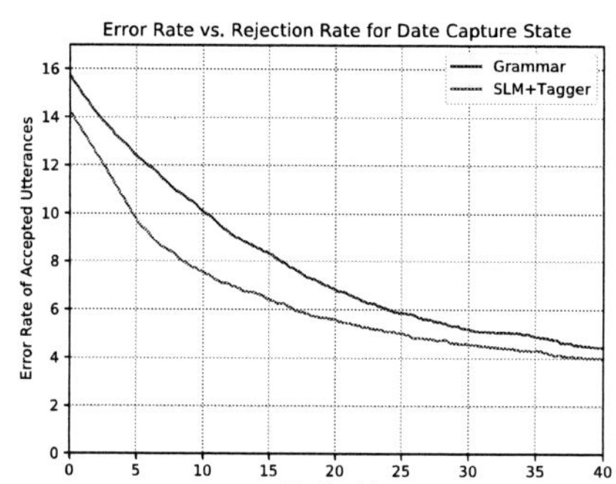

Figure 2: The error rate of accepted utterances versus the percentage of utterances rejected using a confidence-based threshold (FA-Rej curve) for a hand-tuned grammar-based LM compared to the proposed framework for a date capture state in a car rental dialog.

3.1 Generic Date Capture Model

Building out models for new dialog states and applications at scale is challenging under the paradigm of collecting data for training dialog-state specific intent classifiers and entity taggers. To address this issue, we propose a modeling approach that enables deployment of models for new capture states on day zero. First, a representative set of dialog states for a given entity, such as date, are identified and data from those states is aggregated. For example, to build a generic date capture model date capture states pertaining to service start or stop dates, hotel check-in dates, car rental pick-up dates, service appointment dates, and so on are pooled together. Then either rule-based or statistical models for entity extraction are trained using the combined data. There can be a "long tail" of unique dialog state specific intents that may appear in one dialog state from one application but would result in an invalid output that can not be handled by the dialog manager in the dialog state of another application. Thus, a set of fairly "universal" intents for this collection of dialog states must be found. The generic model can then be applied to a new target domain or task that is semantically similar without additional training data. However, the generic model does not generalize to new entity types, meaning that a generic date capture model would be applied to new date capture states only.

The training data for the generic date capture model is aggregated across six date capture states from five different EVA applications. Approximately 1.1 million utterances were used for training the intent classifier and entity extraction pipeline for the generic date capture model. Testing is done on approximately 10K utterances from a held-out date capture state from a novel application whose data never appeared in the training set. The generic intent classifier model supports 38 different intent classes that were determined based on the intents observed in the cross-application training data. The test data from the held-out dialog state contains unique intents that are not covered by the intent classifier because they did not occur in the other states comprising the training data. We compare the generic date capture model having a MEMM sequence tagger to a dialog state specific model having an intent classifier and a BLSTM-CRF sequence tagger trained on 62K utterances from the target dialog state. We use a BLSTM-CRF for the model trained on target dialog state data because it improved performance slightly but we use a MEMM in the case of the generic model because the BLSTM-CRF did not improve performance on that data.

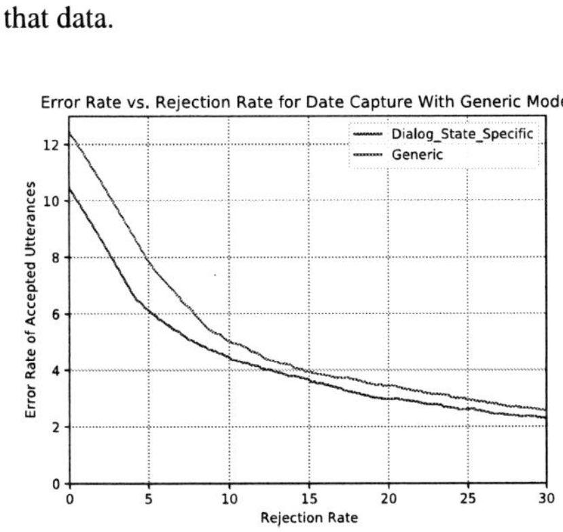

Figure 3: FA-Rej curves for a generic model and a dialog state specific model in a utility start of service date capture state.

FA-Rej curves for both the generic and dialog state specific SLU systems are shown in Figure 3. As expected, there is some loss in performance relative to the dialog state specific model trained on data from the target dialog state. However, analysis of the errors reveals that the performance on entity extraction is unchanged and the loss is largely due to a few specific intents that were not covered in the generic model in this case. Furthermore, the generic model results in a loss of only about 2.5% in automation at an operating point of 5% error, which we believe is reasonable given that this model can be deployed immediately once a new application goes online since data from the target dialog state or application is not required for training.

4 Number Capture

The goal in number capture dialog states is to capture a long sequence of digits, such as phone or account numbers. While the majority of users provide the numeric input as requested by the system prompt, approximately 30% of utterances do not include a digit sequence. Therefore the challenge in such dialog states is two-fold: 1) ensuring that if the user provided a digit sequence, it is captured accurately – a challenge due to ASR errors (even if one digit is substituted or deleted, the entire digit sequence is inaccurate) 2) if the user responds with a non-digit utterance, capture the provided intents in the utterance.

Traditional SLU systems use ASR with a carefully hand-tuned grammar-based LM to capture the digit sequence but a separate grammar needs to be designed and tuned for every new application to cater to that application's intents so it is difficult to scale. In contrast, we demonstrate in Section 4.1 that our proposed pipeline for generic digit sequence models, once trained, can be applied to any utterance with digit sequences. As an alternative to hand-tuned grammar-based models, DNN-based slot-filling models could be applied but they typically require large amounts of domain-specific annotated data for training.

We propose a hybrid grammar-based and statistical approach that overcomes the limitations of grammar-based models alone, yet is scalable and maintains high accuracy. Following the framework described in Section 2, we use an SLM-based ASR system and train a text classifier on the output for intent detection. A `Number` label is used for all utterances that only include a digit sequence, along with a broad set of other intent labels to cover the approximately 30% of utterances that do not include digit sequences. If an utterance is classified as including a digit sequence via the `Number` label, a rule-based system is used to extract and normalize the number. Note that this approach yields the best accuracy for utterances in a specific dialog state since the structure of the digit sequence is predetermined, but for more general number capture an entity tagger could be applied. The rule-based system finds the best digit sequence match in any of the ASR n-best results. Additionally, we trained a confidence model to produce an overall confidence score. An important factor in confidence estimation for number capture is the presence or absence of the digit sequence, and therefore we use that as an additional binary confidence predictor feature. Furthermore, if a digit sequence is detected in the utterance, ASR word scores for the recognized digits, and the length of the digit sequence are used as input features for the number capture confidence model.

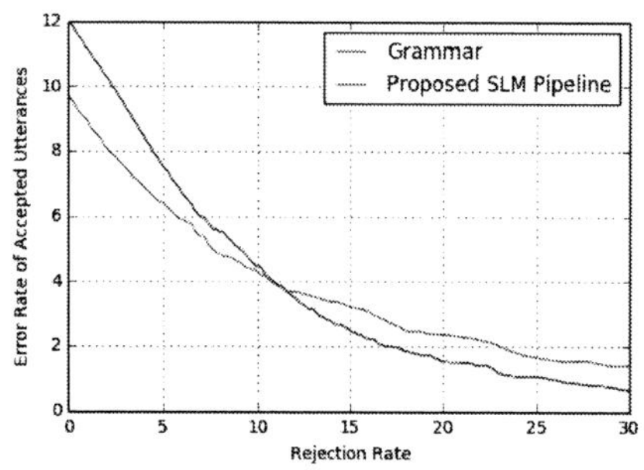

Figure 4: FA-Rej curves for a hand-tuned grammar-based LM compared to the proposed framework for a phone/account number capture state.

We compare the proposed pipeline to a hand-tuned application-specific grammar-based LM approach for account/phone number capture. For this experiment, 2K utterances with reference labels were used for testing, and about 3M utterances for training. Note that only a small subset of the training data (~10%) which had low SLU confidence with an existing grammar-based system were labeled by humans in an online fashion. The data to train the confidence model included about 300K utterances with online human labels. Results are shown in Figure 4. The accuracy (at zero rejection) with the proposed approach has improved by 2.35% absolute, and at an operating point of 5% error, the proposed approach offers 1.2% more automation compared to the grammar-based approach. As shown the grammar-based approach outperforms the SLM-based pipeline for error rates of lower than 4%, which is due to several rounds of careful hand-tuning of the grammar-based LM for some of the less frequent utterances. However, the proposed approach is still superior because of its flexibility to be easily applied to any application.

4.1 Generic Number Capture Model

Following a methodology similar to the one described in Section 3.1, a generic model for digit sequence capture was built. Data for the generic number capture model was pooled from five different applications containing digit capture states with digit sequence lengths ranging from 5-10 digits. In total, 715K utterances were used for training an intent classifier that covered 69 unique intents for these digit capture states, including a label to indicate the presence of a digit sequence. Approximately 67% of the training utterances contained digit sequences and the remaining 33% were only other intents. As before, a rule-based system is used to extract and normalize the number when the intent classifier predicts a digit sequence is present. To train a system-level confidence model, a total of 88k held-out utterances having human-in-the-loop annotated labels from the set of five applications was used. The generic intent and confidence models for digit capture were tested on a test set from one of the five applications included in the model using held-out data and compared to a dialog state specific model trained with data from the target application.

Similar to the results for the generic date capture model in Section 3.1, we observe that the generic model for number capture does perform slightly worse than the dialog state specific model but still offers an acceptable level of automation at an operating point of 5% error. The number capture accuracy of the generic digit capture model is approximately 1% lower than that of dialog state specific model at zero rejection, and less than 2% performance difference at other rejection rates. Error rate versus rejection rate curves for the two models are shown in Figure 5.

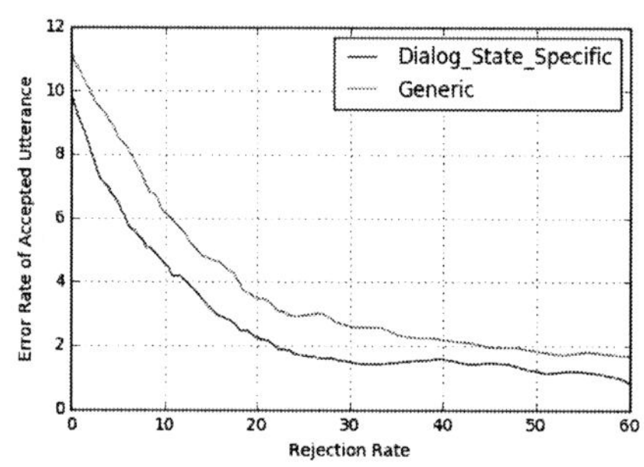

Figure 5: FA-Rej curves comparing a generic model and a dialog state specific model for a number capture dialog state.

5 Name Capture

Person name recognition is a difficult task in spoken language understanding due to the size of the vocabulary and confusions in name pronunciations (Yu et al., 2003; Raghavan and Allan, 2005; Bruguier et al., 2016). In the course of customer care dialogs users are often asked to provide their last name for identification purposes. There are a very large number of last names, some of which are similar sounding like "Stuard", "Stuart", and "Stewart", making it difficult to accurately recognize names in isolation. However, if the user is also asked to provide the spelling as well that can be leveraged to correctly capture the name. We observe that names at the beginning of an utterance are very difficult for ASR to recognise correctly but spelled letters are often recognized more accurately and can be concatenated to capture the name. To recognize potentially hundreds of thousands of last names using a traditional n-gram SLM or grammar, every possible last name and spelling sequence should be encoded, resulting in a very large LM. Instead, we propose a hierarchical language model, which consists of sub language models derived from the beginning sounds of the last names (hereafter, we call this language model *1-layer LM*). This is motivated by the fact that the beginning of a name's pronunciation leads the rest of name and spelling sequence, unlike other ASR tasks (see Figure 6a).

Still, asking the user to also spell their name does not make the recognition task trivial. When spelling a word, there are frequent confusion pairs such as 'f and s', 'b and v', 'p and t' and 'm and n'. To distinguish between such confusion pairs, a common practice is to use the NATO phonetic alphabet - "Sam S as in sierra A as in alpha M as in Mike". However, people tend to use any word they can think of easily for distinguishing the characters in their name, rather than adhering to the NATO phonetic alphabet which may not be familiar to many users. Thus, we added another layer of sub grammar at the bottom of last name sub grammars in the hierarchical language model to cover the NATO phonetic alphabet, as well as a large number of other words people use to distinguish characters (hereafter, *2-layer LM*) shown in Figure 6b. Similar to the date and number capture systems, our approach for last name capture also incorporates an intent classifier covering a set of intents which are likely to occur when last names are not given.

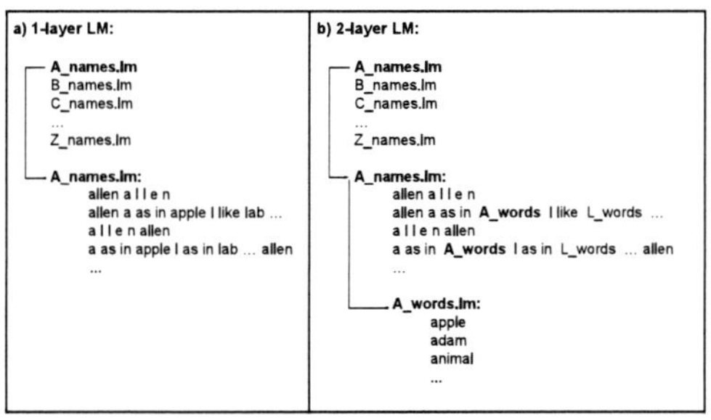

Figure 6: Last name LMs: a) 1-layer LM is trained on name and spell as it is; b) 2-layer LM is trained on names and spells but taking NATO words as another LM component.

We compare four different systems to capture last names in spoken input: 1) *SVM* classifier trained on 170K ASR hypotheses using bi-gram features and human annotated labels for the names; 2) *1-layer LM* with which we decode the utterances and then concatenate the spelled letters to predict the last name. Note that the usual ASR confidence score is used as prediction confidence to draw the rejection curves; 3) *2-layer LM* which is used in the same way as the second system and 4) *2-layer LM with confidence model* which is used in the same way as the third system, but instead a confidence model (described in Section 2.4) is exploited to generate the confidence scores. The confidence model is trained on a 29K data set with features consisting of the ASR-based confidence scores and utterance length.

A test set containing 1K utterances labeled with the last name by human annotators is used for testing. Curves for the various systems on the test set are shown in Figure 7. As expected, the SVM classifier performs very poorly due to the problem of data sparsity in the data set. We selected this approach as one of our baselines for comparison because it shows reasonable performance on a first name capture task where the sparsity of data is less than it is for last names. The second algorithm in which we use the *1-layer LM* to decode the utterances and then concatenate the spelled letters to determine the last names performs better on average but it fails in many cases due to the inclusion of characters that distinguish words in the utterance. However, the *2-layer LM* resolves many of those issues and it significantly improves the accuracy, requiring far fewer utterances to be rejected at an operating point of 5% error. Confidence modeling only marginally helps performance with the simple ASR confidence features used and we suspect more informative features need to be designed.

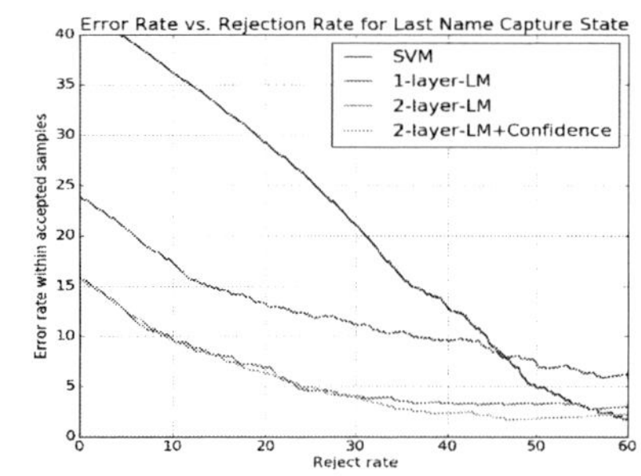

Figure 7: FA-Rej curves for last name capture.

6 Conclusions

SLU for EVAs encompasses a wide-ranging set of practical challenges and investigations into the design of accurate and scalable SLU systems that can quickly be deployed for new applications without requiring much human intervention each time is warranted. In this paper, we have presented an enterprise-grade deployed SLU pipeline for handling intents and entities and demonstrated its effectiveness across several real world subtasks in a deployed customer care virtual agent. We have also highlighted the importance of confidence modeling using features from each component in the pipeline. The proposed approach to create generic date and digit capture models for intents and entities allows for day zero deployment of models for new applications. In the future, we will incorporate word confusion networks and lattices for the different capture tasks presented in this paper.

References

Tony Bruguier, Fuchun Peng, and Françoise Beaufays. 2016. Learning personalized pronunciations for contact names recognition. In *Interspeech*.

Alice Coucke, Alaa Saade, Adrien Ball, Théodore Bluche, Alexandre Caulier, David Leroy, Clément Doumouro, Thibault Gisselbrecht, Francesco Caltagirone, Thibaut Lavril, et al. 2018. Snips voice platform: an embedded spoken language understanding system for private-by-design voice interfaces. *arXiv preprint arXiv:1805.10190*.

James Glass. 1999. Challenges for spoken dialogue systems. In *Proceedings of the 1999 IEEE ASRU Workshop*, volume 696.

Arshit Gupta, AI Amazon, John Hewitt, and Katrin Kirchhoff. 2019. Simple, fast, accurate intent classification and slot labeling for goal-oriented dialogue systems. In *20th Annual Meeting of the Special Interest Group on Discourse and Dialogue*, page 46.

Narendra Gupta, Gokhan Tur, Dilek Hakkani-Tur, Srinivas Bangalore, Giuseppe Riccardi, and Mazin Gilbert. 2005. The at&t spoken language understanding system. *IEEE Transactions on Audio, Speech, and Language Processing*, 14(1):213–222.

Dilek Hakkani-Tür, Frédéric Béchet, Giuseppe Riccardi, and Gokhan Tur. 2006. Beyond asr 1-best: Using word confusion networks in spoken language understanding. *Computer Speech & Language*, 20(4):495–514.

Matthew Henderson, Milica Gašić, Blaise Thomson, Pirros Tsiakoulis, Kai Yu, and Steve Young. 2012. Discriminative spoken language understanding using word confusion networks. In *2012 IEEE Spoken Language Technology Workshop (SLT)*, pages 176–181. IEEE.

Zhiheng Huang, Wei Xu, and Kai Yu. 2015. Bidirectional lstm-crf models for sequence tagging. *arXiv preprint arXiv:1508.01991*.

Yoon Kim. 2014. Convolutional neural networks for sentence classification. In *Proceedings of the 2014 Conference on Empirical Methods in Natural Language Processing (EMNLP)*, pages 1746–1751, Doha, Qatar. Association for Computational Linguistics.

Mingda Li, Weitong Ruan, Xinyue Liu, Luca Soldaini, Wael Hamza, and Chengwei Su. 2020. Improving spoken language understanding by exploiting asr n-best hypotheses. *arXiv preprint arXiv:2001.05284*.

Bing Liu and Ian Lane. 2016. Attention-based recurrent neural network models for joint intent detection and slot filling. In *Interspeech*, pages 685–689.

Loren Lugosch, Mirco Ravanelli, Patrick Ignoto, Vikrant Singh Tomar, and Yoshua Bengio. 2019. Speech Model Pre-Training for End-to-End Spoken Language Understanding. In *Proc. Interspeech 2019*, pages 814–818.

Andrew McCallum, Dayne Freitag, and Fernando CN Pereira. 2000. Maximum entropy markov models for information extraction and segmentation. In *Icml*, volume 17, pages 591–598.

Mahnoosh Mehrabani, David Thomson, and Benjamin Stern. 2018. Practical application of domain dependent confidence measurement for spoken language understanding systems. In *Proceedings of the 2018 Conference of the North American Chapter of the Association for Computational Linguistics: Human Language Technologies, Volume 3 (Industry Papers)*, pages 185–192.

Grégoire Mesnil, Yann Dauphin, Kaisheng Yao, Yoshua Bengio, Li Deng, Dilek Hakkani-Tur, Xiaodong He, Larry Heck, Gokhan Tur, Dong Yu, et al. 2014. Using recurrent neural networks for slot filling in spoken language understanding. *IEEE/ACM Transactions on Audio, Speech, and Language Processing*, 23(3):530–539.

Patti Price. 1990. Evaluation of spoken language systems: The atis domain. In *Speech and Natural Language: Proceedings of a Workshop Held at Hidden Valley, Pennsylvania, June 24-27, 1990*.

Ryan Price. 2020. End-to-end spoken language understanding without matched language speech model pretraining data. In *ICASSP 2020-2020 IEEE International Conference on Acoustics, Speech and Signal Processing (ICASSP)*, pages 7979–7983. IEEE.

Hema Raghavan and James Allan. 2005. Matching inconsistently spelled names in automatic speech recognizer output for information retrieval. In *Proceedings of Human Language Technology Conference and Conference on Empirical Methods in Natural Language Processing*, pages 451–458, Vancouver, British Columbia, Canada. Association for Computational Linguistics.

Rubén San-Segundo, Bryan Pellom, Kadri Hacioglu, Wayne Ward, and José M Pardo. 2001. Confidence measures for spoken dialogue systems. In *2001 IEEE International Conference on Acoustics, Speech, and Signal Processing. Proceedings (Cat. No. 01CH37221)*, volume 1, pages 393–396. IEEE.

Ruhi Sarikaya, Yuqing Gao, Michael Picheny, and Hakan Erdogan. 2005. Semantic confidence measurement for spoken dialog systems. *IEEE Transactions on Speech and Audio Processing*, 13(4):534–545.

Natalia Tomashenko, Antoine Caubrière, and Yannick Estève. 2019. Investigating adaptation and transfer learning for end-to-end spoken language understanding from speech. In *Interspeech 2019*, pages 824–828. ISCA.

Akshit Tyagi, Varun Sharma, Rahul Gupta, Lynn Samson, Nan Zhuang, Zihang Wang, and Bill Campbell. 2020. Fast intent classification for spoken language understanding systems. In *ICASSP 2020-2020 IEEE International Conference on Acoustics, Speech and Signal Processing (ICASSP)*, pages 8119–8123. IEEE.

Sida Wang and Christopher Manning. 2012. Baselines and bigrams: Simple, good sentiment and topic classification. In *Proceedings of the 50th Annual Meeting of the Association for Computational Linguistics (Volume 2: Short Papers)*, pages 90–94, Jeju Island, Korea. Association for Computational Linguistics.

Jason D Williams and Suhrid Balakrishnan. 2009. Estimating probability of correctness for asr n-best lists. In *Proceedings of the SIGDIAL 2009 Conference*, pages 132–135.

Puyang Xu and Ruhi Sarikaya. 2013. Convolutional neural network based triangular crf for joint intent detection and slot filling. In *ieee workshop on automatic speech recognition and understanding*, pages 78–83.

Dong Yu, Kuansan Wang, Milind Mahajan, Peter Mau, and Alex Acero. 2003. Improved name recognition with user modeling. In *Eighth European Conference on Speech Communication and Technology*.

Proteno: Text Normalization with Limited Data for Fast Deployment in Text to Speech Systems

Shubhi Tyagi, Antonio Bonafonte, Jaime Lorenzo-Trueba, Javier Latorre*
Amazon Alexa AI

Abstract

Developing Text Normalization (TN) systems for Text-to-Speech (TTS) on new languages is hard. We propose a novel architecture to facilitate it for multiple languages while using data less than 3% of the size of the data used by the state of the art results on English. We treat TN as a sequence classification problem and propose a granular tokenization mechanism that enables the system to learn majority of the classes and their normalizations from the training data itself. This is further combined with minimal pre-coded linguistic knowledge for other classes. We publish the first results on TN for TTS in Spanish and Tamil and also demonstrate that the performance of the approach is comparable with the previous work done on English. All annotated datasets used for experimentation will be released at `https://github.com/amazon-research/proteno`.

1 Introduction

Text-to-speech synthesis (TTS) consists of a number of processing steps that control the conversion of input text to output speech. Text normalization (TN) is usually the first step for any TTS system. It is defined as the process of mapping of written text to its spoken form. As per Taylor (2009), *semiotic class* denotes things like numbers, dates, times, etc. that are written differently from the way they are verbalized. TN is the process of verbalizing instances of such classes.

Most systems are entirely based on hard coded rules which are neither scalable across languages nor easy to maintain. Many machine learning based techniques have been proposed for TN but they still have heavy dependency on encoded linguistic knowledge or require considerable amount of annotated data making it difficult to scale.

The contributions of this paper are as follows: *i)* Presenting Proteno, a novel architecture for TN with a granular tokenization mechanism, which requires minimal language specific rules, curtails unacceptable errors and is transferable to a large extent to multiple languages, *ii)* Establishing an architecture which can be used to benchmark TN baselines for multiple languages with limited annotated data, *iii)* Release of annotated TN datasets for Tamil and Spanish suitable for TTS systems.

As no benchmark datasets or baselines exist for TN for TTS in Spanish and Tamil, we curated datasets for both and evaluated Proteno on them. We also use the best performing system for TN in English and compare its results with previous work.

2 Related Work

In spite of the success of deep learning approaches in other natural language processing tasks, the problem of TN for TTS systems still remains a challenging one (Sproat and Jaitly, 2016). Work has been done to solve TN by pure encoder-decoder methods particularly Recurrent Neural Networks (Sproat and Jaitly, 2017; Zhang et al., 2019). However, authors have shown that even though such models can perform well overall, occasionally they can make *"unacceptable errors"* like reading "$2" as "two pounds" and thus rendering the system unsuitable for industrial TTS applications.

To curtail such unacceptable errors, previous work based on *semiotic classification* (Sproat et al., 2001; Ebden and Sproat, 2014; Zhang et al., 2019), are encoded with measures like weighted *Finite-state Transducers* (FSTs) introduced by Sproat (1996). FSTs revolve around creating a weak covering grammar which encompasses language specific lexical information. Although such grammars are easier to create as compared to a full blown grammar, they still need prior knowledge of the language and the language specific rules need to be coded in the system (Sodimana et al., 2018). To completely induce FST from training data, as suggested by Zhang et al. (2019), diverse and large

*Work done while at Amazon

Proceedings of NAACL HLT 2021: IndustryTrack Papers, pages 72–79
June 6–11, 2021. ©2021 Association for Computational Linguistics

amount of data is required. The data should represent all the forms a particular token can appear in a given language. Such requirements for all semiotic classes limit the reproducibility of such models for a new language with limited annotated data. Other language-agnostic approaches (A. Conkie and A. Finch, 2020) also need large amounts of data (5M sentences for each language) as parallel corpus and can also result in unacceptable errors.

Our approach curtails such errors by breaking down complex entities like dates into multiple tokens by a granular tokenization mechanism and also by limiting which tokens can be *accepted* into a class. This mechanism, we will see, also enables the system to rely more on data and disambiguate context for normalizations without requiring the knowledge to be specifically coded in the system.

3 Proposed Approach

The target normalization can be directly predicted from unnormalized text with a seq2seq architecture (Sutskever et al., 2014) by treating TN as a *machine translation* task (Zhang et al., 2019; Mansfield et al., 2019) with the previously mentioned limitations. A way to limit the *unacceptable errors* in such systems would be to limit the kind of normalizations the network can generate for a token (Sproat and Jaitly, 2017).

On the other hand, solutions based on semiotic classification convert TN into a sequence tagging problem, where each class has associated mechanisms for normalizing the corresponding unnormalized token(s). It produces verbalizations by first suitably tokenizing the input, then classifying the tokens, and then verbalizing each token according to its corresponding class. These approaches often have a complex tokenization mechanism which is not easily transferable across languages and also need all the possible classes to be exhaustively defined manually.

We solve both these problems by a granular tokenization mechanism which extends the concept of *semiotic classification* to a granular level wherein each unique unnormalized token to normalized token mapping can have a class of its own. The majority of the classes and their appropriate normalizations are automatically learnt from data.

Our classes represent whether a particular token is of a certain type and convert unnormalized tokens into their normalized form. The goal is to manually define the minimum possible set of classes and all the other classes will be automatically learnt from the data. The system learns when each class should be applied. The solution is divided into 4 stages: *i)* Tokenization of unnormalized data, *ii)* Data preparation, *iii)* Classifying unnormalized tokens into correct classes, *iv)* Normalizing tokens using the corresponding class.

3.1 Tokenizer

Typically, TN approaches either assume pre-segmented text by the rule-based standard (Ebden and Sproat, 2014) which identifies multiword sequences as single segment like dates (Jan. 3, 2016) according to pre-defined semiotic classes or train a neural network for tokenization together with a normalization model (Zhang et al., 2019). Proteno's tokenization on the other hand, has elementary rules and is deterministic. The segmentation is done by splitting the sentences on spaces and then further splitting the text when there is a change in the Unicode class. E.g., after splitting on spaces, a token like 'C3PO' will be further split into ['C','3','PO']. Such tokenization enables the system to accurately split complex entities like dates while eliminating the need for a manually defined complex class for them. The same tokenization mechanism was used for all the languages tested. Hence, it is transferable across a large group of languages which have words separated by spaces.

3.2 Data Preparation

While collecting training data, first the unnormalized data is tokenized according to the granular tokenization mechanism described above and then each token is annotated with its corresponding normalized form. Thus, we obtain unnormalized token to normalized token mappings. E.g., a date occurrence '1/1/2020' tokenized as ['1','/','1','/','2020'] is annotated as ['first','of', 'January','','twenty twenty']. For such data annotation, linguistic experts are not needed and this can be done by anyone proficient in the target language.

From our experiments, we observe that for TN the diversity in data is more important than the quantity of data. It is better for the model to see different kinds of normalizations. Hence, while collecting the data, we try to ensure decent coverage of different semiotic classes by having at least 25% of tokens which need normalization (i.e., *non-self*).

3.3 Classes

Each class has 2 functions: *i)* ***Accepts***: This function returns a Boolean value of whether a token is accepted by the class. E.g., *cardinal* class accepts only numeric tokens, *ii) **Normalize***: This is a deterministic function that transforms the unnormalized token into its verbalized form

A token can be classified into a class only if it is *accepted* by it. By restricting the classes a token is accepted into, we limit the kind of normalization output that can be generated. This prevents the model from making *unacceptable errors*. A token can be accepted by multiple classes which can give different normalizations. In such cases, the model is responsible for predicting the appropriate class from the context. If multiple classes give the same normalization for a token, then during inference it doesn't matter which class is chosen.

We have 2 kinds of classes: *i)* **Pre-defined**: We define limited number of classes (~10-15) containing basic normalization rules out of which only a small subset (~5) contain language specific verbalization rules like *cardinal, ordinal* etc. Rules behind the normalization logic for others like *self, sil, digit, roman numerals,* etc. remain similar across many languages, only the surface form of the normalized version changes. E.g., *self* class indicates that the input is to be passed through as it is and it accepts tokens containing only alphabetical characters. *Sil* is used to represent silence, which is typically associated with punctuation. It accepts only punctuation or other kinds of symbols which should not be verbalized. *Roman numerals* also have language agnostic logic to convert the roman number into number form and pass it down to its corresponding cardinal or ordinal class for generating desired normalization. *ii)* **Auto Generated (AG)**: Apart from pre-defined classes, the model learns automatically generated classes from the data by going through the unnormalized to normalized token mappings in the dataset. If none of the existing classes (pre-coded or AG) can generate the target normalization for a token in the training data, then a class is automatically generated which accepts only the token responsible for its generation. Its normalize function returns the target normalization observed in the annotated data for that token. E.g., if "12→December" is observed in the dataset and if none of the existing classes can generate this normalization then a class *"12_to_December_AG"* is created. This class accepts only "12" and its normalize function returns "December". If multiple normalizations are observed for an unnormalized token in the dataset which cannot be generated by existing classes then multiple AGs are stored. AGs enable Proteno to learn majority of the normalizations automatically from data.

3.4 Classification & Normalization

We model TN as a sequence tagging problem where the input is a sequence of unnormalized tokens and the output is the sequence of classes which can generate the normalized text. Before training the classification model, we transform the data to get unnormalized token to class mappings. E.g., ['1','/','1','/','2020'] → [ordinal, /_to_of_AG, 1_to_January_AG, sil, year]. We prepare this data by going over the unnormalized token to normalized token mapping for a sentence and identifying which existing classes can give the target normalization. For a token there can be multiple matching classes. E.g., '2' can be correctly normalized by both cardinal and digit classes. In such cases of multiple matching classes we pick the least frequent class to increase the representation of infrequent classes. This compensates for the imbalance present in the proportion of classes in training set. A more optimum approach to handle cases of multiple matching classes will be explored in the future.

To classify the sequence of unnormalized tokens to their corresponding classes we experimented with 4 classifiers. We first train a first order Conditional Random Fields (CRFs) (Lafferty et al., 2001) and then train neural network (NN) based architectures like Bi-LSTMs (Hochreiter and Schmidhuber, 1997), BiLSTM-CRFs (Huang et al., 2015) and Transformers (Vaswani et al., 2017). We used word embeddings from Mikolov et al. (2018) for NN systems. *i) **CRF***: The features used for each unnormalized token in the model are - part of speech tag, list of classes which accept the token as an input, next token in sequence, suffix of the token (from length 1-4), prefix of the token (from length 1-4), is the token in upper case, is the token numeric and is the token capitalized, *ii) **Bi-LSTM & BiLSTM-CRFs***: Using word embeddings and list of classes which accept the token as input features, *iii) **Transformer***: A Transformer with 6 heads with word embeddings as input features.

For each token we renormalize the probabilities predicted over all classes to only the classes which accept the token. Hence, the model is restricted to classify a token only to one of its few accepted classes. If the system is unable to find a suitable class for the given token (i.e., none of the given classes accept that token) then it gives a empty output instead of an incorrect normalization.

3.5 Aligning tokens in order of verbalization

One of the major challenges in automated TN is handling realignment of tokens which may be required between the written and its spoken form. Our method so far assumes monotonic alignment between the written unormalized tokens and their corresponding spoken normalizations. However, this is not always true. For our chosen languages we saw two exceptions: currency and measure units. E.g., \$3.45 → *'Three dollars forty five cents'* and m^2 → *'squared metres'*. Seq2seq models can naturally learn such kind of realignment from training data (Sproat and Jaitly, 2017). However, they are susceptible to errors specially for limited amount of training data for specific classes.

Thus, to limit errors in such cases we define some rules. Proteno first recognises instances of currency/measure in the text and prevents them from further splitting by the granular tokenizer. The currency/measure classes have the same granular tokenisation logic along with realignment conditions. They further pass the final tokens to their corresponding classes. Thus, an entity like '\$45.18' is transformed into ['45', '\$', '18', '.'] and passed to classes as 45→*cardinal*, \$→*\$_to_dollars_AG*, 18→*cardinal*, . →*_to_cents_AG*.

As all currency symbols have their own AGs automatically generated from the data there will always be a 1:1 mapping between a symbol and its normalized form. As a result, this approach eliminates the possibility of an *unacceptable error* like normalizing \$ → Pounds.

Classes like ***currency*** and ***measure*** contain rules that are responsible for realignment only and hence require limited knowledge to be transferred across languages. The normalization is handled by the already learnt or defined classes. Thus, these classes can be skipped or be used as is for any language which has this kind of realignment.

4 Experiment Protocol

4.1 Datasets

As the goal of Proteno is to be applicable for multiple languages, we evaluate the system across 3 languages. For experimentation with new languages we chose Spanish and Tamil. Further, we evaluate Proteno on English, to see how it compares against a language which has more evolved TN systems available. There are no benchmarked annotated TN for TTS datasets available for Tamil and Spanish. *i)* ***Spanish***: We gathered data from Wikipedia by selecting sentences rich with entities requiring normalization. Due to budget constraints we could collect a dataset of only 135k tokens (5k sentences), *ii)* ***Tamil***: We annotate the data sourced from English-Tamil parallel corpus (Ramasamy et al., 2012) and Comparable Corpora (Eckart and Quasthoff, 2013). From these datasets we sampled 500k tokens (30k sentences) with higher preference towards sentences that needed normalization, *iii)* ***English***: We used a portion of the annotated data from Sproat and Jaitly (2016). First, we run the Proteno tokenizer over the unnormalized section of the dataset and got unnormalized token to normalized token mappings using elementary rules. By doing so, we were able to correctly match only a portion of the dataset due to its different tokenization. And then, from this subset, 300k tokens (24.7k sentences) were randomly sampled to keep the data size comparable to that used for Tamil. This is 1.5% of the data used by Pramanik and Hussain (2019) which used first 20M tokens and 3% of data used by Zhang et al. (2019) which used first 10M tokens.

4.2 Training & Evaluation

Train and test data were split by the ratio of 60:40. We keep a higher test set proportion to have a challenging setting for the systems. Word Error Rate (WER) is used as the evaluation metric for the different classifiers. We use this metric instead of classification accuracy on the classes in order to enable comparison of results from different TN approaches in the future, which may not use the same tokenization mechanism and hence may not have the same classes benchmarked by previous work.

WER is measured as Levenshtein Distance (Levenshtein, 1966) between the model prediction and the desired normalization. Hence, lower WER is desirable. We also report classification accuracy to illustrate that classification accuracy does not directly translate into WER. We first evaluate all the classifiers on Spanish and then choose the classifier with lowest WER for Tamil and English.

5 Results

5.1 Spanish

Due to lack of a standard baseline, we compare the performance of Proteno on Spanish with an existing rule based (RB) system. This is the production TN system containing 1.7k lines of regular expressions code which required extensive linguistic knowledge and programming proficiency.

Normalization was required for **27%** of tokens in both the training and the test set. **10** classes were pre-coded with normalization logic: *self, sil, spell, currency, unit, digit, cardinal, ordinal, roman cardinal and roman ordinal* out of which only **5** had language specific normalization rules (*spell, cardinal_masculine, cardinal_feminine, ordinal_masculine and ordinal_feminine*). **279** AGs were generated from this dataset. The WER results from different models is given in Table 1.

Models	WER(Train)	WER(Test)
RB System	2.3	2.3
CRF	0.3	1.02*
BiLSTM	**0.03**	**0.89***
BiLSTM-CRF	0.04	**0.89***
Transformer	1.2	2.3

Table 1: WER for CRF vs LSTM vs Transformer. Fields in bold are indicative of best model. * signifies statistically significant difference in comparison to RB

On the test set, all models except Transformers showed statistically significant difference ($p<<0.01$) in comparison to the RB system. We can attribute the lower performance of Transformers to lack of *accepted classes* as input features.

Although the numbers suggest that the NN models might be overfitting, we were not able to significantly improve them using regularization techniques. Introducing dropout from 0.1-0.3 increased the train WER from 0.03 to 0.04 but did not impact the test WER. Further increase in dropout increased test WER. We also try replacing the cross entropy loss with the *Weighted Categorical Cross Entropy Loss* to avoid the model's bias towards predicting the dominant class (in this case *'self'*). This loss function decreased the train WER from 0.03 to 0.027 but it did not impact the test WER.

For most of the classes CRFs and NN models performed at par with each other. Classification accuracy by the models is given in Table 2. However, low classification accuracy, though indicative of inaccurate normalization, does not directly translate into higher WERs. Multiple classes can give the same normalization and thus there is no unique correct class. This is particularly prevalent in some cases of number instances where *cardinal_masculine* and *cardinal_feminine* can be used interchangeably.

Even though Transformers give unstable performance in class prediction, they still give a low enough WER. This particular iteration has a bias towards predicting *cardinal_ masculine* over *cardinal_feminine*. This bias changes with different iterations but the WER remains consistent as the normalization output remains unaffected.

5.2 Tamil

For Tamil, we have **8** pre-coded classes *(self_english, self_tamil, sil, spell, currency, digit, cardinal and ordinal)* out of which only **3** are encoded with language specific normalization logic (*cardinal, ordinal and spell*) and **74** AGs were generated from the dataset. To normalize text on Tamil corpus, we trained the system which performed the best on Spanish i.e., BiLSTMs with the same configurations. The model gave a WER=**0.6** on the train set and WER=**3.3** on the test set. The token proportion and high-level classification accuracy results for the tokens are detailed in Table 3.

5.3 English

To evaluate the potential of the approach and benchmark it with existing work we trained Proteno on English. The model had **8** pre-coded classes *(self, sil, spell, cardinal, ordinal, digit, roman, units, year)* out of which only **4** classes contained language specific rules (*spell, cardinal, ordinal, year*). **2658** AGs were generated from the data. The number of AGs in English are significantly higher than the ones generated for Tamil or Spanish as English tends to use much more abbreviations in written form as compared to the other two languages. The model achieved a WER=**0.47** on the train set and a WER=**2.6** on the test set. High level classification accuracies are detailed in Table 3. Out of the 99.26% correctly normalized tokens, 88.2% of the non-self tokens were normalized via AGs i.e., **88.2%** of the normalizations were learnt automatically from data without relying on pre-coded linguistic knowledge.

It is not possible to directly compare our results with previous work done on English TN (Pramanik and Hussain, 2019; Zhang et al., 2019) as these works report classification accuracy on 16 manually defined classes and not WER. Moreover, Proteno does not have the same set of classes due to its granular tokenization mechanism. It also uses only 1.5%-3% of the dataset used by them and further splits it into train and test set. It cannot use the full dataset due to differing tokenization mecha-

	Token Proportion		CRF		BiLSTM		BiLSTM-CRF		Transformers	
	Train	Test	Train	Test	Train	Test	Train	Test	Train	Test
Accuracy			99.7	**99.1**	**99.9**	99.01	99.99	98.9	93.0	92.8
Accuracy per class										
'self'	70.5	70	**100**	**100**	**100**	99.9	**100**	99.9	**100**	99.8
'sil'	13.24	13	99.7	**99.8**	**100**	99.5	99.99	99.6	**100**	98.7
Others			98.0	93.2	**99.9**	93.06	**99.9**	**95.9**	44.2	48.3
'es_num_by_num_cardinal'	2.14	2.1	**99.9**	**99.2**	**99.9**	**99.2**	**99.9**	98.6	3.85	2.4
'es_cardinal_feminine'	3.8	3.8	98.9	**96.7**	**100**	93.5	99.9	92.8	37.7	41.6
'es_ordinal_masculine'	0.38	0.4	95.2	96.7	99.7	96.7	**100**	**97.1**	0	1.9
'spell'	0.62	0.57	98.7	96.0	**100**	75.2	**100**	71.1	99.6	**99.3**
'es_cardinal_masculine'	1.75	2.16	98.2	89.2	**100**	**98.8**	99.8	98.6	87.0	88.1
'es_ordinal_feminine'	0	0.00004	n/a	0.0	n/a	0	n/a	0	n/a	**100**
'mean'	7.63	8	97.6	**92.6**	**99.9**	89.7	**99.9**	88.5	47.9	51.9

Table 2: Token proportions and classification accuracy across systems for Spanish. 'mean' depicts the average accuracy of the remaining pre-coded and all the AG classes. Bold font highlights the best results

Language	**Proportion of self tokens**		**Proportion of other tokens**		**Accuracy on self tokens**		**Accuracy on other tokens**		**Overall Accuracy**	
	Train	Test	Train	Test	Train	Test	Train	Test	Train	Test
Tamil	0.73	0.75	0.27	0.25	99.99	99.99	99.94	96.49	99.98	99.12
English	0.72	0.71	0.28	0.29	99.97	99.99	99.55	97.5	99.85	99.26

Table 3: Token proportions and classification accuracy for Tamil and English

	Plain	**Punct**	**Date**	**Cardinal**	**Verbatim**	**Measure**	**Ordinal**	**Decimal**	**Digit**	**Fraction**	**Letters**
Train Proportion	70.2	18.8	6.13	1.13	0.82	0.21	0.11	0.20	0.04	0.0	2.39
Test Proportion	70.3	18.7	6.08	1.30	0.71	0.19	0.15	0.16	0.04	0.001	2.27
Proteno	99.9	100	98.16	99.08	96.97	96.09	73.05	90.0	41.30	100.0	79.18
P&H	99.4	99.9	99.7	99.4	99.4	97.1	98.0	98.9	79.5	92.3	97.1
Z	99.9	99.9	99.5	99.4	99.9	97.2	98.1	100	86.4	81.3	97.5

Table 4: English Classification Accuracy: Proteno vs Pramanik and Hussain (2019) vs Zhang et al. (2019)

nisms which result into mismatch in the alignment between the unnormalized token and their corresponding normalized forms. However, we extract their pre-defined categories on the dataset we used and evaluate how many tokens within them were normalized correctly. In Table 4 we compare Proteno accuracy with the accuracy reported by Pramanik and Hussain (2019) (P&H) and by Zhang et al. (2019) (Z). It illustrates the token normalization accuracy achieved by Proteno on the test dataset for all the categories which had instances in the small subset we have used.

Proteno performs at par with the other systems for most of the categories in spite of seeing much fewer instances in the train set. For complex entities likes *date* Proteno gave 98.16% accuracy on the 6% tokens available in test set. The system (Z) gives 99.5% accuracy on its set by using a covering grammar learnt from large amounts of data. We observe comparable performance for another complex category like *measure*. On the other hand, we see a significant drop in Proteno's performance when normalizing *ordinal* and *digit*. This is due to low representation of these classes during training and hence during inference the model has a bias towards predicting *cardinal* over them when seen in similar context. This bias can be addressed by having a more equitable representation of instances of *cardinals, ordinals* and *digits* during training.

6 Conclusions

We propose a novel architecture suitable for scaling Text Normalization for TTS across languages using minimal language specific rules, limited annotated dataset and while curbing *unacceptable errors* which makes it suitable for fast deployment in industry applications. We treat Text Normalization as a sequence classification problem while proposing a granular tokenizer which enables majority of normalizations to be automatically learnt from data. We experiment across 3 languages: Spanish, Tamil and English, while pre-coding maximum **5** classes with language specific logic. We also demonstrate that datasets of the order of 135k-500k tokens can give competitive performance while still being of a size practical for hand annotation.

Proteno consists of *i)* a granular tokenizer based on Unicode classes, *ii)* a classifier of tokens into classes, either predefined or added based on the tokenized data, and *iii)* the class verbalizers, either defined by linguists for predefined classes or automatically learnt from the data. BiLSTMs give the best performance with WER=**0.89** for Spanish, WER=**3.3** for Tamil and WER=**2.6** for English. In English, **88.2%** of the normalizations were learnt automatically from data while using less than 3% of the data used in previous work (Zhang et al., 2019; Pramanik and Hussain, 2019) and still showed comparable performance.

Given the simplicity of this architecture, we believe that Proteno can be used to benchmark TN for many languages with limited annotated data. However, languages which are not separated by space or highly inflected languages will be a challenge for the proposed system (Nikulásdóttir and Guðnason, 2019). We leave the adaptation of Proteno to more challenging languages for future work.

Acknowledgements

We would like to thank Denys Savin, Yvonne Flory, Tarek Badr and Anton Nguyen for their foundational contributions to the project and developing the production pipeline.

References

A. Conkie and A. Finch. 2020. Scalable Multilingual Frontend for TTS. In *ICASSP 2020 - 2020 IEEE International Conference on Acoustics, Speech and Signal Processing (ICASSP)*, pages 6684–6688.

Peter Ebden and Richard Sproat. 2014. The Kestrel TTS text normalization system. *Natural Language Engineering*, 21:333–353.

Thomas Eckart and Uwe Quasthoff. 2013. *Statistical Corpus and Language Comparison on Comparable Corpora*, pages 151–165. Springer Berlin Heidelberg, Berlin, Heidelberg.

Sepp Hochreiter and Jürgen Schmidhuber. 1997. Long Short-Term Memory. *Neural Comput.*, 9(8):1735–1780.

Zhiheng Huang, Wei Xu, and Kai Yu. 2015. Bidirectional LSTM-CRF Models for Sequence Tagging. *CoRR*, abs/1508.01991.

John D. Lafferty, Andrew McCallum, and Fernando C. N. Pereira. 2001. Conditional Random Fields: Probabilistic Models for Segmenting and Labeling Sequence Data. In *Proceedings of the Eighteenth International Conference on Machine Learning*, ICML '01, pages 282–289, San Francisco, CA, USA. Morgan Kaufmann Publishers Inc.

Vladimir Iosifovich Levenshtein. 1966. Binary codes capable of correcting deletions, insertions and reversals. *Soviet Physics Doklady*, 10(8):707–710. Doklady Akademii Nauk SSSR, V163 No4 845-848 1965.

Courtney Mansfield, Ming Sun, Yuzong Liu, Ankur Gandhe, and Björn Hoffmeister. 2019. Neural text normalization with subword units. In *Proceedings of the 2019 Conference of the North American Chapter of the Association for Computational Linguistics: Human Language Technologies, Volume 2 (Industry Papers)*, pages 190–196, Minneapolis, Minnesota. Association for Computational Linguistics.

Tomas Mikolov, Edouard Grave, Piotr Bojanowski, Christian Puhrsch, and Armand Joulin. 2018. Advances in Pre-Training Distributed Word Representations. In *Proceedings of the International Conference on Language Resources and Evaluation (LREC 2018)*.

Anna Björk Nikulásdóttir and Jón Guðnason. 2019. Bootstrapping a Text Normalization System for an Inflected Language. Numbers as a Test Case. In *Proc. Interspeech 2019*, pages 4455–4459.

Subhojeet Pramanik and Aman Hussain. 2019. Text normalization using memory augmented neural networks. *Speech Communication*, 109:15–23.

Loganathan Ramasamy, Ondřej Bojar, and Zdeněk Žabokrtský. 2012. Morphological Processing for English-Tamil Statistical Machine Translation. In *Proceedings of the Workshop on Machine Translation and Parsing in Indian Languages (MTPIL-2012)*, pages 113–122.

Keshan Sodimana, Pasindu De Silva, Richard Sproat, A Theeraphol, Chen Fang Li, Alexander Gutkin, Supheakmungkol Sarin, and Knot Pipatsrisawat. 2018. Text normalization for bangla, khmer, nepali, javanese, sinhala, and sundanese tts systems. In *6th International Workshop on Spoken Language Technologies for Under-Resourced Languages (SLTU-2018)*, pages 147–151, 29–31 August, Gurugram, India.

Richard Sproat. 1996. Multilingual text analysis for text-to-speech synthesis. *Natural Language Engineering*, 2(4):369–380.

Richard Sproat, Alan W. Black, Stanley Chen, Shankar Kumar, Mari Ostendorf, and Christopher Richards. 2001. Normalization of Non-standard Words. *Comput. Speech Lang.*, 15(3):287–333.

Richard Sproat and Navdeep Jaitly. 2016. RNN Approaches to Text Normalization: A Challenge. *CoRR*, abs/1611.00068.

Richard Sproat and Navdeep Jaitly. 2017. An RNN Model of Text Normalization. In *Proc. Interspeech 2017*, pages 754–758.

Ilya Sutskever, Oriol Vinyals, and Quoc V. Le. 2014. Sequence to Sequence Learning with Neural Networks. *CoRR*, abs/1409.3215.

Paul Taylor. 2009. *Text-to-Speech Synthesis*. Cambridge University Press.

Ashish Vaswani, Noam Shazeer, Niki Parmar, Jakob Uszkoreit, Llion Jones, Aidan N. Gomez, Lukasz Kaiser, and Illia Polosukhin. 2017. Attention Is All You Need. *CoRR*, abs/1706.03762.

Hao Zhang, Richard Sproat, Axel H. Ng, Felix Stahlberg, Xiaochang Peng, Kyle Gorman, and Brian Roark. 2019. Neural Models of Text Normalization for Speech Applications. *Computational Linguistics*, pages 1–49.

Addressing the Vulnerability of NMT in Input Perturbations

Weiwen Xu[1,2]*, **Ai Ti Aw**[1]†, **Yang Ding**[1], **Kui Wu**[1], **Shafiq Joty**[3]
[1]Institute for Infocomm Research, A*STAR
[2]The Chinese University of Hong Kong
[3]Nanyang Technological University
wwxu@se.cuhk.edu.hk
{aaiti, ding_yang, wuk}@i2r.a-star.edu.sg
srjoty@ntu.edu.sg

Abstract

Neural Machine Translation (NMT) has achieved significant breakthrough in performance but is known to suffer vulnerability to input perturbations. As real input noise is difficult to predict during training, robustness is a big issue for system deployment. In this paper, we improve the robustness of NMT models by reducing the effect of noisy words through a Context-Enhanced Reconstruction (CER) approach. CER trains the model to resist noise in two steps: (1) perturbation step that breaks the naturalness of input sequence with made-up words; (2) reconstruction step that defends the noise propagation by generating better and more robust contextual representation. Experimental results on Chinese-English (ZH-EN) and French-English (FR-EN) translation tasks demonstrate robustness improvement on both news and social media text. Further fine-tuning experiments on social media text show our approach can converge at a higher position and provide a better adaptation.

1 Introduction

Recent techniques (Bahdanau et al., 2014; Wu et al., 2016; Vaswani et al., 2017) in NMT have gained remarkable improvement in translation quality. However, robust NMT that is immune to real input noise remains a big challenge for NMT researchers. Real input noises can exhibit in many forms such as spelling and grammatical errors, homophones replacement, Internet slang, new words or even a valid word used in an unfamiliar or a new context. Unlike humans who can easily comprehend and translate such texts, most NMT models are not robust to generate appropriate and meaningful translations in the presence of such noises, challenging the deployment of NMT system in real scenarios.

Input	通宵打游戏上分贼快
Ref.	It's super-fast to gain scores when playing games over the night.
MT	Play the game all night and take points thief fast.
CER	Play games all night to score points quickly.
Input	我已剪短了我的发,剪断了惩罚,剪一地伤透我的尴尬。。。。
Ref.	I have cut my hair, i cut off the punishment, i away the awkwardness that hurt me.
MT	I got my punishment, got rid of my embarrassment.
CER	I cut short my hair , cut off punishment , and cut off my embarrassment that hurts me.

Table 1: Examples of NMT's vulnerability in translating text containing noisy words ("zei" → "thief", "chengfa" → "punishment"). CER mitigates the effect of noisy words.

Noisy words have long been discussed in previous work. Aw et al. (2006) proposed the normalization approach to reduce the noise before translation. Tan et al. (2020a,b) addressed the character-level noise directly in the NMT model. Though these approaches addressed the effect of noisy words to some extent, they are limited to spelling errors, inflectional variations, and other noises definable during training. In addition, strong external supervision like a parallel corpus of noisy text translation or dictionary containing the translation of those noisy words are hard and expensive to obtain; they are also not practical in handling real noises as noisy words can exhibit in random forms and cannot be fully anticipated during training.

Belinkov and Bisk (2018) pointed out NMT models are sensitive to small input perturbations and if this issue is not addressed, it will continue to bottleneck the translation quality. In such cases, not only the word embeddings of perturbations may cause irregularities with the local context, the contextual representation of other words may also get affected by such perturbations (Liu et al., 2019). This phenomenon applies to valid words in unfamiliar context as well, which will also cause the translation to fail as illustrated in Table 1 (case 2).

*Work was done when the author was a staff in Institute for Infocomm Research, A*STAR.
†Corresponding Author

Proceedings of NAACL HLT 2021: IndustryTrack Papers, pages 80–88
June 6–11, 2021. ©2021 Association for Computational Linguistics

In this paper, we define "noisy word" as a valid or invalid word that is uncommonly used in the context or not observed frequently enough in the training data. When encoding a sentence with such a noisy word, the contextual representation of other words in the sentence are affected by the "less jointly trained" noisy word embeddings. We refer this process as "noise propagation". Noise propagation can extend to the decoder and finally distort the overall translation.

The main intuition of our proposed method is to minimize this noise propagation and reduce the irregularities in contextual representation due to these words via a *Context-Enhanced Reconstruction* (CER) approach. To reduce the sensitivity of contextual towards noisy words in the encoder, we inject made-up words randomly to the source side of the training data to break the text naturalness. We then use a *Noise Adaptation Layer* (NAL) to enable a more stable contextual representation by minimizing the reconstruction loss. In the decoder, we add perturbations with a semantic constraint and apply the same reconstruction loss. Unlike adversarial examples which are crafted to cause the target model to fail, our perturbation process does not have such constraint and does not rely on a target model. Our input perturbations are randomly generated, representing any types of noises that can be observed in real-world usage. This makes the perturbation process generic, easy and fast. Following (Cheng et al., 2018), we generate semantically related perturbations in the decoder to increase the diversity of the translations.

Together with NAL, our model shows its ability to resist noises in the input and produce more robust translations. Results on ZH-EN and FR-EN translation significantly improve over the baseline by +1.24 (MT03) and +1.4 (N15) BLEU on news domain, and +1.63 (*Social*), +1.3 (*mtnt18*) on social media domain respectively. Further fine-tuning experiments on FR-EN social media text even witness an average improvement of +1.25 BLEU over the best approach.

2 Related Work

Robust Training: Robust training has shown to be effective to improve the robustness of the models in computer vision (Szegedy et al., 2013). In Natural Language Processing, it involves augmenting the training data with carefully crafted noisy examples: semantically equivalent word substitutions (Alzantot et al., 2018), paraphrasing (Iyyer et al., 2018; Ribeiro et al., 2018), character-level noise (Ebrahimi et al., 2018b; Tan et al., 2020a,b), or perturbations at embedding space (Miyato et al., 2016; Liang et al., 2020). Inspired by Lei et al. (2017) that nicely captures the semantic interactions in discourse relation, we regard noise as a disruptor to break semantic interactions and propose our CER approach to mitigate this phenomenon. We make up "noisy" words randomly to act as random noise in the input to break the text naturalness. Our experiment demonstrates its superiority in multiple dimensions.

Robust Neural Machine Translation: Methods have been proposed to make NMT models resilient not only to adequacy errors (Lei et al., 2019) but also to both natural and synthetic noise. Incorporating monolingual data into NMT has the capacity to improve the robustness (Sennrich et al., 2016a; Edunov et al., 2018; Cheng et al., 2016). Some non data-driven approaches that specifically designed to address the robustness problem of NMT (Sperber et al., 2017; Ebrahimi et al., 2018a; Wang et al., 2018; Karpukhin et al., 2019; Cheng et al., 2019, 2020) explored effective ways to synthesize adversarial examples into the training data. Belinkov and Bisk (2018) showed a structure-invariant word representation capable of addressing multiple typo noise. Cheng et al. (2018) used adversarial stability training strategy to make NMT resilient to arbitrary noise. Liu et al. (2019) added an additional phonetic embedding to overcome homophone noise.

Meanwhile, Michel and Neubig (2018) released a dataset for evaluating NMT on social media text. This dataset was used as a benchmark for WMT 19 Robustness shared task (Li et al., 2019) to improve the robustness of NMT models on noisy text. We show our approach also benefits the fine-tuning process using additional social media data.

3 Approaches

We propose a Context-Enhanced Reconstruction (CER) approach to learn robust contextual representation in the presence of noisy words through a perturbation step and a reconstruction step in both encoder and decoder during model training. Figure 1 shows the architecture.

The perturbation step automatically inserts made-up words in the input sequence $\mathbf{x}$ to generate a noisy example $\mathbf{x}'$. The noisy example mimics input where text naturalness is broken due to

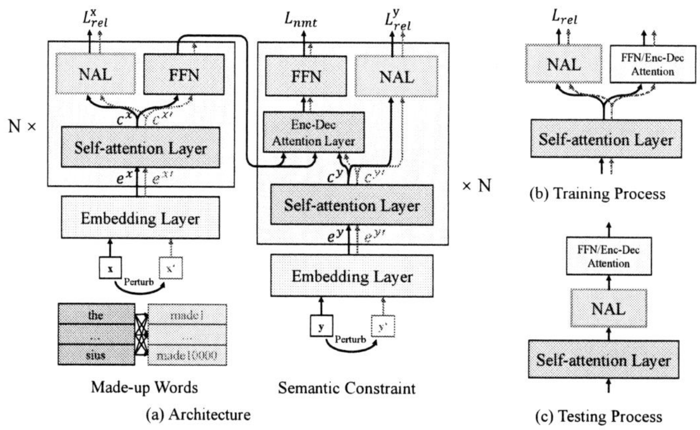

Figure 1: The architecture of CER (a), and the use of NAL in training (b) and testing (c). The solid lines indicate the flow for original input, while the dotted lines for noisy input, generated in the perturbation step.

the noisy words. Similarly, we perturb the output sequence $\mathbf{y}$ to $\mathbf{y}'$ using a semantic constraint to generate noisy examples for the decoder to have more diversity in the translations.

The reconstruction step in the model aims to restore the contextual representation $\mathbf{c}^{\mathbf{x}'}$ of $\mathbf{x}'$ to be similar to its corresponding original contextual representation $\mathbf{c}^{\mathbf{x}}$ in the encoder. Specifically, under the Transformer architecture (Figure 1), the reconstruction step aims to stabilize and minimize the disruption of attention distribution for a word over the whole input in the presence of inserted noise. The stabilization is needed for both clean and noisy words as both of their contextual representations are affected. For a noisy word, reconstruction reduces the attention to itself and encourages the construction of the contextual representation to leverage more on its clean neighbors. For clean words, reconstruction works as a denoise module to mitigate the interference of noisy words. For $\mathbf{c}^{\mathbf{y}'}$ in the decoder, the aim is to generate more examples with similar context as $\mathbf{c}^{\mathbf{y}}$. The reconstruction helps to normalize the contextual representation of semantically similar words.

3.1 Perturbing Input Text with Noise

We insert made-up words, representing any kinds of noise, to disturb the contextual representation during training. To create those words, we build a made-up dictionary $\mathcal{D}_x^-$ with M made-up words. As shown in Figure 1(a), made-up words are simply indexed slots in $\mathcal{D}_x^-$, whose embeddings are randomly initialized with no prior restriction and updated during training just as valid words. During the perturbation step, we randomly select multiple positions in each input sequence based on probability σ_x and replace the words with any arbitrary made-up words in $\mathcal{D}_x^-$.

For the decoder, as the aim is not to insert noise but to increase the diversity of translation, we add small perturbations with a semantic constraint to make the model robust. Specifically, we randomly select multiple positions in each target sequence with a probability σ_y and perturb the corresponding words. For the word y_i chosen to be perturbed, we create a dynamic set $\mathcal{V}_{y_i}$ consisting of m words having the highest cosine similarity with it (excluding y_i). We average the embeddings of the words in $\mathcal{V}_{y_i}$ as the perturbation for y_i.

$$\mathcal{V}_{y_i} = \underset{y_j \in \mathcal{D}_y, j \neq i}{top\_m} \left(cos(e^{y_i}, e^{y_j})\right) \tag{1}$$

$$e^{y_i'} = \frac{1}{m} \sum_{y_j \in \mathcal{V}_{y_i}} e^{y_j} \tag{2}$$

Where $\mathcal{D}_y$ is the target dictionary, e^{y_j} is the target word embedding for y_j and $e^{y_i'}$ is the perturbed embedding for y_i.

3.2 Reconstructing Contextual Representation

As the injected noise in $\mathbf{x}'$ affects the self-attention mechanism in producing correct contextual representation, we regularize the contextual representation using a Noise Adaptation Layer (NAL) immediately after the self-attention layer as depicted in Figure 1(a). This NAL is trained together with the NMT model and used as a reconstruction module during testing (See Figure 1(b),(c)).

Formally, let $\mathbf{c}_l^{\mathbf{x}}$ and $\mathbf{c}_l^{\mathbf{x}'}$ be the outputs of the self-attention in the l-th encoder layer for $\mathbf{x}$ and $\mathbf{x}'$

respectively. We train the NAL by:

$$\mathcal{L}^{x}_{nal}(\boldsymbol{\theta}^{x}_{nal}) = \frac{1}{|S|}\sum_{(\mathbf{x},\mathbf{y})\in S}\sum_{l=1}^{N}||\mathbf{c}^{\mathbf{x}}_{l} - \text{NAL}(\mathbf{c}^{\mathbf{x}'}_{l})||^2 \quad (3)$$

Where $\boldsymbol{\theta}^{x}_{nal}$ are parameters of NAL, S is the training corpus and N is the encoder layer size. Given $\mathbf{c}^{\mathbf{x}'}$, NAL attempts to output a more correct contextual representation guided by $\mathbf{c}^{\mathbf{x}}$. We use a single layer feed-forward network (FFN) in (Vaswani et al., 2017) as our NAL implementation. Similarly, the reconstruction loss for decoder is:

$$\mathcal{L}^{y}_{nal}(\boldsymbol{\theta}^{y}_{nal}) = \frac{1}{|S|}\sum_{(\mathbf{x},\mathbf{y})\in S}\sum_{l=1}^{N}||\mathbf{c}^{\mathbf{y}}_{l} - \text{NAL}(\mathbf{c}^{\mathbf{y}'}_{l})||^2 \quad (4)$$

3.3 Model Training

We apply the perturbation step at the embedding layer, see Figure 1. The inserted noise in $\mathbf{x}'$ and $\mathbf{y}'$ would also receive gradient from the final loss function and update just like other clean words. NAL is added at each Transformer layer where the outputs are only used to calculate the reconstruction loss and not passed to the next layer. On the other hand, the output of FFN is propagated to the next layer as usual. The reconstruction step mainly serves as a stabilizer to prevent the noise from propagating.

The final training objective $\mathcal{L}$ is the combination of the above three loss functions, the original translation loss, the reconstruction loss for the encoder and the reconstruction loss for the decoder. Both λ_x and λ_y are set empirically to count for the relative importance.

$$\mathcal{L} = \mathcal{L}_{nmt}(\boldsymbol{\theta}_{nmt}) + \lambda_x\mathcal{L}^{x}_{nal}(\boldsymbol{\theta}^{x}_{nal}) + \lambda_y\mathcal{L}^{y}_{nal}(\boldsymbol{\theta}^{y}_{nal}) \quad (5)$$

4 Experiment Settings

Experiments are conducted on ZH-EN and FR-EN translation tasks for both news and social media domains. We also use social media text to fine-tune the NMT systems on FR-EN.

4.1 Data

ZH-EN: The training data consists of 1.25M sentence pairs extracted from LDC. For news domain, we use NIST MT02 as the development set and select the best model to test MT03, MT04, MT05, MT06 and MT08 news test sets. For social media domain, we create a test set (*Social*) consisting of 2000 sentences with three human annotated references. The source sentences are collected from public social media platforms in four Chinese-speaking regions: Mainland China, Hong Kong, Taiwan and Singapore [1].

FR-EN: We use the same datasets as Michel and Neubig (2018). The training set consists of 2.16M sentence pairs extracted from *europarl-v7* and *news-commentary-v10*. We use the *newsdiscussdev2015* as development set and evaluate the model on two news test sets, *newstest2014* (N14) and *newsdiscusstest2015* (N15). We also evaluate on two social media test sets: *mtnt18* (Michel and Neubig, 2018) and *mtnt19* (Li et al., 2019).

FR-EN Fine-Tuning: We use the noisy training set (*mtnttrain*) provided by Michel and Neubig (2018) to fine-tune the FR-EN model.

We use fairseq's implementation of Transformer (Ott et al., 2019). In evaluation, we report case-insensitive tokenized BLEU for ZH-EN (Papineni et al., 2002) and `sacre-BLEU` (Post, 2018) for FR-EN. Following Michel and Neubig (2018), we do not use development set but only report best results on three social media test sets.

We segment the Chinese words using THULAC (Li and Sun, 2009) and tokenize both French and English words using `tokenize.perl`[2]. We apply BPE (Sennrich et al., 2016b) to get sub-word vocabularies for the encoder and decoder, both with 20K merge operations.

The hyper-parameters setting is the same as `transformer-base` in (Vaswani et al., 2017) except that we set dropout rate as 0.4 in all our experiments. Our proposed models are trained on top of Transformer baseline for efficiency purpose, where additional parameters from the embeddings of $\mathcal{D}^{-}_{x}$ and ReL are uniformly initialized. The madeup dictionary size M is set to 10,000. The size of dynamic set m is set to 3. The probability σ_x and σ_y are both set to 0.1 and balance coefficient λ_x and λ_y are both set to 1.

4.2 Baseline Models

We use Transformer as our baseline.

ZH-EN: We compare with Wang et al. (2018); Cheng et al. (2018, 2019). Wang et al. (2018) use a data augmentation approach by randomly replacing words in source and target sentences with other in-dictionary words. Cheng et al. (2018) use adversarial stability training to make NMT resilient to noise. Cheng et al. (2019) employ a white-box approach to synthesize adversarial examples.

[1]Available at `https://github.com/wwxu21/CER-MT`.

[2]https://github.com/moses-smt/mosesdecoder

Model	MT02 (DEV)	MT03	MT04	MT05	MT06	MT08	News Ave.	*Social*
		Existing systems						
Wang et al. (2018)	47.13	46.68	47.41	46.66	46.62	38.46	45.17	23.20
Cheng et al. (2018)	46.10	44.07	45.61	43.45	44.44	34.94	42.50	21.27
Cheng et al. (2019)	47.06	46.48	47.39	46.58	46.95	37.38	44.96	22.74
		Our systems						
Transformer	46.98	46.35	47.27	46.35	46.77	38.20	45.00	22.41
+ CER-Enc	47.65	46.72	47.53	47.06	47.04	38.53	45.38	23.81
+ CER	**48.34**	**47.59**	**48.21**	**47.29**	**47.64**	**39.33**	**46.01**	**24.04**

Table 2: Case-insensitive BLEU scores (%) on ZH-EN translation. MT02 is our development set.

Model	N14	N15	*mtnt18*	*mtnt19*
	Exising systems			
Wang et al.	29.2	31.1	25.0	28.1
Michel and Neubig	28.9	30.8	23.3	26.2
Zhou et al.*	N.A.	N.A.	24.5	**30.3**
	Our systems			
Transformer	29.7	31.0	25.2	28.0
+ CER-Enc	30.4	31.7	26.1	28.7
+ CER	**30.7**	**32.4**	**26.5**	29.1

Table 3: `sacreBLEU` (%) on FR-EN translation task. *Zhou et al. use more data to train their model.

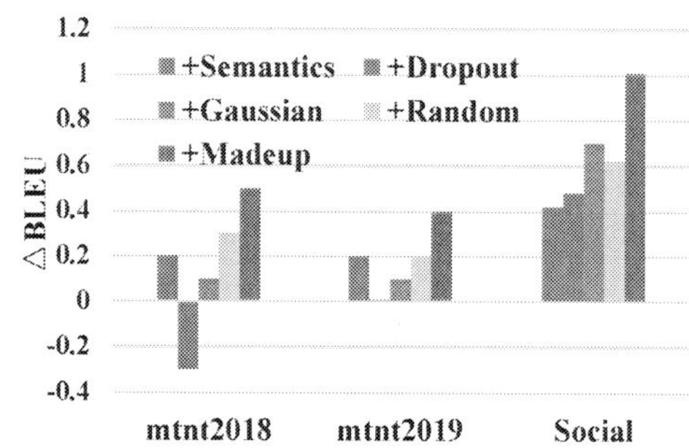

Figure 2: BLEU improvements compared to Transformer baseline shown in Table 2 and Table 3 when applying noise-insertion methods.

FR-EN: In addition to Wang et al. (2018), we compare with Michel and Neubig (2018); Zhou et al. (2019); Vaibhav et al. (2019) on FR-EN or FR-EN Fine-Tuning tasks. Michel and Neubig (2018) do the first benchmark of the noisy text translation tasks in three languages. Vaibhav et al. (2019) leverage effective synthetic noise to make NMT resilient to noisy text. We implement their approach on Transformer backbone. For a fair comparison, we limit the data to train back-translation models only with *mtnttrain*. Zhou et al. (2019) adopt a multitask transformer architecture with two decoders, where the first decoder learns to denoise and the second decoder learns to translate from the denoised text. They adopt the approach proposed by Vaibhav et al. (2019) to synthesize the noisy text for their first decoder.

We do not compare our model with (Berard et al., 2019; Helcl et al., 2019) as they use much more out-domain data, a great number of monolingual data and a bigger Transformer model, and hence not comparable with our experimental settings.

5 Results and Analysis

5.1 Comparison with Baseline Models

Table 2 and Table 3 show the performance on ZH-EN and FR-EN tasks. We show the results of applying CER only to the encoder (+ CER-Enc), and to both the encoder and decoder (+ CER).

As illustrated, our approach improves the news text translations on all test sets for both ZH-EN and FR-EN and outperforms the Transformer baseline in terms of average BLEU by +1.01 and +1.2 on ZH-EN and FR-EN respectively, illustrating the superiority of our approach.

The performance on social media test sets shows significant improvement with up to +1.63 BLEU over Transformer and +0.84 BLEU over the best approach (Wang et al., 2018) on ZH-EN. For FR-EN, our model outperforms Wang et al. (2018) by +1.5 and +1.0 BLEU on *mtnt18* and *mtnt19* respectively. Zhou et al. (2019) use *mtnttrain* and TED (Qi et al., 2018) to synthesize noisy sentences for their first decoder, hence effectively they are exploiting in-domain data during training and thus not quite a fair comparison in the evaluation. Nevertheless, CER still significantly outperforms Zhou et al. (2019) by +2.0 BLEU on *mtnt18*.

5.2 Effect of Noise

We investigate the effect of different noise-insertion methods by dynamically inserting noise into the source side of the original training set using different strategies with a same probability σ_x.

Madeup: Our approach to add made-up words.

Semantics: We test our semantic constraint in the decoder to assess if it benefits the encoder.

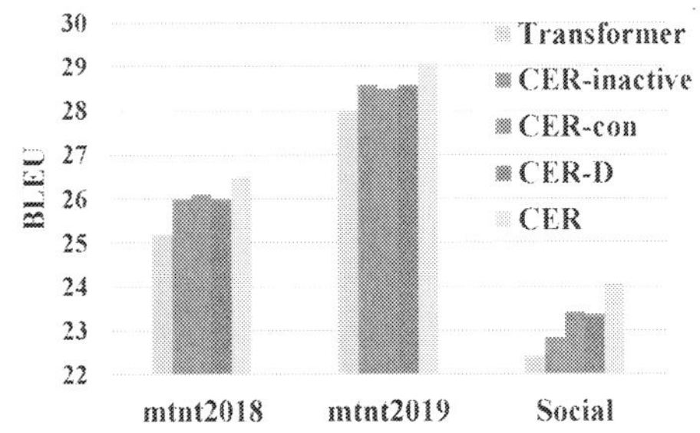

Figure 3: BLEU scores of CER variants.

Dropout: We replace word embeddings with all-0 vectors, similar to enlarging the dropout rate.
Gaussian: Following the feature-level perturbations of Cheng et al. (2018), we add the Gaussian noise to a word embedding to simulate the noise.
Random: We replace a word with an arbitrary word in the dictionary. This would result in a valid word being placed in an unreasonable context.

Figure 2 shows the BLEU improvement of various noise-insertion methods on social media test sets. We find that nearly all kinds of noise-insertion methods improve the robustness of MT with the exception of *Dropout*. Since we have already set the dropout rate to an optimal rate, inserting additional *Dropout* noise does not increase but decreases the performance. As shown, *Madeup* improves the performance nearly twice than the rest of the noise-insertion methods. We conjecture *Semantics*, *Dropout* and *Gaussian* may be small and not diverse enough to simulate the real noisy words. Both *Random* and *Madeup* can break the text coherence. However, *Random* uses a random in-dictionary word, which can place a valid word in an unreasonable context and cause its embedding to update in a wrong direction. In fact, this method improves the robustness of NMT models at the cost of those replaced words. Our *Madeup* can entirely avoid this cost as we use made-up words to work as noisy words and does not cause any context change of all in-dictionary words.

5.3 Effect of NAL

To further gain insights on how NAL helps improve the robustness of NMT models. We create three variants to aid our analysis:
CER-inactive: We do not activate NAL at testing time. The contextual representation is feed directly into later FFN. This variant is to test the effectiveness of NAL.
CER-con: We remove NAL but only add a constraint to ensure $\{\mathbf{c}^{\mathbf{x}}, \mathbf{c}^{\mathbf{x}'}\}$ and $\{\mathbf{c}^{\mathbf{y}}, \mathbf{c}^{\mathbf{y}'}\}$ to be close respectively at training time. This forces the self-attention layer to reconstruct the correct contextual representation itself. This variant is to demonstrate the necessity to set apart the context generation module (self-attention layer) and the reconstruction module (NAL).
CER-D: We borrow the adversarial stability training strategy proposed in Cheng et al. (2018) here. In this variant, NAL is replaced by a discriminator and $\boldsymbol{\theta}^{x}_{nal}$ and $\boldsymbol{\theta}^{y}_{nal}$ are changed to the adversarial learning loss in Cheng et al. (2018). The purpose is to assess the effectiveness of NAL and the discriminator in context reconstruction.

Figure 3 shows the results of the three variants on three social media test sets. From the figure, we make the following observations.

NAL is effective at Test Time. The activation of NAL at test time helps to produce more reliable contextual representation. Notably, NAL gains +1.19 BLEU on *Social*.

NAL needs to be learnt separately. As shown in CER-con, by forcing self-attention layer to do both tasks (context generation and reconstruction), the performance improvement gets affected by at least 0.4 BLEU.

NAL is more effective than a discriminator to guide reconstruction. The improvements are less significant in all test sets when using a discriminator (CER-D) comparing to CER. Therefore, we can conclude that NAL is more effective than a discriminator to reconstruct the perturbed contextual representation and CER outperforms all variants.

Model	mtnt18	mtnt19
Existing systems		
Michel and Neubig	30.3	N/A
Wang et al.	35.1	36.7
Zhou et al.	31.7	32.8
Vaibhav et al.	36.0	37.5
Our systems		
Transformer (Base)	25.2	28.1
+FT	35.2	37.4
+FT w/ CER	**37.3**	**38.7**

Table 4: `sacreBLEU` on FR-EN fine-tuning task.

5.4 FR-EN Fine-Tuning on Social Media Text

We fine-tune the same Transformer model in Table 3 with the social media data *mtnttrain* (*+FT*) and further include CER in the fine-tuning (+FT w/ CER). Table 4 shows our performance (*+FT w/ CER*) with other four fine-tuning approaches on *mtnttrain*. It shows that our CER also bene-

Model		*Social*
Google Translate		38.59
Ours	Baseline	39.01
	+FT	40.56 (+3.97%)
	+FT w/ CER	**40.82 (+4.64%)**

Table 5: Case-insensitive BLEU scores (relative improvement) on large-scale ZH-EN translation system.

fits the fine-tuning process and outperforms all the approaches in two noisy test sets. Specifically, it gains +2.1 and +1.3 BLEU over *+FT* on *mtnt18* and *mtnt19* and outperforms Vaibhav et al. (2019) by +1.3 and +1.2 BLEU respectively.

5.5 Experiments on Large-Scale Datasets

We first train a ZH-EN baseline model using 25M sentence pairs, which are mainly in news domain. Similar to the setting in Table 4, we apply both simple finetuning (+FT) and our CER (+ FT w/ CER) approach using 125K social media training data. We evaluate those models on *Social*. We also include the performance of Google Translate [3] here to show the competitiveness of our baseline model.

As shown in Table 5, our CER approach can still benefit the fine-tuning process even on the strong baseline. It should be noted that the baseline has already maintained high robustness with large-scale training data where improvement in such a model is hard to obtain. In fact, 125K in-domain data can only contribute to 1.55 BLEU improvement. Under this circumstance, the 0.26 BLEU improvement brought by CER should be highly valued considered no additional fine-tuning data is used.

6 Conclusions

In this work, we propose an approach to reduce the vulnerability of NMT models to input perturbations. Our input perturbation is easy, fast and not specific to a target victim model. Experimental results show our proposed approach improves the robustness on both news and social media text and helped to improve the translation of real input.

7 Acknowledgments

The work was supported in part by Defence Science and Technology Agency (DSTA), Singapore.

[3]https://translate.google.com/

References

Moustafa Alzantot, Yash Sharma, Ahmed Elgohary, Bo-Jhang Ho, Mani Srivastava, and Kai-Wei Chang. 2018. Generating natural language adversarial examples. *arXiv preprint arXiv:1804.07998*.

AiTi Aw, Min Zhang, Juan Xiao, and Jian Su. 2006. A phrase-based statistical model for SMS text normalization. In *Proceedings of the COLING/ACL 2006 Main Conference Poster Sessions*, pages 33–40, Sydney, Australia. Association for Computational Linguistics.

Dzmitry Bahdanau, Kyunghyun Cho, and Yoshua Bengio. 2014. Neural machine translation by jointly learning to align and translate. *arXiv preprint arXiv:1409.0473*.

Yonatan Belinkov and Yonatan Bisk. 2018. Synthetic and natural noise both break neural machine translation. In *International Conference on Learning Representations*.

Alexandre Berard, Ioan Calapodescu, and Claude Roux. 2019. Naver labs europe's systems for the wmt19 machine translation robustness task. In *Proceedings of the Fourth Conference on Machine Translation (Volume 2: Shared Task Papers, Day 1)*, pages 526–532, Florence, Italy. Association for Computational Linguistics.

Yong Cheng, Lu Jiang, and Wolfgang Macherey. 2019. Robust neural machine translation with doubly adversarial inputs. In *Proceedings of the 57th Annual Meeting of the Association for Computational Linguistics*, pages 4324–4333, Florence, Italy. Association for Computational Linguistics.

Yong Cheng, Lu Jiang, Wolfgang Macherey, and Jacob Eisenstein. 2020. AdvAug: Robust adversarial augmentation for neural machine translation. In *Proceedings of the 58th Annual Meeting of the Association for Computational Linguistics*, Online. Association for Computational Linguistics.

Yong Cheng, Zhaopeng Tu, Fandong Meng, Junjie Zhai, and Yang Liu. 2018. Towards robust neural machine translation. In *Proceedings of the 56th Annual Meeting of the Association for Computational Linguistics (Volume 1: Long Papers)*, pages 1756–1766, Melbourne, Australia. Association for Computational Linguistics.

Yong Cheng, Wei Xu, Zhongjun He, Wei He, Hua Wu, Maosong Sun, and Yang Liu. 2016. Semi-supervised learning for neural machine translation. In *Proceedings of the 54th Annual Meeting of the Association for Computational Linguistics (Volume 1: Long Papers)*, pages 1965–1974, Berlin, Germany. Association for Computational Linguistics.

Javid Ebrahimi, Daniel Lowd, and Dejing Dou. 2018a. On adversarial examples for character-level neural machine translation. In *Proceedings of the 27th International Conference on Computational Linguistics*, pages 653–663, Santa Fe, New Mexico, USA. Association for Computational Linguistics.

Javid Ebrahimi, Anyi Rao, Daniel Lowd, and Dejing Dou. 2018b. HotFlip: White-box adversarial examples for text classification. In *Proceedings of the 56th Annual Meeting of the Association for Computational Linguistics (Volume 2: Short Papers)*, pages 31–36, Melbourne, Australia. Association for Computational Linguistics.

Sergey Edunov, Myle Ott, Michael Auli, and David Grangier. 2018. Understanding back-translation at scale. In *Proceedings of the 2018 Conference on Empirical Methods in Natural Language Processing*, pages 489–500, Brussels, Belgium. Association for Computational Linguistics.

Jindich Helcl, Jindich Libovick, and Martin Popel. 2019. Cuni system for the wmt19 robustness task. In *Proceedings of the Fourth Conference on Machine Translation (Volume 2: Shared Task Papers, Day 1)*, pages 539–543, Florence, Italy. Association for Computational Linguistics.

Mohit Iyyer, John Wieting, Kevin Gimpel, and Luke Zettlemoyer. 2018. Adversarial example generation with syntactically controlled paraphrase networks. In *Proceedings of the 2018 Conference of the North American Chapter of the Association for Computational Linguistics: Human Language Technologies, Volume 1 (Long Papers)*, pages 1875–1885, New Orleans, Louisiana. Association for Computational Linguistics.

Vladimir Karpukhin, Omer Levy, Jacob Eisenstein, and Marjan Ghazvininejad. 2019. Training on synthetic noise improves robustness to natural noise in machine translation. *arXiv preprint arXiv:1902.01509*.

Wenqiang Lei, Xuancong Wang, Meichun Liu, Ilija Ilievski, Xiangnan He, and Min-Yen Kan. 2017. Swim: A simple word interaction model for implicit discourse relation recognition. In *Proceedings of the Twenty-Sixth International Joint Conference on Artificial Intelligence, IJCAI-17*, pages 4026–4032.

Wenqiang Lei, Weiwen Xu, Ai Ti Aw, Yuanxin Xiang, and Tat Seng Chua. 2019. Revisit automatic error detection for wrong and missing translation – a supervised approach. In *Proceedings of the 2019 Conference on Empirical Methods in Natural Language Processing and the 9th International Joint Conference on Natural Language Processing (EMNLP-IJCNLP)*, pages 942–952, Hong Kong, China. Association for Computational Linguistics.

Xian Li, Paul Michel, Antonios Anastasopoulos, Yonatan Belinkov, Nadir Durrani, Orhan Firat, Philipp Koehn, Graham Neubig, Juan Pino, and Hassan Sajjad. 2019. Findings of the first shared task on machine translation robustness. In *Proceedings of the Fourth Conference on Machine Translation (Volume 2: Shared Task Papers, Day 1)*, pages 91–102, Florence, Italy. Association for Computational Linguistics.

Zhongguo Li and Maosong Sun. 2009. Punctuation as implicit annotations for Chinese word segmentation. *Computational Linguistics*, 35(4):505–512.

Hongru Liang, Wenqiang Lei, Paul Yaozhu Chan, Zhenglu Yang, Maosong Sun, and Tat-Seng Chua. 2020. Pirhdy: Learning pitch-, rhythm-, and dynamics-aware embeddings for symbolic music. In *MM '20: The 28th ACM International Conference on Multimedia, Virtual Event / Seattle, WA, USA, October 12-16, 2020*, pages 574–582. ACM.

Hairong Liu, Mingbo Ma, Liang Huang, Hao Xiong, and Zhongjun He. 2019. Robust neural machine translation with joint textual and phonetic embedding. In *Proceedings of the 57th Annual Meeting of the Association for Computational Linguistics*, pages 3044–3049, Florence, Italy. Association for Computational Linguistics.

Paul Michel and Graham Neubig. 2018. MTNT: A testbed for machine translation of noisy text. In *Proceedings of the 2018 Conference on Empirical Methods in Natural Language Processing*, pages 543–553, Brussels, Belgium. Association for Computational Linguistics.

Takeru Miyato, Andrew M Dai, and Ian Goodfellow. 2016. Adversarial training methods for semi-supervised text classification. *arXiv preprint arXiv:1605.07725*.

Myle Ott, Sergey Edunov, Alexei Baevski, Angela Fan, Sam Gross, Nathan Ng, David Grangier, and Michael Auli. 2019. fairseq: A fast, extensible toolkit for sequence modeling. In *Proceedings of NAACL-HLT 2019: Demonstrations*.

Kishore Papineni, Salim Roukos, Todd Ward, and Wei-Jing Zhu. 2002. Bleu: a method for automatic evaluation of machine translation. In *Proceedings of the 40th annual meeting on association for computational linguistics*, pages 311–318. Association for Computational Linguistics.

Matt Post. 2018. A call for clarity in reporting bleu scores. *arXiv preprint arXiv:1804.08771*.

Ye Qi, Devendra Sachan, Matthieu Felix, Sarguna Padmanabhan, and Graham Neubig. 2018. When and why are pre-trained word embeddings useful for neural machine translation? In *Proceedings of the 2018 Conference of the North American Chapter of the Association for Computational Linguistics: Human Language Technologies, Volume 2 (Short Papers)*, pages 529–535, New Orleans, Louisiana. Association for Computational Linguistics.

Marco Tulio Ribeiro, Sameer Singh, and Carlos Guestrin. 2018. Semantically equivalent adversarial rules for debugging NLP models. In *Proceedings of the 56th Annual Meeting of the Association for Computational Linguistics (Volume 1: Long Papers)*, pages 856–865, Melbourne, Australia. Association for Computational Linguistics.

Rico Sennrich, Barry Haddow, and Alexandra Birch. 2016a. Improving neural machine translation models with monolingual data. In *Proceedings of the 54th Annual Meeting of the Association for Computational Linguistics (Volume 1: Long Papers)*, pages 86–96, Berlin, Germany. Association for Computational Linguistics.

Rico Sennrich, Barry Haddow, and Alexandra Birch. 2016b. Neural machine translation of rare words with subword units. In *Proceedings of the 54th Annual Meeting of the Association for Computational Linguistics (Volume 1: Long Papers)*, pages 1715–1725, Berlin, Germany. Association for Computational Linguistics.

Matthias Sperber, Jan Niehues, and Alex Waibel. 2017. Toward robust neural machine translation for noisy input sequences. In *International Workshop on Spoken Language Translation (IWSLT)*.

Christian Szegedy, Wojciech Zaremba, Ilya Sutskever, Joan Bruna, Dumitru Erhan, Ian Goodfellow, and Rob Fergus. 2013. Intriguing properties of neural networks. *arXiv preprint arXiv:1312.6199*.

Samson Tan, Shafiq Joty, Min-Yen Kan, and Richard Socher. 2020a. It's morphin' time! Combating linguistic discrimination with inflectional perturbations. In *Proceedings of the 58th Annual Meeting of the Association for Computational Linguistics*, pages 2920–2935, Online. Association for Computational Linguistics.

Samson Tan, Shafiq Joty, Lav Varshney, and Min-Yen Kan. 2020b. Mind your inflections! Improving NLP for non-standard Englishes with Base-Inflection Encoding. In *Proceedings of the 2020 Conference on Empirical Methods in Natural Language Processing (EMNLP)*, pages 5647–5663, Online. Association for Computational Linguistics.

Vaibhav Vaibhav, Sumeet Singh, Craig Stewart, and Graham Neubig. 2019. Improving robustness of machine translation with synthetic noise. In *Proceedings of the 2019 Conference of the North American Chapter of the Association for Computational Linguistics: Human Language Technologies, Volume 1 (Long and Short Papers)*, pages 1916–1920, Minneapolis, Minnesota. Association for Computational Linguistics.

Ashish Vaswani, Noam Shazeer, Niki Parmar, Jakob Uszkoreit, Llion Jones, Aidan N Gomez, Ł ukasz Kaiser, and Illia Polosukhin. 2017. Attention is all you need. In I. Guyon, U. V. Luxburg, S. Bengio, H. Wallach, R. Fergus, S. Vishwanathan, and R. Garnett, editors, *Advances in Neural Information Processing Systems 30*, pages 5998–6008. Curran Associates, Inc.

Xinyi Wang, Hieu Pham, Zihang Dai, and Graham Neubig. 2018. SwitchOut: an efficient data augmentation algorithm for neural machine translation. In *Proceedings of the 2018 Conference on Empirical Methods in Natural Language Processing*, pages 856–861, Brussels, Belgium. Association for Computational Linguistics.

Yonghui Wu, Mike Schuster, Zhifeng Chen, Quoc V Le, Mohammad Norouzi, Wolfgang Macherey, Maxim Krikun, Yuan Cao, Qin Gao, Klaus Macherey, et al. 2016. Google's neural machine translation system: Bridging the gap between human and machine translation. *arXiv preprint arXiv:1609.08144*.

Shuyan Zhou, Xiangkai Zeng, Yingqi Zhou, Antonios Anastasopoulos, and Graham Neubig. 2019. Improving robustness of neural machine translation with multi-task learning. In *Proceedings of the Fourth Conference on Machine Translation (Volume 2: Shared Task Papers, Day 1)*, pages 565–571, Florence, Italy. Association for Computational Linguistics.

Cross-lingual Supervision Improves Unsupervised Neural Machine Translation

Mingxuan Wang[1] **Hongxiao Bai**[2] **Hai Zhao**[2] **Lei Li**[1]
[1]ByteDance AI Lab, Beijing, China
{wangmingxuan.89,lileilab}@bytedance.com
[2] Department of ComputeScience and Engineering, Shanghai Jiao Tong University
{baippa, zhaohai} @cs.sjtu.edu.cn

Abstract

We propose to improve unsupervised neural machine translation with cross-lingual supervision (CUNMT), which utilizes supervision signals from high resource language pairs to improve the translation of zero-source languages. Specifically, for training `En-Ro` system without parallel corpus, we can leverage the corpus from `En-Fr` and `En-De` to collectively train the translation from one language into many languages under one model. Simple and effective, CUNMT significantly improves the translation quality with a big margin in the benchmark unsupervised translation tasks, and even achieves comparable performance to supervised NMT. In particular, on WMT'14 `En-Fr` tasks CUNMT achieves 37.6 and 35.18 BLEU score, which is very close to the large scale supervised setting and on WMT'16 `En-Ro` tasks CUNMT achieves 35.09 BLEU score which is even better than the supervised Transformer baseline.

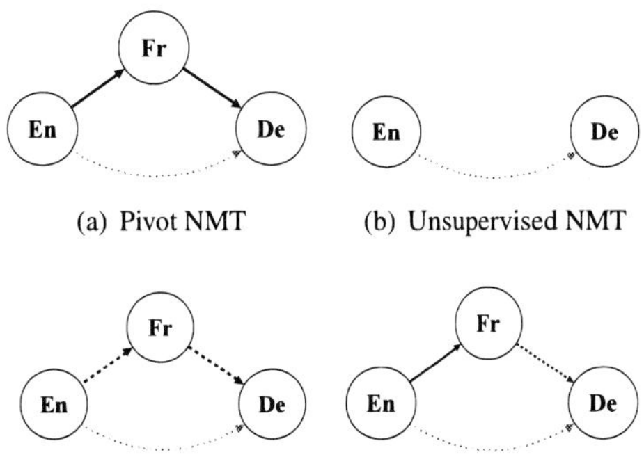

(a) Pivot NMT (b) Unsupervised NMT (c) CUNMT w/o Para. (d) CUNMT w/ Para.

Figure 1: Different settings for zero-resource NMT. Full edges indicate the existence of parallel training data. Dashed blue edges indicate the target translation pair. "CUNMT w/o Para." jointly train several unsupervised pairs in one model with unsupervised cross-lingual supervision. "CUNMT w/ Para." train unsupervised directions with supervised cross-lingual supervision, such as jointly train unsupervised `En-De` with supervised `En-Fr`.

1 Introduction

Neural machine translation (NMT) has achieved great success and reached satisfactory translation performance for several language pairs (Bahdanau et al., 2015; Gehring et al., 2017; Vaswani et al., 2017). Such breakthroughs heavily depend on the availability of colossal amounts of bilingual sentence pairs, such as the some 40 million parallel sentence pairs used in the training of WMT14 English French Task. As bilingual sentence pairs are costly to collect, the success of NMT has not been fully duplicated in the vast majority of language pairs, especially for zero-resource languages. Recently, (Artetxe et al., 2018b; Lample et al., 2018a; **?**) tackled this challenge by training unsupervised neural machine translation (UNMT) models using only monolingual data, which achieves considerably high accuracy, but still not on par with that of the state of the art supervised models.

Most previous works focused on modeling the architecture through parameter sharing or proper initialization to improve UNMT. We argue that the drawback of UNMT mainly stems from the lack of supervised signals, and it is beneficial to transfer multilingual information across languages. In this paper, we take a step towards practical unsupervised NMT with cross-lingual supervision (CUNMT) — making the most of the signal from other language. We investigate two variants of multilingual supervision for UNMT. *a)* CUNMT w/o Para.: a general setting where unrelated monolingual data can be introduced. For example, using monolingual `Fr` data to help the training of `En-De` (Figure 1(c)). *b)* CUNMT w/ Para.: a relatively strict setting where other bilingual language pairs can be introduced. For example, we can naturally leverage parallel `En-Fr` data to facilitate the unsupervised `En-De` transla-

Proceedings of NAACL HLT 2021: IndustryTrack Papers, pages 89–96
June 6–11, 2021. ©2021 Association for Computational Linguistics

tion (Figure 1(d)).

We introduce cross-lingual supervision which aims at modeling explicit translation probabilities across languages. Taking three languages as an example, suppose the target unsupervised direction is `En` $\rightarrow$ `De` and the auxiliary language is `Fr`. Our target is to model the translation probability $p(\texttt{De}|\texttt{En})$ with the support of $p(\texttt{Fr}|\texttt{En})$ and $p(\texttt{De}|\texttt{Fr})$. For forward cross-lingual supervision, the system $\text{NMT}_{\texttt{Fr}\rightarrow\texttt{De}}$ serves as a teacher, translating the `Fr` part of parallel data $(\texttt{En}, \texttt{Fr})$ to `De`. The resulted synthetic data $(\texttt{En}, \texttt{Fr}, \texttt{De})$ can be used to improve our target system $\text{NMT}_{\texttt{En}\rightarrow\texttt{De}}$. For backward cross-lingual supervision, we translate the monolingual `De` to `Fr` with $\text{NMT}_{\texttt{De}\rightarrow\texttt{Fr}}$, and then translate `Fr` to `En` with $\text{NMT}_{\texttt{Fr}\rightarrow\texttt{En}}$. The resulted synthetic bilingual data $(\texttt{De}, \texttt{En})$ can be used for $\text{NMT}_{\texttt{En}\rightarrow\texttt{De}}$ as well.

Our contributions can be summarized as follow: a) Empirical evaluation of CUNMT on six benchmarks verifies that it surpassed individual MT models by a large margin of more than 3.0 BLEU points on average, and also bested several strong competitors. Particularly, on WMT'16 `En-Ro` tasks, CUNMT surpass the supervised baseline by 0.7 BLEU, showing the great potential for UNMT. b) CUNMT is very effective in the use of additional training data. MBART or MASS introduces billions of sentences, while CUNMT only introduces tens of millions of sentences and achieves super or comparable results. It shows the importance of introducing explicit supervision.

2 The Proposed CUNMT

CUNMT is based on a multilingual machine translation model involving supervised and unsupervised methods with a triangular training structure. The original unsupervised NMT depends only on monolingual corpus, therefore the performances of these translation directions cannot be guaranteed.

Formally, given n different languages L_i, x_i denotes a sentence in language L_i. D_i denotes a monolingual dataset of L_i, and $D_{i,j}$ denotes a parallel dataset of (L_i, L_j). We use $\mathcal{E}$ to indicate the set of all translation directions with parallel data and $\mathcal{W}$ to indicate the set of all unsupervised translation directions respectively. The goal of CUNMT is to minimize the log likelihood of both unsupervised and supervised directions:

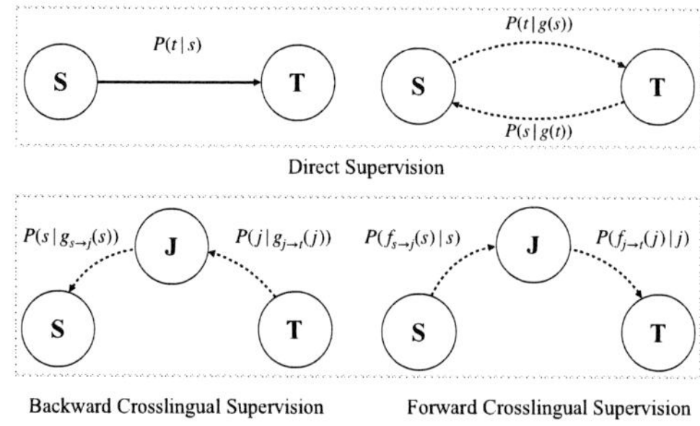

Figure 2: Forward and backward cross lingual translation for auxiliary data. The dashed blue arrow indicates target unsupervised direction. The solid arrow indicates using the parallel data. The dashed black arrow indicates generating synthetic data.

$$\mathcal{L}^{\text{CUNMT}} = \sum_{i,j\in\mathcal{W}} \mathcal{L}^{U}_{i\to j} + \sum_{i,j\in\mathcal{E}} \mathcal{L}^{S}_{i\to j} + \sum_{i,j\in\mathcal{W}+\mathcal{E}} \hat{\mathcal{L}}_{i\to j} \tag{1}$$

where $\mathcal{L}^{U}_{i\to j}$ is the unsupervised direct supervision, and $\mathcal{L}^{S}_{i\to j}$ is the direct supervised supervision, and $\hat{\mathcal{L}}_{i\to j}$ is the indirect supervision.

2.1 Direct & Cross-lingual Supervision

Direct supervision We will first introduce the notion of direct supervision loss, which only consider the translation probability between two different languages.

For supervised machine translation models, given parallel dataset $D_{s,t}$ with source language L_s and target language L_t, we use $\mathcal{L}^{S}_{s\to t}$ to denote the supervised training loss from language L_s to language L_t. The training loss for a single sentence can be defined as:

$$\mathcal{L}^{S}_{s\to t} = \mathbb{E}_{(x_s,x_t)\sim D_{s,t}}[-\log P(x_t|x_s)]. \tag{2}$$

For unsupervised machine translation models, only monolingual dataset D_s and D_t are given. We use $\mathcal{L}^{U}_{s\to t}$ to denote the unsupervised training loss from language L_s to language L_t. We use $\mathcal{B}_{s\to t}$ to denote this back translation procedure. After that, we can use these data to train the model with supervised method from L_s to L_t. The losses of the dual structural are:

$$\begin{aligned}\mathcal{L}^{\mathcal{B}}_{t\to s} =& \mathbb{E}_{x_s\sim D_s}[-\log P(x_s|g_{s\to t}(x_s))],\\ \mathcal{L}^{\mathcal{B}}_{s\to t} =& \mathbb{E}_{x_t\sim D_t}[-\log P(x_t|g_{t\to s}(x_t))],\end{aligned} \tag{3}$$

where $g_{s\to t}(x_s)$ translate the sentence in language L_s to L_t, that is, the back translation of x_s. Then the total loss of an unsupervised machine translation is:

$$\mathcal{L}^U = \mathcal{L}^{\mathcal{B}}_{t\to s} + \mathcal{L}^{\mathcal{B}}_{s\to t}. \quad (4)$$

Cross-lingual supervision When extend to the multilingual scenario, it is natural to introduce indirect supervision across languages. Given n different languages, for each language pair (L_i, L_j), we can easily obtain the translation probability of $P(x_i|x_j)$ through the direct supervised model $\mathcal{L}^S$ or $\mathcal{L}^U$. We use $\hat{\mathcal{L}}_{s\to t}$ to indicate the indirect supervised loss, which can be defined as:

$$\hat{\mathcal{L}}_{s\to t} = \sum_{i=0,i\neq s,t}^{n} \lambda_i \hat{\mathcal{L}}_{s\to i\to t} \quad (5)$$

where λ is the coefficient. T

Due to the lack of triples data (L_i, L_k, L_j), it is difficult to directly estimate the cross translation loss $\hat{\mathcal{L}}_{s\to i\to t}$. We therefor propose the backward and forward indirect supervision to calculate the cross loss:

$$\begin{aligned}\hat{\mathcal{L}}_{s\to j\to t} = \mathbb{E}_{x_t\sim D_t}[-\log P(x_t|g_{t\to j\to s}(x_t))] \\ + \mathbb{E}_{x_s\sim D_s}[-\log P(f_{s\to j\to t}(x_s)|x_s)]\end{aligned} \quad (6)$$

where $g_{t\to j\to s}(x_t)$ is the indirect backward translation which translate x_t to language L_s and $f_{s\to j\to s}(x_t)$ is the indirect forward translation which translate x_s to language L_t.

2.2 Training Procedure of CUNMT

The procedure of CUNMT includes two main steps: multi-lingual pre-training and iterative multi-lingual training.

Multi-lingual Pre-training Due to the ill-posed nature, it is also important to find a good initialization to associate the source side languages and the target side languages. We propose a Multi-lingual Pre-training approach, which jointly train the unsupervised auto-encoder and supervised machine translation. Intuitively, the multi-lingual joint pre-training can take advantage of transfer learning and thus benefit the low resource languages. Apart form the monolingual data, pre-training can also leverage the bilingual parallel data. We suggest the supervised data provides strong signal to optimize the network, which also advantage the unrelated unsupervised NMT pre-training. For example, it is beneficial to use the supervised `En-Fr` model to initialize the unsupervised `De-Fr` model.

Indirect Supervised Training The goal is to train a single system that minimize the jointly loss function of $\mathcal{L}^{\text{CUNMT}}$.

Generally, CUNMT can be applied to a restrict unsupervised scenario where only monolingual are provided, and also can be extended to a unrestricted scenario where parallel data are introduced. For the sake of simplicity, we describe our method on three language pairs, which can be easily extended to more language pairs. Suppose that the three languages are denoted as the triad $(\texttt{En}, \texttt{Fr}, \texttt{De})$, and we have monolingual data for all the three languages and also bilingual data for `En-Fr`. The target is to train an unsupervised `En` $\to$`Fr` system. The detailed method is as follows:

1. Sample batch of monolingual $x_{\texttt{En}}, x_{\texttt{Fr}}, x_{\texttt{De}}$ sentences from $D_{\texttt{En}}, D_{\texttt{Fr}}, D_{\texttt{De}}$
2. Sample batch of parallel sentence from $D_{\texttt{En,Fr}}$ to generate supervised data $\mathcal{S}$
3. Back translate $x_{\texttt{En}}, x_{\texttt{Fr}}, x_{\texttt{De}}$ to generate pseudo data $\mathcal{B}$
4. Indirect back translate $x_{\texttt{En}}, x_{\texttt{Fr}}, x_{\texttt{De}}$ to generate pseudo data $\mathcal{B}^i$
5. Indirect forward translate $x_{\texttt{En}}, x_{\texttt{Fr}}, x_{\texttt{De}}$ to generate pseudo data $\mathcal{F}^i$
6. Merge $\mathcal{B}$, $\mathcal{B}^i$, $\mathcal{F}^i$ and $\mathcal{S}$ to jointly train CUNMT.
7. Repeat 1-6 until convergence.

For indirect or direct supervision, we follow the Equation (6), which will adopts one step forward translation if parallel data is provided. Since we train all directions in one model, the pseudo data will include all directions. In this setting, it contains: `En` $\leftrightarrow$ `Fr`, `En` $\leftrightarrow$ `De`, `Fr` $\leftrightarrow$ `De` with both direct and indirect directions.

3 Experiments

3.1 Datasets and Settings

We conduct experiments including $(\texttt{De}, \texttt{En}, \texttt{Fr})$, $(\texttt{Fr}, \texttt{En}, \texttt{De})$, and $(\texttt{Ro}, \texttt{En}, \texttt{Fr})$. For monolingual data of English, French and German, 20 million sentences from available WMT monolingual News Crawl datasets were randomly selected. For Romanian monolingual data, all of the available Romanian sentences from News Crawl dataset were used and and were supplemented with WMT16 monolingual data to yield a total of in 2.9 million sentences. For parallel data, we use the standard WMT 2014 English-French dataset consisting of about 36M sentence pairs, and the

	(Fr,En,De)		(De,En,Fr)		(Ro,En,Fr)	
	En-Fr	Fr-En	En-De	De-En	En-Ro	Ro-En
Supervised Transformer	41.0	-	34.0	38.6	34.3	34.0
Comparison systems of UNMT						
UNMT (Lample et al., 2018c)	25.1	24.2	17.2	21.0	21.2	19.4
EMB (Lample and Conneau, 2019)	29.4	29.4	21.3	27.3	27.5	26.6
MLM (Lample and Conneau, 2019)	33.4	33.3	26.4	34.3	33.3	31.8
MASS (Song et al., 2019)	37.5	34.9	28.3	**35.2**	**35.2**	33.1
MBART (Liu et al., 2020)	-	-	**29.8**	34.0	35.0	30.5
CUNMT						
CUNMT w/o Para.	32.90	31.93	23.03	31.01	33.23	32.34
CUNMT w/ Para.	34.37	32.77	23.99	31.98	33.95	33.15
CUNMT + Forward	35.88	33.64	26.50	33.11	34.12	33.61
CUNMT + Backward + Forward	**37.60**	**35.18**	27.60	34.10	35.09	**33.95**

Table 1: Main results comparisons. MASS uses large scale pre-training and back translation during fine-tuning. MBART employ large scale multi-lingual pretraining with billions sentences. The last four lines are the results of our method.

standard WMT 2014 English-German dataset consisting of about 4.5M sentence pairs. For analyses, we also introduce the standard WMT 2017 English-Chinese dataset consisting of 20M sentence pairs. Consist with previous work, we report results on newstest 2014 for English-French pair, and on newstest 2016 for English-German and English-Romanian.

In the experiments, CUNMT is built upon Transformer models. We use the Transformer with 6 layers, 1024 hidden units, 16 heads. We train our models with the Adam optimizer, a linear warm-up and learning rates varying from 10^{-4} to 5×10^{-4}. The model is trained on 8 NVIDIA V100 GPUs. We implement all our models in PyTorch based on the code of (Lample and Conneau, 2019)[1]. All the results are evaluated on BLEU score with Moses scripts, which is in consist with the previous studies.

3.2 Main Results

The main results of similar pairs are shown in Table 1. We make comparison with three strong unsupervised methods:

- MLM (Lample and Conneau, 2019) uses large scale cross-lingual data to train the mask language model and then fine-tune on unsupervised NMT.
- MASS (Song et al., 2019) is a sequence to sequence model pre-trained with billions of monolingual data.
- MBART (Liu et al., 2020) introduces tens of billions monolingual data to pre-train a deep Transformer model.

CUNMT *is very efficient in the use of multi-lingual data.* While the pretrained language model is obtained through several hundred times larger monolingual or cross-lingual corpus, CUNMT achieves superior or comparable results with much less cost.

The model was improved by using synthetic data of cross translation that is based on the jointly trained model. The results of "CUNMT + Forward" are from the model tuned by only 1 epoch with about 100K sentences. This method is fast and the performances are surprisingly effective. The "CUNMT + Forward + Backward" denotes that, besides forward translation, we also use monolingual data and cross translate it to the source language. This method yielded the best performance by outperforming the "CUNMT w/o Para." by more than 3 BLEU score on average. The improvements show great potential for introducing indirect cross lingual supervision for unsupervised NMT.

When compared with supervised approaches, CUNMT shows very promising performance. For the large scale WMT14 En-Fr tasks, the gap between CUNMT and supervised baseline is closed to 3.4 BLEU score. And for the medium WMT16 En-Ro task, CUNMT performs even better than the supervised approach.

[1]https://github.com/facebookresearch/XLM

4 Analyses

In this part, we conduct several studies on CUNMT to better understand its setting.

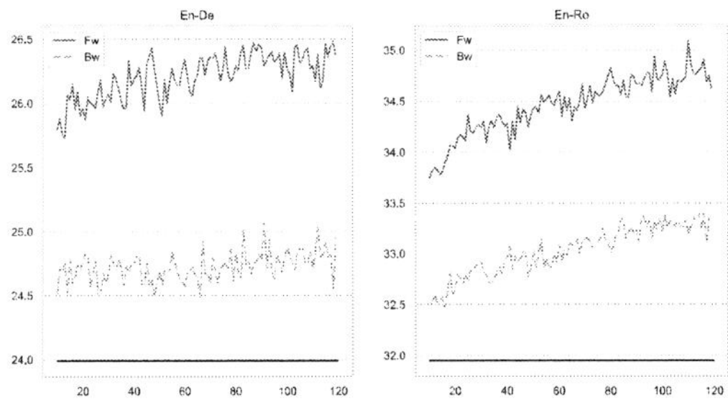

Figure 3: Results comparison for CUNMT fine-tuning with different auxiliary data. "Bw" only adopts cross-lingual backward translation synthetic data, and "Fw" only adopts cross-lingual forward translation synthetic data. The black horizontal is the baseline of UNMT. The horizontal axis is epoch and the vertical axis is the BLEU score. Epoch size is 100K sentences.

Backward or Forward Here we have explored the effect of cross-lingual backward supervision and cross-lingual forward supervision, and plot the performance curves along with the training procedure in Figure 3. The comparison system is CUNMT trained only with monolingual data. To make a fair comparison, we use "CUNMT w/ Para." as the baseline model and fine-tuning it with only indirect forward supervision or indirect backward supervision. We conduct experiments on WMT16 En-De and En-Ro tasks. Clearly, the forward supervision outperforms the backward one with big margins, which shows the importance of introducing the forward supervision for multilingual UNMT. It is still interesting to find that only introducing the indirect backward translation achieves better results than the unsupervised baseline.

We suppose the reasons for the performance gap is that, *a)* The UNMT baseline has included the traditional direct back translation, therefore the information gain from indirect backward translation is limited compared to the forward translation. *b)* The indirect forward translation provides a more direct way to model the relation across different languages. The results in consist with the previous research that pivot translation can help low resource language translation.

Robustness on Parallel Data Scale As shown in Table 4, CUNMT is robust to the parallel data scale. The results also dovetail with the unsupervised En-Fr experiments in Table 1. As it turns out the smaller parallel data of En-De was able to significantly improve the performance of unsupervised En-Fr translation. We then reduce the scale of the parallel data En-De and surprisingly find that even with only 25% supervised data, CUNMT still works well. The experiments demonstrate that CUNMT is robust and has great potential to be applied to practical systems.

Auxiliary Direction	En-Ro	Ro-En
En-De	34.86	33.18
En-De (50%)	34.72	32.85
En-De (25%)	34.52	32.33

Table 2: Robustness of Parallel Data Scale. Mainly evaluated on unsupervised En-Ro direction with different auxiliary parallel data settings.

Auxiliary Direction	En-Ro	Ro-En
En-Fr	35.09	33.95
En-De	34.86	33.18
En-Zh	33.85	32.86
En-De-Fr	35.26	34.20

Table 3: Effects of the Auxiliary Language. Mainly evaluated on unsupervised En-Ro direction with different parallel data settings.En-Fr,En-De and En-Zh are the auxiliary parallel data for training En-Ro. En-De-Fr is the combination of the En-De and En-Fr parallel data.

Importance of the Auxiliary Language Table 3 shows effects of the auxiliary language. We first switch the parallel data from En-Fr to En-De, the performance is almost consistent. We then switch the parallen data to En − Zh, where Zh is dissimilar with Ro, the performance increases. This is in line with our expectations, that similar languages make it easier for transfer learning. Finally, we extend the parallel data to En-De and En-Fr, and achieves further benefits. Compared with , we suggest the language similarity is more important than the auxiliary data scale.

Benefits as All in One Model In table 4, the performance of supervised directions are shown to illustrate the effects on which jointly training a single system has First, we test the baseline supervised system, that is, only $En \rightarrow Fr$ and $Fr \rightarrow En$ are conducted on the model. Due to difference in model architecture, the performance

System	En-Fr	Fr-En
Supervised Training	39.70	36.62
CUNMT + Forward	39.26	36.82
CUNMT + Backward	39.12	36.20

Table 4: Translation performance on supervised directions of CUNMT.

of CUNMT is slightly lower than that of its state of the art counterparts. Also, some techniques such as model average are not applied, and two directions are trained in one model. In CUNMT, the performance of supervised directions drops a little, but in exchange, the performances of zero-shot directions are greatly improved and the model is convenient to serve for multiple translation directions.

Strategies of Synthetic Data Generation For the synthetic data generation, the reported results are from greedy decoding for time efficiency. We compared the effects of sample strategies on the language setting of (Ro, En, De) where En-De is the supervised direction. The results based on beam search generation for En $\rightarrow$ Ro is 34.86, and 33.18 for En $\rightarrow$ Fr in terms of BLEU. Compared with greedy decoding, the performance of beam search is slightly inferior. A possible reason is that the beam search makes the synthetic data further biased on the learned pattern. The results suggest that CUNMT is exceedingly robust to the sampling strategies when performing forward and backward cross translation.

5 Related Work

Multilingual NMT It has been proven low resource machine translation can adopt methods to utilize other rich resource data in order to develop a better system. These methods include multilingual translation system (Firat et al., 2016; Johnson et al., 2017), teacher-student framework (Chen et al., 2017), or others (Zheng et al., 2017). Apart from parallel data as an entry point, many attempts have been made to explore the usefulness of monolingual data, including semi-supervised methods and unsupervised methods which only monolingual data is used. Much work also has been done to attempt to marry monolingual data with supervised data to create a better system, some of which include using small amounts of parallel data and augment the system with monolingual data (Sennrich et al., 2016; He et al., 2016; Wang et al., 2018; Gu et al., 2018; Edunov et al., 2018; Yang et al., 2020). Others also try to utilize parallel data of rich resource language pairs and also monolingual data (Ren et al., 2018; Wang et al., 2019; Al-Shedivat and Parikh, 2019; Lin et al., 2020). (Ren et al., 2018) also proposed a triangular architecture, but their work still relied on parallel data of low resource language pairs. With the joint support of parallel and monolingual data, the performance of a low resource system can be improved.

Unsupervised NMT In 2017, pure unsupervised machine translation method with only monolingual data was proven to be feasible. On the basis of embedding alignment (Artetxe et al., 2017; Lample et al., 2018b), (Lample et al., 2018a) and (Artetxe et al., 2018b) devised similar methods for fully unsupervised machine translation. Considerable work has been done to improve the unsupervised machine translation systems by methods such as statistical machine translation (Lample et al., 2018c; Artetxe et al., 2018a; Ren et al., 2019; Artetxe et al., 2019), pretraining models (Lample and Conneau, 2019; Song et al., 2019), or others (Wu et al., 2019), and all of which greatly improve the performance of unsupervised machine translation.

Our work attempts to utilize both monolingual and parallel data, and combine unsupervised and supervised machine translation through multilingual translation method into a single model CUNMT to ensure better performance for unsupervised language pairs.

6 Conclusion

In this work, we propose a multilingual machine translation framework CUNMT incorporating distant supervision to tackle the challenge of the unsupervised translation task. By mixing different training schemes into one model and utilizing unrelated bilingual corpus, we greatly improve the performance of the unsupervised NMT direction. By joint training, CUNMT can serve all translation directions in one model. Empirically, CUNMT has been proven to deliver substantial improvements over several strong UNMT competitors and even achieve comparable performance to supervised NMT. In the future, we plan to build a universal CUNMT system that is applicable in a wide span of languages.

References

Maruan Al-Shedivat and Ankur Parikh. 2019. Consistency by agreement in zero-shot neural machine translation. In *Proceedings of the 2019 Conference of the North American Chapter of the Association for Computational Linguistics: Human Language Technologies (NAACL:HLT), Volume 1 (Long and Short Papers)*, pages 1184–1197, Minneapolis, Minnesota.

Mikel Artetxe, Gorka Labaka, and Eneko Agirre. 2017. Learning bilingual word embeddings with (almost) no bilingual data. In *Proceedings of the 55th Annual Meeting of the Association for Computational Linguistics (ACL) (Volume 1: Long Papers)*, pages 451–462, Vancouver, Canada.

Mikel Artetxe, Gorka Labaka, and Eneko Agirre. 2018a. Unsupervised statistical machine translation. In *Proceedings of the 2018 Conference on Empirical Methods in Natural Language Processing (EMNLP)*, pages 3632–3642, Brussels, Belgium.

Mikel Artetxe, Gorka Labaka, and Eneko Agirre. 2019. An effective approach to unsupervised machine translation. In *Proceedings of the 57th Annual Meeting of the Association for Computational Linguistics (ACL)*, pages 194–203, Florence, Italy.

Mikel Artetxe, Gorka Labaka, Eneko Agirre, and Kyunghyun Cho. 2018b. Unsupervised neural machine translation. In *International Conference on Learning Representations (ICLR)*.

Dzmitry Bahdanau, Kyunghyun Cho, and Yoshua Bengio. 2015. Neural machine translation by jointly learning to align and translate. In *International Conference on Learning Representations (ICLR)*.

Yun Chen, Yang Liu, Yong Cheng, and Victor O.K. Li. 2017. A teacher-student framework for zero-resource neural machine translation. In *Proceedings of the 55th Annual Meeting of the Association for Computational Linguistics (ACL) (Volume 1: Long Papers)*, pages 1925–1935, Vancouver, Canada.

Sergey Edunov, Myle Ott, Michael Auli, and David Grangier. 2018. Understanding back-translation at scale. In *Proceedings of the 2018 Conference on Empirical Methods in Natural Language Processing (EMNLP)*, pages 489–500, Brussels, Belgium.

Orhan Firat, Baskaran Sankaran, Yaser Al-onaizan, Fatos T. Yarman Vural, and Kyunghyun Cho. 2016. Zero-resource translation with multi-lingual neural machine translation. In *Proceedings of the 2016 Conference on Empirical Methods in Natural Language Processing (EMNLP)*, pages 268–277, Austin, Texas.

Jonas Gehring, Michael Auli, David Grangier, Denis Yarats, and Yann N. Dauphin. 2017. Convolutional sequence to sequence learning. In *Proceedings of the 34th International Conference on Machine Learning (ICML)*, volume 70 of *Proceedings of Machine Learning Research*, pages 1243–1252, International Convention Centre, Sydney, Australia.

Jiatao Gu, Hany Hassan, Jacob Devlin, and Victor O.K. Li. 2018. Universal neural machine translation for extremely low resource languages. In *Proceedings of the 2018 Conference of the North American Chapter of the Association for Computational Linguistics: Human Language Technologies (NAACL:HLT), Volume 1 (Long Papers)*, pages 344–354, New Orleans, Louisiana.

Di He, Yingce Xia, Tao Qin, Liwei Wang, Nenghai Yu, Tie-Yan Liu, and Wei-Ying Ma. 2016. Dual learning for machine translation. In *Advances in Neural Information Processing Systems (NeurIPS) 29*, pages 820–828.

Melvin Johnson, Mike Schuster, Quoc V. Le, Maxim Krikun, Yonghui Wu, Zhifeng Chen, Nikhil Thorat, Fernanda Viégas, Martin Wattenberg, Greg Corrado, Macduff Hughes, and Jeffrey Dean. 2017. Google's multilingual neural machine translation system: Enabling zero-shot translation. *Transactions of the Association for Computational Linguistics (TACL)*, 5:339–351.

Guillaume Lample and Alexis Conneau. 2019. Cross-lingual language model pretraining. *arXiv preprint arXiv:1901.07291*.

Guillaume Lample, Alexis Conneau, Ludovic Denoyer, and Marc'Aurelio Ranzato. 2018a. Unsupervised machine translation using monolingual corpora only. In *International Conference on Learning Representations (ICLR)*.

Guillaume Lample, Alexis Conneau, Marc'Aurelio Ranzato, Ludovic Denoyer, and Hervé Jégou. 2018b. Word translation without parallel data. In *International Conference on Learning Representations (ICLR)*.

Guillaume Lample, Myle Ott, Alexis Conneau, Ludovic Denoyer, and Marc'Aurelio Ranzato. 2018c. Phrase-based & neural unsupervised machine translation. In *Proceedings of the 2018 Conference on Empirical Methods in Natural Language Processing (EMNLP)*, pages 5039–5049, Brussels, Belgium.

Zehui Lin, Xiao Pan, Mingxuan Wang, Xipeng Qiu, Jiangtao Feng, Hao Zhou, and Lei Li. 2020. Pre-training multilingual neural machine translation by leveraging alignment information. *arXiv preprint arXiv:2010.03142*.

Yinhan Liu, Jiatao Gu, Naman Goyal, Xian Li, Sergey Edunov, Marjan Ghazvininejad, Mike Lewis, and Luke Zettlemoyer. 2020. Multilingual denoising pre-training for neural machine translation. *arXiv preprint arXiv:2001.08210*.

Shuo Ren, Wenhu Chen, Shujie Liu, Mu Li, Ming Zhou, and Shuai Ma. 2018. Triangular architecture for rare language translation. In *Proceedings of the*

56th Annual Meeting of the Association for Computational Linguistics (ACL) (Volume 1: Long Papers), pages 56–65, Melbourne, Australia.

Shuo Ren, Zhirui Zhang, Shujie Liu, Ming Zhou, and Shuai Ma. 2019. Unsupervised neural machine translation with smt as posterior regularization. *Proceedings of the AAAI Conference on Artificial Intelligence (AAAI)*, 33:241–248.

Rico Sennrich, Barry Haddow, and Alexandra Birch. 2016. Improving neural machine translation models with monolingual data. In *Proceedings of the 54th Annual Meeting of the Association for Computational Linguistics (ACL) (Volume 1: Long Papers)*, pages 86–96, Berlin, Germany.

Kaitao Song, Xu Tan, Tao Qin, Jianfeng Lu, and Tie-Yan Liu. 2019. MASS: Masked sequence to sequence pre-training for language generation. In *Proceedings of the 36th International Conference on Machine Learning (ICML)*, volume 97 of *Proceedings of Machine Learning Research*, pages 5926–5936, Long Beach, California, USA.

Ashish Vaswani, Noam Shazeer, Niki Parmar, Jakob Uszkoreit, Llion Jones, Aidan N Gomez, Ł ukasz Kaiser, and Illia Polosukhin. 2017. Attention is all you need. In *Advances in Neural Information Processing Systems (NeurIPS) 30*, pages 5998–6008.

Yijun Wang, Yingce Xia, Li Zhao, Jiang Bian, Tao Qin, Guiquan Liu, and Tie-Yan Liu. 2018. Dual transfer learning for neural machine translation with marginal distribution regularization. In *Proceedings of AAAI Conference on Artificial Intelligence (AAAI)*, pages 5553–5560, New Orleans, USA.

Yiren Wang, Yingce Xia, Tianyu He, Fei Tian, Tao Qin, ChengXiang Zhai, and Tie-Yan Liu. 2019. Multi-agent dual learning. In *International Conference on Learning Representations (ICLR)*.

Jiawei Wu, Xin Wang, and William Yang Wang. 2019. Extract and edit: An alternative to back-translation for unsupervised neural machine translation. In *Proceedings of the 2019 Conference of the North American Chapter of the Association for Computational Linguistics: Human Language Technologies (NAACL:HLT), Volume 1 (Long and Short Papers)*, pages 1173–1183, Minneapolis, Minnesota.

Jiacheng Yang, Mingxuan Wang, Hao Zhou, Chengqi Zhao, Weinan Zhang, Yong Yu, and Lei Li. 2020. Towards making the most of bert in neural machine translation. In *Proceedings of the AAAI Conference on Artificial Intelligence*, volume 34, pages 9378–9385.

Hao Zheng, Yong Cheng, and Yang Liu. 2017. Maximum expected likelihood estimation for zero-resource neural machine translation. In *Proceedings of the Twenty-Sixth International Joint Conference on Artificial Intelligence (IJCAI)*, pages 4251–4257.

Should we find another model?: Improving Neural Machine Translation Performance with ONE-Piece Tokenization Method without Model Modification

Chanjun Park[1†], **Sugyeong Eo**[1†], **Hyeonseok Moon**[1†], **Heuiseok Lim**[1*]
[1]Korea University, South Korea
{bcj1210, djtnrud, glee889, limhseok}@korea.ac.kr

Abstract

Most of the recent natural language processing (NLP) studies are based on the pretrain-finetuning approach (PFA). However for small and medium-sized industries with insufficient hardware, there are many limitations in servicing latest PFA based NLP application software, due to slow speed and insufficient memory. Since these approaches generally require large amounts of data, it is much more difficult to service with PFA especially for low-resource languages. We propose a new tokenization method, ONE-Piece, to address this limitation. ONE-Piece combines morphologically-aware subword tokenization and vocabulary communicating method, which has not been carefully considered before. Our proposed method can also be utilized without modifying the model structure. We experiment by applying ONE-Piece to Korean, a morphologically-rich and low-resource language. We revealed that ONE-Piece with vanilla transformer model can achieve comparable performance to the current Korean-English machine translation state-of-the-art model.

1 Introduction

Recent studies using pretrain-finetuning approach (PFA) technique have achieved state-of-the-art (SOTA) performance in many natural language processing (NLP) tasks and are becoming the latest trend (Devlin et al., 2018; Yang et al., 2019; Radford et al., 2019; Brown et al., 2020; Liu et al., 2019; Clark et al., 2020). To utilize the PFA, a large amount of pre-training data and a system with sufficient computing power are required. For example, T5 (Raffel et al., 2019) was trained with 11 B parameters and 1 T tokens in order to get SOTA performance, and for GPT3 (Brown et al., 2020), 170 B parameters were required to train a model to demonstrate the best performance.

The trend of model research based on PFA raises two problems. First, it is hard to expect a similar performance for the low-resource setting. This is because most studies based on the PFA technique rely on large amounts of data (Zoph et al., 2016). But for low-resource languages, it is difficult to provide the comparable amount of data required by recent papers. Second, it is necessary to overturn the existing model and pre-train a new model from scratch to create a PFA-based model that follows the latest research trends.

Since the PFA-based model requires many parameters, companies without adequate server or graphic processing unit (GPU) environments may have many difficulties in configuring the service environment and utilizing the latest model (Park et al., 2020b). Therefore, new approaches are required to ensure high performance for low-resource languages and companies lacking extensive server and GPU environments.

To solve this problem, many researches are being conducted on the way of improving the performance of NLP application software without changing the model through data pre and post-processing, typically in machine translation (Pal et al., 2016; Currey et al., 2017; Banerjee and Bhattacharyya, 2018; Koehn et al., 2018; Kudo, 2018; Park et al., 2020b). Reflecting this trend, we conducted a study on an optimized tokenization that can improve the performance of neural machine translation (NMT) without changing the model.

We propose two perspectives for optimized tokenization. First, we analyze the limitations of byte pair encoding (BPE) (Sennrich et al., 2015) and sentencepiece (Kudo and Richardson, 2018), which can easily be applied to various languages. Due to its language-agnostic characteristic, these methods are currently used as the defaults in language model research and existing tokenization methods. However, there are 7,111 languages around the world. More than 50 million people speak 25 languages

[†] All authors contributed equally.
[*] Corresponding author.

Proceedings of NAACL HLT 2021: IndustryTrack Papers, pages 97–104
June 6–11, 2021.

as their mother tongue that have various morphological characteristics such as isolating language, agglutinative language, and fusional language. Considering this, it seems hard to assert that applying sentencepiece and BPE always produce the best performance.

Second, we focus on the problem that there is not enough discussion about the corpus used in tokenizer training. Several studies that applied BPE and sentencepiece use a merged bilingual corpus, that combines two language corpora into one, when training its tokenizer (Song et al., 2019; Liu et al., 2020). However in these studies, merged bilingual corpus is utilized without sufficient comparative analysis.

In this study, tokenization methods which leveraging merged bilingual corpora and separate bilingual corpora are denoted as Vocabulary Communicating (VC) and Vocabulary Separating (VS), respectively. We denote VC and VS as vocabulary methods and compare the performance of each method in NMT. In other words, we further figure out the optimal tokenization method through comparative experiments on various tokenization methods.

All the experiments are made on a Korean dataset, which is a representative of low-resource and morphologically rich language (MRL). In particular, we propose ONE-Piece that combines the VC method and morphological segmentation followed by sentencepiece. Through comparative experiments with tokenization methods currently used in NLP research, such as BPE and sentencepiece, we revealed that ONE-Piece can encourage the optimal performance in Korean-English machine translation. The contributions of our study are as follows:

- We proposed a new subword tokenization method, ONE-Piece, which leveraging morphological segmentation and vocabulary communicating method. Through ONE-Piece, we can obtain better performance than the existing tokenization methods such as BPE and sentencepiece.
- Based on linguistic analysis, we showed that constructing corpus for training tokenizer is an important factor that has a critical influence on machine translation performance.
- We presented a new viewpoint for pre-processing that can improve translation performance without modifying model structure. Our proposal considered industrial service and demonstrated high speed and performance without using PFA.

2 Proposed Method

This study proposes an optimal tokenization method for improving machine translation performance from the viewpoints of morphological segmentation and vocabulary method. We derive an optimal tokenization method for Korean-English machine translation by conducting a case study that combines the morphological segmentation and vocabulary method.

2.1 Morphologically-Aware SentencePiece

Korean is classified as an agglutinative language according to its type of morphemes. Due to the nature of agglutinative languages, one word can comprises substantive (noun/pronoun/numeral) followed by postposition, or the stem followed by the ending. Table 1 shows the result of tokenizing Korean sentences through BPE (Sennrich et al., 2015), sentencepiece (Kudo and Richardson, 2018), and morphological segmentation using MeCab-ko.

In the case of BPE and sentencepiece, the postpositions '가 (ga), 는 (neun), 를 (leul), 의 (ui), 인 (in)' have not been properly separated from the substantives. This failures in separating the postpositions from the substantives can lead to mistranslation of entities and grammartically incorrect translation. Generally, the postposition indicates the grammatical relationship to the substantive and plays an important role in organizing the meaning of words. Therefore, miss-separating the postpositions can lead to the incorrect translation of the whole sentence, and misunderstanding of the semantic relationship.

Also, in the case of BPE and sentencepiece, the entities (red-common noun, blue-proper noun) are over-tokenized. Both methods tokenize sentences based on frequency and probability without considering linguistic characteristics. This can lead to inappropriate segmentation between substantives and postpositions, or between stems and endings. These problems can be alleviated by employing morphological segmentation. In this study, we quantitatively analyze the effect of morphological segmentation in NMT, and propose the optimal method of leveraging it by combining sentencepiece.

2.2 Why MeCab-ko?

We use Konlpy (Park and Cho, 2014) for morphological segmentation of Korean sentences. Konlpy

Target Sentence	BPE	sentencepiece	MeCab-ko
The number of diagnoses started to soar, just as Lorna and Judith predicted, indeed hoped, that it would	진단/ 숫자는/ 급증@@/했고/ 로@@/나와/ 주@@/디@@/스가/ 예상@@/했고/ 진@@/실로/ 그들이/ 바랬@@/던/ 것처럼	_진단/_숫자는/_급증/했고/_로/나와/_주/디/스가/_예상/했고/_진/실로/_그들이/_바/랬/던/_것처럼'	진단/ 숫자/는/ 급증/했/고/ 로나(**NNP**)/와/주디스(**NNP**)/가/ 예상/했/고/ 진실로/ 그/들/이/ 바랬/던/ 것/처럼
Instead of blaming parents for causing autism, Asperger framed it as a lifelong, polygenetic disability	자폐@@/증을/ 부모의/탓@@/으로/ 돌리는/대신/ 아스@@/퍼@@/거는/ 그것을/ 장기적인/ 다@@/기@@/원의/ 장애@@/로	_자폐/증을/_부모의/_탓/으로/_돌리는/_대신/_아스/퍼/거는/_그것을/_장기적인/_다/기/원의/_장애/로	자폐증/을/ 부모/의/ 탓/으로/ 돌리/는/ 대신/ 아스퍼거(**NNP**)/는/ 그것/을/ 장기/적/인/ 다/기원/의/ 장애/로

Table 1: Comparison of BPE, sentencepiece and MeCab-ko segmentation results.

is an open-source Korean morphological analyzer package which provides 6 morphological analyzers: MeCab-ko, Kkma, Komoran, Hannanum, Okt, and Twitter. In this study, we select an analyzer that shows the best performance among them by experimenting morphological analysis for up to 1 M characters. In particular, since inference speed is a very important factor in the industry field, we focused on the time required for morphological analysis. The inference time required for each analyzer is shown in Figure 1.

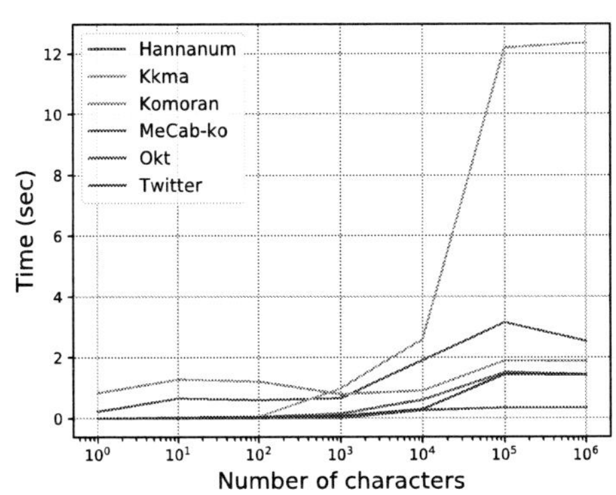

Figure 1: Inference time of morphological analyzer

As shown in Figure 1, MeCab-ko shows the best results compared to other morphological analyzers. It takes 0.3353 secs in processing 1 M characters. Additionally, through experiments on different number of characters, we can see that MeCab-ko conducts analysis of the input sequence at a stable speed despite the exponential increase in the number of characters. For these reasons, we adopt MeCab-ko by its high processing speed and stability in character length.

2.3 Vocabulary Communicating Method

The VC method has been used in several PFA-based models. In MASS (Song et al., 2019), a 60K vocabulary was extracted by composing the source and target language into a merged bilingual corpus. In mBART (Liu et al., 2020), the CC25 corpus was composed of a total of 25 languages extracted from CommonCrawl (CC) (Lample and Conneau, 2019; Wenzek et al., 2019) and used for unified vocabulary extraction. When using the VC method in mBART, there is a generalization effect for unseen languages. However, this effect has not been sufficiently discussed for languages that do not share an alphabet, and no quantitative basis for a generalization effect has been proposed. In this study, we conducted probing for this approach through quantitative analysis.

In practical cases, source and target languages often communicate to each other; source language is contained in target sentences, and vice versa. In the case of our training data, approximately 6.9% of source sentences contains English tokens. For instance, domain specific terms such as "Host IP" can not be replaced by Korean token and constitute Korean sentences in its original form.

For the case of VS method, each language only contributes to the processing of corresponding language corpus, and different tokenizers are applied to the source and target sentences. If a vocabulary is extracted according to the VS method, source language dictionary is composed by reflecting only small fraction of the target languages, which is con-

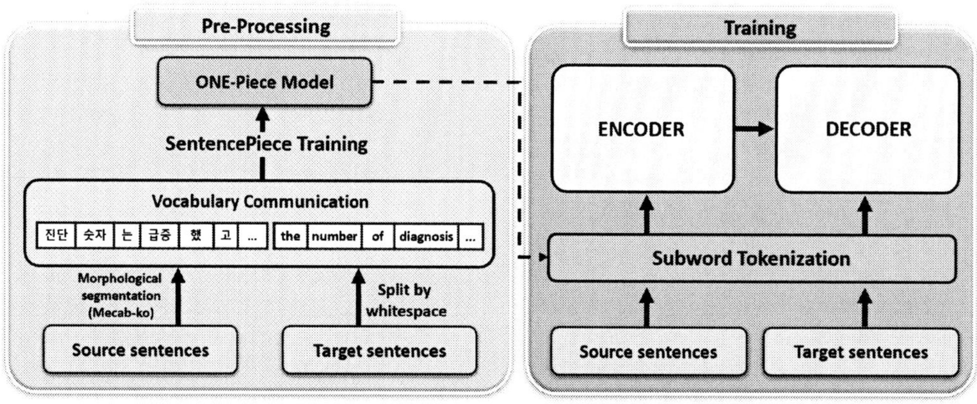

Figure 2: Overall Architecture of NMT training process using ONE-Piece model

tained in source sentences. In this case, target language token, which is not contained in source language dictionary but contained in target language dictionary, is treated as unknown.

The VC method can alleviate this problem. As previously mentioned, the VC method construct a merged corpus and the vocabulary extracted from this merged corpus is identically applied to the source and target sentences. By using VC method, the source and target language can interact within the same vocabulary and are mutually referenceable. Therefore, the source and target language can interact within the same vocabulary and are mutually referenceable. This can lead to full understanding of target language tokens in source sentences and vice verssa.

2.4 ONE-Piece

ONE-Piece is a subword tokenization method that utilizes morphological analysis and the VC method. By applying morphological analysis, characteristics of an agglutinative language, that a single word can comprises multiple morphemes, can be considered. Then by following sentencepiece, applying VC method, can alleviate the out of vocabulary (OOV) problem.

The ONE-piece can be obtained by following processes. First, from a parallel corpus P, which is consist of source sentences $S = \{S_i\}_{i=1}^{N}$ and target sentences $T = \{T_i\}_{i=1}^{N}$, merged corpus M is created. More specifically, this procedures can be described as follows:

$$S_i = \{s_i^j\}_{j=1}^{n_i} \qquad T_i = \{t_i^j\}_{j=1}^{m_i} \tag{1}$$

s_i^j denote j^{th} word of source sentence S_i, which is segmented by whitespace, and n_i indicate the word length of S_i. Similarly, t_i^j denote j^{th} word, and m_i indicate the word length of target sentence T_i, which is segmented by whitespace.

We apply morphological analyzer to agglutinative language. In this paper, source sentences is re-segmented by morpheme-units, through morphological analyer. This can be denoted as equation (2).

$$Seg_i = MA(S_i) = \{seg_i^j\}_{j=1}^{k_i} \tag{2}$$

MA indicates morphological analyzer for source language. By MA, morpheme-unit-segmented sentence Seg_i is generated from source sentence S_i. k_i denotes morpheme-token length of Seg_i. Since a word comprises one or more morphemes, k_i is always equal to or greater than j_i. Then by combining all the Seg_i and T_i into one, merged corpus M is generated as equation (3).

$$M = [T_1, \ldots, T_N, Seg_1, \ldots, Seg_N] \tag{3}$$

M is composed of both source language and target language. As M is created, we can generate ONE-piece by training sentencepiece model by M.

Figure 2 is an overall architecture that describes the process of training NMT model by leveraging ONE-Piece. For Korean sentences in the source part, morphological segmentation is performed with MeCab-ko, and English sentences corresponding to the target side are segmented by whitespace. After combining source sentences and target sentences, we train sentencepiece model by using them. In this process, ONE-Piece model is created. Through ONE-Piece, input sentences are segmented into subwords and fed into the encoder and decoder for training NMT model.

3 Experiments

3.1 Dataset and Experimental Setting

We utilized Korean-English parallel corpora from 3 different data sources for our dataset: the AI Hub Korean-English parallel corpus[1], OpenSubtitles[2], and the IWSLT-17 TED corpus (Cettolo et al., 2017). We constructed 2.7 M sentence pairs from these data sources. For better NMT performance, we applied parallel corpus filtering to our corpus and construct 2.2 M sentence pairs for training. We applied the same filtering method as Park et al. (2020a). We randomly selected 5,000 sentence pairs from our training data for validation and used IWSLT-16 and IWSLT-17 test sets, which is consist of 1,143 and 1,429 sentence pairs, for performance evaluation.

Since our ultimate purpose is to check whether the performance of the NMT model can be improved only by the subword tokenization method without changing the model, we adopt vanilla transformer as our baseline. The performance evaluation of translation results was conducted based on the BLEU score (Papineni et al., 2002). To measure the score, we adopted multi-bleu.perl script[3] in Moses.

3.2 Experimental Results

3.2.1 Verification of the Effectiveness of the VC Method

In this section, we experimentally compare and verify the performance of Korean-English machine translation using VC and VS methods. By applying each method to BPE and sentencepiece, we investigate the impact of the vocabulary method in the performance of NMT. The experimental results are shown in Table 2.

In sentencepiece, the VC method outperforms the VS method by 1.34 BLEU score on the IWSLT-16 test set and 0.99 BLEU score on the IWSLT-17 test set. Conversely for BPE, the VS method outperforms the VC method by 2.78 BLEU score on the IWSLT-16 test set and 2.42 BLEU score on the IWSLT-17 test set. There are some cases where

Tokenization Method	IWSLT-16 (BLEU)	IWSLT-17 (BLEU)
VC SP	21.63	19.11
VS SP	20.29	18.12
VC BPE	17.47	15.42
VS BPE	20.25	17.84

Table 2: Korean-English NMT results applying different vocabulary method in BPE and sentencepiece. SP refers to sentencepiece.

the VS method yields a more superior performance than the VC method, depending on the tokenization algorithm. In other words, the VC method does not show consistently superior performance to the VS method.

Currently, many studies have employed the VC method based tokenizer as a default choice, regardless of the tokenization algorithm. From this experiment, we revealed that the current default option may not be the optimal choice depending on the selection of the tokenization algorithm. We further show that selecting vocabulary method is an important factor that significantly affects machine translation performance. This indicates that the vocabulary method must be considered when adopting a tokenization algorithm to ensure the optimal machine translation performance.

3.2.2 Verification of the Effectiveness of Morphological Segmentation

In this section, we verify the impact of the morphological segmentation. We experimented two tokenization methods using MeCab-ko in Korean corpus. The first method is to segment by morpheme units, and the second method is to add sentencepiece after this process, as first suggested by Park et al. (2019). Whereas Park et al. (2019) used VS method based tokenizers in all of their experiments, we utilized VS method based tokenizers for this experiment. Our results are shown in Table 3.

Tokenization Method	IWSLT-16 (BLEU)	IWSLT-17 (BLEU)
VS SP	20.29	18.12
VS MeCab-ko	19.61	17.08
VS MeCab-ko+SP	19.78	17.49

Table 3: Korean-English NMT results using MeCab-ko. All experiments are implemented using the VS method. sentencepiece is denoted as SP.

[1] https://aihub.or.kr
[2] http://opus.nlpl.eu/OpenSubtitles-v2018.php
[3] https://github.com/moses-smt/mosesdecoder/blob/master/scripts/generic/multi-bleu.perl

Applying sentencepiece after morphological segmentation demonstrates better performance in both the IWSLT-16 and IWSLT-17 test sets compared to the MeCab-ko based segmentation without sentencepiece. However, our results show that applying morphological segmentation for tokenizer training yields overall performance degradation in both test sets. This is contrary to the experimental results of Park et al. (2019), which claim that morphological analysis consistently improves machine translation performance. The main difference between our experiment and Park et al. (2019) is the vocabulary method. From these results, we can infer that the effect of applying morphological segmentation on NMT is relatively different depending on the vocabulary method. This indicates that prior to applying morphological segmentation, the vocabulary method must be considered to get improved NMT performance.

3.2.3 Verification of the ONE-Piece

ONE-Piece differs from existing tokenizers in that it utilizes VC method and the morphological segmentation followed by sentencepiece. In this section, we verify the effectiveness of ONE-Piece by comparing NMT performance using various preprocessing strategies based on the VC method. The results are shown in Table 4.

Tokenization Method	IWSLT-16 (BLEU)	IWSLT-17 (BLEU)
VC Word	7.98	7.16
VC Character	16.39	17.06
VC BPE	17.47	15.42
VC sentencepiece	21.63	19.11
ONE-Piece (ours)	24.95	22.58

Table 4: Korean-English NMT results of different tokenization algorithms. All the experiments are implemented using the VC method.

Compared to the VC-based tokenizer, ONE-Piece produces at least 3.32 BLEU score superior translation performance. This result suggests that further improvement can be made by applying ONE-Piece to other existing sentencepiece-based NMT models.

In sections 3.2.1 and 3.2.2, we revealed that vocabulary method and morphological segmentation significantly affect the NMT performance, but neither of these consistently improve the NMT performance by themselves. However as shown in table 4, by properly combining these two factors, we can derive mutual supplementation effect which lead to a meaningful improvement in the translation performance. This can be viewed as the new criteria for constructing corpus for training tokenizer.

3.2.4 Comparison with Existing Studies

We compare the performance of vanilla transformer model applying ONE-Piece with the performance of mBART(Liu et al., 2020). mBART was trained with 610 M params and 5.6 B tokens from the CC corpus. mBART utilized morpheme based segmentation using MeCab-Ko in the Korean corpus and applied sentencepiece in the English corpus, which is the same tokenization method as VS MeCab-ko in Table 3.

	mBART	MeCab-ko	ONE-Piece
IWSLT-17 (BLEU)	24.6	17.08	22.58
model parameter	610M	32M	32M

Table 5: Comparison of proposed ONE-Piece model with mBART.

As shown in Table 5, when the same tokenization method used in mBART was applied to the baseline model, the performance was 7.52 BLEU lower than that of mBART. However, by applying ONE-Piece to the baseline model, the performance difference narrowed to a 2.02 BLEU score. This shows that applying ONE-Piece enables the vanilla transformer model to have similar performance to the SOTA model. Although the baseline model using ONE-Piece did not exceed the performance of mBART, it is a notable result considering that the number of parameters required by the baseline model is 32 M, approximately 5% of the number of parameters compared to mBART.

The significance of this experiment is that simply by changing the tokenization method, a model with a small number of parameters can achieve a similar performance to SOTA model, which is trained with a more advanced algorithm and larger number of parameters.

4 Conclusion

In this study, we proposed a new tokenization method called ONE-Piece. This can provide the best performance in Korean-English machine translation compared with other tokenization methods.

Our results quantitatively confirmed the effect of the vocabulary method and morphological segmentation on NMT performance. Furthermore, we experimentally proved that the VC method and morphological segmentation cannot consistently improve the performance of NMT by themselves. Our results showed that significant and consistent performance improvement can only be achieved in NMT if they are properly used together. By using ONE-Piece, the vanilla transformer model shows comparable translation performance to the mBART. Accordingly, we expect that companies that have difficulties using the latest PFA-based model, due to an inadequate server environment, will be able to utilize our proposed model to provide sufficiently good performance.

Acknowledgments

This research was supported by the MSIT(Ministry of Science and ICT), Korea, under the ITRC (Information Technology Research Center) support program (IITP-2018-0-01405) supervised by the IITP (Institute for Information & Communications Technology Planning & Evaluation), Institute for Information & communications Technology Planning & Evaluation (IITP), grant funded by the Korean government (MSIT) (No. 2020-0-00368, A Neural-Symbolic Model for Knowledge Acquisition and Inference Techniques) and MSIT(Ministry of Science and ICT), Korea, under the ICT Creative Consilience program(IITP-2021-2020-0-01819) supervised by the IITP(Institute for Information & communications Technology Planning Evaluation).

References

Tamali Banerjee and Pushpak Bhattacharyya. 2018. Meaningless yet meaningful: Morphology grounded subword-level nmt. In *Proceedings of the Second Workshop on Subword/Character LEvel Models*, pages 55–60.

Tom B Brown, Benjamin Mann, Nick Ryder, Melanie Subbiah, Jared Kaplan, Prafulla Dhariwal, Arvind Neelakantan, Pranav Shyam, Girish Sastry, Amanda Askell, et al. 2020. Language models are few-shot learners. *arXiv preprint arXiv:2005.14165*.

Mauro Cettolo, Marcello Federico, Luisa Bentivogli, Niehues Jan, Stüker Sebastian, Sudoh Katsuitho, Yoshino Koichiro, and Federmann Christian. 2017. Overview of the iwslt 2017 evaluation campaign. In *International Workshop on Spoken Language Translation*, pages 2–14.

Kevin Clark, Minh-Thang Luong, Quoc V Le, and Christopher D Manning. 2020. Electra: Pre-training text encoders as discriminators rather than generators. *arXiv preprint arXiv:2003.10555*.

Anna Currey, Antonio Valerio Miceli-Barone, and Kenneth Heafield. 2017. Copied monolingual data improves low-resource neural machine translation. In *Proceedings of the Second Conference on Machine Translation*, pages 148–156.

Jacob Devlin, Ming-Wei Chang, Kenton Lee, and Kristina Toutanova. 2018. Bert: Pre-training of deep bidirectional transformers for language understanding. *arXiv preprint arXiv:1810.04805*.

Philipp Koehn, Huda Khayrallah, Kenneth Heafield, and Mikel L Forcada. 2018. Findings of the wmt 2018 shared task on parallel corpus filtering. In *Proceedings of the Third Conference on Machine Translation: Shared Task Papers*, pages 726–739.

Taku Kudo. 2018. Subword regularization: Improving neural network translation models with multiple subword candidates. *arXiv preprint arXiv:1804.10959*.

Taku Kudo and John Richardson. 2018. Sentencepiece: A simple and language independent subword tokenizer and detokenizer for neural text processing. *arXiv preprint arXiv:1808.06226*.

Guillaume Lample and Alexis Conneau. 2019. Cross-lingual language model pretraining. *arXiv preprint arXiv:1901.07291*.

Yinhan Liu, Jiatao Gu, Naman Goyal, Xian Li, Sergey Edunov, Marjan Ghazvininejad, Mike Lewis, and Luke Zettlemoyer. 2020. Multilingual denoising pre-training for neural machine translation. *arXiv preprint arXiv:2001.08210*.

Yinhan Liu, Myle Ott, Naman Goyal, Jingfei Du, Mandar Joshi, Danqi Chen, Omer Levy, Mike Lewis, Luke Zettlemoyer, and Veselin Stoyanov. 2019. Roberta: A robustly optimized bert pretraining approach. *arXiv preprint arXiv:1907.11692*.

Santanu Pal, Sudip Kumar Naskar, Mihaela Vela, and Josef van Genabith. 2016. A neural network based approach to automatic post-editing. In *Proceedings of the 54th Annual Meeting of the Association for Computational Linguistics (Volume 2: Short Papers)*, pages 281–286.

Kishore Papineni, Salim Roukos, Todd Ward, and Wei-Jing Zhu. 2002. Bleu: a method for automatic evaluation of machine translation. In *Proceedings of the 40th annual meeting of the Association for Computational Linguistics*, pages 311–318.

Chanjun Park, Gyeongmin Kim, and HeuiSeok Lim. 2019. Parallel corpus filtering and korean optimized subword tokenization for machine translation. In *The 31st Annual Conference on Human Cognitive Language Technology*, pages 221–224.

Chanjun Park, Yeonsu Lee, Chanhee Lee, and Heuiseok Lim. 2020a. Quality, not quantity? : Effect of parallel corpus quantity and quality on neural machine translation. In *The 32st Annual Conference on Human Cognitive Language Technology*, pages 363–368.

Chanjun Park, Yeongwook Yang, Kinam Park, and Heuiseok Lim. 2020b. Decoding strategies for improving low-resource machine translation. *Electronics*, 9(10):1562.

Eunjeong L. Park and Sungzoon Cho. 2014. Konlpy: Korean natural language processing in python. In *Proceedings of the 26th Annual Conference on Human Cognitive Language Technology*, Chuncheon, Korea.

Alec Radford, Jeffrey Wu, Rewon Child, David Luan, Dario Amodei, and Ilya Sutskever. 2019. Language models are unsupervised multitask learners. *OpenAI blog*, 1(8):9.

Colin Raffel, Noam Shazeer, Adam Roberts, Katherine Lee, Sharan Narang, Michael Matena, Yanqi Zhou, Wei Li, and Peter J Liu. 2019. Exploring the limits of transfer learning with a unified text-to-text transformer. *arXiv preprint arXiv:1910.10683*.

Rico Sennrich, Barry Haddow, and Alexandra Birch. 2015. Neural machine translation of rare words with subword units. *arXiv preprint arXiv:1508.07909*.

Kaitao Song, Xu Tan, Tao Qin, Jianfeng Lu, and Tie-Yan Liu. 2019. Mass: Masked sequence to sequence pre-training for language generation. *arXiv preprint arXiv:1905.02450*.

Guillaume Wenzek, Marie-Anne Lachaux, Alexis Conneau, Vishrav Chaudhary, Francisco Guzmán, Armand Joulin, and Edouard Grave. 2019. Ccnet: Extracting high quality monolingual datasets from web crawl data. *arXiv preprint arXiv:1911.00359*.

Zhilin Yang, Zihang Dai, Yiming Yang, Jaime Carbonell, Russ R Salakhutdinov, and Quoc V Le. 2019. Xlnet: Generalized autoregressive pretraining for language understanding. In *Advances in neural information processing systems*, pages 5753–5763.

Barret Zoph, Deniz Yuret, Jonathan May, and Kevin Knight. 2016. Transfer learning for low-resource neural machine translation. *arXiv preprint arXiv:1604.02201*.

Autocorrect in the Process of Translation — Multi-task Learning Improves Dialogue Machine Translation

Tao Wang[1,2], Chengqi Zhao[1], Mingxuan Wang[1], Lei Li[1], Deyi Xiong[3]*
[1]ByteDance AI Lab
[2]School of Computer Science and Technology, Soochow University, Suzhou, China
[3]College of Intelligence and Computing, Tianjin University, Tianjin, China
{wangtao.960826, zhaochengqi.d, wangmingxuan.89}@bytedance.com
{lilei.02}@bytedance.com
dyxiong@tju.edu.cn

Abstract

Automatic translation of dialogue texts is a much needed demand in many real life scenarios. However, current neural machine translation systems usually deliver unsatisfying translation results of dialogue texts. In this paper, we conduct a deep analysis of a dialogue corpus and summarize three major issues on dialogue translation, including pronoun dropping (`ProDrop`), punctuation dropping (`PunDrop`), and typos (`DialTypo`). In response to these challenges, we propose a joint learning method to identify omission and typo in the process of translating, and utilize context to translate dialogue utterances. To properly evaluate the performance, we propose a manually annotated dataset with 1,931 Chinese-English parallel utterances from 300 dialogues as a benchmark testbed for dialogue translation. Our experiments show that the proposed method improves translation quality by 3.2 BLEU over the baselines. It also elevates the recovery rate of omitted pronouns from 26.09% to 47.16%. The code and dataset are publicly available at https://github.com/rgwt123/DialogueMT.

1 Introduction

Remarkable progress has been made in Neural Machine Translation (NMT) (Bahdanau et al., 2015; Wu et al., 2016; Lin et al., 2020; Liu et al., 2020) in recent years, which has been widely applied in everyday life. A typical scenario for such application is translating dialogue texts, in particular the record of group chats or movie subtitles, which helps people of different languages understand cross-language chat and improve their comprehension capabilities.

However, traditional NMT models translate texts in a sentence-by-sentence manner and focus on the formal text input, such as WMT news translation

(1)	Nancy怎么了? [她]$_{drop}$是不是哭了啊。
MT	What happened to Nancy? Did you cry?
REF	What happened to Nancy? Did she cry?
(2)	Nancy怎么了[?]$_{drop}$是不是哭了啊。
MT	Did Nancy cry?
REF	What happened to Nancy? Did she cry?
(3)	Nancy怎么[乐]$_{typo}$?
MT	How happy is Nancy?
REF	What happened to Nancy?

Table 1: Examples of `ProDrop` (1), `PunDrop` (2) and `DialTypo` (3). MT is translation results from Google Translate while REF is references.

(Barrault et al., 2020), while the translation of dialogue must take the meaning of context and the input noise into account. Table 1 shows examples of dialogue fragment in Chinese and their translation in English. Example (1) demonstrates that the omission in traditional translation (e.g., dropped pronouns in Chinese) leads to inaccurate translation results.

Despite its vast potential application, efforts of exploration into dialogue translation are far from enough. Existing works (Wang et al., 2016; Maruf et al., 2018) focus on either extracting dialogues from parallel corpora, such as OpenSubtitles (Lison et al., 2019), or leveraging speaker information for integrating dialogue context into neural models. Also, the lack of both training data and benchmark test set makes current dialogue translation models far from satisfying and need to be further improved.

In this paper, we try to alleviate the aforementioned challenges in dialogue translation. We first analyze a fraction of a dialogue corpus and summarize three critical issues in dialogue translation, including `ProDrop`, `PunDrop`, and `DialTypo`. Then we design a Multi-Task Learning (MTLDIAL) approach that learns to self-correct sentences in the process of translating. The model's

*Corresponding author.

Proceedings of NAACL HLT 2021: IndustryTrack Papers, pages 105–112
June 6–11, 2021. ©2021 Association for Computational Linguistics

encoder part automatically learns how to de-noise the noise input via explicit supervisory signals provided by additional contextual labeling. We also propose three strong baselines for dialogue translation, including repair (REPAIRDIAL) and robust (ROBUSTDIAL) model. To alleviate the challenges arising from the scarcity of dialogue data, we use sub-documents in the bilingual parallel corpus to enable the model to learn from cross-sentence context.

Additionally as for evaluation, the most commonly used BLEU metric (Papineni et al., 2001) for NMT is not good enough to provide a deep look into the translation quality in such a scenario. Thus, we build a Chinese-English test set containing sentences with the issues in `ProDrop`, `PunDrop` and `DialTypo`, attached with the human translation and annotation. Finally, we get a test set of 300 dialogues with 1,931 parallel sentences.

The main contributions of this paper are as follows: a) We analyze three challenges `ProDrop`, `PunDrop` and `DialTypo`, which greatly impact the understanding and translation of a dialogue. b) We propose a contextual multi-task learning method to tackle the analyzed challenges. c) We create a Chinese-English test set specifically containing those problems and conduct experiments to evaluate proposed method on this test set.

2 Analysis on Dialogue Translation

There were already some manual analyses of translation errors, especially in the field of discourse translation. Voita et al. (2019) study English-Russian translation and find three main challenges for discourse translation: deixis, ellipsis, and lexical cohesion. For Chinese-English translation, tense consistency, connective mismatch, and content-heavy sentences are the most common issues (Li et al., 2014).

Different from previous works, we mainly analyze the specific phenomena in dialogue translation. We begin with a study on a bilingual dialogue corpus (Wang et al., 2018).[1] We translate source sentences into the target language at sentence level and compare translation results with reference at dialogue level. Around 1,000 dialogues are evaluated, and the results are reported in Table 2. From the statistic, we observe two persistent dialogue translation problems: pronoun dropping (`ProDrop`), punctuation dropping(`PunDrop`). The phenomenon is consistent with the issue we collect in practical Instant Messaging (IM) chat scenarios, except for typos since the analyzed dialogue corpus has been proofread to remove typos.

Types of phenomena	Frequency
Correct	88.1%
`ProDrop`	4.3%
`PunDrop`	3.2%
Incorrect segmentation	2.4%
Other translation errors	2.0%

Table 2: Manual evaluation of dialogue samples.

2.1 Pronoun Dropping

Pronouns are frequently omitted in pro-drop languages (Huang, 1989), such as Chinese, Japanese, Korean, Vietnamese, and Slavic languages. Such phenomenon are more frequent in dialogue, where the interlocutors are both aware of what's omitted in the context. However, when translating a pro-drop language into a non-pro-drop language (e.g., English)[2], it is hard to translate those omitted pronouns, resulting in grammatical errors or semantic inaccuracies in the target language. The first conversation in Table 1 is an example.

2.2 Punctuation Dropping

In dialogue scenarios, such as IM software, punctuation is often omitted and users tend to segment sentences with spaces. The problem becomes much serious in languages with no spaces, such as Chinese, Japanese, Korean, and Thai. Table 1 shows this phenomenon in Example (2).

2.3 Dialogue Typos

Typo repairing is another fundamental but very challenging practical problem. In dialogue translation, typos or misspellings are very common, which dramatically undermine the quality of translation output produced by machine translation. Table 1 shows this phenomenon in Example (3).

3 Approach to NMTDIAL

This section aims to propose a unified framework that facilitates NMT to correct noisy inputs in dialogue neural machine translation (NMTDIAL). The framework includes three different methods, which are REPAIRDIAL, ROBUSTDIAL and MTL-DIAL.

[1]https://github.com/longyuewangdcu/tvsub

[2]https://en.wikipedia.org/wiki/Pro-drop_language

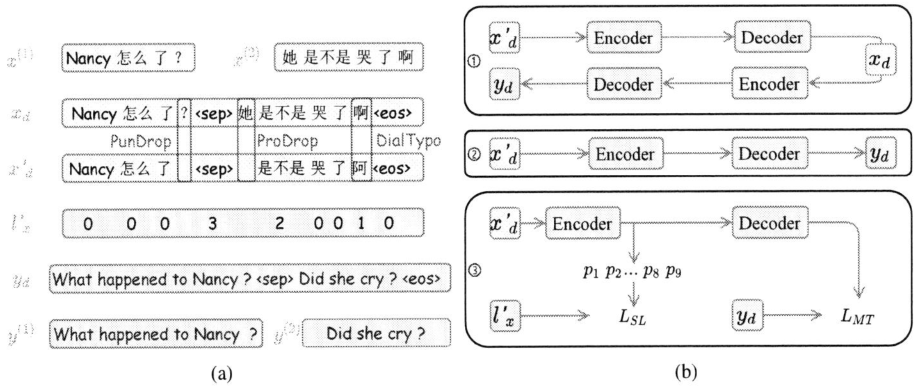

Figure 1: Overall diagram of NMTDIAL. (a) demonstrates the process of data generation, and (b) displays the three proposed methods. ①/②/③ represent REPAIRDIAL, ROBUSTDIAL and MTLDIAL respectively.

3.1 Contextual Perturbation Example Generation

The most challenging problem for NMTDIAL is the data distribution gap between training and inference stage, where the training data are clean sentence-level pairs while the test data are noisy dialogue-level conversations.

To bridge the distribution gap, the first step is to generate perturbation examples based on training instances. The data generation mainly consists of two steps. The first step is to obtain sub-documents with cross-sentence context, and the second step is to generate examples with word perturbations within sub-documents. Figure 1a shows a complete process.

Cross-sentence Context It is difficult to acquire dialog-level parallel training data. As an alternative approach, we use parallel document data to catch dependencies across sentences.

Formally, let $x_d = \{x^{(1)}, x^{(2)}, \cdots, x^{(M)}\}$ be a source-language document containing M source sentences. And $y_d = \{y^{(1)}, y^{(2)}, \cdots, y^{(M)}\}$ is the corresponding target-language document containing the same number of sentences as that of the source document. To get more context information, we randomly sample consecutive sub-document pairs (x_d, y_d) of N sentences (i.e., snippet pairs from aligned documents). We set $N \in [1, 10]$ in this paper.

We use a special token <sep> as the separator to concatenate sentences into a parallel sub-document $\{(x_d, y_d)\}$, as shown in Figure 1a.

Contextual Perturbation We then consider generating perturbation example x'_d from x_d with respect to sub-document context. For `ProDrop`, `PunDrop` and `DialTypo`, we build a Chinese pronoun table $\text{T}_{\texttt{ProDrop}}$, a common punctuation table $\text{T}_{\texttt{PunDrop}}$ and a Chinese homophone table $\text{T}_{\texttt{DialTypo}}$ respectively.

For `ProDrop` and `PunDrop`, we traverse source sentences of x_d, discard pronouns/punctuation in these sentences with a probability of 30% and record deletion positions with corresponding labels (see details below); to construct a typo, we choose a word with a probability of 1%, of which 80% is replaced with one of its homophones according to $\text{T}_{\texttt{DialTypo}}$ and 20% is replaced with another random word. We determine these percentages by observing the generated perturbation data. For annotation labels, we tag correct words with 0, words of `DialTypo` with 1, `ProDrop` words with 2 and `PunDrop` words with 3.

Finally we get x_d, x'_d and their corresponding label sequences ℓ_x, ℓ'_x. ℓ_x is a sequence of all 0s.

3.2 NMTDIAL Base Models

With the created training data, we first introduce two methods for NMTDIAL as our strong baselines, which will be elaborated here for model comparison.

REPAIRDIAL A natural way for NMTDIAL is to train a dialog repair model to transform dialogue inputs into forms that an ordinary NMT system can deal with. REPAIRDIAL involves training a repair model to transform x'_d to x_d and a clean translation model that translates x_d to y_d. As a pipeline method, REPAIRDIAL may suffer from error propagation.

ROBUSTDIAL We extend the robust NMT

(Cheng et al., 2018) to dialogue-level translation. Specifically, we take both the original (x_d, y_d) and the perturbated (x'_d, y_d) bilingual pairs as training instances. So the model is more resilient on dialogue translation. During the inference stage, the robust model directly translates raw inputs into the target language.

3.3 MTLDIAL

ROBUSTDIAL has the potential to handle translation problems caused by noisy dialogue inputs. However, the internal mechanism is rather implicit and in a black box. Therefore, the improvement is limited, and it is not easy to analyze the improvement. To address this issue, we introduce a context-aware multi-task learning method MTLDIAL for NMTDIAL.

As shown in ③ of Figure 1b, the only difference is that we have a contextual labeling module based on the encoder. We denote the final layer output of the Transformer encoder as H. For each token h_i in $H = (h_1, h_2, ..., h_m)$, the probability of contextual labeling is defined as:

$$P(p_i = j|X) = softmax(W \cdot h_i + b)[j] \quad (1)$$

where $X = (x_1, x_2, ..., x_m)$ is the input sequence, $P(p_i = j|X)$ is the conditional probability that token x_i is labeled as j ($j \in 0, 1, 2, 3$ as defined above).

Here we make the labeling module as simple as possible, so that the Transformer encoder can behave like BERT (Devlin et al., 2019), learning more information related to perturbation and guiding the decoder to find desirable translations.

During the training phrase, the model takes $(x_d, x'_d, \ell_x, \ell'_x, y_d)$ as the training data. The learning process is driven by optimizing two objectives, corresponding to sequence labeling as auxiliary loss ($\mathcal{L}_{SL}$) and machine translation as the primary loss ($\mathcal{L}_{MT}$) in a multi-task learning framework.

$$\mathcal{L}_{SL} = -log(P(\ell_x|x_d) + P(\ell'_x|x'_d)) \quad (2)$$
$$\mathcal{L}_{MT} = -log(P(y_d|x_d) + P(y_d|x'_d)) \quad (3)$$

The two objective are linearly combined as the overall objective in learning.

$$\mathcal{L} = \mathcal{L}_{MT} + \lambda \cdot \mathcal{L}_{SL} \quad (4)$$

λ is coefficient. During experiments, we set as follows according the best practice:

$$\lambda = max(1.0 - \frac{update\_num}{10^5}, 0.2) \quad (5)$$

where $update\_num$ is the number of updating steps during training.

We introduce multi-task learning for two reasons: 1) The labeling performance reflects the model's understanding of sentences containing the mentioned phenomena. 2) Contextual Labeling can be seen as a pre-training process based on the BERT-like model, and explicit guidance can enable the encoder to learn more about the information we annotate.

3.4 Modeling Dialogue Context

The modes for exploring dialogue context during decoding can be divided into offline and online. For the offline setting, all sentences in a dialogue are concatenated one by one with <sep>. The concatenated sequence is translated, and the target translation for each sentence can be easily detected according to the separator <sep>.

The offline mode can be used for dialogue translation where the entire source dialogue has already been available before translation (e.g., movie subtitles). However, we continuously get new source sentences for online chat and need to generate corresponding translations immediately. We refer to this mode as the online setting.

We experiment with two online methods. One is *online-cut* where the current sentence is concatenated to the previous context with the separator <sep>. The trained NMTDIAL model then translates the concatenated sequence and the last target segment is used as the translation for the current source sentence. The other is *online-fd*. *Online-fd* is a force decoding method. It forces the decoder to use translated history and continues decoding instead of re-translating the entire concatenated sequence. *Online-fd* brings more consistent translation.

4 Experiments

4.1 Test Set

For better evaluation of NMTDIAL, we create a Chinese-English test set covering all issues discussed above based on the corpus we analyze in the second section. Statistics on the built test set are displayed in Table 3. Building such a test set is hard and time-consuming as we need to perform manual selection, translation and annotation.

As for translation quality evaluation, we use other metrics in addition to BLEU. For `PunDrop` and `DialTypo`, we evaluate BLEU scores on sen-

Item	Count
#dialogues	300
#sentence pairs	1,931
#total tokens	19,155/15,976
#average tokens	9.92/8.27
#ProDrop	299
#PunDrop	542
#DialTypo	203

Table 3: Statistics on the test set. "/" denote numbers in Chinese and English separately.

tences containing missing punctuation or typos according to the annotation information. As for ProDrop, we evaluate the translation quality by the percentage of correctly recovering and translating the dropped pronouns.

4.2 Settings

We adopt the Chinese-English corpus from WMT2020[3], with about 48M sentence pairs, as our bilingual training data D. We select newstest2019 as the development set. After splicing, we get D_{doc} with 1.2M pairs and corresponding perturbated dataset D' and D'_{doc} with 48M and 1.2M pairs respectively.

We use byte pair encoding compression algorithm (BPE) (Sennrich et al., 2016) to process all these data and limit the number of merge operations to a maximum of 30K. In our studies, all translation models are Transformer-big, including 6 layers for both encoders and decoders, 1024 dimensions for model, 4096 dimensions for FFN layers and 16 heads for attention.

During training, we use label smoothing = 0.1 (Szegedy et al., 2016), attention dropout = 0.1 and dropout (Hinton et al., 2012) with a rate of 0.3 for all other layers. We use Adam (Kingma and Ba, 2015) to train the NMT models. $\beta 1$ and $\beta 2$ of Adam are set to 0.9 and 0.98, the learning rate is set to 0.0005, and gradient norm 5. The models are trained with a batch size of 32,000 tokens on 8 Tesla V100 GPUs during training. During decoding, we employ beam search algorithm and set the beam size to 5. We use sacrebleu (Post, 2018) to calculate uncased BLEU-4 (Papineni et al., 2001).

4.3 Results of Offline Setting

The offline mode aims at using the entire source dialogue for translation. We experiment with all the methods in the offline setting, and the results

Methods	Overall BLEU	Details ProDrop	PunDrop	DialTypo
BASE	32.7	26.09%	28.2	24.0
REPAIRDIAL	34.0	29.77%	31.2	27.4
ROBUSTDIAL	34.1	45.48%	33.0	**28.8**
MTLDIAL	**35.9**	**47.16%**	**34.3**	28.7
GOLD+BASE	**36.8**	**97.32%**	**34.6**	**36.8**

Table 4: Experiment results on our constructed dialogue translation test set in offline setting. The GOLD+BASE represents translations of completely correct inputs (without ProDrop, PunDrop or DialTypo) using BASE model, which is used to show the oracle results with Transformer on the test set.

Methods	Overall BLEU	Details ProDrop	PunDrop	DialTypo
BASE	32.8(+0.1)	19.06%(-7.03%)	28.1(-0.1)	22.3(-1.7)
REPAIRDIAL	33.8(-0.2)	24.75%(-5.02%)	32.0(+0.8)	28.3(+0.9)
ROBUSTDIAL	34.2(+0.1)	**36.79%(-8.69%)**	32.7(-0.3)	**28.9(-0.5)**
MTLDIAL	**35.3(-0.6)**	34.78%(-12.38%)	**34.3(-0.0)**	28.6(-0.1)
GOLD+BASE	**37.1(+0.3)**	**96.66%(-0.66%)**	**35.3(+0.7)**	**35.9(-0.9)**

Table 5: Results on our constructed dialogue translation test set in online setting at the sentence level.

are shown in Table 4. BASE is a Transformer-big model trained with D and D_{doc}. GOLD+BASE represents the oracle result on this test set. We can see that MTLDIAL has achieved the best results, reducing the gap between $test_{wrong}$ and $test_{gold}$ from 4.1 to 0.9. Compared with ROBUSTDIAL and MTLDIAL, REPAIRDIAL performs relatively poorly. We believe that this is due to the error propagation caused by the pipeline.

From the specific indicators, we can draw the following conclusions: 1) DialTypo has a very obvious impact on BLEU, and the gap between BASE and GOLD+BASE is more than 12 points; 2) The recovery of ProDrop is a relatively difficult task. Although compared with BASE, the current best result of 47.16% has been greatly improved, but is still far away from the golden result 97.32%; 3) PunDrop seems to be a relatively easy task for each method to address.

4.4 Results of Online Setting

The online mode only makes use of previous context during translation. An extreme situation of online setting is that there is no context, that is, sentence-level translation. We show the results of all the methods on the test set at the sentence level in Table 5. Despite the lack of context, our approaches can still bring general benefits. We find that ProDrop relies heavily on context, especially for MTLDIAL, where the absence of context results in a 12.38% drop in performance. This is in line

[3]This corpus includes News Commentary, Wiki Titles, UN Parallel Corpus, CCMT Corpus, WikiMatrix and Back-translated news.

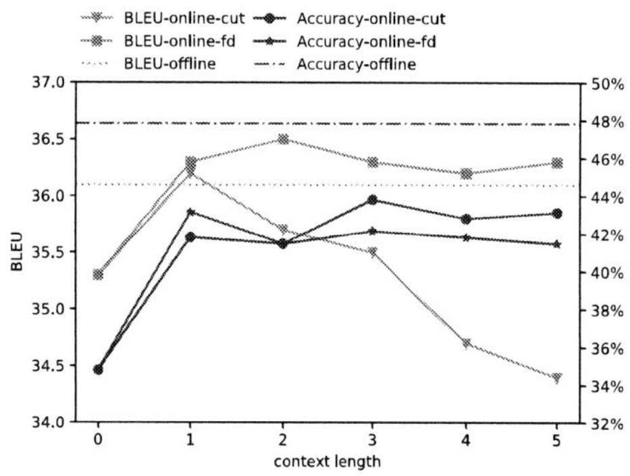

Figure 2: Overall BLEU and `ProDrop` recovery performance (Accuracy) of MTLDIAL with different context length. Dash lines are the offline results.

Data		Precison	Recall	F1
validation	`ProDrop`	**61.3**	**48.7**	**54.3**
	`PunDrop`	80.0	63.6	70.9
	`DialTypo`	**85.3**	**64.2**	**73.2**
test	`ProDrop`	48.6	32.2	38.8
	`PunDrop`	**96.6**	**87.9**	**92.1**
	`DialTypo`	83.3	31.0	45.2

Table 6: Labeling performance on the validation/test set.

with our expectations, as in many cases machine translation system heavily depends on context to fulfill the dropped pronouns.

We further experiment on how context lengths can affect NMTDIAL. The results are shown in Figure 2. In the *online-cut* setting, we can see that using previous few sentences as context may improve overall BLEU score, but continuously adding more preceding texts will lead to a continuous decline. *Online-fd* performs well because using historical translation records to continue decoding can bring more consistent translation results. For the recovery accuracy of `ProDrop`, *online-cut* is better than *online-fd* in contrast, because forced decoding may cause wrong pronoun transmission.

5 Analysis

5.1 Labeling Performance

To better understand how our proposed MTLDIAL make sense, we calculate the labeling performance on both validation and test set. Table 6 shows the overall performance. The validation set follows the same processing progress of training data, while the test set is the real dialogue data set built manually.

The proposed model obtains 54.3% F1 score on the validation set for `ProDrop`, 70.9% for

	zh	en
(1)	艾丽最近怎么样了 她已经不在我的律所了 什么 (**她/she**)为什么走了 (**她/she**)开了自己的律所	What's going on with Ellie? She is no longer in my law firm. What, why are you/is she going? I open my/She opens her own law firm.
(2)	琼斯 (**我/I**)问你件事	Jones asked/, I want to ask you something.
(3)	他上次帮我私下搞 (**他/He**)差点工作都丢了	He helped me out in private last time. I/He nearly lost my/his job.

Table 7: Examples of `ProDrop` recovery errors.

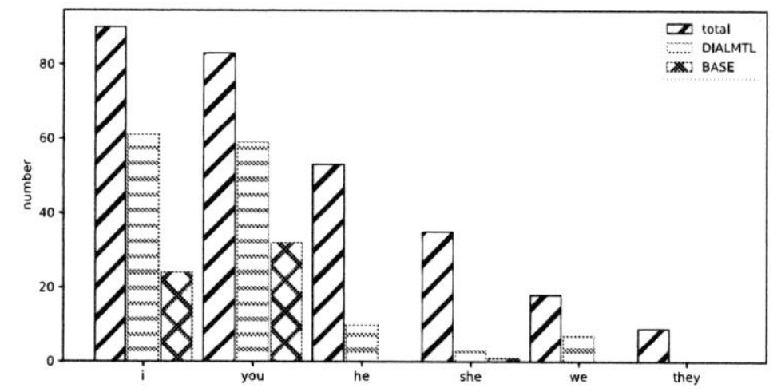

Figure 3: `ProDrop` recovery performance of BASE and contextual MTLDIAL. Total means the total number of occurrence of corresponding pronouns in the test set. We ignore pronouns with a total occurrence number less than 5.

`PunDrop`, and 73.2% for `DialTypo`. When testing on the real test data, the performance on `ProDrop` has declined a lot because of the difference between synthetic training/validation data and real test data. Especially noteworthy is the fact that F1 score of `DialTypo` drops the most, reaching 26%, because of its low recall. It may be due to the considerable difference between the typos generated by our automatic method and the actual distribution.

5.2 Effects of Pronoun Correcting

We further explore the auto-correction of specific pronouns. As shown in Figure 3, we can find that pronouns such as I/you, which occur mostly in the corpus, generally have a higher recovery success rate. We believe this is due to the data imbalance. Compared with BASE, MTLDIAL has a much better performance. While `ProDrop` recovery accuracy has been improved, it still has not achieved 50%. The most common error is that the model does not capture any context or captures previous inappropriate context. We summarize frequently-occurring recovery errors in Table 7.

6 Related Work

Our work is related with both dialogue translation and robust training.

Dialogue Translation

There has been some work on building bilingual dialogue data sets for the translation task in recent years. Wang et al. (2016) propose a novel approach to automatically construct parallel discourse corpus for dialogue machine translation and release around 100K parallel discourse data with manual speaker and dialogue boundary annotation. Maruf et al. (2018) propose the task of translating Bilingual Multi-Speaker Conversations. They introduce datasets extracted from Europarl and Opensubtitles and explore how to exploit both source and target-side conversation histories. Bawden et al. (2019) present a new English-French test set for evaluating of Machine Translation (MT) for informal, written bilingual dialogue. Recently WMT2020 has also proposed a new shared task - machine translation for chats,[4] focusing on bilingual customer support chats (Farajian et al., 2020).

Robust Training

Neural models have been usually affected by noisy issues. Many efforts (Li et al., 2017; Sperber et al., 2017; Vaibhav et al., 2019; Yang et al., 2020) focus on data augmentation to alleviate the problem by adding synthetic noise to the training set. However, generating noise has always been a challenge, as natural noise is always more diversified than artificially constructed noise (Belinkov and Bisk, 2018; Anastasopoulos, 2019; Anastasopoulos et al., 2019).

7 Conclusions

In this paper, we manually analyze challenges in dialogue translation and detect three main problems. In order to tackle these issues, we propose a multi-task learning method with contextual labeling. For deep evaluation, we construct dialogues with translation and detailed annotations as a benchmark test set. Our proposed model achieves substantial improvements over the baselines. What is more, we further analyze the performance of contextual labeling and pronoun recovery errors.

Acknowledgments

We thank the bilingual speakers for test set construction, and the anonymous reviewers for suggestions. Deyi Xiong is partially supported by the Natural Science Foundation of Tianjin (Grant No. 19JCZDJC31400) and the Royal Society (London) (NAF\R1\180122).

[4]http://www.statmt.org/wmt20/chat-task.html

References

Antonios Anastasopoulos. 2019. An analysis of source-side grammatical errors in nmt. In *Proceedings of the 2019 ACL Workshop BlackboxNLP: Analyzing and Interpreting Neural Networks for NLP*, pages 213–223.

Antonios Anastasopoulos, Alison Lui, Toan Q Nguyen, and David Chiang. 2019. Neural machine translation of text from non-native speakers. In *NAACL-HLT (1)*.

Dzmitry Bahdanau, Kyunghyun Cho, and Yoshua Bengio. 2015. Neural machine translation by jointly learning to align and translate. In *3rd International Conference on Learning Representations, ICLR 2015*.

Loïc Barrault, Magdalena Biesialska, Ondřej Bojar, Marta R Costa-jussà, Christian Federmann, Yvette Graham, Roman Grundkiewicz, Barry Haddow, Matthias Huck, Eric Joanis, et al. 2020. Findings of the 2020 conference on machine translation (wmt20). In *Proceedings of the Fifth Conference on Machine Translation*, pages 1–55.

Rachel Bawden, Sophie Rosset, Thomas Lavergne, and Eric Bilinski. 2019. Diabla: A corpus of bilingual spontaneous written dialogues for machine translation. *arXiv preprint arXiv:1905.13354*.

Yonatan Belinkov and Yonatan Bisk. 2018. Synthetic and natural noise both break neural machine translation. In *International Conference on Learning Representations*.

Yong Cheng, Zhaopeng Tu, Fandong Meng, Junjie Zhai, and Yang Liu. 2018. Towards robust neural machine translation. In *Proceedings of the 56th Annual Meeting of the Association for Computational Linguistics, ACL 2018, Melbourne, Australia, July 15-20, 2018, Volume 1: Long Papers*, pages 1756–1766. Association for Computational Linguistics.

Jacob Devlin, Ming-Wei Chang, Kenton Lee, and Kristina Toutanova. 2019. Bert: Pre-training of deep bidirectional transformers for language understanding. In *NAACL-HLT (1)*.

M Amin Farajian, António V Lopes, André FT Martins, Sameen Maruf, and Gholamreza Haffari. 2020. Findings of the wmt 2020 shared task on chat translation. In *Proceedings of the Fifth Conference on Machine Translation*, pages 65–75.

Geoffrey E. Hinton, Nitish Srivastava, Alex Krizhevsky, Ilya Sutskever, and Ruslan R. Salakhutdinov. 2012. Improving neural networks by preventing co-adaptation of feature detectors. *CoRR*, abs/1207.0580.

CT James Huang. 1989. Pro-drop in chinese: A generalized control theory. In *The null subject parameter*, pages 185–214. Springer.

Diederik P. Kingma and Jimmy Ba. 2015. Adam: A method for stochastic optimization. In *Proceedings of ICLR*.

Junyi Jessy Li, Marine Carpuat, and Ani Nenkova. 2014. Assessing the discourse factors that influence the quality of machine translation. In *Proceedings of the 52nd Annual Meeting of the Association for Computational Linguistics (Volume 2: Short Papers)*, pages 283–288.

Yitong Li, Trevor Cohn, and Timothy Baldwin. 2017. Robust training under linguistic adversity. In *Proceedings of the 15th Conference of the European Chapter of the Association for Computational Linguistics: Volume 2, Short Papers*, pages 21–27.

Zehui Lin, Xiao Pan, Mingxuan Wang, Xipeng Qiu, Jiangtao Feng, Hao Zhou, and Lei Li. 2020. Pre-training multilingual neural machine translation by leveraging alignment information. *arXiv preprint arXiv:2010.03142*.

Pierre Lison, Jörg Tiedemann, Milen Kouylekov, et al. 2019. Open subtitles 2018: Statistical rescoring of sentence alignments in large, noisy parallel corpora. In *LREC 2018, Eleventh International Conference on Language Resources and Evaluation*. European Language Resources Association (ELRA).

Yinhan Liu, Jiatao Gu, Naman Goyal, Xian Li, Sergey Edunov, Marjan Ghazvininejad, Mike Lewis, and Luke Zettlemoyer. 2020. Multilingual denoising pre-training for neural machine translation. *Transactions of the Association for Computational Linguistics*, 8:726–742.

Sameen Maruf, André FT Martins, and Gholamreza Haffari. 2018. Contextual neural model for translating bilingual multi-speaker conversations. *WMT 2018*, page 101.

Kishore Papineni, Salim Roukos, Todd Ward, and Wei-Jing Zhu. 2001. Bleu: a method for automatic evaluation of machine translation. In *ACL*.

Matt Post. 2018. A call for clarity in reporting BLEU scores. In *Proceedings of the Third Conference on Machine Translation: Research Papers*, pages 186–191, Belgium, Brussels. Association for Computational Linguistics.

Rico Sennrich, Barry Haddow, and Alexandra Birch. 2016. Neural machine translation of rare words with subword units. In *Proceedings of the 54th Annual Meeting of the Association for Computational Linguistics (Volume 1: Long Papers)*, volume 1, pages 1715–1725.

Matthias Sperber, Jan Niehues, and Alex Waibel. 2017. Toward robust neural machine translation for noisy input sequences. In *International Workshop on Spoken Language Translation (IWSLT)*.

Christian Szegedy, Vincent Vanhoucke, Sergey Ioffe, Jon Shlens, and Zbigniew Wojna. 2016. Rethinking the inception architecture for computer vision. In *Proceedings of the IEEE conference on computer vision and pattern recognition*, pages 2818–2826.

Vaibhav Vaibhav, Sumeet Singh, Craig Stewart, and Graham Neubig. 2019. Improving robustness of machine translation with synthetic noise. In *Proceedings of the 2019 Conference of the North American Chapter of the Association for Computational Linguistics: Human Language Technologies, Volume 1 (Long and Short Papers)*, pages 1916–1920.

Elena Voita, Rico Sennrich, and Ivan Titov. 2019. When a good translation is wrong in context: Context-aware machine translation improves on deixis, ellipsis, and lexical cohesion. In *Proceedings of the 57th Annual Meeting of the Association for Computational Linguistics*, pages 1198–1212.

Longyue Wang, Zhaopeng Tu, Shuming Shi, Tong Zhang, Yvette Graham, and Qun Liu. 2018. Translating pro-drop languages with reconstruction models. In *Thirty-Second AAAI Conference on Artificial Intelligence*.

Longyue Wang, Xiaojun Zhang, Zhaopeng Tu, Andy Way, and Qun Liu. 2016. Automatic construction of discourse corpora for dialogue translation.

Yonghui Wu, Mike Schuster, Zhifeng Chen, Quoc V Le, Mohammad Norouzi, Wolfgang Macherey, Maxim Krikun, Yuan Cao, Qin Gao, Klaus Macherey, et al. 2016. Google's neural machine translation system: Bridging the gap between human and machine translation. *arXiv preprint arXiv:1609.08144*.

Jiacheng Yang, Mingxuan Wang, Hao Zhou, Chengqi Zhao, Weinan Zhang, Yong Yu, and Lei Li. 2020. Towards making the most of bert in neural machine translation. In *Proceedings of the AAAI Conference on Artificial Intelligence*, volume 34, pages 9378–9385.

LightSeq: A High Performance Inference Library for Transformers

Xiaohui Wang, Ying Xiong, Yang Wei, Mingxuan Wang, Lei Li
ByteDance AI Lab
{wangxiaohui.neo, xiongying.taka, weiyang.god}@bytedance.com
{wangmingxuan.89, lileilab}@bytedance.com

Abstract

Transformer, BERT and their variants have achieved great success in natural language processing. Since Transformer models are huge in size, serving these models is a challenge for real industrial applications. In this paper, we propose LightSeq, a highly efficient inference library for models in the Transformer family. LightSeq includes a series of GPU optimization techniques to to streamline the computation of neural layers and to reduce memory footprint. LightSeq can easily import models trained using PyTorch and Tensorflow. Experimental results on machine translation benchmarks show that LightSeq achieves up to 14x speedup compared with TensorFlow and 1.4x compared with FasterTransformer, a concurrent CUDA implementation. The code is available at `https://github.com/bytedance/lightseq`.

1 Introduction

Sequence processing and generation have been fundamental capabilities for many natural language processing tasks, including machine translation, summarization, language modeling, etc (Luong et al., 2015; Qi et al., 2020; Dai et al., 2019). In recent years, with the introduction of Transformer model (Vaswani et al., 2017b), many pre-trained language models such as BERT, GPT, and mRASP have also been widely used in these tasks (Devlin et al., 2019; Radford et al., 2019; Yang et al., 2020; Lin et al., 2020).

However, the parameters of these models become increasingly large, which causes the high latency of inference and brings great challenges to the deployment (Kim and Hassan, 2020). The current popular inference systems are not necessarily the best choice for the online service of sequence processing problems. First, training frameworks, such as TensorFlow and PyTorch, require accommodating flexible model architectures and backward propagation, which introduce additional memory allocation and extra overhead of using fine-grain kernel functions. Therefore, the direct deployment of the training framework is not able to make full use of the hardware resource. Taking an example of machine translation, the Transformer big model currently takes roughly 2 seconds to translate a sentence, which is unacceptable in both academia and industry (Edunov et al., 2018; Hsu et al., 2020). Second, current optimizing compilers for deep learning such as TensorFlow XLA (Abadi et al., 2017), TVM (Chen et al., 2018) and Tensor RT (Vanholder, 2016) are mainly designed for fixed-size inputs. However, most NLP problems enjoy variable-length inputs, which are much more complex and require dynamic memory allocation. Therefore, a high-performance sequence inference library for variable-length inputs is required. There are several concurrent CUDA libraries which share a similar idea with our project, such as FasterTransformer [1] and TurboTransformers (Fang et al., 2021).

We will highlight three innovative features that make LightSeq outperforms similar projects. First, we replace a straightforward combination of fine-grained GPU kernel functions in TensorFlow or PyTorch implementations with coarse-grain fused ones, which avoid high time cost introduced by a mass of kernel function launches and GPU memory I/O for intermediate results. As a result, LightSeq reduces the atomic kernel functions by four times compared with Tensorflow approaches. Second, we specially design a hierarchical auto regressive search method to speed up the auto-regressive search. Third, we propose a dynamic GPU memory reuse strategy. Different from fixed-length inputs, sequence processing tackles the variable-length inputs, which bring difficulty for memory allocation. LightSeq proposes to pre-define the maximal memory for each kernel function and shares the GPU

[1] `https://github.com/NVIDIA/FasterTransformer`

Proceedings of NAACL HLT 2021: IndustryTrack Papers, pages 113–120
June 6–11, 2021.

Inference Libraries	Models					Decoding Methods		
	Transformer	GPT	VAE	BERT	Multilingual	Beam Search	Diverse Beam Search	Sampling
FasterTransformer	✓	✓	✗	✓	✗	✓	✓	✓
TurboTransformers	✓	✗	✗	✓	✗	✗	✗	✗
LightSeq	✓	✓	✓	✓	✓	✓	✓	✓

Table 1: Features for FasterTransformer, TurboTransformers and our proposed LightSeq. LightSeq supports the most features for a comprehensive set of Transformer models.

memory across non-dependent ones. As a result, LightSeq reduces eight times memory allocation without loss of inference speed. As a benefit, LightSeq enjoys several advantages:

Efficient LightSeq shows better inference performance for generation tasks. For example, in machine translation benchmarks, LightSeq achieves up to 14 times speedup compared with TensorFlow and 1.4 times speedup compared with FasterTransformer.

Functional LightSeq supports more architecture variants, such as BERT, GPT, Transformer, and Variational Autoencoders (VAEs). Further, LightSeq provides different search algorithms, such as beam search, diverse beam search and probabilistic sampling (Vijayakumar et al., 2018). Table 1 shows the functional comparison between FasterTransformer[2], TurboTransformers[3], and LightSeq in text generation tasks.

Convenient LightSeq is easy to use, which contains a serving system and efficient CUDA implementations. The popular models, such as BERT, Roberta, GPT, VAEs, MT Transformer, and Speech Transformer can be directly deployed online without code modification. For user-specific architectures, LightSeq supports multiple model reuse, which can be easily adapted with only a few lines of code modification.

2 LightSeq Approach

Transformer-based NLP models mainly consist of two components during inference: the feature calculation layer and the output layer, as shown in Figure 1.

The feature calculation layer is mainly based on self-attention mechanism and feature transformation, which is actually implemented by matrix multiplication and a series of I/O-intensive operations such as element-wise (e.g., reshape) and reduce (e.g., layer normalization).

The output layer slightly changes in different tasks, such as classification in NLU tasks or search (e.g., beam search) in NLG tasks. This layer is usually composed of the `Softmax` over vocabulary, probability sorting, cache refreshing, etc., which are essentially I/O-intensive.

These two components pose challenges for efficient inference:

- The fine-grained call of I/O-intensive GPU kernel function brings a huge amount of GPU memory I/O, which becomes the performance bottleneck of feature calculation.
- Redundant calculations exist due to the fact that we only need a few tokens/labels with the highest probability instead of all in classification or search for the output layer.
- Dynamic shape in variable sequence length and auto-regressive search makes it difficult to achieve memory reuse within or between requests, which leads to a large number of GPU memory allocation during model service.

LightSeq employs a series of innovative methods to address these challenges to accelerate model development, such as fusion of multiple kernel functions to reduce I/O overhead, hierarchical optimization of search algorithms to erase redundant calculations, and reuse of dynamic GPU memory to avoid run-time allocation. The following is a detailed introduction to these methods.

2.1 Operation Fusion

Transformer feature calculation layer needs to be highly optimized since it is ubiquitous in various

[2]As of this writing, we use FasterTransformer v2.1 for comparison.

[3]we use TurboTransformers for comparison at commit 0eae02ebadc8b816cd9bb71f8955a7e620861cd8

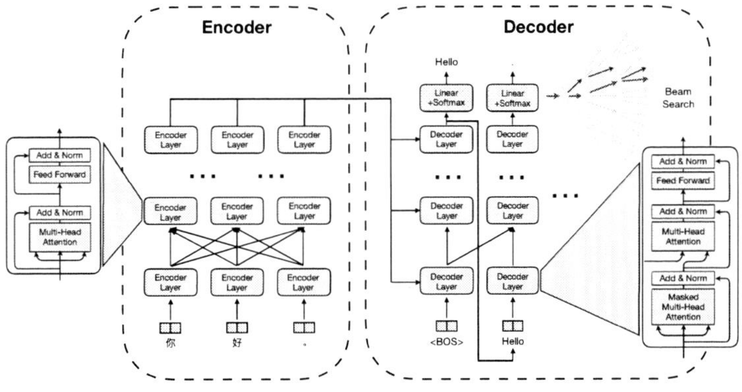

Figure 1: The process of sequence to sequence generation using Transformer model with beam search.

NLP tasks today. In most deep learning frameworks, such as TensorFlow and PyTorch, it is implemented by a straightforward combination of fine-grained kernel functions from standard libraries provided by hardware manufacturers, which introduces high time cost due to a mass of kernel function launches and GPU memory I/O for intermediate results.

Taking layer normalization implemented by TensorFlow as an example, there are still three kernel launches[4] and two intermediate results (mean and variance) even with the help of optimizing compilers like TensorFlow XLA (Abadi et al., 2017). As a comparison, we can write a custom kernel function dedicated to layer normalization based on the CUDA toolkit, which produces only one kernel launch without intermediate results.

LightSeq implements the Transformer feature calculation layer with general matrix multiply (GEMM) provided by cuBLAS[5] and custom kernel functions. The detailed structure is shown in Figure 2. Combination of fine-grained operations between GEMM operations is fused into one custom kernel function. In consequence, there are only six custom kernel functions and six GEMM in a Transformer encoder layer, which is usually more than four times less than its corresponding implementation in common deep learning frameworks like TensorFlow or PyTorch.

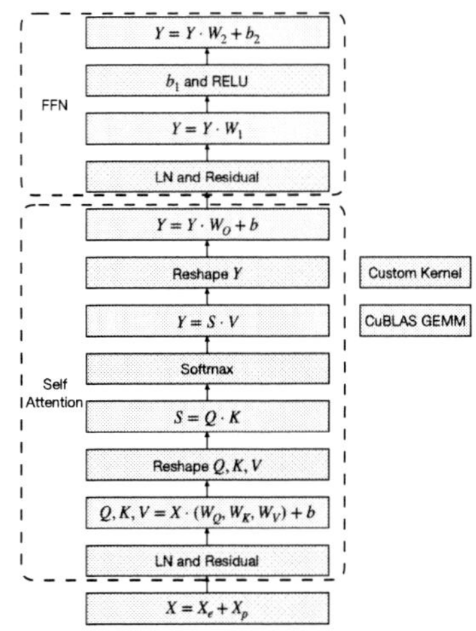

Figure 2: The structure of optimized Transformer encoder layers in LightSeq.

2.2 Hierarchical Auto Regressive Search

LightSeq supports a comprehensive set of output layers, such as sentence-level and token-level classification, perplexity calculation for language models, and auto-regressive search like beam search, diverse beam search and top-*k*/top-*p* sampling (Holtzman et al., 2020). Redundant calculations often exist in these output layers since we only need a few labels/tokens with the highest probability instead of all of them. Auto-regressive search is relatively complicated, and we will discuss it in the next paragraph. For the other types of output layers, we can simply replace `Softmax` with the probability calculation of token/label with the highest `logits`, which brings more obvious benefit when the size of vocabulary or labels is large.

Auto-regressive search is widely used in machine translation and text generation. LightSeq proposes Hierarchical Auto Regressive Search (HARS) method to erase redundant calculations and parallel computing. Here we take the most used beam search method as an example to intro-

[4]Two for `reduce_mean` operations and one for calculation of the final result.

[5]`https://developer.nvidia.com/cublas`

duce the proposed HARS method.

In one step of the beam search process, given the `logits`, we need to perform two calculations over the whole vocabulary:

1. Compute the conditional probability using `Softmax` and write the intermediate result into GPU memory.

2. Read the intermediate result from GPU memory and select the top-k beams and tokens by sequential probability.

These two calculations are highly time-consuming since the vocabulary size is usually in tens of thousands of scales. For example, they account for a latency proportion of 30% in Transformer base models.

In order to reduce the input size of these two calculations, LightSeq introduces a two-stage strategy that is widely employed in the recommended system: retrieve and re-rank.

Before the probability computation and top-k selection, the retrieve is carried out first. For each beam, we calculate as follows:

1. Randomly divide `logits` into k groups.

2. Calculate the maximum of group i, denoted as m_i

3. Calculate the minimum of m_i, denoted as $\mathcal{R}$, which can be regarded as a rough top-k value of `logits`.

4. Select `logits` larger than $\mathcal{R}$ and write them into GPU memory.

The retrieve is co-designed based on GPU characteristics and `logits` distribution. Hence it is efficient and effective:

- Efficient. The retrieve is implemented by one kernel function and can be executed within a dozen instruction cycles.

- Effective. After the retrieve, only dozens of candidates were selected.

After the retrieve, the original two calculations of beam search will be carried out on the small set of candidates, named as Hierarchical Auto Regressive Search.

Figure 3 is a detailed illustration of the proposed hierarchical strategy. In the original beam search method, we need to compute the probability and select the top-k over the whole vocabulary. However, by hierarchical method, we only need to pick a small set of candidates from each beam and then perform probability computation and top-k selection.

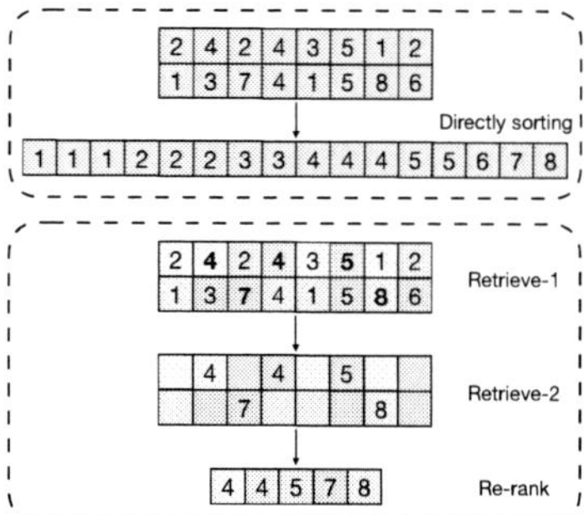

Figure 3: An illustration of the proposed hierarchical strategy. In this case, beam size is 2 and vocabulary size is 8. Each row represents `logits` in a beam.

2.3 Dynamic GPU Memory Reuse

In order to save GPU memory occupancy and avoid allocation of GPU memory during the model serving, LightSeq pre-defines the maximum of dynamic shapes, such as the maximal sequence length. At the start of the service, each intermediate result in the calculation process is allocated GPU memory to its maximum. Besides, GPU memory is shared for non-dependent intermediate results.

Through this memory reuse strategy, on a T4 graphics card, we can deploy up to 8 Transformer big models[6] at the same time, so as to improve graphics card utilization in low frequency or peak-shifting scenarios.

3 Experiments

In this section, we will show the improvements of LightSeq with different GPU hardware and precisions. We first analyze the GPU occupation of LightSeq during inference to investigate if LightSeq can make full use of GPU resources. Then, we make a fair comparison with TensorFlow, PyTorch, FasterTransformer, and TurboTransformers on machine translation and text generation to show the efficiency of LightSeq.

[6]Under the configuration of 8 batch size, 256 sequence length, 4 beam size and 30000 vocabulary size.

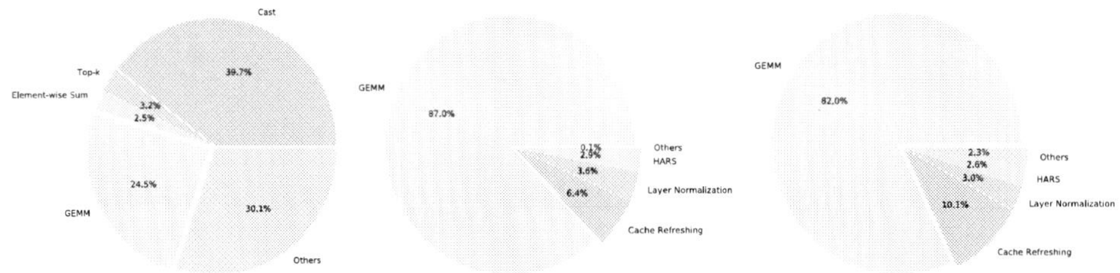

(a) TensorFlow with Float16. (b) LightSeq with Float16. (c) LightSeq with Float32.

Figure 4: Proportion of computation occupation. GEMM is the main indicator and the larger number indicates the higher computation efficiency.

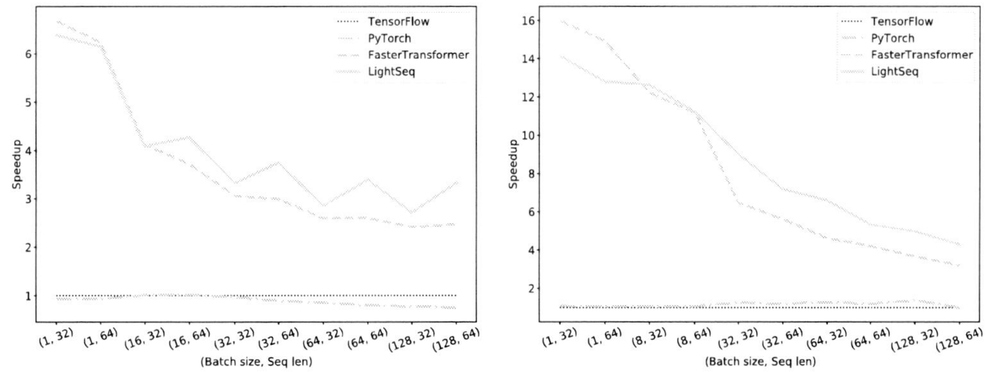

(a) P4 speedup in Float32. (b) T4 speedup in Float16.

Figure 5: Speedup on Transformer with beam search compared with FasterTransformer, TurboTransformers and PyTorch implementation. The baseline is TensorFlow implementation.

3.1 Experiment Settings

We test the generation performance of LightSeq on two latest NVIDIA inference GPU Tesla P4 and T4, choosing TensorFlow, PyTorch, and FasterTransformer implementations as a comparison. Another related library, TurboTransformers, mainly focuses on the Transformer encoder and is not powerful enough for text generation. Its speedup for sequence generation compared to TensorFlow is only about 15%, and it only supports Float32 on GPU. Therefore we do not compare with it.

The experiments on machine translation are conducted on the popular WMT14 English to German translation tasks. The hyper-parameters setting resembles transformer base model (Vaswani et al., 2017a). Specifically, we reduce the vocabulary size of both the source language and target language to 50K symbols using the sub-word technique (Bojanowski et al., 2017).

The experiments on text generation are conducted on a randomly initialized Transformer model and test dataset. Results of Tensorflow and FasterTransformer are obtained from the scripts in the source code of FasterTransformer. The sequence length is used for limiting the total size in the generation test, and the values for top-k and top-p are the most selected settings in our deployments.

3.2 GPU Occupation of LightSeq

We first analyze the GPU occupation to verify the efficiency of LightSeq. The experiments are conducted on Tesla T4 card with the GPU profiling toolkit. The latency of each module is shown in Figure 4 with both Float16 and Float32 precision. We classify the operation into three categories: GEMM, cache refreshing, and others. GEMM latency is the most important indicator, which shows the proportion of matrix calculations occupying the GPU calculation.

After optimization, we can find that:

- GEMM operation in LightSeq accounts for

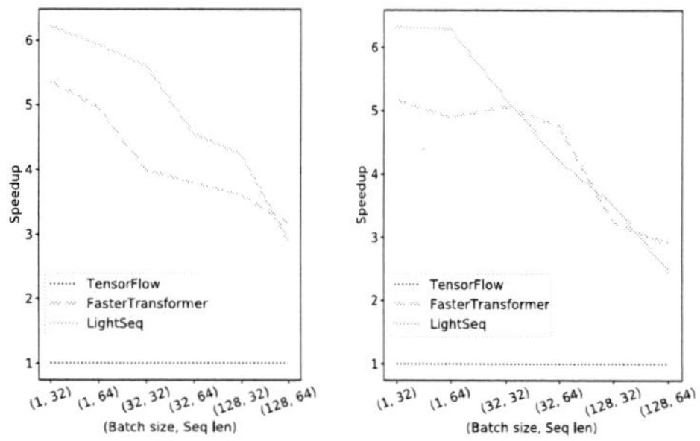

(a) Top-$p = 0.75$. (b) Top-$k = 32$.

Figure 6: T4 speedup on Transformer with sampling compared with FasterTransformer in Float16. LightSeq outperforms FasterTransformer in most cases.

87% and 82% respectively for Float16 and Float32, accounting for most of the inference time. However, in the original TensorFlow model, GEMM operations account for only 25%. This shows that beam search optimization has achieved good results.

- Cast and other operations in TensorFlow are expensive, which launches over 80 different GPU kernels. In LightSeq, we fuse cast operations into weight loading, and other operations into more efficient implementations.
- The latency of cache refreshing in LightSeq accounts for 6% and 10% respectively, which are not negligible but hard to be optimized further. Possible solutions include reducing the amount of cache, such as reducing the number of decoder layers, reducing cache precision, etc.

The results demonstrate that LightSeq has been optimized to a disabling extent and greatly increases the speed of inference. Another interesting finding is that Float16 is more efficient than Float32. A possible explanation is that Float16 occupies less memory. Therefore the cache refreshing and memory I/O operations potentially take less time.

3.3 Comparison on Machine Translation

The comparison between LightSeq, TensorFlow, PyTorch and FasterTransformer are shown in Figure 5. We group the test set into different buckets according to the sequence length and batch size. For example, the x-axis (a, b) indicates that the batch size is a and the sequence length is b. The y-axis is the speedup compared with TensorFlow baseline. The results provide several interesting findings:

- For both LightSeq and FasterTransformer, the speedup gap for smaller batch size or shorter sequence length is much larger.
- The speedup for T4 is larger than P4. The main reason is that T4 is more powerful than P4 and has much room for improvement.
- In most cases, LightSeq performs better than FasterTransformer. For larger batch size and longer sequences, the gap increases. While for smaller batch size, FasterTransformer performs better.
- PyTorch is slightly slower than TensorFlow in P4 and faster in T4, which indicates that LightSeq also greatly outperforms PyTorch in all cases.

The findings provide some guidance for optimization work in the future. There is almost no space to accelerate the inference by fusion of non-computationally intensive operators, especially for small batch size. Future work is recommended to focus on optimizing GEMM operations which account for 80% to 90% of the total computation time.

Finally, we compare TurboTransformers with PyTorch by the translation demo[7]. As of this writing, only decoder layers of MT Transformer in float32 precision is supported, so we only compare the latencies of decoder layers without beam search and cache refreshing. In the final results, TurboTransformers only achieves about 2x speedup for different batch sizes and sequence lengths. So TurboTransformers has no comparability with LightSeq in machine translation tasks (As TurboTransformer repo says, "TurboTransformer will bring 15.9% performance improvements on RTX 2060 GPU. We are still working on decoder model optimization.").

3.4 Comparison on Text Generation

In the text generation scenario, the sampling strategy is applied to improve the diversity of generation. Among which, top-k and top-p sampling strategies are more popular.

[7] `https://github.com/TurboNLP/Translate-Demo/tree/443e6a46fefbdf64282842b6233a8bd0a22d6aeb`

Figure 6 shows the performance comparison of Transformer base with top-k/top-p sampling. The values of top-k and top-p are added in the x-axis. The results provide following findings:

- In most cases, LightSeq achieves greater speedup than FasterTransformer. Unlike results in machine translation, LightSeq performs better for smaller batch size and shorter sequence, while FasterTransformer performs better for larger batch size and longer sequence.

- The speedup in generation tasks are not as large as machine translation. It is mainly because of the lower complexity of sampling methods than beam search, reducing the benefits obtained from operation fusion and HARS.

4 Conclusion

In this paper, we address the deployment problem of expensive sequence models and present an efficient inference library LightSeq for sequence processing and generation, reducing the gap between the performance of big models and the requirement of online services. Comparisons with FasterTransformer show that we perform better in both machine translation and text generation. In future work, we will focus on exploring more techniques to achieve a more significant speedup, including efficient integer-arithmetic-only inference and sparse GEMM computations.

Acknowledgments

We would like to thank the colleagues in machine translation service and advertisement service to support our experiments in online environments and apply LightSeq into real-time systems.

References

Martín Abadi, Michael Isard, and Derek Gordon Murray. 2017. A computational model for tensorflow: an introduction. In *Proceedings of the 1st ACM SIGPLAN International Workshop on Machine Learning and Programming Languages, MAPL@PLDI 2017, Barcelona, Spain, June 18, 2017*, pages 1–7. ACM.

Piotr Bojanowski, Edouard Grave, Armand Joulin, and Tomas Mikolov. 2017. Enriching word vectors with subword information. *Transactions of the Association for Computational Linguistics*, 5:135–146.

Tianqi Chen, Thierry Moreau, Ziheng Jiang, Lianmin Zheng, Eddie Yan, Haichen Shen, Meghan Cowan, Leyuan Wang, Yuwei Hu, Luis Ceze, Carlos Guestrin, and Arvind Krishnamurthy. 2018. TVM: An automated end-to-end optimizing compiler for deep learning. In *13th USENIX Symposium on Operating Systems Design and Implementation (OSDI 18)*, pages 578–594, Carlsbad, CA. USENIX Association.

Zihang Dai, Zhilin Yang, Yiming Yang, Jaime G. Carbonell, Quoc Viet Le, and Ruslan Salakhutdinov. 2019. Transformer-xl: Attentive language models beyond a fixed-length context. In *Proceedings of the 57th Conference of the Association for Computational Linguistics, ACL 2019, Florence, Italy, July 28- August 2, 2019, Volume 1: Long Papers*, pages 2978–2988. Association for Computational Linguistics.

Jacob Devlin, Ming-Wei Chang, Kenton Lee, and Kristina Toutanova. 2019. BERT: pre-training of deep bidirectional transformers for language understanding. In *Proceedings of the 2019 Conference of the North American Chapter of the Association for Computational Linguistics: Human Language Technologies, NAACL-HLT 2019, Minneapolis, MN, USA, June 2-7, 2019, Volume 1 (Long and Short Papers)*, pages 4171–4186. Association for Computational Linguistics.

Sergey Edunov, Myle Ott, Michael Auli, and David Grangier. 2018. Understanding back-translation at scale. In *Proceedings of the 2018 Conference on Empirical Methods in Natural Language Processing, Brussels, Belgium, October 31 - November 4, 2018*, pages 489–500. Association for Computational Linguistics.

Jiarui Fang, Yang Yu, Chengduo Zhao, and Jie Zhou. 2021. Turbotransformers: an efficient GPU serving system for transformer models. In *PPoPP '21: 26th ACM SIGPLAN Symposium on Principles and Practice of Parallel Programming, Virtual Event, Republic of Korea, February 27- March 3, 2021*, pages 389–402. ACM.

Ari Holtzman, Jan Buys, Li Du, Maxwell Forbes, and Yejin Choi. 2020. The curious case of neural text degeneration. In *8th International Conference on Learning Representations, ICLR 2020, Addis Ababa, Ethiopia, April 26-30, 2020*. OpenReview.net.

Yi-Te Hsu, Sarthak Garg, Yi-Hsiu Liao, and Ilya Chatsviorkin. 2020. Efficient inference for neural machine translation. In *Proceedings of SustaiNLP: Workshop on Simple and Efficient Natural Language Processing*, pages 48–53, Online. Association for Computational Linguistics.

Young Jin Kim and Hany Hassan. 2020. FastFormers: Highly efficient transformer models for natural language understanding. In *Proceedings of SustaiNLP: Workshop on Simple and Efficient Natural Language Processing*, pages 149–158, Online. Association for Computational Linguistics.

Zehui Lin, Xiao Pan, Mingxuan Wang, Xipeng Qiu, Jiangtao Feng, Hao Zhou, and Lei Li. 2020. Pre-training multilingual neural machine translation by leveraging alignment information. In *Proceedings of the 2020 Conference on Empirical Methods in Natural Language Processing, EMNLP 2020, Online, November 16-20, 2020*, pages 2649–2663. Association for Computational Linguistics.

Thang Luong, Hieu Pham, and Christopher D. Manning. 2015. Effective approaches to attention-based neural machine translation. In *Proceedings of the 2015 Conference on Empirical Methods in Natural Language Processing, EMNLP 2015, Lisbon, Portugal, September 17-21, 2015*, pages 1412–1421. The Association for Computational Linguistics.

Weizhen Qi, Yu Yan, Yeyun Gong, Dayiheng Liu, Nan Duan, Jiusheng Chen, Ruofei Zhang, and Ming Zhou. 2020. Prophetnet: Predicting future n-gram for sequence-to-sequence pre-training. In *Proceedings of the 2020 Conference on Empirical Methods in Natural Language Processing: Findings, EMNLP 2020, Online Event, 16-20 November 2020*, pages 2401–2410. Association for Computational Linguistics.

Alec Radford, Jeffrey Wu, Rewon Child, David Luan, Dario Amodei, and Ilya Sutskever. 2019. Language models are unsupervised multitask learners. *OpenAI Blog*, 1(8):9.

Han Vanholder. 2016. Efficient inference with tensorrt.

Ashish Vaswani, Noam Shazeer, Niki Parmar, Jakob Uszkoreit, Llion Jones, Aidan N Gomez, Ł ukasz Kaiser, and Illia Polosukhin. 2017a. Attention is all you need. In I. Guyon, U. V. Luxburg, S. Bengio, H. Wallach, R. Fergus, S. Vishwanathan, and R. Garnett, editors, *Advances in Neural Information Processing Systems 30*, pages 5998–6008. Curran Associates, Inc.

Ashish Vaswani, Noam Shazeer, Niki Parmar, Jakob Uszkoreit, Llion Jones, Aidan N. Gomez, Lukasz Kaiser, and Illia Polosukhin. 2017b. Attention is all you need. In *Advances in Neural Information Processing Systems 30: Annual Conference on Neural Information Processing Systems 2017, 4-9 December 2017, Long Beach, CA, USA*, pages 6000–6010.

Ashwin K. Vijayakumar, Michael Cogswell, Ramprasaath R. Selvaraju, Qing Sun, Stefan Lee, David J. Crandall, and Dhruv Batra. 2018. Diverse beam search for improved description of complex scenes. In *Proceedings of the Thirty-Second AAAI Conference on Artificial Intelligence, (AAAI-18), the 30th innovative Applications of Artificial Intelligence (IAAI-18), and the 8th AAAI Symposium on Educational Advances in Artificial Intelligence (EAAI-18), New Orleans, Louisiana, USA, February 2-7, 2018*, pages 7371–7379. AAAI Press.

Jiacheng Yang, Mingxuan Wang, Hao Zhou, Chengqi Zhao, Weinan Zhang, Yong Yu, and Lei Li. 2020. Towards making the most of BERT in neural machine translation. In *The Thirty-Fourth AAAI Conference on Artificial Intelligence, AAAI 2020, The Thirty-Second Innovative Applications of Artificial Intelligence Conference, IAAI 2020, The Tenth AAAI Symposium on Educational Advances in Artificial Intelligence, EAAI 2020, New York, NY, USA, February 7-12, 2020*, pages 9378–9385. AAAI Press.

Practical Transformer-based Multilingual Text Classification

Cindy Wang
Sentropy Technologies
cindy@sentropy.io

Michele Banko
Sentropy Technologies
mbanko@sentropy.io

Abstract

Transformer-based methods are appealing for multilingual text classification, but common research benchmarks like XNLI (Conneau et al., 2018) do not reflect the data availability and task variety of industry applications. We present an empirical comparison of transformer-based text classification models in a variety of practical monolingual and multilingual pretraining and fine-tuning settings. We evaluate these methods on two distinct tasks in five different languages. Departing from prior work, our results show that multilingual language models can outperform monolingual ones in some downstream tasks and target languages. We additionally show that practical modifications such as task- and domain-adaptive pretraining and data augmentation can improve classification performance without the need for additional labeled data.

1 Introduction

While the development of natural language understanding (NLU) applications often begins with high-resource languages such as English, there is a need to create products that are accessible to speakers of the world's nearly 7,000 languages. Only 5% of the world's population is estimated to speak English as a first language.[1]

The growth of NLU-centric products within diverse language markets is evidenced by the increase in language support for popular consumer applications such as virtual assistants, Web search, and social media platforms. As of mid-2020, Google Assistant supported 44 languages on smartphones, followed by Siri (21 languages) and Amazon Alexa (8 languages). At the start of 2021, Google Search and Microsoft Bing supported 149 and 40 languages respectively. Also at this time, Twitter officially supported a total of 45 languages with Facebook reaching over 100 languages.

Advances in multilingual language models such as multilingual BERT (mBERT; Devlin et al., 2019) and XLM-RoBERTa (XLM-R; Conneau et al., 2020) which are trained on massive corpora in over 100 languages, show promise for fast iteration and deployment of NLU applications. In theory, cross-lingual approaches reduce the need for labeled training data in target languages by enabling zero- or few-shot learning. Additionally, they enable simplified model deployment compared to the use of many monolingual models. On the other hand, evaluations show that scaling to more languages causes dilution (Conneau et al., 2020) and consequently cite the relative under-performance of multilingual models on monolingual tasks (Virtanen et al., 2019; Antoun et al., 2020).

Recent studies (Hu et al., 2020; Rust et al., 2020) have explored tradeoffs of multi versus monolingual model paradigms. However, we observe that existing multilingual text classification benchmarks are designed to measure zero-shot cross-lingual transfer rather than supervised learning (Conneau et al., 2018; Yang et al., 2019), though the latter is more applicable to industry settings. Thus, the goal of this paper is to evaluate multilingual text classification approaches with a focus on real applications. Our contributions include:

- A comparison of state-of-the-art language models spanning monolingual and multilingual setups, evaluated across five languages and two distinct tasks;
- A set of practical recommendations for fine-tuning readily available language models for text classification; and
- Analyses of industry-centric challenges such as domain mismatch, labeled data availability, and runtime inference scalability.

2 Multilingual Text Classification

We consider a series of practical components for building multilingual text classification systems.

[1] CIA World Factbook

Proceedings of NAACL HLT 2021: IndustryTrack Papers, pages 121–129
June 6–11, 2021.

Lang.	Model	Pretraining Corpus	Tokenizer	Param.
EN	RoBERTa (Liu et al., 2019)	Various (160GB)	BPE	125M
DE	German BERT (deepset.ai, 2019)	German Wikipedia, OpenLegalData, and news articles (12 GB)	SentencePiece	110M
ES	BETO (Cañete et al., 2020)	Various (18.4GB)	WordPiece	110M
FR	CamemBERT (Martin et al., 2020)	OSCAR (138GB)	SentencePiece	110M
JA	Japanese BERT (Suzuki and Takahashi, 2019)	Japanese Wikipedia (2.6GB)	MeCab+Wordpiece	110M
MULTI	XLM-RoBERTa (Conneau et al., 2019)	CC-100 (2.5 TB) EN (301GB), DE (67GB), ES (53GB), FR (57GB), JA (69GB)	SentencePiece	270M

Table 1: Pretraining corpora, tokenizers, and size (# parameters) of the language models used in our experiments.

2.1 Pretrained Transformer Language Models

Transfer learning using pretrained language models (LMs) which are then fine-tuned for downstream tasks has emerged as a powerful technique for NLU applications. In particular, models using the now-ubiquitous transformer architecture (Vaswani et al., 2017), such as BERT (Devlin et al., 2019) and its variants, have obtained state of the art results in many monolingual and cross-lingual NLU benchmarks (Wang et al., 2019a; Raffel et al., 2020; He et al., 2021).

One drawback of data-hungry transformer models is that they are time- and resource-intensive to train. In our experiments, we consider LMs pretrained on both monolingual and multilingual corpora, and analyze the effects of combining these models with other NLU system components.

For monolingual LMs, we use BERT models pretrained on corpora in each target language. The one exception is English, where we use RoBERTa, a BERT reimplementation that exceeds its performance on an assortment of tasks (Liu et al., 2019).

For multilingual LMs, we use XLM-R, which significantly outperforms mBERT on cross-lingual benchmarks and is competitive with monolingual models on monolingual benchmarks such as GLUE (Wang et al., 2019b). All of the pretrained models used are accessible from the Hugging Face (Wolf et al., 2020) model hub, and their details are summarized in Table 1.

2.2 Domain-Adaptive and Task-Adaptive Pretraining

Though pretrained language models have hundreds of millions of parameters and are trained on diverse corpora, they are not guaranteed to generalize to all tasks and domains. For downstream tasks, a second phase of pretraining on a smaller domain- or task-specific corpus has been shown to provide performance improvements. Gururangan et al. (2020) compare domain-adaptive pretraining (DAPT), which uses a large corpus of unlabeled domain-specific text, and task-adaptive pretraining (TAPT), which uses only the training data of a particular task. The primary difference is that the task-specific corpus tends to be much smaller, but also more task-relevant. Therefore, while DAPT is helpful in both low- and high-resource settings, TAPT is much more resource-efficient and outperforms DAPT when sufficient data is available.

In our experiments, we evaluate both approaches, using the classification task training data as the TAPT corpus and in-domain unlabeled data as the DAPT corpus (see Section 3 for details). BERT and RoBERTa are pretrained with a *masked language modeling* (MLM) objective, a cross-entropy loss on randomly masked tokens in the input sequence. We similarly use the MLM objective when performing DAPT and TAPT.

2.3 Supervised Fine-Tuning

We consider three settings for supervised fine-tuning of language models for downstream classification tasks (N is the number of target languages).

- *mono-target* (N final models): Fine-tune a monolingual LM on the training data in each target language
- *multi-target* (N final models): Fine-tune XLM-R on the training data in each target language
- *multi-all* (one final model): Fine-tune XLM-R on the concatenation of all training data

To represent sequences for classification, we use the final LM hidden vectors $B \in \mathbb{R}^{l \times H}$ corresponding to each of the l input tokens.[2] We then compute average and max pools over the sequence length

[2]Though only the hidden vector for the first (`[CLS]`) token is typically used (Devlin et al., 2019), we find that the pooled sequence summary attains better results on our tasks.

Dataset	Task	Lang.	Unlab.	Train	Test
CLS (AMAZON)	Sentiment	EN	105k	6k	6k
		DE	317k	6k	6k
		FR	58k	6k	6k
		JA	294k	6k	6k
HATEVAL (TWITTER)	Hate speech	EN	-	10k	3k
		ES	-	5k	1.6k

Table 2: The target tasks, languages, and number of training and test examples in each dataset.

Hashtag	Train	Test	Test[†]
#NoDACA	99.36	34.26	99.60
#EndDACA	98.31	33.87	98.39
#BuildThatWall	100.0	24.89	95.99
#BuildTheDamnWall	100.0	62.07	100.0
#NoAmnesty	100.0	48.25	100.0
#SendThemBack	82.02	68.29	87.80
#DeportThemAll	100.0	83.15	99.46

Table 3: Percentage of *hateful* class by anti-immigrant hashtags in HATEVAL (non-exhaustive list). [†]Denotes the relabeled test set.

layer and concatenate them to create the aggregate representation $C \in \mathbb{R}^{2H}$. Finally, the summary vector C is passed to a classification layer where we compute a standard cross-entropy loss.

2.4 Data Augmentation

In real applications, labeled data is often available in high resource languages such as English but sparse or nonexistent in others. We experiment with machine translation[3] as a form of cross-lingual data augmentation, which has been shown to improve performance on multilingual benchmarks (Singh et al., 2019). In single target language settings, we translate training data from other languages into the target language, yielding N times the number of training examples. In the *multi-all* setting, we translate data from every language into every other language, yielding $N(N-1)$ times the number of training examples. At training time, we directly include the translated examples in the training corpus. Following the pretraining convention of XLM-R, we do not use special markers to denote the input language.

3 Data

We choose sentiment analysis and hate speech detection as evaluation tasks due to their relevance to industry applications and the availability of multilingual datasets. An overview of the datasets is shown in Table 2.

3.1 Sentiment Analysis

The Cross-Lingual Sentiment dataset (CLS; Prettenhofer and Stein, 2010)[4] consists of AMAZON product reviews in four languages and three product categories (BOOKS, DVD, and MUSIC). Each review includes title and body text, which we concatenate to create the input example. The dataset contains training and test sets with balanced binary sentiment labels, as well as 50-320k unlabeled examples per language. We sample 10k unlabeled examples from each language for DAPT.

3.2 Hate Speech Detection

The HATEVAL dataset (Basile et al., 2019) contains tweets in English and Spanish annotated for the presence of hate speech targeting women and immigrants. Examples were collected by querying Twitter for users with histories of sending or receiving hateful messages, as well as keywords related to women and immigrants.

Relabeling English Test Data During experimentation, we found that English example labels were inconsistent across the training and test sets. For instance, many test examples containing anti-immigration hashtags were mislabeled as *non-hateful* while similar examples were labeled as *hateful* in the training set (see Table 3). We manually relabeled 641 examples in the test set and release the relabeled data for future research.[5,6]

Unlabeled Twitter Data Since no unlabeled corpus is provided, we collected a sample of 10k random tweets per language from November 2020, which we use for DAPT.

4 Experimental Setup

Preprocessing and Tokenization We apply minimal preprocessing to both datasets, replacing URLs and Twitter usernames with `<url>` and `<user>` tokens. At all stages of training, we use the default tokenizers associated with each pretrained

[3]`https://cloud.google.com/translate`

[4]We use the processed version of this dataset provided by Eisenschlos et al. (2019).

[5]Prior work (Stappen et al., 2020) has also noted this discrepancy and proposed repartitioning the train and test sets. We instead relabeled the test set due to the large number of mislabeled examples.

[6]`https://github.com/sentropytechnologies/hateval2019-relabeled`

Model	DE	FR	JA
mBERT	84.3	86.6	81.2
MultiFiT	92.2	91.4	86.2

Model	EN	ES
Majority label	36.7	37.0
SVM + tf-idf	45.1	70.1
1st place submissions	65.1	73.0

Table 4: Prior results (macro-F1) for CLS (Eisenschlos et al., 2019, top) and HATEVAL (Basile et al., 2019, bottom).

LM (see Table 1) and truncate sequences with more than 512 tokens.

Training We use 80% of each training set for training and the rest for validation. During DAPT and TAPT, we train using the MLM objective for 10 epochs. During supervised fine-tuning, we train for 5 epochs. We use the default hyperparameters for all pretrained LMs and apply dropout of 0.4 to the final classification layer.

Evaluation We report the test set macro-averaged F1 score for both datasets. (For CLS, this is equivalent to accuracy since the classes are balanced.) For reference, prior results on CLS and HATEVAL are shown in Table 4.

5 Results and Analysis

We report results for all experiments in Table 5. For both datasets, **(1)** TAPT and DAPT and **(2)** data augmentation with machine translations improve model performance. These strategies, which require no additional labeled data, improve macro-F1 score by between 0.6-1.5% for CLS and between 0.3-4.3% for HATEVAL. Even without DAPT, which is often the most expensive step, applying TAPT and/or data augmentation alone improves performance in all settings and languages except HATEVAL EN.

CLS For languages where extremely high-resource monolingual LMs are available (EN and FR), models perform best in the *mono-target* setting, in which a monolingual LM is fine-tuned on target language data. This is consistent with prior findings that XLM-R suffers from fixed model capacity and vocabulary dilution (Conneau et al., 2019). However, for DE and JA, which are not low-resource languages but whose monolingual LM pretraining corpora are relatively limited in size and domain (see Table 1), XLM-R models perform better.

HATEVAL On average, XLM-R models perform better on HATEVAL than those fine-tuned from monolingual LMs. Unlike for CLS, this is true even in EN, suggesting that for some classification tasks, the LM pretraining corpus is not as important for downstream task performance as XLM-R's larger model capacity and cross-lingual transfer. Though scores were much higher for the relabeled EN dataset than the original, the effects of LM fine-tuning, TAPT, DAPT, and data augmentation were consistent.

5.1 Not All Classification Tasks Are Created Equal

The two text classification tasks we evaluate are significantly different from both an annotation and a modeling perspective. Sentiment is a well-defined facet of language, and language model representations have even been shown to encode semantic information about it (Radford et al., 2017). Meanwhile, defining and identifying hate speech is much more nuanced, even for humans. Hate speech detection is confounded by many factors that require not only immediate context of the input but also cultural and social contexts (Schmidt and Wiegand, 2017). The difference in the types of information that models need to encode for each task may explain why monolingual LMs, which tend to encode better lexical information than multilingual LMs (Vulić et al., 2020), can outperform XLM-based models when fine-tuned for sentiment analysis but not for hate speech detection.

5.2 Cross-lingual Transfer

Prior work has established that multilingual LMs benefit from the addition of more languages during pretraining up to a point, after which limited model capacity and vocabulary dilution cause performance to degrade on downstream tasks – this is referred to as the *curse of multilinguality* (Conneau et al., 2019). Though this is reflected in the results of CLS EN and FR, other models fine-tuned from XLM-R exhibit gains from cross-lingual transfer. In particular, for CLS JA and HATEVAL EN, the best-performing models benefit not only from multilingual pretraining corpora but also from multilingual task training data.

These results suggest that when fine-tuning LMs for downstream tasks, XLM-R is a robust baseline.

Model	Adapt.	Aug.	CLS EN	CLS DE	CLS FR	CLS JA	CLS AVG	HATEVAL EN	HATEVAL EN†	HATEVAL ES	HATEVAL AVG	HATEVAL AVG†
mono-target												
RoBERTa (EN) / BERT (OTHERS)	×	×	$94.7_{0.4}$	$90.9_{0.6}$	$95.2_{0.0}$	$88.7_{0.3}$	92.4	$44.4_{5.3}$	$58.5_{6.2}$	$75.6_{0.6}$	60.0	67.1
	×	✓	$\mathbf{95.3}_{0.3}$	$92.0_{0.2}$	$95.6_{0.3}$	$89.3_{0.02}$	93.0	$46.1_{2.6}$	$60.6_{3.2}$	$76.0_{1.7}$	61.0	68.3
	TAPT	×	$94.9_{0.1}$	$91.6_{0.1}$	$95.4_{0.1}$	$89.3_{0.3}$	92.8	$45.4_{1.9}$	$59.9_{2.7}$	$76.1_{1.1}$	60.8	68.0
	TAPT	✓	$95.0_{0.4}$	$92.3_{0.4}$	$95.8_{0.2}$	$89.7_{0.4}$	93.2	$44.7_{1.5}$	$59.2_{1.7}$	$76.9_{1.4}$	60.8	68.0
	TAPT+DAPT	×	$94.9_{0.4}$	$91.8_{0.2}$	$95.5_{0.3}$	$89.5_{0.2}$	92.9	$48.0_{1.5}$	$63.1_{2.6}$	$76.3_{1.1}$	62.2	69.7
	TAPT+DAPT	✓	$\mathbf{95.3}_{0.1}$	$93.0_{0.8}$	$\mathbf{95.9}_{0.1}$	$89.9_{0.4}$	**93.5**	$46.0_{4.3}$	$60.2_{4.4}$	$76.9_{0.6}$	61.4	68.5
multi-target												
XLM-RoBERTa	×	×	$92.5_{0.4}$	$93.0_{0.2}$	$92.5_{0.3}$	$90.4_{0.5}$	92.1	$47.2_{2.0}$	$61.4_{1.9}$	$74.8_{0.5}$	61.0	68.1
	×	✓	$93.3_{0.1}$	$94.0_{0.2}$	$93.8_{0.2}$	$90.3_{0.3}$	92.8	$45.6_{1.6}$	$59.3_{2.5}$	$77.0_{1.1}$	61.3	68.1
	TAPT	×	$92.7_{0.5}$	$93.5_{0.5}$	$93.9_{0.3}$	$90.3_{0.1}$	92.6	$47.0_{2.7}$	$62.4_{3.3}$	$76.1_{1.4}$	61.6	69.2
	TAPT	✓	$93.4_{0.6}$	$94.0_{0.3}$	$93.8_{0.5}$	$90.5_{0.4}$	92.9	$47.9_{1.3}$	$63.5_{1.5}$	$77.9_{0.9}$	62.9	70.7
	TAPT+DAPT	×	$93.1_{0.6}$	$93.0_{0.5}$	$93.6_{0.1}$	$90.8_{0.3}$	92.6	$49.9_{2.5}$	$65.6_{2.4}$	$76.5_{1.0}$	63.2	71.0
	TAPT+DAPT	✓	$94.0_{0.3}$	$\mathbf{94.1}_{0.4}$	$93.8_{0.3}$	$91.1_{0.4}$	93.2	$46.6_{2.1}$	$61.7_{2.5}$	$\mathbf{78.1}_{0.8}$	62.3	69.9
multi-all												
XLM-RoBERTa	×	×	$92.4_{0.3}$	$92.6_{0.4}$	$93.3_{0.4}$	$90.4_{0.4}$	92.2	$48.4_{3.5}$	$63.1_{4.5}$	$77.5_{0.4}$	62.9	70.3
	×	✓	$93.4_{0.3}$	$93.3_{0.2}$	$94.0_{0.2}$	$90.4_{0.5}$	92.8	$49.8_{3.5}$	$66.0_{4.6}$	$77.8_{0.9}$	63.8	71.9
	TAPT	×	$92.5_{0.4}$	$93.0_{0.3}$	$93.9_{0.3}$	$90.9_{0.3}$	92.6	$48.4_{2.7}$	$64.2_{3.5}$	$77.4_{0.9}$	62.9	70.8
	TAPT	✓	$93.5_{0.4}$	$93.4_{0.5}$	$94.1_{0.2}$	$91.1_{0.2}$	93.0	$50.0_{2.2}$	$66.5_{2.6}$	$77.8_{0.6}$	63.9	72.2
	TAPT+DAPT	×	$92.7_{0.3}$	$93.3_{0.2}$	$94.0_{0.3}$	$91.2_{0.3}$	92.8	$47.1_{3.9}$	$62.7_{5.3}$	$77.4_{1.0}$	62.3	70.1
	TAPT+DAPT	✓	$93.5_{0.3}$	$93.8_{0.2}$	$94.3_{0.3}$	$\mathbf{91.4}_{0.2}$	93.3	$\mathbf{50.7}_{1.1}$	$\mathbf{67.4}_{1.4}$	$77.7_{0.7}$	**64.2**	**72.6**

Table 5: CLS and HATEVAL results (macro-F1) averaged over five random seeds. The best results for each target language test set are **bolded**, and standard deviations are shown in subscripts. **Model** denotes the supervised fine-tuning setting. **Adapt.** denotes the adaptive pretraining setting: × (no adaptive pretraining), TAPT (task-adaptation only), or TAPT+DAPT (task- and domain-adaptation). **Aug.** denotes whether the training data was augmented with machine-translated examples. For HATEVAL, we report results for both the original and relabeled† test sets.

Model	Data	DE	FR	JA	ES
multi-target	target	94.1	93.8	91.1	78.1
multi-all	all	93.8	94.3	91.4	77.7
zero-shot	EN	92.7	92.6	88.5	72.1

Table 6: Zero-shot learning versus best multilingual approaches. *Data* denotes language of training data. We fine-tune XLM-R and use DAPT, TAPT, and data augmentation for all models shown.

In cases where knowledge transfer from a monolingual LM might be difficult (e.g. due to a limited pretraining corpus or specialized downstream task), XLM-R may even outperform its monolingual competitors.

5.3 Are Target Language Labels Needed?

Zero-shot learning is a topic of significant interest in multilingual NLU research (Conneau et al., 2018, 2019; Artetxe and Schwenk, 2019). In this context, we use *zero-shot learning* to refer to learning a classification task without observing training examples in the target language. Such an approach would allow practitioners to train a classification model using labeled data in a high-resource language such as EN and deploy it in other languages for which labels are not available.

To evaluate the viability of zero-shot approaches for our tasks, we compare the best performing models from the experiments in Table 5 with models trained only on EN training data. We report the test set results for each of the non-EN target languages in Table 6. Zero-shot models are competitive with previously published baselines (Table 4), which demonstrates the effectiveness of cross-lingual transfer in models like XLM-R. However, models trained using target language labels still outperform them by a large margin. Since obtaining a small number of target language labels is straightforward and typically required for validation in real applications, the need for zero-shot learning is reduced in practical scenarios.

5.4 Speed and Memory Usage

The deployment of multilingual NLU systems varies significantly depending on the number of downstream task models trained and the model architectures used. For instance, the *mono-target* and *multi-target* settings induce one model per target

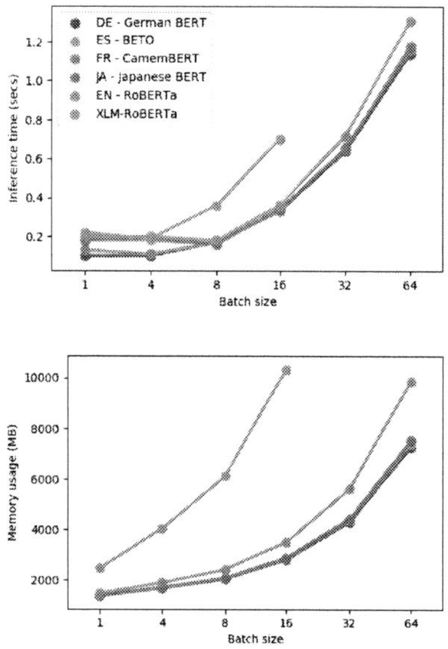

Figure 1: Inference time (top) and memory usage (bottom) benchmarks. XLM-R results not shown at batch sizes 32 and 64 due to GPU memory restraints. Environment details: `transformers v3.1.0, PyTorch v1.4.0, python v3.7.4, Linux. CPU: x86_64 (fp16=False, RAM=15GB). GPU: Tesla P100-PCIE-16GB, RAM=16GB, power=250.0W, perf. state=0)`.

language. Conversely, *multi-all* models have more consistent end-task performance and do not require the added complexity and latency of language detection.

We use the Hugging Face library to benchmark the pretrained transformer models used in our experiments. We measure the inference time and memory usage of a single forward pass on a single Nvidia Tesla P100 GPU. Results are shown in Figure 1.

Monolingual BERT models in different languages are nearly identical in inference speed, but vary slightly at small batch sizes. RoBERTa has more parameters than BERT, but the impact on inference time and memory is small. XLM-R is also comparable with monolingual models at small batch sizes, but its memory usage becomes prohibitively large at batch sizes larger than 32. For certain applications such as those with real-time inference, this may not be important since the most common batch size is 1. Overall, the main tradeoff we observe is between the complexity of deploying N language-specific models and the high parameter count of a single multilingual model.

6 Related Work

6.1 Multilingual Classification Benchmarks

XNLI (Conneau et al., 2018) and PAWS-X (Yang et al., 2019) are commonly used as representative benchmarks for cross-lingual text classification (Hu et al., 2020; Conneau et al., 2019). However, both datasets are designed for evaluating zero-shot cross-lingual transfer. While useful, they do not reflect practical scenarios where (1) a small amount of labeled data obviates zero-shot approaches, and (2) target language test data are not semantically aligned.

Meanwhile, benchmarks for supervised multilingual text classification are limited. Artetxe and Schwenk (2019) propose Language-Agnostic SEntence Representations (LASER) and evaluate them on Multilingual Document Classification Corpus (MLDOC; Schwenk and Li, 2018). Eisenschlos et al. (2019) later show that their multilingual fine-tuning and bootstrapping approach, MultiFit, outperforms LASER and mBERT on CLS and MLDOC. The recently released Multilingual Amazon Reviews Corpus (MARC; Keung et al., 2020) is similar to CLS, but contains a different set of languages and large-scale training sets. Rust et al. (2020) perform a systematic evaluation similar to ours, comparing monolingual and multilingual BERT models on seven monolingual sentiment analysis datasets. Unlike our work, they do not consider multilingual test sets or cross-lingual transfer during training (as in the *multi-all* setting). None of the above evaluate practical training modifications, XLM-R, or tasks with class imbalance.

6.2 Hate Speech Detection

Due to the increased volume and consequence of online content moderation in recent years, there is a growing body of work on multilingual hate speech data and methodology. The Multilingual Toxic Comment Classification Kaggle challenge (Jigsaw, 2019) included a multilingual test set of Wikipedia talk page comments annotated for toxicity. More recently, Glavaš et al. (2020) introduced XHATE-999, an evaluation set of 999 semantically aligned test instances annotated for abusive language in five typologically diverse languages. Similar to our work, they compare state-of-the-art monolingual and multilingual transformer models. However, both the Jigsaw dataset and XHATE-999 are designed for evaluating zero-shot transfer and do not contain multilingual training data.

Other multilingual hate speech studies have largely combined separate existing monolingual datasets for evaluation (Pamungkas and Patti, 2019; Sohn and Lee, 2019; Aluru et al., 2020; Corazza et al., 2020; Zampieri et al., 2020). To avoid domain mismatch effects across languages, we use the HATEVAL dataset (Basile et al., 2019), for which all examples were collected simultaneously.

Previously evaluated approaches include LSTM architectures and feature selection (Pamungkas and Patti, 2019; Corazza et al., 2020), as well as using transformers for fine-tuning (Sohn and Lee, 2019) or feature extraction (Stappen et al., 2020). Aluru et al. (2020) show that fine-tuning from transformer-based language models generally outperforms other methods, including cross-lingual fixed representations like LASER.

7 Conclusion

We conduct an empirical evaluation of transformer-based methods for multilingual text classification in a variety of pretraining and fine-tuning settings. We evaluate our results on two multilingual datasets spanning five languages: CLS (sentiment analysis) and HATEVAL (hate speech detection). Additionally, we contribute a relabeled version of HATEVAL to address mislabeled test examples and enable meaningful comparisons in future work.

Our results and analysis show that practical methods such as task- and domain-adaptive pretraining and data augmentation using machine translations consistently improve model performance without requiring additional labeled data. We further show that multilingual model performance can vary based on task semantics, and that monolingual models are not always guaranteed to outperform massively multilingual models like XLM-R due to its large pretraining corpora and increased capacity.

Our work points to a number of future directions, including cross-domain and cross-task transfer, low-resource and few-shot learning, and practical alternatives to large multilingual models such as distillation.

Acknowledgements

We wish to thank Boya (Emma) Peng, Alexander Wang, and Thomas Boser for discussions and feedback on this work. Thanks also to the anonymous reviewers whose detailed suggestions helped improve its clarity and usefulness.

References

Sai Saket Aluru, Binny Mathew, Punyajoy Saha, and Animesh Mukherjee. 2020. Deep learning models for multilingual hate speech detection. *arXiv preprint arXiv:2004.06465*.

Wissam Antoun, Fady Baly, and Hazem Hajj. 2020. AraBERT: Transformer-based model for Arabic language understanding. In *Proceedings of the 4th Workshop on Open-Source Arabic Corpora and Processing Tools, with a Shared Task on Offensive Language Detection*, pages 9–15, Marseille, France. European Language Resource Association.

Mikel Artetxe and Holger Schwenk. 2019. Massively multilingual sentence embeddings for zero-shot cross-lingual transfer and beyond. *Transactions of the Association for Computational Linguistics*, 7:597–610.

Valerio Basile, Cristina Bosco, Elisabetta Fersini, Debora Nozza, Viviana Patti, Francisco Manuel Rangel Pardo, Paolo Rosso, and Manuela Sanguinetti. 2019. SemEval-2019 task 5: Multilingual detection of hate speech against immigrants and women in Twitter. In *Proceedings of the 13th International Workshop on Semantic Evaluation*, pages 54–63, Minneapolis, Minnesota, USA. Association for Computational Linguistics.

José Cañete, Gabriel Chaperon, Rodrigo Fuentes, Jou-Hui Ho, Hojin Kang, and Jorge Pérez. 2020. Spanish pre-trained bert model and evaluation data. In *PML4DC at ICLR 2020*.

Alexis Conneau, Kartikay Khandelwal, Naman Goyal, Vishrav Chaudhary, Guillaume Wenzek, Francisco Guzmán, Edouard Grave, Myle Ott, Luke Zettlemoyer, and Veselin Stoyanov. 2019. Unsupervised cross-lingual representation learning at scale. *arXiv preprint arXiv:1911.02116*.

Alexis Conneau, Kartikay Khandelwal, Naman Goyal, Vishrav Chaudhary, Guillaume Wenzek, Francisco Guzmán, Edouard Grave, Myle Ott, Luke Zettlemoyer, and Veselin Stoyanov. 2020. Unsupervised cross-lingual representation learning at scale. In *Proceedings of the 58th Annual Meeting of the Association for Computational Linguistics*, pages 8440–8451, Online. Association for Computational Linguistics.

Alexis Conneau, Ruty Rinott, Guillaume Lample, Adina Williams, Samuel R. Bowman, Holger Schwenk, and Veselin Stoyanov. 2018. Xnli: Evaluating cross-lingual sentence representations. In *Proceedings of the 2018 Conference on Empirical Methods in Natural Language Processing*. Association for Computational Linguistics.

Michele Corazza, Stefano Menini, Elena Cabrio, Sara Tonelli, and Serena Villata. 2020. A multilingual evaluation for online hate speech detection. *ACM Trans. Internet Technol.*, 20(2).

deepset.ai. 2019. Open sourcing german bert. `https://deepset.ai/german-bert`.

Jacob Devlin, Ming-Wei Chang, Kenton Lee, and Kristina Toutanova. 2019. BERT: Pre-training of deep bidirectional transformers for language understanding. In *Proceedings of the 2019 Conference of the North American Chapter of the Association for Computational Linguistics: Human Language Technologies, Volume 1 (Long and Short Papers)*, pages 4171–4186, Minneapolis, Minnesota. Association for Computational Linguistics.

Julian Eisenschlos, Sebastian Ruder, Piotr Czapla, Marcin Kadras, Sylvain Gugger, and Jeremy Howard. 2019. Multifit: Efficient multi-lingual language model fine-tuning. In *Proceedings of the 2019 Conference on Empirical Methods in Natural Language Processing and the 9th International Joint Conference on Natural Language Processing (EMNLP-IJCNLP)*, pages 5706–5711.

Goran Glavaš, Mladen Karan, and Ivan Vulić. 2020. XHate-999: Analyzing and detecting abusive language across domains and languages. In *Proceedings of the 28th International Conference on Computational Linguistics*, pages 6350–6365, Barcelona, Spain (Online). International Committee on Computational Linguistics.

Suchin Gururangan, Ana Marasović, Swabha Swayamdipta, Kyle Lo, Iz Beltagy, Doug Downey, and Noah A. Smith. 2020. Don't stop pretraining: Adapt language models to domains and tasks. In *Proceedings of the 58th Annual Meeting of the Association for Computational Linguistics*, pages 8342–8360. Association for Computational Linguistics.

Pengcheng He, Xiaodong Liu, Jianfeng Gao, and Weizhu Chen. 2021. Deberta: Decoding-enhanced bert with disentangled attention.

Junjie Hu, Sebastian Ruder, Aditya Siddhant, Graham Neubig, Orhan Firat, and Melvin Johnson. 2020. Xtreme: A massively multilingual multi-task benchmark for evaluating cross-lingual generalization. *CoRR*, abs/2003.11080.

Jigsaw. 2019. Jigsaw multilingual toxic comment classification. `https://www.kaggle.com/c/jigsaw-multilingual-toxic-comment-classification`.

Phillip Keung, Yichao Lu, György Szarvas, and Noah A. Smith. 2020. The multilingual Amazon reviews corpus. In *Proceedings of the 2020 Conference on Empirical Methods in Natural Language Processing (EMNLP)*, pages 4563–4568, Online. Association for Computational Linguistics.

Yinhan Liu, Myle Ott, Naman Goyal, Jingfei Du, Mandar Joshi, Danqi Chen, Omer Levy, Mike Lewis, Luke Zettlemoyer, and Veselin Stoyanov. 2019. Roberta: A robustly optimized bert pretraining approach. *arXiv preprint arXiv:1907.11692*.

Louis Martin, Benjamin Muller, Pedro Javier Ortiz Suárez, Yoann Dupont, Laurent Romary, Éric de la Clergerie, Djamé Seddah, and Benoît Sagot. 2020. CamemBERT: a tasty French language model. In *Proceedings of the 58th Annual Meeting of the Association for Computational Linguistics*, pages 7203–7219, Online. Association for Computational Linguistics.

Endang Wahyu Pamungkas and Viviana Patti. 2019. Cross-domain and cross-lingual abusive language detection: A hybrid approach with deep learning and a multilingual lexicon. In *Proceedings of the 57th Annual Meeting of the Association for Computational Linguistics: Student Research Workshop*, pages 363–370, Florence, Italy. Association for Computational Linguistics.

Peter Prettenhofer and Benno Stein. 2010. Cross-language text classification using structural correspondence learning. In *Proceedings of the 48th Annual Meeting of the Association for Computational Linguistics*, pages 1118–1127.

Alec Radford, Rafal Józefowicz, and Ilya Sutskever. 2017. Learning to generate reviews and discovering sentiment. *CoRR*, abs/1704.01444.

Colin Raffel, Noam Shazeer, Adam Roberts, Katherine Lee, Sharan Narang, Michael Matena, Yanqi Zhou, Wei Li, and Peter J. Liu. 2020. Exploring the limits of transfer learning with a unified text-to-text transformer. *Journal of Machine Learning Research*, 21(140):1–67.

Phillip Rust, Jonas Pfeiffer, Ivan Vulić, Sebastian Ruder, and Iryna Gurevych. 2020. How good is your tokenizer? on the monolingual performance of multilingual language models.

Anna Schmidt and Michael Wiegand. 2017. A survey on hate speech detection using natural language processing. In *Proceedings of the Fifth International Workshop on Natural Language Processing for Social Media*, pages 1–10, Valencia, Spain. Association for Computational Linguistics.

Holger Schwenk and Xian Li. 2018. A Corpus for Multilingual Document Classification in Eight Languages. In *Proceedings of the Eleventh International Conference on Language Resources and Evaluation (LREC 2018)*, Miyazaki, Japan. European Language Resources Association (ELRA).

Jasdeep Singh, Bryan McCann, Nitish Shirish Keskar, Caiming Xiong, and Richard Socher. 2019. Xlda: Cross-lingual data augmentation for natural language inference and question answering.

Hajung Sohn and Hyunju Lee. 2019. Mc-bert4hate: Hate speech detection using multi-channel bert for different languages and translations. *2019 International Conference on Data Mining Workshops (ICDMW)*, pages 551–559.

Lukas Stappen, Fabian Brunn, and B. Schuller. 2020. Cross-lingual zero- and few-shot hate speech detection utilising frozen transformer language models and axel. *ArXiv*, abs/2004.13850.

Masatoshi Suzuki and Ryo Takahashi. 2019. Pretrained japanese bert models. `https://github.com/cl-tohoku/bert-japanese`.

Ashish Vaswani, Noam Shazeer, Niki Parmar, Jakob Uszkoreit, Llion Jones, Aidan N Gomez, Łukasz Kaiser, and Illia Polosukhin. 2017. Attention is all you need. In *Advances in neural information processing systems*, pages 5998–6008.

Antti Virtanen, Jenna Kanerva, Rami Ilo, Jouni Luoma, Juhani Luotolahti, Tapio Salakoski, Filip Ginter, and Sampo Pyysalo. 2019. Multilingual is not enough: Bert for finnish. *arXiv preprint arXiv:1912.07076*.

Ivan Vulić, Edoardo Maria Ponti, Robert Litschko, Goran Glavaš, and Anna Korhonen. 2020. Probing pretrained language models for lexical semantics. In *Proceedings of the 2020 Conference on Empirical Methods in Natural Language Processing (EMNLP)*, pages 7222–7240.

Alex Wang, Yada Pruksachatkun, Nikita Nangia, Amanpreet Singh, Julian Michael, Felix Hill, Omer Levy, and Samuel Bowman. 2019a. Superglue: A stickier benchmark for general-purpose language understanding systems. In *Advances in Neural Information Processing Systems*, volume 32, pages 3266–3280. Curran Associates, Inc.

Alex Wang, Amanpreet Singh, Julian Michael, Felix Hill, Omer Levy, and Samuel R. Bowman. 2019b. GLUE: A multi-task benchmark and analysis platform for natural language understanding. In the Proceedings of ICLR.

Thomas Wolf, Julien Chaumond, Lysandre Debut, Victor Sanh, Clement Delangue, Anthony Moi, Pierric Cistac, Morgan Funtowicz, Joe Davison, Sam Shleifer, et al. 2020. Transformers: State-of-the-art natural language processing. In *Proceedings of the 2020 Conference on Empirical Methods in Natural Language Processing: System Demonstrations*, pages 38–45.

Yinfei Yang, Yuan Zhang, Chris Tar, and Jason Baldridge. 2019. PAWS-X: A cross-lingual adversarial dataset for paraphrase identification. In *Proceedings of EMNLP 2019*, pages 3685–3690.

Marcos Zampieri, Preslav Nakov, Sara Rosenthal, Pepa Atanasova, Georgi Karadzhov, Hamdy Mubarak, Leon Derczynski, Zeses Pitenis, and Çağrı Çöltekin. 2020. SemEval-2020 task 12: Multilingual offensive language identification in social media (OffensEval 2020). In *Proceedings of the Fourteenth Workshop on Semantic Evaluation*, pages 1425–1447, Barcelona (online). International Committee for Computational Linguistics.

An Emotional Comfort Framework for Improving User Satisfaction in E-Commerce Customer Service Chatbots

Shuangyong Song, Chao Wang, Haiqing Chen, Huan Chen
Alibaba Groups, Hangzhou 311121, China
{shuangyong.ssy,chaowang.wc,haiqing.chenhq,shiwan.ch}
@alibaba-inc.com

Abstract

E-commerce has grown substantially over the last several years, and chatbots for intelligent customer service are concurrently drawing attention. We presented *AliMe* Assist, a Chinese intelligent assistant designed for creating an innovative online shopping experience in E-commerce. Based on question answering (QA), *AliMe* Assist offers assistance service, customer service, and chatting service. According to the survey of user studies and the real online testing, emotional comfort of customers' negative emotions, which make up more than 5% of whole number of customer visits on *AliMe*, is a key point for providing considerate service. In this paper, we propose a framework to obtain proper replies to customers' emotional questions. The framework takes emotion classification model as a core, and the final reply selection is based on topic classification and text matching. Our experiments on real online systems show that the framework is very promising.

1 Introduction

A chatbot is considered as a question answering system in which experts provide knowledge on users' behest. Meanwhile, chatbots are not just question answering systems, since they can carry out a lot of tasks depending on how you design it (Zhu et al., 2018). As chatbot has become an important solution to rapidly increasing customer service demands in recent years, many companies have recently launched their own intelligent customer service (ICS) chatbots for providing customer service, such as Lenovo (Li et al., 2018), Fujitsu (Okuda and Shoda, 2018), JD.com (Zhu, 2019) and Alibaba (Li et al., 2017).

For customers' emotional questions, proper emotional comfort can help improve the service. This is not only applicable to customer service staffs, but also a key point of ICS chatbots, while demonstrating human-like service is the ultimate goal of ICS chatbots. Emotional quotient (EQ) has been a core competence of chatbot (Zhou et al., 2020), and about EQ, we can roughly categorize it into two key components: identifying users' emotions and giving users proper emotional responses. Besides, chatbots' EQ is domain-specific, since it is mainly based on emotion analyzing, and emotion-analyzing technologies are mostly domain specific.

In this paper, we introduce an emotional comfort framework for the e-commerce chatbots. E-commerce customers usually complain of slow delivery, poor quality of goods and difficulty of contacting sellers, etc. Traditional question answering based ICS chatbots may just reply customers with some pieces of 'knowledge' such as 'how to speed up the delivery', 'how to report the quality issues of goods' and 'how to contact sellers'. Without responses that are emotionally appropriate, ICS robots are too 'robotic' to users. Human-like empathy and appropriate emotional reply can help the users regain their confidence and move forward with a positive attitude. Besides, in our framework we don't consider emotional response generation models, such as (Huo et al., 2020) and (Zhou et al., 2018), since we should meet the high Queries-per-second (QPS) needs of real online applications.

Figure 1 gives two simple examples for the comparison of traditional ICS chatbots and emotional ICS chatbots, which are without or with emotional comforts. Without emotional comfort, the response appears abruptly.

2 Related Work

Classification model: classification model training is strongly based on extraction of textual semantic features, and textual semantic features can be roughly separated into word- (or character-) level features (Wang et al., 2018; Song et al., 2017; Kusner et al., 2015) , n-gram level features (Yin et al., 2016; Wan et al., 2016) and sentence level features (Shen et al., 2018; Arora et al., 2016).

Proceedings of NAACL HLT 2021: IndustryTrack Papers, pages 130–137
June 6–11, 2021.

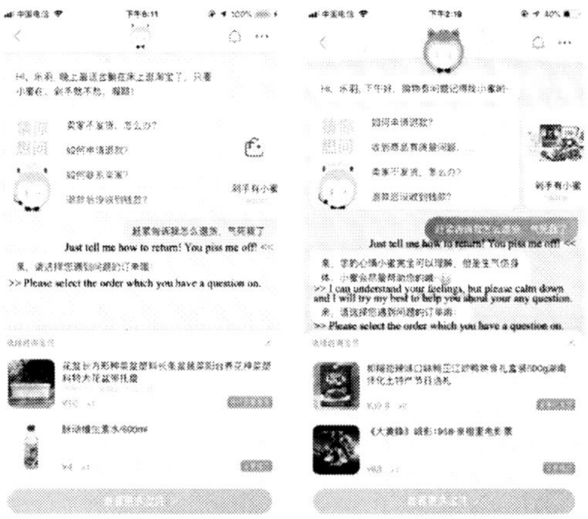

(a) Without comforts (b) With comforts

Figure 1: Comparison of conversations with or without emotional comforts.

1) Word-level features: Kusner et al. (Kusner et al., 2015) proposed word mover's distance (WMD), a distance function between two documents, which measures the minimum traveling distance from the embedded words of one document to another one. WMD achieved good performance in the document classification task (Ma et al., 2018). Referring to WMD, Song et al. (Song et al., 2017) proposed Word Similarity Maximization (WSM), which is a faster method for calculating similarity between two short texts with word embeddings, and WSM can achieve even better results than WMD on short text classification task. Wang et al. (Wang et al., 2018) proposed a novel classification model that considers correlation between embeddings of category labels and word embeddings (LEAM), which has further enriched the word-level features of text classification.

2) N-gram level features: Yin et al. (Yin et al., 2016) proposed Attention based CNN (ABCNN) model to extract n-gram features of each of two texts, and then combine those features as input of Logistic regression model to obtain semantic similarity between two texts. Wan et al. proposed a MV-LSTM model, which utilize Bi-LSTM model to obtain multiple positional sentence representations as a kind of 'dynamic' n-gram features.

3) Sentence level features: Arora et al. (Arora et al., 2016) represent a sentence with a weighted average of word embeddings, with their projection onto the first principal component across all sentences in the corpus removed. Shen et al. (Shen et al., 2018) thoroughly analyzed the effect of pooling mechanisms on representing sentences with simple word embeddings. With those sentence-level features, classification task, text sequence matching task and some other feature based tasks can all achieve good performance.

In our sentiment classification model and topic classification model, we combine those multiple-level features, and prove that our model can achieve significantly improved results.

Emotional chatbot: the most famous emotional chatbot is Xiaoice (Zhou et al., 2020), which was designed about 6 years ago. Understanding and responding to users' emotions are two dimensions of the ability of emotional chatbots. For realizing a human-like customer service chatbot, we try to understand users' emotions with an emotion classification model, and detect topics in user questions with a topic classification model. Then for responding users' emotions, we design an emotional comfort framework including matching based comfort, comfort with considering both emotion and topic, and a base comfort with just considering emotion.

Text matching: text matching needs to capture the rich interaction structures in the matching process, and this process can be conducted between abstract features of two texts (Yin et al., 2016; Hu et al., 2014; Qiu and Huang, 2015) or between word embedding of two texts (Pang et al., 2016; Hu et al., 2014; Lu and Li, 2013) . In papers (Yin et al., 2016; Hu et al., 2014; Qiu and Huang, 2015) (the ARC-I model in (Hu et al., 2014)), they all extract features from each of those two texts and then combine those features as the input of final Logistic regression model. In papers (Pang et al., 2016; Hu et al., 2014; Lu and Li, 2013) (the ARC-II model in (Hu et al., 2014)), they all take the interaction matrix of two texts as input of their models, and extract features from the given interaction matrix to evaluate similarity between two texts. In our matching-based emotional comfort part, we combine a BCNN model (Yin et al., 2016), which is with a text interaction on abstract feature level, and a MatchPyramid model (Pang et al., 2016), which is with a text interaction on word embedding level, to obtain an eligible performance for online service.

3 Framework Description

Our proposed framework consists of two parts (Figure 2), offline part and online part, and each of them consists of three components. With the offline part, we want to realize the ability to understand users' emotions as detailed as possible, and with the online part, we sequentially run increasingly general comfort strategies for responding users' emotions on a larger scale.

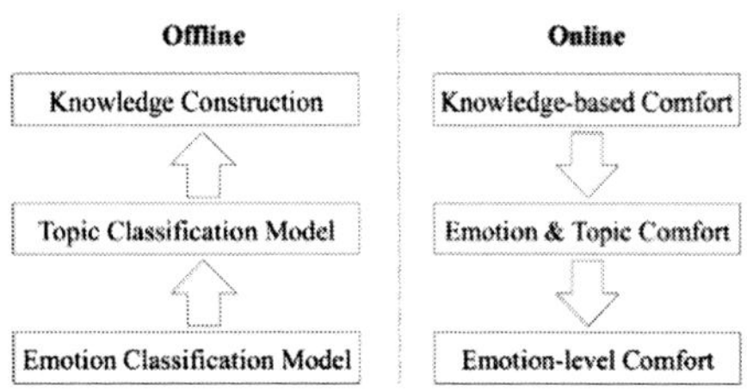

Figure 2: Framework of emotional comfort in ICS chatbots.

Offline Part: 1) Emotion classification model is trained with considering word-level features, n-gram level features and sentence level features. We consider seven different emotions as fear, abuse, disappointed, aggrieved, anxious, anger and grateful. 2) Topic classification model is trained with a same way as the emotion classification model, and we choose 35 high frequency service classes, such as 'complaints about the quality of service' and 'complaints of slow Delivery', etc. 3) Knowledge construction is for collecting some user questions with very specific content that needs to response emotional comforts. Those specific questions are with high frequency, but they are hard to be classified into a topic or cannot get well treated with just topic-level comforts. For each question, our service experts will design a professional reply, and for each 'question-reply' pair we call it as a piece of 'knowledge'.

Online Part: 1) Knowledge-based comfort is for users with specific questions, and we use a text-matching model to match a user's question and the high-frequent questions in collected pieces of knowledge. If we can get a prepared question, which has the biggest similarity with the given user's question and also the similarity value is bigger than a particular threshold, the corresponding reply will be taken as the emotional comfort result to this user. 2) Emotion & topic comfort means the comfort based on both users' emotions and the topics of users' questions. 3) Emotion-level comfort is a backup component to the emotion & topic comfort, since we cannot list all topics. So for other emotional queries without listed topics, we use this component to reply a general emotional response.

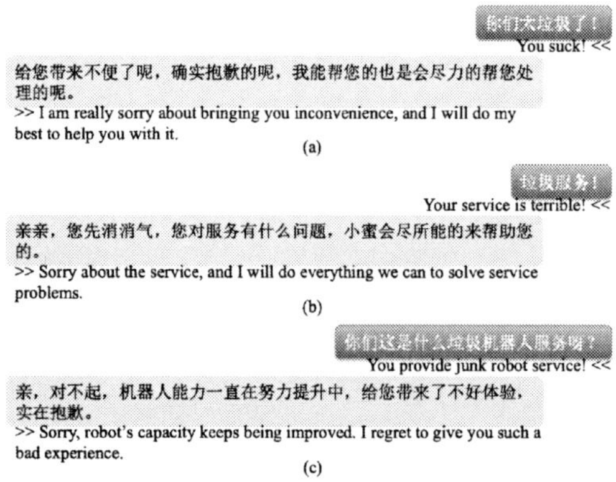

Figure 3: Examples of comforts: (a) emotion-level; (b) emotion & topic level; (c) knowledge-based level

Figure 3 gives examples of online emotional comforts. (a) shows an emotion-level comfort example. This user just complains, without any topic or any reason, so we can just give this user a very general comfort. (b) shows a comfort considering both emotions and topics. This user complains about service, so we can pointedly give a comfort about service. (c) shows a user's complain about bad robot service, and for this kind of questions with very specific content, we utilize knowledge-based matching models to give proper responses.

4 Offline Part

4.1 Emotion Classification

Emotion classification is the base and core of whole emotional comfort framework. We propose an ensemble classification model MLC (Multi-Level feature based Classification), which combines sentence level features, n-gram level features and word-level features. Figure 4 gives the description of this model, and from left to right, sentence level features, n-gram level features and word-level features are respectively obtained. Given the word embedding of which the dimension is set as M, we also define a series of embedding of labels (emotions) of which the dimension is also set as M. Below we discuss the feature extraction steps:

1) Sentence level features: Simple Word-Embedding based Models (SWEM) (Shen et al., 2018), which employs simple pooling strategies operated over word embeddings, shows close performance to some classic CNN- or RNN-based text matching models or classification models. In our work we use those simple pooling strategies to obtain sentence-level features of users' ques-

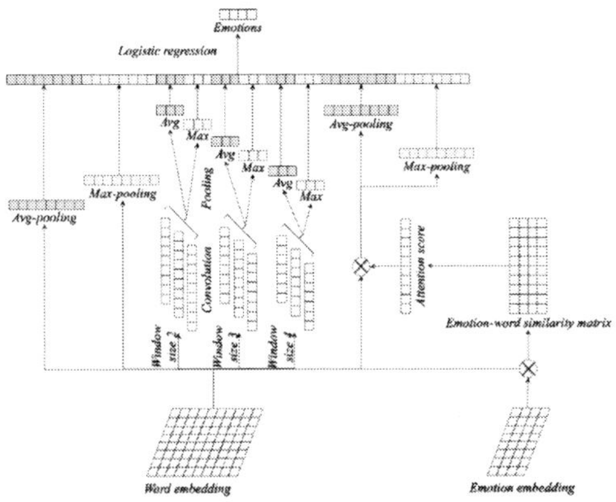

Figure 4: Emotion classification model.

tions for the emotion classification task. For combining the features obtained from average-pooling strategy and max-pooling strategy, two different methods are proposed as concatenating method and hierarchical method. Under the design idea of whole emotion classification model, we choose the SWEM-concat method to combine SWEM-max features and SWEM-avg features.

2) *n*-gram level features: Traditional CNN is used to obtain *n*-gram level features, and *n* is a variate denoting the convolution window size. In this paper, we set *n* as 2, 3 and 4 respectively, and for each window size, 16 convolution kernels are used to extract plentiful information from the original word embedding matrix. Pooling steps are similar as that in extraction of sentence level features.

3) Word-level features: We use the Label-Embedding Attentive Model (LEAM) proposed in (Wang et al., 2018) to extract word-level features. LEAM embeds the words and labels in the same joint space for text classification. It utilizes label descriptions for increasing the interaction between labels and words, which can obtains deeper consideration of semantic information of words. In our model, each 'label' means a kind of emotion, such as 'anger' or 'disappointment', etc. In our online service, 6 negative emotions and a 'grateful' emotion are considered.

Finally, features of different levels are put together for the output layer trained with logistic regression model.

4.2 Topic Classification

We summarize high frequent service topics with referring the experience of service experts, and then use the same model design with the emotion classification step to realize topic classification.

4.3 Knowledge Construction

Besides ICS chatbots, we also have human customer services. For extracting users' high frequent questions and also the high-quality replies, we can all refer to the chat log data of human customer services. We combine the chat log of chatbots and human customer services together, and utilize a self-adapting clustering method proposed in (Song et al.) to cluster similar user questions. With the arrangement of professional service experts, we finally choose 649 high-frequent user questions as basis of constructing 'question-reply' pairs. For each high-frequent user question, we collect referenceable replies from log of human customer services. Then with those referenceable replies, professional service experts can reorganize them to obtain final 649 'question-reply' pairs as our 'knowledge base'.

5 Online Part

5.1 Knowledge-based Comfort

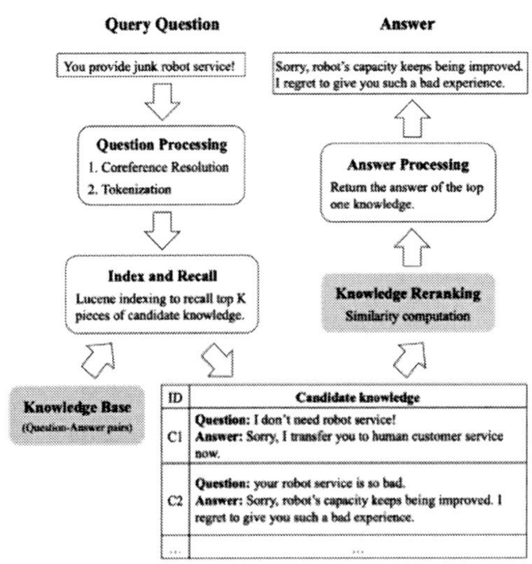

Figure 5: The workflow of retrieval-based QA systems.

We utilize a retrieval-based QA system (Yu et al., 2018) to realize knowledge-based comfort, of which the workflow is shown in figure 5. Collected knowledge base is indexed by Lucene, and for each emotional user question, we recall top K pieces of candidate knowledge from Lucene index, and then rerank those candidates to get a final reply. Similarity computation in 'Knowledge Reranking' module is the key component, and with different situations we have designed different models.

An unsupervised text similarity computation model: For making our framework applicable to some domains with no domain-sensitive labeled data, we use an unsupervised text matching model to rank candidates and decide which is most similar with the given user question. We use Word Similarity Maximization (WSM) (Song et al., 2017), which is an optimization of Word Mover's Distance (WMD) proposed in (Kusner et al., 2015), to realize this unsupervised text matching step. Compared to WMD, WSM can get a normalized similarity value restricted to [0,1] instead of the distance value of WMD of which is not normalized, and computational complexity of WSM can be greatly decreased compared to WMD.

A supervised deep text similarity computation model: With the discussion of 'text matching' in related work section, we choose two well-performing models, MatchPyramid (Pang et al., 2016) and BCNN (Yin et al., 2016), as baselines, and we realize a combined model PBmatch, with considering features in both MatchPyramind and BCNN. Feature extraction steps of MatchPyramind and BCNN are separated and then on the Logistic regressions step, features extracted from both models are combined together, and the whole framework makes a joint training of both models.

5.2 Emotion & Topic Comfort

Emotion classification and topic classification are all run on a given user question, and for each possible 'emotion+topic' combination, our service experts have set different comfortable replies for realizing diversified emotional comfort. These 'emotion+topic' sensitive replies are randomly responded when needed.

5.3 Emotion-level Comfort

Similar with the description in above subsection, with user questions without obvious topical content, we just consider the emotional information contained in questions. For each emotion, our service experts have also set different emotion-level comfortable replies for realizing diversified emotional comfort. Compared with comfortable replies considering both emotion and topic, emotion-level comfortable replies are more general, which are like the example in figure 3(a).

6 Experiments and Evaluations

6.1 Dataset and Evaluation Metric

Dataset: 1) Emotion classification dataset: Since we annotate that just about 5% of user questions are with emotion, a manual labeling on all user questions for emotion classification is a waste. We first extract some suspicious emotional questions with an emotional dictionary, which is empirically collected, and then we published crowdsourcing tasks with checking and revising those dictionary-based labels. Each question was labeled by 3 annotators, with one of the given emotions or 'no emotion'. If 3 annotators give 3 different labels, we delete this question, otherwise we label this question as the emotion labeled by at least 2 annotators. Finally, we got a totally 46,000 labeled questions with 8 different classes: 6 negative emotions, 1 grateful emotion and a class 'other'.

2) Topic classification dataset: Similar with the creation of the emotion classification dataset, we also firstly extract some suspicious topical questions with an empirically collected topical dictionary, which contains 35 topics such as 'poor service attitude', 'recharge slow' and 'urging a refund', and similar crowdsourcing tasks were also published. Finally, we got totally 98,000 labeled questions.

3) Text matching dataset: For creating enough dataset for training the text matching model, we implement following strategies: we randomly select 10,000 user questions from chatbot log, and top 15 candidates for each of them can be obtained with Lucene index. Then 8 service experts labeled those candidates with right/wrong, and some examples are shown in Table 1. Serious data unbalance shows in above labeled data, since just 14.3% candidates are labeled as right ones (positive samples). For balancing the data, we randomly extract about 20% candidates, which are labeled as wrong, of whole dataset as negative samples.

User questions	Candidate knowledge titles	Labels
The seller does not refund, how should I do?	After my application, the seller still won't refund, how should I do?	right
	Seller does not refund shipping charge, how should I do?	wrong
	Buyer does not finish payment after a successful auction.	wrong
Fill a fault phone number	Can I change the phone number if I have filled a fault one?	right
	I filled a fault phone number, how should I do?	right
	I filled a fault phone number. Does it impact my ticket service?	wrong

Table 1: Examples of Labeled Training Dataset (Translated into English).

Evaluation Metric: User Satisfaction.
Same as other kind chatbots, accuracy rating of

single-turn response can also be taken to measure the performance of an ICS chatbot. However, 'User Satisfaction' is a much more important metric for ICS domain and we also take it as a mirror of the performance of our proposed framework. In practice, about 1.5K conversation sessions per day are labeled by users with a satisfaction degree of 1,2 and 3, which respectively mean 'very satisfied', 'so-so' and 'unsatisfied'. We take the percentage of the label '1' as final 'User Satisfaction'.

We choose the final period of data for 'User Satisfaction' evaluation as from Oct. 15, 2020 to Nov. 15, 2020, which consist of almost 20,000 labeled data by user research experts. Besides, our emotional comfort framework was deployed in the online system on Oct. 31, 2020.

6.2 Results and Discussions

	CNN	SWEM	LEAM	MLC
Fear	0.680	0.688	0.652	0.701
Abuse	0.940	0.925	0.889	0.945
Disappointed	0.902	0.921	0.905	0.920
Aggrieved	0.840	0.821	0.812	0.847
Anxious	0.921	0.949	0.911	0.953
Anger	0.930	0.948	0.932	0.955
Grateful	0.955	0.987	0.952	0.997
Total	0.881	0.891	0.865	**0.903**

Table 2: Comparison of emotion classification models

First, we check the performance of the emotion classification model. Table 2 gives an emotion-level performance comparison of different models, which are CNN, SWEM, LEAM and our model. With more diversified features, our model can get better results than all the baseline models. And a total precision of 0.903 has reached the standard of online service when we set an optimum threshold of the classification probability as 0.625. Besides, topic classification is with a same model design of emotion classification. Since the topics are too many to show up all of them, we just give a total precision result comparison in table 3.

	CNN	SWEM	LEAM	MLC
Total	0.801	0.809	0.793	**0.817**

Table 3: Comparison of topic classification models

Table 4 gives the comparison of different models' performance on text matching, and we can see the PBmatch model can get a higher F-value than either BCNN or MatchPyramid models, with setting an optimum threshold. Besides, the two unsupervised models can also get passable experimental results. For the Lucene recalling before the text matching step, we set the maximum number of recalled candidates as 20, considering the high 'query per second' (QPS) demand of our online system.

Models	Threshold	Precision	Recall	F-value
WMD	0.73	0.823	0.782	0.802
WSM	0.75	0.845	0.823	0.834
BCNN	0.87	0.876	0.858	0.862
MatchPyramid	0.93	0.873	0.866	0.869
PBmatch	0.85	0.901	0.878	**0.889**

Table 4: Comparison of Text Matching Models.

Comfort strategies	Knowledge-	Emotion- & topic-	Emotion-
Percentages	21.64%	26.69%	51.67%

Table 5: Percentages of Different Comfort Strategies.

Table 5 gives the coverages of different comfort strategies on emotional user questions. We can see the emotion-level comfort strategy is with the largest percentage, since most of the user questions are usually very short and the emotional expression of users are without specific content or specific topics.

	Without our framework	With our framework
User Satisfaction	0.214	0.301

Table 6: User Satisfaction with or without Our Framework on Negative Emotions.

Table 6 shows the comparison results of user satisfaction with or without our framework on 6 negative emotions. We can see that those chat sessions with users' negative emotions have a very low user satisfaction, and our emotional comfort framework can help slightly raise the user satisfaction with 8.7 percent. Table 7 shows the comparison results of user satisfaction with or without our framework on the grateful emotion. With our framework, users may feel more comfortable and satisfied with the responses to their grateful emotion. So, more human-like service can get more customers' satisfaction.

	Without our framework	With our framework
User Satisfaction	0.589	0.723

Table 7: User Satisfaction with or without Our Framework on the Grateful Emotion.

7 Conclusion

In this paper, we focus on an emotional comfort framework in e-commerce chatbots, and the experiments show such a framework can effectively improve user satisfaction. About the future work, we will consider more emotions in this framework. Besides, we will automatically evaluate users' satisfaction with technologies on emotion analysis and sequence labeling.

References

Sanjeev Arora, Yingyu Liang, and Tengyu Ma. 2016. A simple but tough-to-beat baseline for sentence embeddings.

Baotian Hu, Zhengdong Lu, Hang Li, and Qingcai Chen. 2014. Convolutional neural network architectures for matching natural language sentences. *Advances in neural information processing systems*, 27:2042–2050.

Pei Huo, Yan Yang, Jie Zhou, Chengcai Chen, and Liang He. 2020. Terg: Topic-aware emotional response generation for chatbot. In *2020 International Joint Conference on Neural Networks (IJCNN)*, pages 1–8. IEEE.

Matt Kusner, Yu Sun, Nicholas Kolkin, and Kilian Weinberger. 2015. From word embeddings to document distances. In *International conference on machine learning*, pages 957–966.

Feng-Lin Li, Minghui Qiu, Haiqing Chen, Xiongwei Wang, Xing Gao, Jun Huang, Juwei Ren, Zhongzhou Zhao, Weipeng Zhao, Lei Wang, et al. 2017. Alime assist: An intelligent assistant for creating an innovative e-commerce experience. In *Proceedings of the 2017 ACM on Conference on Information and Knowledge Management*, pages 2495–2498.

Yang Li, Qingliang Miao, Ji Geng, Christoph Alt, Robert Schwarzenberg, Leonhard Hennig, Changjian Hu, and Feiyu Xu. 2018. Question answering for technical customer support. In *CCF International Conference on Natural Language Processing and Chinese Computing*, pages 3–15. Springer.

Zhengdong Lu and Hang Li. 2013. A deep architecture for matching short texts. *Advances in neural information processing systems*, 26:1367–1375.

Yinglong Ma, Peng Zhang, and Jiangang Ma. 2018. An ontology driven knowledge block summarization approach for chinese judgment document classification. *IEEE Access*, 6:71327–71338.

Takuma Okuda and Sanae Shoda. 2018. Ai-based chatbot service for financial industry. *Fujitsu Scientific and Technical Journal*, 54(2):4–8.

Liang Pang, Yanyan Lan, Jiafeng Guo, Jun Xu, Shengxian Wan, and Xueqi Cheng. 2016. Text matching as image recognition. In *Proceedings of the AAAI Conference on Artificial Intelligence*, volume 30.

Xipeng Qiu and Xuanjing Huang. 2015. Convolutional neural tensor network architecture for community-based question answering. In *Twenty-Fourth international joint conference on artificial intelligence*.

Dinghan Shen, Guoyin Wang, Wenlin Wang, Martin Renqiang Min, Qinliang Su, Yizhe Zhang, Chunyuan Li, Ricardo Henao, and Lawrence Carin. 2018. Baseline needs more love: On simple word-embedding-based models and associated pooling mechanisms. *arXiv preprint arXiv:1805.09843*.

Shuangyong Song, Haiqing Chen, and Zhiwei Shi. 2017. Intention classification of user queries in intelligent customer service system. In *2017 International Conference on Asian Language Processing (IALP)*, pages 83–86. IEEE.

Shuangyong Song, Yao Meng, and Zhongguang Zheng. Summarizing microblogging users with existing well-defined hashtags. *International Journal of Asian Language Processing*, 23(2):111–125.

Shengxian Wan, Yanyan Lan, Jiafeng Guo, Jun Xu, Liang Pang, and Xueqi Cheng. 2016. A deep architecture for semantic matching with multiple positional sentence representations. In *Proceedings of the AAAI Conference on Artificial Intelligence*, volume 30.

Guoyin Wang, Chunyuan Li, Wenlin Wang, Yizhe Zhang, Dinghan Shen, Xinyuan Zhang, Ricardo Henao, and Lawrence Carin. 2018. Joint embedding of words and labels for text classification. *arXiv preprint arXiv:1805.04174*.

Wenpeng Yin, Hinrich Schütze, Bing Xiang, and Bowen Zhou. 2016. Abcnn: Attention-based convolutional neural network for modeling sentence pairs. *Transactions of the Association for Computational Linguistics*, 4:259–272.

Jianfei Yu, Minghui Qiu, Jing Jiang, Jun Huang, Shuangyong Song, Wei Chu, and Haiqing Chen. 2018. Modelling domain relationships for transfer learning on retrieval-based question answering systems in e-commerce. In *Proceedings of the Eleventh ACM International Conference on Web Search and Data Mining*, pages 682–690.

Hao Zhou, Minlie Huang, Tianyang Zhang, Xiaoyan Zhu, and Bing Liu. 2018. Emotional chatting machine: Emotional conversation generation with internal and external memory. In *Proceedings of the AAAI Conference on Artificial Intelligence*, volume 32.

Li Zhou, Jianfeng Gao, Di Li, and Heung-Yeung Shum. 2020. The design and implementation of xiaoice, an empathetic social chatbot. *Computational Linguistics*, 46(1):53–93.

Hongyuan Zhu, Qi Liu, Nicholas Jing Yuan, Chuan Qin, Jiawei Li, Kun Zhang, Guang Zhou, Furu Wei, Yuanchun Xu, and Enhong Chen. 2018. Xiaoice band: A melody and arrangement generation framework for pop music. In *Proceedings of the 24th ACM SIGKDD International Conference on Knowledge Discovery & Data Mining*, pages 2837–2846.

Xiaoming Zhu. 2019. Case ii (part a): Jimi's growth path: Artificial intelligence has redefined the customer service of jd. com. In *Emerging Champions in the Digital Economy*, pages 91–103. Springer.

Language Scaling for Universal Suggested Replies Model

Qianlan Ying*[1], Payal Bajaj*[2], Budhaditya Deb[2], Yu Yang[1], Wei Wang†[3], Bojia Lin[1], Milad Shokouhi[2], Xia Song[2], Yang Yang[1], and Daxin Jiang[1]

[1]Microsoft, Beijing, China
[2]Microsoft, Bellevue, Washington, USA
[3]Qualtrics, Seattle, Washington, USA
{qiying,Payal.Bajaj,Budha.Deb,yanyu}@microsoft.com
{bojial,milads,xiaso,yayan,djiang}@microsoft.com
tskatom@gmail.com

Abstract

We consider the problem of scaling automated suggested replies for Outlook email system to multiple languages. Faced with increased compute requirements and low resources for language expansion, we build a single *universal* model for improving the quality and reducing run-time costs of our production system. However, restricted data movement across regional centers prevents joint training across languages. To this end, we propose a multi-task *continual learning* framework, with auxiliary tasks and language adapters to learn universal language representation across regions. The experimental results show positive cross-lingual transfer across languages while reducing *catastrophic forgetting* across regions. Our online results on real user traffic show significant gains in CTR and characters saved, as well as 65% training cost reduction compared with per-language models. As a consequence, we have scaled the feature in multiple languages including low-resource markets.

1 Introduction

Automated suggested replies or smart replies (SR) assist users to quickly respond with a short, generic, and relevant response, without users having to type in the reply. SR is an increasingly popular feature in many commercial applications such as Gmail, Outlook, Skype, Facebook Messenger, Microsoft Teams, and Uber (Kannan et al., 2016; Henderson et al., 2017a; Shang et al., 2015; Deb et al., 2019; Yue Weng, 2019). While the initial versions of this feature mostly targeted English users, making it available in multiple languages and markets is important not only from the perspective of product expansion but also from a linguistic inclusivity point of view.

In this paper we consider the problem of rapid scaling of the SR feature to multiple languages for Outlook. To develop such a system at production scale, we are faced with the following challenges.

- **Model management**: Language scaling increases the effort of training, deploying, and managing per-language models, which needs to be replicated for each language. In addition, one model per language increases the storage and compute requirements for the production servers, which can increase costs and occurrences of run-time issues.

- **Data constraints**: Developing models at production quality requires considerable effort in data collection and management. Due to regional market share and infrastructure constraints, rich and domain-specific data may not be available for all languages.

- **Data privacy and security policies**: Regional policies enforce data to be located in corresponding regions. For example, Spanish and Portuguese data are stored in North American (NAM) clusters while French data is stored in European (EUR) clusters. Data movement across regions is not allowed and this prevents leveraging commonly used multi-lingual co-training methods which require all the data stored to be in the same place.

To reduce the cost of model management, we propose to build a single *universal* SR model, capable of serving multiple languages and markets. To overcome data constraints, we propose to use *augmentation* with machine-translated (MT) data for languages without supervised data. To overcome privacy constraints, we propose a *continual* learning framework, where the model is trained sequentially across regions. To alleviate *catastrophic forgetting* (French, 1999; McCloskey and Cohen, 1989) in the continual learning process, we reinforce the universal properties via multi-task learning approach with public task-agnostic data, and an adapter-based model architecture that leverages domain-specific SR data and MT data.

Our experimental results followed with improvements shown on real user traffic illustrate the ef-

*Both authors contributed equally in the paper.
†Work performed at Microsoft Research.

Proceedings of NAACL HLT 2021: IndustryTrack Papers, pages 138–145
June 6–11, 2021.

fectiveness of the approach. As a consequence, we have rapidly scaled the feature in several languages including low-resource markets. Multilingual training for universal models is often very tricky to work in practice (especially with our data constraints). Thus, we demonstrate a significant accomplishment of a multi-lingual SR system running at production scale on millions of users, which saves resources while improving performance.

2 Core SR Model

The SR feature is similar to open-domain chatbots and task-oriented conversational agents, (Zhou et al., 2020; Henderson et al., 2019b; Fadhil and Schiavo, 2019; Xu et al., 2017; Okuda and Shoda, 2018; Kopp et al., 2018). In terms of usage, SR is closer to the latter, in that it assists users to complete a reply, instead of continuing an open-ended dialog. Following commonly used IR-based models in commercial SR applications (Henderson et al., 2017b; Deb et al., 2019), we use a dual encoder matching model for our SR system.

The matching model has two parallel encoders projecting input message and corresponding reply into a common representation space. Different encoders such as feed-forward and BiLSTM layers can be used here (Henderson et al., 2017a; Deb et al., 2019). More recently, (Devlin et al., 2018; Liu et al., 2019; Yang et al., 2019; Henderson et al., 2019a,b) show considerable improvements with transformer-based pre-trained models. Our English SR model uses a BERT equivalent (Devlin et al., 2018) encoder, while our mono-lingual baselines in other languages use BiLSTM encoders.

The model is trained on one-on-one message-reply (m-r) pairs from commercial email data. We minimize the symmetric loss function. It is a modified softmax on dot products between m-r encoding in equation 1 where $s_{i,j} = e^{\phi(m_i)\cdot\phi(r_j)}$. As described in (Deb et al., 2019), it was shown to improve the relevance by targeting at bi-directional *conversational* constraints.

$$p(m_i, r_i) = \frac{s_{i,i}}{\sum_j s_{i,j} + \sum_k s_{k,i} - s_{i,i}} \tag{1}$$

IR-based model requires a fixed response set. To generate that, we collect differentially private (DP) (Gopi et al., 2020) and anonymized replies, filtered for sensitive content from the training data which preserves user privacy while mining actual user responses. Furthermore, we use human curation

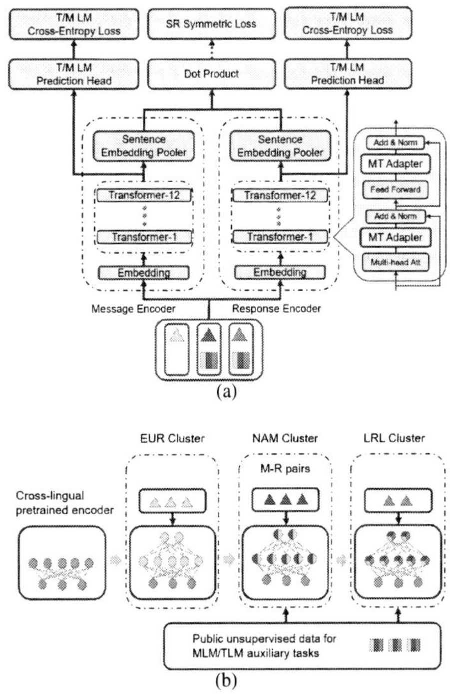

Figure 1: (a) Matching model architecture with symmetric loss and TLM/MLM cross-entropy loss. (b) Multi-task continual training loop for EUR->NAM->LRL clusters.

to edit responses for cultural-sensitivity, gender-neutrality, etc. DP filtration requires a large amount of data due to low yields. For low-resource markets, we translate English responses with human curation for cultural adaptation to languages and locales.

During prediction, we compute the matching score $(\cdot)$ between the message and pre-computed response set vectors. Similar to (Henderson et al., 2017a; Deb et al., 2019), we add a language-model (LM) penalty representing the popularity of responses to bias the predictions towards more common ones. Translated responses inherit the penalty score from the corresponding English responses. Using this score in equation 2 we first select top N_1 responses, and down-select to top N_2 after deduplication using lexical clustering, before presenting to users.

$$Score = \phi(m_i) \cdot \phi_K(r_k)) + \alpha LM_K(r_k) \tag{2}$$

3 Universal SR Model

The universal SR model consists of parallel encoder architecture trained using symmetric loss function similar to the core SR model. We initialize the m-r encoders with InfoXLM (Chi et al., 2020), an XLM-Roberta (Conneau et al., 2019) equivalent multi-lingual model as shown in as Figure 1(a) which creates language-agnostic text representation across 100 languages. The encoder is pre-trained with both publicly available and internal proprietary corpora and has shown good cross-lingual transfer capabilities on benchmarks such as XNLI (Conneau et al., 2018).

Using a universal pre-trained model in itself enables language expansion. However, as we discuss next, data movement constraints made training the universal model tricky, with performance frequently worse than single mono-lingual models.

3.1 Continual Learning

Joint training of universal encoders has led to enormous progress on standard benchmarks and industrial applications such as (Ranasinghe and Zampieri, 2020; Gencoglu, 2020).

However, privacy policies restrict the data movement across geographic clusters. This prevents the joint training at a single compute cluster. As a result, we train the model sequentially in a continual learning fashion by fine-tuning the model in one region, and then continue training in another.

The actual sequence of how this is conducted is important. We observed that keeping English at the last stage provides the best performance. This is likely because English data (which frequently contains bilingual data through code-switching) covers a large proportion in pre-training corpora, thus serving as an anchor in subsequent training stage to maintain the universal properties of the model.

3.2 Multi-task Learning

Training the SR model in multiple stages can lead to catastrophic forgetting, where new knowledge easily supplants old knowledge. This problem can be alleviated to some extent by freezing layers of the pre-trained encoders but is still significant after the model is fine-tuned with large corpora.

Several papers have leveraged self-supervised pre-training tasks based on bi-lingual parallel corpora to create or enhance cross-lingual representations (Devlin et al., 2018; Conneau et al., 2019; Chi et al., 2020). Following such approaches, we experiment with Translation Language Model (TLM) (Lample and Conneau, 2019) in continual learning to preserve the universal properties of the model. A total of $79M$ translation pairs from WikiMatrix (Schwenk et al., 2019) and MultiParaCrawl (Aulamo et al., 2020) data including the languages considered in production are extracted as training data. In addition, we conduct an ablation study on auxiliary task selection by comparing with Masked Language Model (MLM) (Devlin et al., 2018) trained on $370M$ samples from Wikipedia.

The multi-task training alternates between SR and auxiliary tasks according to a set proportion of mini-batches in an epoch. The proportion controls the trade-offs between the tasks, to achieve the desired levels of performance in the system.

3.3 Data Augmentation

Native supervised data (m-r pairs) is currently not available for low-resource languages. In such cases, English data is leveraged to generate pseudo m-r pairs using machine-translation (MT). We utilize MT data in continual learning process with auxiliary tasks, or with adapters (Houlsby et al., 2019) by introducing additional parameters in the transformer layers. When training with adapters, we freeze all parameters except the adapters.

3.4 Universal Model Training Loop

The production system targets 5 high-resource languages (HRL): Spanish (ES), Portuguese (PT), French (FR), German (DE), Italian (IT) with rich native data, and 5 low-resource languages (LRL): Chinese (ZH), Japanese (JA), Dutch (NL), Czech (CS) and Hungarian (HU) without any supervised data. English (EN) serves as pivot language in our experiments. As shown in Table 1, the data is distributed across Europe (EUR), North America (NAM) and a dedicated cluster storing MT data for LRL. Data movement across these regions is not allowed. Public task-agnostic data for auxiliary tasks in 8 languages is accessible in all regions.

Region	Languages	Category
EUR	DE, IT, FR	High-resource
NAM	ES, PT, EN	High-resource
LRL	ZH, JA, NL, CS, HU	Low-resource*

Table 1: Regional distribution of training data for different languages. *: data translated from EN.

We train the model sequentially in 3 stages as shown in Figure 1(b). First, we jointly train the model in EUR for FR, DE, and IT. Next, we move the model to NAM and continue train with EN, ES, and PT along with auxiliary task. Finally, in LRL, we train the model on machine translated m-r pairs along with original EN data in 2 different ways: (1) jointly train with auxiliary task, or (2) infuse the model with low-resource language adapters. In all stages, we freeze the embedding layer of the encoder during fine-tuning. According to previous studies (Lee et al., 2019; Peters et al., 2019), freezing partial layers can maintain the model quality while reducing training time during fine-tuning. We observed that freezing embedding layer provides a good balance between micro-batch size per GPU (low if no layers are frozen) and learning capacity of the model (low if many layers are frozen).

3.5 Universal Model Graph for Serving

For deployment, we create a composite graph with pre-computed response vectors of all languages embedded into the main model. A separate language identifier switches the prediction vectors to the predicted language of the input at run-time. Besides, several auxiliary models are added in online system to decide whether to trigger the universal model according to the characteristics of input message such as length and detected language.

4 Experiments and Results

The training data is collected and processed without any eyes access from commercial users in Outlook email system. To be more specific, we filter 50M m-r pairs from one-to-one conversations for each high-resource language, and translate 20M m-r pairs for each low-resource language. Considering the m-r length distribution, we truncate m-r pairs to (96, 64) tokens as training data, and filter out messages longer than 96 tokens during inference, so that the model is more focused on providing quick responses to short messages. The response set size for each language is 20K, filtered or trans-created from English native data.

In all three stages of training, we use an effective batch size of 16K. We utilize the Adam optimizer (Kingma and Ba, 2014) with weight decay and set peak learning rates as [5e-4, 3e-4, 1e-4] for three stages respectively. We train up to 30 epochs from which the best model is selected based on validation set loss over all languages.

For MLM/TLM objectives, we use single-token masking, the task proportion is set as 0.5. The final loss of the model is sum of symmetric loss and auxiliary task loss. For adapters, we use the hidden dimension of 256 in the bottleneck architecture and initialize these parameters with a normal distribution of mean 0 and standard deviation 0.01. According to our observation, high standard deviation for initialization can cause divergence. All experiments are conducted with 16 Nvidia V100-32GB GPU cards.

During prediction, we pick top $N_1 = 30$ responses according to equation 2, and then cluster the ranked results and down-select $N_2 = 3$ responses as final prediction.

4.1 Offline Evaluation Metrics and Sets

We compute evaluation metrics based on two kinds of evaluation sets. The first test set samples m-r pairs, where reply is contained in the response set (GoldenMR) and is used for computing the ranking metric, Mean Reciprocal Rank: $MRR = \frac{1}{N}\sum_{i=1}^{N}\frac{1}{Rank_i}$, for the top 15 predictions.

The second set consists of general m-r pairs (GenMR) where the reply is not restricted to the response set. *weighted*-ROUGE metrics is computed on final 3 responses with the reference response over uni/bi/tri-grams ($W\_ROUGE = \sum_{i=1}^{3}\frac{1}{w_i}ROUGE_i(Ref, Rep_k)$), with weights of $1:2:3$ proportions.

We use ~50K GoldenMR and 500K GenMR dataset for each language. For languages without native data, an evaluation proxy with MT data is used for model selection before online deployment. We give a higher preference to ROUGE as it showed higher correlation to our online metrics.

4.2 Online Evaluation Metrics

For the deployed models in production, we measure the following online metrics on real user traffic.

Click-through rate (CTR): the ratio of the count of replied emails with SR clicks over all emails that the feature is rendered.

Usage: the ratio of count of replied emails with SR clicks to all replied emails. This captures the contribution of SR to all Email replies.

Char-saved: the average number of characters-saved by clicking the selected reply.

4.3 Results

The model is evaluated on the international markets we are expanding to. English is excluded as EN model is well established. Results on baseline (existing per-language production models) and universal models for high-resource markets are reported in Table 2. Results targeting new markets without any native data are reported in Table 3. Entries in the tables are defined as follows:

BiLSTM: Per-language (mono-lingual) production models for non-EN markets as the baseline and also the control setting of online A/B tests. Here the encoders have shared embedding size of 320 and 2 BiLSTM layers with hidden size of 300.

UniPLM-[*NAM/EUR*]: Universal model created by fine-tuning pre-trained multi-lingual encoders for EUR and NAM regions respectively.

UniPLM-HRL: The model across the first 2 stages with the universal training loop in Figure 1(b). In the second stage, the model is fine-tuned along with TLM auxiliary task with multi-lingual unsupervised data. This is the first universal model candidate that breaks down the data boundary across High-Resource Languages (HRL).

Reg	Lang	Model	MRR	W_ROUGE
EUR	DE	BiLSTM-de	0.3263	0.0685
		UniPLM-EUR	**0.4185**	**0.0698**
		UniPLM-HRL	0.3323	0.0663
	FR	BiLSTM-fr	0.4569	0.0642
		UniPLM-EUR	**0.4721**	**0.0647**
		UniPLM-HRL	0.4135	0.0624
	IT	BiLSTM-it	0.3300	0.0330
		UniPLM-EUR	**0.4819**	**0.0385**
		UniPLM-HRL	0.4186	0.0360
NAM	ES	BiLSTM-es	0.3248	0.0511
		UniPLM-NAM	0.3186	**0.0565**
		UniPLM-HRL	**0.3319**	0.0552
	PT	BiLSTM-pt	**0.4383**	0.0552
		UniPLM-NAM	0.4216	**0.0577**
		UniPLM-HRL	0.4154	0.0563

Table 2: Evaluation on HRL (EUR and NAM) with UniPLM-HRL via continual multi-task learning and production baselines. The best results are in bold.

For new languages without native data, we continue to train the base universal model (UniPLM-HRL) with MT data with two approaches.

UniPLM-All-CL: The UniPLM-HRL model exported to LRL region trained with MT data (and native EN data) with SR and TLM multi-task objectives.

UniPLM-All-ADP: The model trained with MT-adapter, with all parameters frozen except for adapters parameters.

4.4 Model Quality Analysis

Table 2 compares the universal model UniPLM-HRL with both per-language baselines and per-region models. Table 3 shows the results with the low-resource languages, which are trained with data augmentation approach involving MT data, with multi-task learning or adapters.

Reg	Lang	Model	MRR	W_ROUGE
EUR	DE	UniPLM-HRL	**0.3323**	0.0663
		UniPLM-All-CL	0.3103	**0.0686**
	FR	UniPLM-HRL	0.4135	0.0624
		UniPLM-All-CL	**0.4207**	**0.0659**
	IT	UniPLM-HRL	0.4186	0.0360
		UniPLM-All-CL	**0.4274**	**0.0374**
NAM	ES	UniPLM-HRL	**0.3319**	**0.0552**
		UniPLM-All-CL	0.3160	0.0551
	PT	UniPLM-HRL	**0.4154**	**0.0563**
		UniPLM-All-CL	0.3783	0.0561
LRL	ZH	UniPLM-HRL	0.1365	0.0740
		UniPLM-All-CL	0.2638	0.0869
		UniPLM-All-ADP	**0.3024**	**0.0901**
	JA	UniPLM-HRL	0.1475	0.1010
		UniPLM-All-CL	0.3281	0.1106
		UniPLM-All-ADP	**0.3719**	**0.1180**
	NL	UniPLM-HRL	0.0638	0.0371
		UniPLM-All-CL	0.1822	0.0436
		UniPLM-All-ADP	**0.2490**	**0.0480**
	CS	UniPLM-HRL	0.0366	0.0386
		UniPLM-All-CL	0.1312	0.0441
		UniPLM-All-ADP	**0.2612**	**0.0526**
	HU	UniPLM-HRL	0.0420	0.0356
		UniPLM-All-CL	0.0779	0.0776
		UniPLM-All-ADP	**0.2615**	**0.0907**

Table 3: Results with UniPLM-All-CL and UniPLM-All-ADP continually augmented with MT data.

Per-language vs. Universal Model: The BiLSTM production models serve as strong baselines and have comparable MRR for UniPLM-NAM in ES and PT (Table 2). UniPLM-EUR has better performance than the BiLSTM production models. Overall, the Uni-PLM models have comparable or better performance than the monolingual baselines.

UniPLM-NAM/EUR vs. UniPLM-HRL: Table 2 also shows no appreciable difference in ROUGE metrics when training the model in 2 stages. In addition, the model outperforms BiLSTM per-language models on MRR on ES, DE, FR, and IT.

The above two comparisons show that for high-resource languages, we do not suffer significant degradation in quality with single stage and two-stage universal models.

Performance on LRL: Table 3 compares the UniPLM-All-CL and UniPLM-All-ADP with UniPLM-HRL model on low-resource languages. While UniPLM-HRL shows poor ranking performance, UniPLM-All-CL significantly improves on all metrics for LRL, while preserving the ROUGE performance on the other 5 languages. With adapters, UniPLM-All-ADP outperforms other models on all metrics in low-resource languages while keeping the performance unchanged (as a result of freezing the UniPLM-HRL model) in both EUR and NAM.

Overall, the results demonstrate the effectiveness of MT data augmentation in low-resource languages. We observe slight performance degradation on EUR and NAM languages caused by continual training on MT data. This may be due to imperfect translation. However we can mitigate these losses with MT-adapters which are quite promising as they increase the parameters by just 4.3% and even improves training efficiency as we can freeze all other parameters during fine tuning.

Reg	Lang	Model	MRR	W_ROUGE
EUR	DE	UniPLM-HRL	0.3323	0.0663
		-TLM	**0.3643**	**0.0701**
		-TLM+MLM	0.3070	0.0596
	FR	UniPLM-HRL	**0.4135**	**0.0624**
		-TLM	0.3772	0.0583
		-TLM+MLM	0.4126	0.0606
	IT	UniPLM-HRL	0.4186	**0.0360**
		-TLM	**0.4284**	0.0359
		-TLM+MLM	0.4035	0.0343
NAM	ES	UniPLM-HRL	**0.3319**	**0.0552**
		-TLM	0.2958	0.0543
		-TLM+MLM	0.3023	0.0537
	PT	UniPLM-HRL	0.4154	**0.0563**
		-TLM	0.4176	0.0561
		-TLM+MLM	**0.4234**	0.0559

Table 4: Results with variations on UniPLM-HRL. -TLM denotes removing TLM and -TLM+MLM denotes replacing with MLM in continual learning.

Reg	Lang	Model	MRR	W_ROUGE
EUR	DE	UniPLM-HRL	0.3323	0.0663
		+EUR	0.4272	0.0708
	FR	UniPLM-HRL	0.4135	0.0624
		+EUR	0.4818	0.0660
	IT	UniPLM-HRL	0.4186	0.0360
		+EUR	0.4851	0.0388
NAM	ES	UniPLM-HRL	0.3319	0.0552
		+EUR	0.2125	0.0456
	PT	UniPLM-HRL	0.4154	0.0563
		+EUR	0.3298	0.0505

Table 5: Results with 2-stage and replay-based continual learning. +EUR denotes replaying UniPLM-HRL with EUR m-r pairs.

4.5 Ablation Studies

MLM and TLM auxiliary tasks: Table 4 investigates contributions of auxiliary tasks in UniPLM-HRL model. We remove TLM objective as *-TLM* which represents continue training only on SR task, and replace TLM with MLM objective as *-TLM+MLM* which represents joint training with SR and MLM tasks. UniPLM-HRL with TLM task shows improvements over MLM task and also outperforms single SR task for W_ROUGE for all languages except DE. We hypothesize that TLM uses bi-lingual corpora which helps align representations for semantically similar text from different languages in task-specific fine-tuning. Furthermore, TLM objective can be interpreted as maximizing mutual information between cross-lingual contexts implicitly (Chi et al., 2020). It demonstrates that such inductive biases in auxiliary tasks are important for cross-lingual transfer in universal models.

Replay in continual learning: We continue to train the UniPLM-HRL model by rehearsing the old data in EUR as *+EUR*. In Table 5, *+EUR* we see severe regression on NAM languages, despite the improvement on EUR languages. The *replay* concept in continual learning (McClelland, 1998) fails here due to the two reasons. First, forgetting is the quintessential mode of continual learning. Second, EUR iteration doesn't contain the pivot language English training data. Continual learning requires delicately maintaining the universal properties through knowledge anchors which is difficult to achieve in practice.

4.6 Online Results

Based on the offline metrics, we selected UniPLM-HRL as the first candidate for online tests in our production system. Using BiLSTM per-language model as the control, we conducted a 2-week A/B test with 5% user traffic for each model per language/region. Table 6 presents the results for different languages. We observe statistically significant gain in ES (CTR) and FR (Char-saved). While there are regressions in other languages, they are not statistically significant ($p > 0.5$)

Lang	**CTR** (p-val)	**Usage** (p-val)	**Char-saved** (p-val)
ES	**4.20%** (0.0163)	**7.71%** (0.0001)	-0.91% (0.6592)
PT	0.00% (0.3690)	0.00% (0.3264)	3.32% (0.2737)
FR	-3.51% (0.1636)	-3.14% (0.2773)	**5.08%** (0.0495)
IT	-3.62% (0.4506)	-7.59% (0.1515)	7.03% (0.0602)
DE	2.80% (0.5147)	-1.07% (0.8233)	5.39% (0.1193)

Table 6: Online metrics for UniPLM-HRL model. The control model is BiLSTM in each language. The numbers with p-val < 0.05 are in bold.

Overall, the universal model is generally better

or at par compared to their mono-lingual baselines. This has allowed us to deploy the universal model to 100% of users in the 5 languages. An extended universal model supporting low-resource languages is getting deployed during the writing of this paper.

Compared with per-language separate model building, the effort of model training, inference stack and deployment can be substantially reduced, though the process of training data and response collection, and human evaluation for all our targeted languages are still required. Overall, around 65% training and performance improvement time cost can be saved with one single universal model target at 5 languages. We expect even higher amortized serving costs reductions as the approach is scaled to more languages.

5 Conclusions

This paper presents our approach of scaling automated suggested replies with one universal model. Faced with compute resource and data privacy constraints, we propose a multi-task continual learning framework with auxiliary tasks, and data augmentation with adapter-based model architecture. The universal model in production saves significant compute resources and model management overhead, while allowing us to train across regional data boundaries. In addition, the process allows us to *cold-start* in new markets even when no supervised data exists. Based on the promising offline and online results, we have deployed the model in several languages and plan to extend the process for 20 languages around the world.

References

Mikko Aulamo, Umut Sulubacak, Sami Virpioja, and Jörg Tiedemann. 2020. Opustools and parallel corpus diagnostics. In *Proceedings of The 12th Language Resources and Evaluation Conference*, pages 3782–3789.

Zewen Chi, Li Dong, Furu Wei, Nan Yang, Saksham Singhal, Wenhui Wang, Xia Song, Xian-Ling Mao, Heyan Huang, and Ming Zhou. 2020. Infoxlm: An information-theoretic framework for cross-lingual language model pre-training. *arXiv preprint arXiv:2007.07834*.

Alexis Conneau, Kartikay Khandelwal, Naman Goyal, Vishrav Chaudhary, Guillaume Wenzek, Francisco Guzmán, Edouard Grave, Myle Ott, Luke Zettlemoyer, and Veselin Stoyanov. 2019. Unsupervised cross-lingual representation learning at scale. *arXiv preprint arXiv:1911.02116*.

Alexis Conneau, Guillaume Lample, Ruty Rinott, Adina Williams, Samuel R Bowman, Holger Schwenk, and Veselin Stoyanov. 2018. Xnli: Evaluating cross-lingual sentence representations. *arXiv preprint arXiv:1809.05053*.

Budhaditya Deb, P. Bailey, and M. Shokouhi. 2019. Diversifying reply suggestions using a matching-conditional variational autoencoder. In *NAACL-HLT*.

Jacob Devlin, Ming-Wei Chang, Kenton Lee, and Kristina Toutanova. 2018. Bert: Pre-training of deep bidirectional transformers for language understanding. *arXiv preprint arXiv:1810.04805*.

Ahmed Fadhil and Gianluca Schiavo. 2019. Designing for health chatbots. *arXiv preprint arXiv:1902.09022*.

Robert M French. 1999. Catastrophic forgetting in connectionist networks. *Trends in cognitive sciences*, 3(4):128–135.

Oguzhan Gencoglu. 2020. Large-scale, language-agnostic discourse classification of tweets during covid-19. *Machine Learning and Knowledge Extraction*, 2(4):603–616.

Sivakanth Gopi, Pankaj Gulhane, Janardhan Kulkarni, Judy Hanwen Shen, Milad Shokouhi, and Sergey Yekhanin. 2020. Differentially private set union. *arXiv preprint arXiv:2002.09745*.

Matthew Henderson, Rami Al-Rfou', Brian Strope, Yun-Hsuan Sung, László Lukács, Ruiqi Guo, Sanjiv Kumar, Balint Miklos, and Ray Kurzweil. 2017a. Efficient Natural Language Response Suggestion for Smart Reply. *CoRR*, abs/1705.00652.

Matthew Henderson, Rami Al-Rfou, Brian Strope, Yun-Hsuan Sung, László Lukács, Ruiqi Guo, Sanjiv Kumar, Balint Miklos, and Ray Kurzweil. 2017b. Efficient natural language response suggestion for smart reply. *arXiv preprint arXiv:1705.00652*.

Matthew Henderson, Inigo Casanueva, Nikola Mrkšić, Pei-Hao Su, Tsung-Hsien Wen, and Ivan Vulić. 2019a. Convert: Efficient and accurate conversational representations from transformers. *arXiv preprint arXiv:1911.03688*.

Matthew Henderson, Ivan Vuli'c, Daniela Gerz, Iñigo Casanueva, Paweł Budzianowski, Sam Coope, Georgios Spithourakis, Tsung-Hsien Wen, Nikola Mrksi'c, and Pei-Hao Su. 2019b. Training neural response selection for task-oriented dialogue systems. In *Proceedings of ACL*.

Neil Houlsby, Andrei Giurgiu, Stanislaw Jastrzebski, Bruna Morrone, Quentin De Laroussilhe, Andrea Gesmundo, Mona Attariyan, and Sylvain Gelly. 2019. Parameter-efficient transfer learning for NLP. In *Proceedings of the 36th International Conference on Machine Learning*, volume 97 of *Proceedings of Machine Learning Research*, pages 2790–2799. PMLR.

Anjuli Kannan, Karol Kurach, Sujith Ravi, Tobias Kaufmann, Andrew Tomkins, Balint Miklos, Gregory S. Corrado, László Lukács, Marina Ganea, Peter Young, and Vivek Ramavajjala. 2016. Smart Reply: Automated Response Suggestion for Email. In *KDD*.

Diederik P Kingma and Jimmy Ba. 2014. Adam: A method for stochastic optimization. *arXiv preprint arXiv:1412.6980*.

Stefan Kopp, Mara Brandt, Hendrik Buschmeier, Katharina Cyra, Farina Freigang, Nicole Krämer, Franz Kummert, Christiane Opfermann, Karola Pitsch, Lars Schillingmann, et al. 2018. Conversational assistants for elderly users–the importance of socially cooperative dialogue. In *Proceedings of the AAMAS Workshop on Intelligent Conversation Agents in Home and Geriatric Care Applications co-located with the Federated AI Meeting*, volume 2338.

Guillaume Lample and Alexis Conneau. 2019. Cross-lingual language model pretraining. *arXiv preprint arXiv:1901.07291*.

Jaejun Lee, Raphael Tang, and Jimmy Lin. 2019. What would elsa do? freezing layers during transformer fine-tuning. *arXiv preprint arXiv:1911.03090*.

Yinhan Liu, Myle Ott, Naman Goyal, Jingfei Du, Mandar Joshi, Danqi Chen, Omer Levy, Mike Lewis, Luke Zettlemoyer, and Veselin Stoyanov. 2019. Roberta: A robustly optimized bert pretraining approach. *arXiv preprint arXiv:1907.11692*.

James L McClelland. 1998. Complementary learning systems in the brain. a connectionist approach to explicit and implicit cognition and memory. *Annals of the New York Academy of Sciences*, 843:153.

Michael McCloskey and Neal J Cohen. 1989. Catastrophic interference in connectionist networks: The sequential learning problem. In *Psychology of learning and motivation*, volume 24, pages 109–165. Elsevier.

Takuma Okuda and Sanae Shoda. 2018. Ai-based chatbot service for financial industry. *Fujitsu Scientific and Technical Journal*, 54(2):4–8.

Matthew E Peters, Sebastian Ruder, and Noah A Smith. 2019. To tune or not to tune? adapting pretrained representations to diverse tasks. *arXiv preprint arXiv:1903.05987*.

Tharindu Ranasinghe and Marcos Zampieri. 2020. Multilingual offensive language identification with cross-lingual embeddings. *arXiv preprint arXiv:2010.05324*.

Holger Schwenk, Vishrav Chaudhary, Shuo Sun, Hongyu Gong, and Francisco Guzmán. 2019. Wikimatrix: Mining 135m parallel sentences in 1620 language pairs from wikipedia. *arXiv preprint arXiv:1907.05791*.

Lifeng Shang, Zhengdong Lu, and Hang Li. 2015. Neural responding machine for short-text conversation. *arXiv preprint arXiv:1503.02364*.

Anbang Xu, Zhe Liu, Yufan Guo, Vibha Sinha, and Rama Akkiraju. 2017. A new chatbot for customer service on social media. In *Proceedings of the 2017 CHI Conference on Human Factors in Computing Systems*, pages 3506–3510.

Zhilin Yang, Zihang Dai, Yiming Yang, Jaime Carbonell, Russ R Salakhutdinov, and Quoc V Le. 2019. Xlnet: Generalized autoregressive pretraining for language understanding. In *Advances in neural information processing systems*, pages 5753–5763.

Franziska Bell Gokhan Tur Yue Weng, Huaixiu Zheng. 2019. Occ: A smart reply system for efficient in-app communications. *arXiv preprint arXiv:1907.08167*.

Li Zhou, Jianfeng Gao, Di Li, and Heung-Yeung Shum. 2020. The design and implementation of xiaoice, an empathetic social chatbot. *Computational Linguistics*, 46(1):53–93.

Graph-based Multilingual Product Retrieval in E-Commerce Search

Hanqing Lu
Amazon Search
luhanqin@amazon.com

Youna Hu
Amazon Search
ynhu@amazon.com

Tong Zhao
Amazon Personalization
zhaoton@amazon.com

Tony Wu
Amazon Search
tonywu@amazon.com

Yiwei Song
Amazon Search
ywsong@amazon.com

Bing Yin
Amazon Search
alexbyin@amazon.com

Abstract

Nowadays, with many e-commerce platforms conducting global business, e-commerce search systems are required to handle product retrieval under multilingual scenarios. Moreover, comparing with maintaining per-country specific e-commerce search systems, having a universal system across countries can further reduce the operational and computational costs, and facilitate business expansion to new countries. In this paper, we introduce a universal end-to-end multilingual retrieval system, and discuss our learnings and technical details when training and deploying the system to serve billion-scale product retrieval for e-commerce search. In particular, we propose a multilingual graph attention based retrieval network by leveraging recent advances in transformer-based multilingual language models and graph neural network architectures to capture the interactions between search queries and items in e-commerce search. Offline experiments on five countries data show that our algorithm outperforms the state-of-the-art baselines by 35% recall and 25% mAP on average. Moreover, the proposed model shows significant increase of conversion/revenue in online A/B experiments and has been deployed in production for multiple countries.

1 Introduction

Modern e-commerce search engines (Huang et al., 2020; Nigam et al., 2019) typically consist of a retrieval stage and a ranking stage. The retrieval stage is responsible for collecting a set of relevant products with minimum computational resources. The ranking stage then applies sophisticated machine learning (ML) algorithms to determine their impression positions. Traditional retrieval models rely on keyword matching (Manning et al., 2008), which may lead to poor results when the exact term match is unavailable. Recently, semantic matching models (Huang et al., 2013; Pang et al., 2016) have been adopted to improve retrieval performance (Mitra et al., 2018). These models are trained using click/purchase logs and typically separated by countries (Ahuja et al., 2020). However, such per-country specific training schema exposes three major drawbacks. First, maintaining country-specific models increase both operational burden and model iteration risks among countries. Second, the small amount of training data in low traffic countries may limit the ML model performance and this can also block the business expansion to new countries. Third, such models can not handle second language searches well. For example, the training data in US are dominated by English, which produces a model that cannot handle Spanish searches well. To solve above issues, ideally, a multilingual semantic retrieval model should be considered over monolingual retrieval models. However, how to design an effective and scalable multilingual semantic retrieval model for industry grade e-commerce search engine remains unsolved.

Built upon the success of pre-trained transformer-based models (Devlin et al., 2018; Yang et al., 2019b; Liu et al., 2019) such as Bidirectional Encoder Representations from Transformers (BERT) for natural language processing, multilingual BERT (M-BERT) has also demonstrated success for multilingual tasks (Pires et al., 2019). Though the techniques are promising, it is not straightforward to directly apply them to our problem due to the *vocabulary gap* issue (Mandal et al., 2019), i.e., customer searched queries are often short and from spoken input (e.g. 'fancy clothes') but product descriptions are usually in formal written style (e.g. 'formal attire'). There lacks a well established practice for fine-tuning multilingual BERT models on product search retrieval tasks.

In this work, we address the vocabulary gap by sharing information between queries and products in the model via graph convolution networks

Proceedings of NAACL HLT 2021: IndustryTrack Papers, pages 146–153
June 6–11, 2021. ©2021 Association for Computational Linguistics

(GCN). The query-to-product purchase/click logs naturally form a bipartite graph where each clicked product links with searched queries as neighbors. We expect to improve the product representation for retrieval tasks by incorporating information from its neighbor queries. For example, it is difficult for neural networks to directly match the query 'great gifts for child' to the product 'Disney puzzles for kids' given the vocabulary gap. But using the information that the product is connected with query 'children gifts', we can incorporate this information in its final representation, and the product will have a higher chance to be matched with the given query.

This paper presents an end-to-end multilingual retrieval system for e-commerce search engine. Our contributions are three-fold. 1. **Model:** We present a general framework that is compatible with any transformer-based models and any GCN architectures to capture interactions between products and search queries; 2. **Practice:** We provide a principled and practical guide of how to train the proposed model for large-scale product retrieval problem, e.g., how to define effective loss functions, how to feed online model-based hard negative samples to train the model and how to train the multilingual model with a novel one-language-at-a-batch (Sec 2.2) approach; 3. **System:** We discuss how to deploy the model to support product retrievals in multiple countries for e-commerce search.

To validate the effectiveness of our proposed method, we take offline experiments on billion-scale data across five languages and conduct online A/B testing experiments to measure the real traffic impacts. Through experimental results, our model outperforms state-of-the-art baselines by more than 25% and increases revenue and conversion over the current production system.

2 Methodology

We formulate the search retrieval task as follows. Supposed that we have a set of products $P = \{p_1, ..., p_n\}$. Each product p_i has a number of neighbor queries $Q_i = \{q_{i,1}, ..., q_{i,t}\}$ where $(q_{i,j}, p_i)$ appears in the search logs (customers search for $q_{i,j}$ and purchase p_i). For an arbitrary query q, we want to find the top-K relevant products from P. Note that q is not in $Q = \{Q_1, ..., Q_n\}$ when our retrieval system handles unseen queries.

2.1 Model Architecture

The model has two main components: (1) a query encoder that encodes search queries; (2) a product encoder that encodes both the product description and its neighbor queries. The product encoder has a GCN component that encapsulates the neighbor queries and product information.

Query Encoder: The query encoder could be any transformer-based encoder, such as BERT (Devlin et al., 2018), XLNet (Yang et al., 2019b), DistilBERT (Sanh et al., 2019), and RoBERTa (Liu et al., 2019). Choosing these transformer-based encoders over other encoders (e.g. LSTM (Hochreiter and Schmidhuber, 1997)) has several benefits. First, these models employ the word-piece tokenization which is robust to spelling errors and allows us to share vocabulary between different languages. In addition, transformer-based models can be easily parallelized and deployed online. We use the last hidden states of the encoders' [CLS] token as the embeddings for the query. For the other computationally more costly option of using the average pooling of the last hidden states of all tokens, we did not observe significant performance difference.

Product Encoder: The product encoder consists of 1) a transformer based encoder layer to extract the features of a product and its neighbor queries, and 2) a graph convolution layer that aggregates the extracted features to compute the final embeddings for a given product. The transformer-based encoder layer shares its parameters with the query encoder, and we also use the last hidden states of the encoder's [CLS] token as the features. The operations in the graph convolution layer are described in Algorithm 1.

Algorithm 1: Graph Convolution Layer

Input: extracted feature $\mathbf{h}_{p_i}$ of a product p_i, extracted features $\{\mathbf{h}_{q_{i,1}}, ..., \mathbf{h}_{q_{i,t}}\}$ of p_i's neighbor queries $\{q_{i,1}, ..., q_{i,t}\}$
Output: the final product embedding $\mathbf{x}_{p_i}$
Step 1: $\mathbf{h}_{q_i} = \frac{1}{t} \sum_j \text{ReLU}(\mathbf{W_q} \cdot \mathbf{h}_{q_{i,j}} + \mathbf{b_q})$
Step 2: $\mathbf{x}_{p_i} = \text{ReLU}(\mathbf{W_p} \cdot \text{CONCAT}(\mathbf{h}_{p_i}, \mathbf{h}_{q_i}) + \mathbf{b_p})$

The intuition of adding the graph convolution layer to the product encoder is that it can fill the vocabulary gap between queries and product descriptions. With the vocabulary gap and length distribution discrepancy between queries and product descriptions, directly using the transformer-extracted embeddings of queries and products for matching is sub-optimal. By incorporating neighbor query

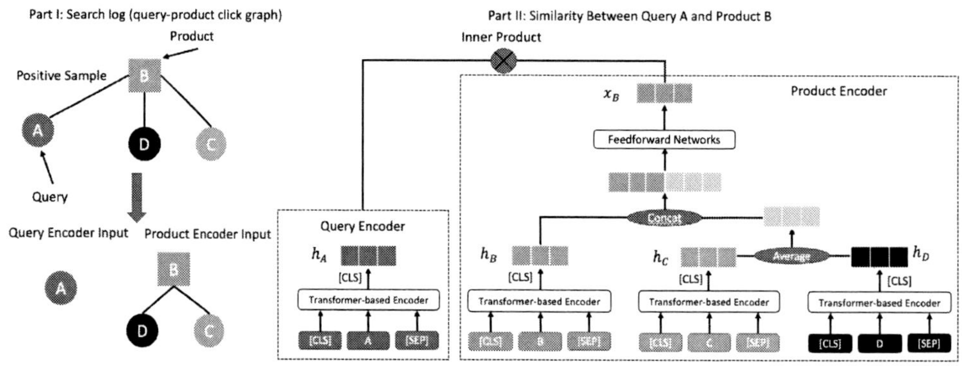

Figure 1: The base architecture of multilingual GCN. Each circle indicates a query and each rectangle represents a product. Query A and product B is a positive pair in the training data, while C and D are the neighbor queries of B. The query encoder takes query A as the input and outputs A's embedding, h_A. The product encoder takes B, C, D as the input and output B's embedding, x_B.

information into the product representation, the matching model not only learns information from query-to-product similarity, but also learns from query-to-query similarity. This is especially helpful to tail queries that have limited behavior signals.

Note that our framework is compatible with any GCN architectures in theory, such as GCN (Kipf and Welling, 2017) and GAT (Veličković et al., 2018), and we will leave those explorations for future work.

Loss Function: In the training stage, we use a pairwise ranking loss to train the model. Specifically, for each query q_i in the training set, we sample a positive product p_{i+} and a negative product p_{i-}. The triplet loss is defined as

$$L = \sum_i \mathrm{Log}(1 + \exp(\mathbf{x}_{q_i} \cdot \mathbf{x}_{p_{i-}} - \mathbf{x}_{q_i} \cdot \mathbf{x}_{p_{i+}})) \quad (1)$$

The intuition of is that we want the inner product of the positive pairs <$\mathbf{x}_{q_i}$, $\mathbf{x}_{p_{i+}}$> to be larger than the inner product of the negative pairs <$\mathbf{x}_{q_i}$, $\mathbf{x}_{p_{i-}}$>and the margin to be as large as possible.

2.2 Training Details

There are two key factors in successfully training the aforementioned framework: 1) how to select proper negative samples for training the model; 2) how to properly feed training data from different languages to the model.

Negative Sampling: Defining negative samples for semantic retrieval tasks is a tricky problem. A widely-adopted method is *random sampling*, where one can randomly sample a product from the product catalog as the negative samples for a given query. However, this simple setting would generate sub-optimal results, since the randomly selected negative samples can be too easily distinguished from the positive samples. Thus, it rarely brings knowledge for model learning and produces a model with low discriminative power for the retrieval task.

Recent research work has indicated that using hard negatives could improve the model performance for retrieval tasks (Ying et al., 2018; Nigam et al., 2019; Huang et al., 2020). The hard negative sample should be the product that is somewhat related to the query but not a exact match. In the search retrieval scenario, we can define the following three kinds of hard negatives.

Behavior-based hard negative: the negative samples are defined by users' behavior and are extracted from the search logs. For a given query, we take those products that were shown to the customer but not clicked as the hard negatives.

Offline model-based hard negative: the negative samples are calculated by the current model in an offline fashion. Specifically, we first use the current model to generate the embeddings for all queries and products in the training set, and then calculate the inner product between all queries and all products. For each query, we sample negatives from its top-200 to top-1000 relevant products.

Online model-based hard negative: the negative samples are generated on-the-fly with model learning. Specifically, we first randomly sample a batch of products. Then we use the current model to calculate the inner product between embeddings of these products and a batch of queries. For each query in the batch, we select the product with highest inner product value as the hard negative sample.

We argue that the online model-based hard negative is the most suitable sampling method to our application. The behavior-based hard negative samples requires additional data collection processes and often yields worse results in the search retrieval task (Huang et al., 2020). In fact, it is more suitable to the ranking task where the candidate pool is more refined. Besides, the offline model-based hard negative is too time-consuming, as we have to compute K-NN for each query in training set when we select/update the hard negatives.

Multilingual Data Fusion: How to properly feed the multilingual data to the model is another crucial factor to the training process. The amount of training data from different languages/countries varies greatly, and therefore low-resource languages would be underrepresented in the neural network model. Inspired by (Devlin et al., 2018), we perform exponentially smoothed weighting of the data. We would take the exponent of the percentage of a language by factor S and then re-normalize. Suppose there are two languages, English and Spanish, which accounts for 90% and 10% of training data respectively. The re-normalized distribution is $\frac{0.9^{0.7}}{0.9^{0.7}+0.1^{0.7}} = 0.82$ for English. Therefore, high-resource languages will be under-sampled, and low-resource languages will be over-sampled.

We also find that mixing training samples from multiple languages in one training batch makes it harder to train the model. Firstly, the negative sampling space is more complicated: we could sample a Spanish product as the negative sample of a English query. These easy negatives provide little knowledge to the model. In addition, different languages of training data appear in the same batch, which makes the batch gradient less stable. We propose to train the model with *one-language-at-a-batch*, and make the negative sampling process language-dependent. In the experiment, we observe that doing so dramatically increases the performance on all languages by 5-6% recall.

3 Deployment

The deployment of the proposed model has two parts: a query encoder and pre-computed product embeddings. As the query encoder is a standard transformer-based model and many papers have talked about the serving of it, this part can be easily deployed online. For the pre-computed product embeddings, we first compute the embeddings for products in our catalog, and incrementally update the product embedding periodically. To avoid repeated computations during the inference time (multiple products might have the same neighbor query), we first use the transformer-based encoder to compute the embeddings for all queries and products in the graph, and then join the products' embeddings with their neighbor queries' embeddings. Lastly, we pass these intermediate embeddings through the GCN layer to generate the final product embeddings. During the search retrieval step, we simply use the query encoder to extract the embedding for an input query. Then, we find the K-nearest neighbors (K-NN) products by calculating the cosine-distance between the query embedding and the pre-computed product embeddings. The K-NN products are used to augment the matchset of the given query.

4 Experiments

We collect the data from a large e-commerce platform that has business in multiple countries. To provide a comprehensive understanding on the role of multilingual queries in a real-world product search system, we select five countries: United States (US), Spain (ES), France (FR), Italy (IT) and Germany (DE). We subsample our data from one year of search log in each country. We organize the collected search log into query-product pairs with different customer behavior signals, e.g. click/purchase. For model offline testing, we first randomly sample 20K queries from each country. We then use our algorithm to rank a sub-corpus of 100K products (in each country) for those queries. The 100K product corpus consists of purchased products for those 20K queries and additional random negatives. Since our work focuses on the retrieval part of a product search engine, we adopt two matching metrics to summarize our results: Recall@10 (recall) and mean Average Precision (mAP). We employ the multilingual DistilBERT (Sanh et al., 2019) with 6 layers and 768 hidden units as our encoder. We set the batch size to 640 and use Adam optimizer (Kingma and Ba, 2014) with $\alpha = 0.0001, \beta_1 = 0.9$, and $\beta_2 = 0.999$. We run all the experiments on an AWS p3dn.24xlarge instance with 768GB memory and 8 NVIDIA V100 GPUs. We train the model on 8 GPUs in a distributed fashion. The model is trained for 140K batches, where the 28K 'warm up' batches are trained with random negatives and remaining batches are trained with online model-based hard negatives.

Table 1: Matching performance for our model and baselines.

method	US		ES		FR		IT		DE	
	recall	mAP	recall	mAP	recall	mAP	recall	mAP	recall	mAP
DSSM	49.53%	34.09%	38.82%	22.26%	38.16%	21.98%	42.51%	24.68%	46.87%	30.16%
Multilingual BERT	38.82%	25.14%	23.06%	12.07%	25.41%	13.67%	24.36%	13.06%	25.31%	15.18%
Our model w/o BERT	79.79%	60.06%	66.53%	39.01%	68.01%	41.43%	70.32%	42.66%	74.69%	51.79%
Our model w/o GCN	80.83%	60.68%	68.98%	41.73%	70.03%	42.28%	72.88%	44.98%	76.69%	53.75%
Our model	**85.86%**	**66.69%**	**73.60%**	**44.40%**	**74.97%**	**47.07%**	**77.16%**	**48.03%**	**81.44%**	**58.33%**

4.1 Comparison Results

We compare against the following baselines:

DSSM (Huang et al., 2013) is an earlier work to extract the semantic representations of queries and documents from large-scale click-through data by leveraging deep neural networks. We train 5 language-specific DSSM models with monolingual training data.

Multilingual BERT (Devlin et al., 2018) is the vanilla BERT without any fine-tuning. We use the *bert-base-multilingual-cased* model from huggingface implementation. We directly use the Multilingual BERT to encode the queries/products, and take the output [CLS] embeddings as the representations of queries/products.

Our model w/o BERT is a variant of our model, where we replace the DistilBERT encoder with a one-layer feed forward neural network and use the same word embedding matrix as the DistilBert. We train this model with exactly the same settings as we train the main model.

Our model w/o GCN is a variant of our model, where we remove the GCN module. It means that we only use product descriptions to get the product embeddings, and there is no graph convolution layer in the product encoder.

Table 1 shows (1) Multilingual BERT without any fine-tuning does not work for multilingual search retrieval tasks. It has the lowest recall and mAP, which proves the necessity of designing proper fine-tuning tasks for BERT-based model; (2) replacing the feed forward neural networks with DistilBERT leads to 6% - 7% recall and 5.5% - 6% mAP improvement on all languages; (3) adding GCN module to the product encoder further achieves significant boosts (5-6% recall improvement and 4.5%-6% mAP improvement), suggesting that GCN help the *vocabulary gap* issue.

4.2 Ablation Study

Negative Sampling: We try three kinds of hard negatives as illustrated in Section 2.2. Table 2 shows the results of training our model with different hard negatives. We observe that the performance of offline model-based hard negatives is similar to that of online model-based hard negatives (< 0.4% recall difference). However, computing the offline model-based hard negatives takes a total of 4x training time. Besides, training with behavior-based hard negatives has worst results (-10% recall, -7% mAP), because behavior-based negatives are not appropriate for retrieval tasks (Huang et al., 2020), since most impressed products are often relevant to the query. Including them as negatives confuses the model from focusing on retrieval tasks.

Multilingual Training Data Fusion: We test three data fusion strategies: 1) sample by unweighted data size + train with one language at a batch (*unweight+separate*); 2) sample by exponentially weighted data size + train with mixed languages in a batch (*weight+mix*); 3) sample by exponentially weighted data size + train with one language at a batch (*weight+separate*). Table 3 shows the results from different multilingual data fusion strategies. By exponentially weighting the training data, we can improve the matching performance in low-resource languages (ES, FR, IT) without hurting the performance in high resource languages (DE and US). Besides, *weighted+separated* beats *weighted+mixed* by 2-3% recall and 1-2% mAP margin on all languages, suggesting that training with one-language-at-a-batch is superior to mixed training.

4.3 Online Experiments

We report our findings from online A/B experiments on a large-scale e-commerce website with our multilingual GCN model. We run online match set augmentation experiments in three countries and two languages. The proposed algorithm significantly improves business metrics in all countries, leading to +1.8% increase in average clicks, +0.3% in revenue, and +0.4% in conversion. We also observe reformulated searches decreased by 1%. This reduction results in customers finding their desired products with less effort, likely from that our model bridges the vocabulary gap between queries and products. All results provide evidence that our

Table 2: Matching performance with different kinds of hard negatives.

	US		ES		FR		IT		DE	
hard negative	recall	mAP	recall	mAP	recall	mAP	recall	mAP	recall	mAP
behavior	76.62%	59.36%	63.28%	38.80%	63.90%	40.31%	66.17%	42.18%	68.44%	49.67%
offline model	85.44%	66.43%	**73.95%**	**44.33%**	74.86%	46.76%	**77.43%**	**48.20%**	**81.52%**	**58.68%**
online model	**85.86%**	**66.69%**	73.60%	44.40%	**74.97%**	**47.07%**	77.16%	48.03%	81.44%	58.33%

Table 3: Matching performance with different multilingual data fusion strategies.

	US		ES		FR		IT		DE	
fusion strategy	recall	mAP	recall	mAP	recall	mAP	recall	mAP	recall	mAP
weight+mix	84.61%	65.24%	70.45%	42.01%	71.41%	44.34%	73.39%	45.46%	78.85%	55.91%
unweight+separate	85.82%	66.60%	71.69%	42.93%	73.29%	45.63%	74.53%	46.66%	80.61%	57.73%
weight+separate	**85.86%**	**66.69%**	**73.60%**	**44.40%**	**74.97%**	**47.07%**	**77.16%**	**48.03%**	**81.44%**	**58.33%**

algorithm leads to better retrieval performance and can help customers fulfill their shopping missions.

5 Related Works

Search engine retrieval has been based on lexical match to identify relevant documents for queries. Recently, major industry search engines (Nigam et al., 2019; Huang et al., 2020; Fan et al., 2019) have incorporated *semantic matching* for improvements. Such algorithms can be classified into *embedding-based models* and *interaction models*. Embedding based models such as DSSM (Huang et al., 2013) and its subsequent works (Shen et al., 2014; Palangi et al., 2016; Hu et al., 2014) convert queries and documents into embeddings for retrieval. Interaction models, like MatchPyramid (Pang et al., 2016) and DRMM (Guo et al., 2016) leverage interaction matrices to capture local term matching. However, they are computationally costly for industry data.

With BERT (Devlin et al., 2018) becoming the state-of-the-art embedding method, it is adopted for various applications (Yang et al., 2019a; Yu et al., 2020; Khattab and Zaharia, 2020; Humeau et al., 2020; Chang et al., 2020). However, how to properly fine-tune BERT for retrieval tasks in product search remains unstudied. Our work fills this gap and provides a practical guide to fine-tune BERT-based models using production-scale search data. Furthermore, M-BERT provides representations for 104 languages and has proven ability to handle multilingual tasks (Pires et al., 2019). Other multilingual embedding models have also been proposed and validated (Schwenk and Douze, 2017; Conneau and Lample, 2019; Conneau et al., 2020). Our method is flexible and so that all these models can serve as a component.

Notably, our multilingual problem is different from the cross-lingual information retrieval (CLIR) problem (Nie, 2010; Jiang et al., 2020) , which refers to the scenario where the query is in one language but document is in other languages. In our problem, product descriptions and search queries are always in the same primary language and except a small fraction in different languages

Graph neural network is gaining prominence in ML applications (Ying et al., 2018; Zhang et al., 2019). The notion of "graph convolutions" is first proposed in (Bruna et al., 2014) with spectral graph theory. Later, GraphSAGE (Hamilton et al., 2017) redefines it to avoid operating on the entire graph. Recent efforts (Wang et al., 2019; Berg et al., 2018) adopt GCN to the user-item interaction graph and leverage the neighbors for recommendation. LightGCN (He et al., 2020) reported that neighborhood aggregation is the only important component of GCN, and weighted-sum of neighbor embeddings yield the best results. Our method leverages GCN to incorporate neighbor queries' information into product embedding, which bridges the vocabulary gap between query and product. Moreover, our framework is compatible with any GCN architectures, so can leverage the advances there.

6 Conclusion

Our paper present a multilingual graph convolution networks model for language-agonistic semantic retrieval in product search engine. Our method not only can handle multilingual text data, but also addresses the *vocabulary gap* issues between queries and product descriptions. We also provide a practical guide of fine-tuning the proposed model on retrieval tasks. We conduct various experiments including offline evaluation on 5 languages and online A/B test in three countries. In all experiments, our model consistently beats the baselines and demonstrates improved product discoverability.

References

Aman Ahuja, Nikhil Rao, Sumeet Katariya, Karthik Subbian, and Chandan K. Reddy. 2020. Language-agnostic representation learning for product search on e-commerce platforms. In *Proceedings of the 13th ACM International Conference on Web Search and Data Mining*, pages 7–15.

Rianne van den Berg, Thomas N Kipf, and Max Welling. 2018. Graph convolutional matrix completion. In *Proceedings of the 24th ACM SIGKDD International Conference on Knowledge Discovery & Data Mining*.

Joan Bruna, Wojciech Zaremba, Arthur Szlam, and Yann LeCun. 2014. Spectral networks and locally connected networks on graphs. In *2nd International Conference on Learning Representations*.

Wei-Cheng Chang, Felix X. Yu, Yin-Wen Chang, Yiming Yang, and Sanjiv Kumar. 2020. Pre-training tasks for embedding-based large-scale retrieval. In *8th International Conference on Learning Representations*.

Alexis Conneau, Kartikay Khandelwal, Naman Goyal, Vishrav Chaudhary, Guillaume Wenzek, Francisco Guzmán, Edouard Grave, Myle Ott, Luke Zettlemoyer, and Veselin Stoyanov. 2020. Unsupervised cross-lingual representation learning at scale. In *Proceedings of the 58th Annual Meeting of the Association for Computational Linguistics*, pages 8440–8451.

Alexis Conneau and Guillaume Lample. 2019. Cross-lingual language model pretraining. In *Advances in Neural Information Processing Systems*, pages 7057–7067.

Jacob Devlin, Ming-Wei Chang, Kenton Lee, and Kristina Toutanova. 2018. Bert: Pre-training of deep bidirectional transformers for language understanding. *arXiv preprint arXiv:1810.04805*.

Miao Fan, Jiacheng Guo, Shuai Zhu, Shuo Miao, Mingming Sun, and Ping Li. 2019. MOBIUS: towards the next generation of query-ad matching in baidu's sponsored search. In *Proceedings of the 25th ACM SIGKDD International Conference on Knowledge Discovery & Data Mining*, pages 2509–2517. ACM.

Jiafeng Guo, Yixing Fan, Qingyao Ai, and W Bruce Croft. 2016. A deep relevance matching model for ad-hoc retrieval. In *Proceedings of the 25th ACM International on Conference on Information and Knowledge Management*, pages 55–64.

Will Hamilton, Zhitao Ying, and Jure Leskovec. 2017. Inductive representation learning on large graphs. In *Advances in Neural Information Processing Systems 30*, pages 1024–1034.

Xiangnan He, Kuan Deng, Xiang Wang, Yan Li, Yong-Dong Zhang, and Meng Wang. 2020. Lightgcn: Simplifying and powering graph convolution network for recommendation. In *Proceedings of the 43rd International ACM SIGIR conference on research and development in Information Retrieval*, pages 639–648.

Sepp Hochreiter and Jürgen Schmidhuber. 1997. Long short-term memory. *Neural computation*, pages 1735–1780.

Baotian Hu, Zhengdong Lu, Hang Li, and Qingcai Chen. 2014. Convolutional neural network architectures for matching natural language sentences. In *Advances in neural information processing systems*, pages 2042–2050.

Jui-Ting Huang, Ashish Sharma, Shuying Sun, Li Xia, David Zhang, Philip Pronin, Janani Padmanabhan, Giuseppe Ottaviano, and Linjun Yang. 2020. Embedding-based retrieval in facebook search. In *Proceedings of the 26th ACM SIGKDD International Conference on Knowledge Discovery & Data Mining*, pages 2553–2561.

Po-Sen Huang, Xiaodong He, Jianfeng Gao, Li Deng, Alex Acero, and Larry P. Heck. 2013. Learning deep structured semantic models for web search using clickthrough data. In *Proceedings of the 22nd ACM International Conference on Information and Knowledge Management*, pages 2333–2338.

Samuel Humeau, Kurt Shuster, Marie-Anne Lachaux, and Jason Weston. 2020. Poly-encoders: Architectures and pre-training strategies for fast and accurate multi-sentence scoring. In *8th International Conference on Learning Representations*.

Zhuolin Jiang, Amro El-Jaroudi, William Hartmann, Damianos G. Karakos, and Lingjun Zhao. 2020. Cross-lingual information retrieval with BERT. In *Proceedings of the workshop on Cross-Language Search and Summarization of Text and Speech@LREC*, pages 26–31.

Omar Khattab and Matei Zaharia. 2020. Colbert: Efficient and effective passage search via contextualized late interaction over BERT. In *Proceedings of the 43rd International ACM SIGIR conference on research and development in Information Retrieval*, pages 39–48.

Diederik P Kingma and Jimmy Ba. 2014. Adam: A method for stochastic optimization. *arXiv preprint arXiv:1412.6980*.

Thomas N. Kipf and Max Welling. 2017. Semi-supervised classification with graph convolutional networks. In *5th International Conference on Learning Representations*. OpenReview.net.

Yinhan Liu, Myle Ott, Naman Goyal, Jingfei Du, Mandar Joshi, Danqi Chen, Omer Levy, Mike Lewis, Luke Zettlemoyer, and Veselin Stoyanov. 2019. Roberta: A robustly optimized bert pretraining approach. *arXiv preprint arXiv:1907.11692*.

Aritra Mandal, Ishita K Khan, and Prathyusha Senthil Kumar. 2019. Query rewriting using automatic synonym extraction for e-commerce search. In *Proceedings of eCOM Workshop@the 42nd International ACM SIGIR Conference on Research and Development in Information Retrieval.*

Christopher D Manning, Hinrich Schütze, and Prabhakar Raghavan. 2008. *Introduction to information retrieval.* Cambridge university press.

Bhaskar Mitra, Nick Craswell, et al. 2018. *An introduction to neural information retrieval.* Now Foundations and Trends.

Jian-Yun Nie. 2010. *Cross-Language Information Retrieval.* Synthesis Lectures on Human Language Technologies. Morgan & Claypool Publishers.

Priyanka Nigam, Yiwei Song, Vijai Mohan, Vihan Lakshman, Weitian Allen Ding, Ankit Shingavi, Choon Hui Teo, Hao Gu, and Bing Yin. 2019. Semantic product search. In *Proceedings of the 25th ACM SIGKDD International Conference on Knowledge Discovery & Data Mining*, pages 2876–2885.

Hamid Palangi, Li Deng, Yelong Shen, Jianfeng Gao, Xiaodong He, Jianshu Chen, Xinying Song, and Rabab Ward. 2016. Deep sentence embedding using long short-term memory networks: Analysis and application to information retrieval. *IEEE/ACM Transactions on Audio, Speech, and Language Processing*, pages 694–707.

Liang Pang, Yanyan Lan, Jiafeng Guo, Jun Xu, Shengxian Wan, and Xueqi Cheng. 2016. Text matching as image recognition. In *Proceedings of the 31st AAAI Conference on Artificial Intelligence.*

Telmo Pires, Eva Schlinger, and Dan Garrette. 2019. How multilingual is multilingual bert? In *Proceedings of the 57th Conference of the Association for Computational Linguistics*, pages 4996–5001.

Victor Sanh, Lysandre Debut, Julien Chaumond, and Thomas Wolf. 2019. Distilbert, a distilled version of bert: smaller, faster, cheaper and lighter. *arXiv preprint arXiv:1910.01108.*

Holger Schwenk and Matthijs Douze. 2017. Learning joint multilingual sentence representations with neural machine translation. In *Proceedings of Rep4NLP@the 55th Annual Meeting of the Association for Computational Linguistics*, pages 157–167.

Yelong Shen, Xiaodong He, Jianfeng Gao, Li Deng, and Grégoire Mesnil. 2014. A latent semantic model with convolutional-pooling structure for information retrieval. In *Proceedings of the 23rd ACM international conference on conference on information and knowledge management*, pages 101–110.

Petar Veličković, Guillem Cucurull, Arantxa Casanova, Adriana Romero, Pietro Lio, and Yoshua Bengio. 2018. Graph attention networks. In *6th International Conference on Learning Representations.*

Xiang Wang, Xiangnan He, Meng Wang, Fuli Feng, and Tat-Seng Chua. 2019. Neural graph collaborative filtering. In *Proceedings of the 42nd international ACM SIGIR conference on Research and development in Information Retrieval*, pages 165–174.

An Yang, Quan Wang, Jing Liu, Kai Liu, Yajuan Lyu, Hua Wu, Qiaoqiao She, and Sujian" Li. 2019a. Enhancing pre-trained language representations with rich knowledge for machine reading comprehension. In *Proceedings of the 57th Annual Meeting of the Association for Computational Linguistics*, pages 2346–2357.

Zhilin Yang, Zihang Dai, Yiming Yang, Jaime G. Carbonell, Ruslan Salakhutdinov, and Quoc V. Le. 2019b. Xlnet: Generalized autoregressive pretraining for language understanding. *arXiv preprint arXiv:1906.08237.*

Rex Ying, Ruining He, Kaifeng Chen, Pong Eksombatchai, William L Hamilton, and Jure Leskovec. 2018. Graph convolutional neural networks for web-scale recommender systems. In *Proceedings of the 24th ACM SIGKDD International Conference on Knowledge Discovery & Data Mining*, pages 974–983.

Juntao Yu, Bernd Bohnet, and Massimo Poesio. 2020. Named entity recognition as dependency parsing. In *Proceedings of the 58th Annual Meeting of the Association for Computational Linguistics*, pages 6470–6476, Online.

Yuan Zhang, Dong Wang, and Yan Zhang. 2019. Neural ir meets graph embedding: A ranking model for product search. In *Proceedings of The Web Conference (WWW)*, pages 2390–2400.

Query2Prod2Vec
Grounded Word Embeddings for eCommerce

Federico Bianchi
Bocconi University
Milano, Italy
f.bianchi@unibocconi.it

Jacopo Tagliabue*
Coveo Labs
New York, USA
jtagliabue@coveo.com

Bingqing Yu
Coveo
Montreal, Canada
cyu2@coveo.com

Abstract

We present **Query2Prod2Vec**, a model that grounds lexical representations for product search in product embeddings: in our model, *meaning* is a mapping between words and a latent space of products in a digital shop. We leverage shopping sessions to learn the underlying space and use merchandising annotations to build lexical analogies for evaluation: our experiments show that our model is more accurate than known techniques from the NLP and IR literature. Finally, we stress the importance of data efficiency for product search outside of retail giants, and highlight how **Query2Prod2Vec** fits with practical constraints faced by most practitioners.

1 Introduction

The eCommerce market reached in recent years an unprecedented scale: in 2020, 3.9 trillion dollars were spent globally in online retail (Cramer-Flood, 2020). While shoppers make significant use of search functionalities, improving their experience is a never-ending quest (Econsultancy, 2020), as outside of few retail giants users complain about sub-optimal performances (Baymard Institute, 2020). As the technology behind the industry increases in sophistication, neural architectures are gradually becoming more common (Tsagkias et al., 2020) and, with them, the need for accurate word embeddings for Information Retrieval (IR) and downstream Natural Language Processing (NLP) tasks (Yu and Tagliabue, 2020; Tagliabue et al., 2020a).

Unfortunately, the success of standard and contextual embeddings from the NLP literature (Mikolov et al., 2013a; Devlin et al., 2019) could not be immediately translated to the product search scenario, due to some peculiar challenges (Bianchi et al., 2020b), such as short text, industry-specific jargon (Bai et al., 2018), low-resource languages; moreover, specific embedding strategies have often been developed in the context of high-traffic websites (Grbovic et al., 2016), which limit their applicability in many practical scenarios. In *this* work, we propose a sample efficient word embedding method for IR in eCommerce, and benchmark it against SOTA models over industry data provided by partnering shops. We summarize our contributions as follows:

1. we propose a method to learn dense representations of words for eCommerce: we name our method **Query2Prod2Vec**, as the mapping between words and the latent space is mediated by the product domain;

2. we evaluate the lexical representations learned by **Query2Prod2Vec** on an analogy task against SOTA models in NLP and IR; benchmarks are run on two independent shops, differing in traffic, industry and catalog size;

3. we detail a procedure to generate synthetic embeddings, which allow us to tackle the "cold start" challenge;

4. we release our implementations, to help the community with the replication of our findings on other shops[1].

While perhaps not fundamental to its industry significance, it is important to remark that grounded lexical learning is well aligned with theoretical considerations on *meaning* in recent (and less recent) literature (Bender and Koller, 2020; Bisk et al., 2020; Montague, 1974).

*Corresponding author. All authors contributed equally and are listed alphabetically.

[1] Public repository available at: https://github.com/coveooss/ecommerce-query-embeddings.

Proceedings of NAACL HLT 2021: IndustryTrack Papers, pages 154–162
June 6–11, 2021. ©2021 Association for Computational Linguistics

2 Embeddings for Product Search: an Industry Perspective

In product search, when the shopper issues a query (e.g. "sneakers") on a shop, the shop search engine returns a list of K products matching the query intent and possibly some contextual factor – the shopper at that point may either leave the website, or click on n products to further explore the offering and eventually make a purchase.

Unlike web search, which is exclusively performed at massive scale, product search is a problem that both big and small retailers have to solve: while word embeddings have revolutionized many areas of NLP (Mikolov et al., 2013a), word embeddings for product queries are especially challenging to obtain at scale, when considering the huge variety of use cases in the overall eCommerce industry. In particular, based on industry data and first-hand experience with dozens of shops in our network, we identify four *constraints* for effective word embeddings in eCommerce:

1. **Short text**. Most product queries are very short – 60% of all queries in our dataset are one-word queries, > 80% are two words or less; the advantage of contextualized embeddings may therefore be limited, while lexical vectors are fundamental for downstream NLP tasks (Yu and Tagliabue, 2020; Bianchi et al., 2020a). For this reason, the current work specifically addresses the quality of *word* embeddings[2].

2. **Low-resource languages**. Even shops that have the majority of their traffic on English domain typically have smaller shops in low-resource languages.

3. **Data sparsity**. In *Shop X* below, only 9% of all shopping sessions have a search interaction[3]. Search sparsity, coupled with vertical-specific jargon and the usual long tail of search queries, makes data-hungry models unlikely to succeed for most shops.

4. **Computational capacity**. The majority of the market has the necessity to strike a good trade-off between quality of lexical representations and the cost of training and deploying models, both as hardware expenses and as additional maintenance/training costs.

The embedding strategy we propose – **Query2Prod2Vec** – has been designed to allow efficient learning of word embeddings for product queries. Our findings are useful to a wide range of practitioners: large shops launching in new languages/countries, mid-and-small shops transitioning to dense IR architectures and the raising wave of multi-tenant players[4]: as A.I. providers grow by deploying their solutions on multiple shops, "cold start" scenarios are an important challenge to the viability of their business model.

3 Related Work

The literature on learning representations for lexical items in NLP is vast and growing fast; as an overview of classical methods, Baroni et al. (2014) benchmarks several count-based and neural techniques (Landauer and Dumais, 1997; Mikolov et al., 2013b); recently, context-aware embeddings (Peters et al., 2018; Devlin et al., 2019) have demonstrated state-of-the-art performances in several semantic tasks (Rogers et al., 2020; Nozza et al., 2020), including document-based search (Nogueira et al., 2020), in which target entities are long documents, instead of product (Craswell et al., 2020). To address IR-specific challenges, other embedding strategies have been proposed: *Search2Vec* (Grbovic et al., 2016) uses interactions with ads and pages as context in the typical context-target setting of skip-gram models (Mikolov et al., 2013b); *QueryNGram2Vec* (Bai et al., 2018) additionally learns embeddings for n-grams of word appearing in queries to better cover the long tail. The idea of using vectors (from images) as an aid to query representation has also been suggested as a heuristic device by Yu et al. (2020), in the context of personalized language models; *this* work is the first to our knowledge to benchmark embeddings on lexical semantics (not

[2]Irrespectively of how the lexical vectors are computed, query embeddings can be easily recovered with the usual techniques (e.g. sum or average word embeddings (Yu et al., 2020)): as we mention in the concluding remarks, investigating compositionality is an important part of our overall research agenda.

[3]This is a common trait verified across industries and sizes: among dozens of shops in our network, 30% is the highest *search vs no-search* session ratio; *Shop Y* below is around 29%.

[4]As an indication of the market opportunity, only in 2019 and only in the space of AI-powered search and recommendations, we witnessed Coveo (Techcrunch), Algolia (Techcrunch, 2019a) and Lucidworks (Techcrunch, 2019b) raising more than 100M USD each from venture funds.

tuned for domain-specific tasks), *and* investigate sample efficiency for small-data contexts.

4 Query2Prod2Vec

In **Query2Prod2Vec**, the representation for a query q is built through the representation of the objects that q refers to. Consider a typical shopper-engine interaction in the context of product search: the shopper issues a query, e.g. "shoes", the engine replies with a noisy set of potential referents, e.g. pairs of shoes from the shop inventory, among which the shopper may select relevant items. Hence, this dynamics is reminiscent of a cooperative language game (Lewis, 1969), in which shoppers give noisy feedback to the search engine on the meaning of the queries. A full specification of **Query2Prod2Vec** therefore involves a representation of the target domain of reference (i.e. products in a digital shop) and a denotation function.

4.1 Building a Target Domain

We represent products in a target shop through a *prod2vec* model built with anonymized shopping sessions containing user-product interactions. Embeddings are trained by solving the same optimization problem as in classical *word2vec* (Mikolov et al., 2013a): *word2vec* becomes *prod2vec* by substituting *words* in a *sentence* with *products* viewed in a *shopping session* (Mu et al., 2018). The utility of *prod2vec* is independently justified (Grbovic et al., 2015; Tagliabue and Yu, 2020) and, more importantly, the referential approach leverages the abundance of browsing-based interactions, as compared to search-based interactions: by learning *product* embeddings from abundant behavioral data first, we sidestep a major obstacle to reliable word representation in eCommerce. Hyperparameter optimization follows the guidelines in Bianchi et al. (2020a), with a total of 26,057 (*Shop X*) and 84,575 (*Shop Y*) product embeddings available for downstream processing[5].

4.2 Learning Embeddings

The fundamental intuition of **Query2Prod2Vec** is treating clicks after q as a noisy feedback mapping q to a portion of the latent product space. In particular, we compute the embedding for q by averaging the product embeddings of all products clicked after it, using frequency as a weighting factor (i.e. products clicked often contribute more). The model has one free parameter, *rank*, which controls how many embeddings are used to build the representation for q: if $rank{=}k$, only the k most clicked products after q are used. The results in Table 1 are obtained with $rank{=}5$, as we leave to future work to investigate the role of this parameter.

The lack of large-scale search logs in the case of new deployments is a severe issue for successful training. The referential nature of **Query2Prod2Vec** provides a fundamental competitive advantage over models building embeddings from past linguistic behavior *only*, as synthetic embeddings can be generated as long as cheap session data is available to obtain an initial *prod2vec* model. As detailed in the ensuing section, the process happens in two stages, event generation and embeddings creation.

4.3 Creating Synthetic Embeddings

The procedure to create synthetic embeddings is detailed in Algorithm 1: it takes as input a list of words, a pre-defined number of sampling iterations, a popularity distribution over products[6], and it returns a list of synthetic search events, that is, a mapping between words and lists of products "clicked". Simulating the *search* event can be achieved through the existing search engine, as, from a practical standpoint, *some* IR system must already be in place given the use case under consideration. To avoid over-relying on the quality of IR and prove the robustness of the method, all the simulations below are not performed with the actual production API, but with a custom-built inverted index over product meta-data, with a simple TF-IDF weighting and Boolean search.

For the second stage, we can treat the synthetic click events produced by Algorithm 1 as a drop-in replacement for user-generated events – that is, for any query q, we calculate an embedding by averaging the product embeddings of the relevant products, weighted by frequency[7]. Putting the two stages together, **Query2Prod2Vec** can not only produce reliable query embeddings based on historical data, but also learn approximate embeddings for a large vocabulary *before* being exposed

[5]Final parameters for *prod2vec* are: $dimension = 50$, $win\_size = 10$, $iterations = 30$, $ns\_exponent = 0.75$.

[6]Please note that data on product popularity can be easily obtained through marketing tools, such as Google Analytics.

[7]Please note that while *this* work focuses on lexical quality, the same strategy can be applied to complex queries in a "cold start" scenario.

Algorithm 1: Generation of synthetic click events.

Data: a list of words W, a pre-defined number N of simulations per word, a distribution D over products.
Result: A dataset of synthetic clicked events: E

```
E ← empty mapping;
foreach word w in W do
    product_list ← Search(w);
    for i = 1 to N do
        p ← Sample(product_list, D);
        append the entry (w, p) to E;
    end
end
return E
```

to any search interaction: in Section 7 we report the performance of **Query2Prod2Vec** when using only synthetic embeddings[8].

5 Dataset and Baselines

5.1 Dataset

Following best practices in the multi-tenant literature (Tagliabue et al., 2020b), we benchmark all models on different shops to test their robustness. In particular, we obtained catalog data, search logs and anonymized shopping sessions from two partnering shops, *Shop X* and *Shop Y*: *Shop X* is a sport apparel shop with Alexa ranking of approximately *200k*, representing a prototypical shop in the middle of the long tail; *Shop Y* is a home improvement shop with Alexa ranking of approximately *10k*, representing an intermediate size between *Shop X* and public companies in the space. Linguistic data is in Italian for both shops, and training is done on random sessions from the period June-October 2019: after sampling, removal of bot-like sessions and pre-processing, we are left with 722,479 sessions for *Shop X*, and 1,986,452 sessions for *Shop Y*.

5.2 Baselines

We leverage the unique opportunity to join catalog data, search logs and shopping sessions to extensively benchmark **Query2Prod2Vec** against a variety of methods from NLP and IR.

- **Word2Vec and FastText**. We train a CBOW (Mikolov et al., 2013a) and a FastText model (Bojanowski et al., 2017) over product descriptions in the catalog;

- **UmBERTo**. We use RoBERTa trained on Italian data – *UmBERTo*[9]. The $\langle s \rangle$ embedding of the last layer of the architecture is the query embedding;

- **Search2Vec**. We implement the skip-gram model from Grbovic et al. (2016), by feeding the model with sessions composed of search queries and user clicks. Following the original model, we also train a time-sensitive variant, in which time between actions is used to weight query-click pairs differently;

- **Query2Vec**. We implement a different context-target model, inspired by Egg (2019): embeddings are learned by the model when it tries to predict a (purchased or clicked) item starting from a query;

- **QueryNGram2Vec**. We implement the model from Bai et al. (2018). Besides learning representations through a skip-gram model as in Grbovic et al. (2016), the model learns the embeddings of *unigrams* to help cover the long tail for which no direct embedding is available.

To guarantee a fair comparison, all models are trained on the same sessions. For all baselines, we follow the same hyperparameters found in the cited works: the dimension of query embedding vectors is set to 50, except that 768-dimensional vectors are used for **UmBERTo**, as provided by the pre-trained model.

As discussed in Section 1, a distinguishing feature of **Query2Prod2Vec** is *grounding*, that is, the relation between words and an external domain – in this case, products. It is therefore interesting not only to assess a possible *quantitative* gap in the quality of the representations produced by the baseline models, but also to remark the *qualitative* difference at the core of the proposed method: if words are *about* something, pure co-occurrence patterns may be capturing only fragments of lexical meaning (Bianchi et al., 2021).

[8] All the experiments are performed with $N = 500$ simulated search events per query.

[9] `https://huggingface.co/Musixmatch/umberto-commoncrawl-cased-v1`

6 Solving Analogies in eCommerce

As discussed in Section 2, we consider evaluation tasks focused on *word meaning*, without using product-based similarity (as that would implicitly and unfairly favor referential embeddings). Analogy-based tasks (Mikolov et al., 2013a) are a popular choice to measure semantic accuracy of embeddings, where a model is asked to fill templates like *man : king = woman : ?*; however, preparing analogies for digital shops presents non trivial challenges for human annotators: these would in fact need to know both the language and the underlying space ("air max" is closer to "nike" than to "adidas"), with the additional complication that many candidates may not have "determinate" answers (e.g. if *Adidas* is to *Gazelle*, then *Nike* is to what exactly?). In building our testing framework, we keep the intuition that analogies are an effective way to test for lexical meaning and the assumption that human-level concepts should be our ground truth: in particular, we programmatically produce analogies by leveraging existing human labelling, as indirectly provided by the merchandisers who built product catalogs[10].

6.1 Test Set Preparation

We extract words from the merchandising taxonomy of the target shops, focusing on three most frequent fields in query logs: *product type*, *brand* and *sport activity* for *Shop X*; *product type*, *brand* and *part of the house* for *Shop Y*. Our goal is to go from taxonomy to analogies, that is, showing how for each pair of taxonomy **types** (e.g. *brand : sport*), we can produce two pairs of **tokens** (*Wilson : tennis*, *Cressi : scubadiving*), and create two analogies: *b1 : s1 = b2 : ? (target: s2)* and *b2: s2 = b1 : ? (target: s1)* for testing purposes. For each **type** in a pair (e.g. *brand : sport*), we repeat the following for all possible values of *brand* (e.g. "Wilson", "Nike") – given a brand B:

1. we loop over the catalog and record all values of *sport*, along with their frequency, for the products made by B. For example, for $B = Nike$, the distribution may be: {"soccer": 10, "basketball": 8, "scubadiving": 0 }; for $B = Wilson$, it may be: {"tennis": 8};
2. we calculate the Gini coefficient (Catalano et al., 2009) over the distribution on the values of *sport* and choose a conservative Gini threshold, i.e. $75th$ percentile: the goal of this threshold is to avoid "undetermined" analogies, such as *Adidas : Gazelle = Nike : ?*. The intuition behind the use of a dispersion measure is that product analogies are harder if the relevant label is found across a variety of products[11].

With all the Gini coefficients and a chosen threshold, we are now ready to generate the analogies, by repeating the following for all values of *brand* – given a brand B we can repeat the following sampling process K times ($K = 10$ for our experiments):

1. if B's Gini value for its distribution of *sport* labels is below our chosen threshold, we skip B; if B's value is *above*, we associate to B its most frequent *sport* value, e.g. *Wilson : tennis*. This is the *source* pair of the analogy; to generate a *target* pair, we sample randomly a brand C with high Gini together with its most frequent value, e.g. *Atomic : skiing*;
2. we add to the final test set two analogies: *Wilson : tennis = Atomic : ?*, and *Atomic : skiing = Wilson : ?*.

The procedure is designed to generate test examples conservatively, but of fairly high quality, as for example *Garmin : watches = Arena : bathing cap* (the analogy relates two brands which sell only one type of items), or *racket : tennis = bathing cap : indoor swimming* (the analogy relates "tools" that are needed in two activities). A total of 1208 and 606 test analogies are used for the analogy task (**AT**) for, respectively, *Shop X* and *Shop Y*: we benchmark all models by reporting Hit Rate at different cutoffs (Vasile et al., 2016), and we also report how many analogies are covered by the lexicon learned by the models (*coverage* is the ratio of analogies for which all embeddings are available in the relevant space).

7 Results

Table 1 reports model performance for the chosen cutoffs. **Query2Prod2Vec** (as trained on real

[10] It is important to note that this categorization is done by product experts for navigation and inventory purposes: all product labels are produced independently from any NLP consideration.

[11] In other words, *Wilson : tennis = Atomic : ? (skiing)* is a better analogy than *Adidas : Gazelle = Nike : ?*.

Model	HR@5,10 for X	HR@5,10 for Y	CV (X/Y)	Acc on ST
Query2Prod2Vec (real data)	**0.332 / 0.468**	**0.277 / 0.376**	0.965/0.924	**0.88**
Word2Vec	0.206 / 0.242	0.005 / 0.009	0.47 / 0.03	0.68
Query2Vec	0.077 / 0.113	0.065 / 0.120	0.97 / 0.93	0.54
QueryNGram2Vec	0.071 / 0.122	0.148 / 0.216	**0.99** / 0.92	0.82
FastText	0.068 / 0.116	0.010 / 0.012	0.52 / 0.03	0.57
UmBERTo	0.019 / 0.042	0.030 / 0.103	0.99 / **1.00**	0.57
Search2Vec (time)	0.018 / 0.025	0.232 / 0.329	0.23 / 0.90	0.17
Search2Vec	0.016 / 0.024	0.095 / 0.150	0.23 / 0.90	0.17

Table 1: Hit Rate (HR) and coverage (CV) for all models and two shops on **AT**; on the rightmost column, Accuracy (Acc) for all models on **ST**.

data) has the best performance[12], while maintaining a very competitive coverage. More importantly, following our considerations in Section 2, results confirm that producing competitive embeddings on shops with different constraints is a challenging task for existing techniques, as models tend to either rely on specific query distribution (e.g. **Search2Vec (time)**), or the availability of linguistic and catalog resources with good coverage (e.g. **Word2Vec**). **Query2Prod2Vec** is the only model performing with comparable quality in the two scenarios, further strengthening the methodological importance of running benchmarks on more than one shop if findings are to be trusted by a large group of practitioners.

7.1 Sample Efficiency and User Studies

To investigate sample efficiency, we run two further experiments on *Shop X*: first, we run **AT** giving only 1/3 of the original data to **Query2Prod2Vec** (both for the *prod2vec* space, and for the denotation). The small-dataset version of **Query2Prod2Vec** still outperforms all other full-dataset models in Table 1 (*HR@5,10 = 0.276 / 0.380*). Second, we train a **Query2Prod2Vec** model *only with simulated data* produced as explained in Section 4 – that is, with *zero* data from real search logs. The entirely simulated **Query2Prod2Vec** shows performance competitive with the small-dataset version (*HR@5,10 = 0.259 / 0.363*)[13], outperforming all baselines.

As a further independent check, we supplement **AT** with a small semantic similarity task (**ST**) on *Shop X*[14]: two native speakers are asked to solve a small set (46) of manually curated questions in the form: "Given the word *Nike*, which is the most similar, *Adidas* or *Wilson*?". **ST** is meant to (partially) capture how much the embedding spaces align with lexical intuitions of generic speakers, independently of the product search dynamics. Table 1 reports results treating human ratings as ground truth and using cosine similarity on the learned embeddings for all models[15]. **Query2Prod2Vec** outperforms all other methods, further suggesting that the representations learned through referential information capture some aspects of lexical knowledge.

7.2 Computational Requirements

As stressed in Section 2, accuracy and resources form a natural trade-off for industry practitioners. Therefore, it is important to highlight that, our model is not just more accurate, but significantly more efficient to train: the best performing **Query2Prod2Vec** takes 30 minutes (CPU only) to be completed for the larger *Shop Y*, while other competitive models such as **Search2Vec(time)** and **QueryNGram2Vec** require 2 to 4 hours[16]. Being able to quickly generate many models allows for cost-effective analysis and optimization; moreover, infrastructure cost is heavily related to ethical and social issues on energy consumption in NLP (Strubell et al., 2019).

[12] HR@20 was also computed, but omitted for brevity as it confirmed the general trend.

[13] A similar result was obtained on *Shop Y*, and it is omitted for brevity.

[14] *Shop X* is chosen since it is easier to find speakers familiar with sport apparel than DIY items.

[15] Inter-rater agreement was substantial, with *Cohen Kappa Score*=0.67 (McHugh, 2012).

[16] Training is performed on a *Tesla V100 16GB* GPU. As a back of the envelope calculation, training **QueryNGram2Vec** on a *AWS p3 large* instance costs around 12 USD, while a standard CPU container for **Query2Prod2Vec** costs less than 1 USD.

8 Conclusion and Future Work

In *this* work, we learned reference-based word embeddings for product search: **Query2Prod2Vec** significantly outperforms other embedding strategies on lexical tasks, and consistently provides good performance in small-data and zero-data scenarios, with the help of synthetic embeddings. In future work, we will extend our analysis to *i*) specific IR tasks, within the recent paradigm of the dual encoder model (Karpukhin et al., 2020), and *ii*) compositional tasks, trying a systematic replication of the practical success obtained by Yu et al. (2020) through image-based heuristics.

When looking at models like **Query2Prod2Vec** in the larger industry landscape, we hope our methodology can help the field broaden its horizons: while retail giants indubitably played a major role in moving eCommerce use cases to the center of NLP research, finding solutions that address a larger portion of the market is not just practically important, but also an exciting agenda of its own[17].

9 Ethical Considerations

Coveo collects anonymized user data when providing its business services in full compliance with existing legislation (e.g. GDPR). The training dataset used for all models employs anonymous UUIDs to label events and sessions and, as such, it does not contain any information that can be linked to shoppers or physical entities; in particular, data is ingested through a standardized client-side integration, as specified in our public protocol.

Acknowledgements

We wish to thank Nadia Labai, Patrick John Chia, Andrea Polonioli, Ciro Greco and three anonymous reviewers for helpful comments on previous versions of this article. The authors wish to thank *Coveo* for the support and the computational resources used for the project. Federico Bianchi is a member of the Bocconi Institute for Data Science and Analytics (BIDSA) and the Data and Marketing Insights (DMI) unit.

[17]Please note that a previous draft of this article appeared on *arxiv* – `https://arxiv.org/abs/2104.02061` – *after* the review process, but before the camera-ready submission.

References

Xiao Bai, Erik Ordentlich, Yuanyuan Zhang, Andy Feng, Adwait Ratnaparkhi, Reena Somvanshi, and Aldi Tjahjadi. 2018. Scalable query n-gram embedding for improving matching and relevance in sponsored search. In *Proceedings of the 24th ACM SIGKDD International Conference on Knowledge Discovery & Data Mining*, KDD '18, pages 52–61, New York, NY, USA. ACM.

Marco Baroni, Georgiana Dinu, and Germán Kruszewski. 2014. Don't count, predict! a systematic comparison of context-counting vs. context-predicting semantic vectors. In *Proceedings of the 52nd Annual Meeting of the Association for Computational Linguistics (Volume 1: Long Papers)*, pages 238–247, Baltimore, Maryland. Association for Computational Linguistics.

Baymard Institute. 2020. *Site Search for Ecommerce.*

Emily M. Bender and Alexander Koller. 2020. Climbing towards NLU: On meaning, form, and understanding in the age of data. In *Proceedings of the 58th Annual Meeting of the Association for Computational Linguistics*, pages 5185–5198, Online. Association for Computational Linguistics.

Federico Bianchi, Ciro Greco, and Jacopo Tagliabue. 2021. Language in a (Search) Box: Grounding Language Learning in Real-World Human-Machine Interaction. In *NAACL-HLT*. Association for Computational Linguistics.

Federico Bianchi, Jacopo Tagliabue, Bingqing Yu, Luca Bigon, and Ciro Greco. 2020a. Fantastic embeddings and how to align them: Zero-shot inference in a multi-shop scenario. In *Proceedings of the SIGIR 2020 eCom workshop*.

Federico Bianchi, Bingqing Yu, and Jacopo Tagliabue. 2020b. Bert goes shopping: Comparing distributional models for product representations. *arXiv preprint arXiv:2012.09807*.

Yonatan Bisk, Ari Holtzman, Jesse Thomason, Jacob Andreas, Yoshua Bengio, Joyce Chai, Mirella Lapata, Angeliki Lazaridou, Jonathan May, Aleksandr Nisnevich, Nicolas Pinto, and Joseph Turian. 2020. Experience grounds language. In *Proceedings of the 2020 Conference on Empirical Methods in Natural Language Processing (EMNLP)*, pages 8718–8735, Online. Association for Computational Linguistics.

Piotr Bojanowski, Edouard Grave, Armand Joulin, and Tomas Mikolov. 2017. Enriching word vectors with subword information. *Transactions of the Association for Computational Linguistics*, 5:135–146.

Michael Catalano, Tanya Leise, and Thomas Pfaff. 2009. Measuring resource inequality: The gini coefficient. *Numeracy*, 2.

Ethan Cramer-Flood. 2020. *Global Ecommerce 2020. Ecommerce Decelerates amid Global Retail Contraction but Remains a Bright Spot.*

Nick Craswell, Bhaskar Mitra, E. Yilmaz, Daniel Fernando Campos, and E. Voorhees. 2020. Overview of the trec 2019 deep learning track. *ArXiv*, abs/2003.07820.

Jacob Devlin, Ming-Wei Chang, Kenton Lee, and Kristina Toutanova. 2019. BERT: Pre-training of deep bidirectional transformers for language understanding. In *Proceedings of the 2019 Conference of the North American Chapter of the Association for Computational Linguistics: Human Language Technologies, Volume 1 (Long and Short Papers)*, pages 4171–4186, Minneapolis, Minnesota. Association for Computational Linguistics.

Econsultancy. 2020. *Site search: retailers still have a lot to learn.*

Alex Egg. 2019. *Query2vec: Search query expansion with query embeddings.*

Mihajlo Grbovic, Nemanja Djuric, Vladan Radosavljevic, Fabrizio Silvestri, Ricardo Baeza-Yates, Andrew Feng, Erik Ordentlich, Lee Yang, and Gavin Owens. 2016. Scalable semantic matching of queries to ads in sponsored search advertising. In *Proceedings of the 39th International ACM SIGIR Conference on Research and Development in Information Retrieval*, SIGIR '16, page 375–384, New York, NY, USA. Association for Computing Machinery.

Mihajlo Grbovic, Vladan Radosavljevic, Nemanja Djuric, Narayan Bhamidipati, Jaikit Savla, Varun Bhagwan, and Doug Sharp. 2015. E-commerce in your inbox: Product recommendations at scale. In *Proceedings of KDD '15.*

Vladimir Karpukhin, Barlas Oguz, Sewon Min, Patrick Lewis, Ledell Wu, Sergey Edunov, Danqi Chen, and Wen-tau Yih. 2020. Dense passage retrieval for open-domain question answering. In *Proceedings of the 2020 Conference on Empirical Methods in Natural Language Processing (EMNLP)*, pages 6769–6781, Online. Association for Computational Linguistics.

Thomas K. Landauer and Susan T. Dumais. 1997. A solution to plato's problem: The latent semantic analysis theory of acquisition, induction, and representation of knowledge.

David Lewis. 1969. Convention. *Mass.: Harvard UP.*

Mary McHugh. 2012. Interrater reliability: The kappa statistic. *Biochemia medica : časopis Hrvatskoga društva medicinskih biokemičara / HDMB*, 22:276–82.

Tomas Mikolov, Kai Chen, Gregory S. Corrado, and Jeffrey Dean. 2013a. Efficient estimation of word representations in vector space. *CoRR*, abs/1301.3781.

Tomas Mikolov, Ilya Sutskever, Kai Chen, Greg Corrado, and Jeffrey Dean. 2013b. Distributed representations of words and phrases and their compositionality. In *Proceedings of the 26th International Conference on Neural Information Processing Systems - Volume 2*, NIPS'13, page 3111–3119, Red Hook, NY, USA. Curran Associates Inc.

Richard Montague. 1974. English as a formal language. In Richmond H. Thomason, editor, *Formal Philosophy: Selected Papers of Richard Montague*, pages 188–222. Yale University Press, New Haven, London.

Cun Mu, Guang Yang, and Zheng Yan. 2018. Revisiting skip-gram negative sampling model with regularization. *CoRR*, abs/1804.00306.

Rodrigo Nogueira, Zhiying Jiang, and Jimmy Lin. 2020. Document ranking with a pretrained sequence-to-sequence model. In *EMNLP*.

Debora Nozza, Federico Bianchi, and Dirk Hovy. 2020. What the [MASK]? making sense of language-specific BERT models. *arXiv preprint arXiv:2003.02912*.

Matthew Peters, Mark Neumann, Mohit Iyyer, Matt Gardner, Christopher Clark, Kenton Lee, and Luke Zettlemoyer. 2018. Deep contextualized word representations. In *Proceedings of the 2018 Conference of the North American Chapter of the Association for Computational Linguistics: Human Language Technologies, Volume 1 (Long Papers)*, pages 2227–2237, New Orleans, Louisiana. Association for Computational Linguistics.

Anna Rogers, Olga Kovaleva, and Anna Rumshisky. 2020. A primer in BERTology: What we know about how BERT works. *Transactions of the Association for Computational Linguistics*, 8:842–866.

Emma Strubell, Ananya Ganesh, and Andrew McCallum. 2019. Energy and policy considerations for deep learning in nlp. In *Proceedings of the 57th Annual Meeting of the Association for Computational Linguistics*, pages 3645–3650.

Jacopo Tagliabue and Bingqing Yu. 2020. Shopping in the multiverse: A counterfactual approach to in-session attribution. In *Proceedings of the SIGIR 2020 Workshop on eCommerce (ECOM 20).*

Jacopo Tagliabue, Bingqing Yu, and Marie Beaulieu. 2020a. How to grow a (product) tree: Personalized category suggestions for eCommerce type-ahead. In *Proceedings of The 3rd Workshop on e-Commerce and NLP*, pages 7–18, Seattle, WA, USA. Association for Computational Linguistics.

Jacopo Tagliabue, Bingqing Yu, and Federico Bianchi. 2020b. The embeddings that came in from the cold: Improving vectors for new and rare products with content-based inference. In *Fourteenth ACM Conference on Recommender Systems*, RecSys '20, page 577–578, New York, NY, USA. Association for Computing Machinery.

Techcrunch. coveo-raises-227m-at-1b-valuation.

Techcrunch. 2019a. Algolia finds $110m from accel and salesforce.

Techcrunch. 2019b. Lucidworks raises $100m to expand in ai finds.

Manos Tsagkias, Tracy Holloway King, Surya Kallumadi, Vanessa Murdock, and Maarten de Rijke. 2020. Challenges and research opportunities in ecommerce search and recommendations. In *SIGIR Forum*, volume 54.

Flavian Vasile, Elena Smirnova, and Alexis Conneau. 2016. Meta-prod2vec: Product embeddings using side-information for recommendation. *Proceedings of the 10th ACM Conference on Recommender Systems*.

Bingqing Yu and Jacopo Tagliabue. 2020. Blending search and discovery: Tag-based query refinement with contextual reinforcement learning. In *EComNLP*.

Bingqing Yu, Jacopo Tagliabue, Ciro Greco, and Federico Bianchi. 2020. An image is worth a thousand features: Scalable product representations for in-session type-ahead personalization. *Companion Proceedings of the Web Conference 2020*.

An Architecture for Accelerated Large-Scale Inference of Transformer-Based Language Models

Amir Ganiev* and **Colt Chapin** and **Anderson de Andrade** and **Chen Liu***
Wattpad
Toronto, ON, Canada
amir.ganiev@mail.utoronto.ca, {colt, anderson}@wattpad.com,
ceciliachen.liu@mail.utoronto.ca

Abstract

This work demonstrates the development process of a machine learning architecture for inference that can scale to a large volume of requests. In our experiments, we used a BERT model that was fine-tuned for emotion analysis, returning a probability distribution of emotions given a paragraph. The model was deployed as a gRPC service on Kubernetes. Apache Spark was used to perform inference in batches by calling the service. We encountered some performance and concurrency challenges and created solutions to achieve faster running time. Starting with 3.3 successful inference requests per second, we were able to achieve as high as 300 successful requests per second with the same batch job resource allocation. As a result, we successfully stored emotion probabilities for 95 million paragraphs within 96 hours.

1 Introduction

As data in organizations becomes more available for analysis, it is crucial to develop efficient machine learning pipelines. Previous work (Al-Jarrah et al., 2015) has highlighted the growing number of data centers and their energy and pollution repercussions. Machine learning models that require less computational resources to generate accurate results reduce these externalities. On the other hand, many machine learning applications also require results in nearly real-time in order to be viable and may also require results from as many data samples as possible in order to produce accurate insights. Hence, there are also opportunity costs associated with missed service-level objectives.

Attention-based language models such as BERT (Devlin et al., 2019) are often chosen for their relative efficiency, and empirical power. Compared to recurrent neural networks (Hochreiter and Schmidhuber, 1997), each step in a transformer layer (Vaswani et al., 2017) has direct access to all other steps and can be computed in parallel, which can make both training and inference faster. BERT also easily accommodates different applications by allowing the fine-tuning of its parameters on different tasks. Despite these benefits, exposing these models and communicating with them efficiently possesses some challenges.

Machine learning frameworks are often used to train, evaluate, and perform inference on predictive models. TensorFlow (Abadi et al., 2016) has been shown to be a reliable system that can operate at a large scale. A sub-component called TensorFlow Serving allows loading models as services that handle inference requests concurrently.

System architectures for inference have changed over time. Initial approaches favored offline settings where batch jobs make use of distributed platforms to load models and data within the same process and perform inference. For example, Ijari, 2017 suggested an architecture that uses Apache Hadoop (Hadoop, 2006) and Apache Pig for large-scale data processing, where results are written to a Hadoop Distributed File System (HDFS) for later consumption. Newer distributed platforms such as Apache Spark (Zaharia et al., 2016) have gained prominence because of their memory optimizations and more versatile APIs, compared to Apache Hadoop (Zaharia et al., 2012).

As part of this architecture, inference services would often be reserved for applications that require faster responses. The batch-based and service-based platforms have different use cases and often run in isolation. Collocating data and models in a batch job has some disadvantages. Loading models in the same process as the data forces them both to scale the same way. Moreover, models are forced to be implemented using the programming languages supported by the distributed data platform. Their APIs often place some limitations on what can be done.

With the evolution of machine learning frame-

*Work done while the author was working at Wattpad.

Proceedings of NAACL HLT 2021: IndustryTrack Papers, pages 163–169
June 6–11, 2021.

works and container-orchestration systems such as Kubernetes,[1] it is now simpler to efficiently build, deploy, and scale models as services. A scalable architecture was presented in (Gómez et al., 2014) that proposes the use of RESTful API calls executed by batch jobs in Hadoop to reach online services that provide real-time inference. Approaches like this simplify the architecture and address the issues discussed previously.

In this work, we present an architecture for batch inference where a data processing task relies on external services to perform the computation. The components of the architecture will be discussed in detail along with the technical challenges and solutions we developed to accelerate this process. Our application is a model for emotion analysis that produces a probability distribution over a closed set of emotions given a paragraph of text (Liu et al., 2019). We present benchmarks to justify our architecture decisions and settings. The proposed architecture is able to generate results for 95 million paragraphs within 96 hours.

2 Architecture design

We deployed our model as a TensorFlow service in a Kubernetes cluster. A sidecar service preprocessed and vectorized paragraphs and forwarded requests to this service. We used gRPC to communicate with the services,[2] which is an efficient communication protocol on HTTP/2. Both nearly real-time and offline use cases made calls to these services. We used Apache Spark for batch processing, which we ran on Amazon's AWS EMR service.[3] Our batch job was developed using Apache Spark's Python API (PySpark). The batch job fetched a dataset of relevant paragraphs, called the inference service, and stored the results. The job had two modes: a backfill mode and a daily mode, which ran on a subset of mutated and new paragraphs. This batch job was part of a data pipeline, scheduled using Apache AirFlow[4] and Luigi.[5] Figure 1 shows the main components of this architecture.

2.1 Kubernetes vs. Apache Spark

One of the key issues we faced in scaling up our inference services was the growing size of the memory footprint of an instance. A standard practice when conducting model inference at scale in a MapReduce program such as Apache Spark is to broadcast an instance of the model to each distributed worker process to allow for parallel processing. However, when the footprint of these instances becomes too large, they begin to compete with the dataset being processed for the limited memory resources of the underlying cluster and, in many cases, exceeding the capacity of the underlying hardware.

While this issue does not preclude the use of Apache Spark for running inferences on large models at scale, it does complicate the process of implementing the job in a cost-efficient manner. It is possible to allocate more resources, but because the clusters are static in size, a lot of work has to go into properly calculating resource allocation to avoid over or under-provisioning. This is where the idea of offloading the model to Kubernetes comes into play.

While our MapReduce clusters struggled to scale and accommodate the larger models being broadcasted, by leveraging Kubernetes we were able to monitor and optimize resource usage as well as define autoscaling behaviors independently of this cluster. That said, while there are clear benefits to isolating your model from your MapReduce job we must now consider the added overhead of the network calls and the effort to build and maintain containerized services.

2.2 Kubernetes node pool

To ensure optimal resource usage, we provisioned a segregated node pool dedicated to hosting instances of our models. A node pool is a collection of similar resources with predefined autoscaling behaviors. We leveraged Kubernetes' built-in taint/toleration functionality to establish the required behavior. In Kubernetes, *Taints* designate resources as non-viable for allocation, unless deployments are specifically annotated as having a *Toleration* for said *Taint*. For this node pool, we selected instance types that offer faster CPUs, but provide an adequate amount of memory to load our models.

2.3 REST vs. gRPC

Once we made the decision to deploy our model as a service, we had to determine which network protocol to use. While representational state transfer (REST) (Pautasso et al., 2013) is a well-known standard, there were two aspects of our use case

[1] `https://kubernetes.io`
[2] `https://grpc.github.io`
[3] `https://aws.amazon.com/emr`
[4] `https://airflow.apache.org`
[5] `https://github.com/spotify/luigi`

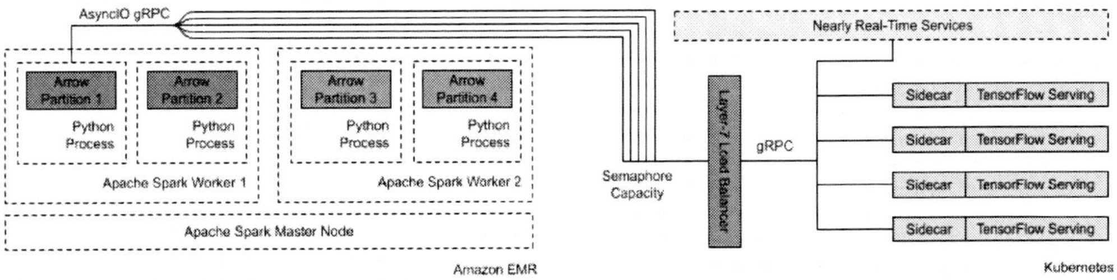

Figure 1: Architecture overview.

that made us consider alternatives. The first is that architecturally, our use case was far more functional in nature than REST. Second, the nature of our data means that request messages can be large. It was for this reason that we found the efficiency offered by the Protobuf protocol a natural fit for our use case.[6]

Having decided to use gRPC and Protobuf, we encountered two issues. First, gRPC uses the HTTP/2 protocol which multiplexes requests over a single persistent TCP connection. Because of this persistent connection, Layer-4 load balancers that can only route connections are not able to recognize requests within them that could be balanced across multiple replicas of a service. To enable this, we rely on a Layer-7 load balancer which is able to maintain persistent connections with all devices, and identify and route requests within these channels accordingly.

The second issue was organizational in nature. REST is a widely accepted standard, but more importantly, it is a protocol that developers are familiar with. The introduction of a different API design has led to significant friction of adoption.

2.4 AWS EMR cluster configuration

The AWS EMR cluster needed to be configured to run a Apache Spark job that makes 95 million inference calls to our micro-service. Due to the unbounded nature of these paragraphs, which can become quite large in our use case, these 95 million records require a significant amount of disk space (in the order of terabytes).

Taking into account the cost constraints of this project, we chose an AWS *r5.xlarge* instance with 200 GiB of disk space as a master node, and 5 AWS *r5.4xlarge* instances with 1,000 GiB of disk space each, as worker nodes. This configuration ensures that there is enough disk capacity to process the data and the number of cores is as high as possible without exceeding the cost constraints. Additionaly, we selected these to be memory-optimized to ensure we provide the job with enough RAM to efficiently process our joins.

The EMR cluster configuration is kept constant as a controlled variable throughout the project and in all of our experiments. This ensures that only the implementation changes affect the performance of the inference job.

2.5 Monitoring

There were two different solutions that monitor different aspects of the proposed architecture: Apache Spark console and DataDog. AWS EMR provided access to the Apache Spark console for its running tasks and a history server for completed tasks. The console displays the execution plan, the running stage, the number of partitions completed in that stage, the number of stages left to execute, as well as statistics and message logs of our inference job. Success or failure of this job and its pipeline was reported using DataDog.[7] DataDog is a cloud based monitoring service that provides helpful visualization tools to monitor applications.

Additionally, our services were instrumented to report the number, latency, and status code of all calls received. We made use of DataDog to aggregate and monitor these metrics. In our implementation, the instrumentation was handled by functional wrappers around our endpoint handlers, as well as a synchronous gRPC Interceptor for the client on our sidecar service. Figure 2 shows an example of our request count on our daily job.

[6] https://developers.google.com/protocol-buffers

[7] https://www.datadoghq.com

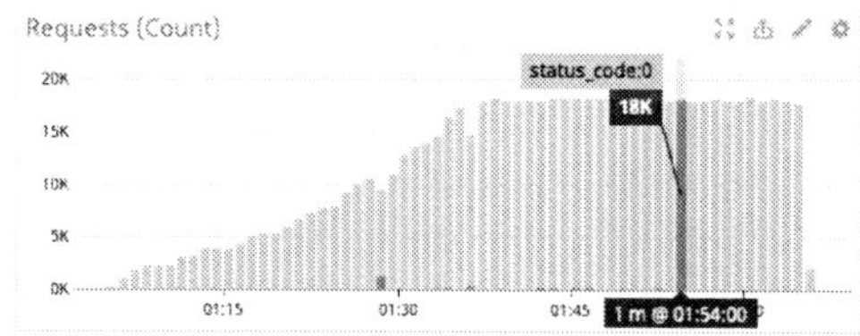

Figure 2: DataDog visualization of a daily job, consisting of 600,000 paragraphs calls to the service. The *X-axis* is the local time starting at 1 a.m. The *Y-axis* is the total number of calls executed within 1 minute. The highlighted vertical bar shows that 18,000 calls were executed within 1 minute (300 per second) at 1:54 a.m. The calls started at around 1 a.m. and reached a peak speed at around 1:40 a.m.

3 Architecture optimization

Our initial approach, which used the configuration in the previous section, was resilient to failures but performed slowly at around 4 requests per second during the inference step. With a backfill target of 95 million paragraphs, running this job was intractable. Our investigations concluded that the issues were rooted in a low request pressure on the backend services. Thus, the sections below describe the steps taken to address these issues and speed up the inference process.

3.1 Scaling model service

Our autoscaling group consisted of instances with Intel's Xeon Platinum 8175M CPUs and 64 GB of RAM. The use of GPUs is not cost-effective without a proper batching mechanism, which is considered to be outside of the scope of this work. Each instance had 8 physical cores and 16 logical cores. To reduce the memory footprint but also allow a fine-grained resource allocation, Kubernetes pods had a limit of 2 physical cores. In our experiments, pods did not consume more than 4 GB of memory under heavy load. Network utilization remained well under 10 Gb/s. We set up an autoscaling policy with a target CPU utilization of 70%.

With a maximum number of 100 pods (25 instances), we achieved a maximum of 300 requests per second, each request being a paragraph with at least 15 characters. Our daily job usually finished within 60 minutes.

3.2 Tuning TensorFlow Serving parameters

We evaluated the performance of TensorFlow Serving with multiple parameter configurations. The only settings that tangibly impacted performance included: enabling Intel's Math Kernel Library (MKL), the OpenMP number of threads for MKL, and the thread pool size for TensorFlow intra-operations. We used TensorFlow Serving version 2.3.0, which uses MKL-DNN version 0.21. Table 1 illustrates performance under different configurations for pods with 2 CPU physical cores and 4 logical cores. In particular, we note that disabling MKL and allocating a thread pool the size of the number of logical cores gave us the best performance for this model.

MKL	OpenMP	Intra-Op	Req/Sec
Yes	2	2	5.207
Yes	2	4	5.931
Yes	4	2	4.786
Yes	4	4	5.714
No	-	2	5.464
No	-	4	**6.452**

Table 1: Average requests per second of the service under different TensorFlow Serving settings: MKL, number of OpenMP threads, and number of intra-operation threads. OpenMP is only used by MKL. Other configurations do not match the number of physical or logical cores available.

3.3 Spark job tuning

Configuring parameters of TensorFlow serving and successfully scaling up BERT micro-service allowed for a faster inference speed. However, adjusting the service alone did not yield better results as the speed remained relatively similar (3.3 complete calls per second). Therefore, a PySpark job reached its limits in the proposed configuration. The micro-service was not receiving enough requests to trigger its autoscaling condition and capped out at 7 pods (far short of our max off 100). To address this, we sought to introduce more load by increasing the rate at which the client makes calls to the micro-service.

Using synchronous calls, the number of requests the batch job can make is bounded by the number of cores assigned to it. Since the computation is done by the service, these cores will be mostly waiting for the service responses.

To address Python's synchronous nature limiting the rate at which a single core can make calls to the service, we leveraged the AsyncIO library[8] within a PySpark User Defined Function (UDF),

[8] `https://www.python.org`

which allowed a single core to implement quasi-concurrent calls and leverage the idle thread awaiting a response. Since AsyncIO was utilized, the gRPC AsyncIO API[9] was imported instead of default gRPC. The async gRPC is compatible with AsyncIO and can create asynchronous channels. Exceptions or errors returned by the call were accessed with *grpc.aio.AioRpcError* method.

Even with everything above implemented within the PySpark UDF, it was not possible to take advantage of AsyncIO yet. By default, a vanilla PySpark UDF receives only one tabular row at a time containing one paragraph. That means that the AsyncIO loop within the UDF was not be able to execute concurrent calls if only one paragraph was available. Apache Spark's Vectorized UDFs (Pandas UDFs) allows us to process partitions in batches and achieve the desired level of concurrency. Each batch is represented in memory using the Apache Arrow format and accessible with the Pandas API.

Apache Arrow is an in-memory columnar data format that facilitates the transference of data between the JVM (Java virtual machine), which runs the Apache Spark job, and Python processes (i.e. Pandas UDFs). It offers zero-copy reads between processes for data access without serialization overhead. In our work, a scalar Pandas UDF was defined to receive paragraphs as a Pandas Series and return a probability distribution of the emotion classes for each paragraph, as a new Pandas Series.[10]

With Python AsyncIO, gRPC Async, and Pandas UDFs using Apache Arrow, the load created by the client (PySpark job) substantially increased. AsyncIO ensured that extra paragraphs were sent to the server while waiting to receive emotion probabilities for outstanding calls. However, as soon as the first one thousand calls were sent to the server (in a matter of seconds), the PySpark job failed. The errors received by the client were canceled, unavailable or the deadline was exceeded (more about gRPC errors in section 3.4). That indicated that the client actually created too much load on the server causing it to respond with errors. The Kubernetes Deployment was overwhelmed and did not have enough time to scale up the micro-service. This led to unavailable and deadline errors.

To limit the maximum number of concurrent calls to the service we utilized Semaphore. Semaphore is a class in the AsyncIO library[11] that implements an internal counter (set by user) to limit the number of concurrent requests as described by Dijkstra, 1968. Number of concurrent requests running in each core can never exceed the maximum Semaphore counter value.

Semaphore Value	Responses Per Second
10	170
25	256.7
50	298.3
75	Service upscaling fails

Table 2: Achieved number of successful gRPC calls per second vs Semaphore value. EMR configuration, table partitions, and paragraphs are kept constant.

To identify the maximum Semaphore value that successfully scales up the number of Kubernetes pods without errors, we conducted tests. Results of the experiments are shown in Table 2.

With the Semaphore value set to 50, PySpark ran successfully and significantly increased the load set by the client to the server. Table 3 summarizes all libraries and tools used to increase the number of calls per second.

3.4 Errors during gRPC calls

As gRPC async calls were made to the service, errors were returned. The most common gRPC response status code exceptions[12] encountered were: *cancelled*, *unavailable*, and *deadline exceeded*. We expected to receive errors when the service was scaling to process the received requests. When an error was received by a running PySpark client, the running job would terminate. Thus, we were unable to produce inference results without a solution that handles errors and keeps running the Spark job.

A Circuit Breaker (Nygard, 2018) was implemented to prevent clients from overwhelming services and a gRPC Interceptor was implemented to wait for services to be available and retry failing calls. Table 4 shows the total number of requests made and the number of errors that were handled by the circuit breaker.

[9] https://grpc.github.io/grpc/python/grpc_asyncio.html

[10] https://spark.apache.org/docs/latest/api/python/user_guide/arrow_pandas.html

[11] https://docs.python.org/3/library

[12] https://grpc.github.io/grpc/core/md_doc_statuscodes.html

Tool	Definition	Description
Async IO	Python Library	Write concurrent requests with coroutines
gRPC AsyncIO	Python Library	GRPC client that works asynchronously
PyArrow with Pandas	Data Format and Python Library	PySpark's tabular data format to pass to UDF as a Pandas table
Semaphore	Class in Async IO	Limits number of running requests
Async Circuit Breaker	Asynchronous Design Pattern	Resends client calls on failure

Table 3: All libraries, design patterns, and data formats imported to PySpark job to accelerate inference speed.

Code	Status	Notes	Amount
0	OK	Returned on success	97.84M
1	CANCELLED	The operation was cancelled, typically by the caller	666
4	DEADLINE_EXCEEDED	The time expired before the operation was complete	469.58K
14	UNAVAILABLE	The service is currently unavailable	27.90K

Table 4: Number of status codes returned in gRPC responses for the entire batch job.

3.5 Asynchronous circuit breaker

A circuit breaker is a software design pattern that was implemented to detect and act upon response failures received by the PySpark client. As discussed in Nygard, 2018, in a closed state the circuit passes through and all gRPC calls are being made. If a number of consecutive failures are received, the circuit opens and subsequent request attempts return a failure immediately. After a time period, the circuit switches to a half-open state to test if the underlying problem still exists. If a call fails in this half-open state, the breaker is once again tripped. When a call finally succeeds, the circuit breaker resets back to the default closed state.

The circuit breaker implementation was taken from an open-source library.[13] Modifications were made to support AsyncIO, so calls running through it are sent concurrently. The state of the circuit breaker is shared across requests that use the the same gRPC client. To open or close the circuit, the circuit breaker only considers the deadline exceeded, unavailable, and cancelled gRPC status codes. Other errors are directly returned to the client.

Finally, a gRPC Interceptor uses this circuit breaker to block requests until the circuit breaker is closed again and retry each request up to 4 times, after which the data point is skipped and the batch job continues. The interceptor gets attached to the gRPC channel on creation. This design pattern allows clients to not overwhelm services with requests and halts our batch job as the service deployment scales up.

4 Results

All steps in Section 3 improve the batch job speed and results in satisfactory performance. The data pipeline is able to produce inference results for more than 95 million paragraphs in around 96 hours with an inference speed of around 300 requests per second. The semaphore value is set to 50.

4.1 Daily runs of the batch job

Once the backfill data is stored, the data pipeline runs daily to find new and updated paragraphs from our S3 datasets. Everyday, around 600,000 (varies daily) paragraphs need to have their inference values stored. The graph in Figure 2 illustrates the typical daily run for the pipeline. It shows that it takes about 40 minutes for the Kubernetes micro-service pods to fully scale up. We limited the maximum number of pods for daily jobs to 100.

4.2 Analytics platform

Inference results were stored in an AWS S3 bucket. This dataset was registered in a AWS Glue Data Catalog.[14] Amazon Athena[15] is a query service that made it possible to run SQL queries on this dataset. Redash[16] is a cloud-based analytics dashboard that we used to visualize insights from the inference

[13] `https://github.com/fabfuel/circuitbreaker`

[14] `https://aws.amazon.com/glue`

[15] `https://aws.amazon.com/athena`

[16] `https://redash.io`

results. In includes a SQL client that makes calls to Amazon Athena and displays the query results. Redash was connected to Amazon Athena as a data source, which enabled us to perform queries to all tables registered in AWS Glue.

5 Conclusion

This paper discussed a successful machine learning architecture for both online and offline inference that centralizes models as services. We present solutions that use concurrency to increase the inference speed of offline batch jobs in Apache Spark. Because of this, the majority of resources are still assigned to these services, and the batch job resources grow at a much smaller rate in comparison.

We used a resource-intensive language model for emotion classification, where we demonstrated how proper tuning of TensorFlow Serving and Kubernetes can improve the service's performance. We also showed that by parallelizing the calls made to the service in PySpark, we can significantly improve inference speed.

Finally, results were presented that provide useful insights into the inference performance. Together, all these components resulted in a satisfactory architecture, which resulted in the emotion probabilities of 95 million paragraphs to be stored within 96 hours. We hope the architecture can be applied to other language tasks or machine learning models.

References

Martín Abadi, Paul Barham, Jianmin Chen, Zhifeng Chen, Andy Davis, Jeffrey Dean, Matthieu Devin, Sanjay Ghemawat, Geoffrey Irving, Michael Isard, Manjunath Kudlur, Josh Levenberg, Rajat Monga, Sherry Moore, Derek G. Murray, Benoit Steiner, Paul Tucker, Vijay Vasudevan, Pete Warden, Martin Wicke, Yuan Yu, and Xiaoqiang Zheng. 2016. Tensorflow: A system for large-scale machine learning. In *12th USENIX Symposium on Operating Systems Design and Implementation (OSDI 16)*, pages 265–283, Savannah, GA. USENIX Association.

Omar Y. Al-Jarrah, Paul D. Yoo, Sami Muhaidat, George K. Karagiannidis, and Kamal Taha. 2015. Efficient machine learning for big data: A review. *Big Data Research*, 2(3):87–93.

J. Devlin, Ming-Wei Chang, Kenton Lee, and Kristina Toutanova. 2019. Bert: Pre-training of deep bidirectional transformers for language understanding. In *NAACL-HLT*.

Edsger W Dijkstra. 1968. Cooperating sequential processes. In *The origin of concurrent programming*, pages 65–138. Springer.

A. Gómez, Esperanza Albacete, Y. Sáez, and P. I. Viñuela. 2014. A scalable machine learning online service for big data real-time analysis. *2014 IEEE Symposium on Computational Intelligence in Big Data (CIBD)*, pages 1–8.

Apache Hadoop. 2006. Apache hadoop. *http://hadoop.apache.org*.

Sepp Hochreiter and Jürgen Schmidhuber. 1997. Long short-term memory. *Neural computation*, 9(8):1735–1780.

Abhish Ijari. 2017. The study of the large scale twitter on machine learning. *International Research Journal of Engineering and Technology (IRJET)*, 4:247–251.

Chen Liu, Muhammad Osama, and Anderson De Andrade. 2019. Dens: a dataset for multi-class emotion analysis. *Proceedings of the EMNLP Conference*.

Michael T Nygard. 2018. *Release it!: design and deploy production-ready software*. Pragmatic Bookshelf.

Cesare Pautasso, Erik Wilde, and Rosa Alarcon. 2013. *REST: advanced research topics and practical applications*. Springer.

Ashish Vaswani, Noam Shazeer, Niki Parmar, Jakob Uszkoreit, Llion Jones, Aidan N Gomez, Lukasz Kaiser, and Illia Polosukhin. 2017. Attention is all you need. *arXiv preprint arXiv:1706.03762*.

Matei Zaharia, Mosharaf Chowdhury, Tathagata Das, Ankur Dave, Justin Ma, Murphy Mccauley, M Franklin, Scott Shenker, and Ion Stoica. 2012. Fast and interactive analytics over hadoop data with spark. *Usenix Login*, 37(4):45–51.

Matei Zaharia, Reynold S Xin, Patrick Wendell, Tathagata Das, Michael Armbrust, Ankur Dave, Xiangrui Meng, Josh Rosen, Shivaram Venkataraman, Michael J Franklin, et al. 2016. Apache spark: a unified engine for big data processing. *Communications of the ACM*, 59(11):56–65.

When and Why does a Model Fail? A Human-in-the-loop Error Detection Framework for Sentiment Analysis

Zhe Liu
IBM Research - Almaden
San Jose, CA, USA
liuzh@us.ibm.com

Yufan Guo *
Amazon Alexa AI
Seattle, WA, USA
gyufan@amazon.com

Jalal Mahmud
IBM Research - Almaden
San Jose, CA, USA
jumahmud@us.ibm.com

Abstract

Although deep neural networks have been widely employed and proven effective in sentiment analysis tasks, it remains challenging for model developers to assess their models for erroneous predictions that might exist prior to deployment. Once deployed, emergent errors can be hard to identify in prediction run-time and impossible to trace back to their sources. To address such gaps, in this paper we propose an error detection framework for sentiment analysis based on explainable features. We perform global-level feature validation with human-in-the-loop assessment, followed by an integration of global and local-level feature contribution analysis. Experimental results show that, given limited human-in-the-loop intervention, our method is able to identify erroneous model predictions on unseen data with high precision.

1 Introduction

Deep learning approaches, especially neural network-based ones, have been widely employed and proven effective in sentiment analysis tasks (Rosenthal et al., 2017; Nakov et al., 2016). These performance improvements, however, have come at the cost of model transparency and accountability (Inkpen et al., 2019). Many times, deep models are being used as black-box tools by users, even without knowing the model's peculiarities as well as limitations (Mojsilovic, 2018). In that sense, users can be easily exposed to impropriety or error predictions made in run time, and thus lose trust towards the sentiment classification system.

Traditional evaluation metrics, such as accuracy and F1-score, can explain the predictive performance of a sentiment model. However, their explanations are from an overall and reactive perspective, as they fail to provide insights into the details on when and why the sentiment models fail in run-time (Nushi et al., 2018). Manual error analysis or heuristics-based error analysis are also common methods for error identification, however, both of them requires either human intervention or domain knowledge, either in the form of labeled data (Stymne, 2011) or declarative information (e.g., heuristics or knowledge bases) (Bassil and Alwani, 2012). However, labeling instances can be time and effort consuming, and pre-defined knowledge applicable to a specific model is difficult to get. To address this concern, researchers and practitioners have recently raised the need for developing more proactive error detection mechanisms to increase the accountability of the sentiment classification systems while in use. Such accountability mechanisms should be able to identify and measure prediction errors as well as to provide prompt notifications and rectification to the users (Crawford et al., 2016).

With this challenge in mind, we introduce in this study an explainable error detection framework with human-in-the-loop for sentiment analysis task. Specifically, as shown in Figure 1, given a pre-trained black-box sentiment model, the error-detection framework first analyzes local feature contributions through a data perturbation process. Next, the local feature contributions are aggregated for global-level feature contributions. Later, humans are brought into the loop to assess the relevance of the top ranked global features to the target sentiment classes, and report errors if any. An erroneous score is calculated based on both global and local features. Instances exhibiting erroneous scores above a specific threshold are flagged as problematic predictions. We demonstrate the error detection framework on two sentiment test datasets. From experimental results, we notice high error detection precision of the proposed framework.

Our contributions are fourfold: First, we present a high precision error detection framework for sen-

* YG was affiliated with IBM Research - Almaden at the time of the work reported in this paper.

Proceedings of NAACL HLT 2021: IndustryTrack Papers, pages 170–177
June 6–11, 2021. ©2021 Association for Computational Linguistics

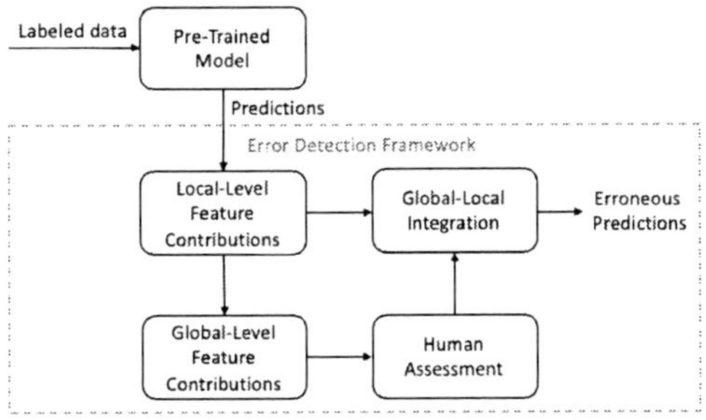

Figure 1: Overview of the explainable error detection framework.

timent analysis task, which can proactively notify users with prediction errors in run-time. Second, the proposed framework calculates the likelihood of concerns on model correctness in even unseen cases. Third, erroneous predictions are identified based on explainable features which allow the users to easily understand why a prediction fails. Fourth, the proposed error detection framework requires little human effort in error detection by labeling on the global feature level, rather than local instance level.

2 Related Work

Error analysis and detection is important to building accountable AI models, as they allow individuals to understand when and how predictions fail (Nushi et al., 2018). The most intuitive error analysis method is to evaluate the algorithms on a broad set of performance metrics, such as, sensitivity and specifity analysis (Harper et al., 2009). But their explanations are from an overall and reactive perspective, as they fail to provide insights on each specific instance level on unseen data. Manual error analysis is another common approach, whereas it requires significant human efforts and time, and is not easy to scale. By taking prior knowledge, such as semantic context, into consideration, heuristic-based method brings context-based errors into practice (Bassil and Alwani, 2012). Comparing to the manual error analysis, heuristic-based method requires no human intervention. However, predefined heuristics applicable to a specific model is difficult to get. Uncertainty sampling (Settles, 2012) based on a model's confidence scores to identify and label potential prediction errors. Although no human effort is needed in this approach, its performance is not always reliable. In addition, a series of methods have recently been introduced to identify model errors in a human-machine interactive manner (Fiebrink et al., 2011; Chen et al., 2018; Nushi et al., 2018). By adding humans into the model evaluation step (Fails and Olsen Jr, 2003), the proposed methods allowed the users to improve the model performance iteratively, by identifying model errors, providing new training data rewardingly, and retraining the model. Common limitations of these human-in-the-loop based methods are that, they require human labeling on the instance level, which can be labor-intensive, and can not be easily generalized to unseen data.

3 Methods

In this section, we present our framework to detect errors in sentiment predictions with human-in-the-loop in detail. Given a blackbox sentiment model and a set of unseen test data, the proposed method runs over the following four steps: 1) "local-level feature contributions" module quantifies the feature contributions to the prediction of each individual target instance. 2) "global-level feature contributions" module characterizes the general effect of a feature to the overall prediction across all instances. 3) "human assessment" module brings human into the loop of error detection by allowing them to manually label on an interpretable feature-level, instead of instance-level, to save the labeling efforts. 4) "global-local integration" module quantifies the erroneous probabilities of instance-level predictions made by the model. With the erroneous probabilities, the framework can send users with failure alerts in prediction run-time on unseen sentiment data.

3.1 Local-Level Explainable Feature Contributions

Local-level feature explanations refers to the interpretations used to justify why the model made a specific decision for a single instance. Many existing approaches (Lundberg and Lee, 2017; Lakkaraju et al., 2017) can be adopted for local interpretations. Among the many existing explanation-generating methods, we adopted LIME (Ribeiro et al., 2016) as an example way for achieving local-level feature importance in the proposed framework. LIME relies on random perturbation to artificially generate datasets around an instance and then using the generated dataset to train local linear interpretable models for single instance level explanations.

In the case of sentiment analysis, we chose unigrams as the explainable feature for LIME, as it is the smallest unit of a text snippet carrying sufficient information that can be reasonably interpreted by human. We implemented linear regression as the base model in LIME and applied it on our dataset, and ranked the explainable features based on their derived coefficients. An example of the local-level feature contributions produced by LIME in our case is presented in Figure 2, where the pre-trained model's prediction for sentence "Panera gives me diarrhea." in 2(a) is "positive". The unigram feature "panera" contributes positively to the positive prediction with a magnitude of 0.576, whereas "diarrhea" contributes negatively to the positive prediction with a magnitude of 0.159. By observing the local-level feature contributions, we can tell that the model makes a prediction error by considering the word "panera" as a significant indicator of the positive polarity, and thus led the model to assign a positive label to the negative sentence.

Panera gives me diarrhea. Positive

Feature	Contribution
panera	0.576
diarrhea	-0.159
gives	0.046

2(a)

Panera is good. Positive

Feature	Contribution
panera	0.153
good	0.152

2(b)

Figure 2: Example of LIME generated local-level feature contributions.

3.2 Global-Level Explainable Feature Contributions

Global-level explainable feature contribution demonstrates how each explainable feature affects the model's prediction with regard to the whole training samples, instead of individual instance level predictions (Molnar, 2019). Achieving global-level feature contributions (Molnar, 2019; Letham et al., 2015; Arguello et al., 2009) can help extract more distilled knowledge for less human efforts and can thus facilitates user's understanding of the whole prediction logic behind the model. In the proposed framework, we ran the perturbation-based analysis first on the local-level for all training samples (although it could be on testing as well (Molnar, 2019)) by masking individual feature j, one at a time, from each data instance d_i, $i \in \{0, 1, \ldots, N\}$, which contains feature j. We then calculated the absolute changes in the model's prediction probabilities associated with each class label $k \in \{0, 1, \ldots, K\}$ as:

$$P_{i,k}^{-j} = |P(y = k|d_i^{-j}) - P(y = k|d_i)|$$

where $P(y = k|d_i)$ is the pre-trained model's prediction probability with feature j, and $P(y = k|d_i^{-j})$ is the probability without j. We denoted the $P_{i,k}^{-j}$ as feature j's local importance associated with class k to data instance d_i. With all N instances containing feature j, we finally aggregated the local level importance of j to all d_i to a global level as:

$$k^* = \arg\max_k \frac{1}{N} \sum_{i=1}^{N} P_{i,k}^{-j}$$

and denoted class label k^* with the maximum average probability change as the direction of feature j's contribution, and the associated P_k^{-j} as its contribution magnitude, where:

$$P_k^{-j} = \frac{1}{N} \sum_{i=1}^{N} P_{k^*}^{-j}$$

The global importance measurement can be viewed as an aggregation of the local contributions. The underlying assumption behind this method is that a feature is important, if removing it can change the prediction probability significantly. Using the unigram feature "underwhelming" as an example, Figure 3 shows how the corresponding feature magnitude and direction are achieved by using the proposed method. Features were ranked in descending order according to their derived global contribution magnitudes. This would allow us next to show the more important features earlier to the human assessors, so as to help them identify the most significant errors in the shortest time.

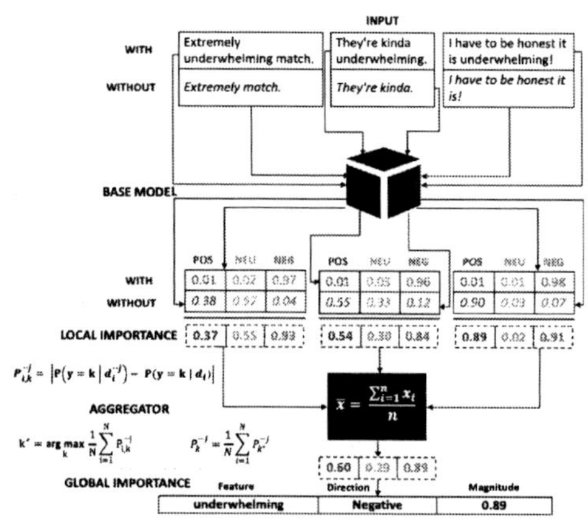

Figure 3: Perturbation-based method for achieving global feature contributions.

3.3 Human-in-the-loop Assessment on Global Errors

The human-in-the-loop assessment module requires human assessors to screen the top N globally contributing features learnt from the previous step with regard to their predicted sentiment labels. Compared with labeling on an instance basis, feature level annotation could be a lot more efficient. Although the top contributing features are not necessarily error-prone, they are more likely to affect the model's overall performance and allow us to zoom into erroneous model predictions in a more efficient manner.

In the proposed algorithm, we asked the human assessors to label on an unigram basis, given the following considerations: First, labeling on unigrams may lead to more generalized outputs as compared to labeling on bigrams/trigrams. Assuming that the same number of erroneous features were identified by the human assessors on both the unigram and the bigram/trigram levels, more potentially erroneous instances containing the identified unigrams could be found as compared to instances containing the identified bigrams/trigrams, as they are often too sparse or too content specific. Second, labeling on unigrams may be less time and effort intensive, as unigrams tend to be more interpretable to human assessors. If we choose any adjacent words as our bigrams/trigrams, under many circumstances we would not get meaningful phrases, on which labeling could be difficult. Third, existing work on constructing polarity lexicons with manual annotation decisions (Mohammad and Turney, 2013; Rouces et al., 2018) were successfully performed on the unigram basis.

To be more specific, in this step, human assessors were asked to rate the correctness of the globally learnt contribution directions (positive, negative or neutral) of the top N unigrams. Given that the top contributing unigrams were not context-specific or sense-disambiguated, we followed the same heuristic as in Rouces et al. (2018) by showing only the definition of the first sense in WordNet (Miller, 1995) to the assessors for annotation purpose, as the first sense is by design the most common meaning of a word. For unigrams that can not be found in WordNet, we showed the top definition from Urban Dictionary [1] instead. An example annotation task would be: for unigram feature "panera", we first displayed the word itself to the assessor, followed by its first definition in Urban Dictionary, and its contribution direction of being "positive" as learnt from the global feature contribution step. We then asked the assessors to rate their agreement on "panera" with the definition "A clean, upscale chain of restaurants primarily located on the eastern coast of America" as of "positive" polarity on a 5-points Likert scale (1: Strongly Disagree, 2: Agree, 3: Neutral, 4: Disagree, 5: Strongly Disagree). As acquiring assessment from experts would be expensive, assessment can be done in a crowd-sourced manner.

[1] https://www.urbandictionary.com

3.4 Global-Local Integration

The erroneous features recognized on the global level could indeed help identify problematic predictions on the unlabeled instances. However, flagging error occurrence on individual instance level only based on these problematic features may also be unreliable. As shown in Figure 2, noticing "panera" being incorrectly learned as "positive" could help us accurately identify the wrong prediction of sentence 2(a). However, its erroneous impact on sentence 2(b) is disguised by the existence of the other positive feature "good", which were actually learned correctly on the global level.

To more accurately identify the problematic predictions on unlabeled instances, in this step we proposed a measurement metric called the local erroneous score e, to determine the relative impact of the global erroneous features on the local level. e was calculated as a normalized version of the accumulated error contributions induced by the globally identified problematic features:

$$e = \frac{\sum_{i=1}^{m} c_j^*}{\sum_{i=1}^{n} c_i^+}$$

where $c_j^* \in [-1, 1]$ represents the local contribution of the erroneous feature j on the specific instance, and m indicates the total number of erroneous features identified from the global perspective. $c_i^+ \in (0, 1]$ represents the local contribution of the feature i, whose contribution direction is the same as the final prediction. n specifies the total number of positively contributed features. The local erroneous score e has the value between $-\infty$ to 1. By applying the proposed equation on the two examples as shown in Figure 2, we can see that sentence 2(a) derived a much higher local erroneous score of 0.926, than sentence 2(b) of score 0.502. This demonstrated the effectiveness of the proposed measurement in terms of error detection. A pre-defined threshold τ is set by the user, and only instances with $e > \tau$ would be retrieved as problematic predictions.

4 Experiment Settings

To test our error detection framework, we first create a three-class sentiment classifier, and later treat it as a black-box "pre-trained" model for error detection. We implemented the classifier using a replication of the multichannel CNN model introduced by Kim (2014), although any algorithm can be applied here as the black-box pre-trained model. The training data contains 2,265,413 positive, 2,704,587 negative, and 2,297,426 neutral cases. They were collected from various sources, ranging from high-quality human-labeled instances to pseudo-labeled instances annotated using emoji or hashtag based indicators (Novak et al., 2015). We evaluated the model on the test dataset of SemEval2016 Task 4 Subtask A (Nakov et al., 2016). Our model achieved a F_1^{PN} of 0.345, and a three-class prediction accuracy of 0.463, which is comparable to many of the SemEval2016 participation systems.

We calculated the local and global feature contributions using the training dataset and performed the human-in-the-loop assessment on Figure Eight [2]. We extracted the top 2,000 non-neutral features with the highest global contribution magnitudes to human assessors to determine their global correctness. We chose only non-neutral features for error assessment as polarity errors, such as predicting positive as negative or vice versa, can greatly impact user's trust towards the model, and we want to focus more on such extreme cases for error detection. 5 unigrams were shown in 1 annotation page and gold questions (easy questions with known answers, e.g. "happy" with the definition "enjoying or showing or marked by joy or pleasure" as "positive" polarity) were embedded on each page for quality check. For each unigram feature, we recruited in total 5 assessors who had to be native English speakers, with the highest level of experience. For all 2,000 unigram features, we collected in total 10,155 judgements within 1 hour. Among them only 155 (1.5%) were from untrusted assessors, who have been excluded during the annotation process. This indicated the relative easiness of feature labeling for sentiment task for even non-expert assessors. We obtained the annotations for 1,725 out of the 2,000 assessed unigrams and converted them into binary cases (agree or disagree, 86.25% inter-rater agreement), where at least 3 assessors agree on the same answer. Among them 161 were found to be wrongly learned by the pre-trained black-box model. Global-level features include "kashmir", "midterm", "dems", "netflix" was being wrongly predicted by the model as "negative", whereas "wingstop", "panera", "minister", "popeyes" as "positive". All 161 global-level problematic features would then be passed to the next step to guide the instance-level error identification.

To assess the method's effectiveness, we applied the proposed error detection framework first on the test dataset of SemEval2016 Task 4 Subtask A. We found 932 instances containing at least one of the globally identified problematic features. Thus, we only calculated the local erroneous score e for the 932 cases. Given that the SemEval dataset only covers a subset (60/161) of the erroneous unigrams, we prepared another dataset customized just for better understanding of the precision of the proposed framework. Specifically, we adopted the 161 problematic unigrams as search keywords to collect tweets using Twitter Search API. For each keyword we collected up to 50 most recent tweets. We cleaned the collected dataset by removing duplicate tweets and tweets with URL, assuming that they have a higher probability of being spam. In total, we collected 3,111 instances in this customized Twitter testing dataset.

For both datasets, we extracted all instances with $e > \tau$. For the self-collected Twitter data, we acquired the ground truth labels from the crowd on Figure Eight. We reported the precision of the proposed method at different settings of the threshold τ, to understand its impacts on the framework's performance.

We adopted uncertainty sampling as the baseline to evaluate the performance of the proposed error detection framework. We adopted the least confidence as the measurement in this experiment, which is based on the difference between the most confident prediction and 100% confidence. In other words, for a three-class classification task, the model is most unconfident when having the maximum prediction probability around 0.33. We applied uncertainty sampling just on the complete SemEval test data, assuming no filtering at all was applied on the original dataset. We extracted in-

[2]https://www.figure-eight.com/

stances with the lowest prediction confidence as under-trained cases and compared the precision@K for both the baseline method and the proposed method.

5 Results

In Figure 4, we plotted the error detection precision for the proposed method on both datasets, along with varied thresholds of τ ranging from 0 to 0.4. We set the upper bound τ to 0.4 instead of 1, since only very limited number of instances (sizes with no or little statistical meaning) were detected for the SemEval dataset when $\tau \geq 0.5$.

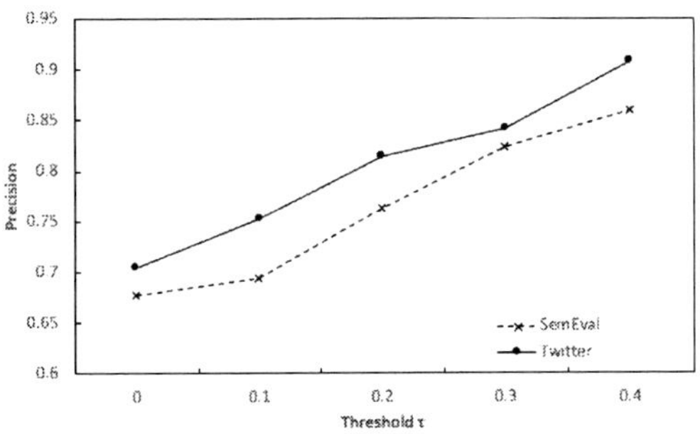

Figure 4: Precision for the error detection framework with varied threshold settings.

As can be seen from Figure 5, even when the threshold τ was set to a low score of 0, the proposed error detection framework can still achieve relatively high precision scores for both datasets. Specifically, for the SemEval dataset, with $\tau = 0$, the proposed framework indicated 48.9% of all prediction instances as erroneous predictions. Among these flagged instances, 67.7% were proved to be truly problematic according to the ground truth labels. The same pattern was also noticed for the self-collected Twitter dataset, when $\tau = 0$, the proposed method detected in total 57.9% suspicious predictions, and 70.5% of them were proved to be truly problematic. Looking further, we observed that the error detection framework became even more precise, as we incrementally increased the value of τ. It reached the highest precision of 85.9% for the SemEval and 90.8% for the Twitter dataset when $\tau = 0.4$. But obviously these increases in precision were achieved with a trade-off of the degradation in the number of detected problematic predictions.

Considering our ultimate goal of altering users of potential prediction errors, we next compared the proposed error detection framework with uncertainty sampling based on precision@K. Precision@K is a widely adopted evaluation metric in information retrieval tasks. It is being defined here as the proportion of identified erroneous cases that are real errors in the top K retrieved results. We chose K ranging from 100 to 400, as only 455 predictions are being identified as problematic with $\tau \geq 0$. Table 1 shows the precision@K for both uncertainty sampling and the proposed approach.

K	*Uncertainty*	*Human-in-the-loop*
100	0.710	0.820
200	0.685	0.805
300	0.686	0.750
400	0.692	0.698

Table 1: Precision@K for uncertainty sampling and the proposed error detection method with human-in-the-loop.

As can be noticed in Table 1, when alerting the users with the top 100 identified error predictions, the proposed error detection method with human-in-the-loop showed significant performance advantage over uncertainty sampling with a 0.110 precision gap. Such advantages gradually decreased as K became larger (more relaxed τ). When $K = 400$, the prediction probability threshold for uncertainty sampling equaled to 0.393, and the precision gap between the two methods decreased to 0.006.

In addition to precision, we were also interested in knowing if the proposed method was able to catch errors that can not be detected by the uncertainty sampling baseline. To achieve this goal, we plotted in Figure 5 the distribution of the prediction probabilities of the erroneous cases identified by the proposed framework when $\tau = 0.4$. From Figure 5, we found that about 40% of the erroneous instances detected by the proposed method were associated with prediction probabilities of larger than 0.7. In other words, this means that the model is quite confident about those predictions and uncertainty sampling would hardly treat them as potential errors. In that sense, we conclude that the proposed framework is able to detect errors even when the prediction confidence is high.

6 Discussion and Conclusion

Our work was motivated by the practical concerns of not knowing the limitations or potential errors of a sentiment model prior to deployment, and not being able to notify or even rectify when erroneous predictions were made once deployed. Driven by

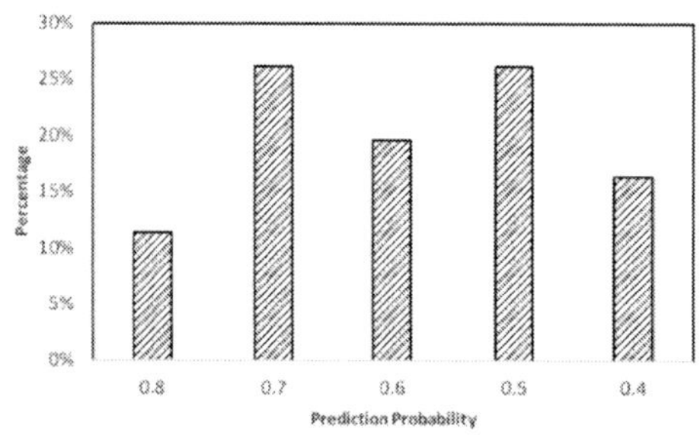

Figure 5: Uncertainty probability distribution for erroneous cases when $\tau = 0.4$.

this demand, in this paper, we presented a framework for identifying prediction errors in an interpretable manner for sentiment analysis tasks. We validated the proposed error detection framework on two different datasets. Results showed that the proposed method can identify problematic model predictions with high precision, which is critical to continuous model refinement. While comparing the proposed approach with the baseline, we noticed that our method can also be adopted as a selective sampling approach, in addition to uncertainty sampling. Besides, given that the proposed error detection framework can be applied on unseen data without ground truth, it can proactively notify users about possible erroneous decisions made by the model in prediction run-time.

In addition to its effectiveness, the proposed error detection framework can also be easily explained to the users. Globally, the proposed framework allows the users to understand the overall contribution of a word to the final predictions made by the black-box sentiment model. Besides, as demonstrated in our results, global-level contributions can also be useful for identifying potential bias existed in the model. For instance, we noticed that "netflix", "dems", and "palestine" were being learned as "negative" in our pre-trained sentiment model. While integrating global-level problematic features with local-level predictions, the proposed erroneous score enables users to know why that specific prediction could be wrong or biased and how much the problematic global feature contributed to the erroneous or biased prediction. Certainly, more work is needed on how the proposed framework can be generalized to the task of bias detection.

Furthermore, the proposed framework efficiently integrated human into the loop of model validation and refinement. Comparing with the previous methods, our approach allows the human annotators to label on the explainable feature level, rather than on the instance level, which can significantly save their time and effort. Regarding the annotation quality of the feature level labeling, our results showed that even non-expert crowd workers can accurately finish the assessment tasks with high inter-rater agreement in a very short period of time.

Finally, our work comes with certain limitations. One of them is the relatively small number of global features (2,000) that were labeled by the human assessors in this work. To some extent, this limited us from evaluating the presented error detection framework from more angels other than precision, although precision is the most important measurement for error detection. Annotations on larger scales will be conducted in later studies and the effectiveness of the proposed framework will be evaluated from more angels. Besides, future works will also be conducted on investigating how these identified erroneous instances or features could be used for further fixing or debugging the pre-trained models.

References

Jaime Arguello, Jamie Callan, and Fernando Diaz. 2009. Classification-based resource selection. In *Proceedings of the 18th ACM conference on Information and knowledge management*, pages 1277–1286. ACM.

Youssef Bassil and Mohammad Alwani. 2012. Ocr post-processing error correction algorithm using google online spelling suggestion. *arXiv preprint arXiv:1204.0191*.

Nan-Chen Chen, Jina Suh, Johan Verwey, Gonzalo Ramos, Steven Drucker, and Patrice Simard. 2018. Anchorviz: Facilitating classifier error discovery through interactive semantic data exploration. In *23rd International Conference on Intelligent User Interfaces*, pages 269–280. ACM.

Kate Crawford, Meredith Whittaker, Madeleine Clare Elish, Solon Barocas, Aaron Plasek, and Kadija Ferryman. 2016. The ai now report: The social and economic implications of artificial intelligence technologies in the near-term. In *AI Now public symposium, hosted by the White House and New York University's Information Law Institute, July 7th*.

Jerry Alan Fails and Dan R Olsen Jr. 2003. Interactive machine learning. In *Proceedings of the 8th international conference on Intelligent user interfaces*, pages 39–45. ACM.

Rebecca Fiebrink, Perry R Cook, and Dan Trueman. 2011. Human model evaluation in interactive supervised learning. In *Proceedings of the SIGCHI Con-*

ference on Human Factors in Computing Systems, pages 147–156. ACM.

F Maxwell Harper, Daniel Moy, and Joseph A Konstan. 2009. Facts or friends?: distinguishing informational and conversational questions in social q&a sites. In *Proceedings of the sigchi conference on human factors in computing systems*, pages 759–768. ACM.

Kori Inkpen, Stevie Chancellor, Munmun De Choudhury, Michael Veale, and Eric PS Baumer. 2019. Where is the human?: Bridging the gap between ai and hci. In *Extended Abstracts of the 2019 CHI Conference on Human Factors in Computing Systems*, page W09. ACM.

Yoon Kim. 2014. Convolutional neural networks for sentence classification. *arXiv preprint arXiv:1408.5882*.

Himabindu Lakkaraju, Ece Kamar, Rich Caruana, and Jure Leskovec. 2017. Interpretable & explorable approximations of black box models. *arXiv preprint arXiv:1707.01154*.

Benjamin Letham, Cynthia Rudin, Tyler H McCormick, David Madigan, et al. 2015. Interpretable classifiers using rules and bayesian analysis: Building a better stroke prediction model. *The Annals of Applied Statistics*, 9(3):1350–1371.

Scott M Lundberg and Su-In Lee. 2017. A unified approach to interpreting model predictions. In *Advances in Neural Information Processing Systems*, pages 4765–4774.

George A Miller. 1995. Wordnet: a lexical database for english. *Communications of the ACM*, 38(11):39–41.

Saif M Mohammad and Peter D Turney. 2013. Crowdsourcing a word–emotion association lexicon. *Computational Intelligence*, 29(3):436–465.

Aleksandra Mojsilovic. 2018. Factsheets for ai services. Retrieved August 22, 2019 from `https://www.ibm.com/blogs/research/2018/08/factsheets-ai/`.

Christoph Molnar. 2019. *Interpretable Machine Learning*. `https://christophm.github.io/interpretable-ml-book/`.

Preslav Nakov, Alan Ritter, Sara Rosenthal, Fabrizio Sebastiani, and Veselin Stoyanov. 2016. Semeval-2016 task 4: Sentiment analysis in twitter. In *Proceedings of the 10th international workshop on semantic evaluation (semeval-2016)*, pages 1–18.

Petra Kralj Novak, Jasmina Smailović, Borut Sluban, and Igor Mozetič. 2015. Sentiment of emojis. *PloS one*, 10(12):e0144296.

Besmira Nushi, Ece Kamar, and Eric Horvitz. 2018. Towards accountable ai: Hybrid human-machine analyses for characterizing system failure. In *Sixth AAAI Conference on Human Computation and Crowdsourcing*.

Marco Tulio Ribeiro, Sameer Singh, and Carlos Guestrin. 2016. Why should i trust you?: Explaining the predictions of any classifier. In *Proceedings of the 22nd ACM SIGKDD international conference on knowledge discovery and data mining*, pages 1135–1144. ACM.

Sara Rosenthal, Noura Farra, and Preslav Nakov. 2017. Semeval-2017 task 4: Sentiment analysis in twitter. In *Proceedings of the 11th international workshop on semantic evaluation (SemEval-2017)*, pages 502–518.

Jacobo Rouces, Nina Tahmasebi, Lars Borin, and Stian Rødven Eide. 2018. Generating a gold standard for a swedish sentiment lexicon. In *Proceedings of the Eleventh International Conference on Language Resources and Evaluation (LREC 2018)*.

Burr Settles. 2012. Active learning. *Synthesis Lectures on Artificial Intelligence and Machine Learning*, 6(1):1–114.

Sara Stymne. 2011. Blast: A tool for error analysis of machine translation output. In *Proceedings of the 49th Annual Meeting of the Association for Computational Linguistics: Human Language Technologies: Systems Demonstrations*, pages 56–61. Association for Computational Linguistics.

Technical Question Answering across Tasks and Domains

Wenhao Yu[†], Lingfei Wu[‡], Yu Deng[‡], Qingkai Zeng[†],
Ruchi Mahindru[‡], Sinem Guven[‡], Meng Jiang[†]
†University of Notre Dame, Notre Dame, IN, USA
‡IBM Thomas J. Watson Research Center, Yorktown Heights, NY, USA
†{wyu1, qzeng, mjiang2}@nd.edu
‡{wuli, dengy, rmahindr, sguven}@us.ibm.com

Abstract

Building automatic technical support system is an important yet challenge task. Conceptually, to answer a user question on a technical forum, a human expert has to first retrieve relevant documents, and then read them carefully to identify the answer snippet. Despite huge success the researchers have achieved in coping with general domain question answering (QA), much less attentions have been paid for investigating technical QA. Specifically, existing methods suffer from several unique challenges (i) the question and answer rarely overlaps substantially and (ii) very limited data size. In this paper, we propose a novel framework of deep transfer learning to effectively address technical QA across tasks and domains. To this end, we present an adjustable joint learning approach for document retrieval and reading comprehension tasks. Our experiments on the TechQA demonstrates superior performance compared with state-of-the-art methods.

1 Introduction

Recent years have seen a surge of interests in building automatic technical support system, partially due to high cost of training and maintaining human experts and significant difficulty in providing timely responses during the peak season. Huge successes have been achieved in coping with open-domain QA tasks (Chen and Yih, 2020), especially with advancement of large pre-training language models (Devlin et al., 2019). Among them, two-stage retrieve-then-read framework is the mainstream way to solve open-domain QA tasks, pioneered by (Chen et al., 2017): a retriever component finding a document that might contain an answer from a large collection of documents, followed by a reader component finding the answer snippet in a given paragraph or a document. Recently, various pre-training language models (e.g., BERT) have dominated the encoder design for solving different open-domain QA tasks (Karpukhin et al., 2020; Xiong et al., 2020).

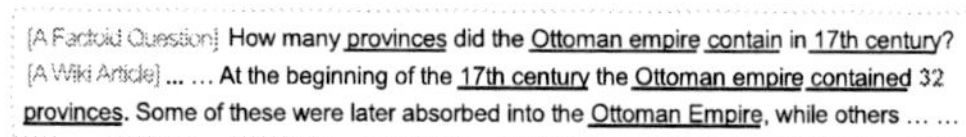

(a) A factoid QA example in the SQuAD dataset.

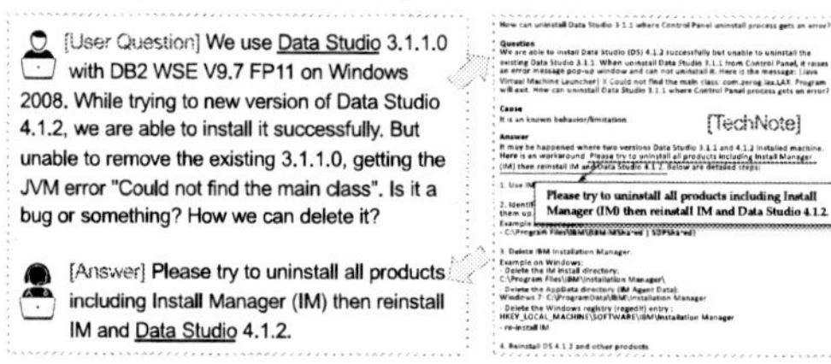

(b) A non-factoid QA example in the TechQA dataset.

Figure 1: Factoid QA is semantic aligned but non-factoid QA has few overlapping words. Semantic similarities between such non-factoid QA is not indicative.

Despite the tremendous successes achieved in general QA domain, technical QA have not yet been well investigated due to several unique challenges. First, technical QAs are non-factoid. The question and answer can hardly overlap substantially, because the answer typically fills in missing information and actionable solutions to the question such as steps for installing a software package and configuring an application. Different from factoid questions that are typically aligned with a span of text in document (Rajpurkar et al., 2016, 2018), semantic similarities between such non-factoid QA pairs could have a large gap as shown in Fig.1. Therefore, the retrieval module in retrieve-then-read framework might find documents that do not contain correct answers due to the semantic gap in non-factoid QAs (Karpukhin et al., 2020; Lee et al., 2019; Yu et al., 2020b). Second, compared to SQuAD (with more than 100,000 QA pairs), technical domain datasets typically have a much smaller number of labelled QA pairs (e.g., about 1,400 in TechQA), partially due to the prohibitive cost of creating labelled data. In addition, there are limited real user questions and technical support documents, especially for some new tech products and

Proceedings of NAACL HLT 2021: IndustryTrack Papers, pages 178–186
June 6–11, 2021.

communities. Since the pre-trained language models are mainly trained on general domain corpora, directly fine-tuning pre-trained language models may lead to unsatisfying performance due to the large discrepancy between source tasks (general domains) and target tasks (technical domains) (Chang et al., 2020; Gururangan et al., 2020).

To address the aforementioned challenges, we propose a novel deep transfer learning framework that explores knowledge transfer across tasks and domains (TransTD). TransTD consists of two components: TransT (knowledge transfer across tasks) and TransD (knowledge transfer across domains). TransTD jointly learns snippet prediction (reading comprehension) task and matching prediction (document retrieval) task simultaneously, applying it on both general domain QA and target domain QA.

To address the first challenge of non-factoid QAs, TransT leverages a joint learning model that directly ranks all predicted snippets by reading each pair of query and candidate document. It optimizes matching prediction and snippet prediction in parallel. Compared to two-stage retrieve-then-read methods that only read most semantically related documents, TransT considers potential snippets in every candidate document. When jointly training these two tasks, snippet prediction pays attention to local correspondence and matching prediction helps understand the semantic relationship from a global perspective, allowing the multi-head attentions in BERT-based encoders to jointly attend to information from different representation subspaces at different positions. Besides, the weights of two training objectives can be dynamically learned to pay more attention on the more difficult task when training different data samples.

To address the second challenge of learning with limited data, TransD leverages a deep transfer learning model to transfer knowledge from general domain QAs to technical domain QAs. General domain QA dataset like SQuAD has a much larger data size and a similar task setting (i.e., snippet prediction). Though knowledge is different between two domains, by learning the ability to answer questions in general domains, the model can quickly adapt and learn efficiently when changing into a new domain, reflected in faster convergence and better performance. Transfer learning helps avoid overfitting on technical QAs with limited size of data. Specifically, our model first applies the multi-task joint learning in general domain QAs (SQuAD), then transfers model parameters to initialize the training in the target domain QAs (TechQA), making knowledge transfer across domains to address data limitation.

We conducted extensive experiments on the TechQA dataset and utilized BERT as basic models. Experiments show that TransTD can provide superior performance than models with no knowledge transfer and other state-of-the-art methods.

2 Related Work

Open-Domain QA Open-domain textual question answering is a task that requires a system to answer factoid questions using a large collection of documents as the information source, without the need of pre-specifying topics or domains (Chen and Yih, 2020). Two-stage retriever-reader framework is the mainstream way to solve open-domain QA, pioneered by (Chen et al., 2017). Recent work has improved this two-stage open-domain QA from different perspectives such as novel pre-training methods (Lee et al., 2019; Guu et al., 2020), semantic alignment between question and passage (Lee et al., 2019; Karpukhin et al., 2020; Wu et al., 2018), cross-attention based BERT retriever (Yang et al., 2019; Gardner et al., 2019), global normalization between multiple passages (Wang et al., 2019).

Transfer Learning Transfer learning studies how to transfer knowledge from auxiliary domains to a target domain (Pan and Yang, 2009; Jiang et al., 2015; Yao et al., 2019). Recent advances of deep learning technologies with transfer learning has achieved great success in a variety of NLP tasks (Ruder et al., 2019). Several research work in this domain greatly enrich the application and technology of transfer learning on question answering from different perspectives (Min et al., 2017; Deng et al., 2018; Castelli et al., 2020; Yu et al., 2020a). Although transfer learning has been successfully applied to various QA applications, its applicability to technical QA has yet to be investigated. In this work, we focus on leveraging transfer learning to enhance QA in tech domain.

3 Research Problem

In the technical support domain, suppose we have a set of questions $\mathcal{Q}$ and a large collection of documents $\mathcal{D}$. For each question $Q \in \mathcal{Q}$, we aim at finding a relevant document $D \in \mathcal{D}$ and extracting the snippet answer $S = (D_{start}, D_{end})$ in the document D. Note that the answer may not exist, and so, the relevant document may not exist, either. All predicted snippets are ranked by a specific span score calculation method, and (usually) the top-1[1] answer span is chosen to answer the given question.

4 Proposed Framework

In this section, we present our proposed framework for technical QA. Given a query, we first obtain 50 Technotes by issuing the query to the search engine Elasticsearch[2]. Instead of using a document retriever based on semantic similarity between the query and each document, our proposed TransTD jointly optimizes snippet prediction and matching prediction in a parallel style. Figure 2 illustrates the design of the framework. It has a multi-task learning method to transfer knowledge across the snippet prediction (reading comprehension) and matching prediction (document retrieval) tasks. This method is further applied to pre-train the model on auxiliary domain QAs[3]. Furthermore, the weights of two training objectives are dynamically adjusted by calculating the difference between real answer snippet and predicted snippet. So, the model can focus on optimizing the more difficult task when training different data samples. Lastly, Our model has a novel snippet ranking function that uses snippet prediction to obtain an alignment score and linearly combines it with the matching prediction score.

4.1 Knowledge Transfer across Tasks

We build our model upon BERT (Devlin et al., 2019) to jointly optimize on the RC and DR tasks. Suppose Θ has the BERT encoder parameters. When we apply domain knowledge transfer, which will be introduced in the following section, we initialize it with the parameters $\Theta^{(aux)}$ trained on the auxiliary domain; when we do not apply the transfer, we initialize it with the original pre-trained BERT parameters. We have two multi-layer perceptron (MLP) classifiers for the two tasks, whose parameters are denoted by θ_{RC} and θ_{DR}, respectively. Both classifiers are randomly initialized. More specifically, the RC classifier is to predict answer snippets, and the DR classifier is to predict document matching. The joint loss is as follows:

$$\begin{aligned}\mathcal{L}^{(aux)} &= \mathcal{L}_{RC}(\Theta^{(aux)}, \theta_{RC}^{(aux)}) \\ &\quad + \lambda^{(aux)} \cdot \mathcal{L}_{DR}(\Theta^{(aux)}, \theta_{DR}^{(aux)}), \quad (1)\end{aligned}$$

where λ is a hyper-parameter for the weight of the DR task over RC task.

Calculate adjustment factor As shown in Eq.(1), the weights between two training objectives are only adjusted by a pre-determined hyper-parameter λ. However, for different samples in the dataset, the difficulty of learning snippet prediction and matching prediction is different. The weight of two training objectives should be dynamically adjusted so that the model can focus on optimizing the more difficult task when training different data samples. Since non-factoid questions are open-ended questions that often require complex answers that are mostly sentence-level texts, positional relationships between start token and end token in answer snippets have more fluctuations than factoid answers. Therefore, we take the difference between real answer snippet and predicted snippet to measure the difficulty of snippet prediction. Intuitively, when the predicted answer snippet is significantly different from the actual answer snippet (much larger or much smaller), it indicates snippet prediction is difficult for the current data sample. So, the model should focus on optimizing the reading comprehension part. On the contrary, the model should focus on optimizing the document retrieval part. Formally, the weight-adjustable joint learning loss function is defined as:

$$\begin{aligned}\mathcal{L}^{(aux)} &= w \cdot \mathcal{L}_{RC}(\Theta^{(aux)}, \theta_{RC}^{(aux)}) \\ &\quad + \lambda^{(aux)} \cdot \mathcal{L}_{DR}(\Theta^{(aux)}, \theta_{DR}^{(aux)}), \quad (2)\end{aligned}$$

$$w = \exp\left(\frac{|(D_{end} - D_{start}) - (\hat{D}_{end} - \hat{D}_{start})|}{D_{end} - D_{start}}\right). \quad (3)$$

4.2 Knowledge Transfer across Domains

Besides transferring across tasks, in our framework, we employ knowledge transfer across domains. We identify a dataset from an auxiliary domain (not a technical support domain) for technical question answering like SQuAD. We apply the multi-task learning to the auxiliary domain. The goal is to learn BERT encoder parameters $\Theta^{(aux)}$ and two MLP classifiers $\theta_{RC}^{(aux)}$ and $\theta_{DR}^{(aux)}$:

$$\begin{aligned}\mathcal{L}^{(aux)} &= \mathcal{L}_{RC}(\Theta^{(aux)}, \theta_{RC}^{(aux)}) \\ &\quad + \lambda^{(aux)} \cdot \mathcal{L}_{DR}(\Theta^{(aux)}, \theta_{DR}^{(aux)}), \quad (4)\end{aligned}$$

[1] Since technical domain RC is extremely difficult, we also evaluate performance on top-5 predictions in our experiments.

[2] Elasticsearch – https://www.elastic.co/elasticsearch/

[3] In our work, auxiliary domain QAs are from general domain QAs, so we use these two words interchangeably.

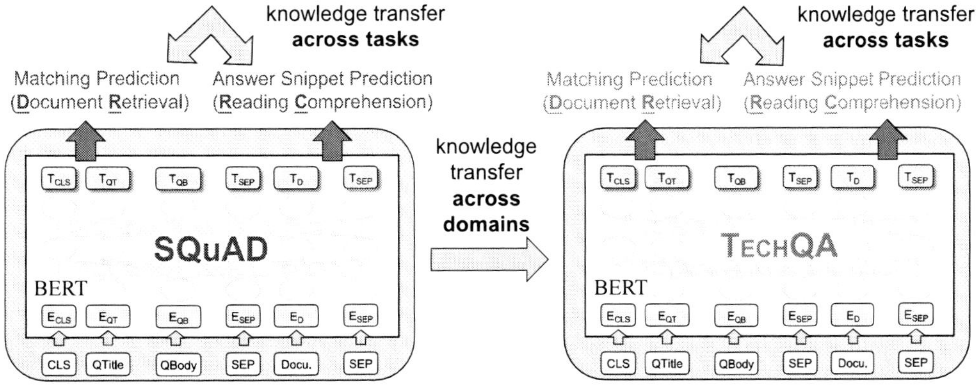

Figure 2: Our framework performs knowledge transfer across tasks and domains. It explores the mutual enhancement between the snippet prediction (reading comprehension) and matching prediction (document retrieval), applying multi-task learning to the BERT models on both auxiliary domain (SQuAD) and target domain (TechQA).

Here the encoder is initialized by the original pretrained BERT parameters. We will initialize the BERT encoder in the target domain Θ with $\Theta^{(aux)}$ (used in TransTD-Mean and TransTD-CLS). When $\lambda^{(aux)} = 0$, we apply the single RC task on the auxiliary domain (used in TransTD-single).

4.3 Framework Components

Question and Document Encoder Given a pair of question Q and document D, we first build a concatenation by $[[\text{CLS}], Q, [\text{SEP}], D, [\text{SEP}]]$, where [CLS] stands for a classification token and [SEP] separates components in the sequence. The BERT_Θ encoder generates contextualized representations of every token X in the input sequence q, which is denoted by $\text{BERT}_\Theta(q)[X] \in \mathbb{R}^d$, where $d = 1024$. So we have a matrix of token representations $\mathbf{H} \in \mathbb{R}^{m \times d}$, where $H(k) = \text{BERT}_\Theta(q)[q[k]]$ (k is the index of the token).

Reader MLP This classifier reads the representation matrix $\mathbf{H}$ and computes the score of each token being the start token in the answer snippet $\mathbf{p}_{start} \in \mathbb{R}^m$ and the score of each token being the end token $\mathbf{p}_{end} \in \mathbb{R}^m$.

$$\mathbf{p}_{start} = \mathbf{w}_{start} \cdot \mathbf{H}^{\mathrm{T}}, \ \mathbf{p}_{end} = \mathbf{w}_{end} \cdot \mathbf{H}^{\mathrm{T}}, \quad (5)$$

where $\mathbf{w}_{start}, \mathbf{w}_{end} \in \mathbb{R}^d$ are trainable parameters. We have the snippet $S_{RC} = (\hat{D}_{start}, \hat{D}_{end})$ as

$$\hat{D}_{start} = \text{argmax}_{k \in \{1,\ldots,m\}} p_{start}[k], \quad (6)$$

$$\hat{D}_{end} = \text{argmax}_{k \in \{1,\ldots,m\}} p_{end}[k]. \quad (7)$$

Matching MLP Suppose we have the representation of the sequence q. It can be denoted by $\mathbf{h} \in \mathbb{R}^d$. The classifier is to predict whether the question Q and document D are aligned, which is a binary variable projected from $\mathbf{h}$:

$$p_{DR} = \sigma(\mathbf{w}_{DR} \cdot \mathbf{h}), \quad (8)$$

where σ is the sigmoid function and $\mathbf{w}_{DR} \in \mathbb{R}^d$ are trainable parameters. We have two options to produce $\mathbf{h}$ from the input sequence q. The first option is to apply mean pooling to the representations of all tokens (used in TransTD-Mean):

$$\mathbf{h} = \text{MEAN}(\{\text{BERT}_\Theta(q)[X] | X \in q\}). \quad (9)$$

The second option is to use the classification token [CLS] (used in TransTD-CLS):

$$\mathbf{h} = \text{BERT}_\Theta(q)[\text{CLS}]. \quad (10)$$

Joint Inference The reading MLP takes question and document pairs and predicts a reading score,

$$S_{reader} = (p_{start}[D_s] + p_{end}[D_e]) - (p_{start}[0] + p_{end}[0]). \quad (11)$$

where $p_{(\cdot)}[0]$ denotes the probability of taking first token of the sequence as the start position or end position of the snippet. The joint ranking score of a (Q, D) pair is a linear combination of reading score and matching score,

$$S = \alpha \cdot p_{DR} + (1 - \alpha) \cdot S_{reader}. \quad (12)$$

It should be noted that different from previous work that only leverages the first term in reading score, i.e.,

Table 1: Statistics of TechQA. The test set is not publicly available, only allowing people to submit models for evaluation. The length of *TechNotes* is much bigger than that of question and answer texts.

	#Ques. (answerable/non-ans.)	#TechNotes	Len-Ques.	Len-Ans.	Len-Notes
Train	600 (450 / 150)	30,000	52.1±31.6	48.1±38.7	433.9±320.6
Dev.	310 (160 / 150)	15,500	53.1±30.4	41.2±27.7	449.1±351.2
Test	490	24,500	-	-	-

Table 2: Ablation study on knowledge transfer across tasks and across domains on TechQA. TransTD transfers knowledge across both tasks and domains, and TransTD$^+$ is further improved by the adjustable weight.

Methods		Adjustable	Source task(s)	Target task(s)	Reading Comprehension			Document Retrieval		
					Ma-F1	HA-F1@1	HA-F1@5	MRR	R@1	R@5
BERT$_{DR}$	-	✘	-	DR	-	-	-	55.80	45.58	58.23
BERT$_{RC}$	-	✘	-	RC	52.49	24.92	37.26	51.20	48.13	56.25
TransD	-	✘	RC	DR	-	-	-	60.63	58.13	64.38
	-	✘	RC	RC	55.31	34.69	50.52	64.60	60.63	68.23
TransT	CLS	✘	-	RC+DR	53.43	26.83	38.50	51.19	46.88	56.88
	Mean	✘	-	RC+DR	52.30	26.28	41.50	52.68	47.50	59.35
TransTD	CLS	✘	RC+DR	RC+DR	56.43	39.12	52.30	66.79	64.38	70.63
	Mean	✘	RC+DR	RC+DR	56.88	37.96	49.83	67.55	**67.50**	69.38
TransTD$^+$	CLS	✔	RC+DR	RC+DR	56.66	38.33	50.95	67.80	65.00	72.50
	Mean	✔	RC+DR	RC+DR	**58.58**	**40.28**	**52.57**	**67.98**	66.88	**73.13**

Table 3: TransTD outperforms two-stage retrieve-then-read methods that retrieve document based on semantic alignment. k is the number of retrieved documents.

Method	Setting	Ma-F1	HA-F1@1	R@1
BERTserini (Yang et al., 2019) (with BM25 as retriever)	k=1	51.34	15.23	30.00
	k=5	56.60	28.31	48.75
DPR (Karpukhin et al., 2020) (w/o pre-trained retriever)	k=1	53.22	15.57	26.25
	k=5	56.47	30.40	47.50
DPR (Karpukhin et al., 2020) (with pre-trained retriever)	k=1	54.82	19.46	30.63
	k=5	58.56	33.03	53.13
TransTD-Mean$^+$ (Ours, S_{with})	-	**58.58**	**40.28**	**66.88**

Table 4: Our proposed snippet ranking function can bring additional improvements. Using $(p_s[0] + p_e[0])$ reflects the degree of misalignment between Q and D.

Snippet ranking method	Ma-F1	HA-F1@1	R@1
MP-BERT (Wang et al., 2019) ($S_{\text{MP-BERT}} = p_{DR} \cdot p_s \cdot p_e$)	49.45	24.65	43.75
WKLM (Xiong et al., 2020) ($S_{\text{BERT}} = \alpha \cdot p_{DR} + p_s + p_e$)	57.82	39.71	66.25
Ours (w/o document score) ($S_{w/o} = p_s + p_e - p_s[0] - p_e[0]$)	**58.58**	**40.28**	65.00
Ours (with document score) ($S_{with} = \alpha \cdot p_{DR} + S_{w/o}$)	**58.58**	**40.28**	**66.88**

$S_{reader} = (p_{start}[D_s] + p_{end}[D_e])$ (Xiong et al., 2020; Qu et al., 2020), our added second term improved inference performance. This is because during the training time, the span label of a document that does not contain an answer is set to $(0, 0)$, and such negative documents are the majority. Therefore, $(p_{start}[0] + p_{end}[0])$ reflects the probability that Q and D is not aligned. See Table 4 for experimental comparisons.

5 Experiments

5.1 TechQA Dataset

The TechQA dataset (Castelli et al., 2020) contains actual questions posed by users on the IBM DeveloperWorks forums. TechQA is designed for machine reading comprehension tasks, Each question is associated with a candidate list of 50 *Technotes* obtained by issuing a query on the search engine Elasticsearch[4]. A question is answerable if an answer snippet exists in the 50 *Technotes*, or is unanswerable otherwise. Data statistics are given in Table 1. In TechQA, the training set has 600 questions in which 450 questions are answerable; the validation set has 310 questions in which 160 questions are answerable; the test set has 490 questions. The Technotes are usually of greater length than question and answer texts.

[4]https://www.elastic.co/elasticsearch/

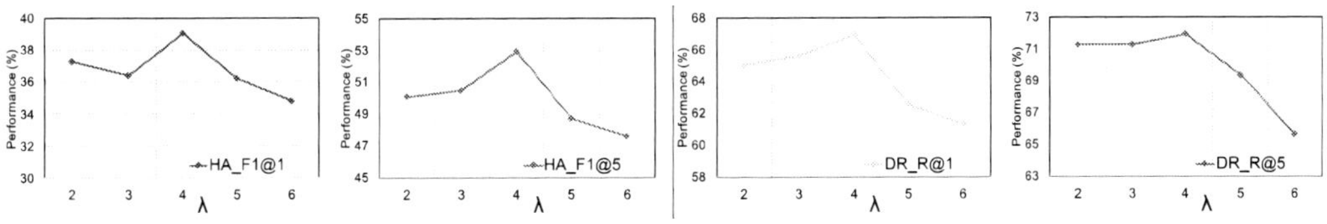

Figure 3: λ is the weight of the DR task loss over the RC task loss. When $\lambda = 4.0$, TransTD achieves the best performance for both RC (left two) and DR (right two) tasks.

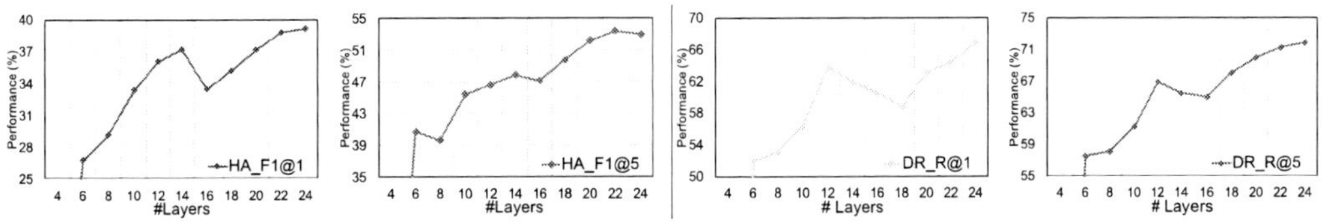

Figure 4: The more layers being fine-tuned in the target domain, the better performance we can have. However, it shows the pattern but not always true in the middle of the range.

5.2 Evaluation methods

The accuracy of the extracted snippets is evaluated by Ma-F1[5] and HA_F1@K. Ma-F1 is the macro average of the F1 scores computed on the first of the K answers provided by the system for each given question:

$$\text{Ma-F1} = \frac{\sum_{i=1}^{K} \text{F1@}K}{K}, \tag{13}$$

where F1@K computes F1 scores for top-K answer snippets, selects the maximum F1 score, and computes the macro F1 score average over all questions. HA_F1@K calculates macro F1 score average over all answerable questions. Besides, models are evaluated on retrieving and ranking document by mean reciprocal rank (MRR) and recall at K (R@K). R@K is the percentage of correct answers in top K out of all the relevant answers. MRR represents the average of the reciprocal ranks of results for a set of queries.

5.3 Ablation Study

TranT transfers knowledge across tasks on the target domain, with multi-tasks of RC and DR.

TranD transfers knowledge from source domain RC to target domain RC w/o multi-task learning.

TransTD transfers knowledge across both tasks and domains. TransTD$^+$ is further improved by the adjustable weight.

[5]To avoid confusion between F1 (used on the TechQA leaderboard) and F1@K, we use Ma-F1 instead of F1.

5.4 Experimental Analysis

5.4.1 Knowledge transfer across domains

In Table 2, the model first fine tuning on the source domain QA (SQuAD) then further fine tuning on the target domain QA (TechQA) makes superior performance than only fine tuning on the target domain QA. This indicates knowledge transfer from general domain QA is crucial for technical QA.

5.4.2 Knowledge transfer across tasks

In Table 2, transferring knowledge across tasks better capture local correspondence and global semantic relationship between the question and document. Compared with BERT$_{\text{RC}}$, TransT improves Ma-F1 by +0.94% and HA_F1@1 by +1.91%.

5.4.3 Across both tasks and domains

In Table 2, transferring knowledge across both tasks and domains further improve model performance. TransTD fine tunes on SQuAD, then further fine tunes on the TechQA with both RC and AR tasks. It performs better than TransD and TransT. TransTD$^+$ makes adjustable joint learning, which further brings +1.7% and +2.32% improvements on Ma-F1 and HA_F1@1 compared to TransTD.

5.4.4 Comparison with retrieve-then-read (two-stage) methods

Using semantic similarity to predict alignment between query and document in open-domain QA is an efficient and accurate method. It can be statistical-based (e.g., BM25) (Yang et al., 2019) or neural-based that can be jointly optimized with snippet prediction (Karpukhin et al., 2020; Lee et al., 2019). However, as shown in Table 3, in

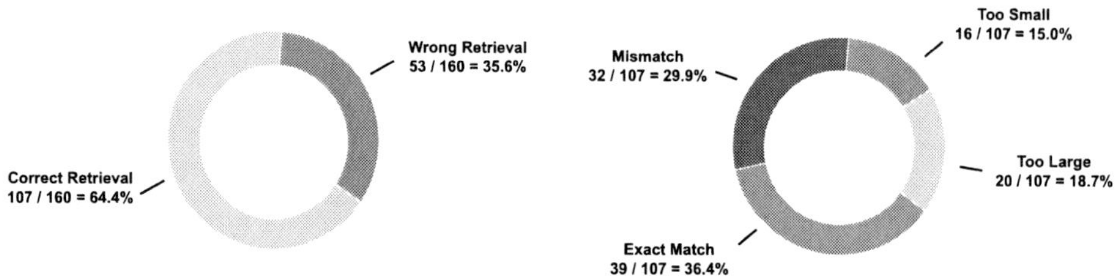

Figure 5: Error analysis. The left figure represents the proportions between correct and wrong prediction on DR. The right figure represents the proportion of RC results when the retrieval phase already predicts the correct document. (Here, "too small" means that if the prediction is $S_{RC} = (D^{(pred)}_{start}, D^{(pred)}_{end})$ and the truth is $S = (D_{start}, D_{end})$, we have $D^{(pred)}_{start} > D_{start}$ and $D^{(pred)}_{end} < D_{end}$; on the contrary, "too large" means we have $D^{(pred)}_{start} < D_{start}$ and $D^{(pred)}_{end} > D_{end}$.)

the case of the same encoder (i.e., BERT), our proposed TransTD with novel snippet ranking function can identify answers more accurately than above methods. This means that our method is more effective in the context of non-factoid QAs whose semantics of query and document are not aligned.

5.5 Parameter Analysis

Loss ratio In Figure 3, we compare performance with loss ratio between the RC and DR tasks, λ in Eq.(1). We observe that when $\lambda = 4.0$, TransTD achieves the best performance for both RC and DR tasks. If the loss ratio becomes more than 4.0, the performance decreases significantly. This is because RC helps DR more than DR helps RC, which is consistent with results in Table 2.

Number of fine tuning layers As shown in Figure 4, we compare performance on different numbers of fine tuning layers. Fine tuning all layers (24 layers) makes the best performance. However, the model performance and the number of fine tuning layers are not an absolute linear relationship. For example, only fine tuning 12 to 14 layers achieves better performance than having 16 or 18 layers, making a good reference for training with limited GPU memories.

5.6 Error Analysis

As shown in Figure 5, we manually categorize the predictive results of 160 answerable question instances in the development set. First of all, there are 107 (64.4%) questions that can be correctly matched with corresponding documents through the joint inference by Eq.(12), however, 53 (35.6%) questions are mismatched with the documents that do not contain desirable answers. Additionally, among 107 correct predictions, only 39 (36.4%) of them are given with the correct answer snippet in the best matching document. Among 68 wrong predictions, 32 (47.1%) of them are mismatched with the answer span. Besides, 16 (23.5%) of them are provided with a smaller span of answer snippet than the actual span, in which the average length of answer snippet is 44 words. On the contrary, 20 (29.4%) of them are provided with a larger span of answer snippet than the actual span, in which their average length is 16 words. We observe that the TechQA dataset offers a challenging yet interesting problem, where the answers have a wide range of the number of words. Some long answers are across multiple sentences.

6 Conclusion

In this paper, we studied QA in the technical domain, which was not well investigated. Technical QA faces two unique challenges: (i) the question and answer rarely overlaps substantially (on-factoid questions) and (ii) very limited data size. To address the challenges, we propose a novel framework of deep transfer learning to effectively address TechQA across tasks and domains. To this end, we present an adjustable joint learning approach for document retrieval and reading comprehension tasks. Our experiments on the TechQA dataset demonstrates superior performance compared with non-transfer learning state-of-the-art methods.

Acknowledgements

The authors would like to thank the anonymous referees for their valuable comments and suggestions. This work is supported by National Science Foundation grants, IIS-1849816 and CCF-1901059.

References

Vittorio Castelli, Rishav Chakravarti, Saswati Dana, Anthony Ferritto, Radu Florian, Martin Franz, Dinesh Garg, Dinesh Khandelwal, Scott McCarley, Mike McCawley, et al. 2020. The techqa dataset. *Proceedings of the 58th Annual Meeting of the Association for Computational Linguistics (ACL).*

Wei-Cheng Chang, Felix X Yu, Yin-Wen Chang, Yiming Yang, and Sanjiv Kumar. 2020. Pre-training tasks for embedding-based large-scale retrieval. *In Proceedings of 8th International Conference for Learning Representation (ICLR).*

Danqi Chen, Adam Fisch, Jason Weston, and Antoine Bordes. 2017. Reading wikipedia to answer open-domain questions. In *Proceedings of the 55th Annual Meeting of the Association for Computational Linguistics (Volume 1: Long Papers).*

Danqi Chen and Wen-tau Yih. 2020. Open-domain question answering. In *Proceedings of the 58th Annual Meeting of the Association for Computational Linguistics: Tutorial Abstracts*, pages 34–37.

Yang Deng, Ying Shen, Min Yang, Yaliang Li, Nan Du, Wei Fan, and Kai Lei. 2018. Knowledge as a bridge: Improving cross-domain answer selection with external knowledge. In *Proceedings of the 27th international conference on computational linguistics*, pages 3295–3305.

Jacob Devlin, Ming-Wei Chang, Kenton Lee, and Kristina Toutanova. 2019. Bert: Pre-training of deep bidirectional transformers for language understanding. In *Proceedings of the 2019 Conference of the North American Chapter of the Association for Computational Linguistics: Human Language Technologies, Volume 1 (Long and Short Papers).*

Matt Gardner, Jonathan Berant, Hannaneh Hajishirzi, Alon Talmor, and Sewon Min. 2019. On making reading comprehension more comprehensive. In *Proceedings of the 2nd Workshop on Machine Reading for Question Answering*, pages 105–112.

Suchin Gururangan, Ana Marasović, Swabha Swayamdipta, Kyle Lo, Iz Beltagy, Doug Downey, and Noah A Smith. 2020. Don't stop pretraining: Adapt language models to domains and tasks.

Kelvin Guu, Kenton Lee, Zora Tung, Panupong Pasupat, and Ming-Wei Chang. 2020. Realm: Retrieval-augmented language model pre-training. *arXiv preprint arXiv:2002.08909.*

Meng Jiang, Peng Cui, Xumin Chen, Fei Wang, Wenwu Zhu, and Shiqiang Yang. 2015. Social recommendation with cross-domain transferable knowledge. *IEEE transactions on knowledge and data engineering*, 27(11):3084–3097.

Vladimir Karpukhin, Barlas Oğuz, Sewon Min, Ledell Wu, Sergey Edunov, Danqi Chen, and Wen-tau Yih. 2020. Dense passage retrieval for open-domain question answering. *arXiv preprint arXiv:2004.04906.*

Kenton Lee, Ming-Wei Chang, and Kristina Toutanova. 2019. Latent retrieval for weakly supervised open domain question answering. In *Proceedings of the 57th Annual Meeting of the Association for Computational Linguistics.*

Sewon Min, Minjoon Seo, and Hannaneh Hajishirzi. 2017. Question answering through transfer learning from large fine-grained supervision data. In *Proceedings of the 55th Annual Meeting of the Association for Computational Linguistics (Volume 2: Short Papers)*, pages 510–517.

Sinno Jialin Pan and Qiang Yang. 2009. A survey on transfer learning. *IEEE Transactions on knowledge and data engineering*, 22(10):1345–1359.

Chen Qu, Liu Yang, Cen Chen, Minghui Qiu, W Bruce Croft, and Mohit Iyyer. 2020. Open-retrieval conversational question answering. *SIGIR Conference on Research and Development in Information Retrieval.*

Pranav Rajpurkar, Robin Jia, and Percy Liang. 2018. Know what you don't know: Unanswerable questions for squad. In *Proceedings of the 56th Annual Meeting of the Association for Computational Linguistics (Volume 2: Short Papers)*, pages 784–789.

Pranav Rajpurkar, Jian Zhang, Konstantin Lopyrev, and Percy Liang. 2016. Squad: 100,000+ questions for machine comprehension of text. In *Proceedings of the 2016 Conference on Empirical Methods in Natural Language Processing*, pages 2383–2392.

Sebastian Ruder, Matthew E Peters, Swabha Swayamdipta, and Thomas Wolf. 2019. Transfer learning in natural language processing. In *Proceedings of the 2019 Conference of the North American Chapter of the Association for Computational Linguistics: Tutorials*, pages 15–18.

Zhiguo Wang, Patrick Ng, Xiaofei Ma, Ramesh Nallapati, and Bing Xiang. 2019. Multi-passage bert: A globally normalized bert model for open-domain question answering. In *Proceedings of the 2019 Conference on Empirical Methods in Natural Language Processing and the 9th International Joint Conference on Natural Language Processing (EMNLP-IJCNLP)*, pages 5881–5885.

Lingfei Wu, Ian EH Yen, Kun Xu, Fangli Xu, Avinash Balakrishnan, Pin-Yu Chen, Pradeep Ravikumar, and Michael J Witbrock. 2018. Word mover's embedding: From word2vec to document embedding. *arXiv preprint arXiv:1811.01713.*

Wenhan Xiong, Jingfei Du, William Yang Wang, and Veselin Stoyanov. 2020. Pretrained encyclopedia: Weakly supervised knowledge-pretrained language model. *International Conference for Learning Representation (ICLR).*

Wei Yang, Yuqing Xie, Aileen Lin, Xingyu Li, Luchen Tan, Kun Xiong, Ming Li, and Jimmy Lin. 2019. End-to-end open-domain question answering with bertserini. In *Proceedings of the 2019 Conference of the North American Chapter of the Association for Computational Linguistics (Demonstrations)*.

Huaxiu Yao, Chuxu Zhang, Ying Wei, Meng Jiang, Suhang Wang, Junzhou Huang, Nitesh V Chawla, and Zhenhui Li. 2019. Graph few-shot learning via knowledge transfer. *arXiv preprint arXiv:1910.03053*.

Wenhao Yu, Lingfei Wu, Yu Deng, Ruchi Mahindru, Qingkai Zeng, Sinem Guven, and Meng Jiang. 2020a. A technical question answering system with transfer learning. In *Proceedings of the 2020 Conference on Empirical Methods in Natural Language Processing (EMNLP)*.

Wenhao Yu, Lingfei Wu, Qingkai Zeng, Yu Deng, Shu Tao, and Meng Jiang. 2020b. Crossing variational autoencoders for answer retrieval. *Proceedings of the 58th Annual Meeting of the Association for Computational Linguistics (ACL)*.

Cost-effective Deployment of BERT Models in a Serverless Environment

Katarína Benešová *
Slido
kbenesova@slido.com

Andrej Švec *
Slido
asvec@slido.com

Marek Šuppa *
Slido
msuppa@slido.com

Abstract

In this study we demonstrate the viability of deploying BERT-style models to serverless environments in a production setting. Since the freely available pre-trained models are too large to be deployed in this way, we utilize knowledge distillation and fine-tune the models on proprietary datasets for two real-world tasks: sentiment analysis and semantic textual similarity. As a result, we obtain models that are tuned for a specific domain and deployable in serverless environments. The subsequent performance analysis shows that this solution results in latency levels acceptable for production use and that it is also a cost-effective approach for small-to-medium size deployments of BERT models, all without any infrastructure overhead.

1 Introduction

Machine learning models are notoriously hard to bring to production environments. One of the reasons behind is the large upfront infrastructure investment it usually requires. This is particularly the case with large pre-trained language models, such as BERT (Devlin et al., 2018) or GPT (Radford et al., 2019) whose size requirements make them difficult to deploy even when infrastructure investment is not of concern.

At the same time, the serverless architecture with minimal maintenance requirements, automatic scaling and attractive cost, is becoming more and more popular in the industry. It is very well suited for stateless applications such as model predictions, especially in cases when the prediction load is unevenly distributed. Since the serverless platforms have strict limits, especially on the size of the deployment package, it is not immediately obvious it may be a viable platform for deployment of models based on large pre-trained language models.

In this paper we describe our experience with deploying BERT-based models to serverless environments in a production setting. We consider two tasks: sentiment analysis and semantic textual similarity. While the standard approach would be to fine-tune the pre-trained models, this would not be possible in our case, as the resulting models would be too large to fit within the limits imposed by serverless environments. Instead, we adopt a knowledge distillation approach in combination with smaller BERT-based models. We show that for some of the tasks we are able to train models that are an order of magnitude smaller while reporting performance similar to that of the larger ones.

Finally, we also evaluate the performance of the deployed models. Our experiments show that their latency is acceptable for production environments. Furthermore, the reported costs suggest it is a very cost-effective option, especially when the expected traffic is small-to-medium in size (a few requests per second) and potentially unevenly distributed.

2 Related work

Despite a number of significant advances in various NLP approaches over the recent years, one of the limiting factors hampering their adoption is the large number of parameters that these models have, which leads to large model size and increased inference time. This may limit their use in resource-constrained mobile devices or any other environment in which model size and inference time is the limiting factor, while negatively affecting the environmental costs of their use (Strubell et al., 2019)
.

This has led to a significant body of work focusing on lowering both the model size and inference time, while incurring minimal performance penalty. One of the most prominent approaches include Knowledge Distillation (Buciluă et al., 2006; Hinton et al., 2015), in which a smaller model (the

*Equal contribution

Proceedings of NAACL HLT 2021: IndustryTrack Papers, pages 187–195
June 6–11, 2021.

"student") is trained to reproduce the behavior of a larger model (the "teacher"). It was used to produce smaller BERT alternatives, such as:

- **TinyBERT** (Jiao et al., 2019), which appropriates the knowledge transfer method to the Transformer architecture and applies it in both the pretraining and downstream fine-tuning stage. The resulting model is more than 7x smaller and 9x faster in terms of inference.
- **MobileBERT** (Sun et al., 2020), which only uses knowledge distilation in the pre-training stage and reduces the model's width (layer size) as opposed to decreasing the number of layers it consists of. The final task-agnostic model is more than 3x smaller and 5x faster than the original $\text{BERT}_{\text{BASE}}$.

When decreasing the model size leads to decreased latency, it can also have direct business impact. This has been demonstrated by Google, which found out that increasing web search latency from 100 ms to 400 ms reduced the number of searches per user by 0.2 % to 0.6 % (Brutlag, 2009). A similar experiment done by Booking.com has shown that an increase in latency of about 30 % results in about 0.5 percentage points decrease in conversion rates, which the authors report as a *"relevant cost for our business"* (Bernardi et al., 2019).

Each serverless platform has its specifics, which can have different impact on different use cases. Various works, such as (Back and Andrikopoulos, 2018; Wang et al., 2018; Lee et al., 2018), provide a comparison of performance differences between the available platforms. In order to evaluate specific use cases, various benchmark suites have been introduced such as FunctionBench (Kim and Lee, 2019), which includes language generation as well as sentiment analysis test case.

Possibly the closest published work comparable to ours is (Tu et al., 2018), in which the authors demonstrate the deployment of neural network models, trained for short text classification and similarity tasks in a serverless context. Since at the time of its publication the PyTorch deployment ecosystem has been in its nascent stages, the authors had to build it from source, which complicates practical deployment.

To the best of our knowledge, our work is the first to show the viability of deploying large pretrained language models (such as BERT and its derivatives) in the serverless environment.

	AWS	**Azure**	**GCP**
Function size	250MB[1]	-	500MB
Execution time	15min	-	9min
Memory	10GB	14GB	8GB
Request size	6MB	100MB	10MB

Table 1: Limitations of the three main serverless providers: Amazon Web Services (AWS), Microsoft Azure (Azure) and Google Cloud Platform (GCP).

3 Serverless environments

Serverless environments offer a convenient and affordable way of deploying a small piece of code. A survey by O'Reilly Media (O'Reilly Media, Inc, 2019) shows that the adoption of serverless was successful for the majority of the respondents' companies. They recognize reduced operational costs, automatic scaling with demand and elimination of concerns for server maintenance as the main benefits.

Since the functions deployed in a serverless environment share underlying hardware, OS and runtime (Lynn et al., 2017), there are naturally numerous limitations to what can be run in such environment. The most pronounced ones include:

- **Maximum function size**, mostly limited to a few hundreds of MBs (although some providers do not have this limitation). In the context of deployment of a machine learning model, this can significantly limit the model size as well as the selection of libraries to be used to execute the model.
- **Maximum memory** of a few GBs slows down or makes it impossible to run larger models.
- **No acceleration.** Serverless environments do not support GPU or TPU acceleration which can significantly increase the inference time for larger models.

A more detailed list of the main limitations of the three most common serverless providers can be found in Table 1. It suggests that any model deployed in this environment will need to be small in size and have minimal memory requirements. These requirements significantly limit the choice of models appropriate for this environment and warrants a specific training regimen, which we describe in the next section.

[1] Recently, a new way of deployment was added, allowing

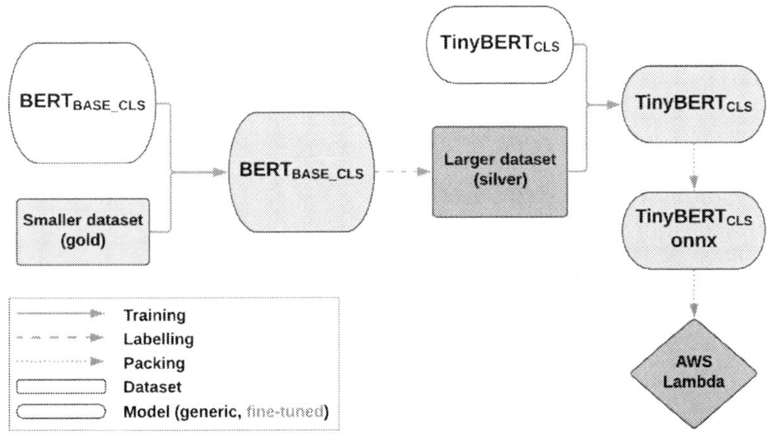

Figure 1: Schema of the distillation pipeline of BERT$_{BASE}$ for sentiment analysis. BERT$_{BASE_CLS}$ is fine-tuned on the gold dataset and then used for labelling a large amount of data (silver dataset) that serves as a training set for distillation to TinyBERT. The distilled model is exported to the ONNX format and deployed to AWS Lambda (see Section 5). The same pipeline was executed for MobileBERT.

4 Model training

In the two case studies presented in this section, we first consider BERT-provided classification token (`[CLS]` token) an aggregate representation of a short text (up to 300 characters) for the sentiment analysis task. Secondly, we utilize the embeddings produced by Sentence-BERT (SBERT) (Reimers and Gurevych, 2019) for estimating the semantic similarity of a pair of short texts.

Since deploying even the smaller BERT$_{BASE}$ with over 400MB in size is not possible in our setup, in the following cases studies we explore several alternative approaches, such as knowledge distillation into smaller models or training a smaller model directly. To do so, we use TinyBERT (Jiao et al., 2019) and MobileBERT (Sun et al., 2020) having about 56 MB and 98 MB in size, respectively.

4.1 BERT for sentiment analysis

One of the direct applications of the special `[CLS]` token of BERT is the analysis of sentiment (Li et al., 2019). We formulate this problem as classification into three categories: *Positive*, *Negative* and *Neutral*.

The task is divided into two stages: first, we fine-tune BERT$_{BASE}$ using a labelled domain-specific dataset of 68K training examples and 9K examples for validation. Then we proceed with knowledge distillation into a smaller model with faster inference: we label a large amount of data by the fine-tuned BERT$_{BASE}$ and use the dataset to train a smaller model with a BERT-like architecture. The distillation pipeline is illustrated in Figure 1.

4.1.1 Fine-tuning BERT$_{BASE}$

To utilize BERT$_{BASE}$ for a classification task, an additional head must be added on top of the Transformer blocks, i.e. a linear layer on top of the pooled output. The additional layer typically receives only the representation of the special `[CLS]` token as its input. To obtain the final prediction, the output of this layer is passed through a Softmax layer producing the probability distribution over the predicted classes.

We fine-tuned BERT$_{BASE}$ for sequence classification (BERT$_{BASE_CLS}$) with this adjusted architecture for our task using a labelled dataset of size 68K consisting of domain-specific data. We trained the model for 8 epochs using AdamW optimizer with small learning rate 3×10^{-5}, L2 weight decay of 0.01 and batch size 128.

To cope with the significant class imbalance[2] and to speed up the training, we sampled class-balanced batches in an under-sampling fashion, while putting the examples of similar length together (for the sake of a more effective processing of similarly padded

to deploy a container of size up to 10 GB.

[2]About 82% of the dataset were *Neutral* examples, 10% *Negative* and 8% *Positive*.

data). Using this method, we were able to at least partially avoid over-fitting on the largest class and reduce the training time about 2.5 times.

We also tried an alternative fine-tuning approach by freezing $\text{BERT}_{\text{BASE}}$ layers and attaching a small trainable network on top of it. For the trainable part, we experimented with 1-layer bidirectional GRU of size 128 with dropout of 0.25 plus a linear layer and Softmax output. $\text{BERT}_{\text{BASE\_CLS}}$ outperformed this approach significantly.

The accuracy evaluation of both fine-tuned $\text{BERT}_{\text{BASE}}$ models on the validation dataset can be found in Table 2. In order to meet the function size requirements of the target serverless environments, we proceed to the knowledge distillation stage.

4.1.2 Knowledge distillation to smaller BERT models

Having access to virtually unlimited supply of unlabelled domain-specific examples, we labelled almost 900K of them by the fine-tuned $\text{BERT}_{\text{BASE\_CLS}}$ "teacher" model and used them as ground truth labels for training a smaller "student" model. We experimented with MobileBERT and even smaller TinyBERT as the student models since these are, in comparison to $\text{BERT}_{\text{BASE}}$, 3 and 7 times smaller in size, respectively.

During training, we sampled the batches in the same way as in Section 4.1.1, except for a smaller batch size of 64. We trained the model for a small number of epochs using AdamW optimizer with learning rate 2×10^{-5}, weight decay 0.01 and early stopping after 3 epochs in case of TinyBERT and one epoch for MobileBERT (in the following epochs the models no longer improved on the validation set).

For evaluation we used the same validation dataset as for the fine-tuned $\text{BERT}_{\text{BASE\_CLS}}$ described in 4.1. The performance comparison is summarized in Table 2. We managed to distill the model knowledge into the significantly smaller TinyBERT with only 0.02 points decrease in F1 score (macro-averaged). In case of MobileBERT we were able to match the performance of $\text{BERT}_{\text{BASE\_CLS}}$. These results suggest that the large language models might not be necessary for classification tasks in a real-life scenario.

Model	**Size** (MB)	**F1**
$\text{BERT}_{\text{BASE}}$ + GRU	426	0.75
$\text{BERT}_{\text{BASE\_CLS}}$	420	**0.84**
TinyBERT (distilled)	56	0.82
MobileBERT (distilled)	98	**0.84**

Table 2: Comparison of fine-tuned BERT models and smaller distilled models on the validation dataset (macro-averaged F1 score). The slight decrease in TinyBERT's performance is an acceptable trade-off for the significant size reduction.

4.2 Sentence-BERT for semantic textual similarity

The goal of our second case study was to train a model that would generate dense vectors usable for semantic textual similarity (STS) task in our specific domain and be small enough to be deployed in a serverless environment. The generated vectors would then be indexed and queried as part of a duplicate text detection feature of a real-world web application. To facilitate this use-case, we use Sentence-BERT (SBERT) (Reimers and Gurevych, 2019).

While the SBERT architecture currently reports state-of-the-art performance on the sentence similarity task, all publicly available pre-trained SBERT models are too large for serverless deployment. The smallest one available is $\text{SDistilBERT}_{\text{BASE}}$ with on-disk size of 255 MB. We therefore had to train our own SBERT model based on smaller BERT alternatives. We created the smaller SBERT models by employing the TinyBERT and MobileBERT into the SBERT architecture, i.e. by adding an embedding averaging layer on top of the BERT model.

In order to make the smaller SBERT models perform on the STS task, we fine-tune them in two stages. Firstly, we fine-tune them on standard datasets to obtain a smaller version of the generic SBERT model and then we fine-tune them further on the target domain data. The fine-tuning pipeline is visualized in Figure 2.

4.2.1 Generic SBERT fine-tuning

To obtain a smaller version of SBERT, we followed the the SBERT training method as outlined in (Reimers and Gurevych, 2019). We first fine-tuned a smaller SBERT alternative on a combination of SNLI (Bowman et al., 2015) (dataset of sentence pairs labeled for entailment, contradiction, and semantic independence) and Multi-Genre NLI

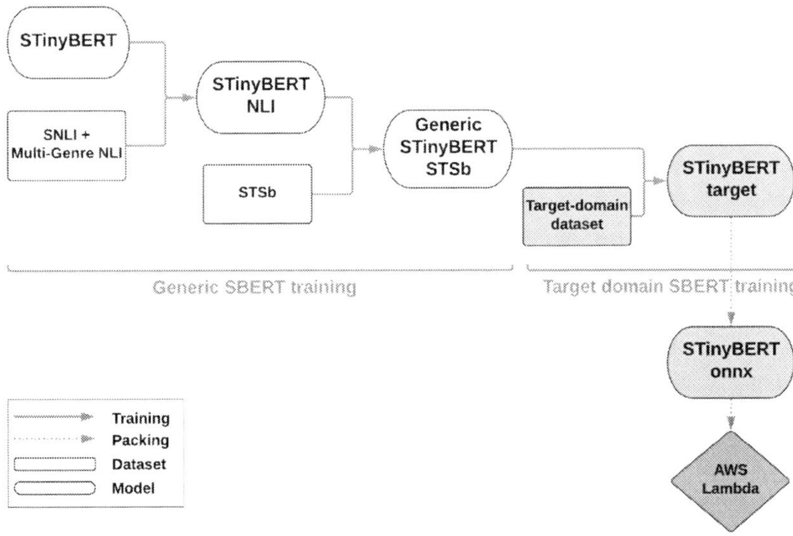

Figure 2: Schema of the fine-tuning pipeline of STinyBERT for STS task. In the first stage, STinyBERT is fine-tuned on NLI and STSb datasets to obtain Generic STinyBERT. In the second phase, the model is trained further on the target-domain dataset, exported to the ONNX format and deployed to AWS Lambda (see Section 5). The same pipeline was executed for SMobileBERT. $\text{SBERT}_{\text{BASE}}$ was only fine-tuned on target domain dataset.

(Williams et al., 2018) (dataset of both written and spoken speech in a wide range of styles, degrees of formality, and topics) datasets.

We observed the best results when fine-tuning the model for 4 epochs with early stopping based on validation set performance, batch size 16, using Adam optimizer with learning rate 2×10^{-5} and a linear learning rate warm-up over 10 % of the total training batches.

Next, we continued fine-tuning the model on the STSbenchark (STSb) dataset (Cer et al., 2017) using the same approach, except for early stopping based on STSb development set performance and a batch size of 128.

4.2.2 Target domain fine-tuning

Once we obtained a small enough generic SBERT model, we proceeded to fine-tune it on examples from the target domain. We experimented with two approaches: fine-tuning the model on a small gold dataset and generating a larger silver dataset.

Dataset. We worked with a balanced training set of 2856 pairs. Each pair was assigned to one of three classes: *duplicate* (target cosine similarity 1), *related* (0.5) or *unrelated* (0). The classes were assigned semi-automatically. *Duplicate* pairs were created by back-translation (Sennrich et al., 2016) using the translation models released as part of the OPUS-MT project (Tiedemann and Thottingal, 2020). *Related* pairs were pre-selected and expertly annotated and *unrelated* pairs were formed by pairing random texts together.

Validation and test sets were composed of 665 and 696 expertly annotated pairs, respectively. These sets were not balanced due to the fact that finding *duplicate* pairs manually is far more difficult than finding *related* or *unrelated* pairs, which stems from the nature of the problem. That is why *duplicate* class forms only approximately 13 % of the dataset, whereas *related* and *unrelated* classes each represent roughly 43 %.

Fine-tuning on plain dataset. We first experimented with fine-tuning the generic SBERT model on the train set of the target domain dataset. We call the output model SBERT target. We fine-tuned it for 8 epochs with early stopping based on validation set performance, batch size 64, Adam optimizer with learning rate 2×10^{-5} and a linear learning rate warm-up over 10 % of the total training batches.

Extending the dataset. Since we had a lot of data without annotations available, we also experimented with extending the dataset and fine-tuning

Augmented SBERT (Thakur et al., 2020).

We pre-selected 379K duplicate candidates using BM25 (Amati, 2009) and annotated them using a pre-trained cross-encoder based on $\text{RoBERTa}_{\text{LARGE}}$. In the annotated data, low similarity values were majorly prevalent (median similarity was 0.18). For this reason, we needed to balance the dataset by undersampling the similarity bins with higher number of samples to get to a final balanced dataset of 32K pairs. We refer to the original expert annotations as gold data and to the cross-encoder annotations as silver data.

After creating the silver dataset, we first fine-tuned the model on the silver data and then on the gold data. We call the model fine-tuned on augmented target dataset AugSBERT. Correct hyperparameter selection was crucial for a successful fine-tuning. It was especially necessary to lower the learning rate for the final fine-tuning on the gold data and set the right batch sizes. For the silver dataset we used a learning rate of 2×10^{-5} and batch size of 64. For the final fine-tuning on the gold dataset we used a lower learning rate of 2×10^{-6} and a batch size of 16.

4.2.3 Results

As we can see in Table 3, smaller BERT alternatives can compete with $\text{SBERT}_{\text{BASE}}$. AugSMobileBERT manages to reach 93 % of the performance of $\text{SBERT}_{\text{BASE}}$ on the target dataset while being more than 3 times smaller in size.

We believe that the lower performance of smaller models is not only caused by the them having less parameters, but it also essentially depends on the size of the model's output dense vector. TinyBERT's output embedding size is 312 and MobileBert's is 512, whereas $\text{BERT}_{\text{BASE}}$ outputs embeddings of size 768. This would in line with the findings published in (Wieting and Kiela, 2019) which state that even random projection to a higher dimension leads to increased performance.

5 Deployment

As described in Section 3, numerous limitations must be satisfied when deploying a model to a serverless environment, among which the size of the deployment package is usually the major one. The deployment package consists of the function code, runtime libraries and in our case a model.

Model	STSb	Target
STinyBERT NLI	72.86	46.29
SMobileBERT NLI	78.29	52.08
$\text{SBERT}_{\text{BASE}}$ NLI	77.03	52.44
STinyBERT STSb	76.76	53.89
SMobileBERT STSb	81.52	59.05
$\text{SBERT}_{\text{BASE}}$ STSb	85.35	65.87
STinyBERT target	75.49	53.29
SMobileBERT target	79.56	59.27
$\text{SBERT}_{\text{BASE}}$ target	82.52	64.20
AugSTinyBERT target	73.88	54.34
AugSMobileBERT target	**80.47**	**61.75**
$\text{AugSBERT}_{\text{BASE}}$ target	82.98	64.14

Table 3: Spearman rank correlation between the cosine similarity of dense vectors and true labels measured for individual models on the test set of the STSbenchmark dataset (STSb column) and on the test set of the target domain dataset (Target column). The values are multiplied by 100 for convenience. We also present $\text{SBERT}_{\text{BASE}}$ performance as baseline. The model with the best performance on the target domain dataset, that is also deployable in serverless environment, is highlighted.

5.1 Model inference engine

In order to fit all of the above in a few hundreds of MBs allowed in the serverless environments, standard deep learning libraries cannot be used: the standard PyTorch wheel has 400 MB (Paszke et al., 2019) and TensorFlow is 850 MB in size (Abadi et al., 2015).

ONNX Runtime. We therefore used a smaller model interpreter library called ONNX Runtime (Bai et al., 2019), which is mere 14 MB in size, leaving a lot of space for the model. Prior to executing the model by the ONNX Runtime library, it needs to be converted to the ONNX format. This can be done using off-the-shelf tools, for instance the Hugging Face `transformers` library (Wolf et al., 2020) is shipped with a simple out-of-the-box script to convert BERT models to ONNX.

TensorFlow Lite. It is also possible to use the TensorFlow Lite interpreter library (Abadi et al., 2015), which is 6 MB in size. However, we only used ONNX in our deployments as we had problems converting more complex BERT models to TensorFlow Lite format.

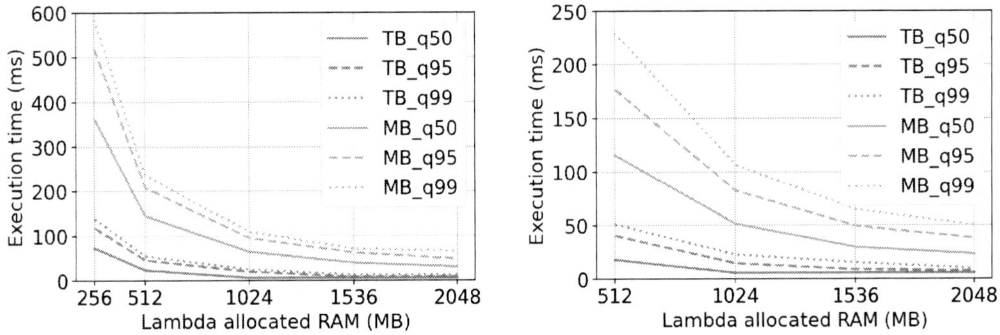

(a) Sentiment analysis.

(b) SBERT encoding.

Figure 3: Results of performance tests of trained models deployed in AWS Lambda. Execution time is denoted in miliseconds (ms). TB stands for TinyBERT, MB for MobileBERT. q50, q95 and q99 denote the 0.5, 0.95 and 0.99 quantiles, respectively.

	AWS			GCP		
	q50	q95	q99	q50	q95	q99
Sentiment TinyBERT	6.63	19.20	24.77	10.47	100.71	110.31
Sentiment MobileBERT	64.67	89.00	105.84	27.58	125.04	176.46
STinyBERT	5.71	13.03	21.24	10.93	101.32	111.80
SMobileBERT	50.08	80.14	102.65	58.88	175.14	213.56

Table 4: Performance comparison between the Amazon Web Services (AWS) and Google Cloud Platform (GCP) serverless environments. Numbers denote execution time in miliseconds with 1GB of RAM allocated for the deployed function. q50, q95 and q99 denote the 0.5, 0.95 and 0.99 quantiles, respectively.

5.2 Serverless deployment

After training the models and converting them into the ONNX format, we deployed them to different serverless environments.

6 Deployment evaluation

We measured the performance of deployed models in scenarios with various amounts of allocated memory by making them predict on more than 5000 real-world examples. Before recording measurements we let the deployed model evaluate a small subsample of data in order to keep the infrastructure in a "warm" state. This was done in order to estimate the real-life inference time, i.e. to avoid biasing the inference results by initialization time of the service itself.

From the results described in Table 4 we can see that using both the AWS and GCP platforms, we can easily reach the 0.99 quantile of execution time on the order of 100 ms for both tasks and models. Figure 3 also lets us observe that the execution time in AWS Lambda decreases with increasing RAM. This is expected, as both AWS Lambda and GCP Cloud Functions automatically allocate more vCPU with more RAM.

The serverless deployments are also cost-effective. The total costs of 1M predictions, taking 100 ms each and using 1 GB of RAM, are around $2 on both AWS and GCP, whereas the cheapest AWS EC2 virtual machine with 1 GB of RAM costs $8 per month.

7 Conclusion

We present a novel approach of deploying domain-specific BERT-style models in a serverless environment. To fit the models within its limits, we use knowledge distillation and fine-tune them on domain-specific datasets. Our experiments show that using this process we are able to produce much smaller models at the expense of a minor decrease in their performance. The evaluation of the deployment of these models shows that it can reach latency levels appropriate for production environments, while being cost-effective.

Although there certainly exist platforms and deployments that can handle much higher load (often times with smaller operational cost (Zhang et al., 2019)), the presented solution requires minimal infrastructure effort, making the team that trained these models completely self-sufficient. This makes it ideal for smaller-scale deployments, which can be used to validate the model's value. The smaller, distilled models created in the process can then be used in more scalable solutions, should the cost or throughput prove inadequate during test deployments.

References

Martín Abadi et al. 2015. TensorFlow: Large-scale machine learning on heterogeneous systems. Software available from tensorflow.org.

Giambattista Amati. 2009. *BM25*, pages 257–260. Springer US, Boston, MA.

Timon Back and Vasilios Andrikopoulos. 2018. Using a microbenchmark to compare function as a service solutions. In *European Conference on Service-Oriented and Cloud Computing*, pages 146–160. Springer.

Junjie Bai et al. 2019. Onnx: Open neural network exchange. `https://github.com/onnx/onnx`.

Lucas Bernardi et al. 2019. 150 successful machine learning models: 6 lessons learned at booking. com. In *Proceedings of the 25th ACM SIGKDD International Conference on Knowledge Discovery & Data Mining*, pages 1743–1751.

Samuel R. Bowman, Gabor Angeli, Christopher Potts, and Christopher D. Manning. 2015. A large annotated corpus for learning natural language inference. In *Proceedings of the 2015 Conference on Empirical Methods in Natural Language Processing*, pages 632–642, Lisbon, Portugal. Association for Computational Linguistics.

Jake Brutlag. 2009. Speed matters for google web search.

Cristian Buciluă, Rich Caruana, and Alexandru Niculescu-Mizil. 2006. Model compression. In *Proceedings of the 12th ACM SIGKDD international conference on Knowledge discovery and data mining*, pages 535–541.

Daniel M. Cer, Mona T. Diab, Eneko Agirre, Iñigo Lopez-Gazpio, and Lucia Specia. 2017. Semeval-2017 task 1: Semantic textual similarity - multilingual and cross-lingual focused evaluation. *CoRR*, abs/1708.00055.

Jacob Devlin et al. 2018. Bert: Pre-training of deep bidirectional transformers for language understanding. *arXiv preprint arXiv:1810.04805*.

Geoffrey Hinton, Oriol Vinyals, and Jeff Dean. 2015. Distilling the knowledge in a neural network. *arXiv preprint arXiv:1503.02531*.

Xiaoqi Jiao et al. 2019. Tinybert: Distilling bert for natural language understanding. *arXiv preprint arXiv:1909.10351*.

Jeongchul Kim and Kyungyong Lee. 2019. Functionbench: A suite of workloads for serverless cloud function service. In *2019 IEEE 12th International Conference on Cloud Computing (CLOUD)*, pages 502–504. IEEE.

Hyungro Lee et al. 2018. Evaluation of production serverless computing environments. In *2018 IEEE 11th International Conference on Cloud Computing (CLOUD)*, pages 442–450. IEEE.

Xin Li et al. 2019. Exploiting bert for end-to-end aspect-based sentiment analysis. *arXiv preprint arXiv:1910.00883*.

Theo Lynn et al. 2017. A preliminary review of enterprise serverless cloud computing (function-as-a-service) platforms. In *2017 IEEE CloudCom*, pages 162–169. IEEE.

O'Reilly Media, Inc. 2019. O'Reilly serverless survey 2019: Concerns, what works, and what to expect. `https://www.oreilly.com/radar/oreilly-serverless-survey-2019-concerns-what-works-and-what-to-expect/`. Accessed: 2021-01-12.

Adam Paszke et al. 2019. Pytorch: An imperative style, high-performance deep learning library. In H. Wallach, H. Larochelle, A. Beygelzimer, F. d'Alché-Buc, E. Fox, and R. Garnett, editors, *Advances in Neural Information Processing Systems 32*, pages 8024–8035. Curran Associates, Inc.

Alec Radford, Jeffrey Wu, Rewon Child, David Luan, Dario Amodei, and Ilya Sutskever. 2019. Language models are unsupervised multitask learners. *OpenAI blog*, 1(8):9.

Nils Reimers and Iryna Gurevych. 2019. Sentence-bert: Sentence embeddings using siamese bert-networks. *arXiv preprint arXiv:1908.10084*.

Rico Sennrich, Barry Haddow, and Alexandra Birch. 2016. Improving neural machine translation models with monolingual data. In *Proceedings of the 54th Annual Meeting of the Association for Computational Linguistics (Volume 1: Long Papers)*, pages 86–96, Berlin, Germany. Association for Computational Linguistics.

Emma Strubell et al. 2019. Energy and policy considerations for deep learning in nlp. *arXiv preprint arXiv:1906.02243*.

Zhiqing Sun et al. 2020. Mobilebert: a compact task-agnostic bert for resource-limited devices. *arXiv preprint arXiv:2004.02984*.

Nandan Thakur, Nils Reimers, Johannes Daxenberger, and Iryna Gurevych. 2020. Augmented sbert: Data augmentation method for improving bi-encoders for pairwise sentence scoring tasks. *arXiv preprint arXiv:2010.08240*.

Jörg Tiedemann and Santhosh Thottingal. 2020. OPUS-MT — Building open translation services for the World. In *Proceedings of the 22nd Annual Conferenec of the European Association for Machine Translation (EAMT)*, Lisbon, Portugal.

Zhucheng Tu, Mengping Li, and Jimmy Lin. 2018. Pay-per-request deployment of neural network models using serverless architectures. In *Proceedings of the 2018 Conference of the North American Chapter of the Association for Computational Linguistics: Demonstrations*, pages 6–10.

Liang Wang et al. 2018. Peeking behind the curtains of serverless platforms. In *2018 {USENIX} Annual Technical Conference ({USENIX}{ATC} 18)*, pages 133–146.

John Wieting and Douwe Kiela. 2019. No training required: Exploring random encoders for sentence classification. *arXiv preprint arXiv:1901.10444*.

Adina Williams, Nikita Nangia, and Samuel Bowman. 2018. A broad-coverage challenge corpus for sentence understanding through inference. In *Proceedings of the 2018 Conference of the North American Chapter of the Association for Computational Linguistics: Human Language Technologies, Volume 1 (Long Papers)*, pages 1112–1122, New Orleans, Louisiana. Association for Computational Linguistics.

Thomas Wolf, Lysandre Debut, Victor Sanh, Julien Chaumond, Clement Delangue, Anthony Moi, Pierric Cistac, Tim Rault, Rémi Louf, Morgan Funtowicz, Joe Davison, Sam Shleifer, Patrick von Platen, Clara Ma, Yacine Jernite, Julien Plu, Canwen Xu, Teven Le Scao, Sylvain Gugger, Mariama Drame, Quentin Lhoest, and Alexander M. Rush. 2020. Transformers: State-of-the-art natural language processing. In *Proceedings of the 2020 Conference on Empirical Methods in Natural Language Processing: System Demonstrations*, pages 38–45, Online. Association for Computational Linguistics.

Chengliang Zhang, Minchen Yu, Wei Wang, and Feng Yan. 2019. Mark: Exploiting cloud services for cost-effective, slo-aware machine learning inference serving. In *2019 {USENIX} Annual Technical Conference ({USENIX}{ATC} 19)*, pages 1049–1062.

Noise Robust Named Entity Understanding for Voice Assistants

Deepak Muralidharan[*], **Joel Ruben Antony Moniz**[*], **Sida Gao**[*], **Xiao Yang**[*†]
**Justine Kao, Stephen Pulman, Atish Kothari, Ray Shen, Yinying Pan,
Vivek Kaul, Mubarak Seyed Ibrahim, Gang Xiang, Nan Dun, Yidan Zhou,
Andy O, Yuan Zhang, Pooja Chitkara, Xuan Wang, Alkesh Patel,
Kushal Tayal, Roger Zheng, Peter Grasch, Jason D. Williams, Lin Li** [‡]
Apple

Abstract

Named Entity Recognition (NER) and Entity Linking (EL) play an essential role in voice assistant interaction, but are challenging due to the special difficulties associated with spoken user queries. In this paper, we propose a novel architecture that jointly solves the NER and EL tasks by combining them in a joint reranking module. We show that our proposed framework improves NER accuracy by up to 3.13% and EL accuracy by up to 3.6% in F1 score. The features used also lead to better accuracies in other natural language understanding tasks, such as domain classification and semantic parsing.

1 Introduction

Understanding named entities correctly when interacting with virtual assistants (e.g. "Call Jon", "Play Adele hello", "Score for Warrior Kings game") is crucial for a satisfying user experience. However, NER and EL methods that work well on written text often perform poorly in such applications: utterances are relatively short (with just 5 tokens, on average), so there is not much context to help disambiguate; speech recognizers make errors ("Play Bohemian raspberry" for "Play Bohemian Rhapsody"); users also make mistakes ("Cristiano Nando" for "Cristiano Ronaldo"); non-canonical forms of names are frequent ("Shaq" for "Shaquille O'Neal"); and users often mention new entities unknown to the system.

In order to address these issues we propose a novel Named Entity Understanding (NEU) system that combines and optimizes NER and EL for noisy spoken natural language utterances. We pass multiple NER hypotheses to EL for reranking, enabling NER to benefit from EL by including information from the knowledge base (KB).

[*] **Equal contributions.**
[†] graceyx.scut@gmail.com
[‡] lli9@apple.com

We also design a retrieval engine tuned for spoken utterances for retrieving candidates from the KB. The retrieval engine, along with other techniques devised to address fuzzy entity mentions, lets the EL model be more robust to partial mentions, variation in named entities, use of aliases, as well as human and speech transcription errors.

Finally, we demonstrate that our framework can also empower other natural language understanding tasks, such as domain classification (a sentence classification task) and semantic parsing.

2 Related Work

There have been a few attempts to explore NER on the output of a speech pipeline (Ghannay et al., 2018; Abujabal and Gaspers, 2018; Coucke et al., 2018). Among these, our NER model is closest to Abujabal and Gaspers (2018) and Coucke et al. (2018); however, unlike the former, we use a richer set of features rather than phonemes as input, and unlike the latter, we are able to use a deep model because of the large volume of data available.

EL has been well explored in the context of clean (Martins et al., 2019; Kolitsas et al., 2018; Luo et al., 2015) and noisy text inputs (Eshel et al., 2017; Guo et al., 2013; Liu et al., 2013), but as with NER, there have been only a few efforts to explore EL in the context of transcribed speech (Benton and Dredze, 2015; Gao et al., 2017), although crucially, both these works assume gold standard NER and focus purely on the EL component.

Traditionally, a pipelined architecture of NER followed by EL has been used to address the entity linking task (Lin et al., 2012; Derczynski et al., 2015; Bontcheva et al., 2017; Bowden et al., 2018). Since these approaches rely only on the best NER hypothesis, errors from NER propagate to the EL step. To alleviate this, joint models have been proposed: Sil and Yates (2013) proposed an NER+EL model which re-ranks candidate mentions and entity links produced by their base model. Our work

Proceedings of NAACL HLT 2021: IndustryTrack Papers, pages 196–204
June 6–11, 2021. ©2021 Association for Computational Linguistics

differs in that we use a high precision NER system, while they use a large number of heuristically obtained Noun Phrase (NP) chunks and word n-grams as input to the EL stage. Luo et al. (2015) jointly train an NER and EL system using a probabilistic graphical model. However, these systems are trained and tested on clean text and do not address the noise problems we are concerned with.

3 Architecture Design

For a given utterance, we first detect and label entities using the NER model and generate the top-l candidate hypotheses using beam search. The EL model consists of two stages: (i) candidate retrieval and (ii) joint linking and re-ranking. In the retrieval stage, for each NER hypothesis, we construct a structured search query and retrieve the top-c candidates from the retrieval engine. In the ranking stage, we use a neural network to rank these candidate entity links within each NER hypothesis while simultaneously using rich signals (entity popularity, similarity between entity embeddings, the relation across multiple entities in one utterance, etc.) from these entity links as additional features to re-rank the NER hypotheses from the previous step, thus jointly addressing both the NER and EL tasks.

3.1 NER

For the NER task, following Lample et al. (2016) we use a combination of character and word level features. They are extracted by a bi-directional LSTM (biLSTM) (Hochreiter and Schmidhuber, 1997), and then concatenated with pre-trained GloVe word embeddings [1] (Pennington et al., 2014) to pass through another biLSTM and fed into a CRF model to produce the final label prediction based on a score $s(\tilde{\mathbf{y}}_\mathbf{i}, \mathbf{x}; \theta)$ that jointly optimizes the probability of labels for the tokens and the transition score for the entire sequence $\tilde{\mathbf{y}}_\mathbf{i} = (y_1, \ldots, y_T)$ given the input $\mathbf{x}$:

$$s(\tilde{\mathbf{y}}_\mathbf{i}, \mathbf{x}; \theta) = \sum_{t=0}^{T} \left(\psi_{t,\theta}(y_t) + \phi_{t,t+1}(y_t, y_{t+1})\right),$$

where $\psi_{t,\theta}$ is the biLSTM prediction score from the label y_t of the tth token, and $\phi(j,k)$ is the transition score from label j to label k.

During training, we maximize the probability of the correct label sequence p_{seq}, which is defined as

$$p_{seq}(\tilde{\mathbf{y}}_\mathbf{i}, \mathbf{x}; \theta) = \frac{\exp(s(\tilde{\mathbf{y}}_\mathbf{i}, \mathbf{x}; \theta))}{\sum_{\tilde{\mathbf{y}}_\mathbf{j} \in S} \exp\left(s(\tilde{\mathbf{y}}_\mathbf{j}, \mathbf{x}; \theta)\right)},$$

where $\tilde{\mathbf{y}}_\mathbf{i}$ is the label sequence for hypothesis i, and S is the set of all possible label sequences.

During inference, we generate up to 5 NER alternatives for each utterance using beam search. We also calculate a mention level confidence p_{men} for each entity mention $\mathbf{m_k}$. p_{men} is computed by aggregating the sequence level confidence for all the prediction sequences that share the same mention sub-path $\mathbf{m_k}$:

$$p_{men}(\mathbf{m_k}, \mathbf{x}; \theta) = \frac{\sum_{\tilde{\mathbf{y}}_\mathbf{i} \in S_{\mathbf{m_i}}} \exp(s(\tilde{\mathbf{y}}_\mathbf{i}, \mathbf{x}; \theta))}{\sum_{\tilde{\mathbf{y}}_\mathbf{j} \in S} \exp(s(\tilde{\mathbf{y}}_\mathbf{j}, \mathbf{x}; \theta))},$$

where S_{m_i} is the set of prediction sequences that all have $\mathbf{m_k}$ as the prediction for the corresponding tokens. Both p_{seq} and p_{men} are computed by dynamic programming, and serve as informative features in the EL model.

3.2 Joint Linking and Re-ranking

The entity linking system follows the NER model and consists of two steps: candidate retrieval, and joint linking and re-ranking.

To build the candidate retrieval engine, we first index the list of entities in our knowledge base, which can be updated daily to capture new entities and change of their popularity. To construct the index, we iterate through the flattened list of entities and construct token-level unigram, bigram and trigram terms from the surface form of each entity. Apart from using the original entity names, we also use common aliases, harvested from usage logs, for popular entities (e.g. LOTR as an alias for "Lord of the Rings") to make the retrieval engine more robust to commonly occurring variations. Next, we create an inverted index which maps the unique list of n-gram terms to the list of entities that these n-grams are part of, also known as posting lists. Further, to capture cross-entity relationships in the knowledge base (such as relationships between an artist and a song or two sports teams belonging to the same league), we assign a pointer[2] for each

[1] We also tried more recent contextual embeddings such as BERT (Devlin et al., 2019), and empirically observed very little difference in performance when compared to GloVe. So we adopt GloVE, which is substantially more efficient in terms of inference time required.

[2] Each entity in our knowledge base consists of metadata (for example, a song entry in our knowledge base would contain metadata such as the music artist, album, year the song was released in etc.) that we leverage to automatically construct these relationship pointers.

entity in the knowledge base to its related entities and this relational information is leveraged by the EL model for entity disambiguation (described in 5.2). We then compute the tf-idf score for all the n-gram terms present in the entities and store them in the inverted index.

For each hypothesis predicted by the NER model we query the retrieval engine with the corresponding text. We first send the query through a high-precision seq-to-seq correction model (Schmaltz et al., 2017; Ge et al., 2019) trained using common errors observed in usage. Next, we construct n-gram features from the corrected query in a similar way to the indexing phase and retrieve all entities matching these n-gram features in our inverted index. Additionally, we use synonyms derived from usage for each term in the query to expand our search criteria: for example, our synonym list for "Friend" contains "Friends", which matches the TV show name which would have been missed if only the original term was used.

For each entity retrieved, we get the tf-idf score for the terms present in the query chunk from the inverted index. We then aggregate the tf-idf scores of all the terms present in the query for this entity and linearly combine this aggregate score with other attributes such as popularity (i.e. prior usage probability) of the entity to generate a final score for all retrieved entity candidates for this query. Finally, we perform an efficient sort across all the entity candidates based on this score and return a top-c (in our case $c = 25$) list filtered by the entity type detected by the NER model for that hypothesis. These entity candidates coupled with the original NER hypothesis are sent to the ranker model described below for joint linking and re-ranking.

Following the candidate retrieval step, we introduce a neural model to rerank the candidate entities, aggregating features from both the NER model and the candidate retrieval engine.

The EL model scores each entity linking hypothesis separately. An entity linking hypothesis consists of a prediction from the NER model (which consists of named entity chunks in the input utterance and their types), and the candidate retrieval results for each chunk. Formally, we define an entity linking hypothesis $\mathbf{y}$ with k entity predictions as:

$$\mathbf{y} = \{\mathbf{f}_{\text{utter}}, \mathbf{f}_{\text{NER}}, \mathbf{f}_{\text{CR}}, \{j \in \{1 \ldots k\} : (\mathbf{m}_j, \mathbf{e}_j)\}\}$$

where $\mathbf{m}_j$ is the j-th mention in the utterance, and $\mathbf{e}_j$ is the entity name associated with this mention from the knowledge base. $\mathbf{f}_{\text{utter}}$, $\mathbf{f}_{\text{NER}}$, $\mathbf{f}_{\text{CR}}$ are features derived from the original utterance text, the NER model and the candidate retrieval system respectively. In our system, $\mathbf{f}_{\text{utter}}$ is a representation of the utterance from averaging the pre-trained word embeddings for the tokens in the utterance. Intuitively, having a dense representation of the full utterance can help the EL model better leverage signals from the utterance context. $\mathbf{f}_{\text{NER}}$ includes the type of each mention, as well as the sequence and mention confidence computed by the NER model. $\mathbf{f}_{\text{CR}}$ includes popularity, and whether a relation exists between the retrieved entities in $\mathbf{y}$.

To be robust to noise, the EL model adopts a pair of CNNs to compare each entity mention $\mathbf{m}_j$ and its corresponding knowledge base entity name $\mathbf{e}_j$. The CNN learns a name embedding with one-dimensional convolution on the character sequence, and the kernel parameters are shared between the CNN used for user mention and the one used for the canonical name. A character-based text representation model is better at handling mis-transcriptions or mis-pronounced entity names. While a noisy entity name may be far from the canonical name in the word embedding space when they are semantically different, they are usually close to each other in the character embedding space due to similar spellings. To model the similarity between CNN name embeddings of $\mathbf{m}_j$ and $\mathbf{e}_j$, we use the standard cosine similarity as a baseline, we experiment with an MLP that takes the concatenated name embeddings as input. We are able to model more expressive interactions between the two name embeddings with the MLP, and in turn better handle errors. Finally, we concatenate the similarity features with other features as input to another MLP that computes the final score for $\mathbf{y}$. Formally, the scoring function is defined in Equation 1, where $\oplus$ means concatenation.

$$s(\mathbf{y}) = \mathbf{MLP}(\mathbf{f}_{\text{utter}} \oplus \mathbf{f}_{\text{NER}} \oplus \mathbf{f}_{\text{CR}} \bigoplus_{j=1}^{k} [\mathbf{MLP}(\mathbf{CNN}(\mathbf{m}_j), \mathbf{CNN}(\mathbf{e}_j)) \oplus \mathbf{CNN}(\mathbf{m}_j) \oplus \mathbf{CNN}(\mathbf{e}_j)]) \quad (1)$$

In our data, the number of entity mentions in an utterance averages less than 3. We pad the entity feature sequence to length 5, which provides a good coverage. In the scoring model above, we use a simple concatenation to aggregate the embedding similarities of multiple entity mentions which empirically performs as well as sequence models like LSTM, while being much cheaper in computation.

To train the EL model, we use the standard max-margin loss for ranking tasks. If for the i-th example, we denote the ground truth as $\mathbf{y}^*{}_i$ and an incorrect prediction as $\hat{\mathbf{y}}_i$, and the scoring function $s(\cdot)$ is as defined in Equation 1, the loss function is

$$\mathcal{L} = \frac{1}{N}\sum_{i=1}^{N}[\gamma(\hat{\mathbf{y}}_i, \mathbf{y}^*{}_i) + s(\hat{\mathbf{y}}_i) - s(\mathbf{y}^*{}_i)]_+. \quad (2)$$

The max-margin loss encourages the ground truth score to be at least a margin γ higher than the score of an incorrect prediction. The margin is defined as a function of the ground truth and the incorrect prediction, thus adaptive to the quality of prediction. A larger margin is needed when the incorrect prediction is further away from the ground truth. For our reranking task, we set a smaller margin when only the resolved entities are incorrect but the NER result is correct, and a larger margin when the NER result is wrong. This adaptive margin helps rerank NER hypotheses even when the model cannot rank the linking results correctly. During training, we uniformly sample the negative predictions from the candidates retrieved by the retrieval engine.

3.3 Improvement on Other Language Understanding Tasks

We also explore the impact of our NEU feature encoding on two tasks: a domain classifier and a domain-specific shallow semantic parser.

3.3.1 Domain Classification

Domain classification identifies which domain a user's request falls into: sports, weather, music, etc., and is usually done by posing the task as sequence classification: our baseline uses word embeddings and gazetteer features as inputs to an RNN, in a manner similar to Chen et al. (2019).

Consider a specific token t. Let a be the number of alternatives used from the NER model in the domain classifier (which we treat as a hyperparameter), p_i represent the (scalar) sequence level confidence score $p_{seq}(\bar{\mathbf{y}}_i, \mathbf{x}; \theta)$ of the ith NER alternative defined in Section 3.1, c_i represent an integer for the entity type that NER hypothesis i assigns to the token t, and $\mathbf{o}(.)$ represent a function converting an integer into its corresponding one-hot vector. Then the additional NER feature vector $\mathbf{f_r}$ concatenated to the input vector fed into token t as part of the domain classifier can be written as:

$$\mathbf{f_r} = \bigoplus_{i=1}^{i=a} p_i\mathbf{o}(c_i). \quad (3)$$

Likewise, for the featurization that uses both NER and EL, let a be the number of alternatives used from the NER+EL system in the domain classifier (also a hyperparameter); these a alternatives are now sorted by the scores from the EL hypotheses, as opposed to the sequence level confidence scores from NER. Let s_i be the ith re-ranked alternative's cosine similarity score between the mention and knowledge base entity name as output by the EL model. p_i and c_i are consistent with our earlier notation, except that they now correspond to the ith NER alternative after re-ranking. Then the additional NER+EL feature vector $\mathbf{f_u}$ concatenated to the input fed into token t as part of the domain classifier can be written as:

$$\mathbf{f_u} = \bigoplus_{i=1}^{i=a} p_i\mathbf{o}(c_i) \oplus s_i\mathbf{o}(c_i). \quad (4)$$

3.3.2 Semantic Parsing

Our virtual assistant also uses domain-specific shallow semantic parsers, running after domain classification, responsible both for identifying the correct intent that the user expects (such as the "play" intent associated with a song) and for assigning semantic labels to each of the tokens in a user's utterance (such as the word "score" and "game" respectively being tagged as tokens related to a sports statistic and sports event respectively in the utterance "What's the score of yesterday's Warriors game?"). Each semantic parser is structured as a multi-task sequence classification (for the intent) and sequence tagging (for the token-level semantic labelling) task, with our production baseline using word embeddings and gazetteer features as inputs into an RNN similar to our domain classifier. Here, $\mathbf{f_r}$ and $\mathbf{f_u}$ are featurized as described above. Note that in contrast to the NEU system, the semantic parser uses a domain-specific ontology, to enable each domain to work independently and to not be encumbered by the need to align ontologies.

4 Datasets and Training Methodology

To create our datasets, we randomly sampled around $600k$ unique anonymous English transcripts (machine transcribed utterances), and annotated them with NER and EL labels. Utterances are subject to Apple's baseline privacy practices with respect to Siri requests, including that such requests are not associated with a user's Apple ID, email address, or other data Apple may have from a user's use of other Apple services, and have been filtered as described in Section 7. We then split the annotated data into 80/10/10 for train, development and test sets. For both the NER and EL tasks, we report our results on test sets sampled from the "music", "sports" and "movie & TV" domains. These are popular domains in the usage and have a high percentage of named entities: with an average of 0.6, 1.1 and 0.7 entities for each utterance in the 3 domains respectively. To evaluate model performance specifically on noisy user inputs, we select queries from the test sets that are marked as containing speech transcription or user errors by the annotators and report results on this "noisy" subset, which constitutes 13.5%, 12.7% data for movie&TV and music domain respectively when an entity exists. [3] To evaluate the relation feature, we also look at the "related" subset where a valid relation exists in the utterance. This subset consists 13.4% and 5.3% of data for the music and sports domain with at least one entity. [4]

We first train the NER model described in Section 3.1. Next, for every example in our training dataset, we run inference on the trained NER model and generate the top-5 NER hypotheses using beam search. Following this, we retrieve the top 25 candidates for each of these hypotheses using our search engine combined with the ground truth NER and EL labels and fed to the EL model for training.

To measure the NER model performance, we use the standard NER F1 metric used for the CoNLL-2003 shared task (Tjong Kim Sang and De Meulder, 2003). To measure the quality of the top-5 NER hypotheses, we compute the oracle top-5 F1 score by comparing and choosing the best alternative hypothesis among the 5 and calculate its F1 score, for each test utterance. In this manner, we also know the upper bound that EL can reach from reranking NER hypotheses. As described in section 3.2, the EL model is optimized to perform two tasks simultaneously: entity linking and reranking of NER hypotheses. Hence to evaluate the performance of the EL model, we use two metrics: reranked NER-F1 score and the EL-F1 score. The reranked NER F1 score is measured on the NER predictions according to the top EL hypothesis, and is defined in the same way as the previous NER task. To evaluate entity linking quality, we adopt a strict F1 metric similar to the one used for NER. Besides entity boundary and entity type, the resolved entity also needs to be correct for the entity prediction to be counted as a true positive.

For NER model training, we use standard mini-batch gradient descent using the Adam optimizer with an initial learning rate of 0.001, a scheduled learning rate decay of 0.99, LSTM with a hidden layer of size 350 and a batch size of 256. We apply a dropout of 0.5 to the embedding and biLSTM layers, and include token level gazetteer features (Ratinov and Roth, 2009) to boost performance in recognizing common entities. We linearly project these gazetteer features and concatenate the projection with the 200 dimensional word embeddings and 100 dimensional character embeddings which are then fed into the biLSTM followed by the CRF.

For EL, the character CNN model we use has two layers, each with 100 convolution kernels of size 3, 4, and 5. Character embedding are 25 dimensional and trained end to end with the entity linking task. The MLP for embedding similarity takes the concatenation of two name embeddings, as well as their element-wise sum, difference, minimum, maximum, and multiplication. It has two hidden layers of size 1024 and 256, with output dimension 64. Similarity features of mentions in the prediction are averaged, while the other features like NER confidence and entity popularity are concatenated to the representation. The final MLP for scoring has two hidden layers, with size 256 and 64. We train the model on 4 GPUs with synchronous SGD, and for each gradient step we send a batch of 100 examples to each GPU.

5 System Evaluation

5.1 Results

We present F1 scores in different domains of the NER and EL model in Table 1. Since the EL model takes 5 NER hypotheses as input, it also acts as a reranker of the NER model, and we show substantial

[3] Sports domain does not have the annotation for noisy data available when this experiment was conducted.

[4] Our KB does not have relation information for movie&TV domain.

improvements on top-1 NER F1 score consistently over all test sets.

	NER F1 top-1/top-5	reranked NER F1	EL F1
movie&TV	78.76 / 96.83	81.62	79.67
music	84.27 / 97.26	87.40	84.95
sports	92.97 / 99.15	93.48	91.13

Table 1: Results for the best model setting. NER F1 are reported on the top-1 and top-5 NER prediction from the NER model that provides features for EL. Reranked NER F1 and EL F1 are reported on top-1 prediction from the best EL model selected by development sets.

In Table 2, we show improvements achieved by several specific model design choices and features on entity linking performance. Table 2(a) shows the MLP similarity substantially improves entity linking accuracy with its capacity to model text variations, especially on utterances with noisy entity mentions. The relation feature is powerful for disambiguating entities with similar names, and we show a considerable improvement in EL F1 on the subset of utterances that have related entities in Table 2(b). Table 2(c) shows utterance embeddings brought improvements in the music, and media & TV domains. The improvement brought by log-scale popularity feature is the largest for the movie & TV domain as shown in Table 2(d), where the popularity distribution has extremely long tails compared to other domains.

5.2 Qualitative Analysis

We provide a few examples to showcase the effectiveness of our NEU system. Firstly, the EL model is able to link noisy entity mentions to the corresponding entity canonical name in the knowledge base. For instance, when the transcribed utterance is "play Carla Cabello", the EL model is able to resolve the mention "Carla Carbello" to the correct artist name "Camila Cabello".

Secondly, the EL model is able to recover from errors made by the NER system by leveraging the knowledge base to disambiguate entity mentions. The reranking is especially powerful when the utterance contains little context of the entity for the NER model to leverage. For example, for "Doctor Strange", the top NER hypothesis labels the full utterance as a generic "Person" type, and after reranking, EL model is able to leverage the popularity information ("Doctor Strange" is a movie that was recently released and has a high popularity in our knowledge base) and correctly label the utterance as "movieTitle". Reranking is also effective when the entity mentions are noisy, which will cause mismatches for the gazetteer features that NER uses. For "play Avengers Age of Ultra", the top NER hypothesis only predicts "Avengers" as "movieTitle", while after reranking, the EL model is able to recover the full span "Avengers Age of Ultra" as a "movieTitle", and resolve it to "Avengers: Age of Ultron", the correct canonical title.

The entity relations from the knowledge base are helpful for entity disambiguation. When the user refers to a sports team with the name "Giants", they could be asking for either "New York Giants", a National Football League (NFL) team, or "San Francisco Giants", a Major League Baseball team. When there are multiple sports team mentions in an utterance, the EL model leverages a relation feature from the knowledge base indicating whether the teams are from the same sports league (as the user is more likely to mention two teams from the same league and the same sport). Knowing entity relations, the EL model is able to link the mention "Giants" in "Cowboys versus Giants" to the NFL team, knowing that "Cowboys" is referring to "Dallas Cowboys".

To validate the utility of our proposed NEU framework, we illustrate performance improvements in the Domain Classifier and the Semantic Parsers corresponding to the three domains (music, movies & TV and sports) as described in Section 3.3. Table 3 reports the classification accuracy for the Domain Classifier and the parse accuracies for the Semantic Parsers (the model is said to have predicted the parse correctly if all the tokens are tagged with their correct semantic parse labels). We observe substantial improvements in all 4 cases when NER features are used as additional input, given all the other components of the system being the same. In turn, we observe further improvements when our NER+EL featurization is used.

6 Conclusion

In this work, we have proposed a Named Entity Understanding framework that jointly identifies and resolves entities present in an utterance when a user interacts with a voice assistant. Our proposed architecture consists of two modules: NER and EL, with the EL serving the additional task of possibly correcting the recognized entities from NER

	(a) + MLP
movie&TV	+3.58
(noisy)	+9.67
music	+2.05
(noisy)	+10.03

	(b) + Relation
music	+0.86
(related)	+1.97
sports	+0.07
(related)	+0.81

	(c) + Utterance Embedding	(d) + Log-scale Popularity
movie&TV	+0.25	+0.27
music	+0.39	+0.02
sports	-0.07	+0.08

Table 2: EL mean F1 relative % improvements, reported on 10 runs average.

	A	B	C
DC	88.95	89.46	**90.04**
SP [movie&TV]	89.62	90.99	**91.67**
SP [music]	83.97	84.26	**84.42**
SP [sports]	86.37	**86.47**	86.46

Table 3: Results for domain classifier (first row) and semantic parser. A is the baseline, B is A+NER, C is A+NER+EL.

by leveraging rich signals from entity links in the knowledge base while simultaneously linking these entities to the knowledge base. With several design strategies in our system targeted towards noisy natural language utterances, we have shown that our framework is robust to speech transcription and user errors that occur frequently in spoken dialog systems. We have also shown that featurizing the output of NEU and feeding these features into other language understanding tasks substantially improves the accuracy of these models.

7 Ethical Considerations

We randomly sampled transcripts from Siri production datasets over a period of months, and we believe it to be a representative sample of usage in the domains described. In accordance with Apple's privacy practices with respect to Siri requests, Siri utterances are not associated with a user's Apple ID, email address, or other data Apple may have from a user's use of other Apple services. In addition to Siri's baseline privacy guarantees, we filtered the sampled utterances to remove transcripts that were too long, contained rare words, or contained references to contacts before providing the dataset to our annotators.

Acknowledgements

We would like to thank Alex Acero, Anmol Walia, Arjun Rangarajan, Barry-John Theobald, Bhagyashree Shekawat, Christopher Klein, Dhivya Piraviperumal, Hong Yu, Jianpeng Cheng, Jiarui Lu, John Giannandrea, John Keesling, Katy Linsky, Lanqing Wang, Ryan Templin, Robert Daland, Shruti Bhargava, Xi Chen and Yvonne Xiao for discussions and for their help and feedback. We also want to thank all the anonymous reviewers for the helpful feedback and suggestions on this work.

References

Abdalghani Abujabal and Judith Gaspers. 2018. Neural named entity recognition from subword units. *arXiv preprint arXiv:1808.07364*.

Adrian Benton and Mark Dredze. 2015. Entity linking for spoken language. In *Proceedings of the 2015 Conference of the North American Chapter of the Association for Computational Linguistics: Human Language Technologies*, pages 225–230, Denver, Colorado. Association for Computational Linguistics.

Kalina Bontcheva, Leon Derczynski, and Ian Roberts. 2017. Crowdsourcing named entity recognition and entity linking corpora. In *Handbook of Linguistic Annotation*, pages 875–892. Springer.

Kevin Bowden, Jiaqi Wu, Shereen Oraby, Amita Misra, and Marilyn Walker. 2018. SlugNERDS: A named entity recognition tool for open domain dialogue systems. In *Proceedings of the Eleventh International Conference on Language Resources and Evaluation (LREC 2018)*, Miyazaki, Japan. European Language Resources Association (ELRA).

Xi C Chen, Adithya Sagar, Justine T Kao, Tony Y Li, Christopher Klein, Stephen Pulman, Ashish Garg, and Jason D Williams. 2019. Active learning for domain classification in a commercial spoken personal assistant. *Proc. Interspeech 2019*, pages 1478–1482.

Alice Coucke, Alaa Saade, Adrien Ball, Théodore Bluche, Alexandre Caulier, David Leroy, Clément Doumouro, Thibault Gisselbrecht, Francesco Caltagirone, Thibaut Lavril, et al. 2018. Snips voice platform: an embedded spoken language understanding system for private-by-design voice interfaces. *arXiv preprint arXiv:1805.10190*.

Leon Derczynski, Diana Maynard, Giuseppe Rizzo, Marieke Van Erp, Genevieve Gorrell, Raphaël

Troncy, Johann Petrak, and Kalina Bontcheva. 2015. Analysis of named entity recognition and linking for tweets. *Information Processing & Management*, 51(2):32–49.

Jacob Devlin, Ming-Wei Chang, Kenton Lee, and Kristina Toutanova. 2019. Bert: Pre-training of deep bidirectional transformers for language understanding. In *Proceedings of the 2019 Conference of the North American Chapter of the Association for Computational Linguistics: Human Language Technologies, Volume 1 (Long and Short Papers)*, pages 4171–4186.

Yotam Eshel, Noam Cohen, Kira Radinsky, Shaul Markovitch, Ikuya Yamada, and Omer Levy. 2017. Named entity disambiguation for noisy text. In *Proceedings of the 21st Conference on Computational Natural Language Learning (CoNLL 2017)*, pages 58–68, Vancouver, Canada. Association for Computational Linguistics.

Ning Gao, Douglas W. Oard, and Mark Dredze. 2017. Support for interactive identification of mentioned entities in conversational speech. In *Proceedings of the 40th International ACM SIGIR Conference on Research and Development in Information Retrieval*, SIGIR '17, page 953–956, New York, NY, USA. Association for Computing Machinery.

Tao Ge, Xingxing Zhang, Furu Wei, and Ming Zhou. 2019. Automatic grammatical error correction for sequence-to-sequence text generation: An empirical study. In *Proceedings of the 57th Annual Meeting of the Association for Computational Linguistics*, pages 6059–6064, Florence, Italy. Association for Computational Linguistics.

Sahar Ghannay, Antoine Caubrière, Yannick Estève, Nathalie Camelin, Edwin Simonnet, Antoine Laurent, and Emmanuel Morin. 2018. End-to-end named entity and semantic concept extraction from speech. In *2018 IEEE Spoken Language Technology Workshop (SLT)*, pages 692–699. IEEE.

Stephen Guo, Ming-Wei Chang, and Emre Kiciman. 2013. To link or not to link? a study on end-to-end tweet entity linking. In *Proceedings of the 2013 Conference of the North American Chapter of the Association for Computational Linguistics: Human Language Technologies*, pages 1020–1030, Atlanta, Georgia. Association for Computational Linguistics.

Sepp Hochreiter and Jürgen Schmidhuber. 1997. Long short-term memory. *Neural computation*, 9(8):1735–1780.

Nikolaos Kolitsas, Octavian-Eugen Ganea, and Thomas Hofmann. 2018. End-to-end neural entity linking. In *Proceedings of the 22nd Conference on Computational Natural Language Learning*, pages 519–529, Brussels, Belgium. Association for Computational Linguistics.

Guillaume Lample, Miguel Ballesteros, Sandeep Subramanian, Kazuya Kawakami, and Chris Dyer. 2016. Neural architectures for named entity recognition. In *Proceedings of the 2016 Conference of the North American Chapter of the Association for Computational Linguistics: Human Language Technologies*, pages 260–270, San Diego, California. Association for Computational Linguistics.

Thomas Lin, Mausam, and Oren Etzioni. 2012. Entity linking at web scale. In *Proceedings of the Joint Workshop on Automatic Knowledge Base Construction and Web-scale Knowledge Extraction (AKBC-WEKEX)*, pages 84–88, Montréal, Canada. Association for Computational Linguistics.

Xiaohua Liu, Yitong Li, Haocheng Wu, Ming Zhou, Furu Wei, and Yi Lu. 2013. Entity linking for tweets. In *Proceedings of the 51st Annual Meeting of the Association for Computational Linguistics (Volume 1: Long Papers)*, pages 1304–1311, Sofia, Bulgaria. Association for Computational Linguistics.

Gang Luo, Xiaojiang Huang, Chin-Yew Lin, and Zaiqing Nie. 2015. Joint entity recognition and disambiguation. In *Proceedings of the 2015 Conference on Empirical Methods in Natural Language Processing*, pages 879–888.

Pedro Henrique Martins, Zita Marinho, and André F. T. Martins. 2019. Joint learning of named entity recognition and entity linking. In *Proceedings of the 57th Annual Meeting of the Association for Computational Linguistics: Student Research Workshop*, pages 190–196, Florence, Italy. Association for Computational Linguistics.

Jeffrey Pennington, Richard Socher, and Christopher Manning. 2014. Glove: Global vectors for word representation. In *Proceedings of the 2014 Conference on Empirical Methods in Natural Language Processing (EMNLP)*, pages 1532–1543, Doha, Qatar. Association for Computational Linguistics.

Lev Ratinov and Dan Roth. 2009. Design challenges and misconceptions in named entity recognition. In *Proceedings of the Thirteenth Conference on Computational Natural Language Learning (CoNLL-2009)*, pages 147–155, Boulder, Colorado. Association for Computational Linguistics.

Allen Schmaltz, Yoon Kim, Alexander Rush, and Stuart Shieber. 2017. Adapting sequence models for sentence correction. In *Proceedings of the 2017 Conference on Empirical Methods in Natural Language Processing*, pages 2807–2813, Copenhagen, Denmark. Association for Computational Linguistics.

Avirup Sil and Alexander Yates. 2013. Re-ranking for joint named-entity recognition and linking. In *Proceedings of the 22nd ACM international conference on Information and Knowledge Management*, pages 2369—2374, San Francisco, USA.

Erik F. Tjong Kim Sang and Fien De Meulder. 2003. Introduction to the CoNLL-2003 shared task: Language-independent named entity recognition. In *Proceedings of the Seventh Conference on Natural Language Learning at HLT-NAACL 2003*, pages 142–147.

Goodwill Hunting: Analyzing and Repurposing Off-the-Shelf Named Entity Linking Systems

Karan Goel*
Stanford University

Laurel Orr
Stanford University

Nazneen Fatema Rajani
Salesforce Research

Jesse Vig
Salesforce Research

Christopher Ré
Stanford University

Abstract

Named entity linking (NEL) or mapping "strings" to "things" in a knowledge base is a fundamental preprocessing step in systems that require knowledge of entities such as information extraction and question answering. In this work, we lay out and investigate two challenges faced by individuals or organizations building NEL systems. Can they directly use an off-the-shelf system? If not, how easily can such a system be repurposed for their use case? First, we conduct a study of off-the-shelf commercial and academic NEL systems. We find that most systems struggle to link rare entities, with commercial solutions lagging their academic counterparts by 10%+. Second, for a use case where the NEL model is used in a sports question-answering (QA) system, we investigate how to close the loop in our analysis by repurposing the best off-the-shelf model (BOOTLEG) to correct sport-related errors. We show how tailoring a simple technique for patching models using weak labeling can provide a 25% absolute improvement in accuracy of sport-related errors.

1 Introduction

Named entity linking (NEL), the task of mapping from "strings" to "things" in a knowledge base, is a fundamental component of commercial systems such as information extraction and question answering (Shen et al., 2015). Given some text, NEL systems perform contextualized linking of text phrases, called *mentions*, to a knowledge base. If a user asks her personal assistant "How long would it take to drive a Lincoln to Lincoln", the NEL system underlying the assistant should link the first mention of "Lincoln" to the car company, and the second "Lincoln" to Lincoln in Nebraska, in order to answer correctly.

As NEL models have direct impact on the success of downstream products (Peters et al., 2019), all major technology companies deploy large-scale NEL systems; e.g., in Google Search, Apple Siri and Salesforce Einstein. While these companies can afford to build custom NEL systems at scale, we consider how a smaller organization or individual could achieve the same objectives.

We start with a simple question: how would someone, starting from scratch, build an NEL system for their use case? Can existing NEL systems be used off-the-shelf, and if not, can they be repurposed with minimal engineer effort? Our "protagonist" here must navigate two challenging problems, as shown in Figure 1:

1. **Off-the-shelf capabilities.** Industrial NEL systems provide limited transparency into their performance, and the majority of academic NEL systems are measured on standard benchmarks biased towards popular entities (Steinmetz et al., 2013). However, prior works suggest that NEL systems struggle on so-called "tail" entities that appear infrequently in data (Jin et al., 2014; Orr et al., 2020). As the majority of user queries are over the tail (Bernstein et al., 2012; Gomes, 2017), it is critical to understand the extent to which NEL systems struggle on the tail in off-the-shelf academic and commercial systems.

2. **Repurposing systems.** If off-the-shelf systems are inadequate on the tail or other relevant subpopulations, how difficult is it for our protagonist to develop a customized solution without building a system from scratch? Can they treat an existing NEL model as a black box and still modify its behavior? When faced with designing a NEL system with desired capabilities, prior work has largely focused on developing new systems (Sevgili et al., 2020; Shen et al., 2014; Mudgal et al., 2018). The question of how to guide or "patch" an existing NEL system without changing its architecture, features, or training strategy—what we call *model*

* E-mail: kgoel@cs.stanford.edu

Proceedings of NAACL HLT 2021: IndustryTrack Papers, pages 205–213
June 6–11, 2021. ©2021 Association for Computational Linguistics

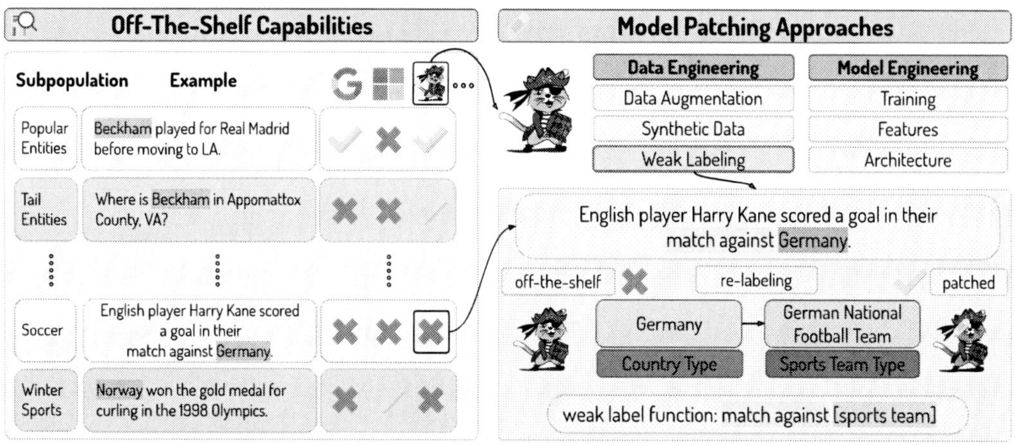

Figure 1: Challenges faced by individuals or small organizations in building NEL systems. *(left)* the fine-grained performance of off-the-shelf NEL systems varies widely—struggling on tail entities and sports-relevant subpopulations—making it likely that they must be repurposed for use; *(right)* for a sports QA application where no off-the-shelf system succeeds, the best-performing model (BOOTLEG) can be treated as a black box and successfully patched using weak labeling. In the example, a simple rule re-labels training data to discourage the BOOTLEG model from predicting a country entity ("Germany") when a clear sports-relevant contextual cue ("match against") is present.

engineering—remains unaddressed.

In response to these questions, we investigate the limitations of existing systems and the possibility of repurposing them:

1. **Understanding failure modes (Section 3).** We conduct the first study of open-source academic and commercially available NEL systems. We compare commercial APIs from MICROSOFT, GOOGLE and AMAZON to open-source systems BOOTLEG (Orr et al., 2020), WAT (Piccinno and Ferragina, 2014) and REL (van Hulst et al., 2020) on subpopulations across 2 benchmark datasets of WIKIPEDIA and AIDA (Hoffart et al., 2011). Supporting prior work, we find that most systems struggle to link rare entities, are sensitive to entity capitalization and often ignore contextual cues when making predictions. On WIKIPEDIA, commercial systems lag their academic counterparts by 10%+ recall, while MICROSOFT outperforms other commercial systems by 16%+ recall. On AIDA, a heuristic that relies on entity popularity (POP) outperforms all commercial systems by 1.5 F1. Overall, BOOTLEG is the most consistent system.

2. **Patching models (Section 3.2).** Consider a scenario where our protagonist wants to use a NEL system as part of a downstream QA model answering sport-related queries; e.g., "When did England last win the FIFA world cup?". All models underperform on sport-relevant subpopulations of AIDA; e.g., BOOTLEG can fail to predict national sports teams despite strong sport-relevant contextual cues, favoring the country entity instead. We therefore take the best system, BOOTLEG, and show how to correct undesired behavior using *data engineering* solutions—model agnostic methods that modify or create training data. Drawing on simple strategies from prior work in weak labeling, which uses user-defined functions to weakly label data (Ratner et al., 2017), we relabel standard WIKIPEDIA training data to patch these errors and finetune the model on this relabeled dataset. With this strategy, we achieve a 25% absolute improvement in accuracy on the mentions where a model predicts a country rather than a sports team.

We believe these principles of understanding fine-grained failure modes in the NEL system and correcting them with data engineering apply to large-scale industrial pipelines where the NEL model or its embeddings are used in numerous downstream products.

2 Named Entity Linking

Given some text, NEL involves two steps: the identification of all entity mentions (*mention ex-*

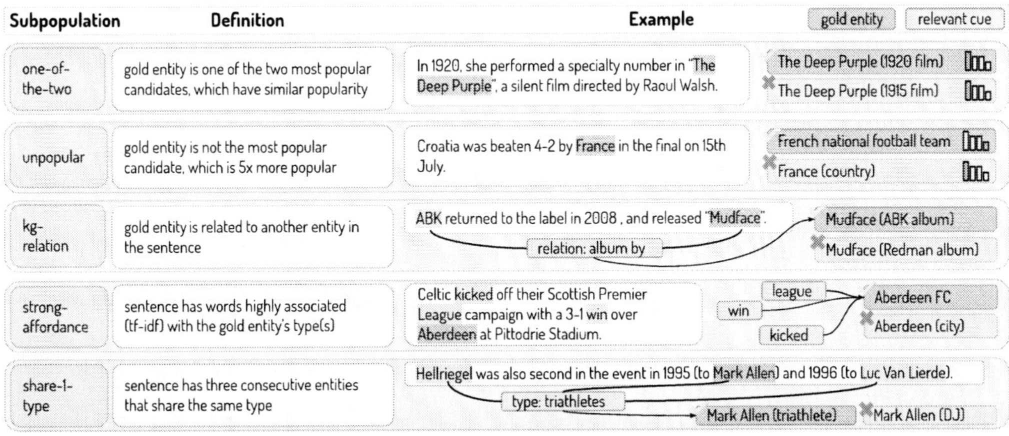

Figure 2: Subpopulations analyzed on the WIKIPEDIA dataset, along with their definitions and examples. We consider five subpopulations inspired by Orr et al. (2020).

traction), and contextualized linking of these mentions to their corresponding knowledge base entries (*mention disambiguation*). For example, in "What ingredients are in a Manhattan", the mention "Manhattan" links to `Manhattan (cocktail)`, not `Manhattan (borough)` or `The Manhattan Project`. Internally, most systems have an intermediate step that generates a small set of possible candidates for each mention (*candidate generation*) for the disambiguation model to choose from.

Given the goal of building a NEL system for a specific use case, we need to answer two questions: (1) what are the failure modes of existing systems, and (2) can they be repurposed, or "patched", to achieve desired performance.

3 Understanding Failure Modes

We begin by analyzing the fine-grained performance of off-the-shelf academic and commercial systems for NEL.

Setup. To perform this analysis, we use Robustness Gym (Goel et al., 2021b), an open-source evaluation toolkit for analyzing natural language processing models. We evaluate all NEL systems by considering their performance on *subpopulations*, or subsets of data that satisfy some condition.

Systems. We use 3 commercially available APIs: (i) GOOGLE Cloud Natural Language API (Google) , (ii) MICROSOFT Text Analytics API (Microsoft) , and (iii) AMAZON Comprehend API (Amazon)[1]. We compare to 3 state-of-the-art systems: (i) BOOTLEG, a self-supervised system, (ii) REL, which combines existing state-of-the-art approaches, (iii) WAT an extension of the TAGME (Ferragina and Scaiella, 2010) linker. We also compare to a simple heuristic (iv) POP, which picks the most popular entity among candidates provided by BOOTLEG.

Datasets. We compare methods on examples drawn from two datasets: (i) WIKIPEDIA, which contains $100,000$ entity mentions mined from gold anchor links across $37,492$ sentences from a November 2019 Wikipedia dataset, and (ii) AIDA, the AIDA test-b benchmark dataset[2].

Metrics. As WIKIPEDIA is sparsely labeled (Ghaddar and Langlais, 2017), we compare performance on recall. For AIDA, we use Macro-F1, since AIDA provides a more dense labeling of entities.

Results. Our results for WIKIPEDIA and AIDA are reported in Figures 3, 4 respectively.

3.1 Analysis on WIKIPEDIA

Subpopulations. In line with Orr et al. (2020), we consider 4 groups of examples — *head, torso, tail and toe* — that are based on the popularity of the entities being linked. Intuitively, head examples involve resolving popular entities that occur frequently in WIKIPEDIA, torso examples have medium popularity while tail examples correspond to entities that are seen rarely. Toe entities are a subset of the tail that are almost never seen. We con-

[1] AMAZON performs named entity recognition (NER) to identify entity mentions in text, so we use it in conjunction with a simple string matching heuristic to resolve entity links.

[2] REL uses AIDA for training, so we exclude it.

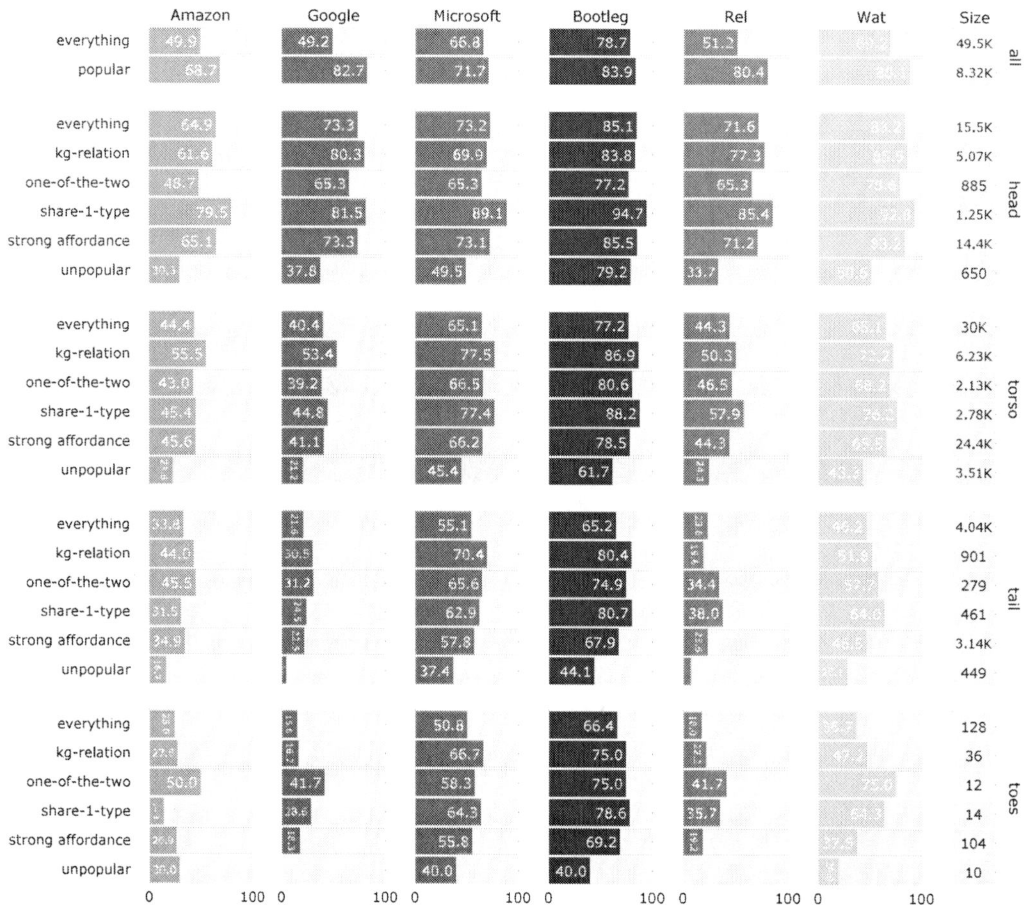

Figure 3: Robustness Report (Goel et al., 2021b) for NEL on Wikipedia, measuring recall.

sider 5 subpopulations inspired by Orr et al. (2020), described in Figure 2 with examples. These subpopulations require close attention to contextual cues such as relations, affordances and types.

We also consider aggregate performance on the entire dataset (**everything**), and **globally popular** entities, which are examples where the entity mention is in the top 800 most popular entity mentions.

BOOTLEG is best overall. Overall, BOOTLEG outperforms other systems by a wide margin, with a 12-point gap to the next best system (MICROSOFT), while MICROSOFT in turn outperforms other commercial systems by more than 16 points.

Performance degrades on rare entities. For all systems, performance on head slices is substantially better than performance on tail/toe slices. BOOTLEG is the most robust across the set of slices that we consider. Among commercial systems, GOOGLE and AMAZON struggle on tail and torso entities e.g. GOOGLE from 73.3 points on *head* to 21.6 points on *tail*, while MICROSOFT's performance degrades more gracefully. GOOGLE is adept at globally popular entities, where it outperforms MICROSOFT by more than 11 points.

3.2 Analysis on AIDA

Subpopulations. We consider subpopulations that vary by: (i) fraction of capitalized entities, (ii) average popularity of mentioned entities, (iii) number of mentioned entities; (iv) sports-related topic.

Overall performance. Similar to WIKIPEDIA, BOOTLEG performs best, beating WAT by 1.3%, with commercial systems lagging by 11%+.

Sensitivity to capitalization. Both GOOGLE and MICROSOFT are sensitive to whether the entity mention is capitalized. GOOGLE's performance goes from 54.1% on sentences where all mentions

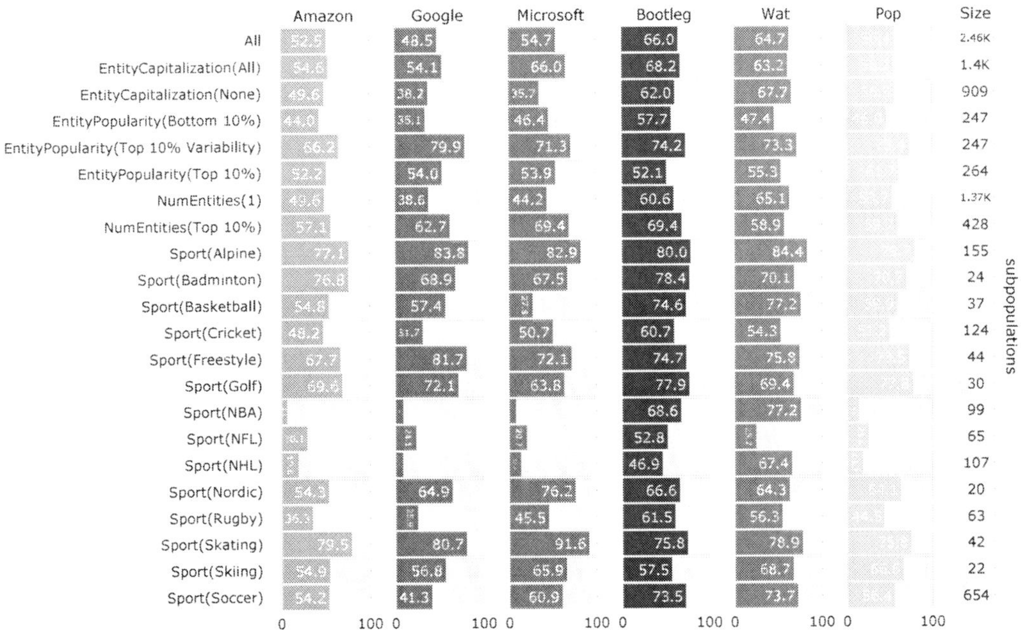

Figure 4: Robustness Report (Goel et al., 2021b) for NEL on AIDA, measuring Macro-F1.

are capitalized to 38.2% on sentences where none are capitalized. Similarly, MICROSOFT degrades from 66.0% to 35.7%. This suggests that mention extraction in these models is capitalization sensitive. In contrast, AMAZON, BOOTLEG and WAT appear insensitive to capitalization artifacts.

Performance on topical entities. Interestingly, all models struggle on some topics, e.g. on NHL examples, all models degrade significantly, with WAT outperforming others by 20%+. GOOGLE and MICROSOFT display strong performance on some topics, e.g., GOOGLE on alpine sports (83.8%) and MICROSOFT on skating (91.6%).

Popularity heuristic outperforms commercial systems. Somewhat surprisingly, POP outperforms all commercial systems by 1.7%. In fact, we note that the pattern of errors for POP is very similar to those of the commercial systems, e.g., performing poorly on NBA, NFL and NHL slices. This suggests that commercial systems sidestep the difficult problem of disambiguating ambiguous entities in favor of returning the more popular answer. Similar to WIKIPEDIA, GOOGLE performs best among commercial systems on examples with globally popular entities (top 10% entity popularity).

Our results suggest that state-of-the-art academic systems outperform commercial APIs for NEL.

Next, we explore whether it is possible to simply "patch" an off-the-shelf NEL model for a specific downstream use case. Standard methods for designing models with desired capabilities require technical expertise to engineer the architecture and features. As these skills are out of reach for many organizations and individuals, we consider patching models where they are treated as a black-box.

We provide a proof-of-concept that we can use data engineering to patch a model. For our grounding use case, we consider the scenario where the NEL model will be used as part of a sports question-answering (QA) system that uses a knowledge graph (KG) to answer questions. For example, given the question "When did England last win the FIFA world cup?", we would want the NEL model to resolve the *metonymic* mention "England" to the English national football team, and not the country. This makes it easy for the QA model to answer the question using the "winner" KG-relationship to the 1966 FIFA World Cup, which applies only to the team and not the country.

3.3 Predicting the Wrong Granularity

Our off-the-shelf analysis revealed that all models struggle on sport-related subpopulations of AIDA. For instance, BOOTLEG is biased towards predicting countries instead of sport teams, even with strong contextual cues. For example, in the sentence "...the years I spent as manager of the Republic of Ireland were the best years of my life", BOOTLEG predicts the country "Republic of Ireland" instead of the national sports team. In general, this makes it undesirable to directly use off-the-shelf in our sports QA system scenario.

We explore repurposing in a controlled environment using BOOTLEG, the best-performing off-the-shelf NEL model. We train a small model, called BOOTLEGSPORT, over a WIKIPEDIA subset consisting only of sentences with mentions referring to both countries and national sport teams. We define a subpopulation, *strong-sport-cues*, as mentions directly preceded by a highly correlated sport team cue[3]. Examining *strong-sport-cues* reveals two insights into BOOTLEGSPORT's behavior:

1. BOOTLEGSPORT misses some strong sport-relevant textual cues. In this subpopulation, 5.8% examples are mispredicted as countries.

2. In this supopulation, an estimated 5.6% of mentions are *incorrectly* labeled as countries in WIKIPEDIA. As WIKIPEDIA is hand labeled by users, it contains some label noise.

In our use case, we want to guide BOOTLEGSPORT to always predict a sport team over a country in sport-related sentences.

3.4 Repurposing with Weak Labeling

While there are some prior data engineering solutions to "model patching", including augmentation (Sennrich et al., 2015; Wei and Zou, 2019; Kaushik et al., 2019; Goel et al., 2021a), weak labeling (Ratner et al., 2017; Chen et al., 2020), and synthetic data generation (Murty et al., 2020), due to the noise in WIKIPEDIA, we repurpose BOOTLEGSPORT using weak labeling to modify training labels and correct for this noise. Our weak labeling technique works as follows: any existing mention from *strong-sport-cues* that is labeled as a country is relabeled as a national sports team for that country. We choose the national sport team to be consistent with other sport entities in the sentence. If there are none, we choose a random national sport team. While this may introduce noise, it allows us to guide BOOTLEGSPORT to prefer sport teams over countries.

[3]We mine these textual cues by looking at the most commmon two-grams proceeding a national sport team in the training data. The result is phrases such as "scored against", "match against", and "defending champion".

Subpop.	Gold Label	Pred. Label	Size (Off-The-Shelf → Patched)	
All	Country	Country	90885 → 90591	(↓)
		Team	201 → 254	(↑)
	Team	Country	216 → 161	(↓)
		Team	4057 → 4120	(↑)
Weak Sport Cues	Country	Country	15225 → 15139	(↓)
		Team	154 → 190	(↑)
	Team	Country	151 → 106	(↓)
		Team	3393 → 3447	(↑)

Table 1: BOOTLEGSPORT prediction matrix before and after model patching. The weak sport cues subpopulation contains sentences with more generic sport related keywords.

Results. After performing weak labeling, we fine-tune BOOTLEGSPORT over this modified dataset. As WIKIPEDIA ground truth labels are noisy and do not reflect our goal of favoring sport teams in sport sentences, we examine the distribution of predictions before and after guiding. In Table 1 we see that our patched model shows an increased trend in predicting sport teams. Further, the patched BOOTLEGSPORT model now only predicts countries in 4.0% of the *strong-sport-cues* subpopulation, a 30% relative reduction.

For examples where the gold entity is a sports team that BOOTLEGSPORT predicts is a country, weak labeling improves absolute accuracy by 24.54%. Weak-labeling "shifts" probability mass from countries towards teams by 20% on these examples, and 1.8% overall across all examples where the gold entity is a sports team. It does so without "disturbing" probabilities on examples where the true answer is indeed a country, where the shift is only 0.07% towards teams.

4 Related Work

Identifying Errors. A key step in assessing off-the-shelf systems is *fine-grained evaluation*, to determine if a system exhibits undesirable behavior. Prior work on fine-grained evaluation in NEL (Rosales-Méndez et al., 2019) characterizes how to more consistently evaluate NEL models, with an analysis that focuses on academic systems. By contrast, we consider both academic and industrial off-the-shelf systems, and describe how to assess them in the context of a downstream use-case. We use Robustness Gym (Goel et al., 2021b), an open-source evaluation toolkit for performing the analysis, although other evaluation toolkits (Ribeiro et al., 2020; Morris et al., 2020) are possible to use, depending on the objective of the assessment.

Patching Errors. If a system is assessed to have some undesirable behavior, the next step is to correct its errors and repurpose it for use. The key challenge lies in how to correct these errors. Although similar to the related fields of domain adaptation (Wang and Deng, 2018) and transfer learning (Zhuang et al., 2020) where the goal is to transfer knowledge from a pretrained, source model to a related task in a potentially different domain, our work focuses on user-guided behavior correction when using a pretrained model on the same task.

For industrial NEL applications, Orr et al. (2020) describe how to use data management techniques such as augmentation (Sennrich et al., 2015; Wei and Zou, 2019; Kaushik et al., 2019; Goel et al., 2021a), weak supervision (Ratner et al., 2017), and slice-based learning (Chen et al., 2019) to correct underperforming, user-defined sub-populations of data. Focusing on image data Goel et al. (2021a) use domain translation models to generate synthetic augmentation data that improves underperforming subpopulations.

NEL. NEL has been a long standing problem in industrial and academic systems. Standard, pre-deep-learning approaches to NEL have been rule-based (Aberdeen et al., 1996), but in recent years, deep learning systems have become the new standard (see Mudgal et al. (2018) for an overview of deep learning approaches to NEL), often relying on contextual knowledge from language models such as BERT (Févry et al., 2020) for state-of-the-art performance. Despite strong benchmark performance, the long tail of NEL (Bernstein et al., 2012; Gomes, 2017) in industrial workloads has remained a challenge. Recent papers Orr et al. (2020); Wu et al. (2019) have begun to measure and improve performance on unseen entities, but it remains an open problem.

5 Conclusion

We studied the performance of off-the-shelf NEL models and how to repurpose them for a downstream use case. In line with prior work, we found that off-the-shelf models struggle to disambiguate rare entities. Using a sport QA system as a case study, we showed how to use a data engineering solution to patch a BOOTLEG model from mispredicting countries instead of sports teams. We hope that our study of data engineering to effectuate model behavior inspires future work in this direction.

Acknowledgements

CR gratefully acknowledges the support of NIH under No. U54EB020405 (Mobilize), NSF under Nos. CCF1763315 (Beyond Sparsity), CCF1563078 (Volume to Velocity), and 1937301 (RTML); ONR under No. N000141712266 (Unifying Weak Supervision); the Moore Foundation, NXP, Xilinx, LETI-CEA, Intel, IBM, Microsoft, NEC, Toshiba, TSMC, ARM, Hitachi, BASF, Accenture, Ericsson, Qualcomm, Analog Devices, the Okawa Foundation, American Family Insurance, Google Cloud, Swiss Re, Total, the HAI-AWS Cloud Credits for Research program, the Salesforce AI Research grant and members of the Stanford DAWN project: Facebook, Google, and VMWare. The U.S. Government is authorized to reproduce and distribute reprints for Governmental purposes notwithstanding any copyright notation thereon. Any opinions, findings, and conclusions or recommendations expressed in this material are those of the authors and do not necessarily reflect the views, policies, or endorsements, either expressed or implied, of NIH, ONR, or the U.S. Government.

References

John Aberdeen, John D Burger, David Day, Lynette Hirschman, David D Palmer, Patricia Robinson, and Marc Vilain. 1996. Mitre: Description of the alembic system as used in met. In *TIPSTER TEXT PROGRAM PHASE II: Proceedings of a Workshop held at Vienna, Virginia, May 6-8, 1996*, pages 461–462.

Amazon. Amazon comprehend api.

Michael S Bernstein, Jaime Teevan, Susan Dumais, Daniel Liebling, and Eric Horvitz. 2012. Direct answers for search queries in the long tail. In *SIGCHI*.

Mayee F. Chen, Daniel Y. Fu, Frederic Sala, Sen Wu, Ravi Teja Mullapudi, Fait Poms, Kayvon Fatahalian, and Christopher Ré. 2020. Train and you'll miss it: Interactive model iteration with weak supervision and pre-trained embeddings. *arXiv preprint arXiv:2006.15168*.

Vincent Chen, Sen Wu, Alexander J Ratner, Jen Weng, and Christopher Ré. 2019. Slice-based learning: A programming model for residual learning in critical data slices. In *Advances in neural information processing systems*, pages 9392–9402.

P. Ferragina and Ugo Scaiella. 2010. Tagme: on-the-fly annotation of short text fragments (by wikipedia entities). *ArXiv*, abs/1006.3498.

Thibault Févry, Nicholas FitzGerald, Livio Baldini Soares, and Tom Kwiatkowski. 2020. Empirical evaluation of pretraining strategies for supervised entity linking. In *AKBC*.

Abbas Ghaddar and Philippe Langlais. 2017. Winer: A wikipedia annotated corpus for named entity recognition. In *Proceedings of the Eighth International Joint Conference on Natural Language Processing (Volume 1: Long Papers)*, pages 413–422.

Karan Goel, Albert Gu, Yixuan Li, and Christopher Ré. 2021a. Model patching: Closing the subgroup performance gap with data augmentation. In *The International Conference on Learning Representations (ICLR)*.

Karan Goel, Nazneen Rajani, Jesse Vig, Samson Tan, Jason Wu, Stephan Zheng, Caiming Xiong, Mohit Bansal, and Christopher Ré. 2021b. Robustness gym: Unifying the nlp evaluation landscape.

Ben Gomes. 2017. Our latest quality improvements for search. `https://blog.google/products/search/our-latest-quality-improvements-search/`.

Google. Google cloud natural language api.

Johannes Hoffart, Mohamed Amir Yosef, Ilaria Bordino, Hagen Fürstenau, Manfred Pinkal, Marc Spaniol, Bilyana Taneva, Stefan Thater, and Gerhard Weikum. 2011. Robust disambiguation of named entities in text. In *Proceedings of the 2011 Conference on Empirical Methods in Natural Language Processing*, pages 782–792.

Johannes M. van Hulst, F. Hasibi, K. Dercksen, K. Balog, and A. D. Vries. 2020. Rel: An entity linker standing on the shoulders of giants. *Proceedings of the 43rd International ACM SIGIR Conference on Research and Development in Information Retrieval*.

Yuzhe Jin, Emre Kıcıman, Kuansan Wang, and Ricky Loynd. 2014. Entity linking at the tail: sparse signals, unknown entities, and phrase models. In *Proceedings of the 7th ACM international conference on Web search and data mining*, pages 453–462.

Divyansh Kaushik, Eduard Hovy, and Zachary C Lipton. 2019. Learning the difference that makes a difference with counterfactually-augmented data. *arXiv preprint arXiv:1909.12434*.

Microsoft. Microsoft text analytics api.

John X Morris, Eli Lifland, Jin Yong Yoo, and Yanjun Qi. 2020. Textattack: A framework for adversarial attacks in natural language processing. *arXiv preprint arXiv:2005.05909*.

Sidharth Mudgal, Han Li, Theodoros Rekatsinas, An-Hai Doan, Youngchoon Park, Ganesh Krishnan, Rohit Deep, Esteban Arcaute, and Vijay Raghavendra. 2018. Deep learning for entity matching: A design space exploration. In *Proceedings of the 2018 International Conference on Management of Data*, pages 19–34.

Shikhar Murty, Pang Wei Koh, and Percy Liang. 2020. Expbert: Representation engineering with natural language explanations. *arXiv preprint arXiv:2005.01932*.

L. Orr, Megan Leszczynski, Simran Arora, Sen Wu, N. Guha, Xiao Ling, and C. Ré. 2020. Bootleg: Chasing the tail with self-supervised named entity disambiguation. *CIDR*.

Matthew E Peters, Mark Neumann, Robert L Logan IV, Roy Schwartz, Vidur Joshi, Sameer Singh, and Noah A Smith. 2019. Knowledge enhanced contextual word representations. *arXiv preprint arXiv:1909.04164*.

Francesco Piccinno and P. Ferragina. 2014. From tagme to wat: a new entity annotator. In *ERD '14*.

Alexander Ratner, Stephen H Bach, Henry Ehrenberg, Jason Fries, Sen Wu, and Christopher Ré. 2017. Snorkel: Rapid training data creation with weak supervision. In *Proceedings of the VLDB Endowment. International Conference on Very Large Data Bases*, volume 11, page 269. NIH Public Access.

Marco Tulio Ribeiro, Tongshuang Wu, Carlos Guestrin, and Sameer Singh. 2020. Beyond accuracy: Behavioral testing of nlp models with checklist. In *Association for Computational Linguistics (ACL)*.

Henry Rosales-Méndez, Aidan Hogan, and Barbara Poblete. 2019. Fine-grained evaluation for entity linking. In *Proceedings of the 2019 Conference on Empirical Methods in Natural Language Processing and the 9th International Joint Conference on Natural Language Processing (EMNLP-IJCNLP)*, pages 718–727.

Rico Sennrich, Barry Haddow, and Alexandra Birch. 2015. Improving neural machine translation models with monolingual data. *arXiv preprint arXiv:1511.06709*.

Ozge Sevgili, Artem Shelmanov, Mikhail Arkhipov, Alexander Panchenko, and Chris Biemann. 2020. Neural entity linking: A survey of models based on deep learning. *arXiv preprint arXiv:2006.00575*.

Wei Shen, Jianyong Wang, and Jiawei Han. 2014. Entity linking with a knowledge base: Issues, techniques, and solutions. *IEEE Transactions on Knowledge and Data Engineering*, 27(2):443–460.

Wei Shen, Jianyong Wang, and Jiawei Han. 2015. Entity linking with a knowledge base: Issues, techniques, and solutions. *IEEE Transactions on Knowledge and Data Engineering*, 27:443–460.

Nadine Steinmetz, Magnus Knuth, and Harald Sack. 2013. Statistical analyses of named entity disambiguation benchmarks. In *NLP-DBPEDIA@ ISWC*.

Mei Wang and Weihong Deng. 2018. Deep visual domain adaptation: A survey. *Neurocomputing*, 312:135–153.

Jason W Wei and Kai Zou. 2019. Eda: Easy data augmentation techniques for boosting performance on text classification tasks. *arXiv preprint arXiv:1901.11196*.

Ledell Wu, Fabio Petroni, Martin Josifoski, Sebastian Riedel, and Luke Zettlemoyer. 2019. Scalable zero-shot entity linking with dense entity retrieval. *arXiv preprint arXiv:1911.03814*.

Fuzhen Zhuang, Zhiyuan Qi, Keyu Duan, Dongbo Xi, Yongchun Zhu, Hengshu Zhu, Hui Xiong, and Qing He. 2020. A comprehensive survey on transfer learning. *Proceedings of the IEEE*, 109(1):43–76.

Intent Features for Rich Natural Language Understanding

Brian Lester[♠*] and **Sagnik Ray Choudhury**[◇†] and **Rashmi Prasad**[♠] and **Srinivas Bangalore**[♠]
[♠]Interactions, 41 Spring Street, New Providence, NJ 07974
[◇]University of Copenhagen, Denmark
{blester,rprasad,sbangalore}@interactions.com, src@di.ku.dk

Abstract

Complex natural language understanding modules in dialog systems have a richer understanding of user utterances, and thus are critical in providing a better user experience. However, these models are often created from scratch, for specific clients and use cases, and require the annotation of large datasets. This encourages the sharing of annotated data across multiple clients. To facilitate this we introduce the idea of *intent features*: domain and topic agnostic properties of intents that can be learned from the syntactic cues only, and hence can be shared. We introduce a new neural network architecture, the Global-Local model, that shows significant improvement over strong baselines for identifying these features in a deployed, multi-intent natural language understanding module, and, more generally, in a classification setting where a part of an utterance has to be classified utilizing the whole context.

1 Introduction

While generic dialog systems, or chatbots, such as Amazon Alexa or Google Assistant, are increasingly popular, to date, most industrial dialog systems are built for specific clients and use cases. Typically, these systems have the following: 1. A natural language understanding (NLU) module to analyze the user utterance, 2. A dialog manager module to reason over the analyzed utterance and decide on an action, and 3. A natural language generation module to generate an appropriate response based on the action.

Typically, an NLU module has two purposes: understanding the intent or goal of an utterance (classification) and identifying the entities in the utterance (slot filling). As dialog managers have evolved from simple flow-based systems to information state update systems (Traum and Larsson, 2003), NLU modules have progressed past simple single intent detection and flat slot filling to multiple intents and nested entities (Chen et al., 2018). As these dialog systems need to be rebuilt for each client, the NLU module faces a significant data bottleneck; it is time-consuming and expensive to collect data, develop a domain-specific annotation scheme, and annotate data. Therefore, it is imperative that the data is shared across clients as much as possible.

In a production dialogue system, there are often similar situations that require drastically different responses. For example, "I want to cancel my subscription." and "I am thinking about canceling my subscription." are very similar. They are both about the canceling of a subscription. However, they differ in the users conviction. The latter user is much more likely to not cancel if offered a discount. Making this distinction is critical for creating sophisticated and nuanced dialogue systems. A common approach to solve this problem would be to split the intent space so the dialogue manager can differentiate between these examples, creating a `cancel` and a `think-cancel` intent. Using intents to recognize specific situations leads to data sparsity as each intent is broken into many subcategories like present vs. past tense, how certain a user is in their actions, and if the user has tried an action or not. There would be very few examples of each intent. Additionally, the combinations of different sub-categories would cause a combinatorial explosion of intents. Another short-coming of fine-grained intents is the loss of compositionality. Fundamentally the `cancel` and `think-cancel` intents are very similar, but because they are modeled as independent output classes, there is not a shared representation of these labels the model can lean on.

In order to avoid these shortcomings, and allow for many examples per intent, we factor out these small differences in situations into what we call

*Now an AI Resident at Google
†Work done while at Interactions

Proceedings of NAACL HLT 2021: IndustryTrack Papers, pages 214–221
June 6–11, 2021. ©2021 Association for Computational Linguistics

intent features. Intent features are a set of domain-independent properties for intents that can primarily be understood from the syntax of the utterance. These intent features represent specifics of situation, such as tense, without having a massive intent space. By decoupling these small differences, we can keep the intent categories general, while still providing the dialogue manager with the information it needs for nuanced, human-like responses.

In a multi-intent setting where each clause in the utterance has an intent, intent features reduce to the problem of classification of a span embedded within a larger utterance. We propose a new model, the Global-Local model, for this problem which shows significant improvement over strong baselines.

2 Intent Features

Table 1 shows a sample utterance with its intents and features. This is a multi-intent setting where non-overlapping spans of an utterance have different intents. Each intent span has the following features:

Communicative functions: The communicative functions (cf) captures what kind of response (or action) the user is trying to elicit from the system. We define five such functions:

- `inform`: The user is informing the system about something. Typically, these intents are a response to a question or they represent background information surrounding the main purpose of the utterance. For example, in the utterance, "I am installing X but it keeps saying I have an error", the first clause has a communicative function of `inform`. The user provides background information about installing something on a device and then presents a problem with the install procedure, which would have a communicative function of `issue`.
- `issue`: The user is saying that something has gone against their expectations (see above for an example).
- `request-action`: The user requests for some action to be undertaken in response to the request, or requests help with something. For example, "I would like to install X."
- `request-confirm`: The user is requesting confirmation, or disconfirmation, of their belief. Often this warrants a yes/no answer. For example, one expects a yes or no from, "Was my installation successful?"
- `request-info`: The user is requesting some information about something. These are typically expressed as "wh/how" questions, such as: "How can I install X?"

All of our running examples above share the intent of installing software; however, differences in phrasing warrants different responses. An `inform` does not typically require a targeted reply from the system, whereas for an `issue`, the system should start the response with "I am sorry you are having trouble."

Attribution: Attribution is concerned with *agency*. There are two types of attribution. The first type is the of attribution of the communicative function (**attr-cf**) and it deals with who is the primary source of the content of the topic. The second type is the attribution of the event/action (**attr-ev**) of a topic and describes who is the agent of the event or action. This is perhaps best elucidated by an example. In Table 2, we see multiple utterances that all have the intent `payment`, but we can see how the attribution features change as both the payer and the informer of the payment change. Both **attr-cf** and **attr-ev** take values `self` (when the agent is the user) and `other`.

Negation: Topics of many intents are represented in their negated versions, as well. For example, in the software domain, the `compatibility` intent models whether a piece of software is compatible with some device. A negation feature would denote incompatibility. The negation feature takes values `positive` and `negative`.

Tense: Events and actions can occur in the past, present, or future, which is modeled by the tense feature using values of `past`, `present`, or `future`. The steps to solve a problem as it occurs are often quick-fixes, whereas the first step when fixing a problem that occurred in the past is often information gathering. The tense feature allows the dialogue manager to distinguish between these two possibilities. Tense information is common in the annotation of event extraction, such as in ACE 2005 dataset (Consortium, 2005).

Modality: The real-world actions and events represented by an intent can also be viewed in terms of a modality of certainty, that is, whether or not the event or action actually occurred, and to what degree. We consider two types of modality. The first

text	topic/intent	attr-cf	attr-ev	cf	modality	negation	tense
I am trying to install	install	self	self	inform	modal-try	positive	present
and	-	-	-		-	-	-
I see a problem	general	self	self	issue	other	positive	present

Table 1: A sample utterance from our dataset with multiple intents and features. Each row represents an intent span and the columns are the features that apply to that particular intent. We see that intents are general categories of actions like "install", while intent features yield specifics of the current state of the user. Given the "modality" and "tense" features, we see that the user is currently in the middle of installing the program, rather than telling us they installed it last week. "cf" stands for communicative function.

Utterance	Attribution CF	Attribution Ev
I have paid $$	self	self
I got an email confirming I paid $$	other	self
I was charged $$	self	other
I got an email confirming that I was charged $$	other	other

Table 2: Different types of attribution with the same `payment` intent. The dialogue manager would react differently depending on whether the user paid voluntarily vs she was charged or if she was only informed that she was charged.

is *possibility*—the expression of the event as hypothetical, or being possible, rather than certain, as in, "I am *planning/going* to install X on my laptop." We also consider *attempts at action*. An expression can imply that it is unclear whether the action was completed or is in the attempted stage. This is expressed with modifying verbs, such as, "try", as in, "I am *trying* to install X." This feature takes the values `modal-poss`, `modal-try`, and `other`. A version of Modality is present in event extraction datasets like ACE 2005 (Consortium, 2005), but instead of just marking an event as "Asserted" or "Other", our version of Modality distinguishes between different aspects of hypothetical events.

3 Modeling

There are four different model types we explored for intent features that we detail below. However, before we can annotate an intent with a feature, we need to have an intent span. First, we describe our intent span extraction model whose predictions are used as intent spans.

3.1 Multi-Intent as Annotatable Spans

The intents in our system are often conditionally dependent. Some intents even appear sequentially, for example, the `cancel` intent is often followed by the `refund` intent, as users tend to request a cancellation first and then ask for a refund. Therefore, we modeled our multi-intent system as a sequence tagging problem, where intent spans are encoded as token level annotations with the IOBES tagging scheme (Ratinov and Roth, 2009). We used a standard BiLSTM-CRF architecture following Ma and Hovy (2016). Each input token is represented both as a character composition, by running a small convolutional neural network with a filter size of 3 over the characters and doing max-over-time pooling as in Dos Santos and Zadrozny (2014), and as a word embedding. We use the concatenation of multiple word embeddings, GloVe embeddings (Pennington et al., 2014), as well as 100 dimensional, in-domain embeddings trained in-house, following Lester et al. (2020a). The token sequence is then fed into an bidirectional LSTM (Graves et al., 2005), where the LSTM (Hochreiter and Schmidhuber, 1997) in each direction has a size of 200, and projected to the final label space. Finally a Conditional Random Field (CRF) (Lafferty et al., 2001) with constrained decoding (Lester et al., 2020b) is used to produce the final sequence of intents. This model was trained using SGD with momentum using 0.0015 as the learning rate, 0.9 for momentum, and a batch size of 10. Model results were satisfactory, but not the focus of this paper. Instead, intent spans are the atomic unit of text that can be annotated with intent features and can be used as features for a downstream intent feature model.

3.1.1 Convolutional Baseline

The first approach was to assume that the feature labels for an intent are local to that intent span, and, therefore, each intent span can be fed into a classifier independently of the other intent spans. Under this assumption, we used a convolutional neural network with parallel filters (Kim, 2014), as it is a strong baseline used in several of our production systems. We used parallel filters of size 3, 4, and 5 with 100 filters each. Max-over-time pooling was used to produce a final span representation, which is projected into the label space. This model was trained using Adadelta (Zeiler, 2012) with an initial learning rate of 1.0 and a batch size of 50. However, this approach misses possible dependencies across spans. Some features (such as "tense") are naturally co-dependent among spans; the use of a past tense verb in one span dictates that all spans in the utterance are past tense, even when there is no explicit signal from the span itself. While less intuitive, the "communicative function" features are conditional as well: an utterance such as, "I would like to order a pizza, but I am having a problem" (a `request-action` followed by an `issue`) is far more common than an utterance like "I am having a problem, I would like to order a pizza" (an `issue` followed by a `request-action`). It follows that the "independence of intent spans" assumption will become problematic and a contextual model that takes other spans into account will be needed.

3.1.2 Contextual Features with a BiLSTM-CRF

This motivated us to reuse the BiLSTM-CRF architecture we used for intents for the intent features, as well. This model takes the utterance as input, just like the intent model. This approach has a potential pitfall, the intent model and the feature model may produce different boundaries which need to be heuristically merged. A small modification to this approach is to use a cascading tagger where the output of the intent tagger is used in the input to the feature tagger. This is done by creating an embedding that represents the span each token is within and concatenating it to the token representation. This gives the feature tagger information about the span boundaries and should keep the spans synced between the intent and feature models. However, the actual intent labels need to be masked. Instead of seeing `intent=issue` as a feature, the feature model will just see `intent`. This is required because we want the feature labels to be reusable and therefore unconditioned on exact intent label. Intent features are applied to intent spans within an utterance, meaning our BiLSTM-CRF tagger is a natural baseline that considers the global context of an utterance.

3.1.3 Global-Local Model

Our fourth approach is a new model architecture we call the Global-Local model. This model aims to create a targeted representation for a subsection of an utterance while also infusing information derived from the whole utterance. An utterance U of n tokens and a subsequence of k tokens from U, are first encoded into matrices of dimension n x e and k x e, respectively, where e is the dimension of some shared embedding space. This encoding can be as simple as word embeddings or more complex like a BiLSTM encoder. A "global" pooling function $g : \mathbb{R}^{n \text{ x } e} \mapsto \mathbb{R}^e$ then collapses the global sentence matrix to a sentence vector and another "local" pooling function $l : \mathbb{R}^{k \text{ x } e} \mapsto \mathbb{R}^e$ reduces the span matrix to a span vector (both with dimension e). The local vector is a representation based solely on the span, while the global vector is a representation of the span that takes the whole utterance into account. These vectors are concatenated to create the final representation for the span S. This representation is then projected into the output space. The pooling functions can be as simple as max or mean pooling, or as complicated as self-attention (Vaswani et al., 2017). Each example is represented as a sequence of tokens and a mask. The mask is a sequence of zeros and ones, aligned to the tokens, that marks a token as part of the local span (a one) or not (a zero). A diagram of the model architecture can be found in Figure 1.

Our implementation uses lookup-table based word embeddings, the same embeddings used in our convolutional baseline, to create a sequence of vectors representing the input. Then a convolutional neural network with multiple parallel filters, followed by max-over-time pooling, is used as both the local and global pooling functions. We found that when g and l share parameters, results were a bit worse compared to when they are learned separately. Like our convolutional baseline, we use filter sizes of 3, 4, and 5 with 100 filters each. This model was trained with a cross-entropy loss using the Adadelta optimizer with an initial learning rate of 1.0 and a batch size of 50.

4 Dataset

The data consists of customer utterances. They were collected from the first customer turn in web-chat conversations between customers and agents

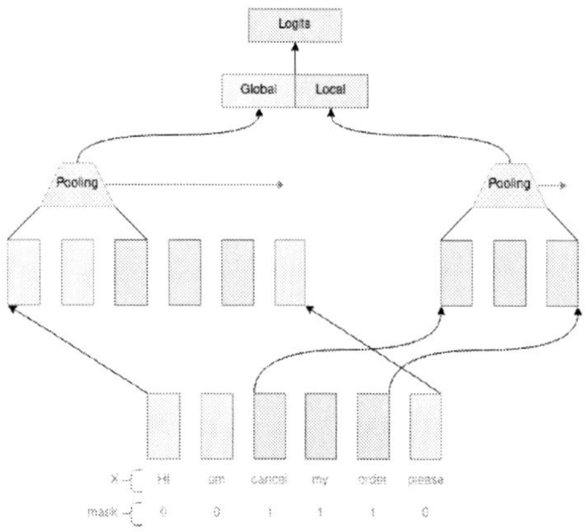

Figure 1: The architecture of our Global-Local model. There are four distinct phases of the model. First, the input is encoded into a sequence of vector representations. This can be as simple as word embeddings or it can use a more complex encoding like a BiLSTM. Then, the local span is extracted from the sequence using the input mask. Global and Local pooling functions are applied to create two vectors, which are joined by concatenation. The local vector encodes the features of the span while the global vector encodes the features of the span as contextualized by the whole input. Finally, this joint representation is used for classification.

from a software company after filtering out low content first turns such as "Hi", "Hello", and "Hey". Our training, validation, and testing datasets have 36,725; 9,256; and 4,993 examples respectively. The data was annotated by a team of six (non-overlapping) commercial annotators over a period of a month and then corrected by an expert annotator. A small subset of the data was annotated (before the error correction) by two expert annotators. The agreement was 53% between two expert annotators and 42% between one expert and the other non-expert annotators.

5 Experiments

The F1 scores for these models are reported in Table 3. The BiLSTM-CRF tagger without any information about the intent boundaries has the lowest performance. Our analysis suggests that it is difficult for the tagger to learn the span boundaries for the features. When that information is supplied—as seen in the cascaded tagger column—the results improve by a large margin. The span-level convolutional model, which is agnostic to the tokens of the other spans, performs much worse than the Global-Local model, which clearly validates our hypothesis that global information is valuable.

We further ablate the Global-Local model to understand the reasons for the performance gain in Table 4. To test if the performance improvement is only due to the larger parameter count, and not the global cues, we use *only* the span as the input (as opposed to *both* the utterance and the span), but the same Global-Local Model. If the Global-Local model is only stronger because it is larger, we should not see a drop in performance. As we can see in the "– Global Context" row, limiting the model to only see the span causes large performance drops across the board. This model is even worse than the simple convolutional model. This implies that the global context is critical.

The current implementation has a shared encoder step where the entire utterance in encoded into a sequence of vectors before the span is extracted and processed by the local pooling function separately. Doing this efficiently in a batched computing environment, like TensorFlow (Abadi et al., 2015), is slightly tricky to implement. A much simpler model would feed the global utterance and the span separately, to be encoded and processed independently. Our ablations in the "– Shared Embedding" row of Table 4 shows that using a shared embedding space does yield performance gains, but it can be removed for the sake of easier model deployment and still maintain superior performance over the span-level model.

All models were trained with Mead-Baseline (Pressel et al., 2018), an open-source library for the development, training, and export for deep neural networks for NLP.

6 Deployment

We have deployed a NLU component of a task-oriented, production dialogue system that produces intent features. The dialogue system deals with customer service in the retail software domain. The dialogue manager currently makes use of several intent features. The easier feature to use is negation and it is critical to understand user intent. It also uses the tense feature to understand if it needs to wait because a user is currently performing an action or if it can ask about the result because the action had already been performed. The next feature the dialogue manager plans to leverage is the modality features. Understanding the user's convection in an action, like canceling, can help make decisions about whether an upsale or discount would be effective.

Feature	BiLSTM-CRF	BiLSTM-CRF Cascaded Tagger	Span-level Convolutional	Global-Local
Attribution CF	78.63	91.90	95.37	**97.69**
Attribution EV	80.06	92.27	95.86	**98.16**
Communicative Function	69.07	89.22	90.12	**91.92**
Modality	79.31	92.61	96.60	**99.36**
Tense	73.49	86.01	89.31	**92.59**
Negation	78.47	94.45	95.86	**98.73**

Table 3: F1 score of intent features using various models. BiLSTM-CRF is the feature tagger that was not given intent boundaries. Cascaded Tagger is the same BiLSTM-CRF model, except the intent boundaries are fed into the model. Span-level Convolutional is our model that classifies each intent span independently, and Global-Local is our new model that encodes both the span and a global view of the sentence. We see that our Global-Local model shows consistent improvements over other model types.

Model	Attribution CF	Attribution Ev	CF	Modality	Tense	Negation
Global-Local	**97.69**	**98.16**	**91.91**	**99.36**	**92.59**	**98.73**
– Global Context	93.55	95.47	90.14	96.74	87.18	95.74
– Shared Embedding	97.65	96.63	91.43	98.34	90.17	96.36

Table 4: Ablation of the Global-Local model. We see that removing the global context causes a large degradation in F1 score, implying that the strong performance of the Global-Local model is due to the global feature, not just the increased parameter count. We also see the removing the shared embedding hurts model performance but to a much smaller degree.

In designing these intent features, we hoped they would be general enough to be transferable across domains without retraining a model on the new domain. Recent work with a new client in the general retail domain gave the opportunity for a small scale test. We were given approximately 500 sample utterances that had been annotated with general labels like, "Is this utterance equivalent to an FAQ?" This is very similar to our `request-info` intent feature. We ran our intent feature model on this new data and compared how many FAQ questions were labeled with `request-info`. We found that our model had high precision, 83.3% of `request-info` utterances were in fact FAQ questions, but had low recall, only 40.5%. This small scale experiment suggests that our intent features are general, but the low recall means our specific model is probably overfit to the lexical features in our original domain.

7 Previous Work

Most popular intent taxonomies such as ATIS (Price, 1990) are domain-specific. Dialog Acts (DA) (Stolcke et al., 2000) are more formalized and generalized versions of intents. The international standard for DA annotations (Bunt et al., 2010, 2012, 2016) defined the concept of communicative functions in a dialog act. However, these functions are defined for a wide range of use cases. We note that a very restrictive and reworked subset of these suffices for our use cases. We believe the other features in the annotation scheme are novel or have an expanded range of possible values.

The Global-Local model draws inspiration from the Lee et al. (2017) model for end-to-end neural coreference resolution. Like us, they have regions on interest embedded in a larger context. However, our models differ in several key ways: their span representation is a hand-crafted combination of token features while ours is a learned pooling of token representations. Also, their model is restricted to operating on contiguous spans (possibly due to unavailability of spans a priori, or that non-contiguous spans would lead to a combinatorial explosion), while our model has no such restriction.

8 Conclusion

Improvements in the complexity of conversations that a dialogue system can handle have put tremendous pressure on NLU systems to capture fine-grained and domain-specific information. Difficulty in the data generation process means the ability to share data across clients is critical. We define intent features, a core set of general annotations, on intents that provide context and clarity on the exact nature of the user requests, and allow for a more natural and intelligent response from the dialogue manager. A NLU system that produces these intent features has been deployed in a production system with a dialogue manager that makes use of them.

To extract these intent features from an utterance, we propose a new neural network architecture, the Global-Local model, that fuses the representation of the content of a span of text and its global context through learned pooling functions. This model shows large improvements over several strong baselines.

9 Ethical Considerations

The largest ethical concern about our work stems from our goal to share these intent features, and the models that identify them, across clients. It is critical to ensure that models trained for one client do not leak private user information to other clients. Given that our model is a simple classifier, opposed to a generative model, we do not believe information is leaking, but we are working on verifying this fact.

In addition to user privacy concerns, it is also important that our models do not underperform on a specific population of people. An internal tech report has investigated differences in performance based on user gender and has found none. This method will be applied to future models, as well as our currently deployed feature intent models, to make sure our models remain un-biased.

References

Martín Abadi, Ashish Agarwal, Paul Barham, Eugene Brevdo, Zhifeng Chen, Craig Citro, Greg S. Corrado, Andy Davis, Jeffrey Dean, Matthieu Devin, Sanjay Ghemawat, Ian Goodfellow, Andrew Harp, Geoffrey Irving, Michael Isard, Yangqing Jia, Rafal Jozefowicz, Lukasz Kaiser, Manjunath Kudlur, Josh Levenberg, Dandelion Mané, Rajat Monga, Sherry Moore, Derek Murray, Chris Olah, Mike Schuster, Jonathon Shlens, Benoit Steiner, Ilya Sutskever, Kunal Talwar, Paul Tucker, Vincent Vanhoucke, Vijay Vasudevan, Fernanda Viégas, Oriol Vinyals, Pete Warden, Martin Wattenberg, Martin Wicke, Yuan Yu, and Xiaoqiang Zheng. 2015. TensorFlow: Large-scale machine learning on heterogeneous systems. Software available from tensorflow.org.

Harry Bunt, Jan Alexandersson, Jean Carletta, Jae-Woong Choe, Alex Chengyu Fang, Koiti Hasida, Kiyong Lee, Volha Petukhova, Andrei Popescu-Belis, Laurent Romary, Claudia Soria, and David Traum. 2010. Towards an ISO standard for dialogue act annotation. In *Proceedings of the Seventh International Conference on Language Resources and Evaluation (LREC'10)*, Valletta, Malta. European Language Resources Association (ELRA).

Harry Bunt, Jan Alexandersson, Jae-Woong Choe, Alex Chengyu Fang, Koiti Hasida, Volha Petukhova, Andrei Popescu-Belis, and David Traum. 2012. ISO 24617-2: A semantically-based standard for dialogue annotation. In *Proceedings of the Eighth International Conference on Language Resources and Evaluation (LREC'12)*, pages 430–437, Istanbul, Turkey. European Language Resources Association (ELRA).

Harry Bunt, Volha Petukhova, Andrei Malchanau, Kars Wijnhoven, and Alex Fang. 2016. The DialogBank. In *Proceedings of the Tenth International Conference on Language Resources and Evaluation (LREC'16)*, pages 3151–3158, Portorož, Slovenia. European Language Resources Association (ELRA).

J. Chen, R. Prasad, S. Stoyanchev, E. Selfridge, S. Bangalore, and M. Johnston. 2018. Corpus and annotation towards nlu for customer ordering dialogs. In *2018 IEEE Spoken Language Technology Workshop (SLT)*, pages 707–713.

Linguistic Data Consortium. 2005. Ace (automatic-content extraction) english annotation guidelines for events.

Cícero Nogueira Dos Santos and Bianca Zadrozny. 2014. Learning Character-level Representations for Part-of-speech Tagging. In *Proceedings of the 31st International Conference on International Conference on Machine Learning - Volume 32*, ICML'14, pages II–1818–II–1826. JMLR.org.

Alex Graves, Santiago Fernández, and Jürgen Schmidhuber. 2005. Bidirectional lstm networks for improved phoneme classification and recognition. In *Proceedings of the 15th International Conference on Artificial Neural Networks: Formal Models and Their Applications - Volume Part II*, ICANN'05, page 799–804, Berlin, Heidelberg. Springer-Verlag.

Sepp Hochreiter and Jürgen Schmidhuber. 1997. Long short-term memory. *Neural Comput.*, 9(8):1735–1780.

Yoon Kim. 2014. Convolutional Neural Networks for Sentence Classification. In *Proceedings of the 2014 Conference on Empirical Methods in Natural Language Processing (EMNLP)*, pages 1746–1751, Doha, Qatar. Association for Computational Linguistics.

John D. Lafferty, Andrew McCallum, and Fernando C. N. Pereira. 2001. Conditional random fields:

Probabilistic models for segmenting and labeling sequence data. In *Proceedings of the Eighteenth International Conference on Machine Learning*, ICML '01, page 282–289, San Francisco, CA, USA. Morgan Kaufmann Publishers Inc.

Kenton Lee, Luheng He, Mike Lewis, and Luke Zettlemoyer. 2017. End-to-end Neural Coreference Resolution. In *Proceedings of the 2017 Conference on Empirical Methods in Natural Language Processing*, pages 188–197, Copenhagen, Denmark. Association for Computational Linguistics.

Brian Lester, Daniel Pressel, Amy Hemmeter, Sagnik Ray Choudhury, and Srinivas Bangalore. 2020a. Multiple word embeddings for increased diversity of representation. *arXiv preprint arXiv:2009.14394*.

Brian Lester, Daniel Pressel, Amy Hemmeter, Sagnik Ray Choudhury, and Srinivas Bangalore. 2020b. Constrained decoding for computationally efficient named entity recognition taggers. In *Findings of the Association for Computational Linguistics: EMNLP 2020*, pages 1841–1848, Online. Association for Computational Linguistics.

Xuezhe Ma and Eduard Hovy. 2016. End-to-end Sequence Labeling via Bi-directional LSTM-CNNs-CRF. In *Proceedings of the 54th Annual Meeting of the Association for Computational Linguistics (Volume 1: Long Papers)*, pages 1064–1074, Berlin, Germany. Association for Computational Linguistics.

Jeffrey Pennington, Richard Socher, and Christopher Manning. 2014. GloVe: Global Vectors for Word Representation. In *Proceedings of the 2014 Conference on Empirical Methods in Natural Language Processing (EMNLP)*, pages 1532–1543, Doha, Qatar. Association for Computational Linguistics.

Daniel Pressel, Sagnik Ray Choudhury, Brian Lester, Yanjie Zhao, and Matt Barta. 2018. Baseline: A library for rapid modeling, experimentation and development of deep learning algorithms targeting nlp. In *Proceedings of Workshop for NLP Open Source Software (NLP-OSS)*, pages 34–40. Association for Computational Linguistics.

P. J. Price. 1990. Evaluation of spoken language systems: The atis domain. In *Proceedings of the Workshop on Speech and Natural Language*, HLT '90, page 91–95, USA. Association for Computational Linguistics.

Lev Ratinov and Dan Roth. 2009. Design Challenges and Misconceptions in Named Entity Recognition. In *Proceedings of the Thirteenth Conference on Computational Natural Language Learning (CoNLL-2009)*, pages 147–155, Boulder, Colorado. Association for Computational Linguistics.

Andreas Stolcke, Klaus Ries, Noah Coccaro, Elizabeth Shriberg, Rebecca Bates, Daniel Jurafsky, Paul Taylor, Rachel Martin, Carol Van Ess-Dykema, and Marie Meteer. 2000. Dialogue act modeling for automatic tagging and recognition of conversational speech. *Computational Linguistics*, 26(3):339–374.

David R. Traum and Staffan Larsson. 2003. The Information State Approach to Dialogue Management. In Jan van Kuppevelt and Ronnie W. Smith, editors, *Current and New Directions in Discourse and Dialogue*, Text, Speech and Language Technology, pages 325–353. Springer Netherlands, Dordrecht.

Ashish Vaswani, Noam Shazeer, Niki Parmar, Jakob Uszkoreit, Llion Jones, Aidan N Gomez, Łukasz Kaiser, and Illia Polosukhin. 2017. Attention is All you Need. In I. Guyon, U. V. Luxburg, S. Bengio, H. Wallach, R. Fergus, S. Vishwanathan, and R. Garnett, editors, *Advances in Neural Information Processing Systems 30*, pages 5998–6008. Curran Associates, Inc.

Matthew D. Zeiler. 2012. Adadelta: An adaptive learning rate method. *ArXiv*, abs/1212.5701.

Development of an Enterprise-Grade Contract Understanding System

A. Agarwal[2], L. Chiticariu[3], P. Chozhiyath Raman[3], M. Danilevsky[1], D. Ghazi[5*], A. Gupta[2], S. Guttula[2], Y. Katsis[1], R. Krishnamurthy[3], Y. Li[1], S. Mudgal[3], V. Munigala[2], N. Phan[6*], D. Sonawane[3], S. Srinivasan[3], S. Thitte[3], M. Vasa[3], R. Venkatachalam[3], V. Yaski[4*], H. Zhu[1]

[1] IBM Research - Almaden [2] IBM Research - India [3] IBM Data and AI
[4] Amazon [5] Google LLC [6] Visa

{arvagarw, ankushgupta, shguttul, vmunig10}@in.ibm.com; {chiti, pchozhi, mdanile, rajase, yunyaoli, srthitte, mitesh.vasa, venkatra, huaiyu}@us.ibm.com; {yannis.katsis, shubham.mudgal, dhaval.sonawane1, sneha.srinivasan1130}@ibm.com; dimanghazi@google.com; thefryingphan@gmail.com; vinitha.yaski@gmail.com

Abstract

Contracts are arguably the most important type of business documents. Despite their significance in business, legal contract review largely remains an arduous, expensive and manual process. In this paper, we describe the Transparent and Expert Contract Understanding System (TECUS): a commercial system designed and deployed for contract understanding and used by a wide range of enterprise users for the past few years. We reflect on the challenges and design decisions when building TECUS. We also summarize the data science life cycle of TECUS and share lessons learned.

1 Introduction

A *contract* is an agreement between businesses and/or individuals to create mutual obligations enforceable by law (Cornell Law School). Written contracts are also used by companies to safeguard their resources and as such, legal advice is sought prior to participating in a binding contract. Currently, legal review remains an arduous and expensive process. For instance, a procurement contract requires 5 hours of legal review on average, contributing to thousands of dollars in total cost (Cummins, 2017).

While contract reviewing is a well-established legal process, building an enterprise-grade system for *Contract Understanding* (CU) to facilitate this process poses three major challenges:

C1: Model CU as an NLP Problem. CU does not have a corresponding standard NLP definition. The underlying processes and the associated requirements for CU need to be well understood to translate it to concrete NLP tasks.

Table 1: Example Contract Understanding Use-cases

Context	Application
Quote to Cash	Identify non-standard, risky terms
Accounts Receivable	Prevent leakage, improve cash-flow
Procurement	Analyze numerous contracts in negotiation
Global Accounting	Assist with numerous compliance checklists
Mergers & Acquisitions	Identify early termination notice period, penalty amount etc.

C2: Lack of Representative Data. Contracts, while often proprietary, also vary significantly across domains and businesses. Thus, one cannot assume the presence of representative contracts towards building models. Moreover, Subject Matter Experts (SMEs) qualified to label ground truth are expensive[1]. As such, NLP models may need to be developed with limited non-representative labeled data but still be able to generalize well over previously unseen data.

C3: Need for Model Stability. CU models are integrated into existing business processes to drive decisions. As the models evolve over time (e.g. due to availability of new data, updates to existing labeled data, etc.), users expect the models to behave in a stable manner and produce no surprising results (Kearns and Ron, 1997).

* Work done while author was working at IBM.

[1]According to https://www.zippia.com/contract-attorney-jobs/salary/, the average annual salary for a contract attorney is $86,000 ($41.35/hour).

Proceedings of NAACL HLT 2021: IndustryTrack Papers, pages 222–229
June 6–11, 2021.

Problem	Example	Task	Concepts	Sample Supported Question
Nature & Party Classification	**Obligation - Supplier**	Multi-Label Classification	Nature: Definition, Disclaimer, Exclusion, Obligation, Right, ... Party: Buyer, End User, Supplier, ...	"Is Tenant allowed to install additional fixtures?" *(Right - Tenant)*
Category Classification	This is **Warranties**	Multi-Label Classification	Category: Amendments, Asset Use, Assignments, Audits, Business Continuity, Communication, Confidentiality, Deliverables, ...	"Is there an additional charge for services and utilities?" *(Pricing & Taxes)*
Attribute Extraction	**Location: New York**	Element-level Extraction	Attributes: Currency, DateTime, DefinedTerm, Duration, Location, Number, Organization, ...	"Where will disputes regarding this agreement be settled?" *(Location)*
Metadata Extraction	**Effective Date: 1/1/2016**	Document-level Extraction	Metadata: Contract Types, Effective Dates, Termination Dates, Contract Amounts, Contract Terms, ...	"What is the effective & termination date of this agreement?" *(Effective Date, Termination Date)*

Figure 1: TECUS' Sub-Problems (see (IBM, b) for complete list of supported concepts)

To overcome the above challenges, we designed and developed the **Transparent and Expert Contract Understanding System (TECUS)**, a commercial system that enables legal professionals to review contracts with minimal effort.

TECUS first models CU as a series of text classification and extraction tasks, defined collaboratively with SMEs, to capture the information that legal experts seek when reviewing contracts.

Second, it leverages SystemT, a state-of-the-art declarative text understanding engine for the enterprise (Chiticariu et al., 2010, 2018), towards developing transparent models on top of syntactic and semantic linguistic features, to mitigate a possible lack of representative labeled data and to satisfy model stability requirements. This approach enables (1) the development of stable models that explicitly capture domain knowledge without requiring large amounts of labeled data or representative samples; and (2) a data science workflow that supports systematic error analysis and incorporation of user feedback towards continuous model improvement (Section 3).

TECUS is available as part of multiple commercial products including IBM Watson® Discovery (IBM, a) and IBM Watson® Compare and Comply [2]. As part of these products, it has been in use by enterprise customers since 2017 to support a variety of contract understanding use-cases (Table 1). While several other commercial offerings, such as Cognitiv+ (Cog), Kira (Kir), LawGeex (Law), LegalSifter (Leg), and Lexion (Lex) use NLP to analyze contracts, their internals are not publicly disclosed. Thus, TECUS is to the best of our knowledge the first commercial automated contract understanding system ever presented to the scientific community in such detail.

In addition to assisting in the understanding of a single contract, as described in this paper, TECUS also allows legal professionals to compare two contracts, identifying similarities and differences along multiple dimensions; another critical task in the contract reviewing process. TECUS models this problem as a clause-level comparison problem, identifying (i) clauses that are identical between two contracts, (ii) clauses that are on the same topic but have changed, and (iii) clauses that appear in one contract but not in the other. The comparison component, similar to the contract understanding component, leverages syntactic and semantic linguistic features provided by SystemT and an associated data science workflow tuned towards a systematic and stable model development. However, for space reasons, this work focuses on single contract analysis, enabled by TECUS' Contract Understanding (CU) component.

2 Modeling CU as an NLP Problem

Working with legal experts, we first define the CU problem as a combination of Multi-class Multi-label[3] Classification and Entity Extraction tasks, as depicted in Figure 1.

Clause Classification. A business contract consists of thousands of sentences, each defining one or more clauses, such as *Obligation*, *Exclusion*, etc. At the core of the legal review process are identi-

[2]IBM and IBM Watson are trademarks of International Business Machines Corporation, registered in many jurisdictions worldwide.

[3]The classification problems correspond to multi-label classification, as elements are often complex and cover multiple Categories/Natures/Parties.

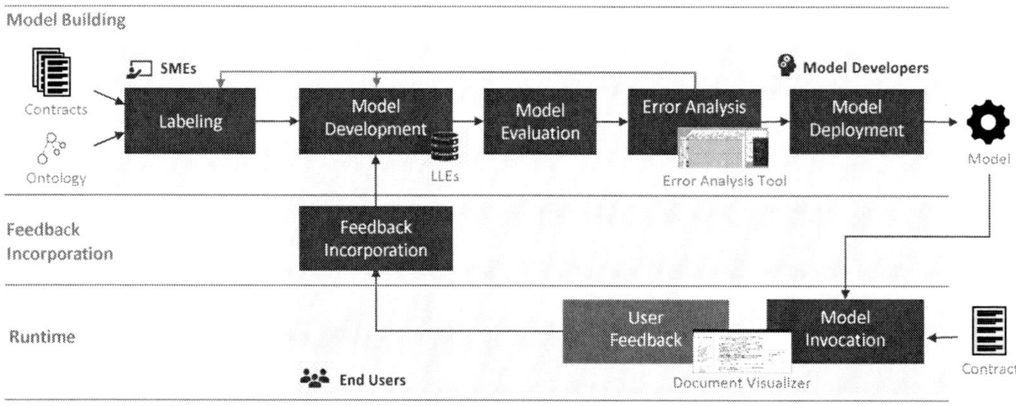

Figure 2: TECUS' Architecture

fying, classifying and reviewing individual clauses to spot potential risks. For example, the sentence

> *"Purchaser will purchase the Assets by a cash payment of FOUR HUNDRED FIFTEEN THOUSAND US DOLLARS."*

is a clause related to *Pricing & Taxes* that describes an *Obligation* for the *Purchaser*. To help legal professionals focus on relevant parts of the contract, we classify contract sentences (henceforth known as *elements* [4]) according to three dimensions of interest to domain experts:

• **Category**: the topic associated with the element, such as *Pricing & Taxes* in our example.

• **Nature**: the action described by the element, such as *Obligation* in our example.

• **Party**: the individual or entity affected by the action, such as *Supplier* in our example.

A consistent ontology (shown in Figure 1) was defined in the early stages of the project, in collaboration with SMEs via an iterative process, and reflecting the prevailing views of legal experts. However, to also accommodate users who adopt slight variations of the definitions (which we discovered can be common due to the subtle nature of legal terms), users can also customize TECUS through user feedback, as described in Section 3.3.

Attribute and Metadata Extraction. In addition to classifying elements, legal teams are also interested in extracting entities of particular importance to corporate law. These fall into two categories:

• **Attributes**: general entities of interest, such as *Organizations* and *Persons* involved in a contract, *Dates*, *Locations* and *Currencies*. Attributes are extracted from individual elements.

• **Contract Metadata**: document-level legal entities of interest, such as the *Effective Dates*, *Termination Dates*, and *Contract Amounts*. Contract Metadata are extracted from across a contract, and are thus applicable to the entire contract.

3 System Overview

As can be seen in Figure 2, TECUS consists of three main components, which we subsequently describe in detail: *Runtime*, *Model Building*, and *Feedback Incorporation*.

3.1 Runtime

As shown in Figure 3, users can analyze their contracts by interacting with TECUS's *Document Visualizer*, via the following two panes:

The *Faceted Exploration Pane* (#1) allows users to quickly acquire an overview of the contract's contents and drill down into specific categories/natures/parties of interest. In our example, a user interested in *Pricing & Taxes*, focuses on such clauses by selecting the corresponding checkbox.

The *Contract View Pane* (#2) allows users to see the selected elements within the contract (#3) and for each of them inspect the *Category/Nature/Party* and *Attributes* identified by CU (#4). It also includes a *Metadata View* showing the metadata extracted from the contract, such as *Contract Amounts*, *Effective Dates*, *Termination Dates*, etc. (omitted in the interest of space).

At any point in time, users can provide feedback on the CU results through the "Suggest changes" feature (#5). User feedback is then further analyzed and incorporated as described in Section 3.3.

[4]TECUS supports classification of elements beyond sentences, including bulleted list items and table content, which often appear in contracts.

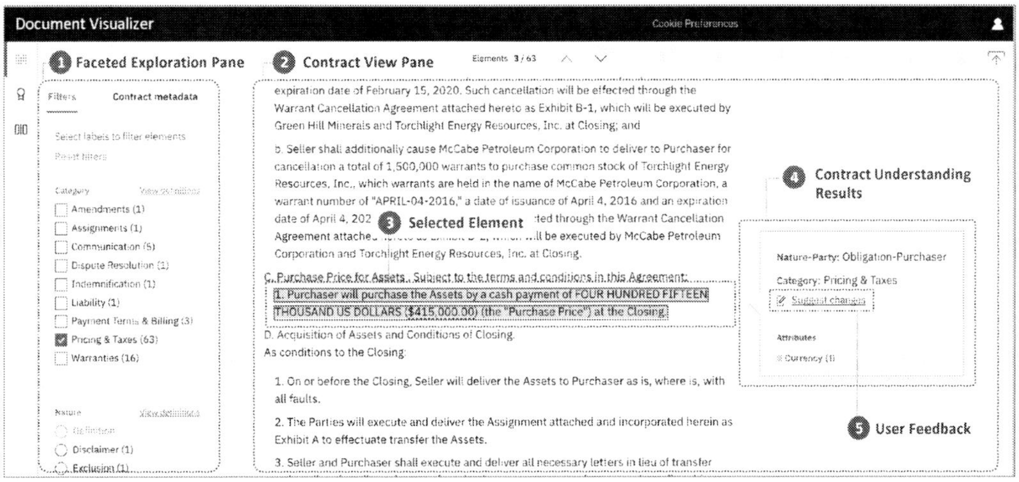

Figure 3: Reviewing a Contract through TECUS' Document Visualizer

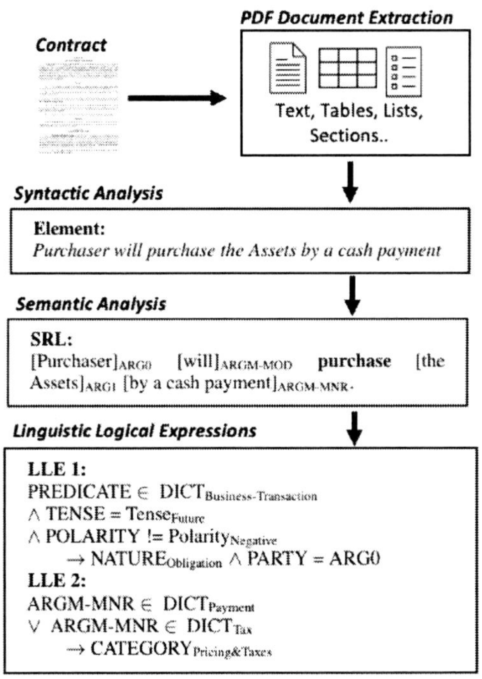

Figure 4: Contract Understanding Components

3.2 Model Building

3.2.1 Model Development

Figure 4 illustrates the sequence of model components used by TECUS to accomplish the tasks in Figure 1. TECUS uses declarative models towards both classification and extraction tasks [5]:

(1) Once text and document structures such as lists, sections, tables etc. are extracted from a contract PDF document [6], sentences/elements (for classification) and tokens/phrases (for extraction) are identified using syntactic analysis.

(2) Next, extended Semantic Role Labels (SRL) (Palmer et al., 2010), provided by SystemT (Chiticariu et al., 2010, 2018) [7]are identified in elements. As shown in Figure 4, SRL captures *who did what to whom, when, where, and how* from the example element.

(3) A collection of logical formulae, called *Linguistic Logical Expressions (LLEs)*, are constructed using these SRLs to perform logical reasoning using linguistic patterns in contracts, similar to reasoning by legal experts. For instance, the two LLEs [8] in Figure 4 identify the Category, Nature, and Party concerning the example element.

Each classification model in TECUS consists of a collection of such LLEs. Such a model not only yields a transparent understanding of a contract along the concepts outlined in Figure 1, it is also uniquely positioned to handle the challenges outlined in Section 1 for the following reasons:

Generalizability. LLEs are manually built by model developers on top of SRL[9], to explicitly

[5]Here, we focus on classification due to its challenging aspects. Attribute and Metadata extraction are performed using entity extraction, enabled by SystemT.

[6]Here, we use PDF as the business document format for ease of exposition. The presented techniques apply also to other document formats, such as Microsoft Word.

[7]SystemT also provides additional information, such as tense and voice; please refer to (Zhu et al., 2019) for details.

[8]Simplified from the actual product LLEs for readability.

[9]Potentially aided by machine learning (Sen et al., 2019)

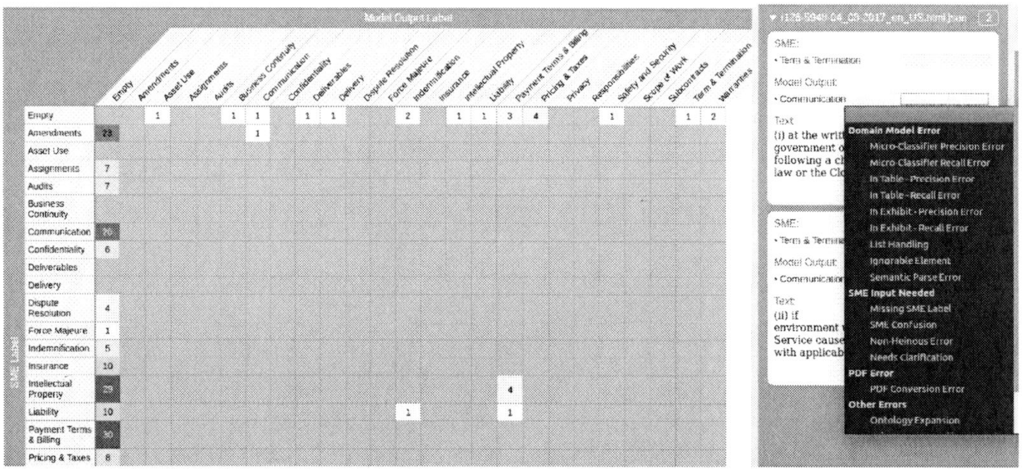

Figure 5: Analyzing CU Errors through the ModelLens Error Analysis Tool

capture domain knowledge. Each LLE reflects patterns from not only the documents used during the development process, but also unseen contracts where similar semantic patterns appear. As a result, the CU model generalizes much better to yet unseen contracts than state-of-the-art black-box models (see Section 4 for more details).

Enabling systematic model improvement workflow. Use of LLEs enable a fine-grained association of CU model output with highly specific, lower-level constructs of the model. This transparency allows a team of developers to make localized updates and develop models with stable and explainable behavior, aided by a carefully created data science workflow of *model evaluation*, *error analysis* and *feedback incorporation*, as described next.

3.2.2 Model Evaluation

As the CU model in TECUS evolves over time, it is regularly evaluated for: (1) quality, in terms of precision, recall and accuracy towards both Nature-Party and Category classification tasks, and (2) performance, in terms of throughput, memory consumption and behavior profile.

We measure model quality over in-domain and out-of-domain data split into the usual train (dev) and test (hold-out) subsets. Similarly, we profile runtime performance upon multiple in-domain and out-of-domain sets, allowing developers to preemptively rectify potentially problematic runtime behaviors, prior to deployment.

Beyond the typical global measurements, the transparent nature of the CU model permits evaluation at finer granularity: across classes, per-class and per-LLE towards both quality and runtime performance. Such detailed model evaluation along with a systematic model improvement workflow together enable TECUS to provide reliable guarantees of consistency and robustness of its results.

3.2.3 Error Analysis

While evaluation provides an overview of model performance, model improvement requires delving deeper and analyzing individual errors to understand their root causes and inform further model development efforts (Ribeiro et al., 2020).

TECUS supports root cause identification of errors through the *ModelLens* error analysis tool shown in Figure 5 and the associated error analysis workflow (Katsis and Wolf, 2019). Specifically, ModelLens allows model developers to perform the following error analysis tasks:

(1) Acquire a high-level overview of the errors through a confusion matrix that depicts the types of misclassifications made by the model, to help prioritize errors for further analysis.

(2) Inspect erroneous instances in context. For a chosen misclassification type, developers can drill down and inspect all elements that exhibit it (shown on the right side of the screen). For each element, ModelLens also provides additional context, such as the surrounding text, the SRL output, and the provenance of the model output, to help model developers identify the error root cause.

(3) Annotate errors with their root causes. Once a developer identifies the root cause of an error, they can record it through the drop-down next to the

corresponding label.

This error analysis process classifies errors based on their root causes, separating true model errors from other errors that have to be treated differently (e.g., labeling errors, errors from preceding models, such as PDF conversion errors, and others). Additionally, ModelLens exploits the transparent nature of the model to allow developers to identify specific LLEs that need to be revised to address model errors. Moreover, by providing contextual information for each error, it also assists in identifying additional linguistic patterns that could be translated into new LLEs.

3.3 Feedback Incorporation

User feedback is essential for TECUS: First, it enables model improvement, by communicating to the development team cases not captured by the current model. This is especially important given the lack of representative labeled data discussed in Section 1. Second, it allows the customization of models. Custom models allow TECUS to adapt to the needs of individual customers, who may adopt slightly different definitions of the Category/Nature/Party classes from our SMEs, as described in Section 2. Feedback is enabled by the following human-in-the-loop process:

(1) Users review model results and suggest the exclusion of incorrect labels or the inclusion of missing labels through the Document Visualizer.

(2) The system locates other elements that share a similar linguistic pattern (i.e., LLE) with the ones on which feedback was provided, and asks the user whether they would like to propagate the suggested label updates to those. This capability is to reduce user efforts in providing feedback.

(3) The system associates user feedback to the corresponding LLEs, allowing model changes to be localized to a small part of the model.

The localized nature of the changes enable the model to remain stable over time; in contrast, black box models may regress in unexpected ways when globally retrained over time with additional ground truth data. Results on model stability and the effectiveness of feedback incorporation are presented in the next section.

4 Results & Discussion

We next present evaluation results, showing how TECUS addresses the challenges discussed above.

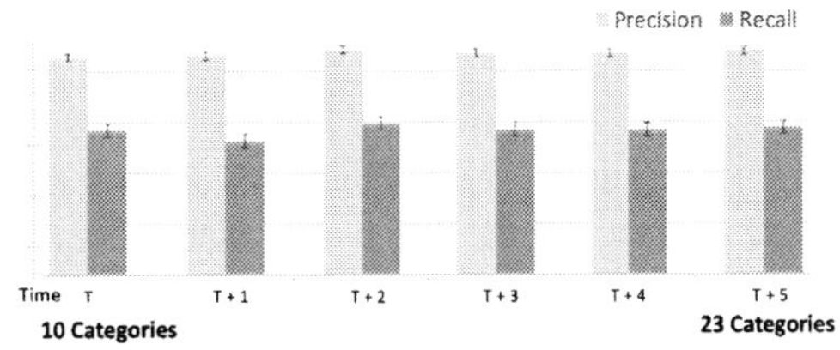

Figure 6: Model Stability with Increasing Complexity

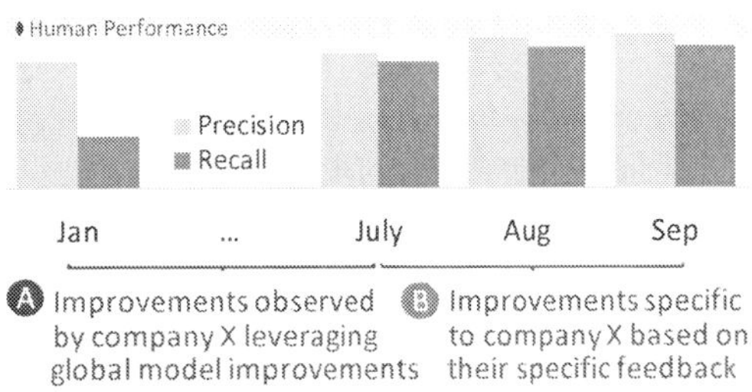

Figure 7: Effectiveness of Feedback Incorporation

Model generalizability. To verify our intuition that the transparent nature of the CU model helps it generalize to unseen contracts, we compare it to state of the art black box ML models. In our experiments, when trained on procurement contracts (PCs) sourced from within IBM (in-domain) and tested on PCs sourced randomly from the web (out-of-domain), the CU model significantly outperforms the alternatives, with 1.3x, 2.09x, and 2.58x higher micro-$F1$ score over a Bidirectional Long Short-Term Memory (BiLSTM), Convolutional Neural Network (CNN), and Logistic Regression (LR) model, respectively.

For reference, prior state-of-the-art results of nature identification in contracts (Chalkidis et al., 2018) and financial legislation (Neill et al., 2017) were based on different BiLSTM-based architectures, which we have found in our experiments to perform well on contracts similar to the ones on which they were trained (e.g., contracts that follow similar templates) but generalize poorly to other unseen contracts.

Model stability. To verify the stability of model performance over time, we capture in Figure 6 the CU model's precision and recall on category classification across six consecutive development sprints (each two weeks long). During this time period, the development team added support for additional categories, increasing the supported categories from 10 to 23. Despite a quick addition of new categories (with 2.25 new categories added per sprint on average), the model's quality remained stable across all categories, old and new. This can be attributed (a) to the transparent nature of the model, which allows changes to be localized and (b) to the data science process which allows quick additions of new categories without compromising on quality.

Effectiveness of feedback incorporation. To verify the effectiveness of TECUS's feedback incorporation mechanism, we capture in Figure 7 the CU model's precision and recall for category classification on data of interest for an individual customer X over 9 months. During this period the model development team incorporated two types of feedback: in the first few months (January-July), they leveraged feedback solely from other customers, while in the last few months (July-Sep), they incorporated focused feedback from customer X. As shown in the chart, customer X benefited both from the feedback given by other customers, as well as its own feedback, which further improved quality. Moreover, the model quality increased consistently towards human performance (calculated internally based on evaluation of inter-annotator agreement among SMEs).

5 Conclusion

We have presented TECUS, a commercial system that effectively assists and supplements legal experts in understanding and reviewing contracts. TECUS' effectiveness is based on (a) the transparent nature of the CU model, comprised of Linguistic Logical Expressions on top of SRL, which in turn enables (b) a systematic data science workflow towards swift yet stable model development. This leads to models that can be developed with limited, non-representative labeled data and remain stable and predictable over time; traits that are essential not just in the contract understanding domain but the wider legal domain as well. Finally, while the system was developed for the CU problem, we believe that its design and associated insights could inform efforts in other areas that pose similar requirements of generalizability and stability.

References

Cognitiv+ (Accessed: 2021-04-09). http://www.cognitivplus.com.

a. IBM Watson Discovery (Accessed: 2021-04-09). https://www.ibm.com/cloud/watson-discovery.

b. IBM Watson Discovery: Understanding Contract Analysis (Accessed: 2021-04-09). https://cloud.ibm.com/docs/discovery-data?topic=discovery-data-contract_parsing.

Kira (Accessed: 2021-04-09). https://kirasystems.com.

LawGeex (Accessed: 2021-04-09). https://www.lawgeex.com.

LegalSifter (Accessed: 2021-04-09). https://www.legalsifter.com.

Lexion (Accessed: 2021-04-09). https://lexion.ai.

Ilias Chalkidis, Ion Androutsopoulos, and Achilleas Michos. 2018. Obligation and Prohibition Extraction Using Hierarchical RNNs. In *Proceedings of the 56th Annual Meeting of the Association for Computational Linguistics (Volume 2: Short Papers)*, pages 254–259, Melbourne, Australia. Association for Computational Linguistics.

Laura Chiticariu, Marina Danilevsky, Yunyao Li, Frederick Reiss, and Huaiyu Zhu. 2018. SystemT: Declarative Text Understanding for Enterprise. In *Proceedings of the 2018 Conference of the North American Chapter of the Association for Computational Linguistics: Human Language Technologies, Volume 3 (Industry Papers)*, pages 76–83. Association for Computational Linguistics.

Laura Chiticariu, Rajasekar Krishnamurthy, Yunyao Li, Sriram Raghavan, Frederick R. Reiss, and Shivakumar Vaithyanathan. 2010. SystemT: An Algebraic Approach to Declarative Information Extraction. In *Proceedings of the 48th Annual Meeting of the Association for Computational Linguistics. ACL '10*, pages 128–137. Association for Computational Linguistics.

Cornell Law School (Accessed: 2021-04-09). Contract. https://www.law.cornell.edu/wex/contract.

Tim Cummins. 2017. Cost of processing a basic contract soars to $6900 (accessed: 2021-04-09). https://blog.lawgeex.com/contractcosts/.

Yannis Katsis and Christine T. Wolf. 2019. ModelLens: an interactive system to support the model improvement practices of data science teams. In *Conference Companion Publication of the 2019 on Computer Supported Cooperative Work and Social Computing*, CSCW '19, page 9–13, New York, NY, USA. Association for Computing Machinery.

Michael Kearns and Dana Ron. 1997. Algorithmic stability and sanity-check bounds for leave-one-out cross-validation. In *Proceedings of the Tenth Annual Conference on Computational Learning Theory*, COLT '97, page 152–162, New York, NY, USA. Association for Computing Machinery.

James O' Neill, Paul Buitelaar, Cecile Robin, and Leona O' Brien. 2017. Classifying Sentential Modality in Legal Language: A Use Case in Financial Regulations, Acts and Directives. In *Proceedings of the 16th Edition of the International Conference on Articial Intelligence and Law*, ICAIL '17, page 159–168, New York, NY, USA. Association for Computing Machinery.

Martha Palmer, Daniel Gildea, and Nianwen Xue. 2010. *Semantic Role Labeling*. Synthesis Lectures on Human Language Technology Series. Morgan and Claypool.

Marco Tulio Ribeiro, Tongshuang Wu, Carlos Guestrin, and Sameer Singh. 2020. Beyond accuracy: Behavioral testing of NLP models with CheckList. In *Proceedings of the 58th Annual Meeting of the Association for Computational Linguistics*, pages 4902–4912, Online. Association for Computational Linguistics.

Prithviraj Sen, Yunyao Li, Eser Kandogan, Yiwei Yang, and Walter Lasecki. 2019. HEIDL: Learning linguistic expressions with deep learning and human-in-the-loop. In *Proceedings of the 57th Annual Meeting of the Association for Computational Linguistics: System Demonstrations*, pages 135–140, Florence, Italy. Association for Computational Linguistics.

Huaiyu Zhu, Yunyao Li, and Laura Chiticariu. 2019. Towards universal semantic representation. In *Proceedings of the First International Workshop on Designing Meaning Representations*, pages 177–181, Florence, Italy. Association for Computational Linguistics.

Discovering Better Model Architectures for Medical Query Understanding

Wei Zhu[1,2] *, **Yuan Ni**[2], **Xiaoling Wang**[1], **Guotong Xie**[2,3,4], **Fang Zhang**[5]
[1] East China Normal University, China
[2] PingAn Health Technology, China
[3] Ping An Health Cloud Company Limited, China
[4] Ping An International Smart City Technology Co., Ltd, China
[5] Shanghai Municipal Center for Disease Control and Prevention, China

Abstract

In developing an online question-answering system for the medical domains, natural language inference (NLI) models play a central role in question matching and intention detection. However, which models are best for our datasets? Manually selecting or tuning a model is time-consuming. Thus we experiment with automatically optimizing the model architectures on the task at hand via neural architecture search (NAS). First, we formulate a novel architecture search space based on the previous NAS literature, supporting cross-sentence attention (cross-attn) modeling. Second, we propose to modify the ENAS method to accelerate and stabilize the search results. We conduct extensive experiments on our two medical NLI tasks. Results show that our system can easily outperform the classical baseline models. We compare different NAS methods and demonstrate that our approach provides the best results.

1 Introduction

Nowadays, online medical question answering (QA) systems are becoming more and more popular. Since the breakout of COVID-19, people grapple with going to the hospital, and hospitals' emergency rooms in some cities are even empty during the daytime.[1] Thus, medical QA systems are of essential importance. NLI models play a central role in such a QA system (Xie et al., 2020). In our QA scenario, we usually use NLI models to determine whether a query has the same intention as some of our labeled questions. For in-domain tasks like ours, modeling experiences are scarce, so selecting a suitable model for our medical NLI tasks becomes a time-consuming procedure. From our experience, different datasets have different optimal models. Thus when a new dataset comes, our engineers usually devote 4 to 5 days experimenting on model tuning and hyper-parameter search with multiple GPU cards.

To speed up the development of our medical QA system and free up the NLP engineers from laborious work, we propose developing a neural architecture search (NAS) framework. Neural architecture search (NAS) has recently attracted intensive attention, both in computer vision and NLP. New RNN models are learned in NASNet (Zoph and Le, 2017), ENAS (Pham et al., 2018), DARTS (Liu et al., 2018), improved DARTS(Jiang et al., 2019) for language modeling. Evolved transformer (So et al., 2019) use the evolution-based NAS algorithm to search for better transformer architectures. TextNAS (Wang et al., 2020) design a new search space for NLU tasks. We will refer to our system as NASQU, shorted for Neural Architecture Search for Query Understanding.

NASQU consists of two parts. First, we design a search space that is suited for NLI tasks. The search space is an extension of the search spaces of TextNAS (Wang et al., 2020). First, for sentence pair modeling, cross-sentence attention plays a central role in aligning the two sentences' contexts and providing a more in-depth understanding of the semantic relations between two sentences (Chen et al., 2016). We add cross-sentence attention operations in the search space, enabling NASQU to search for models with cross-sentence attention mechanisms. Second, aggregating the encoder's outputs to a fixed vector is essential for an NLI model's performance. In this work, we use NAS to decide which layers' outputs are fed into the aggregator and the specific operation in the aggregator layer.

Second, for improving the search results, we employ two modifications to the search method. Our search method mainly follows ENAS (Pham et al., 2018), a reinforcement learning (RL) based search approach. An LSTM controller is employed

*Contact: 52205901018@stu.ecnu.edu.cn.

[1] https://www.cbc.ca/news/health/covid-19-emergency-departments-canada-1.5510778

Proceedings of NAACL HLT 2021: IndustryTrack Papers, pages 230–237
June 6–11, 2021. ©2021 Association for Computational Linguistics

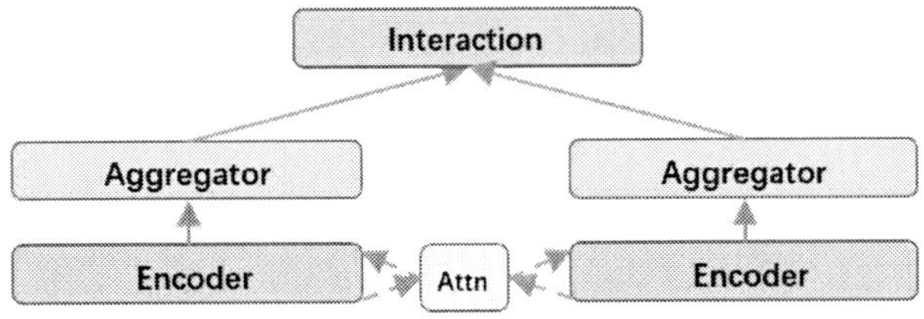

Figure 1: The sentence vector-based framework for the NLI task.

to generate a novel child model, and it will receive a reward based on the child model's performance. Then the controller can update its parameters to improve its ability to generate better child models. A key ingredient for ENAS is weight sharing. We propose further to enhance the weight sharing strategies during architecture search. Besides, we suggest that search warm-ups can stabilize the search processes and provide better search results.

We conduct experiments on two medical NLI datasets designated for intent identification in our medical QA system. The experimental results show that NASQU can learn novel models that perform better than baseline models and meet efficiency requirements. Also, a comparison among the search methods shows that our NASQU obtains better results than other search methods. Besides, we show that the search space design of NASQU is essential.

Our work contributes to the field by the following aspects:

- We extend the search space for neural architecture search in NLP tasks by including cross-sentence attention modules and many design choices.
- We experiment on more in-depth parameter sharing strategies than ENAS, which are proven to provide better search results within less time.

2 NASQU

In this section, we first describe the architecture framework of NLI tasks. Then we extend the search space of TextNAS to support cross-attn modeling and aggregator search. And Finally, we elaborate on the search algorithm in NASQU.

2.1 Architecture framework

We adopt the sentence vector-based framework (Bowman et al., 2015) for NLI tasks. The framework is illustrated in Figure 1. The two sentences (i.e., hypothesis and premise) are encoded and aggregated in siamese network architecture. After obtaining the sentence embedding vector u and v, the final feature vector is $[u; v; |u - v|; u \cdot v]$, where [] is concatenation operation.

Note that our framework is different from TextNAS in two ways. First, we enable attention to flow between the two sentences, which we will elaborate on in the next subsection. Second, we add the search space for aggregators, where TextNAS (Wang et al., 2020) fixes the aggregator to the self-attention aggregator.

2.2 Encoder Search space

To ensure efficiency, we do not stack blocks of the same structure in the encoder. Thus the micro and macro search space are the same. The search space for the encoder is depicted as a fully connected DAG. As is shown in Figure 2, the encoder has K (= 5) layers. Node i in the DAG is a neural network layer, and edge $<i, j>$ means the output of layer i is fed into layer j. If a layer has multiple inputs, then the inputs will be summed.

For each node, the controller first decides whether the node encodes the sentence itself (self-encoding layer), or it encodes the attention from one sentence to each other (cross-attention layer).

If layer i is a cross-sentence layer, it will make its input attend to its counterpart's input in the other sentence's encoder. For example, in Figure 2, layer 2 of the premise encoder is a cross-sentence attention layer. So its input will attend to the input of layer 2 in the hypothesis encoder. In addition to the dot product attention used in the multi-head attention of Transformers (denote as **dot**), we incorporate the four attention functions in Tan et al. (2018), referred to as **p_dot**[2], **concat**, **add**, **minus**.

[2]Note that the dot attention in Tan et al. (2018) (denoted as **p_dot** by us) is not the same as the dot product attention in MHA, where the former is a pointwise product ('A * B' in

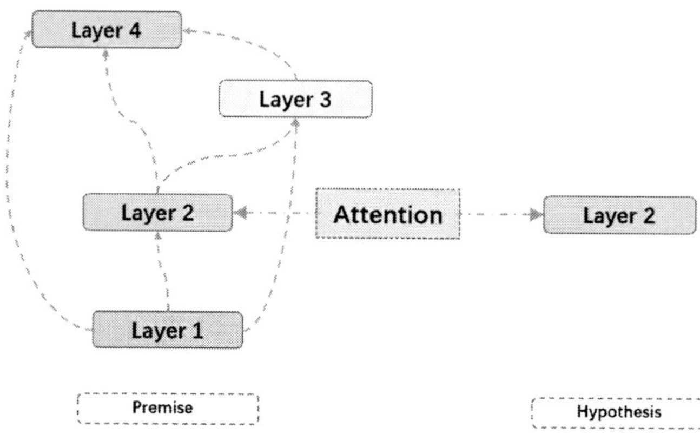

Figure 2: The DAG for the encoder. The layers can be self-encoding layers or cross-attention layers. If layer i is a cross-sentence layer, it will make its input attend to its counterpart's input in the other sentence's encoder.

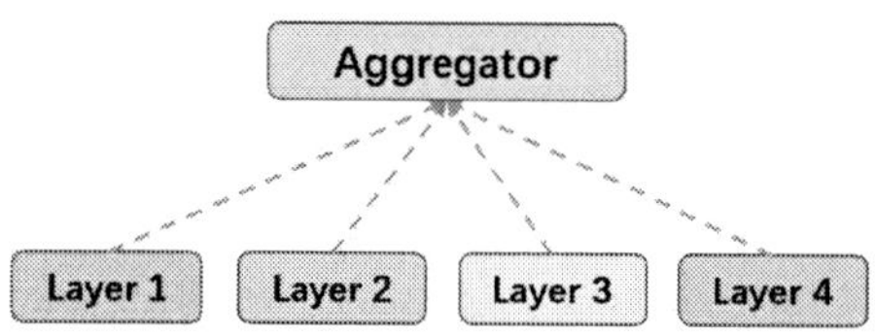

Figure 3: The DAG for the aggregation layer.

For the self-encoding layer, we incorporate four categories of candidate layers which are commonly used for text representation, namely convolutional layers with kernel size 1, 3, 5 (denoted as **conv1**, **conv3**, **conv5**), recurrent layers such as LSTM/GRU (**lstm**, **gru**), max pooling layers with window size 3 and 5 (denoted as **pool_3**, **pool_5**), and multi-head self-attention layers with number of heads 4 and 8 (**mha_4**, **mha_8**). Skip connection (**skip**) is also included to support residual layers. Zero layer (**zero**), which is to output zero tensors, is also included, so that the final model can be sparser than is shown in Figure 2.

2.3 Aggregator search space

As depicted in Figure 3, the DAG for aggregator is much simpler. One has to decide whether each layer's output in the encoder DAG should be fed into the aggregation layer. If multiple layers are selected, their outputs are summed. There are several different aggregation operations. The most common two are the max-pooling aggregator (**max_agg**) and the average-pooling aggregator (**avg_agg**). The self-attention (**sa_agg**) technique is also used for aggregation (Gong et al., 2018; Chen et al., 2018) . We also include dynamic routing (Gong et al., 2018) (henceforth *dr_agg*) into our aggregator operation space.[3]

2.4 Architecture search algorithm

We adopt the ENAS (Pham et al., 2018) framework for search since it is one of the most effective and efficient among all state-of-the-art search algorithms. ENAS searches for the best network architecture via reinforcement learning with weight sharing. ENAS leverages an LSTM as the controller. In each step, the controller samples several child networks from the search space. The child networks share the same set of parameters with the global super-graph to accelerate the evaluation procedure. After child models' performances are obtained, they are fed back to the controller as reward signals. The parameters of the controller are updated through policy gradients based on REINFORCE (Williams, 1992). We implement ENAS via NNI[4].

In this work, we try to improve the search results by deeper parameter sharing and search warm-up. First, the parameter sharing in ENAS is relatively shallow. The parameters are shared only when precisely the same operation is used in the same position of the DAG. We share the parameters across related operations. For convolutional layers, we use depthwise separable convolution networks since they are more parameter efficient. And the point-

PyTorch), and the latter is (batch-wise) matrix multiplication ('torch.matmul(A, B)').

[3]Following Gong et al. (2018), we set the number of capsules as 4 and the number of iterations as 3.

[4]https://github.com/microsoft/nni

wise convolution inside each convolutional layer is shared across **conv1**, **conv3**, and **conv5**. The key, query and value matrices inside **mha_4** and **mha_8** are shared for multi-head attention layers. The key, query, and value matrices for cross-attn modules of different attention functions are shared.

Second, we add a search warm-up phase before the search begins, and the learning rate of the RL controller is also gradually increased to the maximum value and follows a linear decay schedule. The intuition is that when the shared parameters are trained for pre-specified steps, the controller can receive much more reliable reward signals.

To make the model efficient enough for online deployment, we add efficiency constraints to the generated child models, which will be specified in the next section. Child models that fail these requirements will be assigned a zero reward so that the controller will learn how to generate models that meet the requirements.

3 Experiments and Discussion

3.1 Datasets

We conduct experiments on two medical NLI datasets we build for developing our medical dialogue system, whose statistics and metrics for evaluation are shown in Table 1.

Chinese Medical Frequent Asked Queries (CMFAQ). These datasets contain pairs of Chinese medical frequently asked questions (FAQs), and the model has to determine whether the two queries contain the same meaning. The dataset is collected from the logs of an online medical consultation provider. The sentences in this dataset are usually general health-related questions.[5]

Chinese Medical Query Patterns (CMQP). This dataset is designated for semantic matching of the query patterns. The model has to determine whether two patterns have the same intention. We collect queries that are related to medical entities and annotate their NER tags. Then we replace the named entities with special tokens that reflect the entity types in the sentence and transform the query into a query pattern.[6]

The train/valid/test split is defined by randomly splitting the whole annotated dataset with a ratio 7:1:2.

3.2 Experimental settings

To improve the performances of models that are not pre-trained on a large corpus, we will distill knowledge from a pre-trained large teacher model both during search and model evaluation. The knowledge distillation method follows Liu et al. (2019), and the distillation temperature is set to be 10. We select the Chinese BERT-wwm-ext (Cui et al., 2019) as the teacher model. To make it more suitable for our domain applications (Gu et al., 2020), we further pre-train it on our 2.3GB medical corpus.

In our experiments, the encoder has five layers at most. The 128d word embedding vectors are initialized by a pre-trained Word2Vec (Mikolov et al., 2013) model trained on our medical corpus and are fine-tuned during training. The hidden dimension is kept to 256 in the model. During the architecture search, the batch size is 128, max input length is 64 for both premise and hypothesis, the dropout ratio is 0.2, and the weight decay is 2e-6. For both model weights and controller, we utilize Adam optimizer and learning rate decay with cosine annealing. The maximum learning rate l_{max} is 3e-3, and the minimum learning rate l_{min} is 1e-6, and the cosine cycle is 10. For model weights, at the beginning of training, the learning rate is linearly warmed up for 0.8 of one epoch to l_{max}. For search warm-up, in the first 3 epochs, the controller is not updated, and at the beginning of the fourth epoch, the controller learning rate is also linearly warmed up for 0.8 of one epoch to l_{max}.

After each epoch, ten candidate architectures are generated by the controller and evaluated on the validation set. The inference batch size is 1, which mimic the scenario for online deployment. When obtaining the validation performance, we also calculate the inference speed and memory consumption. The efficiency requirement is that the model's GPU memory consumption is less than 1 GB, and the per-sample inference time is lower than 20ms. If the efficiency requirements are not satisfied, the child model's reward is set to be zero. After train-

[5]For examples, "现在在居家隔离，我要怎么保持健康？" (Now in isolation at home, how can I keep healthy?) is a quite popular query during the breakout of COVID-19, and it is matched to one of our collected FAQs, "居家隔离如何养生？" (How to keep healthy when quarantined at home?)

[6]For example, a common question we received is "立普妥是饭前吃吗？" (Is Lipitor taken before meals?). In this sentence, "立普妥" (Lipitor) is a drug entity, so the query is transformed into a query pattern "<drug>是饭前吃吗?" (<drug> should be taken before meals?), and it is matched to one of our collected query patterns "<drug>应该饭前吃还是饭后吃？" (<drug> should be taken before meals or after meals?).

Dataset	avg seq_len	Train #	Dev #	Test #	Label #	Metrics
CMFAQ	32.5	37676	5382	10764	2	F1
CMQP	19.6	32476	4639	9279	2	F1

Table 1: Overview of medical NLI datasets in experiments.

ing 150 epochs, the architecture with the highest evaluation F1 is chosen as the final network. And this model is retrained from scratch with optimal hyper-parameters tuned using NNI's implementation of Bayesian optimization. We mainly focus on three hyper-parameters: (1) batch size, (2) learning rate, (3) dropout rate.

We assign 2 CPU cores, 8G memory, and 1 Tesla V100 GPU card for each search or evaluation in our experiments. The search lasts 12 hours and 4 hours for CMFAQ and CMQP, respectively.

3.3 Baseline methods

The best learned architectures are evaluated by training from scratch (with hyper-parameter search). The baseline models include: (a) LSTM + *max_agg*; (b) LSTM + *sa_agg*, which are evaluated by Wang et al. (2018); (c) LSTM/Transformer + *dr_agg* (Gong et al., 2018); (d) ESIM (Chen et al., 2016); (e) Decomposable attention (DecompAttn) model (Parikh et al., 2016). The number of encoder layers is treated as a hyper-parameter and are tuned together with other parameters. We also compare our search space with that in TextNAS. We also compare different search algorithms that have similar time complexities as ENAS, including DARTS (Liu et al., 2018), One-Shot (Luo et al., 2019), and Random Search with Weight Sharing (RandomSA) (Li and Talwalkar, 2019). [7] The BERT-wwm-ext teacher model's performances are also reported.

3.4 Search Results

As depicted in Figure 4(a) and 4(b), the learned architectures consist of different layers categories. For convenience, we will refer to the best model learned on CMFAQ as NASQU-1 and the best model learned on CMQP as NASQU-2. NASQU-1's encoder has 3 self-encoding encoders, 2 of which are two convolutional layers, and the other one is a MHA layer, and it has a cross-attn layer with the **add** attention function. Note that NASQU-1 discards the 4th layer in the DAG since it is **zero**

[7]Unless specified, the default settings of their open-source codes are used.

MODEL	CMFAQ	CMQP
Baseline models		
GRU + *max_agg*	81.8	83.6
LSTM + *max_agg*	82.3	84.6
LSTM + *sa_agg*	83.6	85.4
LSTM + *dr_agg*	85.3	**87.7**
Transformer + *dr_agg*	84.3	86.8
ESIM	**85.8**	87.6
DecompAttn	84.5	86.9
NAS models		
DARTS	**86.4**	87.9
One-Shot	86.3	88.1
RandomSA	85.5	87.2
TextNAS	86.3	**88.6**
Our models		
NASQU-1	**87.1***	88.5
NASQU-2	86.2	**89.5***
BERT-wwm-ext	88.9	90.5

Table 2: Results of the two medical NLI dataset. For each dataset, we conduct a significance test against the best reproducible model, and * means that the improvement is significant at the level of 0.05 significance level.

operation. The aggregator of NASQU-1 takes layers 2 and 4 as input, and the aggregator is **sa_agg**. Meanwhile, NASQU-2 is more lightweight than NASQU-1 since it discards the 3rd and 5th layer. NASQU-2's encoder has a GRU layer, a conv layer, and a cross-attn layer with **p_dot** attention function. The aggregator of NASQU-2 takes all valid layers as input, and the aggregator is **dr_agg**.

Although the learned model seems to be more involved than manual architectures, we still find that there are some design principles in line with the commonsense and previously established observations:

- Convolution layers are combined with GRU and multi-head self-attention layers, which are similar to C-LSTM (Zhou et al., 2015) and Transformer (Vaswani et al., 2017). Intuitively, convolution operations extract local features similar to n-gram, which complement long-term dependency features captured by GRU/self-attention.

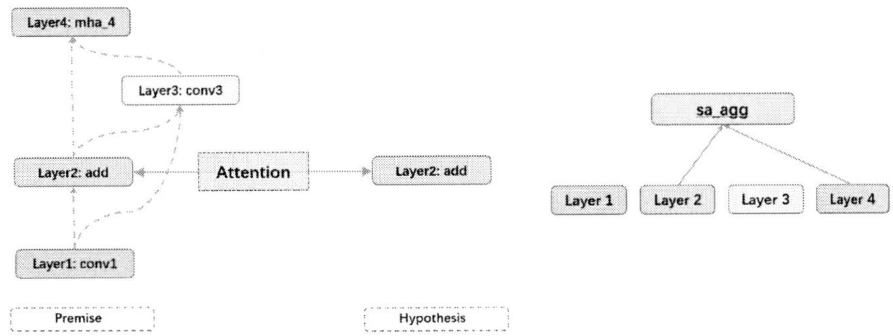

(a) NASQU_1

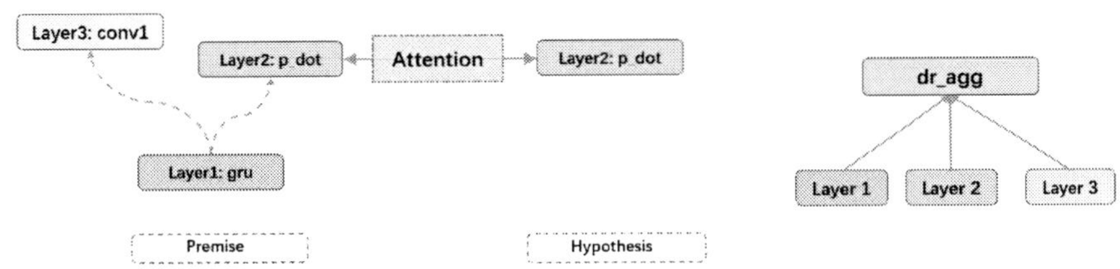

(b) NASQU_2

Figure 4: Learned architectures on the two medical NLI datasets.

- We find that the best learned architectures include cross-attn modules, which are in line with observations in the previous literature (Parikh et al., 2016; Chen et al., 2016). Cross sentence attention can align the semantics of two text inputs and provide better feature extraction for NLI tasks.
- Different tasks result in quite different architectures, emphasizing the importance of task specificity. Besides, a smaller dataset size prefers a more light-weighted architecture, since intuitively, a heavier architecture is more prone to over-fitting on a small dataset.

The performance results are shown in Table 2. The learned architecture discovered by NASQU achieves higher average F1 scores than all the baseline models. Also, it outperforms other network architectures found automatically by other search spaces and algorithms. Note that on CMQP, the improvement over different baselines is statistically significant. We also evaluate the transferring ability of the two best learned architectures. Although NASQU-1 also performs well on CMQP compared with baselines, it is significantly worse than NASQU-2. This observation also stands for NASQU-2 on the CMFAQ dataset. These observations validate the importance of customizing different architecture for different tasks.

Model	GPU memory	inference speed
BERT-wwm-ext	4.8 GB	66ms/it
NASQU-1	0.84 GB	14ms/it
NASQU-2	0.71 GB	11ms/it
LSTM + *dr_agg*	0.72GB	15ms/it
ESIM	1.12GB	21ms/it

Table 3: Comparison of GPU memory consumption and inference speed between the teacher model BERT Large and NASQU-1, and NASQU-2.

Table 2 also shows that the performances of the two learned models is close to the BERT teacher. We now compare the inference speed and GPU memory consumptions of BERT and the learned models. The results are reported in Table 3. We can see that the learned models achieve significant speed-up over the BERT teacher models without too much performance loss, and they are more efficient than ESIM. LSTM + **dr_agg** has comparable efficiency, but the performance is significantly worse.

3.5 Ablation studies

We now conduct extensive ablation studies to demonstrate our search space design, and modi-

strategies	test F1
NASQU	**87.1***
- deeper weight sharing	85.9
- search warm-up	84.5

Table 4: Results for ablations studies on the strategies we propose for search.

search space	test F1
NASQU	**87.1***
- cross sentence attention	86.2
- aggregator search space	84.6

Table 5: Results for ablations studies on the search space we construct for architecture search for NLI tasks.

fications to the search algorithm are essential. The ablation studies are performed on CMFAQ.

First, we conduct ablation on the proposed modifications to the search method. As we can see from Table 4, deeper weight sharing is beneficial. Intuitively, deeper parameter sharing reduces the number of shared parameters during the search phase, making the reward signal more reliable. The results also show that the search warm-up also contributes to better search results.

We now conduct an ablation study on our entire search space. The results are shown in Table 5. Note that for our NLI tasks, when we drop the cross attention mechanism from the search space, the search results drop from 87.1 to 86.2. And we can see that dropping the aggregator search space (fixing the aggregator to be **sa_agg**) also results in worse performances.

4 Conclusion and Future Work

In this work, we experiment on modeling NLI tasks via NAS on our medical NLI tasks. Our search space is an extension to TextNAS and ENAS, which enable us to search for novel models with cross sentence attention and suitable aggregators. To improve the search results, we also propose a more in-depth weight sharing strategy than ENAS and search warm-up steps. Experiments on our NLI tasks demonstrate that our search space is beneficial for NLI tasks.

References

Samuel R. Bowman, Gabor Angeli, Christopher Potts, and Christopher D. Manning. 2015. A large annotated corpus for learning natural language inference. In *Proceedings of the 2015 Conference on Empirical Methods in Natural Language Processing*, pages 632–642, Lisbon, Portugal. Association for Computational Linguistics.

Qian Chen, Zhen-Hua Ling, and Xiaodan Zhu. 2018. Enhancing sentence embedding with generalized pooling. In *Proceedings of the 27th International Conference on Computational Linguistics*, pages 1815–1826, Santa Fe, New Mexico, USA. Association for Computational Linguistics.

Qian Chen, Xiaodan Zhu, Zhenhua Ling, Si Wei, Hui Jiang, and Diana Inkpen. 2016. Enhanced lstm for natural language inference. *arXiv preprint arXiv:1609.06038*.

Yiming Cui, W. Che, T. Liu, B. Qin, Ziqing Yang, S. Wang, and G. Hu. 2019. Pre-training with whole word masking for chinese bert. *ArXiv*, abs/1906.08101.

Jingjing Gong, Xipeng Qiu, Shaojing Wang, and Xuanjing Huang. 2018. Information aggregation via dynamic routing for sequence encoding. *arXiv preprint arXiv:1806.01501*.

Yu Gu, Robert Tinn, Hao Cheng, Michael Lucas, Naoto Usuyama, Xiaodong Liu, Tristan Naumann, Jianfeng Gao, and Hoifung Poon. 2020. Domain-specific language model pretraining for biomedical natural language processing.

Yufan Jiang, Chi Hu, Tong Xiao, Chunliang Zhang, and Jingbo Zhu. 2019. Improved differentiable architecture search for language modeling and named entity recognition. In *Proceedings of the 2019 Conference on Empirical Methods in Natural Language Processing and the 9th International Joint Conference on Natural Language Processing (EMNLP-IJCNLP)*, pages 3585–3590, Hong Kong, China. Association for Computational Linguistics.

Liam Li and Ameet Talwalkar. 2019. Random search and reproducibility for neural architecture search. *ArXiv*, abs/1902.07638.

H. Liu, K. Simonyan, and Y. Yang. 2018. Darts: Differentiable architecture search. *arXiv preprint arXiv:1806.09055*.

Xiaodong Liu, Pengcheng He, W. Chen, and Jianfeng Gao. 2019. Multi-task deep neural networks for natural language understanding. In *ACL*.

Renqian Luo, Tao Qin, and E. Chen. 2019. Understanding and improving one-shot neural architecture optimization. *ArXiv*, abs/1909.10815.

Tomas Mikolov, Ilya Sutskever, Kai Chen, Greg S Corrado, and Jeff Dean. 2013. Distributed representations of words and phrases and their compositionality. In *NIPS*.

Ankur P Parikh, Oscar Täckström, Dipanjan Das, and Jakob Uszkoreit. 2016. A decomposable attention model for natural language inference. *arXiv preprint arXiv:1606.01933*.

H. Pham, M.Y. Guan, B. Zoph, Q.V. Le, and J. Dean. 2018. Efficient neural architecture search via parameter sharing. *arXiv preprint arXiv:1802.03268*.

Hieu Pham, Melody Y. Guan, Barret Zoph, Quoc V. Le, and Jeff Dean. 2018. Efficient Neural Architecture Search via Parameter Sharing. *arXiv e-prints*, page arXiv:1802.03268.

David R So, Chen Liang, and Quoc V Le. 2019. The evolved transformer. *arXiv preprint arXiv:1901.11117*.

Chuanqi Tan, Furu Wei, Wenhui Wang, Weifeng Lv, and Ming Zhou. 2018. Multiway attention networks for modeling sentence pairs. In *IJCAI*, pages 4411–4417.

Ashish Vaswani, Noam Shazeer, Niki Parmar, Jakob Uszkoreit, Llion Jones, Aidan N Gomez, Łukasz Kaiser, and Illia Polosukhin. 2017. Attention is all you need. In *NIPS*.

Alex Wang, Amanpreet Singh, Julian Michael, Felix Hill, Omer Levy, and Samuel R Bowman. 2018. Glue: A multi-task benchmark and analysis platform for natural language understanding. *arXiv preprint arXiv:1804.07461*.

Yujing Wang, Yaming Yang, Yiren Chen, Jing Bai, Ce Zhang, Guinan Su, Xiaoyu Kou, Yunhai Tong, Mao Yang, and Lidong Zhou. 2020. Textnas: A neural architecture search space tailored for text representation. *Proceedings of the AAAI Conference on Artificial Intelligence*, 34(05):9242–9249.

Ronald J Williams. 1992. Simple statistical gradient-following algorithms for connectionist reinforcement learning. *Machine learning*, 8(3-4):229–256.

Ruobing Xie, Yanan Lu, F. Lin, and Leyu Lin. 2020. Faq-based question answering via knowledge anchors. In *NLPCC*.

Chunting Zhou, Chonglin Sun, Zhiyuan Liu, and F. C. M. Lau. 2015. A c-lstm neural network for text classification. *ArXiv*, abs/1511.08630.

B. Zoph and Q.V. Le. 2017. Neural architecture search with reinforcement learning. In *ICLR*.

OodGAN: Generative Adversarial Network for Out-of-Domain Data Generation

Petr Marek*
Czech Technical University in Prague
Prague, Czech Republic
marekp17@fel.cvut.cz

Vishal Ishwar Naik
Amazon Alexa AI
Sunnyvale, California
naikvish@amazon.com

Vincent Auvray
Amazon Alexa AI
Sunnyvale, California
vauvray@amazon.de

Anuj Goyal
Amazon Alexa AI
Sunnyvale, California
anujgoya@amazon.com

Abstract

Detecting an Out-of-Domain (OOD) utterance is crucial for a robust dialog system. Most dialog systems are trained on a pool of annotated OOD data to achieve this goal. However, collecting the annotated OOD data for a given domain is an expensive process. To mitigate this issue, previous works have proposed generative adversarial networks (GAN) based models to generate OOD data for a given domain automatically. However, these proposed models do not work directly with the text. They work with the text's latent space instead, enforcing these models to include components responsible for encoding text into latent space and decoding it back, such as auto-encoder. These components increase the model complexity, making it difficult to train.

We propose OodGAN, a sequential generative adversarial network (SeqGAN) based model for OOD data generation. Our proposed model works directly on the text and hence eliminates the need to include an auto-encoder. OOD data generated using OodGAN model outperforms state-of-the-art in OOD detection metrics for ROSTD (67% relative improvement in FPR 0.95) and OSQ datasets (28% relative improvement in FPR 0.95) (Zheng et al., 2020).

1 Introduction

OOD detection is an essential task in AI voice assistants like Alexa, Siri, or Google Assistant. The task is to recognize whether a given user utterance belongs to the in-domain (IND) distribution or not. Users usually do not know the limitations of a voice application and assign requests which the system can not act upon. These requests are referred to as OOD since these do not belong to the application's domain. Voice assistants should be able to handle OOD utterances robustly by not taking unintended action or giving wrong or nonsensical responses leading to a poor user experience.

Intent classification (IC) is one of the main tasks in a conversational system that selects the best intent given a user input. IC can be extended to support OOD detection in two different ways. The first one is to add OOD as another intent to the IC model, but this requires annotated OOD data for training. The second method is to use a threshold on the classifier's output probability distribution during the runtime. This method does not require OOD data for training necessarily. Nevertheless, it proves difficult to select the threshold in practice without it.

The state-of-the-art IC algorithms are trained using neural networks to produce probability distribution over output classes and use cross-entropy loss. However, Lakshminarayanan et al. (2017), and Guo et al. (2017) pointed out that the neural network classifier tends to be overconfident in its classification. This means that the classifier tends to assign a high probability for one class, even when the example was not seen in the training phase. Thus, such a classifier cannot correctly recognize if an example belongs to an IND or OOD distribution during runtime with any reasonable threshold value. In this paper, we focus on improving the performance of the threshold-based OOD detection method with the help of generated OOD data.

Zheng et al. (2020) proposed to use negative entropy as an additional loss for the classification task in a neural network. The negative entropy loss trains the network to flatten the produced probability distribution as opposed to cross-entropy, which teaches the network to maximize the correct class probability. Thus, the idea is to apply cross-entropy loss on IND data and negative entropy loss on OOD data. The result is that IND data receives a high

* Research conducted during an internship at Amazon Alexa AI

Proceedings of NAACL HLT 2021: IndustryTrack Papers, pages 238–245
June 6–11, 2021.

probability for the correct class, and OOD data receives low probabilities for all classes. Thanks to this fact, we can select a reasonable threshold on the output probability that will classify both IND and OOD data correctly. We need OOD data to train models in this way. However, the collection of OOD data is a manual and expensive process.

The IND data forms a small distribution cluster in the space of vector text representation. In principle, the rest of that space is covered by OOD data. Also, in real-world scenarios, most OOD data share patterns with IND data. Nevertheless, Zheng et al. (2020) demonstrated that training IC model with OOD data that are just outside IND distribution should be sufficient to handle most of the OOD requests during runtime.

In this paper, we propose a novel OOD data generation model OodGAN, which is an extension of SeqGAN (Yu et al., 2017). We use GAN to generate OOD data that share the same patterns as IND and are very close to IND distribution.

Our proposed model aims to be deployed to Natural Language Understanding (NLU) frameworks offered by popular voice assistants like Amazon Alexa and Google Assistant. These NLU frameworks are offered to third-party developers to create voice applications. Third-party developers can define any number of IND intents and provide sample utterances for each to build voice applications. These voice applications should recognize OOD requests during run time without additional developer effort to provide OOD training data. The proposed model can be deployed in a NLU framework to generate application-specific OOD data that the IC model can use during training to recognize OOD requests robustly and improve the end-user experience.

Our main contributions are:

(1) We propose a novel and simple OOD data generation model OodGAN that improves on the model proposed by Zheng et al. (2020). It works with a sequence of words directly unlike the previously proposed models, which work on latent space represented by auto-encoder. Our model eliminates the need for the auto-encoder, which reduces the overall size of the model.

(2) We evaluate our model on the ROSTD and OSQ datasets, and we show that OOD examples generated by OodGAN achieved state-of-the-art results.

2 Related Work

There are three research areas relevant to our work: OOD detection, text generation and OOD generation.

Out-of-Domain Detection

Larson et al. (2019) introduced a dataset for intent classification that includes OOD queries. They propose three baseline approaches for OOD detection that rely on OOD training data. Gangal et al. (2019) created a ROSTD dataset and explored likelihood ratio based approaches. Lee and Shalyminov (2019) proposed an OOD detection method that does not require OOD data by utilizing counterfeit OOD turns in the context of a dialog. Ryu et al. (2018) proposed an OOD detection system that uses only IND sentences to build a generative adversarial network in which the discriminator generates low scores for OOD sentences.

Text Generation

Donahue and Rumshisky (2018) proposed a two-step solution to text generation using auto-encoder and GAN that works with a low-dimensional representation of sentences. Yu et al. (2017) proposed a sequence generation framework SeqGAN that works directly on the text and hence eliminates the need for an auto-encoder.

Out-of-Domain Data Generation

Zheng et al. (2020) proposed a GAN based model to generate pseudo-OOD examples that are akin to IND input utterances. The model uses a denoising auto-encoder that is trained to map an input example into a latent code. The functions of the auto-encoder's parts are the following. The encoder learns to create a latent representation of the examples. The decoder learns to convert the vector of the latent representation into text. The model's generator produces vectors in the latent space. The discriminator evaluates the closeness of latent space vectors generated by the generator to real latent space vectors created by the encoder. Discriminator sends a training signal to the generator to force it to generate indistinguishable vectors from vectors encoded by the encoder. An auxiliary classifier trained on IND examples is introduced to force the generator to generate latent code belonging to OOD. The resulting utterances share patterns with IND examples but belong to OOD.

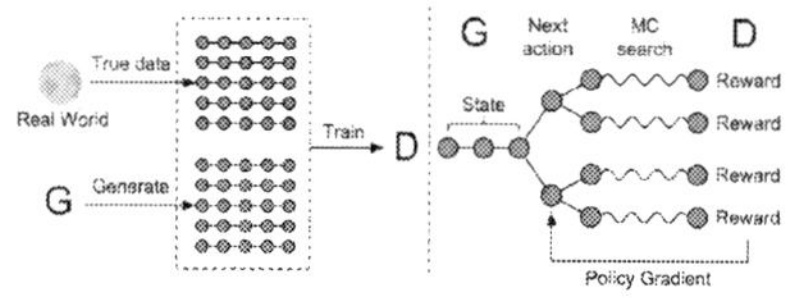

Figure 1: The illustration of SeqGAN (Yu et al., 2017). Left: Discriminator D is trained over the real data and the data generated by generator G. Right: Generator is trained by policy gradient where the final reward signal is provided by the discriminator and is passed back to the intermediate action value via Monte Carlo search.

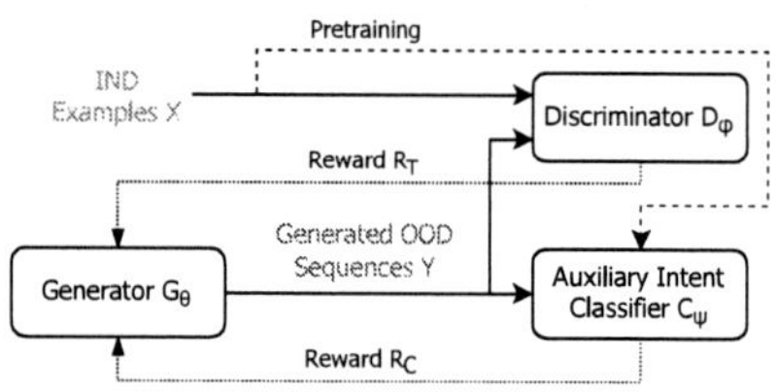

Figure 2: The overall architecture of the OodGAN. C_ψ is pretrained to recognize intent classes for IND examples. D_ϕ is trained to distinguish between IND and generated OOD examples during adversarial training. G_θ is trained by the REINFORCE algorithm during adversarial training to generate OOD sequences. The training is guided by rewards originating in C_ψ and D_ϕ.

3 Generative Adversarial Networks for Out-of-Domain Data Generation

3.1 SeqGAN

The SeqGAN model proposed by Yu et al. (2017) is a starting point for the proposed OodGAN. SeqGAN is a sequence generation framework illustrated in Figure 1. Yu et al. (2017) denote the problem of sequence generation as follows. Given a dataset of real-world structured sequences, train a θ-parameterized generative model G_θ to produce a sequence $Y_{1:T} = (y_1, ..., y_t, ...y_T), y_t \in Y$ where Y is the vocabulary of candidate tokens. They apply reinforcement learning to this problem. In timestep t, the state s is the current produced tokens $(y_1, ..., y_{t-1})$ and the action a is the next token y_t to select.

They propose to additionally train a ϕ-parameterized discriminative model D_ϕ that provides guidance for improving generator G_θ. D_ϕ produces a probability $D_\phi(Y_{1:T})$ representing the probability of $Y_{1:T}$ being a real sequence vs. a generated one. The discriminative model D_ϕ is trained with real sequence data, labeled as positive examples, and synthetic sequences from the generative model G_θ, labeled as negative examples.

SeqGAN uses the REINFORCE algorithm (Williams, 1992) to train generative model G_θ. Parameters of generative model G_θ are updated at the same time by a policy gradient and Monte Carlo search based on the expected end reward received from the discriminative model D_ϕ for the generated sequence. The reward is represented by a likelihood that the generated sequence will fool the discriminative model D_ϕ. Thus the generator's goal is to generate a sequence that would fool the discriminator into considering it as real.

3.2 OodGAN

We propose OodGAN based on SeqGAN. There are two benefits of SeqGAN for our task of OOD data generation. SeqGAN produces sequences similar to the training data, and it works directly on input sequence unlike earlier model (Zheng et al., 2020), which works on latent space. Eliminating the auto-encoder responsible for converting a sequence of words into latent space reduces the overall model size. Also, our experiments with Zheng et al. (2020) show a degradation in the overall performance due to the auto-encoder component (see the Results section for details).

Since our task is to generate OOD data, we have the additional criterion that generated sequences should be close to the training IND sequences. However, we also want them not to belong to any IND intent class. We propose the OodGAN to achieve the two criteria.

The main difference between SeqGAN and OodGAN is the introduction of an auxiliary intent classifier. The auxiliary intent classifier C_ψ estimates the probability $C_\psi(z_i|Y)$ of example Y belonging into intent class z_i. The task of the auxiliary intent classifier is to produce an additional reward signal. The reward signal guides the generator to produce a sequence not belonging to any IND intent class. The reward R_{C_ψ} coming from the auxiliary intent classifier for each generated example is defined as Shannon's Entropy $R_{C_\psi} = -\sum_{i=1}^{m} C_\psi(z_i|Y) \cdot log(C_\psi(z_i|Y))$, where m is the number of IND intent classes. The intuition for using Shannon's Entropy is that we want to reward a generator for producing examples for which the auxiliary intent classifier cannot clearly assign one of IND classes. In other words, the auxiliary classifier should assign a nearly uniform distribution across all intent classes for a good generated example. The generator obtains a high reward for such examples because the uniform distribution has the highest Shannon's Entropy.

We train the auxiliary intent classifier to predict one of the classes $z_{1...m}$ for each training IND example $X_{1...n}$ during the pre-training step. We do not have to retrain it during adversarial training because IND intent classes' distribution does not change.

The goal of the generator is to generate a sequence that maximizes the expected sum of rewards from discriminator D_ϕ (the estimated probability of the sequence being real), and auxiliary intent classifier C_ψ (Shannon's Entropy calculated using estimated probabilities of sequence belonging to IND intent classes by auxiliary intent classifier).

Empirically, we evaluated different training strategies. We found that optimizing generator G using only the discriminator's reward first, followed by using only the auxiliary intent classifier reward, and then repeating the process for each training batch produced the most stable results. This worked better than summing up the rewards from the discriminator and auxiliary intent classifier. When we tried summing up the two rewards, we noticed that the generator tended to collapse into a state in which it generated a single sequence highly rewarded by the auxiliary intent classifier, even though this did not happen for all training runs. We observed this situation even when we normalized rewards to a value between 0 and 1.

We also observed that part of the examples generated by OodGAN is semantically similar to some IND training example or is generated multiple times. Examples that are identical or too close to IND examples are problematic and confuse the OOD classifier. Duplicated examples do not represent the OOD distribution effectively. For those reasons, we removed with an automatic filter the generated OOD examples that are identical or similar to IND examples or that are generated repeatedly.

To summarize, OodGAN's training procedure has the following steps.

(1) Train Auxiliary classifier: First train auxiliary classifier to predict the classes $z_{1...m}$ for IND data $X_{1...n}$ until convergence.

(2) Train Generator as Language Model: Next, train the generator on the IND data $X_{1...n}$ as a language model until it converges. Thanks to this step, it is easier for the generator to fool the discriminator from the start of the adversarial training.

(3) Train Discriminator: Generate adversarial examples from the generator. This training step helps the discriminator to provide a useful reward signal from the start of adversarial training.

(4) Adversarial Training: Perform adversarial training of generator and discriminator. There are three optimization steps for each training batch. First, optimize the generator using reward from discriminator as proposed by Yu et al. (2017). Next, optimize the generator using a reward from the auxiliary classifier. Lastly, optimize the discriminator.

4 Experiments

4.1 Datasets

We conducted experiments on ROSTD (Gangal et al., 2019) and OSQ (Larson et al., 2019) datasets.

- **ROSTD** contains three categories (alarm, reminder, and weather), each consisting of four intents. The dataset consists of 30,000 training, 4,000 validation and 8,000 testing IND examples. OOD examples were selected in a way that they do not belong to any category and do not share patterns with any IND examples. There are also no OOD examples in the training set of the dataset. The testing set contains 4,500 OOD examples. IND and OOD examples from ROSTD are listed in Table 5.

- **OSQ** consists of 150 intents. The datases consists of 15,000 training, 3,000 validation and 4,500 testing IND examples. The dataset was created using Mechanical Turk. The turkers were given the name of the intent, and they were supposed to write intent examples fitting into the intent. The dataset authors manually went through examples and moved examples not fitting into the given intent class to the OOD class. In this way, OOD examples share the same patterns as IND examples. The OSQ dataset contains 100 training OOD examples. However, we decided not to use them for training due to the nature of our experiments. There are also 100 validation and 1,000 testing OOD examples.

4.2 Evaluation Process

We evaluate the model on the downstream task of OOD data detection and measure the change in

OOD data detection metrics. We designed experiments in the following way. We train the OodGAN on IND training examples as a first step. Next, we generate the OOD examples using the trained model of OodGAN. We generate the same number of OOD examples as a number of IND examples in the training set. In a third step, we train the threshold-based OOD detection model using cross-entropy loss on training IND examples and negative entropy loss on generated OOD examples. In the last step, we evaluate both IND and OOD metrics.

4.3 Metrics

We evaluate the OodGAN by measuring metrics on the downstream task of OOD detection. We measure AUROC, AUPR, and FPR*N* metrics (Ren et al., 2019; Hendrycks and Gimpel, 2017; Hendrycks et al., 2019) to evaluate OodGAN's ability to generate OOD data that helps IC to distinguish IND and OOD input utterances. We treat OOD examples as the positive class.

- **AUROC** The area under the receiver operating characteristic (ROC) curve. The score says the probability that a randomly selected OOD example will have a higher predicted probability of being an OOD than a randomly selected IND example. Higher AUROC score is better.
- **AUPR** The area under the precision-recall curve when OOD inputs are treated as positive samples. AUPR calculates the average precision score for all recall values. Intuitively, the higher the classification threshold we select, the more OOD will be classified as OOD. However, we risk that more IND will be classified as OOD. AUPR expresses this risk. Higher AUPR score is better.
- **FPR*N*** The false-positive rate (FPR) when the true positive rate (TPR) is N%. FPR*N* metric is a practical value in real-world application since it evaluates an OOD detection performance at a particular threshold. Lower FPR*N* means there is a smaller chance of IND examples triggering false alarm (IND getting classified as OOD) when the model's performance on OOD example is N%. We report FPR when TPR is 0.95 and 0.90. Lower FPR*N* score is better.

We consider FPR*N* metric as the most practical value in real-world application since it evaluates an OOD detection performance at a particular threshold. Lower FPR*N* means there is a smaller chance of IND examples triggering false alarm (IND getting classified as OOD) when the model correctly recognizes N% of OOD examples.

We also measure IND accuracy that evaluates generated OOD data's influence on the IC's ability to recognize the intents of IND data correctly.

- **IND accuracy** The percentage of IND data that have assigned correct intent label. We expect that generated OOD examples cannot improve the IC's ability to recognize intent labels for ID. However, generated OOD examples can degrade the IC's ability to recognize IND intents. Thus, we measure the IND accuracy to evaluate whether generated OOD negatively impacts the IC. Higher IND accuracy is better.

4.4 Implementation

We based our implementation on the Github repository[1] of SeqGAN implemented in PyTorch. The generator is one layer GRU recurrent neural network trained using Adam optimizer with a learning rate set to 0.001. Input to the generator is embedded with fastText embeddings (Joulin et al., 2016) trained on Wikipedia. The generator uses negative log-likelihood loss during LM training and policy gradient loss during GAN training. The discriminator is a two-layer bidirectional GRU recurrent neural network with a tanh activation function. Adagrad optimization is used for training the discriminator with a learning rate set to 0.1 and binary cross-entropy loss is optimized. The auxiliary classifier uses the convolutional neural network proposed by Kim (2014), which has filters of size 2, 3, 4, and 5, and for each size, there are 256 filters. We used the LeakyReLU activation function and 0.5 dropout in output dense layers. The auxiliary classifier is trained using the Adam optimizer with a learning rate set to 0.0001 and cross-entropy loss is optimized.

We show the comparison of number of parameters between OodGAN, SeqGAN, and Zheng et al. (2020) in Table 1.

5 Results

5.1 Results on Zheng et al. (2020)

We first conducted experiments to replicate results reported by Zheng et al. (2020) on the OSQ dataset.

[1] https://github.com/suragnair/seqGAN

	# Parameters
Zheng et al. (2020)	7M
SeqGAN (Yu et al., 2017)	800k
OodGAN	2M

Table 1: Number of parameters

OSQ (Larson et al., 2019)	AUROC ↑	AUPR ↑	FPR 0.95 ↓	FPR 0.90 ↓	IND Acc. ↑
Results reported by Zheng et al. (2020)	95.4	98.9	25.0	10.1	93.3
Our implementation of Zheng et al. (2020)	88.79	58.22	36.49	26.87	88.00

Table 2: OOD detection performance on the OSQ dataset with model proposed by Zheng et al. (2020)

We created our implementation according to the paper's description because there is no publicly accessible implementation of their proposed model. We report results in Table 2.

We could not reproduce the number reported by Zheng et al. (2020) even though we implemented the model as was described in the paper. The experiments showed that the denoising auto-encoder is a weak part of the architecture. Its token accuracy of text reconstruction on the validation set was only 0.37%. Thus, the low performance of the auto-encoder is the reason why the generator generates poor quality examples.

5.2 Results on proposed model OodGAN

First, we want to compare OodGAN with baselines. We selected two baselines to evaluate improvements of our proposed OodGAN. Our baselines for the ROSTD dataset is our implementation of Zheng et al. (2020) and the work of Gangal et al. (2019). The baseline for the OSQ dataset is our implementation of Zheng et al. (2020).

Table 3 shows results on ROSTD dataset and Table 4 shows results on OSQ dataset. Results on ROSTD data are promising. They show around 65% relative improvement in FPR 0.95 compared to baseline of our implementation of Zheng et al. (2020) and around 5% absolute improvement in FPR 0.95 compared to baseline of Gangal et al. (2019). For the more challenging OSQ dataset, there is around 28% relative improvement in both FPR 0.95 and FPR 0.90 compared to the baseline.

To evaluate whether OodGAN helps the threshold-based OOD detection model to discriminate between OOD and IND examples, we plotted the histogram of the test data's maximum intent probability for system trained with and without generated OOD examples. Figure 3 shows the histogram for ROSTD dataset. Probability scores for IND (blue) and OOD (red) data are spread out over all probability values when there are no OOD data used for model training. Thus it is hard to select

ROSTD (Gangal et al., 2019)	AUROC ↑	AUPR ↑	FPR 0.95 ↓	FPR 0.90 ↓	IND Acc. ↑
w.o. OOD	97.64	93.86	8.10	5.56	**99.05**
Our implementation of Zheng et al. (2020)	88.67	54.84	37.82	26.04	88.00
Gangal et al. (2019)	98.22	**96.47**	7.41	-	-
OodGAN	**98.99**	96.26	**2.59**	**1.37**	98.31

Table 3: OOD detection performance on the ROSTD dataset

OSQ (Larson et al., 2019)	AUROC ↑	AUPR ↑	FPR 0.95 ↓	FPR 0.90 ↓	IND Acc. ↑
w.o. OOD	90.89	**97.99**	28.11	20.98	89.04
Our implementation of Zheng et al. (2020)	88.79	58.22	36.49	26.87	88.00
OodGAN	**91.24**	97.79	**26.07**	**19.29**	**90.11**

Table 4: OOD detection performance on the OSQ dataset

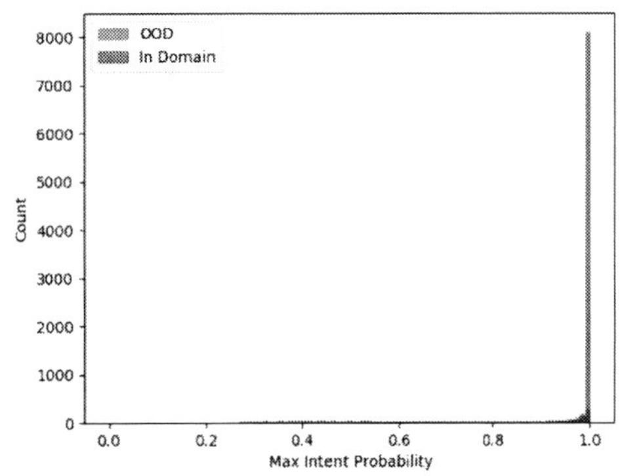

(a) Model trained with no OOD

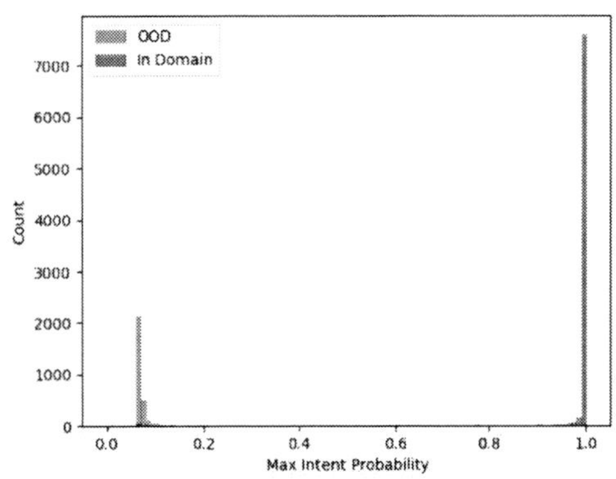

(b) Model trained with generated OOD

Figure 3: Distributions of detection scores corresponding to the IND and OOD examples of the ROSTD dataset

a well discriminating threshold. The result of the model trained with OOD data is significantly better. The graph shows a clear separation between IND and OOD data, with IND data receiving high intent score and OOD data receiving a low score.

The OOD detection model is combined with IC in many real-world applications. For this reason, the joint accuracy of OOD detection and IND intent recognition is an important metric. We show how the joint accuracy depends on the selected threshold in Figure 4. To draw this graph, we select different thresholds, and we tag examples having an intent score below the threshold as OOD. We classify the intent for the rest. Our proposed approach leads to high joint accuracy of OOD detection and IND intent recognition with low threshold values. That confirms that models trained with generated OOD assign low scores to OOD and high scores to IND examples.

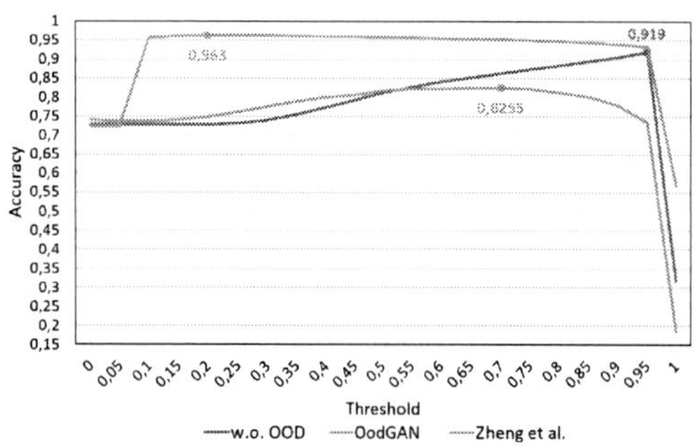

Figure 4: Joint accuracy for ROSTD data across different threshold value. Points mark the highest joint accuracy of OOD detection and IND intent recognition.

The separation between generated OOD examples and IND examples is visible in t-SNE (Hinton and Roweis, 2002) visualization as well. Figure 5 shows the t-SNE visualization of IND and generated OOD data. We can notice that generated data create recognizable clusters close to IND data but do not mix with it. Finally, we list OOD examples generated by OodGAN in table 5.

6 Conclusion

This paper proposed a novel OOD data generation model OodGAN that generates OOD examples that improved OOD detection performance in a dialog system. The model does not require any OOD training examples. Moreover, the model does not rely on the auto-encoder to map utterances into latent space, reducing the model size. It models the data

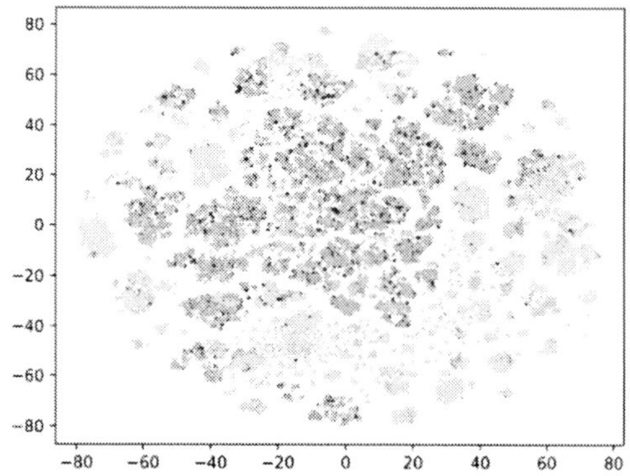

Figure 5: t-SNE visualization of the BERT feature vectors associated with the examples from the ROSTD dataset. IND examples are blue, testing OOD examples are red, and examples generated by OodGAN are green.

IND Examples	Should I be expecting rain today I need a new alarm for 8:30 am Show my reminders Show me the extended forecast please Snooze alarm for 5 more minutes
OOD Examples	Why do people watch television Where do pineapples grow Should I go to the mall today or tomorrow Tell me how to install a pool Transfer my PayPal balance to my bank
Generated by OodGAN	Remind me of my 4pm and Game of Thrones alarm When should I unpack Add day at workout please Give me my Sarasota appointment Do I need to pack to Galway this umbrella

Table 5: Examples sampled from the IND and OOD test set of the ROSTD dataset and OOD utterances generated using OodGAN model.

generator as a stochastic policy in reinforcement learning instead. The model uses two rewards for the generator. The discriminator's reward guides the generator to generate examples as close to the IND data as possible. The auxiliary intent classifier's reward guides the generator to generate examples with low probabilities for all intent classes. Our experiments show that OOD examples generated by OodGAN improve the performance of the OOD detection problem.

References

David Donahue and Anna Rumshisky. 2018. Adversarial text generation without reinforcement learning. *arXiv preprint arXiv:1810.06640*.

Varun Gangal, Abhinav Arora, Arash Einolghozati, and Sonal Gupta. 2019. Likelihood ratios and generative classifiers for unsupervised out-of-domain detection in task oriented dialog. *arXiv preprint arXiv:1912.12800.*

Chuan Guo, Geoff Pleiss, Yu Sun, and Kilian Q Weinberger. 2017. On calibration of modern neural networks. *arXiv preprint arXiv:1706.04599.*

Dan Hendrycks and Kevin Gimpel. 2017. A baseline for detecting misclassified and out-of-distribution examples in neural networks. *ArXiv*, abs/1610.02136.

Dan Hendrycks, Mantas Mazeika, and Thomas G. Dietterich. 2019. Deep anomaly detection with outlier exposure. *ArXiv*, abs/1812.04606.

Geoffrey E Hinton and Sam Roweis. 2002. Stochastic neighbor embedding. *Advances in neural information processing systems*, 15:857–864.

Armand Joulin, Edouard Grave, Piotr Bojanowski, and Tomas Mikolov. 2016. Bag of tricks for efficient text classification. *arXiv preprint arXiv:1607.01759.*

Yoon Kim. 2014. Convolutional neural networks for sentence classification. *arXiv preprint arXiv:1408.5882.*

Balaji Lakshminarayanan, Alexander Pritzel, and Charles Blundell. 2017. Simple and scalable predictive uncertainty estimation using deep ensembles. In *Advances in neural information processing systems*, pages 6402–6413.

Stefan Larson, Anish Mahendran, Joseph J Peper, Christopher Clarke, Andrew Lee, Parker Hill, Jonathan K Kummerfeld, Kevin Leach, Michael A Laurenzano, Lingjia Tang, et al. 2019. An evaluation dataset for intent classification and out-of-scope prediction. *arXiv preprint arXiv:1909.02027.*

Sungjin Lee and Igor Shalyminov. 2019. Contextual out-of-domain utterance handling with counterfeit data augmentation. In *ICASSP 2019-2019 IEEE International Conference on Acoustics, Speech and Signal Processing (ICASSP)*, pages 7205–7209. IEEE.

J. Ren, Peter J. Liu, E. Fertig, Jasper Snoek, Ryan Poplin, Mark A. DePristo, Joshua V. Dillon, and Balaji Lakshminarayanan. 2019. Likelihood ratios for out-of-distribution detection. In *NeurIPS*.

Seonghan Ryu, Sangjun Koo, Hwanjo Yu, and Gary Geunbae Lee. 2018. Out-of-domain detection based on generative adversarial network. In *Proceedings of the 2018 Conference on Empirical Methods in Natural Language Processing*, pages 714–718.

Ronald J Williams. 1992. Simple statistical gradient-following algorithms for connectionist reinforcement learning. *Machine learning*, 8(3-4):229–256.

Lantao Yu, Weinan Zhang, Jun Wang, and Yong Yu. 2017. Seqgan: Sequence generative adversarial nets with policy gradient. In *Thirty-first AAAI conference on artificial intelligence.*

Yinhe Zheng, Guanyi Chen, and Minlie Huang. 2020. Out-of-domain detection for natural language understanding in dialog systems. *IEEE/ACM Transactions on Audio, Speech, and Language Processing*, 28:1198–1209.

Coherent and Concise Radiology Report Generation via Context Specific Image Representations and Orthogonal Sentence States

Litton J Kurisinkel, Ai Ti Aw, Nancy F. Chen
Institute for Infocomm Research, A*STAR, Singapore
litton_kurisinkel, aaiti, nfychen@i2r.a-star.edu.sg

Abstract

Neural models for text generation are often designed in an end-to-end fashion, typically with zero control over intermediate computations, limiting their practical usability in downstream applications. In this work, we incorporate explicit means into neural models to ensure topical continuity, content comprehensiveness and informativeness of automatically generated radiology reports. We propose a method to compute image representations specific to each sentential context to minimize hallucination caused by sequence-to-sequence approaches and to further eliminate redundant content by exploiting diverse sentence states. We conduct experiments to generate radiology reports from medical images of chest x-rays using MIMIC-CXR. Our model outperforms baselines by up to 18% and 29% respective in the evaluation for informativeness and content ordering respectively on objective metrics and 16% on human validations.

1 Introduction

Presenting information in text format has been critical to the development of human civilizations. Thus text generation is an important field in artificial intelligence and natural language processing, where the input to such natural language generation models could take on the form of text, graphs, images or database records (Koncel-Kedziorski et al., 2019; See et al., 2017; Kinghorn et al., 2018).

Recent advancements in natural language generation has been propelled by end-to-end neural models (e.g. (Chopra et al., 2016)), which has strong capabilities to learn associations within large-scale datasets. However, since it is challenging to exert control over the neural generation process and the corresponding output, the usability of such models in practical scenarios are limited, as the generated content could be erroneous, incoherent, or even socially inappropriate (Liu et al., 2020; Wiseman et al., 2017). It is therefore ideal to include explicit provisions in neural text generation to better model characteristics such as informativeness and topical continuity. It has also been shown that informativeness and textual cohesion are important properties in clinical texts to make them more easily comprehensible (Smith et al., 2011; Liu and Rawl, 2012).

Image to text generation is a natural language generation task that has been popular in communities beyond NLP (e.g. computer vision, machine learning). A general approach is to construct the representation of the entire input image and decode the output text conditioned on the image representation (You et al., 2016). Such approaches work well for scenarios where only a short generated sentence is needed in the output (e.g. image captioning), as typically what is needed is to identify individual objects and fill in the most probable words to describe the overall situation. However, such approaches might not generalize to scenarios where complex semantics embodied in the input images need further inferencing or where the generated outputs need to articulate detailed or specific information, logical reasoning, or recommendations — all of these cases typically require at least multiple sentences (to form a report) (Jing et al., 2017). Medical reports are a classic example of such a scenario where each sentence in a report describes very precise clinical observations or inferences.

We present a neural approach for producing radiology reports from images in a sentence-by-sentence order to pinpoint more targeted and precise medical information from the input images and at the same time minimize hallucination from neural text generation. The modeling components ensures the generated report is informative, coherent, and concise via gated mechanisms to model topical continuity, orthogonality criteria in sentence state selection to reduce redundancy, and a neural architecture that is pretrained to predict domain entities during each context of sentence generation in order to encourage induction bias.

Proceedings of NAACL HLT 2021: IndustryTrack Papers, pages 246–254
June 6–11, 2021. ©2021 Association for Computational Linguistics

2 Related Work

2.1 Natural Language Generation

Quests for more efficient methods arising from machine translation using dense sentence representations resulted in the development of neural text-to-text generation models (Bahdanau et al., 2014; Cho et al., 2014; Srivastava et al., 2014; Wiseman et al., 2018). Subsequently, neural approaches for text-to-text generation for summarization tasks also started to gain traction (Cheng and Lapata, 2016; Nallapati et al., 2017; See et al., 2017; Paulus et al., 2017). A major interest in the medical NLP community focuses on information extraction (see Wang et al. (2018) for a review). There has been work in areas such as automatic ICD code assignment (Zhang et al., 2017; Scheurwegs et al., 2017; Mullenbach et al., 2018), risk prediction (Ma et al., 2018), and dialogue comprehension (Liu et al., 2019), and text generation (Buchanan et al., 1995; Moradi and Ghadiri, 2018; Pauws et al., 2019).

2.2 Image to Text

There has been much work in image to text generation, which typically constructs a representation of the input image using CNN and generates the output text using RNN (Fang et al., 2015; Krause et al., 2017; Vinyals et al., 2015). Such work has been improved further by incorporating the attention mechanism on input representations (Xu et al., 2015; You et al., 2016). Xu et al. (2015) used visual spatial attention for improving text generation while You et al. (2016) introduced semantic attention on concepts. All of the aforementioned work demonstrated effectiveness on single sentence generation such as captions. Image to text generation becomes more challenging when considering multi-sentence outputs. Some recent work generated multi-sentence outputs using hierarchical decoding (Krause et al., 2017; Liang et al., 2017). Jing et al. (2017) adapted this approach for radiology report generation by incorporating co-attention. Yuan et al. (2019) further improved the design by incorporating concept prediction and leveraging the predicted concept for guiding generation. In our work, the network is pre-trained to predict context entities so that each sentence generation is implicitly guided by domain entities. In addition, our system explicitly models informativeness and topical continuity to improve coherence while reducing redundancy to increase factual correctness and readability.

3 Method

In this section we delineate the following: (1) The proposed neural architecture and the corresponding network computations; (2) How we pre-train the network to predict the context entities from each sentence representation using a multi-label classifier; (3) How we further train the neural architecture to decode the corresponding sentences from each sentence representation to form the report.

3.1 Neural Architecture

Each input to our network is a set of images S_I with different views of the chest from the same patient and an indication text Q, which is a short sentence or phrase describing the purpose of the radiology investigation (e.g. intense coughing)[1]. Figure 1 depicts the architecture of our neural model, consisting of components for image encoding, indication text encoding, image feature selection for informativeness, sentential content creation for topical continuity and redundancy reduction and for decoding individual sentences in the report. Before the network computations commence, content creation RNN is initialized with a zero vector hidden state. We elaborate each component in the following subsections.

3.1.1 Image Encoding and Sentential Content Creation

Our network is designed to generate the radiology report in a sentence-by-sentence manner from the input set of images, guided by the indication text. The sentence-by-sentence design allows the report generation to focus on specific and important details in the medical image and reduces possible pitfalls of hallunciation in neural text generation. The Image encoder is a ResNet152 network with pretrained weighs (He et al., 2016). Using the encoder, each of the image matrix i in the input image set is converted to $I_i \epsilon R^n$, as depicted on the left hand side of Figure 1. The network updates the image representations during each context of sentence generation. The network employs gates for informative content selection and topical continuity weighted by a control gate.

Informative Content Selection: The content selection gate is represented by the trapezium on the top of Figure 1. Gate gc selects the

[1] An example of indication text: `male with cough and rib pain`.

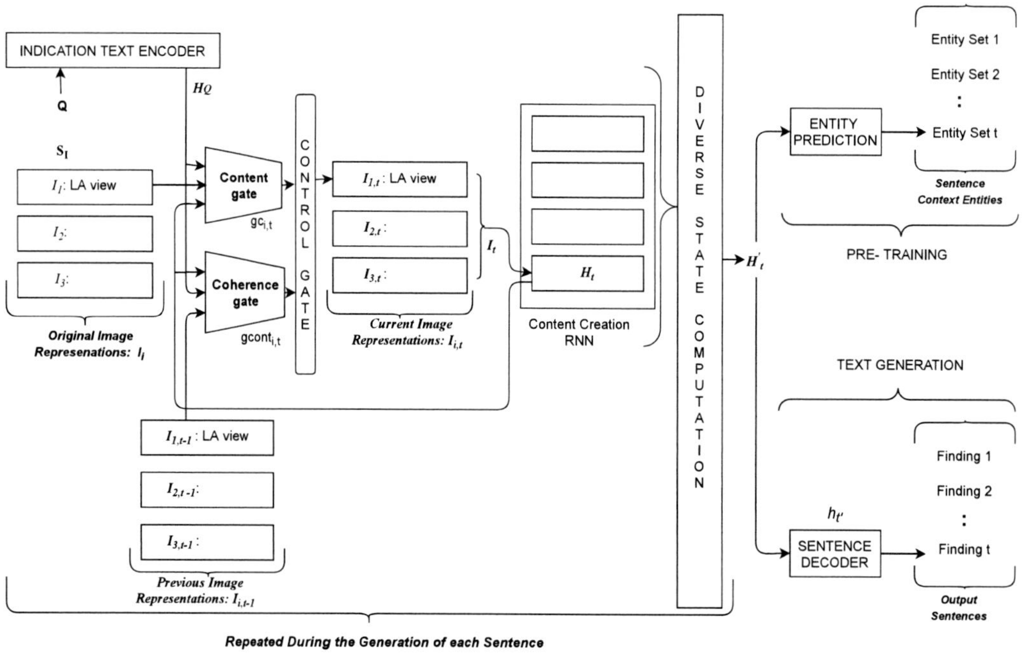

Figure 1: Proposed Neural Architecture

informative content from the original image representations during each time-step t of the content creation RNN. Gate gc filters the features of the input image representation I_i as follows:

$$gc_{i,t} = \text{sigmoid}(\mathbf{W_{gc}}[I_i; H_{t-1}; H_Q])$$
$$Ic_{i,t} = gc_{i,t} \odot I_i$$

where W_{gc} is the parameter matrix, H_{t-1} is the previous hidden state of content creation RNN and H_Q is the indication text encoded using a transformer network. The presence of H_{t-1} ensures that features are selected in the context of previously generated sentences.

Content Selection for Topical Continuity: The gate $gcont$ selects the content for topical continuity at time- step t from the image representations computed for the previous time- step $t-1$. In Figure 3.1, the continuity gate is represented by the trapezium at the bottom. The Gate $gcont$ selects the content for topical continuity as follows:

$$gcont_{i,t} = \text{sigmoid}(\mathbf{W_{gcont}}[I_{i,t-1}; H_{t-1}; H_Q]) \quad (1)$$

$$Icont_{i,t} = gcont_{i,t} \odot I_{i,t-1} \quad (2)$$

W_{gcont} is a parameter matrix and $I_{i,t-1}$ is the representation of the ith image in the input set computed at time-step $t-1$.

Control Gate: The control gate is represented by the first vertical rectangle in Figure 1. Control gate weighs and creates the representation of the ith image for time step t as follows.

$$\alpha_{i,t} = \text{sigmoid}(\mathbf{W_{cont}}[H_{t-1}]) \quad (3)$$
$$I_{i,t} = \alpha_{i,t} * Ic_{i,t} + (1-\alpha_{i,t}) * Icont_{i,t}, \quad (4)$$

where W_{cont} is a parameter matrix.

3.1.2 Sentence Content Creation

The content creation RNN is represented by the vertical rectangle, encompassing smaller rectangles corresponding to different states as depicted in the middle of Figure 3.1. Content Creation RNN computes the content for the sentence to be decoded at time step t by taking final representations for the images in the input set into account. The input I_t at the current time step t of content creation RNN is computed as follows:

$$I_t = \frac{\sum_i I_{i,t}}{m} \quad (5)$$

where m is the number of images in the input set. The hidden state H_t for content creation RNN at time step t is computed as below.

$$H_t = \textbf{GRU}(I_t, H_{t-1}), \quad (6)$$

3.1.3 Reducing Redundancy via Orthogonal Sentence States

Avoiding redundant content generation is a problem to be explicitly addressed by text generation systems (Nema et al., 2017). Hidden states of content creation RNN represents the content corresponding to each sentence in the final report. Enforcing diversity among these hidden representations can reduce the redundant content in the resultant report. We ensure that each hidden state of content creation RNN used to initialize decoder to be orthogonal to the mean of previous hidden states. In the purview of this orthogonality H_t of content creation RNN is updated as follows.

$$H_t^{'} = H_t - \frac{H_t^T H_{t-1}^M}{(H_{t-1}^M)^T H_{t-1}^M} (7)$$

where H_{t-1}^M is the mean of previous hidden states.

3.2 Pre-Training via Entity Prediction

For the purpose of pre-training we predict context entities from the constructed content $H_t^{'}$ using a multi-label classifier:

$$\begin{aligned} H_t^{''} &= NN(H_t^{'}) \\ Scores_t &= \text{softmax}(H_t^{''}) \quad (8) \\ Ent_t^k &= arg\,max_k(Scores_t) \end{aligned}$$

NN is a two layered fully connected neural network where the individual layer computations are a linear transformation followed by a ReLU activation. Ent_t^k represents the set of top k ranking context entities, which are intended to contain the entities to be mentioned in the sentence to be generated at time-step t of content creation RNN. The pre- training is done using binary cross entropy loss.

3.3 Training the Sentence Decoder

We use a decoder with beam search decoding to generate sentences. The sentence decoder RNN is initialized with $H_t^{'}$, which represents the content to be materialized at time step t. At each time step $t^{'}$ of decoder RNN, a word in the sentence under construction is generated as follows:

$$P(w_{t'}|w_{<t'}) = \text{softmax}(\mathbf{W_o}(h_{t'}) + b_o), \quad (9)$$

where $h_{t'}$ is the hidden state of decoder RNN at time-step $t^{'}$. Negative log likelihood is used for training the network to generate sentences.

4 Results

4.1 Data Setup

A subset of 19,800 entries were selected from the MIMIC-CXR Database[2] for generating radiology reports from medical images of chest X-rays (Johnson et al., 2019), where each entry is represented by a triplet (S_I, Q, SEQ_F). S_I is a set of m input radiology images where there are one or more images corresponding to different views of a patient's chest, Q is a short text span specifying the purpose of the radiology investigation, and SEQ_F represents the sentences written by a radiologist in the context of S_I and Q. SEQ_F is a sequence of sentences $f_1, .., f_n$, each representing an individual finding.

We reformulate the dataset so that each entry record is (S_I, Q, SEQ_F, SEQ_E). SEQ_E represents a sequence of entity sets $ent_1, ..., ent_n$, where ent_i represents the set of entities mentioned in sentence f_i. We extracted entities from individual sentences[3] and identified a frequently occurring set of 1,060 entity clusters[4] suitable for learning to predict context entities and subsequent sentence generation. Sentences that do not consist a single mention of any of these entities were removed because they were evaluated to be subject to information not included in the corresponding images. Our dataset consists of 18,000, 900 and 900 training, test and development records respectively.

4.2 Experimental Setup

- **Img + RNN :** The entire radiology report is decoded as a single sequence from the mean of image representations (Fang et al., 2015).

- **Img + Attn :** The decoder RNN attends over the input image representation to generate a single sequence that constitutes the report (You et al., 2016).

[2]https://physionet.org/content/mimic-cxr/2.0.0/

[3]A pilot study was conducted to compare the effectiveness of entities extracted from https://spacy.io/ and https://ctakes.apache.org/, which showed no obvious difference between the two named entity recognition tools. The former was thus chosen due to ease of integration into our existing codebase.

[4]Entities that refer to the same medical phenomenon (e.g. *acute pneumonia* and *pneumonia*) were clustered to further streamline the modeling process.

Experimental Setting	Text Gen R -1	R - 2	B -2	B - 4	Cont Order P	R	F
Img + RNN	0.241	0.070	0.200	0.070	0.040	0.050	0.045
Img + Attn	0.270	0.079	0.200	0.075	0.060	0.070	0.064
Img + Pred + Co-Attn	0.291	0.093	0.250	0.091	0.081	0.110	0.093
Img + Ent + Attn	0.300	0.096	0.273	0.102	0.080	0.100	0.089
Img + IC	0.291	0.090	0.261	0.100	0.070	0.090	0.772
Img + IC + TC	0.310	0.097	0.291	0.109	0.090	0.126	0.100
Img + IC + TC + O	0.318	**0.109**	0.328	0.117	**0.120**	0.135	**0.127**
Img + IC+ TC + O + PT	**0.323**	0.106	**0.334**	**0.120**	0.117	**0.137**	0.126

Table 1: Report Generation Performance Comparison. Text Generation: R-1, R-2, B-2, B-4 denote ROUGE-1, ROUGE-2, BLEU-2, BLUE-4, respectively. Content Ordering: P: Precision, R:Recall, F: F-Measure.

Experimental Setting	HR mean	std
Img + RNN	2.70	2.07
Img + Attn	3.51	1.70
Img + Pred + Co-Attn	6.16	1.46
Img + Ent + Attn	6.02	1.53
Img + IC	4.50	1.65
Img + IC + TC	6.10	1.45
Img + IC + TC + O	**7.02**	1.26
Img + IC+ TC + O + PT	6.71	1.33

Table 2: Human Ratings is denoted as HR; the mean and standard deviation (denoted as std) are computed for each setting, and the overall Pearson Coefficient is 0.67.

- **Img+ Pred + Co-Attn :** A multi-image variant of the co-attention based method (Jing et al., 2017), in which sentence context vectors by co-attending over input images and entities.
- **Img + Ent+Attn :** This setting is a variant of (Yuan et al., 2019), where the decoder attends over a predicted set of entities to generate sentences.
- **Our Method:** We experiment with different settings of our approach depicted in Figure 3.1 with different combinations of Informative Content selection **(IC)**, Topical Continuity **(TC)**, Orthogonal Sentence States **(O)** and Pre-Training **(PT)**.

Encoded image size is 900 after linear transformation of ResNet output, $H_t \epsilon R^{900}$ and $h_{t'} \epsilon R^{900}$. Other parameters are adjusted accordingly. For all settings, a beam size of 9 is set for the decoder. For all the settings and for each of the test record we generate five sentences as the average number of sentences in development set reports is approximately five. The set of parameters which gave maximum recall for entity prediction in the development set during pre- training is used initialize the network during training.

4.3 Text Generation and Content Ordering

We evaluated the quality of text generation using BLEU and ROUGE metrics as shown in Table 1. The setting $Img + IC$ did not perform well with respect to other counterparts. This suggests that just informative content selection gate and hidden state of content ordering RNN alone is insufficient for defining the context of a sentence. However $Img + IC + TC$ achieves an incremental accuracy by employing the efficient gated mechanism for sentence content creation. $Img+IC+TC+O$ performs consistently well on all metrics, especially using BLEU-4, implying the approach of eliminating redundant content in long text generation via enforcing topic diversity with orthogonal sentence states is effective. The setting with pre-training on entity prediction ($Img + IC + TC + O + PT$) achieved a slight incremental improvement in accuracy. We observe that for a large set of 1,060 domain entities, our training data is not dense enough for a significant improvement through pre-training. However the incremental improvement is encouraging.

Coherent reading results from accurate content ordering. For evaluating content ordering we relied on the method used by Kurisinkel and Chen (2019). They utilize the bigrams constituted by words in preceding and succeeding sentences irrespective of their positions within text in order to measure

ImgEnc + Ent + Attn
1) The lungs are clear without airspace consolidation.
2) Lungs are hyperinflated with no pleural effusion or pneumothorax is seen.
3) Lungs are hyperinflated with no pleural effusion or pneumothorax is seen.
4) The lungs are clear without focal consolidation.
5) No evidence of pleural effusion, pulmonary edema, pneumothorax, or focal airspace consolidation.
Img + IC+ TC
1) The lungs are clear without airspace consolidation.
2) No pleural effusion, pulmonary edema, pneumothorax, or focal consolidation.
3) Lungs are hyperinflated with no pleural effusion or pneumothorax is seen.
4) Lungs are hyperinflated with no pleural effusion or pneumothorax is seen.
5) Degenerative changes of the thoracic spine with calcification of the anterior longitudinal ligament are present.
Img + IC + TC + O + PT (Proposed)
1) The lungs are clear without focal consolidation.
2) Lungs are hyperinflated with no pleural effusion, pulmonary edema or pneumothorax is seen.
3) Interstitial prominence is chronic.
4) The cardiac and mediastinal silhouettes are stable.
5) Degenerative changes of the thoracic spine with calcification of the anterior longitudinal ligament are present.
Radiologist Report Written by Physicians
1) PA and lateral views of the chest demonstrate the lungs are well expanded, with no evidence of pleural effusion, pulmonary edema, pneumothorax, or focal airspace consolidation.
2) Mild interstitial prominence is chronic, and unchanged.
3) Previously demonstrated bilateral fat-containing Bochdalek hernias are better assessed on prior CT of the chest.
4) The heart is mildly enlarged, Otherwise, the cardiomediastinal silhouette is unremarkable.
5) Multilevel degenerative changes are noted throughout the thoracic spine, with calcification. of the anterior longitudinal ligament

Table 3: Text generated from different experimental setups. Capital letters and dots are manually added for ease of reading. Red text: redundancy; blue text: named entities; green text: content that cannot be inferred from the given medical images in the dataset.

the accuracy of ordering. Accuracy depends on the overlap of such bigrams in generated and reference texts, measured using Precision, Recall and F- Measure. The results of content ordering are shown on the right side of Table 1. It is evident that adding explicit means for topical continuity (TC) and Redundancy reduction (O) increased the quality of content ordering at each phase.

4.4 Human Evaluation

We resort to human evaluation for rating the factual accuracy of radiology reports with respect to the reference report in hand. Four human evaluators were asked to rate the reports generated by all settings in Table 2 for a set of 100 test records that were randomly chosen. Reports were presented to the evaluators in a random order to minimize potential bias. The rating of a sentence is the sum of individual ratings of all the sentences in a report. Sentences describing an abnormal condition is weighed more than a sentence explaining a normal condition as they are clinically more relevant. A non-redundant sentence explaining an accurate normal condition is given a rating of 1.5 while that explaining an abnormal condition is given a rating of 3. A factually incorrect or redundant sentence receives a score of 0. The mean and standard deviation for each experimental setting are shown in the rightmost column of Table 1. The Pearson Coefficient is 0.67, suggesting that the agreement among the human evaluators are reasonably consistent (Benesty et al., 2009). The settings with content selection and continuity gates and diverse state computation achieved a clear advantage over the other settings implying it is effective to generate specific content for each sentence while explicitly eliminating redundancy in our proposed approach.

4.5 Qualitative Comparisons

Examples of radiology reports generated by different settings for the same set of images are shown in Table 3 to give readers more qualitative context of the generation results. Settings which used the gated mechanism for sentence content creation and orthogonal state computation better emulate human written reports in terms of informativeness and content ordering. There is an adequate number of domain entities in the generated report. which are found to be clinically relevant when compared with the corresponding human written report. There are portions of text in the human written report which are subjective to the situation and are irrelevant in the objective scheme of text generation.

5 Conclusion

We presented a technical approach on radiology report generation which ensures global text properties such as informativeness, topical continuity for coherence while reducing redundant content. Both objective metrics and human evaluations showed significant performance over competitive baselines.

6 Acknowledgements

The authors would like to thank the insightful discussions with I. Ho Mien, Z. Liu, P. Krishnaswamy, M. Nguyen, R. Puduppully, B. Unnikrishnan, and Y. Zhang. This research was supported by grant funding from A*STAR, Singapore (CR-2020-001, SSF A1818g0044, IAF H19/01/a0/023).

References

Dzmitry Bahdanau, Kyunghyun Cho, and Yoshua Bengio. 2014. Neural machine translation by jointly learning to align and translate. *arXiv preprint arXiv:1409.0473*.

Jacob Benesty, Jingdong Chen, Yiteng Huang, and Israel Cohen. 2009. Pearson correlation coefficient. In *Noise reduction in speech processing*, pages 1–4. Springer.

Bruce G Buchanan, Johanna D Moore, Diana E Forsythe, Giuseppe Carenini, Stellan Ohlsson, and Gordon Banks. 1995. An intelligent interactive system for delivering individualized information to patients. *Artificial intelligence in medicine*, 7(2):117–154.

Jianpeng Cheng and Mirella Lapata. 2016. Neural summarization by extracting sentences and words. In *Proceedings of the 54th Annual Meeting of the Association for Computational Linguistics (Volume 1: Long Papers)*, pages 484–494.

Kyunghyun Cho, B van Merrienboer, Dzmitry Bahdanau, and Yoshua Bengio. 2014. On the properties of neural machine translation: Encoder-decoder approaches. In *Eighth Workshop on Syntax, Semantics and Structure in Statistical Translation (SSST-8), 2014*.

Sumit Chopra, Michael Auli, and Alexander M Rush. 2016. Abstractive sentence summarization with attentive recurrent neural networks. In *Proceedings of the 2016 Conference of the North American Chapter of the Association for Computational Linguistics: Human Language Technologies*, pages 93–98.

Hao Fang, Saurabh Gupta, Forrest Iandola, Rupesh K Srivastava, Li Deng, Piotr Dollár, Jianfeng Gao, Xiaodong He, Margaret Mitchell, John C Platt, et al. 2015. From captions to visual concepts and back.

In *Proceedings of the IEEE conference on computer vision and pattern recognition*, pages 1473–1482.

Kaiming He, Xiangyu Zhang, Shaoqing Ren, and Jian Sun. 2016. Deep residual learning for image recognition. In *Proceedings of the IEEE conference on computer vision and pattern recognition*, pages 770–778.

Baoyu Jing, Pengtao Xie, and Eric Xing. 2017. On the automatic generation of medical imaging reports. *arXiv preprint arXiv:1711.08195*.

Alistair EW Johnson, Tom J Pollard, Seth J Berkowitz, Nathaniel R Greenbaum, Matthew P Lungren, Chih-ying Deng, Roger G Mark, and Steven Horng. 2019. Mimic-cxr, a de-identified publicly available database of chest radiographs with free-text reports. *Scientific Data*, 6.

Philip Kinghorn, Li Zhang, and Ling Shao. 2018. A region-based image caption generator with refined descriptions. *Neurocomputing*, 272:416–424.

Rik Koncel-Kedziorski, Dhanush Bekal, Yi Luan, Mirella Lapata, and Hannaneh Hajishirzi. 2019. Text generation from knowledge graphs with graph transformers. In *Proceedings of the 2019 Conference of the North American Chapter of the Association for Computational Linguistics: Human Language Technologies, Volume 1 (Long and Short Papers)*, pages 2284–2293.

Jonathan Krause, Justin Johnson, Ranjay Krishna, and Li Fei-Fei. 2017. A hierarchical approach for generating descriptive image paragraphs. In *Proceedings of the IEEE conference on computer vision and pattern recognition*, pages 317–325.

Litton J Kurisinkel and Nancy Chen. 2019. Set to ordered text: Generating discharge instructions from medical billing codes. In *Proceedings of the 2019 Conference on Empirical Methods in Natural Language Processing and the 9th International Joint Conference on Natural Language Processing (EMNLP-IJCNLP)*, pages 6166–6176.

Xiaodan Liang, Zhiting Hu, Hao Zhang, Chuang Gan, and Eric P Xing. 2017. Recurrent topic-transition gan for visual paragraph generation. In *Proceedings of the IEEE International Conference on Computer Vision*, pages 3362–3371.

Chiung-Ju Liu and Susan M Rawl. 2012. Effects of text cohesion on comprehension and retention of colorectal cancer screening information: A preliminary study. *Journal of health communication*, 17(sup3):222–240.

Haochen Liu, Zhiwei Wang, Tyler Derr, and Jiliang Tang. 2020. Chat as expected: Learning to manipulate black-box neural dialogue models. *arXiv preprint arXiv:2005.13170*.

Zhengyuan Liu, Hazel Lim, Nur Farah Ain Suhaimi, Shao Chuen Tong, Sharon Ong, Angela Ng, Sheldon Lee, Michael R Macdonald, Savitha Ramasamy, Pavitra Krishnaswamy, et al. 2019. Fast prototyping a dialogue comprehension system for nurse-patient conversations on symptom monitoring. In *Proceedings of the 2019 Conference of the North American Chapter of the Association for Computational Linguistics: Human Language Technologies, Volume 2 (Industry Papers)*, pages 24–31.

Fenglong Ma, Jing Gao, Qiuling Suo, Quanzeng You, Jing Zhou, and Aidong Zhang. 2018. Risk prediction on electronic health records with prior medical knowledge. In *Proceedings of the 24th ACM SIGKDD International Conference on Knowledge Discovery & Data Mining*, pages 1910–1919. ACM.

Milad Moradi and Nasser Ghadiri. 2018. Different approaches for identifying important concepts in probabilistic biomedical text summarization. *Artificial intelligence in medicine*, 84:101–116.

James Mullenbach, Sarah Wiegreffe, Jon Duke, Jimeng Sun, and Jacob Eisenstein. 2018. Explainable prediction of medical codes from clinical text. In *Proceedings of the 2018 Conference of the North American Chapter of the Association for Computational Linguistics: Human Language Technologies, Volume 1 (Long Papers)*, pages 1101–1111.

Ramesh Nallapati, Feifei Zhai, and Bowen Zhou. 2017. Summarunner: A recurrent neural network based sequence model for extractive summarization of documents. In *Thirty-First AAAI Conference on Artificial Intelligence*.

Preksha Nema, Mitesh Khapra, Anirban Laha, and Balaraman Ravindran. 2017. Diversity driven attention model for query-based abstractive summarization. *arXiv preprint arXiv:1704.08300*.

Romain Paulus, Caiming Xiong, and Richard Socher. 2017. A deep reinforced model for abstractive summarization. *arXiv preprint arXiv:1705.04304*.

Steffen Pauws, Albert Gatt, Emiel Krahmer, and Ehud Reiter. 2019. Making effective use of healthcare data using data-to-text technology. In *Data Science for Healthcare*, pages 119–145. Springer.

Elyne Scheurwegs, Boris Cule, Kim Luyckx, Léon Luyten, and Walter Daelemans. 2017. Selecting relevant features from the electronic health record for clinical code prediction. *Journal of biomedical informatics*, 74:92–103.

Abigail See, Peter J Liu, and Christopher D Manning. 2017. Get to the point: Summarization with pointer-generator networks. In *Proceedings of the 55th Annual Meeting of the Association for Computational Linguistics (Volume 1: Long Papers)*, pages 1073–1083.

Catherine Arnott Smith, Scott Hetzel, Prudence Dalrymple, and Alla Keselman. 2011. Beyond readability: investigating coherence of clinical text for consumers. *Journal of Medical Internet Research*, 13(4):e104.

Nitish Srivastava, Geoffrey Hinton, Alex Krizhevsky, Ilya Sutskever, and Ruslan Salakhutdinov. 2014. Dropout: a simple way to prevent neural networks from overfitting. *The Journal of Machine Learning Research*, 15(1):1929–1958.

Oriol Vinyals, Alexander Toshev, Samy Bengio, and Dumitru Erhan. 2015. Show and tell: A neural image caption generator. In *Proceedings of the IEEE conference on computer vision and pattern recognition*, pages 3156–3164.

Yanshan Wang, Liwei Wang, Majid Rastegar-Mojarad, Sungrim Moon, Feichen Shen, Naveed Afzal, Sijia Liu, Yuqun Zeng, Saeed Mehrabi, Sunghwan Sohn, et al. 2018. Clinical information extraction applications: a literature review. *Journal of biomedical informatics*, 77:34–49.

Sam Wiseman, Stuart Shieber, and Alexander Rush. 2017. Challenges in data-to-document generation. In *Proceedings of the 2017 Conference on Empirical Methods in Natural Language Processing*, pages 2253–2263, Copenhagen, Denmark. Association for Computational Linguistics.

Sam Wiseman, Stuart Shieber, and Alexander Rush. 2018. Learning neural templates for text generation. In *Proceedings of the 2018 Conference on Empirical Methods in Natural Language Processing*, pages 3174–3187.

Kelvin Xu, Jimmy Ba, Ryan Kiros, Kyunghyun Cho, Aaron Courville, Ruslan Salakhudinov, Rich Zemel, and Yoshua Bengio. 2015. Show, attend and tell: Neural image caption generation with visual attention. In *International conference on machine learning*, pages 2048–2057.

Quanzeng You, Hailin Jin, Zhaowen Wang, Chen Fang, and Jiebo Luo. 2016. Image captioning with semantic attention. In *Proceedings of the IEEE conference on computer vision and pattern recognition*, pages 4651–4659.

Jianbo Yuan, Haofu Liao, Rui Luo, and Jiebo Luo. 2019. Automatic radiology report generation based on multi-view image fusion and medical concept enrichment. In *International Conference on Medical Image Computing and Computer-Assisted Intervention*, pages 721–729. Springer.

Danchen Zhang, Daqing He, Sanqiang Zhao, and Lei Li. 2017. Enhancing automatic icd-9-cm code assignment for medical texts with pubmed. In *BioNLP 2017*, pages 263–271.

An Empirical Study of Generating Texts for Search Engine Advertising

Hidetaka Kamigaito[*1], **Zhang Peinan**[*2], **Hiroya Takamura**[3] **and Manabu Okumura**[1]
[1]Tokyo Institute of Technology, [2]CyberAgent, Inc.
[3]National Institute of Advanced Industrial Science and Technology (AIST)
kamigaito@lr.pi.titech.ac.jp, zhang_peinan@cyberagent.co.jp
takamura.hiroya@aist.go.jp, oku@lr.pi.titech.ac.jp

Abstract

Although there are many studies on neural language generation (NLG), few trials are put into practice, particularly in the advertising domain. Generating ads with NLG models can help copywriters in their creation. However, few studies have adequately evaluated the effect of generated ads with actual serving because this requires a large amount of training data and a particular environment. In this study, we demonstrate a practical use case of generating ad-text with an NLG model. Particularly, we show how to improve the ads' impact, deploy models to a product, and evaluate the generated ads.

1 Introduction

Search engine advertising (SEA) displays ads relevant to the queries that users have searched on search engines as a part of the search results. On the ad creation side, ad copywriters develop keywords and ad-texts that are likely to be searched by users, and ad-texts are attractive to users based on the keywords and landing page (LP) contents. Advertisers or advertising agencies then submit these keywords and ad-texts to the ad delivery service. After submission, if the user's search queries and the submitted keywords match, the service selects an ad-text from the submissions through an auction and displays it to the user. SEA plays an important role in the advertising market because it can mutually satisfy users' and advertisers' respective demands. Advertising agencies have many copywriters on staff; however, manual creation will eventually reach its limit with the ever-increasing content. Therefore, auto-generating ads are expected to be a great support for ad creation.

Fill templates with words and phrases extracted from web search results or LPs are commonly used in ad-text generation (Bartz et al. (2008), Fujita et al. (2010), Fujita et al. (2011), Thomaidou et al. (2013)). These approaches create limited ad-text because they strongly rely on a pre-built list of templates or an LP containing ad-related texts. Hughes et al. (2019) proposed a method to incorporate a reinforcement learning (RL) framework into an end-to-end sequence-to-sequence (Seq2Seq) model for generating effective search engine ad-text considering feedback regarding ad effectiveness from ad delivery services.

Input	**LP Content**: Introducing popular insurance services in a ranking format! You can compare insurance services in the largest domestic comparison site of insurance A operated by B in various forms, such as by the order of request for information and the order of application by type of insurance. **Keyword**: [insurance, comparison] **Query**: [comparison of insurance services]
Output	**Title**: Which insurance is the best deal? Latest rankings. **Description**: This is the largest insurance comparison site. It is recommended for you from the top of the ranking order.

Table 1: Example of an input and its ad-text.

However, unlike typical natural language generation tasks, ad-texts are determined from input and characteristics such as previous ad delivery performance, the contexts in overall ads, and the relevance between the search queries and the results. Diversity is also an importance factor in this task because readers can be bored if a model generates ad-text that has already been used. Therefore, to make ad-texts more attractive, the model must generate ad-texts that were not used previously. In addition, the model must consider the ad-text's length because ads are presented in a limited space, which imposes a limitation on the length in practical usage. The addition of important keywords in the ad-text is also necessary to enhance user engagement because the search result page highlights the searched keyword in the user query and the ad-text. Furthermore, few ad-text generation models are used in real-world applications notwithstanding the commercial domain of advertising. Therefore, few studies have evaluated all end-to-end processes from generation to actual delivery.

Considering these requirements, we propose a

*Equal contribution.

Proceedings of NAACL HLT 2021: IndustryTrack Papers, pages 255–262
June 6–11, 2021. ©2021 Association for Computational Linguistics

method for generating ad-text by utilizing RL with rewards. This approach enables using ad-texts not included in the original training dataset through sampling from the training model. Therefore, we can expect improvements in diversity for generated ad-texts. We compared models specifically constructed for ad-text generation to determine the important factors for this task. We investigated our models in a real-world application, and performed an ad-delivery evaluation. The evaluation results showed that the proposed method improved the both human-rated attractiveness and relevance scores and the ad-delivery results compared to other approaches, while also maintaining diversity of the generated ad-texts.

Our contributions are as follows.

- We present a case study of ad-text generation as a real-world application. This study confirmed that the automatic generation of ad-texts using the RL-based encoder-decoder model is effective in actual advertisement creation.
- We propose a method for generating ad-text that utilizes RL with rewards to improve advertising performance. We performed automated evaluations on different types of metrics, as well as human evaluations involving crowdsourcing workers and professional copywriters. The results showed the usefulness of the methods.
- We describe how to incorporate our model into an ad-delivery service and performed an online evaluation to compare the performance of ad-texts generated by the model with traditional ads written by a human.

2 Generating Ad-text with RL

As shown in Table 1, Seq2Seq generates ad-texts from the given keywords and contents of LPs. Note that we concatenated these elements as sequences for each side by a separator symbol <SEP>. Figure 1 presents an overview of the proposed ad-text generation method. We use a model proposed by Paulus et al. (2018) as our Seq2Seq. In our method, Seq2Seq is trained using RL to capture useful features for generating effective ad-texts. In Sections 2.1 and 2.2, we describe each part of the proposed ad-text generation method.

2.1 RL for Seq2seq

In Seq2Seq, for the input sequence $\mathbf{x} = x_1 \cdots x_n$, the ad-text $\mathbf{y} = y_1 \cdots y_m$ is generated by maximizing the output probability, which is calculated by the following formula:

$$\mathbf{y} = \arg\max_{\mathbf{y}} \prod_{t=1}^{m} P(y_t|\mathbf{x}, y_{t-1} \cdots y_1). \quad (1)$$

For training Seq2Seq in consideration of the characteristics of an effective ad, we use RL in training. Because considering all possible outputs in the decoder is intractable, we use an approach based on a policy gradient method called self-critical sequence training (SCST) (Rennie et al., 2017), which can train models on sampled output sequences. In SCST, using $\mathbf{y}^s = y_1^s \cdots y_t^s$ (a sequence sampled from Seq2Seq) and $\hat{\mathbf{y}} = \hat{y}_1 \cdots \hat{y}_t$ (a sequence obtained by greedy decoding), the RL loss L_{rl} is calculated as follows:

$$L_{rl} = (r(\hat{\mathbf{y}}) - r(\mathbf{y}^s)) \sum_{t=1}^{m} logP(y_t^s|y_{t-1}^s \cdots y_1^s, \mathbf{x}), \quad (2)$$

where $r(\hat{\mathbf{y}})$ and $r(\mathbf{y}^s)$ are the rewards of $\hat{\mathbf{y}}$ and $\mathbf{y}^s$, respectively. It is difficult to optimize the model using only RL owing to its instability. We must, therefore, use maximum likelihood estimation (MLE), which maximizes the probability of the reference sequence $y_t^\star \cdots y_1^\star$ as follows:

$$L_{mle} = -\sum_{t=1}^{m} logP(y_t^\star|y_{t-1}^\star \cdots y_1^\star, \mathbf{x}). \quad (3)$$

Considering L_{rl} and L_{mle}, our final loss function L_{mix} is defined as follows:

$$L_{mixed} = \gamma L_{rl} + (1-\gamma) L_{mle}, \quad (4)$$

where γ is a hyperparameter weighting the importance of L_{rl}.

2.2 Rewards

To explicitly capture the characteristics of effective ad-text, we use the following three rewards: fluency, relevance, and ad quality. These rewards are summed and incorporated in the loss function of Eq.(2) to enhance the effectiveness of the ad. Thus, the reward for the generated text $\mathbf{y}$ is calculated as follows:

$$r(\mathbf{y}) = r^F(\mathbf{y}) + r^R(\mathbf{x}, \mathbf{y}) + r^Q(\mathbf{x}, \mathbf{y}), \quad (5)$$

where $r^F(\mathbf{y})$ is a reward for fluency, $r^R(\mathbf{y})$ is a reward for relevance, and $r^Q(\mathbf{y})$ is a reward for ad quality. In Sections 2.2.1 through 2.2.3, we discuss these rewards in detail.

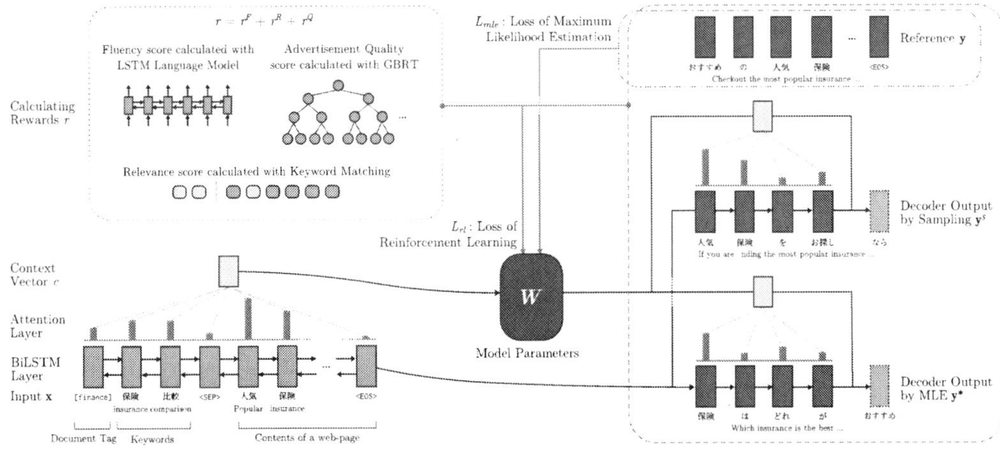

Figure 1: Overview of proposed ad-text generation method

2.2.1 Fluency

Fluency is an essential factor in generating natural language texts. In addition, the length limitation of the text must be considered, as space for advertising is limited. If the ad-text is truncated owing to space limitations, its fluency is significantly degraded. To address these problems, our fluency reward consists of two types of scores as follows:

$$r^F = s^{LM}(\mathbf{y}) + s^{Len}(\mathbf{y}), \quad (6)$$

where $s^{LM}(\mathbf{y})$ is a grammatical score and $s^{Len}(\mathbf{y})$ scores the fidelity of $|\mathbf{y}|$ to the given desired length. We use the function described in Eq. (10) of Zhang and Lapata (2017) as the first score $s^{LM}(\mathbf{y})$.

The second score, $s^{Len}(\mathbf{y})$, measures the appropriateness of the length of the generated text. The length of the generated text must not exceed the length limit. However, to maintain informativeness, it should not be significantly shorter than the limit. We incorporate these factors into s^{Len}. Let $\mathbf{y}_{title}$ be the title part of $\mathbf{y}$, $\mathbf{y}_{desc}$ be the description part of $\mathbf{y}$, C_{title} be the length limit of the title part, C_{desc} be the length limit of the description part, and s^l be a score function for each part of the generated text. The score s^{Len} is calculated as follows:

$$s^{Len}(\mathbf{y}) = \frac{s^l(\mathbf{y}_{title}, C_{title}) + s^l(\mathbf{y}_{desc}, C_{desc})}{2}, \quad (7)$$

where $s^l(\bar{\mathbf{y}}, C)$ is a function that returns $\exp(|\bar{\mathbf{y}}| - C)$ when $|\bar{\mathbf{y}}| \leq C$, whereas it returns 0 when $|\bar{\mathbf{y}}| > C$.

2.2.2 Relevance

Effective ad-text is generally consistent with what it advertises. Therefore, we consider the relevance between the input text and output ad-text as a reward. In ad-text generation, the input text includes important keywords that should be emphasized in the generated ad-text. For the generated ad-text to be relevant to the input, the ad-text should contain keywords from the input text as important words[1]. Therefore, we focus on the use of important keywords in the generated ad-text for building a reward to measure relevance. In addition to the coverage of keywords, the positions of keywords in the generated ad-text are also important, because keywords should appear at the beginning of ad-text. Considering these factors, we calculate $r^R(\mathbf{x}, \mathbf{y})$, the reward of the relevance for input $\mathbf{x}$ and the generated ad-text $\mathbf{y}$ as follows:

$$r^R(\mathbf{x}, \mathbf{y}) = s^{cov}(\mathbf{x}, \mathbf{y}) + s^{pos}(\mathbf{x}, \mathbf{y}), \quad (8)$$

where $s^{cov}(\mathbf{x}, \mathbf{y})$ scores the coverage of keywords in $\mathbf{x}$ and $s^{pos}(\mathbf{x}, \mathbf{y})$ scores the position of keywords in $\mathbf{y}$. The first score $s^{cov}(\mathbf{x}, \mathbf{y})$ calculates the proportion of keywords in $\mathbf{x}$ that are covered by $\mathbf{y}$. The second score $s^{pos}(\mathbf{x}, \mathbf{y})$ calculates the average position of keywords in $\mathbf{y}$. To prevent this reward from reducing the coverage of keywords, we impose the length of the generated ad-text as a score of a keyword not included in the ad-text. Then,

[1] Actually, Google Ads recommends to include at least one of advertisement keywords as described in the support page: `https://support.google.com/google-ads/answer/1704392?hl=en`

$s^{pos}(\mathbf{x}, \mathbf{y})$ is calculated as follows:

$$s^{pos}(\mathbf{x}, \mathbf{y}) = \exp\left(-\frac{1}{|K|}\sum_{k \in K} s^{p}(k, \mathbf{y})\right), \quad (9)$$

where K is a set of keywords included in $\mathbf{x}$ and $s^p(k, \mathbf{y})$ is a function that returns a character-based position of k in $\mathbf{y}$ if $k \in \mathbf{y}$, whereas it returns $|\mathbf{y}|$ if $k \notin \mathbf{y}$.

2.2.3 Ad Quality

Ad quality score (QS) is an important factor indicating ad-text quality based on the delivery performance and keyword relevance. Because QS is reported by the ad delivery service as the effectiveness of the delivered ad-text, we cannot use it directly to evaluate the generated ad-text. Thus, we predict the QS from $\mathbf{x}$ and $\mathbf{y}$ in accordance with previous research (Hughes et al., 2019). We treat the predicted QS as $r^Q(\mathbf{x}, \mathbf{y})$, the reward of the ad-text's quality. To train a classifier to predict QS from the given $\mathbf{x}$ and $\mathbf{y}$, we prepare an ad dataset from our ad-text databases. This dataset consists of a title, description, and score that represent the quality of each ad. The QS ranges from 1 to 10, where a lower score corresponds to lower ad quality and a higher score indicates higher ad quality.

We develop a simple regression model to predict the QS from the title and description. In the model, the title and description are joined and encoded into embeddings by fastText (Bojanowski et al., 2017) and max-pooling of simple word embedding (SWEM) (Shen et al., 2018). After the encoding, we use the gradient boosting regression tree (GBRT) (Ke et al., 2017) to predict the QS. We developed a simple model because that the predicted quality score is used as a reward in RL, which requires a large computational time; therefore, efforts should be made to shorten it.

3 Experimental Settings

3.1 Dataset

We prepared a dataset that contained pairs consisting of an input and ad-text in Japanese for training and evaluating our models. This dataset consisted of eight clients (one real estate company, one health food company, one media service company, two cosmetic companies, one job recruiting company, and three financial companies). We carefully split the dataset into 713,928, 8,000, and 8,000 pairs for training, development, and the test set, respectively. In this dataset, we used the meta-description as the content of the LP. In addition to the ad-texts, we prepared Japanese Wikipedia articles[2] to pre-train the language model. The fine-tuning of LM was performed on the ad-text dataset. All texts in this dataset were tokenized by MeCab[3] with the Neologd dictionary (Sato et al., 2017).

3.2 Models

The baselines are as follows:

Separated (Sep): This baseline trains the models for different clients separately. Therefore, it is necessary to build as many models as the number of clients, which can be significantly high. In addition, the diversity of the ad-text generated from this model was considerably low. Such unpractical features are not suitable for automatic ad-text generation; however, this model can generate ad-text that is highly similar to the given dataset. Therefore, we treated this model as a type of upper limit for generating ad-texts.

Mixed without Domain Tags (Mix w/o tag): This model was trained on the entire dataset with the MLE loss of Eq. (3).

Mixed (Mix): Similar to **Mix w/o tag**, this model was trained on the entire dataset with the MLE loss of Eq. (3). However, in this model, we included additional labels to identify the domain and the client of the input in both the training and the prediction steps. Particularly, we added the tags <domain_id> and <client_id> to the beginning of the input.

The methods employed are as follows:

Mixed with Rewards (Mix+[Rewards]): This model was trained on the mixed loss function, which is a combination of the RL loss and MLE loss, as defined in Eq. (4). The data format used in this model is similar to that in the **Mixed** model. We combined several rewards: reward of the fluency r^F in Eq. (6) (**Flu**), the reward of the relevance r^R in Eq. (8) (**Rel**), and reward of the ad quality r^Q discussed in Section 2.2.3 (**QS**). The combinations of **Flu**, **Rel**, and **QS** are represented by the + symbol. It should be noted that **Mix+QS** is the model proposed by Hughes et al. (2019); thus, it is categorized as a baseline.

Table 2 presents the parameter settings. We adapted to the settings used in previous research (Paulus et al., 2018) and choose λ as 0.98 for the re-

[2] https://dumps.wikimedia.org/jawiki/

[3] https://github.com/taku910/mecab

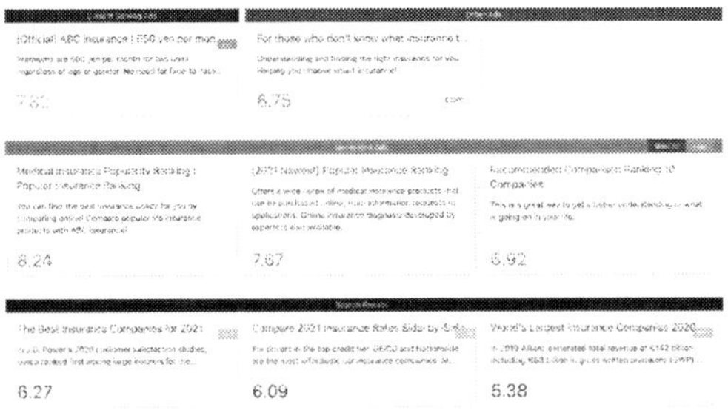

Figure 2: Screenshot of the ad-text generation tool displaying the current serving ads, generated ads, and search results corresponding to the keyword "insurance comparison." The scores in the figure are examples for clarity and are not equivalent to the scores used in the actual tool.

Seq2Seq	Dim	200	**LM**	Dim	200
	Vocab	cut word its freq. <2		Vocab	50,000
	Optimizer	Adam		Optimizer	SGD
	Learning rate	0.0001		Learning rate (LR)	20
	LR decay	-		LR decay	0.25
	Gradient normalization	0.5		Gradient normalization	0.25
	Dropout	0.3		Dropout	0.2
	Batch size	50		Batch size	20
	Epoch	10		Epoch (pretrain)	40
	γ	0.98		Epoch (fine-tuning)	10
	C_{title}	60		Max length	300
	C_{desc}	180			

Table 2: Parameter settings.

inforcement learning. If the method does not have any reward, we set λ as 0.0.

3.3 Automatic Evaluation

We used BLEU, F_1 scores of Rouge-1 (**R-1**), Rouge-2 (**R-2**), Rouge-L (**R-L**), and the following metrics for our automatic evaluation:

Estimated Quality Score (EQ): To measure ad quality for the generated ad-text, we used $r^Q(x, y)$ as discussed in Section 2.2.3.

Language Model Score (LM): To evaluate how a generated ad-text is grammatical, we used the language model for calculating s_{LM}.

Coverage of Keywords (Cov): To evaluate whether the keywords were included in the generated ad-text, we used the coverage score $s^{cov}(\mathbf{x}, \mathbf{y})$ defined in Section 2.2.2.

Position of Keywords (Pos): To investigate if important keywords appeared at the beginning of the generated ad-text, we used the position score $s^p(\mathbf{x}, \mathbf{y})$ used in Eq. (9).

Format Correctness (FC): This metric measures the number of generated ad-texts that followed the appropriate format. We verified whether the generated ad-texts contained the title and description parts, and that the lengths of these parts did not exceed the length limit. The percentage of ad-texts with the appropriate format was reported.

Diversity (Div): This metric evaluates the diversity of the generated ad-text by calculating the percentage of generated ad-texts excluded from the training dataset for each model.

3.4 Human Evaluation

We hired 10 annotators through Lancers[4], a crowdsourcing service in Japan, and 3 professional copywriters to evaluate the quality of ad-texts that were generated by the seven models: ad-text written by a human (**Reference**), **Sep**, **Mix**, **Mix+QS**, **Mix+Flu+QS**, **Mix+Flu+Rel**, and **Mix+Flu+QS+Rel**. It should be noted that, for this human evaluation, we omitted some models that performed poorly in the automatic evaluation.

We generated ad-texts from randomly sampled 240 ads in the test set and performed two tasks to evaluate three criteria: (i) fluency, (ii) attractiveness, and (iii) relevance. In the first task, annotators were instructed to evaluate the fluency of a displayed single ad-text.In the second task, the annotators were instructed to select one of the two ad-texts displayed side-by-side from the perspective of the ad-texts' attractiveness and relevance to the keywords[5]. We generated 11,760 questions in total, including 1,680 questions for the first task and 10,080 questions for the second task.

In the first task, fluency scores were obtained by calculating the percentage of annotators who answered "yes" to all questions. All answers were represented as a relation of each pair such as "win," "lose," and "tie" in the second task. We then scored each method's performance through these relation pairs using TrueSkill™(Herbrich et al., 2007), a widely used rating system that incorporates a Bayesian inference algorithm[6]. This algorithm treats the performance of each method as a standard distribution, where the mean μ represents the performance, and variance σ represents confidence. These are updated by repeating the pairwise comparison through the annotators' evaluations. We used the μ value of each method as the final result.

3.5 Deployment and Ad-delivery Evaluation

We deployed the baselines and our models to an ad-text generation tool, as shown in Figure 2. In

[4] `https://www.lancers.jp`

[5] There was also the option "same," but it was explicitly stated in the tutorial that this was deprecated.

[6] Following the official settings, the parameters were initialized as follows: $\mu = 25.0, \sigma = 8.33$. The draw probability was set to the ratio of the number of "same" options selected out of all answers.

Model	**R-1**	**R-2**	**R-L**	**BLEU**	**EQ**	**LM**	**Cov**	**Pos**	**FC**	**Div**
Sep	36.4	20.2	36.4	44.2	64.1	10.6	55.7	11.0	99.2	19.7
Mix w/o tag	36.8	17.9	36.8	43.7	64.0	10.4	51.6	10.4	99.3	36.0
Mix	35.6	18.5	35.6	44.7	64.3	12.4	**55.6**	10.6	99.5	40.6
Mix+QS	35.8	18.0	35.8	44.2	64.6	**13.4**	53.1	**10.2**	**99.6**	42.0
Mix+Flu	36.8	17.9	36.8	44.9	64.2	12.1	54.4	10.8	**99.6**	35.3
Mix+Rel	34.6	17.3	34.6	42.9	64.6	12.2	52.8	11.3	99.3	**45.1**
Mix+Flu+QS	36.3	16.9	36.3	**45.4**	64.5	12.9	52.2	10.8	99.3	37.4
Mix+Flu+Rel	**37.5**	**20.5**	**37.5**	44.4	**64.9**	13.3	53.2	11.9	99.4	40.8
Mix+Flu+Rel+QS	35.3	18.4	35.2	43.1	**64.9**	13.1	55.2	11.8	99.4	42.7

Table 3: Results of automatic evaluation.

	Copywriter			Crowdsourcing		
Model	(1) Flu.	(2) Att.	(3) Rel.	(1) Flu.	(2) Att.	(3) Rel.
Reference	87.5	25.5	24.4	75.6	26.8	29.1
Sep	82.1	25.2	24.0	65.7	24.6	28.4
Mix	**83.3**	25.1	23.7	**64.5**	23.8	26.1
Mix+QS	80.8	25.0	23.7	64.0	23.2	26.5
Mix+Flu+QS	81.7	**25.3**	22.8	64.3	24.4	26.6
Mix+Flu+Rel	77.5	24.2	23.7	60.9	24.8	26.2
Mix+Flu+QS+Rel	81.2	23.9	**24.3**	62.7	**25.4**	**26.9**

Table 4: Results of human evaluation. Flu., Att., and Rel. refer to Fluency, Attractiveness, and Relevance, respectively.

addition to the generated ad-texts, the tool also displays currently serving ads, other ads in the search result, and the non-ad search results on the same screen. Besides, we predict the quality scores for all items using the method described in Section 2.2.3. This tool aids copywriters to edit the generated ad-text effectively and obtain a comprehensive understanding of market trends.

We also performed an ad-delivery evaluation using the deployed tool. We gathered the ad-texts generated by the different models[7], including those written by copywriters, into the same ad-group per product and served each ad-group for one to two weeks. In total, we served 104 ads, 11 ad-groups, and 1,568 keywords for three weeks. In the result section, we show the number of impressions, click-through rates (CTRs), and costs averaged by ad-groups from the serving result. The Impression is the number of times an ad is displayed, the CTR is the percentage of clicks that out of impressions, and the Cost is the budget spent; the higher, the better for all metrics.

[7] **Mix+Flu+QS** was not included because it had a high percentage of output overlap with the other models, and we filtered out ad-texts that could cause legal problems.

4 Results and Discussions

4.1 Automatic Evaluation

Table 3 presents the results of the automatic evaluation. **Mix** achieved the best diversity among the three models **Sep**, **Mix**, and **Mix w/o tag**. The diversity of **Mix w/o tag** was also better than that of **Sep**. This result indicates that a dataset covering many domains is useful for improving diversity. Furthermore, a comparison between **Mix** and **Mix w/o tag** illustrated that discriminating domains and clients is useful in terms of diversity. **Mix+Flu+Rel** improved **R-1**, **R-2**, and **R-L** by 0.7, 2.0, and 0.7 points, respectively, whereas **Mix+Flu+QS** achieved the best BLEU score. Because Rouge uses the F_1 score and BLEU uses the precision of overlapped words between references and system outputs, we conclude that **Rel** generated ad-texts with words that were not included in the references. This is consistent with the improvements of **Mix+Rel** and **Mix+Flu+Rel** in **Div**. In **EQ**, **Rel** improved **EQ** similar to **QS**. This result is consistent with our expectation that Rel is an important factor for the effectiveness of ad-texts. In both **LM** and **Pos**, **QS** achieved the best scores. This result indicates that **LM** and **Pos** are correlated with **EQ**. In **Cov**, only **Mix+Flu+Rel+QS** achieved a score comparable to that of **Mix**. The results for each metric suggest the importance of a combination of rewards. However, the importance of each metric in ad-text generation is uncertain. To clarify this concept, we performed additional human evaluations.

4.2 Human Evaluation

Table 4 presents the results of these human evaluations. Our methods achieved better scores than all other methods in terms of the attractiveness and relevance criteria by both the copywriter's and crowdsourcing's evaluations. Particularly, **Mix+Flu+QS+Rel** improved attractiveness and relevance scores by 1.6 and 0.4 points, respectively. Considering the attractiveness evaluation results, there are some differences between the annotations by copywriters and crowdsourcing workers. This is due to the stance of each annotator, where copywriters evaluate ad-texts as editable sources. By contrast, crowdsourcing workers treat ad-texts as a part of completed ads. In other words, copywriters rate an ad-text highly if they regard that they can fix it to a good one, whereas crowdsourcing workers evaluate ad-texts in their current form. This trend also appears in the fluency task, as presented in Table 4; overall, the score of the fluency task in the copywriter section is higher than that in the crowdsourcing section. **Mix** produced the best score for the fluency task; however, the proposed **Mix+Flu+QS** had a highly competitive result with a difference of just 0.2 points.

4.3 Ad-Delivery Evaluation

Table 5 presents the result of the ad-delivery evaluation. **Mix+Flu+Rel** achieved the best score in terms of impression and cost, whereas **Sep** achieved the best score in CTR. Because **Sep** and **Reference** have similar ad-texts, their CTRs are almost identical. These results indicate that considering the relevance between ad-texts and user queries is important to enhance user recognition for the ad-texts.

Based on these results, we used linear regression to investigate if the evaluation metrics are related to each ad-delivery evaluation metric. Figure 3 shows the results. With regard to impression and cost, considering the coverage of keywords in generated ad-texts is important. In CTR, it is necessary to focus on the fluency rated by crowdsourcing workers. The attractiveness of crowdsourcing workers is counterproductive. This is because people avoid clicking on an ad-text that looks like an ad-text. Based on the result, we conclude that the keyword-related automatic evaluation metric and evaluations via crowdsourcing are important for generating effective ad-texts.

Model	Impression	CTR (%)	Cost
Reference	1.33	7.82	23.79
Sep	3.96	7.98	47.43
Mix	4.71	5.18	78.80
Mix+QS	2.77	**7.01**	51.89
Mix+Flu+Rel	**5.06**	4.10	**86.01**
Mix+Flu+QS+Rel	1.75	5.53	61.48

Table 5: Results of ad-delivery evaluation.

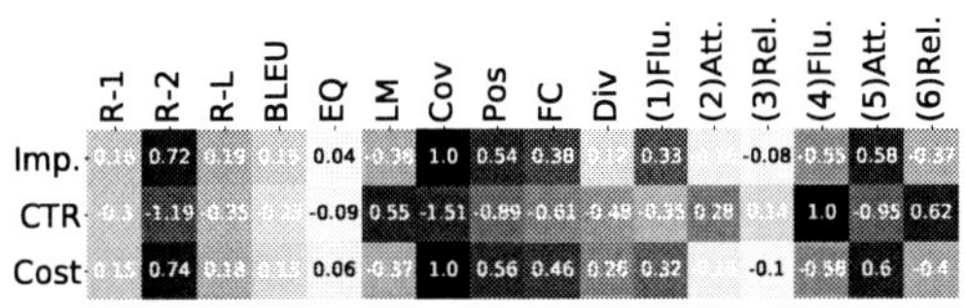

Figure 3: The weights for each metric. All weights are scaled by maximum values for each row.

5 Conclusion

In this paper, we proposed several rewards based on RL, which can consider the various characteristics of ad-texts. In experiments, ad-texts generated from Seq2Seq incorporated with these rewards achieved better automatic, human, and ad-delivery evaluation results than the basic Seq2Seq methods. Our analysis showed that considering results from the keyword-related automatic evaluation metric and the fluency by crowdsourcing workers is important for generating effective ad-texts. As further work, we plan to consider diversity as a reward to generate more diverse ad-texts.

Acknowledgement

The ad-delivery results used in this paper were served and aggregated by the AI Tech Studio of CyberAgent, Inc. We would like to take this opportunity to thank them.

[7] CW and CS denote the copywriter and the crowdsourcing results, respectively.

References

Kevin Bartz, Cory Barr, and Adil Aijaz. 2008. Natural language generation for sponsored-search advertisements. In *Proceedings of the 9th ACM Conference on Electronic Commerce*, EC '08, page 1–9, New York, NY, USA. Association for Computing Machinery.

Piotr Bojanowski, Edouard Grave, Armand Joulin, and Tomas Mikolov. 2017. Enriching word vectors with subword information. *Transactions of the Association for Computational Linguistics*, 5:135–146.

Atsushi Fujita, Katsuhiro Ikushima, and Satoshi Sato. 2011. Automatic generation of listing ads and assessment of their performance on attracting customers: a case study on restaurant domain. *Journal of Information Processing*, 56(6):2031–2044.

Atsushi Fujita, Katsuhiro Ikushima, Satoshi Sato, Ryo Kamite, Ko Ishiyama, and Osamu Tamachi. 2010. Automatic generation of listing ads by reusing promotional texts. In *Proceedings of the 12th International Conference on Electronic Commerce: Roadmap for the Future of Electronic Business*, ICEC '10, page 179–188, New York, NY, USA. Association for Computing Machinery.

Ralf Herbrich, Tom Minka, and Thore Graepel. 2007. Trueskill™ : A bayesian skill rating system. In B. Schölkopf, J. C. Platt, and T. Hoffman, editors, *Advances in Neural Information Processing Systems 19*, pages 569–576. MIT Press.

J. Weston Hughes, Keng-hao Chang, and Ruofei Zhang. 2019. Generating better search engine text advertisements with deep reinforcement learning. In *Proceedings of the 25th ACM SIGKDD International Conference on Knowledge Discovery and Data Mining*, KDD '19, page 2269–2277, New York, NY, USA. Association for Computing Machinery.

Guolin Ke, Qi Meng, Thomas Finley, Taifeng Wang, Wei Chen, Weidong Ma, Qiwei Ye, and Tie-Yan Liu. 2017. Lightgbm: A highly efficient gradient boosting decision tree. In I. Guyon, U. V. Luxburg, S. Bengio, H. Wallach, R. Fergus, S. Vishwanathan, and R. Garnett, editors, *Advances in Neural Information Processing Systems 30*, pages 3146–3154. Curran Associates, Inc.

Romain Paulus, Caiming Xiong, and Richard Socher. 2018. A deep reinforced model for abstractive summarization. In *International Conference on Learning Representations*.

S. J. Rennie, E. Marcheret, Y. Mroueh, J. Ross, and V. Goel. 2017. Self-critical sequence training for image captioning. In *2017 IEEE Conference on Computer Vision and Pattern Recognition (CVPR)*, pages 1179–1195, Los Alamitos, CA, USA. IEEE Computer Society.

Toshinori Sato, Taiichi Hashimoto, and Manabu Okumura. 2017. Implementation of a word segmentation dictionary called mecab-ipadic-neologd and study on how to use it effectively for information retrieval (in japanese). In *NLP*, pages NLP2017–B6–1. The Association for Natural Language Processing.

Dinghan Shen, Guoyin Wang, Wenlin Wang, Martin Renqiang Min, Qinliang Su, Yizhe Zhang, Chunyuan Li, Ricardo Henao, and Lawrence Carin. 2018. Baseline needs more love: On simple word-embedding-based models and associated pooling mechanisms. In *Proceedings of the 56th Annual Meeting of the Association for Computational Linguistics (Volume 1: Long Papers)*, pages 440–450, Melbourne, Australia. Association for Computational Linguistics.

Stamatina Thomaidou, Ismini Lourentzou, Panagiotis Katsivelis-Perakis, and Michalis Vazirgiannis. 2013. Automated snippet generation for online advertising. In *Proceedings of the 22nd ACM International Conference on Information and Knowledge Management*, CIKM '13, page 1841–1844, New York, NY, USA. Association for Computing Machinery.

Xingxing Zhang and Mirella Lapata. 2017. Sentence simplification with deep reinforcement learning. In *Proceedings of the 2017 Conference on Empirical Methods in Natural Language Processing*, pages 584–594, Copenhagen, Denmark. Association for Computational Linguistics.

Ad Headline Generation using Self-Critical Masked Language Model

Yashal Shakti Kanungo
yashalk@amazon.com

Sumit Negi
suminegi@amazon.com

Aruna Rajan
rajarna@amazon.com

Abstract

For any E-commerce website it is a nontrivial problem to build enduring advertisements that attract shoppers. It is hard to pass the creative quality bar of the website, especially at a large scale. We thus propose a programmatic solution to generate product advertising headlines using retail content. We propose a state of the art application of Reinforcement Learning (RL) Policy gradient methods on Transformer (Vaswani et al., 2017) based Masked Language Models (Devlin et al., 2019). Our method creates the advertising headline by jointly conditioning on multiple products that a seller wishes to advertise. We demonstrate that our method outperforms existing Transformer and LSTM + RL methods in overlap metrics and quality audits. We also show that our model-generated headlines outperform human submitted headlines in terms of both grammar and creative quality as determined by audits.

1 Introduction

There are a various types of ads. A set of example ads that showcase products selected by sellers along with headlines that advertise them are shown in Figure 1. Sellers create multiple ad campaigns for multiple products, bid in an auction to advertise and pay for clicks on the ad.

An E-Commerce product catalog may have millions of products which can be advertised. To ease the ad headline writing process, humans resort to programmatically padding keywords, or repasting the retail catalog content in the advertisement.

Templated creatives such as "Save Now on ..." or "Buy more (product) of (brand)" save the creative effort but fail to create any excitement or brand identity in the minds of shoppers. High quality headlines are more attractive to shoppers and offer better value proposition. In this paper, we describe how we built a Natural Language Generation (NLG) system to generate instantaneous, attractive and brand identity building headlines for advertisements that intend to promote a wide range of products offered by a brand.

The content associated with a retail product has challenging characteristics. Some product titles have poor structure, grammatical issues, or partial phrases. The product titles also include varying number of product features such as *"Hyper Tough 18V Cordless Drill, 3/8 inch Chuck, Variable Speed, with 1.2Ah Nickel Cadmium Battery, Charger, Bit Holder LED Light"* along with titles such as *"ZIPIT Grillz Backpack, Camo Grey"*.

The generated headlines need to capture the information present in the retail attributes and at the same time be different and uniquely attractive. Advertisers select multiple related products that are advertised as part of a single ad campaign. The ad campaign headline is then shared across all of these related products. Thus, the headline also needs to generalize the shared characteristics of the products and cannot be specific to a single product within the campaign.

The key contributions of our work are:

- We use Masked Language Model (MLM) for the generation of advertisement headlines using multiple products at the same time. Extensive test-set metrics, quality and grammar audits show that the proposed model outperforms all the baselines and the human-submitted headlines in terms of quality and grammar.
- The novel usage of RL for the training of MLM allows us to directly optimize the MLM for improved headline quality metrics without changing inference setup or latency. Our method can also be applied to any other NLG task such as summarization, translation etc.
- Our model reduces the extensive effort and time that is required to manually create headlines and has low latency.

Proceedings of NAACL HLT 2021: IndustryTrack Papers, pages 263–271
June 6–11, 2021.

Figure 1: Examples of different product ads from multiple websites across the internet. A variety of ad headlines accompany the products in these ads.

2 Related Work

Natural Language Understanding (NLU) using Language Models (LM) has observed great leaps in recent years. LMs have evolved from using word level models (Joulin et al., 2016) to to a variety of extensions to the Transformer (Vaswani et al., 2017). The BERT (Devlin et al., 2019) employs Transformer in a pre-training setting and introduced the MLM training objective.

Ramachandran et al. (2016) first demonstrated textual generation by using auto-regressive prediction in a seq2seq architecture. Transformer based auto-regressive methods such as GPT2 (Radford et al., 2019) and BART (Lewis et al., 2019) which predict one word at a time have also shown good results. Zhu et al. (2020) concatenated BERT representations with the Encoder and Decoder layers of another LM to incorporate pre-trained LM. Another model (Dong et al., 2019) combines BERT-based Transformer Encoder with attention masking from the Transformer decoder. Rothe et al. (2019) combined pre-trained BERT Encoder with GPT decoder for NLG.

Ranzato et al. (2016) framed NLG as an RL problem and the generation quality as a reward. The Self-Critical Sequence Training (SCST) approach (Rennie et al., 2017) replaces the learned baseline from other approaches (Bahdanau et al., 2017) with the model's own inference time algorithm to normalize the rewards.

For advertising, recent works (Xu et al., 2019; Hughes et al., 2019) have combined LSTM based pointer network (See et al., 2017) with RL methods to generate advertisement headlines. While these methods improve the results, they fail to utilize extensive pre-training of Transformer based models and their various well-demonstrated advantages.

Our method extends BERT based generation (Dong et al., 2019) by using Self-Critical policy gradient method (Rennie et al., 2017) and jointly conditioning the generated sentence on multiple products at the same time. This allows us to use pre-trained BERT based LMs that can be trained to optimize various inference time metrics that are typically non-differentiable such as BLEU, Rouge, Readability etc.

3 Self-Critical Masked Language Model

3.1 Masked Language Model

The BERT model takes an unlabeled input sequence $x = (x_1, x_2, ..., x_{|x|})$ and randomly masks some positions M_x by replacing them with a special mask token [MASK], to produce a sequence like $(x_1, \text{[MASK]}, ..., x_{|x|})$. All the tokens are embedded and added to special positional embeddings. It then uses N identical Transformer layers to generate contextualized representation, with each layer employing self-attention by taking in the output of the previous layer. To compute self-attention, the output of the previous layer is projected into triplets of vectors named Query, Key and Value (Q, K, V) of dimensions d. The attention A is then given as:

$$A = \text{softmax}(\frac{QK^T}{\sqrt{d}})V \tag{1}$$

After the final Transformer layer the model uses a feed forward layer followed by a softmax over the vocabulary to predict the masked tokens. The MLM loss for the sequence x is then calculated as:

$$\mathcal{L}_{MLM} = -\log \prod_{m \in M_x} p(x_m | (x_{m'} \in x \setminus M_x)) \tag{2}$$

where $(x_{m'} \in x \setminus M_x)$ represents all the tokens in x that are not masked and $m \in M_x$ are all the masked positions.

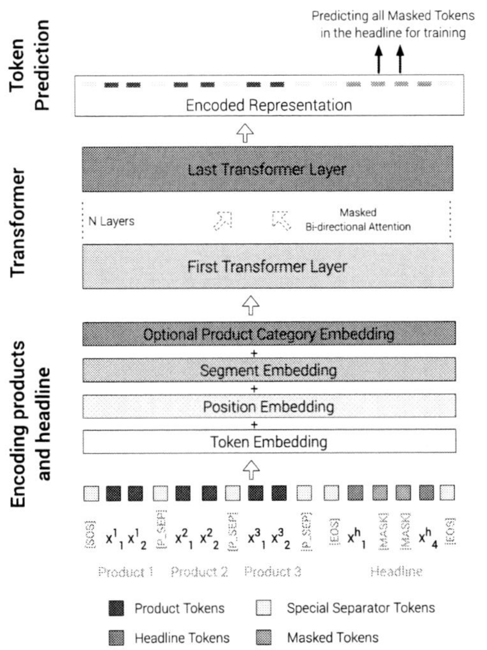

Figure 2: The sub-tokens from the product titles and headline are embedded and added with other embeddings that encode the positional and segment information. We also optionally add an embedding that represents the category of the product. During training, the masked tokens are predicted using Transformer layers and the cross-entropy (Eq. 2) loss and Self-Critical (Eq. 9) gradient is used to optimize the model. During inference, we predict one word at a time (left-to-right) in an auto-regressive manner using Beam Search.

3.2 Encoding multiple products and common headline for Proposed MLM

During training, for a given advertising campaign, our model takes as input it's headline $x^h = (x_1^h, ..., x_{|x^h|}^h)$ and a set P of one or more products. Each product p is represented by its title $x^p = (x_1^p, ..., x_{|x^p|}^p)$. The titles and the headline are tokenized to sub-word tokens.

To encode using the model that only accepts a single product, we simply append '[EOS]' $\in \mathbb{V}$ to both the title and the headline and concatenate their tokens. The entire concatenated sequence is prepended with '[SOS]' $\in \mathbb{V}$.

We encode multiple products by concatenating the tokens from different products using a special token '[P_SEP]' $\in \mathbb{V}$. We replace a token '[UNUSED_0]' $\in \mathbb{V}$ that remains unused during pre-training, with this special token during multi-product fine-tuning. This makes a distinction between different titles as well as the source and target sub-sequences. It also yields individual embeddings for each product for other tasks.

Only the tokens from the headline x^h are randomly masked with token '[MASK]' $\in \mathbb{V}$. We discuss results for the model that additionally also masks the source tokens in section 5.1.

The complete process for an example such that all products in the ad have two tokens and the headline has 4 tokens is illustrated in Figure 2.

We also experimented with adding of category based embeddings. The category labels for each product such as "Cell Phones and Accessories" are tokenized to subword units, encoded using the same embedding matrix as that of the title tokens, averaged and added to the title token embeddings.

3.3 Generation using Self-Critical Masked Language Model

The BERT MLM framework with multi-directional attention discussed in Section 3.1 cannot be used for auto-regressive generation directly. This is because, during training, the masked headline words may condition on the future words which are not available during auto-regressive inference. For MLM auto-regressive generation, we employ masked attention (Dong et al., 2019) that modifies the attention from equation 1 as below:

$$A_{masked} = \text{softmax}(\frac{QK^T}{\sqrt{d}} + \Phi_{ij})V \quad (3)$$

where Φ_{ij} represents the attention mask between the positions i and j. The elements are set to 0 if attention is allowed and $-\infty$ if it is not allowed. Figure 3 illustrates the attention mask for headline generation using multiple input products.

The BERT MLM uses log-likelihood (Equation 2) of masked words during training to optimize the model parameters. The likelihood is predicted using other ground-truth words during training and other predicted words during inference. This causes exposure bias (Ranzato et al., 2016; Rennie et al., 2017) and accumulates error during inference. Moreover, the training is optimized for log-likelihood, while we actually care about other more evolved measures of headline quality such as overlap metrics BLEU (Papineni et al., 2002) and ROUGE (Lin, 2004).

To overcome these issues and improve the quality of the generated headlines, we frame the MLM

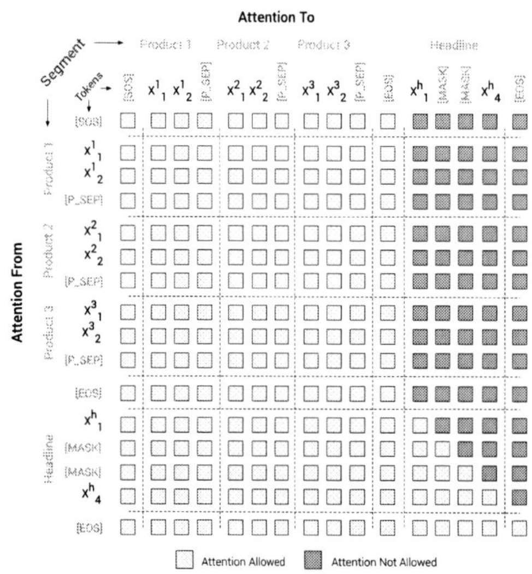

Figure 3: Masked attention partially restricts attention for some token pairs. It prevents attention to headline tokens that would not be accessible during each step of generation during inference.

as an RL problem. The model is an 'agent' that takes the 'action' of predicting masked words and updates the 'state' such as the self-attention weights. The MLM follows a policy π_θ defined by the parameters θ of the model. It receives a reward that is proportional to the quality of the generated headline. This quality may either be the overlap with ground truth headlines that have been approved by internal subject-matter-experts or be predicted by another model. Our goal is to maximize the reward corresponding to a generated headline $\hat{x}^h$ during training, with the tokens at some masked positions M_{x^h} sampled from the model.

We thus minimize the negative expected reward defined by any reward function $r(\cdot)$ for headline quality $r(\hat{x}^h)$ as:

$$\mathcal{L}_{RL} = -\mathbb{E}_{\hat{x}^h \sim \pi_\theta}[r(\hat{x}^h)] \tag{4}$$

We can compute the gradient $\nabla_\theta \mathcal{L}_{RL}$ using the REINFORCE algorithm (Williams, 1992). It is defined as:

$$\nabla_\theta \mathcal{L}_{RL} = -\mathbb{E}_{\hat{x}^h \sim \pi_\theta}[r(\hat{x}^h)\nabla_\theta P] \tag{5}$$

where,

$$P = \sum_{m \in M_{\hat{x}^h}} \log p_\theta(\hat{x}^h_m | (\hat{x}^h_{m'} \in \hat{x}^h \setminus M_{\hat{x}^h}) \tag{6}$$

such that $M_{\hat{x}^h}$ are the masked positions and $\hat{x}^h \setminus M_{\hat{x}^h}$ are all the unmasked tokens.

To reduce the variance without changing the expected gradient, the algorithm proposes to use a baseline b that does not depend on the generated headline $\hat{x}^h$. b is used to normalize the reward along with P from equation 6 as:

$$\nabla_\theta \mathcal{L}_{RL} = -\mathbb{E}_{r(\hat{x}^h) \sim \pi_\theta}[(r(\hat{x}^h) - b)\nabla_\theta P] \tag{7}$$

A single Monte-Carlo sample for each set of products and headline can be used to approximate the gradient. Using the definition of P from equation 6, we have the approximate gradient:

$$\nabla_\theta \mathcal{L}_{RL} \approx -(r(\hat{x}^h) - b)\nabla_\theta P \tag{8}$$

Instead of using other models to estimate the expected baseline reward (Ranzato et al., 2016; Bahdanau et al., 2017), we employ Self-Critical training (Rennie et al., 2017) that involves generating two headlines using the same underlying MLM. The first headline $\hat{x}^h$ is generated by sampling from the vocabulary distributions generated by the model for the masked tokens. The second headline $\hat{z}^h$ is generated using the inference time strategy, which uses the token with the maximum probability at each step rather than sampling. The difference in the reward achieved by these two headlines is used to compute the gradient:

$$\nabla_\theta \mathcal{L}_{SC\_MLM} \approx -(r(\hat{x}^h) - r(\hat{z}^h))\nabla_\theta P \tag{9}$$

where P is defined by equation 6.

Thus, this method maximizes both the reward of the headlines generated by MLM and the likelihood of correct words by incorporating both the likelihood and the reward in the loss function.

3.4 Inference

During inference, we generate the headline autoregressively using beam search until we reach the predetermined max length or each beam generates the end token. We have employed a modified version of Length Normalization (Wu et al., 2016) to better adapt to our headline lengths and training setup. This is necessary as the default beam search setup uses the log probability of each word to select the best headline. However, this biases the results as longer headlines would have lower probability of generation. We thus use the following normalized scores for each word to select the best headline:

$$\text{score}(\hat{x}_i^h) = \text{log-likelihood}(\hat{x}_i^h) * \frac{(2+1)^\alpha}{(2+i)^\alpha} \quad (10)$$

where α is the length normalization coefficient and $\hat{x}_i^h$ is the ith word of the generated headline in each beam. We also include additional Regular Expression based post-processing to remove extra spaces around various symbols such as '-,+()' etc.

4 Experiments

4.1 Training and Inference

We used over 500,000 ad campaigns that were created on Amazon by sellers who have signed-up for advertising. Each campaign contains a set of related products along with an ad headline. We only selected the campaigns that contained English headlines and products with English titles. They were also de-duplicated to only have unique products-headline pairs. The mean product title length is 19.6 words and the mean headline length is 6.16 words. The entire dataset was divided into train (85%), validation (5%) and test (10%) sets. For training, we only selected the campaigns that comply with ad policies as verified by internal experts.

We use the HuggingFace (Wolf et al., 2020) implementation of the Transformer BERT 'Large' models as the base for our experiments. The models are pre-trained on WikiPedia and BookCorpus (Devlin et al., 2019; Dong et al., 2019). We first fine-tune the pre-trained model for up-to 15 epochs with early stopping using $\mathcal{L}_{MLM}$ and Adam (Kingma and Ba, 2014). We then further fine-tune the model for another 15 epochs with early stopping using Adam with $\nabla \mathcal{L}_{SC\_MLM}$ (Equation 9). We use the Rouge L F1 (Lin, 2004) overlap with the approved headlines as the headline quality reward. For a fair comparison, the MLM-only model is fine-tuned for upto 30 epochs.

The model training is very time expensive with a single fine-tuning sub-experiment of 30 epochs taking over 20 days on an Nvidia v100. We thus only performed the essential experiments that help to determine the contribution of different sub-experiments and proposals. We estimated post-experiment that a single fine-tuning sub-experiment of 30 epochs would consume approximately 150 kWh of energy based on the GPU's power draw.

4.2 Baseline

We used a Pointer Network (See et al., 2017) based bi-LSTM with intra-decoder and temporal attention. We also used Self-Critical training with the bi-LSTM, similar to other ad headline generation methods (Xu et al., 2019; Hughes et al., 2019) methods for a fair comparison to Self-Critical MLM.

4.3 Ablations

We trained a model with the same architecture, number of parameters and input as the proposed models but without MLM pre-training and separately without Self-Critical loss to study the impact of the proposals.

We also trained a model with MLM pre-training but fine-tuning only using the primary first product from each campaign instead of using all the products. This is interesting since some of the campaigns are cohesive to a degree with similar products and using only one product improves training time and inference latency.

We also report overlap metrics for model that does not use length normalization and post-processing discussed in equation 10. We also include results for model that uses BERT Base as the base model instead of BERT Large.

5 Results

5.1 Overlap with Approved Headlines

The first evaluation criterion we adopt is overlap (Sharma et al., 2017) of model headlines with subject-matter-experts approved human-submitted headlines from the test set (Table 1).

Masking the source product title words reduces the performance as the titles and headlines do not follow the same sentence structure and distribution. Adding product category embedding reduces performance and our hypothesis is that this is because the base model cannot be pre-trained with these embeddings. Only using one title achieves lesser but respectable performance, highlighting the efficacy of multi-product conditioning.

"No pre-training of MLM" highlights the advantage of using non-pretrained Transformer based architecture over bi-LSTM. 'Proposed MLM' shows the advantage of using pre-training, BERT Large and only masking the headline. 'Proposed Self-Critical MLM' achieves the best scores across all the metrics and highlights the applicability of our proposed approach.

Model	Rouge-L	CIDEr	BLEU-4	METEOR	Avg. Cos. Sim.
Baseline bi-LSTM Pointer Network model					
bi-LSTM	-	-	-	-	-
Self Critical bi-LSTM	0.62	0.01	1.06	0.42	-4.31
MLM Baselines and Ablations (Single Product and No Self Critical Training)					
First Product Only	2.14	0.19	5.03	3.55	0.36
First Product and Category embedding	1.52	0.13	4.18	2.938	0.15
Proposed MLM and Ablations (Multiple Products and No Self Critical Training)					
Using BERT Base instead of BERT Large	2.85	0.22	4.96	3.58	1.53
No pre-training of MLM (Training from scratch)	3.38	0.27	5.72	3.79	-0.04
Additional Source Titles Masking	4.13	0.29	4.42	5.41	-2.09
Proposed MLM	5.08	0.42	7.49	5.46	1.31
Proposed Self-Critical MLM (SC-MLM) and Ablation					
No beam search normalization and post-processing	5.37	0.43	7.81	5.61	1.96
Proposed Self-Critical MLM	**6.33**	**0.55**	**9.11**	**6.14**	**3.75**

Table 1: Absolute improvement over baseline in terms of overlap measures with over 50,000 manually approved human-submitted headlines from the test set. We have reported the **differences** in the F1 of Rouge-L and BLEU-4 scores to the baseline bi-LSTM model. 'Avg. Cos. Sim.' is the average cosine similarity of model headlines to the human-submitted headlines measured using an independently pre-trained Language Model.

	SC-biLSTM	MLM - Single Product	Proposed MLM	Proposed SC-MLM
% improvement in mean rating over human-submitted headlines				
	-9.87%	0.40%	1.15%	**2.07%**
% improvement in number of headlines				
Rated $\geq$ 2 out of 3	-4.99%	**2.75%**	2.42%	2.37%
Rated 3 out of 3	-42.96%	-0.06%	1.22%	**6.53%**

Table 2: Comparison of model-generated headlines to human-submitted headlines on a 3-point scale quality audit of a random blind test set (N $\approx$ 5000).

5.2 Quality and Grammar Audits

We also conducted large scale crowd-sourced evaluation studies of the headlines with over 150,000 judgments. All headlines are shuffled and each headline is rated by 3 random and double-blind crowd-sourced auditors. The quality is judged on a 3-point scale of [1. Incorrect or Irrelevant, 2. Correct, 3. Correct and Attractive] and we use the mode of the 3 judgments.

In this double-blind audit, the auditors were not aware of the source of the headlines and we were not aware of the identity or demographics of any auditor. More details about the workforce may be found in the platform documentation (Ground Truth, 2021). In order to determine the compensation for the crowd-sourced workers, we used the guideline provided by the crowd-sourcing platform to "choose a price consistent with the approximate time it takes to complete a task" (Visible in the Console while creating the Labeling (2021) job). We thus first conducted an internal audit by volunteers across our organization to determine the time required to complete the task (average 21.59s) and then used the remuneration recommended for the corresponding time range ($0.12 for 20s - 22s).

Table 2 summarizes the quality audits. The SC-biLSTM model performed worse compared to human-submitted headlines. The proposed SC-MLM model achieves the highest average rating and the most number of perfectly rated headlines. Using just a single product does produce correct headlines with 8% faster inference latency but fails to produce attractive headlines due to lack of input from multiple products.

We also conducted Grammar specific audits (N $\approx$ 10000) in which the grammar of the headlines is judged independently. 98.13% of SC-MLM and 98.12% of MLM generated headlines were judged to have correct grammar against 93.14% of human submitted headlines.

Table 3 shows a sample of headlines for campaigns in the blind test-set. Excessive keyword stuffing in source product titles does hamper headline quality at times and post-filtering using beam

One of the source product's title	Human Submitted Headline	Proposed MLM	Proposed SC-MLM
BEST Natural Hair Growth Oil for GUARANTEED Hair Strength, Thickening, Hair Gro...	All Natural Hair care products	Natural Hair Growth & Beard Care Products	Protect Your Hair and Beard With All Natural Oils
Royal 310DX Thermal Print Electronic Cash Register	Affordable Reliable Cash Management from Royal	Royal Cash Registers - Retail & Event Supplies	Secure your cash with Royal Cash Registers
Blue Copper 5 Anti-Aging Body Lift, Pregnancy Stretch Marks Prevention and Removal Cream 5 Oz	Blue Copper 5 Anti-Aging Products	Discover Osmotics Best Selling Products	Say Goodbye to Stretch Marks
Cosy House Collection Twin Size Bed Sheets - Cream Bedding Set - Deep Pocket - Extra Soft Luxury...	Soft & Hypoallergenic Twin Sheets	Luxury Twin Sheets - These Will Change Your Life.	Soft Luxury Sheets - These Will Change Your Life.
Carson Dellosa I Valentine's Day Heart Stickers I 1-inch x 1-inch, 216ct	Share the Love with this Classroom Decor	Valentine's Day Celebrations	Show your Valentine some love this Valentine's Day
Canon GI-20 PGBK Ink Bottle, Compatible to PIXMA G6020 and G5020 MegaTank Printers	Print more for less with SuperTank printers. Canon	All-in-one solution for professional grade prints.	All-in-one solution for professional grade prints.
LABILUS iPhone Xs MAX case, (Rugged Armor Series) TPU Soft Stripe Designed Protective Cover Case...	360° Protection Heavy Duty for iPhone Xs Max	Rugged Protective Case for iPhone Xs MAX	Rugged Armor Protective Case for iPhone Xs Max
Biscotti Cookie Gift Basket, Gourmet Gift Basket, Delicious Biscotti Artfully Decorated 18 Count...	Valentines Gifts	Gourmet Chocolate Gift Baskets	Gourmet Holiday Gift Baskets
Le Angelique Tapered Curling Iron Wand with Glove And 2 Clips - 3/4 to 1 Inch (18-25mm) Conical ...	Tapered Curling Wands with Glove and 2 Clips	Le Angelique Tapered Curling Iron Wand	Le Angelique Tapered Curling Iron Wand
JUNK Brands London Fog-BBL London Fog Big Bang Lite Headband	Headbands for Every Adventure	Headbands for Every Adventure	BBL Headbands for Adventure
Jump&Go Portable Car Battery Jump Starter set -16,000mAh, 600A Peak, Mini Automotive Power Boost...	Portable Jump and go Jumpstarter	Jump and Go Portable Car Jump Starter	Jump and Go Portable Jump Starters
decanit Silver Metal Thin Edge 5x7 Picture Frames, Silver Thin Profile Photo Frames 5 by 7 Inch,...	Life-Style-Living	Metal Thin Edge Picture Frames	Thin Edge Picture Frames
CARSYS Coating Thickness Gauge DPM-816 Extended Range Precision Probe Fe/NFe Paint Meter for Car...	Coating Thickness Gauges	Coating Thickness Gauge - Range Precision	Coating Thickness Gauge
Rich & Creamy Buttermilk Syrup Original Flavor by Uncle Bob's Butter Country 16 fl oz/1 Pack	Fresh and Premium Buttermilk Syrup	Rich and Creamy Buttermilk Syrup	Rich and Creamy Buttermilk Syrup - Taste Great
Sesame Street Ernie Face Tee Funny Humor Pun Adult Mens Graphic T-Shirt Apparel (Small), Orange	Sesame Street Tees for Adults	Sesame Street Men's Shirts	Sesame Street Men's Shirts
Agvee Unbreakable End Tip [3 Pack 6ft] 4A Heavy Duty USB Phone Charger Cable, Durable Charging for iPhone 11 Pro Max X XS XR, i-Phone 10x 10xs	AGVEE Fast Lightning Charging Cable for iPhone	AGVEE Fast iPhone 11 X 10s 10s XR Cable	AGVEE Heavy Duty iPhone 11 Xs XS XR Cable

Table 3: Some samples of model generated headlines from subsets rated 3, 2 and 1. The frequency of headlines is not indicative of true distribution of headline quality.

search score helps to filter them out.

We do observe cases where both the models generate the same headline. This is an artifact of the fact that both the models share the first 15 epochs. The SC-MLM model generates more descriptive headlines and both models are able to abstract the product qualities.

6 Conclusion

Ad headline generation is a difficult problem owing to the varying nature of retail product attributes. A lot of historical methods focus on template based creation of ad headlines that are not very expressive.

We demonstrated a new NLG based method to generate headlines for multiple products. Our method achieves highest score in overlap metrics, quality audits and grammar audits compared to the baselines and human-submitted headlines.

Masked Language Models were relatively unexplored for ad headline generation and we were able to demonstrate their utility. We further extended the performance of the model by using Reinforcement Learning. The method only changes the training procedure without impacting inference latency. Thus, our work contributes to both SOTA and practical business applications.

The approach can also be used for any other NLG task.

References

Dzmitry Bahdanau, Philemon Brakel, Kelvin Xu, Anirudh Goyal, Ryan Lowe, Joelle Pineau, Aaron Courville, and Yoshua Bengio. 2017. An Actor-Critic Algorithm for Sequence Prediction. *arXiv:1607.07086 [cs]*. ArXiv: 1607.07086.

Jacob Devlin, Ming-Wei Chang, Kenton Lee, and Kristina Toutanova. 2019. BERT: Pre-training of Deep Bidirectional Transformers for Language Understanding. *arXiv:1810.04805 [cs]*. ArXiv: 1810.04805.

Li Dong, Nan Yang, Wenhui Wang, Furu Wei, Xiaodong Liu, Yu Wang, Jianfeng Gao, Ming Zhou, and Hsiao-Wuen Hon. 2019. Unified Language Model Pre-training for Natural Language Understanding and Generation. *arXiv:1905.03197 [cs]*. ArXiv: 1905.03197.

Using MTurk with Ground Truth. 2021. [link].

J. Weston Hughes, Keng-hao Chang, and Ruofei Zhang. 2019. Generating Better Search Engine Text Advertisements with Deep Reinforcement Learning. In *Proceedings of the 25th ACM SIGKDD International Conference on Knowledge Discovery & Data Mining*, KDD '19, pages 2269–2277, Anchorage, AK, USA. Association for Computing Machinery.

Armand Joulin, Edouard Grave, Piotr Bojanowski, and Tomas Mikolov. 2016. Bag of tricks for efficient text classification. *arXiv preprint arXiv:1607.01759*.

Diederik Kingma and Jimmy Ba. 2014. Adam: A method for stochastic optimization. *International Conference on Learning Representations*.

Ground Truth Labeling. 2021. Create a labeling job.

Mike Lewis, Yinhan Liu, Naman Goyal, Marjan Ghazvininejad, Abdelrahman Mohamed, Omer Levy, Ves Stoyanov, and Luke Zettlemoyer. 2019. BART: Denoising Sequence-to-Sequence Pretraining for Natural Language Generation, Translation, and Comprehension. *arXiv:1910.13461 [cs, stat]*. ArXiv: 1910.13461.

Chin-Yew Lin. 2004. ROUGE: A Package for Automatic Evaluation of Summaries. In *Text Summarization Branches Out*, pages 74–81, Barcelona, Spain. Association for Computational Linguistics.

Kishore Papineni, Salim Roukos, Todd Ward, and Wei-Jing Zhu. 2002. Bleu: a method for automatic evaluation of machine translation. In *Proceedings of the 40th Annual Meeting of the Association for Computational Linguistics*, pages 311–318, Philadelphia, Pennsylvania, USA. Association for Computational Linguistics.

Sponsored Advertising policies. [link].

Alec Radford, Jeffrey Wu, Rewon Child, David Luan, Dario Amodei, and Ilya Sutskever. 2019. Language models are unsupervised multitask learners. *OpenAI Blog*, 1(8):9.

Prajit Ramachandran, Peter J. Liu, and Quoc V. Le. 2016. Unsupervised pretraining for sequence to sequence learning. *arXiv preprint arXiv:1611.02683*.

Marc'Aurelio Ranzato, Sumit Chopra, Michael Auli, and Wojciech Zaremba. 2016. Sequence Level Training with Recurrent Neural Networks. *arXiv:1511.06732 [cs]*. ArXiv: 1511.06732.

Steven J. Rennie, Etienne Marcheret, Youssef Mroueh, Jarret Ross, and Vaibhava Goel. 2017. Self-critical Sequence Training for Image Captioning. *arXiv:1612.00563 [cs]*. ArXiv: 1612.00563.

Sascha Rothe, Shashi Narayan, and Aliaksei Severyn. 2019. Leveraging Pre-trained Checkpoints for Sequence Generation Tasks. *arXiv:1907.12461 [cs]*. ArXiv: 1907.12461.

Abigail See, Peter J. Liu, and Christopher D. Manning. 2017. Get To The Point: Summarization with Pointer-Generator Networks. In *Proceedings of the 55th Annual Meeting of the Association for Computational Linguistics (Volume 1: Long Papers)*, pages 1073–1083, Vancouver, Canada. Association for Computational Linguistics.

Shikhar Sharma, Layla El Asri, Hannes Schulz, and Jeremie Zumer. 2017. Relevance of Unsupervised Metrics in Task-Oriented Dialogue for Evaluating Natural Language Generation. *arXiv:1706.09799 [cs]*. ArXiv: 1706.09799.

Ashish Vaswani, Noam Shazeer, Niki Parmar, Jakob Uszkoreit, Llion Jones, Aidan N Gomez, Łukasz Kaiser, and Illia Polosukhin. 2017. Attention is All you Need. In I. Guyon, U. V. Luxburg, S. Bengio, H. Wallach, R. Fergus, S. Vishwanathan, and R. Garnett, editors, *Advances in Neural Information Processing Systems 30*, pages 5998–6008. Curran Associates, Inc.

Ronald J. Williams. 1992. Simple statistical gradient-following algorithms for connectionist reinforcement learning. *Machine Learning*, 8(3):229–256.

Thomas Wolf, Lysandre Debut, Victor Sanh, Julien Chaumond, Clement Delangue, Anthony Moi, Pierric Cistac, Tim Rault, Rémi Louf, Morgan Funtowicz, and Jamie Brew. 2020. HuggingFace's Transformers: State-of-the-art Natural Language Processing. *arXiv:1910.03771 [cs]*. ArXiv: 1910.03771.

Yonghui Wu, Mike Schuster, Zhifeng Chen, Quoc V. Le, Mohammad Norouzi, Wolfgang Macherey, Maxim Krikun, Yuan Cao, Qin Gao, Klaus Macherey, Jeff Klingner, Apurva Shah, Melvin Johnson, Xiaobing Liu, Łukasz Kaiser, Stephan Gouws, Yoshikiyo Kato, Taku Kudo, Hideto Kazawa, Keith Stevens, George Kurian, Nishant Patil, Wei Wang, Cliff Young, Jason Smith, Jason Riesa, Alex Rudnick, Oriol Vinyals, Greg Corrado, Macduff Hughes, and Jeffrey Dean. 2016. Google's Neural Machine Translation System: Bridging the Gap between Human and Machine Translation. *arXiv:1609.08144 [cs]*. ArXiv: 1609.08144.

Peng Xu, Chien-Sheng Wu, Andrea Madotto, and Pascale Fung. 2019. Clickbait? Sensational Headline Generation with Auto-tuned Reinforcement Learning. In *Proceedings of the 2019 Conference on Empirical Methods in Natural Language Processing and the 9th International Joint Conference on Natural Language Processing (EMNLP-IJCNLP)*, pages 3065–3075, Hong Kong, China. Association for Computational Linguistics.

Jinhua Zhu, Yingce Xia, Lijun Wu, Di He, Tao Qin, Wengang Zhou, Houqiang Li, and Tie-Yan Liu. 2020. Incorporating BERT into Neural Machine Translation. *arXiv:2002.06823 [cs]*. ArXiv: 2002.06823.

LaTeX-Numeric: Language-agnostic Text attribute eXtraction for E-commerce Numeric Attributes

Kartik Mehta
India Machine Learning
Amazon
kartim@amazon.com

Ioana Oprea
Retail Business Services
Amazon
ioanao@amazon.com

Nikhil Rasiwasia
India Machine Learning
Amazon
rasiwasi@amazon.com

Abstract

In this paper, we present LaTeX-Numeric - a high-precision fully-automated scalable framework for extracting E-commerce numeric attributes from product text like product description. Most of the past work on attribute extraction is not scalable as they rely on manually curated training data, either with or without the use of active learning. We rely on distant supervision for training data generation, removing dependency on manual labels. One issue with distant supervision is that it leads to incomplete training annotation due to missing attribute values while matching. We propose a multi-task learning architecture to deal with missing labels in the training data, leading to F1 improvement of 9.2% for numeric attributes over single-task architecture. While multi-task architecture benefits both numeric and non-numeric attributes, we present automated techniques to further improve the numeric attributes extraction models. Numeric attributes require a list of units (or aliases) for better matching with distant supervision. We propose an automated algorithm for alias creation using product text and attribute values, leading to a 20.2% F1 improvement. Extensive experiments on real world dataset for 20 numeric attributes across 5 product categories and 3 English marketplaces show that LaTeX-numeric achieves a high F1-score, without any manual intervention, making it suitable for practical applications. Finally, we show that the improvements are language-agnostic and LaTeX-Numeric achieves 13.9% F1 improvement for 3 Romance languages[1].

1 Introduction

E-commerce websites often sell billions of products. These websites provide information in form of product images, product text (such as title and product description) and structured information, henceforth, termed as product attributes[2]. These attributes often act as a concise summary of product information and are useful in product discovery, comparison and purchase decisions. They are usually provided by selling partners at the time of product listing and can be missing or invalid, even though they might be present in product text sources. Extracting attribute values from these product text sources can be used to populate the missing attribute values and is the focus of this work.

Attribute Extraction from free form text can be posed as a Named Entity Recognition (NER) problem (Zheng et al., 2018). Recently, deep learning models (Lample et al., 2016; Ma and Hovy, 2016; Huang et al., 2015) have shown remarkable performance on NER tasks, eliminating the need of manually curated features. However, these approaches still require large amount of labelled data. While active learning can be used to efficiently curate training data (Zheng et al., 2018), however gathering data for hundreds of product categories and attributes is a resource extensive task. One solution is to use distant supervision to create training data. Distant supervision has been extensively used to curate training set without manual effort for relation extraction (Mintz et al., 2009). In context of attribute extraction for E-commerce, we can curate training data by using attribute values and matching them with tokens in product text. However, if attribute values are missing, distant supervision leads to missing annotations, a phenomenon not studied in literature.

In this work, we present an automated framework for building high-precision attribute extraction models for numeric attributes using distant supervision. Multiple works in literature (Madaan et al., 2016; Ibrahim et al., 2016) argue that distant

[1]https://www.britannica.com/topic/Romance-languages

[2]E.g. RAM, weight and front_camera are some of the product attributes for mobile phone. We use the terminologies 'product attributes' and 'attributes' interchangeably in this paper.

Proceedings of NAACL HLT 2021: IndustryTrack Papers, pages 272–279
June 6–11, 2021.

supervision for numeric attributes poses unique challenges and have given separate treatment to numeric attributes. Highlighted below are some interesting challenges that distant supervision poses for numeric attribute extraction models:

Partial Annotations: Distant supervision leads to incorrect annotations when attribute is present in the text field but structured attribute value is missing.

Diverse surface forms: There are multiple ways that attributes are mentioned in product text (e.g. resolution of '2' can be mentioned as '2 mp', '2 mpix' or '2 megapixels'). We term these different surface forms as alias.

Confusing attributes: Many attributes have common units and may have confusing mention in the text (e.g. '16 GB memory' refers to RAM while '128 GB memory storage' refers to 'Hard Disk')

Use of different units: Seller may use diverse units for numeric attributes (e.g. '1.5 kg' as attribute value and '3.3 pounds' in product text).

Addressing these challenges in automated manner is the primary focus of this work. Our paper has the following contributions: (1) We propose a multi-task architecture to deal with partial annotations introduced due to missing attributes. This multi-task architecture leads to F1 improvement of 9.2% for numeric and 7.4% for non-numeric attributes over single task architecture. (2) We propose a fully automated algorithm for alias creation using product text and attribute values. These alias improve the quality of training annotation in distant supervision, leading to models with 20.2% F1 improvement for numeric attributes. We demonstrate the effectiveness of our proposed approach using a real-world dataset of 20 numeric attributes across 5 categories and 3 English marketplaces. Models trained using our proposed framework achieve a high F1-score without any manual intervention, making them suitable for practical applications. We show that our proposed approach is language agnostic. Experiments of using our framework on 3 Romance languages show 13.9% F1 improvement. To the best of our knowledge, this is first successful attempt at building automated attribute extraction for numeric attributes at E-commerce scale. Rest of the paper is organized as follows. We describe our proposed framework and its components in Section 3. We describe the 'Multi Task' architecture in Section 3.1 and 'automated alias creation' component in Section 3.2. We describe datasets, experimental setup and results in Section 4. Lastly, we summarize our work in Section 5.

2 Related Work

2.1 Attribute Extraction for E-commerce

Early works on information extraction focused on extracting facts from generic web pages (Oren et al., 2005; Yates et al., 2007; Etzioni et al., 2008). With rise of E-commerce, multiple works focused on extracting attributes from product pages. Ghani et al. (2006) proposed use of supervised learning to extract attributes from E-commerce product descriptions. Putthividhya and Hu (2011) formulated attribute extraction from short titles as NER problem, using multiple base classifiers and a CRF layer. The training data was created by matching entries from a seed dictionary. More (2016) proposed use of distant supervision for attribute extraction. They used token-wise string matching (henceforth referred as exact match) based on attribute values to annotate title tokens and train an NER model with manually defined features. They used manual intervention to improve the training annotations e.g. dealing with spelling mistakes and different surface forms of brand. Majumder et al. (2018) extended this work with use of recurrent neural networks, excluding use of manually defined features. Zheng et al. (2018) proposed OpenTag using bidirectional LSTM, Conditional Random Fields (CRF) and attention mechanism. But the training data for OpenTag is manually created with use of active learning, making it challenging to use at E-commerce scale.

2.2 Distant supervision of numeric attributes

Getting manual training data has always been a resource intensive and expensive task and distant supervision has been explored as an alternative. Distant supervision for numeric attributes has been used for relation extraction (Hoffmann et al., 2010; Madaan et al., 2016), question answering (Davidov and Rappoport, 2010), entity linking (Ibrahim et al., 2016). Madaan et al. (2016) argued that distant supervision for numerical attributes presents peculiar challenges not found for non-numeric attributes, such as high noise due to matching out of context, low recall due to different rounding level, and importance of units. Ibrahim et al. (2016) constructed a KB from freebase.com, keeping a list of units and conversion rules for numeric quantities. While these works have established the im-

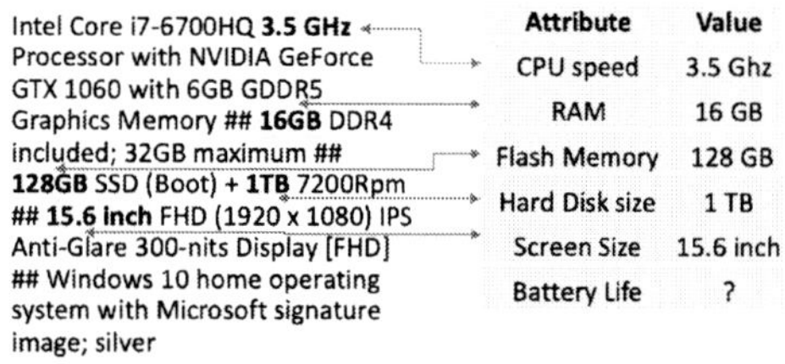

Figure 1: Illustration of E-commerce attribute extraction problem.

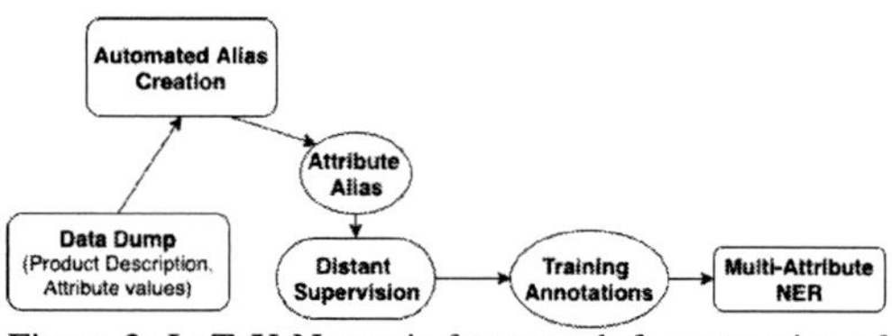

Figure 2: LaTeX-Numeric framework for extraction of E-commerce numeric attributes.

portance of units for distant supervision of numeric attributes, but the list of units is manually curated.

2.3 NER with partial annotation

Distant supervision may lead to noisy training data due to partial annotations. Tsuboi et al. (2008) argued that partial annotations may happen due to ambiguous annotation and proposed CRF-PA to alleviate the issue of partial annotations. Yang et al. (2018) studied partial annotations introduced due to incomplete dictionary and extended CRF-PA to NER models. Jie et al. (2019) proposed learning the probability distribution of all possible label sequences compatible with given incomplete annotation, and using this probability to clean the training annotations. For E-commerce attribute extraction, partial annotations may happen due to missing attribute value. Our paper is the first work to establish this phenomenon for attribute extraction and provide a systematic way to alleviate this problem. We compare our proposed approach with Jie et al. (2019) in Section 4.2.

3 LaTeX-Numeric Framework

We pose the attribute extraction problem (refer Figure 1) as a NER problem, where product attributes are treated as named entities. Formally, we are given a text X with a particular tokenization (x_1, x_2,.....x_m) and a set of attributes A: ($\alpha_1, \alpha_2 \ldots\ldots \alpha_n$). The task is to extract $v_i = \alpha_k$ for i ∈ [1, m] where k ∈ [0, n] and α_0 represents 'Other' entity.

Figure 2 gives an overview of our proposed *LaTeX-Numeric* framework. We are given a list of pre-defined numeric attributes, dump of products consisting of product text and existing attribute values. The attribute values are decimals (e.g. 16) and have an underlying unit (e.g. GB). We term this underlying unit as the canonical unit. For creating distant supervision-based training annotations, we use these canonical units and combine them with attribute values for matching with product text. This serves as the 'canonical aliasing' baseline for our comparisons. We use BIO tagging scheme for our experiments as it is a popular format. For training, we use the recently proposed BiLSTM-CNN-CRF model (Ma and Hovy, 2016). This model consists of CNN architecture to encode character information, LSTM-based encoder to model contextual information of each token and a CRF based tag decoder, which exploits the labels of neighboring tokens for improved classification. Unlike OpenTag (Zheng et al., 2018), we don't use attention as we didn't observe any improvements with use of attention in our initial experiments.

Creating training annotations using distant supervision may lead to partial annotations due to missing attribute values. In Section 3.1, we describe our proposed multi-task learning architecture to deal with such partial annotations. Additionally, we have observed that sellers use multiple surface forms to mention attributes in product text (e.g. '3mp', '3mpix', '3 megapixels' for resolution) and hence, distant supervision with just canonical units (e.g. 'mp') may lead to suboptimal training annotations. Curating a list of these diverse surface forms will help improve the quality of training annotations. We describe an automated approach for curating such diverse units and improving training annotations of numeric attributes in Section 3.2.

3.1 Multi Attribute Joint Extraction

To jointly extract multiple attributes, the tagging strategy can be modified to consider an output label with tags for all attributes. With 'BIO' tagging, each attribute has its own ('B' and 'I') tags with 'O' common for all attributes, leading to total $2K + 1$ tags for K attributes. Based on this modified tagging, a single NER model can be trained for multi-attributes extraction. We term this setting of training 'Multi Attribute Single Task' model as MAST-NER (refer Figure 3). MAST-NER is the commonly used strategy for attributes extraction (Zheng et al., 2018; Sawant et al., 2017; Shen et al., 2017; Joshi et al., 2015).

Under distant supervision, attribute value is used to find matches in product text tokens. However, if the attribute value is missing, no match will be found even when attribute value is mentioned in text and hence, the corresponding tokens are incorrectly tagged as 'O'. We term this partial annotation due to missing attribute as Missing-PA problem. Table 1 shows an illustration of this problem. Missing-PA is generic to distant supervision for multi-attributes and exists for non-numeric attributes as well. To the best of our knowledge, this problem has not received attention in literature.

	Display	**RAM**	**Weight**	**BatteryLife**
Attribute Value	12.3	16	missing	10
Canonical Unit	inches	gb	kg	hours
The high performance Chromebook. Features 7th Gen Intel Core i7 processor, **16 GB** RAM and 512 GB for storage. The long lasting battery provides up to **10 hours** of use and its fast charging so you can get 2 hours of use in 15 minutes ## Pixelbook's super thin and lightweight design measures 10.3 mm and weighs **1.2 kg** Features a **12.3 inches** 360 touchscreen display				

Table 1: Illustration of Missing-PA for distant supervision. 1.2kg will be incorrectly tagged as 'O' as value for weight attribute is missing.

To alleviate Missing-PA problem, one can train separate models for each attribute, by excluding samples where the corresponding attribute value is missing. However, such an approach requires training and managing a large number of models and separate computation for each attribute at evaluation time. Due to these practical challenges, this strategy is not suitable for practical applications. Another way to alleviate missing-PA is to use MAST-NER setting, and to exclude all samples where atleast one attribute has missing value. However, this approach may significantly reduce the size of training data as some attributes may have high missing rate, leading to a suboptimal model. To alleviate this problem, we propose a multi-task learning architecture with separate output layers for each attribute as separate tasks. We term this architecture of training 'Multi Attribute Multi Task' model as MAMT-NER (Refer Figure 3). MAMT-NER consists of shared character encoder, word encoder and BiLSTM layers. For each training sample, loss is deactivated (using masking) for tasks where corresponding attribute value is missing and activated only for remaining tasks where corresponding attribute values are non-missing. Loss for all activated tasks are weighted uniformly and weights of those tasks (including shared weights) are updated for the given sample. Note that the proposed MAMT-NER architecture is generic and can be used for non-numeric attributes as well as any underlying NER architecture, including recently proposed BERT (Devlin et al., 2019).

3.2 Automated Alias Creation

As argued earlier, the canonical unit is often not sufficient to capture diverse surface forms that sellers use to mention attributes in product text. E.g. '13 inch', '13 inches', '13 in', are multiple ways to mention display_size. One can analyze the mention of attribute values in product text and leverage that to create a list of commonly used surface forms. While, such an algorithm will detect common surface forms, it will miss out on units which require a multiplicative factor (e.g. 'pounds', 'lbs' and 'ounces' for weight where attribute values are in 'kg'). To detect such units, we can analyze all numeric mentions in product texts (in isolation from attribute value) and filter out noisy candidates by using similarity with canonical units in embedding space. Additionally, we have observed that some numeric attributes have units which are specific to those attributes (e.g. 'mah' for battery_power and 'hertz' for refresh_rate). One can detect such attributes and use this information while creating training annotations using distant supervision. Based on these learnings, we propose an approach for generating a more exhaustive list of aliases, in an automated fashion (Figure 4).

3.2.1 Creation of alias_dw

We create attribute-specific alias_dw using product text and attribute values. We use a regex matching function, $\mathcal{M}$[3], to find candidate alias which are preceded by numeric attribute value in text. Though this matching function may lead to instances of collision (e.g. *5* for RAM attribute may match with *5 ghz* in text), we ignore cases where more than one match is found in text, to prevent impact of collisions. Alias_dw leads to common surface form of attribute units (e.g. 'in', 'inches', 'inch' for display_size and 'gb', 'gigabyte' for hard_disk).

3.2.2 Creation of alias_bp

We create a single alias_bp (common across attributes) using product text data. We use a regex function $\mathcal{F}$[4] to find candidate alias, which are to-

[3] $\mathcal{M} = re.findall(\text{“ ”} + <value> + r\text{“}[\ -]*[a-zA-Z]+\ '', <text>)$, where <value> is attribute value (e.g. 8 for RAM) and <text> is product text.

[4] $\mathcal{F} = re.findall(\text{“ ”} + r\text{“}[\backslash d\backslash .]*[\backslash d][\ -]*[a-zA-Z]+\ '', <text>)$, where <text> is product text.

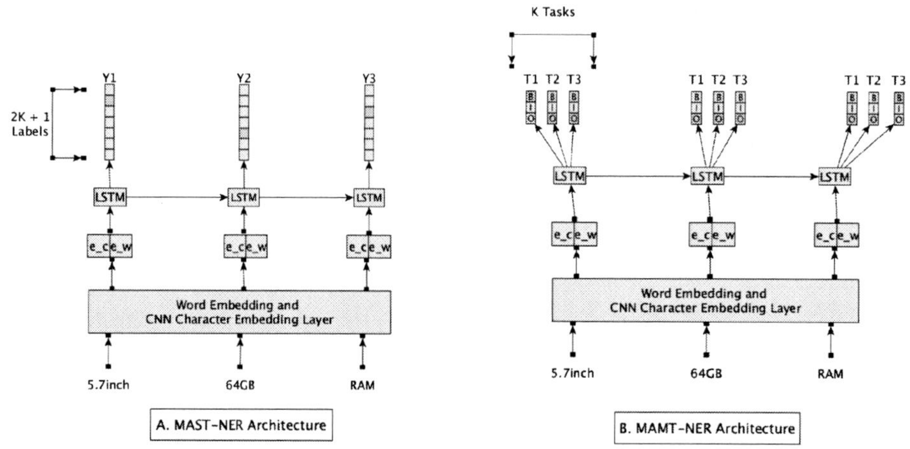

Figure 3: Figure showing different architectures for Multi Attributes Extraction models. We assume BIO-tagging of attributes with only 3 tags possible - B, I and O. For MAST-NER, we have two possible tags for each attribute and one others tag. For MAMT-NER, each attribute extraction is considered a separate task with weights shared for character embeddings, word embeddings and BiLSTM layer

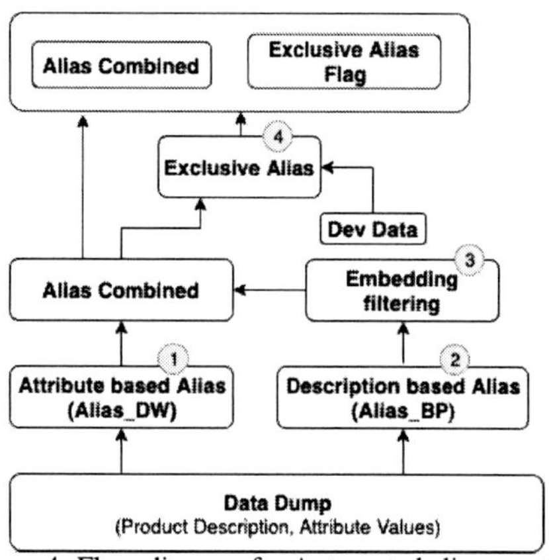

Figure 4: Flow-diagram for Automated alias creation.

kens preceeded by any numeric mention in product text. Alias_bp may contain noisy candidates which are not units for any attribute. We use word embeddings to match alias_bp candidates with attributes and exclude noisy candidates.

3.2.3 Embedding based filtering

To remove noisy candidates and match alias_bp candidates to attributes, we leverage canonical units and Glove embeddings. For each attribute, we calculate similarity of each alias_bp candidate with its canonical unit in embedding space and keep only those candidates where similarity is greater than a pre-determined threshold. Thus, we obtain alias_bp_filter, which is attribute specific. E.g. we filter out 'inches' and select 'pounds' and 'lbs' for weight attribute having 'kg' as canonical unit.

Alias_dw and alias_bp_filter complement each other. Alias_bp_filter misses out on units which have low similarity using embeddings (e.g. 'in' for display_size as 'in' has a low similarity with 'inch'). Alternately, alias_dw misses out on cases where the unit mentioned in product text may require a multiplicative factor (e.g. alias_dw for item_weight misses out on 'pounds' and 'lbs'). We concatenate alias_dw and alias_bp_filter to obtain alias_combined for each attribute (shown for four attributes in Table 2).

With small manual effort, one can get the multiplicative factor for converting values in canonical units to units in alias_combined and vice versa, which can further improve training annotations. As focus of current work is to build a fully automated attribute extraction system, we leave this as future work to be explored.

Category	Attribute	Alias_combined
Laptop	Hard_Disk	[gb, mb, gigabyte, tb, x]
Laptop	Display	[inches, inch, mm, cm, ft, centimeter, feet, in]
Tablet	Weight	[kilograms, kgs, kg, grams, lbs, pounds, ounces, g]
TV	Refresh_Rate	[hertz, hz]

Table 2: Alias values shown for few attributes

3.2.4 Exclusive Alias Flag

We use a small manually labelled dev set (created for hyper-parameters tuning) to create a flag indicating which attributes have exclusive alias. We evaluate precision of extracting any mention of alias for a given attribute and if this precision is above a threshold, we consider that attribute to have exclusive alias. For attributes having an exclusive alias, we use regex-based matching for training annotations, tagging any numeric value followed by the corresponding unit, irrespective of the attribute value.

We refer our proposed approach of using 'alias_combined' and 'exclusive alias flag' for creating training data of numeric attributes as 'auto-aliasing' henceforth. We discuss experiments of using 'auto-aliasing' as compared to other distant supervision techniques for numeric attributes in Section 4.1.

4 Experimental Setup and Results

We picked five product categories and their 20 numeric attributes for three English marketplaces (IN, US and UK). We extracted product data (product description and attribute values) for these categories and split this data into two parts (80% train and 20% test). The train part is used for automated alias creation and creation of training annotations with distant supervision. From the test part, we randomly picked products for each category and label the mention of category-specific numeric attributes in text. Out of the total labelled attribute-product pairs, we observed mention of 6.9K attributes in product text. We term training data for English as 'Train-EN' and audited test dataset as 'Test-EN' (details in Table 3). To evaluate applicability of our proposed LaTeX-Numeric framework for non-English languages, we did a similar analysis with one product category for three Romance languages of French (FR), Spanish (SP) and Italian (IT). We term this training data as 'Train-Romance' and audited test dataset as 'Test-Romance'. Similar to (Zheng et al., 2018), we use F1-score for evaluation. Predictions are given full credit if correct value is extracted, but extracting more values than actual is considered incorrect (e.g. for a mobile phone with '4 gb' RAM, extracting either '4' or '4 gb' is considered correct prediction, but extracting two values of '4 gb' and '16 gb' is considered incorrect prediction).

4.1 Evaluation of Matching Techniques

In this section, we study improvements with our proposed alias creation. For comparison, we use two baselines of creating training annotation a) using lexical matching of numeric attribute value and product text ('exact match'), and b) matching based on canonical units ('canonical aliasing'). For each strategy, we use CNN-BiLSTM-CRF with MAST-NER architecture. Table 4 shows F1 score for using different matching techniques. 'Canonical aliasing' approach shows better F1 score than 'exact match', but it still suffers from low recall due to missing out on different surface forms mentioned in product text. With our proposed auto-aliasing, we address this limitation of 'canonical aliasing' and observe an average F1 improvement of 20.2%, establishing 'auto-aliasing' as best technique for distant supervision of numeric attributes. We use the training data created using 'auto-aliasing' for all subsequent experiments (unless otherwise specified).

Product Category	IN	US	UK
A (6)	14K (854)	241K (966)	70K (468)
B (4)	11K (396)	57K (493)	171K (320)
C (6)	43K (1027)	112K (623)	76K (559)
D (2)	3K (201)	14K (146)	32K (90)
E (2)	11K (246)	89K (266)	41K (244)
Total (20)	83K (2724)	514K (2494)	391K (1681)
Product Category	**FR**	**IT**	**ES**
A (6)	93K (727)	70K (508)	74K (559)

Table 3: Stats for training and test data. Number of training products are shown with unit 'K' (K=1000) and number of labelled attributes mention in test data is shown in adjacent parenthesis. Number of attributes is shown in parenthesis adjacent to each category.

Matching Technique	IN	US	UK	Avg
exact match	78.0	86.5	93.3	85.5
canonical aliasing	100.0	100.0	100.0	100.0
auto aliasing (our)	**113.1**	**120.3**	**128.5**	**120.2**

Table 4: Comparison of various matching techniques for training data generation using distant supervision (all numbers are relative to using canonical units).

4.2 Evaluation of MAMT Architecture

In this section, we perform a quantitative evaluation of our proposed MAMT architectures. Table 5 shows results of using MAST and MAMT architecture with CNN-BiLSTM-CRF. As compared to MAST-NER architecture, we observe 9.2% F1 improvement with our proposed MAMT architecture. Additionally, we observe that Jie et al. (2019) [5] shows better F1 score than MAST due to higher recall. However, Jie et al. (2019) leads to drop in precision due to confusion between close attributes

[5] We use implementation of https://github.com/allanj/ner_incomplete_annotation. We show results only for IN as we get memory error when training for US and UK datasets which have larger training size.

Model + Architecture	IN	US	UK	Avg
BiLSTM-MAST	113.1	120.3	128.5	120.2
BiLSTM (Jie et al. (2019))	114.4	NA	NA	NA
BiLSTM-MAMT	124.4	131.4	139.0	131.2
BERT-MAST	117.7	122.9	128.8	122.8
BERT-MAMT	120.4	127.8	134.3	127.1

Table 5: Study of multi-task architecture for numeric attributes. BERT uses softmax as output layer, while, BiLSTM refers to CNN-BiLSTM model with crf as output layer. All numbers are relative to using canonical units in Table 4.

Model	Archi- tecture	Precision	Recall	F1
BiLSTM	MAST	100.0	100.0	100.0
BiLSTM	MAMT	93.6	117.8	**107.4**

Table 6: Study of multi-task architectures for textual attributes (all numbers are relative). BiLSTM refers to CNN-BiLSTM model with crf as output layer.

(e.g. front-camera and back-camera for mobile.) Our proposed MAMT shows 8.7% better F1 score than Jie et al. (2019) for IN.

Further, we do comparison of MAST and MAMT architectures with BERT[6] as underlying model and observed 3.5% F1 improvement with MAMT, demonstrating its applicability to multiple underlying models. To establish the effectiveness of MAMT architecture for non-numeric attributes, we curated a test dataset of 600 samples per attribute for 8 textual attributes across 4 product categories. As shown in Table 6, we observe 7.4% F1 improvement on this dataset with our proposed MAMT-NER architecture, showing its effectiveness on textual attributes as well.

4.3 Evaluation on non-English Languages

Architecture + Matching	FR	IT	ES	Avg
MAST + canonical-aliasing	100	100	100	100
MAST + auto-aliasing	103.0	107.1	108.4	106.0
MAMT + auto-aliasing	**104.0**	**118.4**	**121.6**	**113.9**

Table 7: Comparison of auto-aliasing and multi-task architecture on Romance languages (numbers are relative to using canonical-aliasing).

In this section, we study the applicability of LaTeX-Numeric for three Romance languages. We train a separate (Category-A) model for each Romance language replacing English word embeddings with language specific fastText (Lample et al., 2018) embeddings. Table 7 shows results on Test-Romance dataset. We observe 6.0% F1 improvement with our proposed auto-aliasing and additional 7.9% improvement with use of MAMT-NER architecture, showing effectiveness of our proposed approaches across languages.

[6]We use implementation of https://github.com/namisan/mt-dnn, which uses bert-base and softmax as output layer.

5 Conclusion

In this paper, we described 'LaTeX-Numeric', a high-precision fully-automated framework for training attribute extraction models for E-commerce numeric attributes. We characterized the problem of Missing-PA that arises with distant supervision due to missing attribute values and proposed a multi-task learning architecture to alleviate the Missing-PA problem, leading to 9.2% F1 improvement for numeric attributes. We established the applicability of our proposed multi-task architecture for textual attributes and BERT as underlying model as well. Additionally, we proposed an automated algorithm for alias creation, to deal with variations of numeric attribute mentions, leading to models with 20.2% F1 improvement. Our evaluation on three Romance languages establishes that these improvements are applicable across non-English languages as well. Models trained using our proposed LaTeX-Numeric framework achieve high F1 score, making them suitable for practical applications.

References

Dmitry Davidov and Ari Rappoport. 2010. Extraction and approximation of numerical attributes from the web. In *48th Annual Meeting of ACL*, pages 1308–1317.

Jacob Devlin, Ming-Wei Chang, Kenton Lee, and Kristina Toutanova. 2019. Bert: Pre-training of deep bidirectional transformers for language understanding. In *NAACL-HLT (1)*.

Oren Etzioni, Michele Banko, Stephen Soderland, and Daniel S Weld. 2008. Open information extraction from the web. *Communications of the ACM*, 51(12):68–74.

Rayid Ghani, Katharina Probst, Yan Liu, Marko Krema, and Andrew Fano. 2006. Text mining for product attribute extraction. *ACM SIGKDD Explorations Newsletter*, 8(1):41–48.

Raphael Hoffmann, Congle Zhang, and Daniel S Weld. 2010. Learning 5000 relational extractors. In *48th Annual Meeting of the ACL*, pages 286–295.

Zhiheng Huang, Wei Xu, and Kai Yu. 2015. Bidirectional lstm-crf models for sequence tagging. *arXiv*.

Yusra Ibrahim, Mirek Riedewald, and Gerhard Weikum. 2016. Making sense of entities and quantities in web tables. In *25th CIKM*, pages 1703–1712. ACM.

Zhanming Jie, Pengjun Xie, Wei Lu, Ruixue Ding, and Linlin Li. 2019. Better modeling of incomplete annotations for named entity recognition. In *Proceedings of the 2019 Conference of the North American Chapter of the Association for Computational Linguistics: Human Language Technologies, Volume 1 (Long and Short Papers)*, pages 729–734, Minneapolis, Minnesota. Association for Computational Linguistics.

Mahesh Joshi, Ethan Hart, Mirko Vogel, and Jean-David Ruvini. 2015. Distributed word representations improve ner for e-commerce. In *1st Workshop on Vector Space Modeling for Natural Language Processing*, pages 160–167.

Guillaume Lample, Miguel Ballesteros, Sandeep Subramanian, Kazuya Kawakami, and Chris Dyer. 2016. Neural architectures for named entity recognition. In *Proceedings of the 2016 Conference of the NAACL-HLT*, pages 260–270, San Diego, California. Association for Computational Linguistics.

Guillaume Lample, Alexis Conneau, Marc'Aurelio Ranzato, Ludovic Denoyer, and Hervé Jégou. 2018. Word translation without parallel data. In *International Conference on Learning Representations*.

Xiaodong Liu, Pengcheng He, Weizhu Chen, and Jianfeng Gao. 2019. Multi-task deep neural networks for natural language understanding. In *Proceedings of the 57th Annual Meeting of the Association for Computational Linguistics*, pages 4487–4496.

Xuezhe Ma and Eduard Hovy. 2016. End-to-end sequence labeling via bi-directional LSTM-CNNs-CRF. In *Proceedings of the 54th Annual Meeting of the Association for Computational Linguistics (Volume 1: Long Papers)*, pages 1064–1074, Berlin, Germany. Association for Computational Linguistics.

Aman Madaan, Ashish Mittal, Ganesh Ramakrishnan, Sunita Sarawagi, et al. 2016. Numerical relation extraction with minimal supervision. In *Thirtienth AAAI*.

Bodhisattwa Prasad Majumder, Aditya Subramanian, Abhinandan Krishnan, Shreyansh Gandhi, and Ajinkya More. 2018. Deep recurrent neural networks for product attribute extraction in ecommerce. *arXiv*.

Mike Mintz, Steven Bills, Rion Snow, and Dan Jurafsky. 2009. Distant supervision for relation extraction without labeled data. In *Joint Conference of the 47th Annual Meeting of the ACL and the 4th IJCNLP of the AFNLP*, pages 1003–1011.

Ajinkya More. 2016. Attribute extraction from product titles in ecommerce. *CoRR*, abs/1608.04670.

Etzioni Oren, Cafarella Michael, Downey Doug, Popescu Ana-Maria, Shaked Tal, Soderland Stephen, Weld Daniel S, and Yates Alexander. 2005. Unsupervised named-entity extraction from web: An experimental study. *Artificial intelligence*, 165(1):91–134.

Duangmanee Pew Putthividhya and Junling Hu. 2011. Bootstrapped named entity recognition for product attribute extraction. In *EMNLP*, pages 1557–1567. ACl.

Nils Reimers and Iryna Gurevych. 2017. Optimal hyperparameters for deep lstm-networks for sequence labeling tasks. *arXiv*.

Uma Sawant, Vijay Gabale, and Anand Subramanian. 2017. E-fashion product discovery via deep text parsing. In *26th International Conference on WWW*, pages 837–838.

Yanyao Shen, Hyokun Yun, Zachary Lipton, Yakov Kronrod, and Animashree Anandkumar. 2017. Deep active learning for named entity recognition. In *Proceedings of the 2nd Workshop on Representation Learning for NLP*, pages 252–256, Vancouver, Canada. Association for Computational Linguistics.

Anders Søgaard and Yoav Goldberg. 2016. Deep multi-task learning with low level tasks supervised at lower layers. In *54th Annual Meeting of the ACL (Volume 2: Short Papers)*, pages 231–235.

Yuta Tsuboi, Hisashi Kashima, Hiroki Oda, Shinsuke Mori, and Yuji Matsumoto. 2008. Training conditional random fields using incomplete annotations. In *22nd COLING*, pages 897–904. ACL.

Yaosheng Yang, Wenliang Chen, Zhenghua Li, Zhengqiu He, and Min Zhang. 2018. Distantly supervised ner with partial annotation learning and reinforcement learning. In *27th COLING*.

Alexander Yates, Michael Cafarella, Michele Banko, Oren Etzioni, Matthew Broadhead, and Stephen Soderland. 2007. Textrunner: open information extraction on the web. In *Human Language Technologies: The Annual Conference of the NAACL: Demonstrations*, pages 25–26. ACL.

Guineng Zheng, Subhabrata Mukherjee, Xin Luna Dong, and Feifei Li. 2018. Opentag: Open attribute value extraction from product profiles. In *24th ACM SIGKDD*, pages 1049–1058. ACM.

Training Language Models under Resource Constraints for Adversarial Advertisement Detection

Eshwar Shamanna Girishekar **Shiv Surya** **Nishant Nikhil*** **Dyut Kumar Sil**
Sumit Negi **Aruna Rajan**
Amazon
{geshwar, shisurya, dyut, suminegi, rajarna}@amazon.com *i.nishantnikhil@gmail.com

Abstract

Advertising on e-commerce and social media sites deliver ad impressions at web scale on a daily basis driving value to both shoppers and advertisers. This scale necessitates programmatic ways of detecting unsuitable content in ads to safeguard customer experience and trust. This paper focusses on techniques for training text classification models under resource constraints, built as part of automated solutions for advertising content moderation. We show how weak supervision, curriculum learning and multi-lingual training can be applied effectively to fine-tune BERT and its variants for text classification tasks in conjunction with different data augmentation strategies. Our extensive experiments on multiple languages show that these techniques detect adversarial ad categories with a substantial gain in precision at high recall threshold over the baseline.

1 Introduction

All advertisements on e-commerce and social media platforms must be moderated to ensure regulatory and ethical standards in countries where they are being served. A tiered moderation workflow with automated components like cached lookup, ML models, rule based annotators complement human experts to ensure reliable content moderation for ads created by advertisers while scaling to e-commerce advertising volumes. The advertising platform currently enables ads to be created in various media formats like text, images and videos. In this work, we focus on detecting adversarial ads in one broad class of ads, where engagement is driven primarily through text and images. Such ads on e-commerce site serve as a casing for the product being advertised. The casing includes product text and image attributes along with optional custom captions provided by the advertiser. It is under the purview of moderation to check whether an ad contains prohibited content. Any ad containing prohibited content can have an adverse impact on the shopper experience and hence needs to be prevented from showing up. See Section 2.1 for a broad overview of the adversarial ad categories.

In this paper, we focus on techniques we use to train NLP models built as a part of this system. Training any ML model requires a good quality dataset that is representative of the policy being enforced. The quality of data available to train models targeting a defect, say detection of "adult and objectionable content" depends on several factors. Typically occurrences of such products are rare but the impact of such an ad on shopper experience is adverse. The uncommonness of these violations makes curating large in-domain monolingual corpora difficult. This problem is compounded in low resource languages where there are limited linguistic resources and the rarity of these violations are even more skewed. Further, it is expensive and time consuming to gather more labeled data.

Through this paper, we show different ways to train generalised language models when we have limited labeled data. We suggest various ways for data augmentation and empirically provide evidence suggesting when each of the approaches works best. We explore how we can leverage the product catalogue and user behaviour in weak and semi-weak supervision, curriculum learning and multilingual training strategies to train generalised language models like BERT (Devlin et al., 2019) and its variants. Our experiments show :

- Weak supervision for unlabelled data in the target domain provides an average gain of 10.88% in precision across languages.
- Curriculum strategies to augment labeled data from resource rich language by translation improves average true negative rate(TNR) by 24.25% in low resource setting.
- Multilingual training using labeled data in any

*Work done when at Amazon

Proceedings of NAACL HLT 2021: IndustryTrack Papers, pages 280–287
June 6–11, 2021. ©2021 Association for Computational Linguistics

available languages provides average gain of 24.32% in TNR over the baselines.

2 Background: Content moderation

2.1 Scope of content moderation

Online advertising platforms typically enable advertisers to create ads in various media formats like text, images and videos. Here we provide an overview of the broad categories which are generally restricted from advertising across these platforms.

Sculley et al. (2011) describe some of the adversarial categories which can compromise the user safety. These include ads which promote unsafe and illegal content or products. In addition to these categories, promotion of adult, profane, hate inciting and tobacco related products/content are restricted as well. All of these adversarial categories are under the purview for content moderation.

We primarily featurise the text attributes of the product in catalogue such as product title, description and optional custom text provided by the advertiser to detect aforementioned unsuitable content.

2.2 Dataset

A very small fraction of ads belong to the restricted categories referenced in Section 2.1. We perform all experiments on 5 such semantic categories shown in Table 1. For the positive class(defective ad), we consider all ads labelled by human experts. We split this data into train and validation set using multi-label stratification (Sechidis et al. (2011); Szymański and Kajdanowicz (2017)) on catalogue categorisation of the product. To enable training, we restrict the size of negative class by restricting the sample size to utmost 100 times the size of the positive class and augment it with 10% of hard negative samples that were caught by existing signals but approved by human experts. The validation set is used to tune model hyperparameters and determine the stopping criterion. We maintain a separate temporally distinct test set replicating production setting. A similar approach is taken when creating train and test set for low resource languages.

2.3 Baselines

BERT and M-BERT For all the experiments we make use of BERT (Bidirectional Encoder Representations from Transformers)(Devlin et al., 2019), a transformer based attention model that encodes an entire sequence at once using multiple attention based encoder layers. We use a linear classification layer applied on max-pooled version of last four attention layer outputs of BERT and finetune the model on limited labeled data. Because of the skew in the labels, we weight the binary cross entropy loss inversely based on label frequency and clip the scaling factor to improve stability of training. The model is trained using textual attributes of the products. Adam (Kingma and Ba, 2014) optimiser is used and the maximum sequence length is restricted to 512 during training and inference. For low resource languages we make use of M-BERT. We decide the hyper-parameters of the models by their performance on the validation set and maintain these hyper parameters across ablative experiments.

Word embedding based text classifier In the multi-lingual setting, we use another baseline. This is a linear classifier based on word embeddings similar to the setup in (Shen et al., 2018). We use fastext (Bojanowski et al., 2017) embeddings for German to get the word embeddings and combine them by taking a weighted average of the embeddings as described in Arora et al. (2017). This removes the special direction to generate the sentence embedding. We also obtain max-pooled embeddings that extracts salient features along vector dimensions. This is later stacked to the reference weighted average embedding and used to train a logistic regression classifier with the limited labeled data. We refer to this model as BOE_LIN.

3 Finetuning BERT under low resource constraints

We explore various techniques that can be used to train generalised language models(GLM) like BERT and multilingual variants with significant performance gains over baseline models described in Section 2.3. We look at resource constraints during training of machine learning models in a supervised setting attributed to the following cases:

- Lack of labeled data.
- Lack of large in-domain monolingual corpora.
- Linguistic resources insufficient for building reliable statistical NLP applications.

We leverage product catalog to source data for weak and semi-weak supervision training in monolingual setting. We also explore how curriculum strategies and multilingual training can benefit training text classifiers for low resource languages.

Our experiment show that generalised language models like BERT or multilingual variants like M-BERT can be trained using these techniques with significant performance gains over baseline model described in Section 2.3.

3.1 Semi-Supervision and Semi-Weak-Supervision

We employ two approaches as described in Yalniz et al. (2019) One is the conventional semi-supervised approach using teacher-student paradigm. The teacher model is trained using the limited labelled data (or strong data) and then used to get predictions for the unlabelled data. Top k% of the predicted samples for each of the class are used to pre-train the new student model. The student model is further fine-tuned using the limited labelled data. The second approach is semi-weakly-supervised approach. Here, the sourced data associated with weak labels is used to pre-train the teacher model before fine-tuning on the limited labelled data. Again top k% predicted samples by the this teacher model is used to pre-train student network prior to fine-tuning on the strong data. Yalniz et al. (2019) apply these two techniques for image and video classification tasks and achieve SOTA results using semi-weak-supervision. We explore these approaches applied to text classification task using a GLM like BERT.

3.1.1 Semi-Supervised(SS) Methodology

In this section we describe how we augment unlabelled/weakly labeled data. We leverage user behavioural data by using internal search engine to source products relevant to different categories from huge product catalog. We can query search using generic text phrases and pre-existing catalogue categorisation (CC). So we design relevant text phrases and pre-existing catalogue categorisation for a defect of interest. These attributes are filtered by a keyword list which is a combination of a curated list and word list sourced from models that use BoW as a feature. Table 1 provides the statistics of the proportion of number of products sourced using different approaches.

We use the augmentation for only defective class since the class skew is several orders larger. Once we have the augmented data for the defective category we treat it as unlabelled for semi-supervised setup. The teacher model which is BERT is trained only on the strong data. In case of very limited data like CAT4–5 we make use of fasttext classifier as teacher. The teacher model is used to score the augmented samples. Top k% of the augmented data based on model scores are picked to pre-train the new student BERT model. Later the student BERT model is fine-tuned using the strong labelled data. When training both teacher and student models we validate the model after each epoch on the same validation set and use the validation score as the stopping criteria.

Table 1: Statistics of deny list keywords, catalogue categorisation labels (CC) and relative scale of data for each label category

Defect category	CAT1	CAT2	CAT3	CAT4	CAT5
Count of keywords	315	240	36	45	50
Count of CC	26	111	27	1	20
Scale of Data	10	100	5	2	1

Table 2: Precision over Baseline, BERT(B) trained with limited labeled data, at our high Recall threshold for all models across defects.

Precision improvement at high Recall threshold over Baseline					
Method	CAT1	CAT2	CAT3	CAT4	CAT5
B_SS	+40.46	**+11.6**	+ 2.12	+4.85	+2.93
B_SWS	**+40.48**	+10.99	**+6.44**	**+8.02**	**+7.09**

3.1.2 Semi-Weak-Supervised(SWS) Methodology

Here we treat the augmented data as weakly labeled data and use it to pre-train teacher model before fine-tuning it with strong labeled data. This teacher model is used to score the top k% samples of the weakly labeled data which is used to pre-train new student model which is later fine-tuned using strong data. Here again while pre-training and fine-tuning teacher and student models we validate the model after each epoch on the same validation set and use the validation score as the stopping criteria.

3.1.3 Extension to low resource languages

We take the exact same approach of augmenting data for low resource languages and train the M-BERT model. With low resource languages we face two challenges. First, labelled data available here is less compared to English(EN). In German(DE) and French(FR), the scale of the positive class is of order 0.02-0.15 compared to scale of different defect categories for EN reported in Table 1. Second, keywords available for sourcing weakly labeled data is less which affects quality of sourcing weak data. To address these challenges we explore curriculum learning and multilingual training for low resource setting.

3.2 Curriculum for leveraging resource rich domains

In the above section we discussed augmenting data using weak signals. Here we explore how we can utilise large amounts of labeled data available in resource rich languages such as EN. We translate the ad creatives available in EN to the target language. Hence forth, this data is referred to as translated data. A trivial approach to utilise this data for tuning the model is to combine the strong and translated data and randomly sample mini-batches (B_TL_{RS}) from the unified set while training. Another possibility is to use the translated data to pretrain the classifier and fine-tune it with the strong data in target domain (B_TL_{FT}). Here, during every epoch, we initially train the model with the mini-batches sampled from the translated data followed by sampling mini-batches from strong data. This clearly has an advantage over the earlier approach as it helps model adapt to the target domain and avoid domain shift arising from the translation engine employed.

We also explore an approach leveraging curriculum learning that is agnostic of the distinction between translated and strong data for training the M-BERT model. Curriculum learning(Hacohen and Weinshall, 2019) involves using the prior knowledge of the difficulty of the training samples to sample training mini-batch. To rank the difficulty of the training sample (x_i, y_i) we need a scoring function. Scoring function $f : X \rightarrow R$ is any function which scores the difficulty of a given training sample. If $f(x_i, y_i) > f(x_j, y_j)$ then (x_i, y_i) is more difficult than (x_j, y_j). We also use a pacing function (Hacohen and Weinshall, 2019) which determines the sequence of subsets $X_1, .., X_m \subseteq X$ of size g_i from which mini-batches $\{B_i\}_{i=1}^{M}$ are sampled. These are generally monotonically increasing functions so the likelihood of the easier samples decrease over time.

In our case, we use BOE_LIN (See Section 2.3) as our scoring function- a proxy for hardness of the sample. Samples with confident predictions by BOE_LIN for positive and negative classes are considered easy while hardness increases as the samples are closer to boundary of separation. We initially pick the easier samples for the first x iterations. We augment the training samples with difficult samples progressively for every x iterations till all the data is seen by the model. In our case, we consider $x = 2$ and split the data into 5 sets of increasing difficulty. Iterations 1–2 are trained using the set having the most easy samples defined by the scoring function f. In iterations 3–4, we take the initial two sets of easy samples. In such a progression, the model sees the entire dataset in iterations 9–10. We use early stopping to choose the model at iteration i.

3.3 Multi-Lingual training of M-BERT

In Section 3.1 - 3.2, we explored methods of augmenting data from external sources for the same language i.e they were trained on monolingual data. However, in weak supervision, the quality of weak data is contingent on sourcing technique used. Using translated data from source domains risks introducing semantic drift due to inaccuracies in the translation engine used. Advertisers create ads for different markets and we have limited data in French(FR), Spanish(ES), Italian(IT) apart from English(EN) and German(DE). To mitigate these challenges, we explore multilingual training of M-BERT leveraging data from different languages to train a classifier for the target DE language thus avoiding sourcing technique to augment data.

Pires et al. (2019) show that M-BERT is good at zero shot cross lingual transfer where task specific text in one language is used for fine-tuning the model for a different target language. They further show that the transfer is more pronounced when there is more lexical overlap between the languages. They also show that transfer works with zero lexical overlap when the two languages are typologically similar i.e the ordering of subject, object and verbs among other parts of speech in a sentence. In our experiments we mainly rely on the lexical similarity between languages for training M-BERT. Table 4 (Wikipedia contributors, 2004) provides the lexical similarity between the languages for which we have labeled data. Lexical similarity score of 1 would mean total overlap between vocabularies and 0 would mean no overlap between vocabularies.

From entries for lexical similarity in Table 4, we observe that DE is lexically most similar to EN followed by FR. In case of missing values, we consider the corresponding languages as lexically farthest to the target language. Since M-BERT is trained on monolingual corpora and the above-mentioned 5 languages are among them, the vocabulary of M-BERT would have all the alphabets from these languages. On the basis of results evidenced in Pires et al. (2019), we hypothesise that

Table 3: Precision and TNR improvements at our high recall threshold for all the explored models for DE and FR languages using different training strategies and for ablation studies in Section 4.1 over BOE_LIN. Here B refers to M-BERT finetuned with limited labeled data.

		Model Type							Ablation Type			
		B	B_SS	B_SWS	B_TL_{RS}	B_TL_{FT}	B_TL_{CL}	B_ML_{LEX}	B_TL_{ACL}	B_TL_{RCL}	$B\_ML_{LEX}^{REV}$	$B\_ML_{LEX}^{RAND}$
DE	TNR	+14.35	+23.15	+24.79	+13.84	+23.76	+26.40	**+29.08**	+25.7	+21.0	+14.17	+26.90
	Prec.	+0.76	+1.69	+1.95	+0.72	+1.78	+2.24	**+2.83**	+2.11	+1.4	+0.75	+2.34
FR	TNR	+15.29	+19.16	+20.05	+15.10	+20.41	**+22.11**	+19.57	+21.02	+20.68	+12.71	+18.80
	Prec.	+0.77	+1.10	+1.19	+0.75	+1.23	**+1.43**	+1.14	+1.30	+1.26	+0.59	+1.07

Table 4: Lexical Similarity scores between languages of interest taken from Wikipedia.

Language	EN	DE	FR	ES	IT
EN	1	0.6	0.27	-	-
DE	0.6	1	0.29	-	-
FR	0.27	0.29	1	0.75	0.89
ES	-	-	0.75	1	0.82
IT	-	-	0.89	0.82	1

the zero shot transfer is more likely among similar lexical languages and devise our multi-language training of M-BERT in the following manner. We take the labeled data available in 5 languages and sort them based on increasing lexical similarity with the target language. For target language DE, the ordering would be ES, IT, FR, EN, DE. We feed all the data in the aforementioned ordering and progressively drop the lexically farthest language every x iterations until we are only left with the target language. In our case we set $x = 2$ and train the M-BERT. We generally stop training the model after 10 iterations since we do not observe significant gains beyond this.

4 Results

In all experiments, we track model performance using precision and recall. Precision indicates the fraction of ads correctly rejected by model. Recall indicates the fraction of true defective products rejected by the model for a particular category.

SS and SWS for EN Table 2 shows the improvement in precision for all the models built using the semi-supervision and semi-weak-supervised approaches. We see semi-supervision(B_SS) consistently perform better than the baseline, BERT finetuned with strong data, across all categories. For CAT1–2, we observe a substantial lift in precision over baseline compared to other categories. This is attributed to strong sourcing characteristics for these categories observed in Table 1. We observe significant gains by SWS(B_SWS) models especially in low resource categories like CAT3–5. For CAT3, CAT4 and CAT5 we see 6–8% better precision respectively.

Results for low resource languages In case of low resource languages the amount of defective ads is much lesser and is of order 0.02-0.15 as called out earlier. Since the quantity of positive class is drastically low, precision does not always indicate the true gains seen by our models. Hence we also report true negative rate(TNR) which is the % of non-defective ads rightly approved by our models.

Table 3 provides the relative improvements in metrics of all the models in comparison to baseline BOE_LIN. The complex and heavily parameterised M-BERT(B) model achieves a significant increase in TNR despite dearth of training data. From performance numbers in Table 3, we see that fine-tuning(B_TL_{FT}) the model with target domain after pre-training with translated data is better than random sampling(B_TL_{RS}) of mini-batches across strong and translated data. Plain augmentation of data through translation without any curriculum during training the model might not always show gains as indicated by M-BERT's performance. However, introducing a curriculum(B_TL_{CL}) based on the difficulty of the training samples outperforms the initial two approaches.

Table 3 also shows performance of weak supervision techniques (see Section 4.1). Models trained using both SS(B_SS) and SWS(B_SWS) approaches outperform the model which was trained only using the strong data.

We observe the best performance for the model (B_ML_{LEX}) leveraging data from multiple languages and trained in lexical order fashion. Since DE is lexically similar to EN, the larger training data in EN aided the model performance in this setting. We also rerun the experiments with FR with same setting and results are provided in Table 3. If we observe the lexical similarity in Table 4, FR is most similar to IT and ES and farther away from EN which has the most amount of labeled data. Hence, we do not see the similar kind of gains for FR as seen in DE which is lexically closer to EN. For FR the model trained using curriculum (B_TL_{CL}) based on the hardness of the sample performs the best. We observe a similar trend in FR for rest of the approaches.

4.1 Ablations

We ablate the effects of curriculum learning based on increasing difficulty using models trained in two control conditions. (a) Anti-curriculum learning (B_TL_{ACL}) using scoring function $f' = -f$ where harder samples are fed first and (b) random curriculum (B_TL_{RCL}) where scoring function randomly scores the training samples. As seen from the Table 3 anti-curriculum and random curriculum are not as effective as the curriculum of increasing hardness. Further, random scoring function results in significant degradation of performance when compared to approaches employing a curriculum. Similar trends are observed for respective models trained in FR as well.

We further conduct ablations to rule out any other factors contributing to the gain in recall from curriculum based on lexical similarity. We perform two other experiments where we train the model in similar manner but feed the languages in reverse lexical similarity order($B\_ML_{LEX}^{REV}$) and random order ($B\_ML_{LEX}^{RAND}$). However, in both the experiments we feed the target language at the end to minimise domain shift. We see that the model trained in the lexical similarity order beats the performance of the other two models in Table 3. We validate statistical significance of gains from both lexical and hardness curricula using the McNemar's Test (Dietterich, 1998; McNemar, 1947) (Raschka, 2018). The gains through both curriculum are statistically significant as p-value is < 0.05 for both DE and FR.

5 Conclusion

We have explored multiple ways of training a GLM and it's multilingual variant in low resource settings. When large in-domain monolingual corpora is present but labeled data is limited, sourcing weak data applied in semi and semi-weak supervision training improves model performance consistently. Curricula are useful in resource constrained settings. Multilingual training on a lexical similarity based curriculum is useful when target language is lexically closer to resource rich languages. Alternate curriculum like sample hardness is useful in low resource languages which are lexically distant to resource rich language such as EN.

6 Related Work

Lately, there has been exponential progress in generating efficient embeddings for various natural language processing(NLP) tasks using language models (Radford et al. (2019); Liu et al. (2019)). BERT (Devlin et al., 2019) based embeddings achieved SOTA results in eleven NLP tasks at the time of its release. Devlin et al. (2019) also release a multilingual version of BERT(M-BERT), pre-trained using monolingual corpora of 104 different languages. M-BERT is also surprisingly good at zero shot transfer between languages as shown by Pires et al. (2019). Prior to and in parallel to M-BERT multiple works have been done for multilingual NLP tasks (Ruder et al., 2019). LASER described in Artetxe and Schwenk (2019) achieve language independent representation by having a single encoder and decoder which are shared by all language pairs for the translation task. Conneau and Lample (2019) propose using parallel data to train translation language model as an extension to M-BERT. Conneau et al. (2019) release XLM-R which is pretrained using 100 languages using much larger corpus compared to M-BERT.

Most of the recently launched language models have millions of parameters which demands huge amount of labelled data for training robust models. However, obtaining large amount of labeled data is a laborious and expensive process. Semi-supervised approaches involve efficiently incorporating huge quantity of unlabelled data along with limited labelled data. There has been a lot of work in this area in image and text domain. Yalniz et al. (2019) propose a teacher-student paradigm for incorporating both unlabelled and weakly labelled data for training a image classifier. Karamanolakis et al. (2019) also make use of teacher-student approach for leveraging weak signals for aspect detection in text. Variational auto encoders (Yang et al. (2017); Gururangan et al. (2019)) and virtual adversarial training(Miyato et al., 2016) have been extensively used in semi-supervised setting. Recently interpolations in textual hidden space(Chen et al., 2020) have been used for semi-supervised learning as well.

Multiple prior works (Sculley et al. (2011); Sanzgiri et al. (2018)) detect adversarial ads in online advertising platforms. While Sculley et al. (2011) provide a holistic view of creating an adversarial ad detection system, Sanzgiri et al. (2018) look at techniques for detecting sensitive content in images.

Our work focuses on techniques we leverage to train state of the art language models for detecting adversarial advertising content in text. However, the uncommon nature of these violations pose a challenge, often compounded in low resource languages. We leverage related work in semi-weak supervision and curriculum learning to overcome these challenges. We also show how data available in multiple languages can be used for training classifiers for a given target language.

References

Sanjeev Arora, Yingyu Liang, and Tengyu Ma. 2017. A simple but tough-to-beat baseline for sentence embeddings.

Mikel Artetxe and Holger Schwenk. 2019. Massively multilingual sentence embeddings for zero-shot cross-lingual transfer and beyond. *Transactions of the Association for Computational Linguistics*, 7:597–610.

Piotr Bojanowski, Edouard Grave, Armand Joulin, and Tomas Mikolov. 2017. Enriching word vectors with subword information. *Transactions of the Association for Computational Linguistics*, 5:135–146.

Jiaao Chen, Zichao Yang, and Diyi Yang. 2020. Mixtext: Linguistically-informed interpolation of hidden space for semi-supervised text classification. *arXiv preprint arXiv:2004.12239*.

Alexis Conneau, Kartikay Khandelwal, Naman Goyal, Vishrav Chaudhary, Guillaume Wenzek, Francisco Guzmán, Edouard Grave, Myle Ott, Luke Zettlemoyer, and Veselin Stoyanov. 2019. Unsupervised cross-lingual representation learning at scale. *arXiv preprint arXiv:1911.02116*.

Alexis Conneau and Guillaume Lample. 2019. Cross-lingual language model pretraining. In *Advances in Neural Information Processing Systems*, pages 7059–7069.

Jacob Devlin, Ming-Wei Chang, Kenton Lee, and Kristina Toutanova. 2019. BERT: Pre-training of deep bidirectional transformers for language understanding. In *Proceedings of the 2019 Conference of the North American Chapter of the Association for Computational Linguistics: Human Language Technologies, Volume 1 (Long and Short Papers)*, pages 4171–4186, Minneapolis, Minnesota. Association for Computational Linguistics.

Thomas G. Dietterich. 1998. Approximate statistical tests for comparing supervised classification learning algorithms. *Neural Comput.*, 10(7):1895–1923.

Suchin Gururangan, Tam Dang, Dallas Card, and Noah A Smith. 2019. Variational pretraining for semi-supervised text classification. *arXiv preprint arXiv:1906.02242*.

Guy Hacohen and Daphna Weinshall. 2019. On the power of curriculum learning in training deep networks. *CoRR*, abs/1904.03626.

Giannis Karamanolakis, Daniel Hsu, and Luis Gravano. 2019. Leveraging just a few keywords for fine-grained aspect detection through weakly supervised co-training. *arXiv preprint arXiv:1909.00415*.

Diederik P Kingma and Jimmy Ba. 2014. Adam: A method for stochastic optimization. *arXiv preprint arXiv:1412.6980*.

Yinhan Liu, Myle Ott, Naman Goyal, Jingfei Du, Mandar Joshi, Danqi Chen, Omer Levy, Mike Lewis, Luke Zettlemoyer, and Veselin Stoyanov. 2019. Roberta: A robustly optimized bert pretraining approach. *arXiv preprint arXiv:1907.11692*.

Quinn McNemar. 1947. Note on the sampling error of the difference between correlated proportions or percentages. *Psychometrika*, 12(2):153–157.

Takeru Miyato, Andrew M Dai, and Ian Goodfellow. 2016. Adversarial training methods for semi-supervised text classification. *arXiv preprint arXiv:1605.07725*.

Telmo Pires, Eva Schlinger, and Dan Garrette. 2019. How multilingual is multilingual BERT? In *Proceedings of the 57th Annual Meeting of the Association for Computational Linguistics*, pages 4996–5001, Florence, Italy. Association for Computational Linguistics.

Alec Radford, Jeffrey Wu, Rewon Child, David Luan, Dario Amodei, and Ilya Sutskever. 2019. Language models are unsupervised multitask learners. *OpenAI blog*, 1(8):9.

Sebastian Raschka. 2018. Mlxtend: Providing machine learning and data science utilities and extensions to python's scientific computing stack. *Journal of Open Source Software*, 3(24):638.

Sebastian Ruder, Ivan Vulić, and Anders Søgaard. 2019. A survey of cross-lingual word embedding models. *Journal of Artificial Intelligence Research*, 65:569–631.

Ashutosh Sanzgiri, Daniel Austin, Kannan Sankaran, Ryan Woodard, Amit Lissack, and Sam Seljan. 2018. Classifying sensitive content in online advertisements with deep learning. In *2018 IEEE 5th International Conference on Data Science and Advanced Analytics (DSAA)*, pages 434–441. IEEE.

D Sculley, Matthew Eric Otey, Michael Pohl, Bridget Spitznagel, John Hainsworth, and Yunkai Zhou. 2011. Detecting adversarial advertisements in the wild. In *Proceedings of the 17th ACM SIGKDD international conference on Knowledge discovery and data mining*, pages 274–282.

Konstantinos Sechidis, Grigorios Tsoumakas, and Ioannis Vlahavas. 2011. On the stratification of multi-label data. *Machine Learning and Knowledge Discovery in Databases*, pages 145–158.

Dinghan Shen, Guoyin Wang, Wenlin Wang, Martin Renqiang Min, Qinliang Su, Yizhe Zhang, Chunyuan Li, Ricardo Henao, and Lawrence Carin. 2018. Baseline needs more love: On simple word-embedding-based models and associated pooling mechanisms. In *Proceedings of the 56th Annual Meeting of the Association for Computational Linguistics (Volume 1: Long Papers)*, pages 440–450, Melbourne, Australia. Association for Computational Linguistics.

Piotr Szymański and Tomasz Kajdanowicz. 2017. A network perspective on stratification of multi-label data. In *Proceedings of the First International Workshop on Learning with Imbalanced Domains: Theory and Applications*, volume 74 of *Proceedings of Machine Learning Research*, pages 22–35, ECML-PKDD, Skopje, Macedonia. PMLR.

Wikipedia contributors. 2004. Plagiarism — Wikipedia, the free encyclopedia. [Online; accessed Feb-2020].

I. Zeki Yalniz, Hervé Jégou, Kan Chen, Manohar Paluri, and Dhruv Mahajan. 2019. Billion-scale semi-supervised learning for image classification. *CoRR*, abs/1905.00546.

Zichao Yang, Zhiting Hu, Ruslan Salakhutdinov, and Taylor Berg-Kirkpatrick. 2017. Improved variational autoencoders for text modeling using dilated convolutions. *arXiv preprint arXiv:1702.08139*.

Combining Weakly Supervised ML Techniques for Low-Resource NLU

Victor Soto and **Konstantine Arkoudas**
Amazon Alexa AI
New York, NY, USA
{nvmartin, arkoudk}@amazon.com

Abstract

Recent advances in transfer learning have improved the performance of virtual assistants considerably. Nevertheless, creating sophisticated voice-enabled applications for new domains remains a challenge, and meager training data is often a key bottleneck. Accordingly, unsupervised learning and SSL (semi-supervised learning) techniques continue to be of vital importance. While a number of such methods have been explored previously in isolation, in this paper we investigate the synergistic use of a number of weakly supervised techniques with a view to improving NLU (Natural Language Understanding) accuracy in low-resource settings. We explore three different approaches incorporating anonymized, unlabeled and automatically transcribed user utterances into the training process, two focused on data augmentation via SSL and another one focused on unsupervised and transfer learning. We show promising results, obtaining gains that range from 4.73% to 7.65% relative improvements on semantic error rate for each individual approach. Moreover, the combination of all three methods together yields a relative improvement of 11.77% over our current baseline model. Our methods are applicable to any new domain with minimal training data, and can be deployed over time into a cycle of continual learning.

1 Introduction

Virtual assistants are becoming ubiquitous, their expansion fueled by third-party developers who build voice-enabled applications for an increasingly diverse array of domains. However, oftentimes these independent developers don't have the wherewithal to produce sufficient amounts of labeled data, and consequently their applications suffer from poor NLU performance. Large pre-trained language models have mitigated but not eliminated the need for domain-specific training data, and therefore unsupervised and SSL techniques continue to form an important direction of work in the field. While a number of such methods have been previously tried in isolation, in this paper we explore the synergistic use of a number of SSL techniques with a view to improving NLU accuracy in low resource settings, specifically for third-party (3P) applications. NLU in our setting is understood as the joint task of Intent Classification (IC) and Named Entity Recognition (NER).

Alexa is an AI virtual assistant developed by Amazon. By default, Alexa is enabled to work across many Amazon-built domains, including news, music, calendar, weather, etc. But Alexa also includes a third-party *skill toolkit*, which enables external developers to implement new voice-enabled functionality in the form of external skills, such as quiz and trivia games, food-ordering skills, voice interfaces to a host of devices ranging from vacuum cleaners to automobiles, and so on. Developers can build skills by creating skill definitions, consisting of carrier phrases annotated with intent labels and slot labels (a.k.a named entities). For example, for a pizza ordering skill, a developer could provide the following carrier phrase: *I would like a* **Size** *pizza with* **Topping** *and* **Topping**, with an intent such as **OrderPizza**. The values of the **Size** and **Topping** slots are specified in the form of catalogs:

$$\begin{aligned} \text{Catalog}(\textbf{Size}) &= \{large, medium, \ldots\} \\ \text{Catalog}(\textbf{Topping}) &= \{bacon, peppers, \ldots\} \end{aligned}$$

A full utterance can be realized from the carrier phrase and the slot catalogs, e.g., *I would like a medium pizza with peppers and bacon*. Every token in this utterance would be labeled with an **Other** slot, except for the tokens corresponding to the slots in the carrier phrase, which would be labeled as **Size**, **Topping** and **Topping** respectively.

In most cases, skill definitions only contain a few carrier phrases per intent, resulting in very small training datasets that lack linguistic diversity and

Proceedings of NAACL HLT 2021: IndustryTrack Papers, pages 288–295
June 6–11, 2021.

do not always resemble user queries. The main goal of this paper is to improve NLU model performance by incorporating unlabeled, anonymized and automatically transcribed user utterances from skills into the training pipeline, without human intervention or annotators. We explored three different methods: 1) Data augmentation via maximal FST-matching; 2) Data augmentation via tri-training ensembles; and 3) Injecting auto-encoder sentence embeddings into our baseline DNN (Deep Neural Network) model architecture.

The first two techniques automatically obtain labels for live user utterances, which are then used to augment the baseline training data. The third technique performs unsupervised pre-training of an auto-encoder (AE) on user traffic, and this AE is then used to inject sentence embeddings into our models as additional signals. The NLU task we focus on in this paper is the joint task of Intent Classification (IC) and Named Entity Recognition (NER), also referred to as Slot Labeling.

The rest of this paper is organized as follows: Section 2 gives an overview of data augmentation for NLU skills; Section 3 introduces the three methods; Section 4 details our experimental design; Section 5 summarizes the results for all skills, including cumulative results for the three methods. Finally, Section 6 presents our conclusions.

2 Related Work

Learning strategies focused on addressing the scarcity of labeled data within a specific domain can be grouped into two approaches: one focused on leveraging models and resources from other domains for which there is a wealth of resources; and approaches that aim to leverage unannotated data for the target domain.

In the first group, **Transfer Learning** strategies (McCann et al., 2017; Peters et al., 2018) focus on pre-training unsupervised models on large amounts of unlabeled data and then fine-tuning that model on a small quantity of labeled data. The most recent successful example of transfer learning are BERT models (Devlin et al., 2019), where a large transformer language model is pre-trained on either the task of masked language modeling or next sentence prediction, and whose encoder can be later fine-tuned as a feature extractor on other NLU tasks (Peshterliev et al., 2019).

In the second group, **Active Learning** algorithms use individual classifiers or ensembles of classifiers to select data points for human annotation based on different criteria: Least-confidence for examples that are assigned low confidence scores by the classifiers (Lewis and Catlett, 1994), query-by-committee for examples that are assigned a diverse set of labels by the individual classifiers in the ensemble (Freund et al., 1997), or, more recently, a Majority-CRF that relies on majority voting from an ensemble of binary classifiers (Peshterliev et al., 2019) to select data for new NLU domains. Similarly, **Semi-Supervised Learning** (SSL) (Chapelle et al., 2009) algorithms aim to use models trained on small amounts of annotated data to assign soft labels to unseen examples which can later be incorporated into the training set. Self-training (Scudder, 1965; Yarowsky, 1995; Lee, 2013) does this by using the same classifier or a teacher-student pair of classifiers to select and annotate data, whereas tri-training (Zhou and Li, 2005) creates an ensemble of three diverse classifiers that augments unlabeled datasets during an iterative process based on classifier agreement.

In this paper, we use (a) transfer learning to pre-train an auto-encoder that is later used to inject sentence embeddings into our IC-NER models (Section 3.2) and (b) SSL to augment data with IC-NER annotations obtained by maximal FST-matching and tri-training ensembles (Sections 3.1 and 3.3 respectively). On the topic of data augmentation via partial parses, similar to our maximal FST-matching approach, (Kim et al., 2015) proposes to extract slot tagging annotations from web logs using a weakly supervised approach based on Conditional Random Fields; and in (Augenstein et al., 2016) the authors use regular expressions to augment training data for the task of Stance Detection. More recently, (Karamanolakis et al., 2021) has proposed a semi-supervised framework to leverage unlabelled data and weak classification rules for improved text classification.

3 Methods

3.1 Maximal FST-Matching

The carrier phrases given by a developer are arranged into a finite-state transducer (FST), which can take an arbitrary utterance u and either (a) accept it, if u is an instance of a carrier phrase, while emitting the corresponding slot labeling and intent as its output; or (b) reject it, if u is not an exact match for any of the given carrier phrases. This FST is then sampled to generate the training data for the DNN. Depending on the number and linguistic diversity of the carrier phrases, the resulting training set can range from complete enough for a good NLU model (given smart use of transfer learning and model adaptation techniques) to severely underspecified.

With the SSL method described in this section, which we call *maximal FST matching*, we aim to augment the training set with automatically transcribed user utterances that are close in form and meaning to the ones provided by the skill developers, and which inject greater language diversity into the training. Specifically, while only a minority of user utterances are perfect FST matches (i.e., completely match developer-provided carrier phrases), many more of them are *partial* or imperfect matches. The intuition here is to compute the maximal part of a user utterance that matches a carrier phrase and then superimpose the semantics (intent and NER labeling) of that matched carrier phrase to the entire utterance. To take a simple example, the utterance *Hi, I would like a large pizza with peppers and mushrooms please* does not match the earlier carrier phrase *I would like a* **Size** *pizza with* **Topping** *and* **Topping**, due to the initial *Hi* and the trailing *please*. However, it is a partial match, since there is an internal segment of the utterance that is a perfect instance of the carrier phrase. Thus, the entire utterance can receive the intent and NER labeling of the internal segment (with tokens outside of the matching segment receiving the label **Other**) and become part of the training data.

We use a greedy approach to extract maximal internal FST matches from a user utterance: we first run the full span of the utterance through the FST, then every sub-utterance of length $n-1$, and so on down to length 1. The FST matching is stopped as soon as a match is found, at which point the intent and slot labels output from the FST are transferred to the full utterance as described above.

For each extracted match, we compute its span ratio, which is the fraction of the length of the FST-matched sub-utterance over the length of the full utterance. We treat this ratio as a tunable hyperparameter. In Section 5.1 we perform data augmentation by only keeping maximally FST-matched utterances whose span ratio exceeds a certain threshold, both globally and on a skill-specific basis.

Maximal FST-matching can introduce mislabeled utterances in several ways: a) it can ignore important semantic information if this is outside of the scope of the FST match (e.g. "(Do not) include pepperoni in the pizza."), which can potentially change the intent of the utterance (in our example, from ExcludeTopping to AddTopping); and b) it can miss slot entities that fall out of the scope of the match (e.g. "Add pepperoni (and green peppers)"). Both risks can be mitigated by filtering out utterances with low match span ratios.

This method has important advantages. It is easy to productize, since changes made to the NLU skill and its carrier phrases can be accommodated by rerunning the new FST on the already matched FST utterances, which is relatively inexpensive; and the resulting augmented training set will better reflect the true distribution of live user traffic.

3.2 Sentence Embeddings via Seq2Seq Auto-Encoder

Our baseline NLU model consists of a shared component that is pre-trained on the MLM task on Alexa traffic and other large NLP corpora, and a specific component that jointly models IC and NER, trained from scratch for every skill separately. We add to this architecture a component that is pre-trained on large amounts of automatically-transcribed traffic and optionally fine-tuned.

In particular, we experiment with seq-2-seq auto-encoder (s2s-AE) architectures. We pre-train several s2s-AE models with different features and data sources to obtain an encoder, and we plug the encoder's output into the baseline NLU model as a new component. The impact of this new feature on NLU performance (measured on a test set of 86 skills) is detailed in Section 5.2.

3.3 Tri-training

In an effort to obtain more realistic training data, we use SSL to compute high-quality labels for automatically-transcribed live user traffic. Specifically, we build a series of tri-training ensembles that we use to annotate live utterances. We show that by adding this newly annotated data to our regular training data, our baseline NLU models attain very significant improvements on SemER (Semantic Error Rate).

Tri-training (Zhou and Li, 2005) is a SSL technique that relies on three independently trained classifiers. It fine-tunes the three models by pulling examples from a pool of unlabeled data. On each iteration of the algorithm, if a pair of classifiers agree on an unlabeled example, that example is

Algorithm 1 Generalized Tri-Training

```
L = grammar utterances
U = live utterances
Train M1, M2 on L
while not criterion do
    U12 = Utts in U that M1 & M2 agree on
    M3 = Train(L + U12)
    U13 = Utts in U that M1 & M3 agree on.
    M2 = Train(L + U13)
    U23 = Utts in U that M2 & M3 agree on.
    M1 = Train(L + U23)
end while
Obtain labelled examples from U for examples
  that M1, M2 and M3 agree on.
```

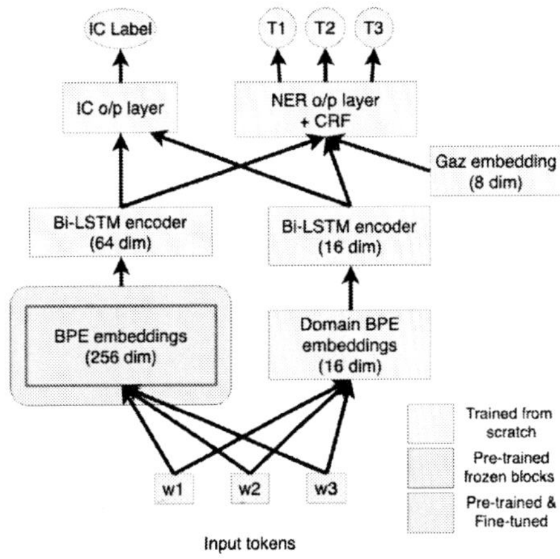

Figure 1: The Baseline NLU model.

then labeled and added to the training set of the third classifier. Algorithm 1 shows an implementation of the Generalized Tri-Training algorithm (Søgaard and Rishøj, 2010), that we also expanded to an arbitrary number of a classifiers.

Section 5.3 discusses our tri-training experiments.

4 Experiment Design

We compare our methods against our production 3P DNN model, which is depicted in Figure 1. It consists of a pre-trained shared component and a skill-specific component. The shared component is pre-trained on Alexa unsupervised traffic and external NLP corpora and computes BPE embeddings. The specific component consists of a large Bi-LSTM encoder whose input is the shared embeddings and a small BPE embedding followed by a short Bi-LSTM encoder. The IC layer output takes the summary vectors from both encoders and outputs an IC prediction. The NER layer takes as input a sequence of vectors, where each vector is composed of the concatenation of the two encoder representations and the gazetteer feature of each token. Gazetteer features are mappings from sequences of strings to Named Entities, e.g., the sequence *The Beatles* would be mapped to *Artist_Name*. This model is referred to as Base in what follows.

This study was carried out on 86 English skills from the top 100 Alexa skills with the highest amount of user traffic. Baseline training datasets for 3P skills consist of ten thousand carrier phrases sampled with repetition. For the 26 skills that include an out-of-domain (OOD) intent in their skill definition, we sample the training sets to contain 50% of OOD intent examples. For the 86 skills included in this study, the average number of unique carrier phrases in a baseline dataset for a skill is 3,302. Our test sets for every skill are comprised of live user traffic annotated in-house with Intent and Slot labels. On average, the number of utterances in a skill test set is 816, with 425 of those being unique.

5 Results

We use two different metrics, SemER (Semantic Error Rate) and IRER (Interpretation Recognition Error Rate) (Su et al., 2018). SemER combines intent and slot classification accuracy into a single score. It computes a modified edit distance that takes into account the number of substitutions (S), incorrect predictions (I), and deletions (D) in the sequence of slots, and the intent prediction. For a sequence of L tokens, SemER is defined as (S + I + D) / (L + 1). The IRER of a single utterance is 1 if all the slots and intent are correctly recognized, and 0 otherwise. The IRER of a dataset is the fraction of utterances whose IRER is 1.

5.1 Data Augmentation via Maximal FST-Matching

We collected a dataset of live automatically-transcribed user traffic spanning four months across 86 skills, and split it in two: we use one set for selecting a Maximal Span Ratio (MSR) threshold, and the second one for testing the MSR threshold selection (and vice versa). All live user traffic used in this study was de-identified. When using a global threshold across all 86 skills, the best global threshold is 0.8. Under this scheme, a newly labeled live utterance is retained only if its maximal FST match spans at least 80% of the utterance. Using this policy, the relative improvement on SEMER with respect to our baseline DNN model (i.e., the SEMER improvement that we obtain by adding those utterances to our training data) is 1.14%.

When performing skill-specific thresholding (by using part of the skill's test data as a dev set for selecting a threshold, and the rest of the test set to compute metrics), we obtained a 10.14% relative improvement on SEMER and 6.2% improvement on IRER with respect to our baseline DNN. Another set of experiments where MSR threshold selection was performed on two months of data and tested on five months of data obtained relative improvements on SEMER and IRER of 5.01% and 1.44% respectively.

5.2 Sentence Embedding Injection

We collected automatically transcribed live traffic from the last six months of 2019. After deduping the utterances, we split them into an unsupervised training set of 60K hours of speech, and validation and test sets of 1.6K hours each.

We trained and evaluated s2s-AE models with different architectural features, as in LSTM and Transformer layers for their encoder or decoder, encoder and decoder depth (2 or 3 hidden layers), number of hidden units per layer (256, 512, or 1,024 units per layer), number of epochs for training, vocabulary token types (words or BPE), vocabulary size (20k or 50K) and size of training set (16.6K, 33K and 60K hours of transcribed speech). The best performing model, measured both on validation perplexity and on SEMER on an annotated test set that spanned September to December 2019, was a s2s-AE model with two transformer layers on both encoder and decoder, 512 units per layer, trained on 60K hours of automatically transcribed speech using a BPE vocabulary of 50k tokens.

The s2s-AE is hooked into our baseline NLU model by discarding the decoder and passing the latent code (sentence embedding) into the Intent Classification (IC) block; and by passing the sequence of hidden states into the Named Entity Recognition (NER) block. A block diagram for the resulting NLU model can be seen in Figure 2. Injecting the s2s-AE into the baseline model without any skill-specific fine-tuning yields SEMER relative improvements of 1.53% on our seven month anno-

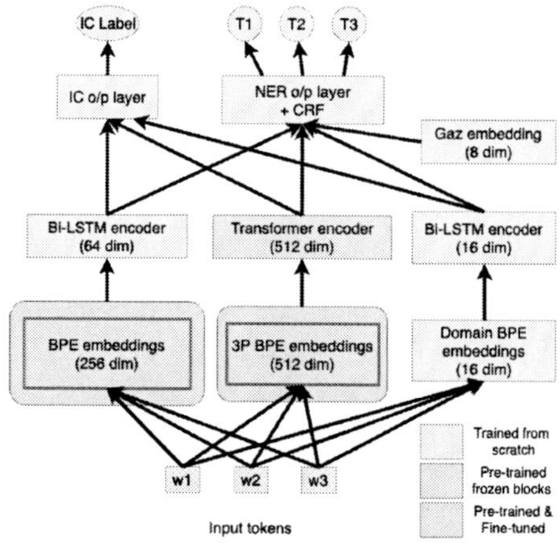

Figure 2: A Baseline 3P NLU model with a Sentence Embedding from the s2q-AE.

tated test set. Using an additional annotated test set that spanned September to December 2019, and by trying several learning rate multipliers (LRMs) for our seq2seq encoder, we found the overall best LRM was 0.0 (no fine-tuning), followed by 0.1 (which caused a -0.31% relative regression on SEMER). This indicates that for fine-tuning to work, it needs to be done in a skill-specific fashion.

Following the same steps for skill-specific fine-tuning as for maximal FST-matching and for the MSR threshold parameter, we use one annotated dataset from September to December 2019 for LRM selection and an annotated test set that spans January to July 2020 for evaluation. We choose the best LRM for each of the 86 skills on the first dataset, obtain SEMER values on the second one, and average them, observing a 4.73% relative improvement.

5.3 Data Augmentation via Tri-training Ensembles

We start by training a tri-training ensemble of three identical NLU models with different seeds to diversify the initial training/validation sets and the training algorithm. The tri-training stopping criterion was set to either reaching an average SEMER on the validation sets of 0.0 or run for a maximum of three iterations. Upon finishing, we obtained live utterances labeled with high-precision labels. These are utterances that all three models had complete agreement on IC and NER annotations (not majority vote agreement). On average, each skill had their training set size increased by 138.54%, ranging from 7.11% to 1089.57%.

We trained NLU models on new training sets formed by the baseline 10k training utterances and up to another 10k utterances from the live utterances with high-precision labels. The average training set went up to 16K utterances per skill and the average SEMER was improved with a 2.56% relative improvement. Without capping the amount of live data added to the training set, the SEMER is further improved with a 2.91% relative improvement on SEMER, and a 4.45% relative improvement on IRER. Despite the good initial results, 28 skills suffered SEMER degradation.

The second ensemble we tried consists of a baseline NLU model, the NLU model with an additional encoder pre-trained as an auto-encoder model on live utterances from Section 5.2, and an NLU BERT-based model. We use the same stopping criterion. By the end of tri-training, we obtained high-quality labels that increased the domain training sets for an average of 99.15% per skill.

Again, we trained NLU models without a maximum training size, with a validation set of 10% of these utterances. This time we obtained a relative improvement of 7.65% on SEMER. The IRER relative improvement is 9.67%. A total of 18 skills suffered SEMER degradation with this ensemble.

We used our trained tri-ensemble to infer high-precision labels on the test set and measure how accurate the high-precision labels really are. Using a setting where an utterance is only retrieved with complete agreement in the ensemble, the average coverage was 63.88%.

Tri-training theory assumes that the ensemble classifiers are independently trained. Here we explore the addition of an altogether different type of classifier to our collections of neural classifiers, namely SVMs for IC and NER. Both use BPE word embeddings as features. For IC, we extract the BPE embeddings and concatenate the max, min, sum and mean vector of the embedding sequence for a total of 1024 dimensions. For NER, we map every word to the sum of its BPE embeddings. Both models use linear kernels, since the size of our datasets and the need to perform grid search make non-linear kernels impractical.

We built a 4-classifier ensemble by adding the SVM classifiers to the previous ensemble composed of a NLU model, a NLU model with an additional encoder pre-trained as an auto-encoder model on live utterances, and an NLU BERT-based model. In this occasion the addition of the SVM model causes the test coverage ratio to be greatly reduced to 55%.Furthermore, the NLU DNN model trained on the additional data labeled by this ensemble achieves 7.27% and 8.32% relative improvements on SEMER and IRER, which is small reduction from the previous best ensemble.

Model	SEMER Δ%	IRER Δ%
+M-FST	5.01	1.44
+Tri	7.65	9.67
+M-FST&Tri	10.54	11.49

Table 1: NLU Performance for Base Model with three Data Augmentation options. Relative improvement values are computed with respect to the Base Model without data augmentation.

5.4 Cumulative Experiments

In this section we present some cumulative results obtained by applying combinations of the three techniques. We start by analyzing the performance of our baseline NLU model (Base) by itself; b) after adding fine-tuned maximally FST-matched data (FT-FST); c) after adding SSL data from tri-training (Tri); and d) after adding both FST-matched data and tri-training data (Table 1). Fine-tuned FST-matched data yields relative improvements of 5.01% and 1.44% on SEMER and IRER respectively, tri-training data yields 7.65% and 9.67% relative improvements on SEMER and IRER, and both combined deliver 10.54% and 11.49% relative improvements.

Next, we analyze the performance of the NLU model that incorporates a sentence embedding from an auto-encoder fine-tuned specifically for every skill (Base+SE). By adding fine-tuned maximally FST-matched data, SEMER and IRER improve by 8.23% and 7.73%, respectively. Adding tri-training data yields 8.33% and 10.81% relative improvements on SEMER and IRER, respectively, while both combined deliver relative improvements of 11.77% and 12.94% on SEMER and IRER. All these relative improvements are with respect to the baseline NLU model (without data augmentation). See Table 2.

6 Conclusions

We presented three different approaches to improving NLU performance for skills that have limited amounts of annotated data. The two data augmentation approaches, based on maximal fst-matching and tri-training ensembles, yield considerable relative improvements of 5.01 and 7.65%. A third

Model	SEMER Δ%	IRER Δ%
Base+SE	4.73	4.51
+M-FST	8.23	7.73
+Tri	8.33	10.81
+M-FST&Tri	11.77	12.94

Table 2: NLU Performance for Base+SE Model with three Data Augmentation options. Relative improvement values are computed with respect to the Base Model performance.

approach, based on injecting sentence embeddings obtained from an auto-encoder pre-trained on live traffic, gave 4.73%. The combination of the three techniques attained a total relative improvement of 11.77%. Overall, adding these three methods into our pipeline improves NLU performance, leverages automatically transcribed user traffic for all skills, lessens the need for developers to provide annotated data, and eliminates the need for internal human-based annotations for training better models.

Acknowledgments

The authors are thankful to Saleh Soltan and the rest of the DeepNLU team for some of the pretrained models and components that have been used in this study, and to Lisheng Fu, Matthew Trager and Sandesh Swamy for their assistance.

References

Isabelle Augenstein, Tim Rocktäschel, Andreas Vlachos, and Kalina Bontcheva. 2016. Stance detection with bidirectional conditional encoding. In *Proceedings of the 2016 Conference on Empirical Methods in Natural Language Processing*, pages 876–885, Austin, Texas. Association for Computational Linguistics.

Olivier Chapelle, Bernhard Scholkopf, and Alexander Zien. 2009. Semi-supervised learning. *IEEE Transactions on Neural Networks*, 20(3):542–542.

Jacob Devlin, Ming-Wei Chang, Kenton Lee, and Kristina Toutanova. 2019. BERT: Pre-training of deep bidirectional transformers for language understanding. In *Proceedings of the 2019 Conference of the North American Chapter of the Association for Computational Linguistics: Human Language Technologies, Volume 1 (Long and Short Papers)*, pages 4171–4186, Minneapolis, Minnesota. Association for Computational Linguistics.

Yoav Freund, H Sebastian Seung, Eli Shamir, and Naftali Tishby. 1997. Selective sampling using the query by committee algorithm. *Machine learning*, 28(2-3):133–168.

Giannis Karamanolakis, Subhabrata (Subho) Mukherjee, Guoqing Zheng, and Ahmed H. Awadallah. 2021. Self-training with weak supervision. In *NAACL 2021*. NAACL 2021.

Young-Bum Kim, Minwoo Jeong, Karl Stratos, and Ruhi Sarikaya. 2015. Weakly supervised slot tagging with partially labeled sequences from web search click logs. In *Proceedings of the 2015 Conference of the North American Chapter of the Association for Computational Linguistics: Human Language Technologies*, pages 84–92.

Dong-Hyun Lee. 2013. Pseudo-label: The simple and efficient semi-supervised learning method for deep neural networks. In *Workshop on challenges in representation learning, ICML*.

David D Lewis and Jason Catlett. 1994. Heterogeneous uncertainty sampling for supervised learning. In *Machine learning proceedings 1994*, pages 148–156. Elsevier.

Bryan McCann, James Bradbury, Caiming Xiong, and Richard Socher. 2017. Learned in translation: Contextualized word vectors. In *Advances in neural information processing systems*, pages 6294–6305.

Stanislav Peshterliev, John Kearney, Abhyuday Jagannatha, Imre Kiss, and Spyros Matsoukas. 2019. Active learning for new domains in natural language understanding. In *Proceedings of the 2019 Conference of the North American Chapter of the Association for Computational Linguistics: Human Language Technologies, Volume 2 (Industry Papers)*, pages 90–96, Minneapolis, Minnesota. Association for Computational Linguistics.

Matthew Peters, Mark Neumann, Mohit Iyyer, Matt Gardner, Christopher Clark, Kenton Lee, and Luke Zettlemoyer. 2018. Deep contextualized word representations. In *Proceedings of the 2018 Conference of the North American Chapter of the Association for Computational Linguistics: Human Language Technologies, Volume 1 (Long Papers)*, pages 2227–2237, New Orleans, Louisiana. Association for Computational Linguistics.

H Scudder. 1965. Probability of error of some adaptive pattern-recognition machines. *IEEE Transactions on Information Theory*, 11(3):363–371.

Anders Søgaard and Christian Rishøj. 2010. Semi-supervised dependency parsing using generalized tri-training. In *Proceedings of the 23rd International Conference on Computational Linguistics (Coling 2010)*, pages 1065–1073, Beijing, China. Coling 2010 Organizing Committee.

C. Su, R. Gupta, S. Ananthakrishnan, and S. Matsoukas. 2018. A re-ranker scheme for integrating large scale nlu models. In *2018 IEEE Spoken Language Technology Workshop (SLT)*, pages 670–676.

David Yarowsky. 1995. Unsupervised word sense disambiguation rivaling supervised methods. In *33rd Annual Meeting of the Association for Computational Linguistics*, pages 189–196, Cambridge, Massachusetts, USA. Association for Computational Linguistics.

Zhi-Hua Zhou and Ming Li. 2005. Tri-training: Exploiting unlabeled data using three classifiers. *IEEE Trans. on Knowl. and Data Eng.*, 17(11):1529–1541.

Label-Guided Learning for Item Categorization in E-commerce

Lei Chen
Rakuten Institute of Technology
Boston, MA
lei.a.chen@rakuten.com

Hirokazu Miyake
Rakuten Institute of Technology
Boston, MA
hirokazu.miyake@rakuten.com

Abstract

Item categorization is an important application of text classification in e-commerce due to its impact on the online shopping experience of users. One class of text classification techniques that has gained attention recently is using the semantic information of the labels to guide the classification task. We have conducted a systematic investigation of the potential benefits of these methods on a real data set from Rakuten, a major e-commerce company in Japan. We found that using pre-trained word embeddings specialized to specific categories of items performed better than one obtained from all available categories despite the reduction in data set size. Furthermore, using a hyperbolic space to embed product labels that are organized in a hierarchical structure led to better performance compared to using a conventional Euclidean space embedding. These findings demonstrate how label-guided learning can improve item categorization systems in the e-commerce domain.

1 Introduction

Natural language processing (NLP) techniques have been applied extensively to solve modern e-commerce challenges (Malmasi et al., 2020; Zhao et al., 2020). One major NLP challenge in e-commerce is *item categorization* (IC) which refers to classifying a product based on textual information, typically the product title, into one of numerous categories in the product category taxonomy tree of online stores. Although significant progress has been made in the area of text classification, many standard open-source data sets have limited numbers of classes which are not representative of data in industry where there can be hundreds or even thousands of classes (Li and Roth, 2002; Pang and Lee, 2004; Socher et al., 2013)To cope with the large number of products and the complexity of the category taxonomy, an automated IC system is needed and its prediction quality needs to be high enough to provide positive shopping experiences for customers and consequently drive sales. Figure 1 shows an example diagram of the product category taxonomy tree for the IC task. In this example, a tin of Japanese tea [1] needs to be classified into the leaf level category label "Japanese tea."

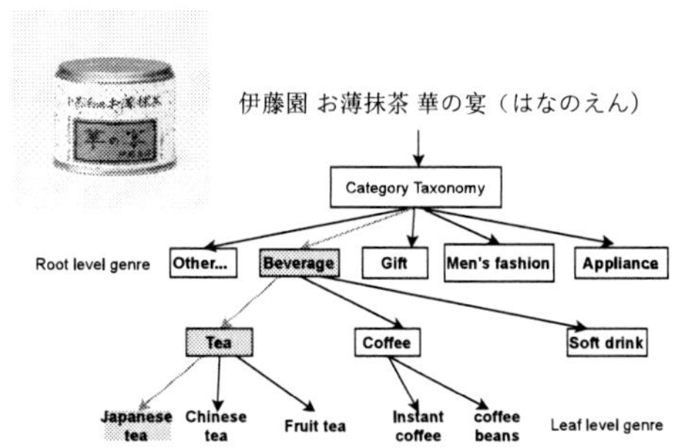

Figure 1: Subset of the product taxonomy tree for item categorization.

As reviewed in Section 2, significant progress has been made on IC as a deep learning text classification task. However, much of the progress in text classification does not make use of the semantic information contained in the labels. Recently there have been increasing interest in taking advantage of the semantic information in the labels to improve text classification performance (Wang et al., 2018; Liu et al., 2020; Du et al., 2019; Xiao et al., 2019; Chai et al., 2020). For the IC task, labels in a product taxonomy tree are actively maintained by human experts and these labels bring rich semantic information. For example, descriptive genre information like "clothes" and "electronics" are used rather than just using a numeric index for the class labels. It is reasonable to surmise that leveraging the semantics of these category labels will improve the IC models.

Although label-guided learning has been shown

[1] Image from https://item.rakuten.co.jp/kusurinokiyoshi/10016272/

Proceedings of NAACL HLT 2021: IndustryTrack Papers, pages 296–303
June 6–11, 2021. ©2021 Association for Computational Linguistics

to improve classification performance on several standard text classification data sets, its application to IC on real industry data has been missing thus far. Compared to standard data sets, e-commerce data typically contain more complicated label taxonomy tree structures, and product titles tend to be short and do not use standard grammar. Therefore, whether label-guided learning can help IC in industry or not is an open question worth investigating.

In this paper, we describe our investigation of applying label-guided learning to the IC task. Using real data from Rakuten[2], we tested two models: Label Embedding Attentive Model (LEAM) (Wang et al., 2018) and Label-Specific Attention Network (LSAN) (Xiao et al., 2019). In addition, to cope with the challenge that labels in an IC task tend to be similar to each other within one product genre, we utilized label embedding methods that can better distinguish labels which led to performance gains. This included testing the use of hyperbolic embeddings which can take into account the hierarchical nature of the taxonomy tree (Nickel and Kiela, 2017).

The paper is organized as follows: Section 2 reviews related research on IC using deep learning-based NLP and the emerging techniques of label-guided learning. Section 3 introduces the two label-guided learning models we examined, namely LEAM and LSAN, as well as hyperbolic embedding. Section 4 describes experimental results on a large-scale data set from a major e-commerce company in Japan. Section 5 summarizes our findings and discusses future research directions.

2 Related works

Deep learning-based methods have been widely used for the IC task. This includes the use of deep neural network models for item categorization in a hierarchical classifier structure which showed improved performance over conventional machine learning models (Cevahir and Murakami, 2016), as well as the use of an attention mechanism to identify words that are semantically highly correlated with the predicted categories and therefore can provide improved feature representations for a higher classification performance (Xia et al., 2017).

Recently, using semantic information carried by label names has received increasing attention in text classification research, and LEAM (Wang et al., 2018) is one of the earliest efforts in this direction that we are aware of. It uses a joint embedding of both words and class labels to obtain label-specific attention weights to modify the input features. On a set of benchmark text classification data sets, LEAM showed superior performance over models that did not use label semantics. An extension of LEAM called LguidedLearn (Liu et al., 2020) made further modifications by (a) encoding word inputs first and then using the encoded outputs to compute label attention weights, and (b) using a multi-head attention mechanism (Vaswani et al., 2017) to make the attention-weighting mechanism have more representational power. In a related model, LSAN (Xiao et al., 2019) added a label-specific attention branch in addition to a self-attention branch and showed superior performance over models that did not use label semantics on a set of multi-label text classification tasks.

Alternatively, label names by themselves may not provide sufficient semantic information for accurate text classification. To address this potential shortcoming, longer text can be generated based on class labels to augment the original text input. Text generation methods such as using templates and reinforcement learning were compared, and their effectiveness were evaluated using the BERT model (Devlin et al., 2019) with both text sentence and label description as the input (Chai et al., 2020).

Finally, word embeddings such as word2vec (Mikolov et al., 2013) and GloVe (Pennington et al., 2014) are generated in Euclidean space. However, embeddings in non-Euclidean space called hyperbolic embeddings have been developed (Nickel and Kiela, 2017; Chen et al., 2020a,b) and have been shown to better represent the hierarchical relationship among labels.

3 Model

For a product title $\mathcal{X}$ consisting of L words $\mathcal{X} = [w_1, \ldots, w_L]$, our goal is to predict one out of a set of K labels, $y \in \mathcal{C} = \{c_1, \ldots, c_K\}$. In a neural network-based model, the mapping $\mathcal{X} \to y$ generally consists of the following steps: (a) *encoding step* (f_0), converting $\mathcal{X}$ into a numeric tensor representing the input, (b) *representation step* (f_1), processing the input tensor to be a fixed-dimension feature vector $\mathbf{z}$, and (c) *classification step* (f_2), mapping $\mathbf{z}$ to y using a feed-forward layer.

Among label-guided learning models, we chose both LEAM (Wang et al., 2018) and LSAN (Xiao

[2]https://www.rakuten.co.jp

Step	LEAM	LSAN
f_0	Word embedding	Word embedding + Bi-LSTM encoding
f_1	Only label-specific attention	Both self- and label-specific attentions + adaptive interpolation
f_2	Softmax with CE loss	Softmax with CE loss

Table 1: Comparison of LEAM (Wang et al., 2018) and LSAN (Xiao et al., 2019) with respect to the three modeling steps.

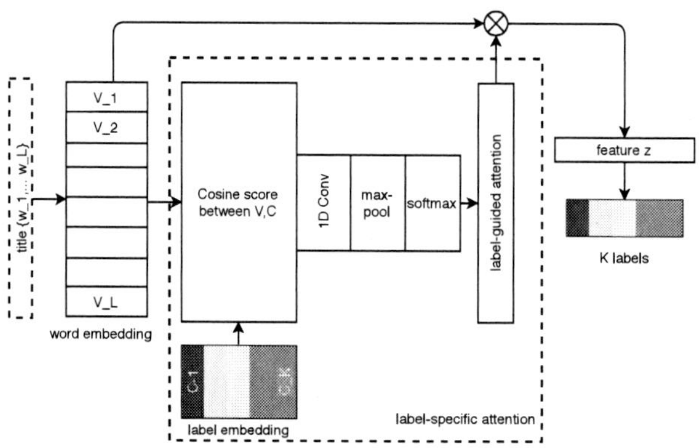

Figure 2: Architecture of LEAM (Wang et al., 2018).

et al., 2019) for our experiments. Table 1 shows a comparison between these models.

3.1 LEAM

The LEAM architecture is shown in Figure 2 (Wang et al., 2018). First a product title of length L is encoded as $V = [v_1, \ldots, v_L]$ where $v_l \in \mathbb{R}^D$ is determined through word embedding and $V \in \mathbb{R}^{D \times L}$. The class labels are also encoded via label embedding as $C = [c_1, ..., c_K]$ where K is the total number of labels, $c_k \in \mathbb{R}^D$ and $C \in \mathbb{R}^{D \times K}$. The label embeddings are title-independent and is the same across all titles for a given set of labels. We can then compute the compatibility of each word-label pair based on their cosine similarity to obtain a compatibility tensor $G \in \mathbb{R}^{L \times K}$.

The compatibility tensor is transformed into an attention vector through the following steps, (a) apply a 1D convolution to refine the compatibility scores by considering its context, (b) apply max pooling to keep the maximum score, and (c) apply a softmax operation to obtain the label-guided attention weights β. These attention weights containing the label semantic information are used in the f_1 step to compute a new representation,

$$z = \sum_l \beta_l v_l. \tag{1}$$

After obtaining z, we use a fully-connected layer with softmax to predict $y \in \mathcal{C}$. The entire process $f_2(f_1(f_0(\mathcal{X})))$ is optimized by minimizing the cross-entropy loss between y and $f_2(z)$.

3.2 LSAN

The LSAN architecture is shown in Figure 3 (Xiao et al., 2019). As shown in Table 1, LSAN has a few modifications compared to LEAM. First, a bi-directional long short-term memory (Bi-LSTM) encoder is used to better capture context semantic cues in the representation. The resulting concatenated tensor is $H = [\overrightarrow{H}, \overleftarrow{H}]$ where $\overrightarrow{H}$ and $\overleftarrow{H}$ represent LSTM encoding outputs from forward and backward directions and $H \in \mathbb{R}^{L \times 2P}$ where P is the dimension of the LSTM hidden state. For model consistency we typically set $P = D$.

Additional features of LSAN which extend LEAM include (a) using self-attention on the encoding H, (b) creating a label-attention component from H and C, and (c) adaptively merging the self- and label-attention components.

More specifically, the self-attention score $A^{(s)}$ is determined as

$$A^{(s)} = \text{softmax}(W_2 \tanh(W_1 H^T)), \tag{2}$$

where $W_1 \in \mathbb{R}^{d_a \times 2P}$ and $W_2 \in \mathbb{R}^{K \times d_a}$ are self-attention tensors to be trained, d_a is a hyperparameter, $A^{(s)} \in \mathbb{R}^{K \times L}$ and each row $A_{j\cdot}^{(s)}$ is an L-dimensional vector representing the contributions

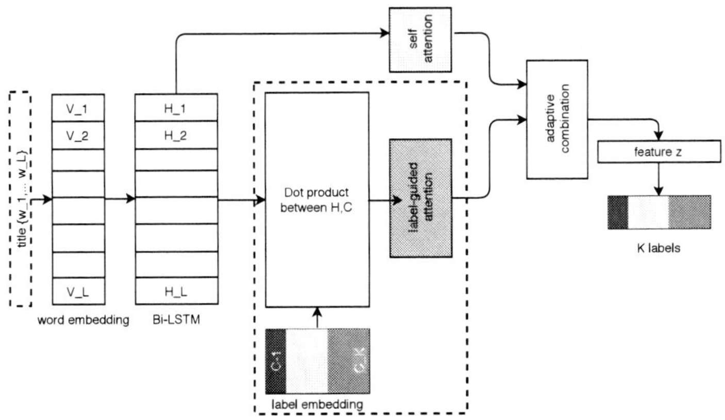

Figure 3: Architecture of LSAN (Xiao et al., 2019).

of all L words to label j. Therefore,

$$M^{(s)} = A^{(s)}H \tag{3}$$

is a representation of the input text weighted by self-attention where $M^{(s)} \in \mathbb{R}^{K\times 2P}$.

From the title encoding H and the label embedding C, compatibility scores between class labels and title words can be computed as the product

$$\overleftarrow{A^{(l)}} = C^T\overleftarrow{H}^T \tag{4}$$

$$\overrightarrow{A^{(l)}} = C^T\overrightarrow{H}^T, \tag{5}$$

where $A^{(l)} \in \mathbb{R}^{K\times L}$ and each row $A^{(l)}_{j\cdot}$ is a L-dimensional vector representing the contributions of all L words to label j. The product title can be represented using label attention as

$$M^{(l)} = [\overleftarrow{A^{(l)}}\overleftarrow{H}, \overrightarrow{A^{(l)}}\overrightarrow{H}] \tag{6}$$

where $M^{(l)} \in \mathbb{R}^{K\times 2P}$.

The last procedure in the f_1 step of LSAN is to adaptively combine the self- and label-attention representations $M^{(s)}$ and $M^{(l)}$ as

$$M_{j\cdot} = \alpha_j M^{(s)}_{j\cdot} + \beta_j M^{(l)}_{j\cdot}, \tag{7}$$

where the two interpolation weight factors ($\alpha, \beta \in \mathbb{R}^K$) are computed as

$$\alpha = \sigma(M^{(s)}W_3) \tag{8}$$

$$\beta = \sigma(M^{(l)}W_4), \tag{9}$$

with the constraint $\alpha_j + \beta_j = 1$, $W_3, W_4 \in \mathbb{R}^{2P}$ are trainable parameters, $\sigma(x) \equiv 1/(1+e^{-x})$ is the element-wise sigmoid function, and $M \in \mathbb{R}^{K\times 2P}$.

Although the original LSAN model proposed multiple additional layers in its f_2 step, in our implementation we performed average pooling along the label dimension and then to a fully-connected layer with softmax output, similar to LEAM. Finally, the cross entropy loss is minimized.

3.3 Hyperbolic Embedding

In e-commerce item categorization we tend to use a more complicated label structure with a large number of labels organized as a taxonomy tree compared to standard text classification data sets. One immediate issue is that hundreds of labels can exist at the leaf level, some with very similar labels like "Japanese tea" and "Chinese tea," and the difference in label embedding vectors in Euclidean space can be too small to be distinguished by machine learning models. Such issues become more severe with increasing taxonomy tree depth as well. Hyperbolic embedding is one technique that has been developed which can address these issues (Nickel and Kiela, 2017; Chen et al., 2020a,b).

Hyperbolic space is different from Euclidean space by having a negative curvature. Consequently, given a circle, its circumference and disc area grow exponentially with radius. In contrast, in Euclidean space the circumference and area grow only linearly and quadratically, respectively. For representing hierarchical structures like trees, this property can ensure that all leaf nodes which are closer to the edge of the circle maintain large enough distances from each other.

As a specific application, Poincaré embedding uses the Poincaré ball model which consists of points within the unit ball $\mathbb{B}^d$ where the distance

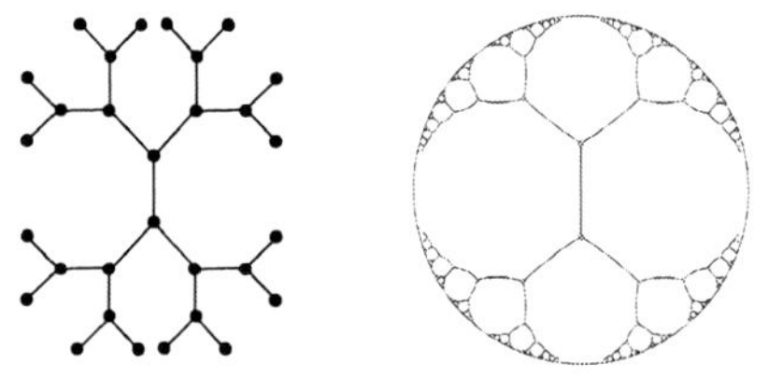

Figure 4: (a) Tree with a branching factor of 2 in Euclidean space. (b) Embedding a hierarchical tree with a branching factor of 2 in a Poincaré disk. Figure from Figure 1(b) in (Nickel and Kiela, 2017).

between two points, $\mathbf{u}, \mathbf{v} \in \mathbb{B}^{\mathbf{d}}$ is defined as

$$d(\mathbf{u}, \mathbf{v}) = \cosh^{-1}\left(1+2\frac{\|\mathbf{u}-\mathbf{v}\|^2}{(1-\|\mathbf{u}\|^2)(1-\|\mathbf{v}\|^2)}\right). \quad (10)$$

The Poincaré embedding is obtained by minimizing a loss function depending only on $d(\mathbf{u}, \mathbf{v})$ for all pairs of labels $(\mathbf{u}, \mathbf{v})$ using Riemannian optimization methods.

Figure 4 illustrates the differences between using an Euclidean space and a Poincaré ball model when representing nodes organized in a tree. Using a hyperbolic embedding has the potential to maintain large enough distances when our models aim to distinguish subtle differences among these labels.

4 Experiments and Results

4.1 Experimental Setup

Data set: Our data set consisted of more than one million products in aggregate from Rakuten, a large e-commerce platform in Japan, focusing on four major product categories which we call root-level genres. Our task, a multi-class classification problem, was to predict the leaf-level product categories from their Japanese titles. Further details of our data set are shown in Table 2.

Evaluation metric: We used the macro-averaged F-score F to evaluate model performance. This is defined in terms of the per-class F-score F_k as

$$F = \frac{1}{K}\sum_{k=1}^{K} F_k, \quad (11)$$

$$F_k = \frac{2P_kR_k}{P_k + R_k}, \quad (12)$$

where K is the total number of classes, and P_k and R_k are the precision and recall for class k.

Pre-trained embedding methods: We tested the following three methods:

- All genre: Word embedding pre-trained on all of the data across different root-level genres; for the label embedding, the average of the word embedding from all word tokens in a label is used to initialize the label embedding C and this is further updated in the model training process.

- Genre specific: Word embedding pre-trained from data specific to each root-level genre; label embeddings were obtained similarly to the all-genre method.

- Poincaré: Label embedding pre-trained on the Poincaré ball taking into account the full hierarchical taxonomy tree.

Models: We compared a number of variants of LEAM and LSAN as described below.

- LEAM: Described in Section 3 (Wang et al., 2018), using all-genre pre-trained word embeddings.

- $LEAM_{\text{base}}$: LEAM without the label embedding attention component (effectively fixing $\beta_l = 1/L$ in Eq. 1), using all-genre pre-trained word embeddings.

- LSAN: Described in Section 3 (Xiao et al., 2019), using all-genre pre-trained word embeddings.

- $LSAN_{\text{base}}$: LSAN without the label-specific attention component (effectively fixing $\beta = 0$ in Eq. 7) which is similar to AttentionXML (You et al., 2019), and using all-genre pre-trained word embeddings.

- $LSAN_{\text{genre}}$: LSAN using genre-specific pre-trained word embeddings.

- $LSAN_{\text{Poincaré}}$: LSAN using genre-specific pre-trained word embeddings for the titles and pre-trained Poincaré embeddings for the labels.

Experimental parameters: Our models were implemented in TensorFlow 2.3 using a GPU for training and evaluation. Since Japanese text does not have spaces to indicate individual words, tokenization was performed with MeCab, an open source

Root genre	Class size	Train size	Dev size	Test size	Mean words/title
Catalog Gifts & Tickets	29	11,369	1,281	559	31
Beverages	32	205,107	22,805	10,315	21
Appliances	286	399,584	44,529	18,478	20
Men's Fashion	71	593,126	65,939	43,243	23

Table 2: Summary of our data set obtained from a large e-commerce platform in Japan.

Root genre	$LEAM_{\text{base}}$	LEAM	$LSAN_{\text{base}}$	LSAN
Catalog Gifts & Tickets	0.341	0.289↓	0.241	0.338
Beverages	0.719	0.755	0.759	0.773
Appliances	0.682	0.654↓	0.667	0.686
Men's Fashion	0.696	0.657↓	0.685	0.686

Table 3: Macro F-score of LEAM and LSAN without and with label attention.

Japanese part-of-speech and morphological analyzer using conditional random fields (CRF).[3] Once the text was tokenized, we fixed our input length to $L = 60$ words by truncating the title if it was longer than L and zero-padding the title if it was shorter than L. If a word appeared less than three times, it was discarded and replaced with an out-of-vocabulary token.

Pre-trained word embeddings of dimension $D = 100$ using just product titles were obtained with fastText, which uses a skipgram model with bag-of-character n-grams (Bojanowski et al., 2016). No external pre-trained embeddings were used. After initialization of word and label embeddings with pre-trained values, they were jointly trained with the remaining parameters of the model.

For Poincaré embedding of labels, we used an embedding dimension of 300. Pre-trained Poincaré embeddings of labels were obtained by representing the genre taxonomy tree as (child, parent) pairs and minimizing a loss function which depends only on inter-genre distances as defined in Eq. 10 (Nickel and Kiela, 2017). These pre-trained Poincaré label embeddings were used to initialize the label embeddings in LSAN but during training were allowed to vary according to the standard loss optimization process in Euclidean space.

For LEAM, we used a 1D convolution window size of 5. For LSAN, we set $d_a = 50$, and when we experimented with the Poincaré embedding we set the LSTM hidden state dimension $P = 300$ to match the Poincaré embedding dimension.

The models were trained by minimizing the cross-entropy loss function using the Adam optimizer with an initial learning rate of 0.001 (Kingma and Ba, 2015). We used early stopping with a patience of 10 to obtain the final models.

4.2 Results and Discussions

Impact of label attention: We examined the impact of label attention by comparing performance without and with label attention for LEAM and LSAN for each of the four root-level genres using all-genre pre-trained word embeddings. The result is shown in Table 3. For LEAM, we do not observe consistent improvements by including the label attention component, contrary to what was previously reported on standard text classification data sets (Wang et al., 2018). On the other hand for LSAN we do observe consistent improvements over all root-level genres by including the label attention component of the model. Since we did not observe a consistent improvement for LEAM in using label attention, for the remainder of this section we focus on variations of LSAN.

Impact of different pre-trained embeddings: We next evaluated the impact of using different pre-trained embeddings for the title embeddings as well as the label embeddings for each of the four root-level genres. This is shown in Table 4. We observed that different pre-trained embeddings can consistently have a significant effect on model performance. In particular, using genre-specific embeddings outperformed all-genre embeddings for all genres. This is particularly notable for the smallest genre where we used more than 10 times the data to obtain the all-genre embeddings.

We believe this is because words that occur in the same root-level genre will tend to be embedded closer to each other in the full embedding space,

[3] https://taku910.github.io/mecab/

Root genre	LSAN	$LSAN_{\text{genre}}$	$LSAN_{\text{Poincaré}}$
Catalog Gifts & Tickets	0.338	0.403	**0.438**
Beverages	0.773	0.784	**0.789**
Appliances	0.686	0.697	**0.701**
Men's Fashion	0.686	0.701	**0.722**

Table 4: Macro F-score of LSAN with various pre-trained title and label embeddings.

which then makes it more difficult for the label attention to distinguish between different but similar labels such as "Japanese tea" and "Chinese tea." By using pre-trained embeddings obtained from specific genres, the embeddings become spaced farther apart and therefore the label attention is able to better distinguish labels with similar names.

Poincaré embeddings take this further by requiring the embedding space distance between all leaf-genre labels to be far apart from each other, and our results show that this leads to the best model performance. This supports our hypothesis that the distance between labels in the label embedding space is an important factor in ensuring that label attention improves model performance.

Compared to models using only the product titles, we see that models using label-guided learning can significantly improve the F-score. In particular, LSAN using a Poincaré label embedding shows the following F-score increases compared to LSAN base: 19.7% for "Catalog Gifts & Tickets," 3.0% for "Beverages," 3.4% for "Appliances," and 3.7% for "Men's Fashion." Note that the largest increase was achieved on the genre with the fewest training instances.

5 Conclusions

Since 2018, there have been increasing interest in the field of NLP to use the semantic information of class labels to further improve text classification performance. On the item categorization task in e-commerce, a taxonomy organized in a hierarchical structure already contains rich meaning and provides an ideal opportunity to evaluate the impact of label-guided learning. In this paper, we used real industry data from Rakuten, a leading Japanese e-commerce platform, to evaluate the benefits of label-guided learning.

Our experiments showed that LSAN is superior to LEAM because of its usage of context encoding and adaptive combination of both self- and label-attention. We also found that using genre-specific pre-trained embeddings led to better model performance than pre-trained embeddings obtained from all product genres. This is likely because pre-training on specific genres allows the embedding to focus on differences between similar genres and the label embeddings are able to take advantage of this. Finally, we showed that using hyperbolic embedding, more specifically Poincaré embedding, can improve model performance further by ensuring that all class labels are sufficiently separated to allow label-guided learning to work well.

One possible limitation of our current work is that although the label embedding is initialized using a hyperbolic embedding, the rest of the training process proceeds in Euclidean space. Future work could explore the possibility of training the entire model in hyperbolic space. Another direction is to incorporate the label-attention mechanism into the BERT model (Devlin et al., 2019), which has proven to be a powerful approach to text encoding. In addition, more advanced approaches to obtaining better representations of labels on top of our existing approach of using word tokens in labels could be explored.

Acknowledgements

The authors would like to thank Yandi Xia for introducing hyperbolic embeddings to us and pre-training the Poincaré embeddings.

References

Piotr Bojanowski, Edouard Grave, Armand Joulin, and Tomas Mikolov. 2016. Enriching word vectors with subword information. *arXiv preprint arXiv:1607.04606*.

Ali Cevahir and Koji Murakami. 2016. Large-scale multi-class and hierarchical product categorization for an E-commerce giant. In *Proceedings of COLING 2016, the 26th International Conference on Computational Linguistics: Technical Papers*, pages 525–535, Osaka, Japan. The COLING 2016 Organizing Committee.

Duo Chai, Wei Wu, Qinghong Han, Fei Wu, and Jiwei Li. 2020. Description based text classification with reinforcement learning. In *Proceedings of the 37th*

International Conference on Machine Learning, volume 119 of *Proceedings of Machine Learning Research*, pages 1371–1382. PMLR.

Boli Chen, Xin Huang, Lin Xiao, Zixin Cai, and Liping Jing. 2020a. Hyperbolic interaction model for hierarchical multi-label classification. *Proceedings of the AAAI Conference on Artificial Intelligence*, 34(05):7496–7503.

Boli Chen, Xin Huang, Lin Xiao, and Liping Jing. 2020b. Hyperbolic capsule networks for multi-label classification. In *Proceedings of the 58th Annual Meeting of the Association for Computational Linguistics*, pages 3115–3124, Online. Association for Computational Linguistics.

Jacob Devlin, Ming-Wei Chang, Kenton Lee, and Kristina Toutanova. 2019. BERT: Pre-training of Deep Bidirectional Transformers for Language Understanding. *arXiv:1810.04805 [cs]*. ArXiv: 1810.04805.

Cunxiao Du, Zhaozheng Chen, Fuli Feng, Lei Zhu, Tian Gan, and Liqiang Nie. 2019. Explicit interaction model towards text classification. *Proceedings of the AAAI Conference on Artificial Intelligence*, 33(01):6359–6366.

Diederik P. Kingma and Jimmy Ba. 2015. Adam: A method for stochastic optimization. In *3rd International Conference on Learning Representations, ICLR 2015, San Diego, CA, USA, May 7-9, 2015, Conference Track Proceedings*.

Xin Li and Dan Roth. 2002. Learning question classifiers. In *COLING 2002: The 19th International Conference on Computational Linguistics*.

Xien Liu, Song Wang, Xiao Zhang, Xinxin You, Ji Wu, and Dejing Dou. 2020. Label-guided Learning for Text Classification. *arXiv preprint arXiv:2002.10772*.

Shervin Malmasi, Surya Kallumadi, Nicola Ueffing, Oleg Rokhlenko, Eugene Agichtein, and Ido Guy, editors. 2020. *Proceedings of The 3rd Workshop on e-Commerce and NLP*. Association for Computational Linguistics, Seattle, WA, USA.

Tomas Mikolov, Kai Chen, Greg Corrado, and Jeffrey Dean. 2013. Efficient estimation of word representations in vector space. *arXiv preprint arXiv:1301.3781*.

Maximillian Nickel and Douwe Kiela. 2017. Poincaré embeddings for learning hierarchical representations. In *Advances in Neural Information Processing Systems*, volume 30. Curran Associates, Inc.

Bo Pang and Lillian Lee. 2004. A sentimental education: Sentiment analysis using subjectivity summarization based on minimum cuts. In *Proceedings of the 42nd Annual Meeting of the Association for Computational Linguistics (ACL-04)*, pages 271–278, Barcelona, Spain.

Jeffrey Pennington, Richard Socher, and Christopher Manning. 2014. GloVe: Global vectors for word representation. In *Proceedings of the 2014 Conference on Empirical Methods in Natural Language Processing (EMNLP)*, pages 1532–1543, Doha, Qatar. Association for Computational Linguistics.

Richard Socher, Alex Perelygin, Jean Wu, Jason Chuang, Christopher D. Manning, Andrew Ng, and Christopher Potts. 2013. Recursive deep models for semantic compositionality over a sentiment treebank. In *Proceedings of the 2013 Conference on Empirical Methods in Natural Language Processing*, pages 1631–1642, Seattle, Washington, USA. Association for Computational Linguistics.

Ashish Vaswani, Noam Shazeer, Niki Parmar, Jakob Uszkoreit, Llion Jones, Aidan N. Gomez, Łukasz Kaiser, and Illia Polosukhin. 2017. Attention is all you need. In *Proceedings of the 31st International Conference on Neural Information Processing Systems*, NIPS'17, page 6000–6010, Red Hook, NY, USA. Curran Associates Inc.

Guoyin Wang, Chunyuan Li, Wenlin Wang, Yizhe Zhang, Dinghan Shen, Xinyuan Zhang, Ricardo Henao, and Lawrence Carin. 2018. Joint embedding of words and labels for text classification. In *Proceedings of the 56th Annual Meeting of the Association for Computational Linguistics (Volume 1: Long Papers)*, pages 2321–2331, Melbourne, Australia. Association for Computational Linguistics.

Yandi Xia, Aaron Levine, Pradipto Das, Giuseppe Di Fabbrizio, Keiji Shinzato, and Ankur Datta. 2017. Large-scale categorization of Japanese product titles using neural attention models. In *Proceedings of the 15th Conference of the European Chapter of the Association for Computational Linguistics: Volume 2, Short Papers*, pages 663–668, Valencia, Spain. Association for Computational Linguistics.

Lin Xiao, Xin Huang, Boli Chen, and Liping Jing. 2019. Label-specific document representation for multi-label text classification. In *Proceedings of the 2019 Conference on Empirical Methods in Natural Language Processing and the 9th International Joint Conference on Natural Language Processing (EMNLP-IJCNLP)*, pages 466–475, Hong Kong, China. Association for Computational Linguistics.

Ronghui You, Zihan Zhang, Ziye Wang, Suyang Dai, Hiroshi Mamitsuka, and Shanfeng Zhu. 2019. Attentionxml: Label tree-based attention-aware deep model for high-performance extreme multi-label text classification. In *Advances in Neural Information Processing Systems*, volume 32, pages 5820–5830. Curran Associates, Inc.

Huasha Zhao, Parikshit Sondhi, Nguyen Bach, Sanjika Hewavitharana, Yifan He, Luo Si, and Heng Ji, editors. 2020. *Proceedings of Workshop on Natural Language Processing in E-Commerce*. Association for Computational Linguistics, Barcelona, Spain.

Benchmarking Commercial Intent Detection Services with Practice-Driven Evaluations

Haode Qi†*, Lin Pan†*, Atin Sood†, Abhishek Shah†
Ladislav Kunc†, Mo Yu‡, Saloni Potdar†
†IBM Watson
‡MIT-IBM Watson AI Lab
{Haode.Qi,Abhishek.Shah1,lada}@ibm.com
{panl,asood,yum,potdars}@us.ibm.com

Abstract

Intent detection is a key component of modern goal-oriented dialog systems that accomplish a user task by predicting the intent of users' text input. There are three primary challenges in designing robust and accurate intent detection models. First, typical intent detection models require a large amount of labeled data to achieve high accuracy. Unfortunately, in practical scenarios it is more common to find small, unbalanced, and noisy datasets. Secondly, even with large training data, the intent detection models can see a different distribution of test data when being deployed in the real world, leading to poor accuracy. Finally, a practical intent detection model must be computationally efficient in both training and single query inference so that it can be used continuously and re-trained frequently. We benchmark intent detection methods on a variety of datasets. Our results show that Watson Assistant's intent detection model outperforms other commercial solutions and is comparable to large pretrained language models while requiring only a fraction of computational resources and training data. Watson Assistant demonstrates a higher degree of robustness when the training and test distributions differ.

1 Introduction

Intent detection and entity recognition form the basis of the Natural Language Understanding (NLU) components of a task-oriented dialog system. The intents and entities identified in a given user utterance help trigger the appropriate conditions defined in a dialog tree which guides the user through a predetermined dialog-flow. These task-oriented dialog systems have gained popularity for designing applications around customer support, personal assistants, and opinion mining, etc.

The Conversational AI market is expected to grow to an estimated USD 13.9 billion by 2025 as reported by Markets & Markets [1]. There are several solutions in the market that help enterprises build and deploy chatbots quickly to automate large portions of their customer service interactions. Hence, a commercial conversational AI solution needs to adapt to a variety of use cases, accurately identify users' intents and resolve their queries.

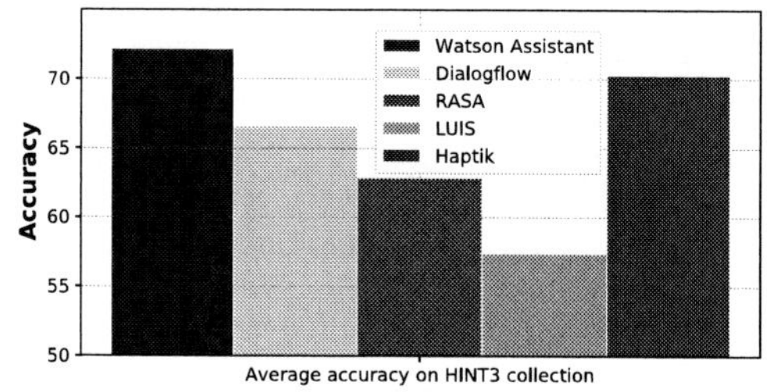

Figure 1: **Accuracy of commercial solutions** on the HINT3 collection of datasets. Results are averaged across the *Full* versions of the three datasets and their *Subset* versions. The in-scope accuracy is reported on a threshold of 0.1. Watson Assistant achieves the best results on average. Results for all methods except Watson Assistant are obtained from Arora et al. (2020).

There are three primary challenges in designing intent detection models that power real-world dialog systems: (1) **Limitations in training data**: while typical machine learning models are trained on large, balanced, labeled datasets, practical intent detection systems rely on customer provided data. These datasets are usually small, probably noisy, unbalanced, and contain classes with overlapping semantics, etc. The relatively poor quality of training data makes it hard to train accurate models. (2) **Robustness to non-standard user inputs**: when the intent detection models are deployed in real-world settings, they often operate on test data that differs significantly from the training data. The mismatch in train and test data distributions mainly

*Equal contribution

[1]https://customerthink.com/conversational-ai-in-2021-3-top-trends-to-look-out-for

Proceedings of NAACL HLT 2021: IndustryTrack Papers, pages 304–310
June 6–11, 2021. ©2021 Association for Computational Linguistics

comes from the free-form of input user queries. These real world queries express the same intents with their non-standard paraphrases, which are difficult to fully cover during training. The lack of large and clean training data makes this problem worse. (3) **Computational efficiency**: the intent detection models should be computationally efficient for both training and inference. On one hand, efficient inference is crucial since it allows for faster query resolution times for the users.[2] On the other hand, a real-world dialog system is frequently updated according to customer needs, so faster training time becomes an important consideration for real-world conversational AI solutions.

In this work, taking the aforementioned three realistic challenges into consideration, we evaluate multiple intent detection models and focus on their accuracy, data efficiency, robustness, and computational efficiency. We compare the performance of various commercial intent detection models on three datasets in the HINT3 collection (Arora et al., 2020). We also evaluate pretrained Language Models (LM) on three commonly used public datasets for benchmarking intent detection - CLINC150 (Larson et al., 2019), BANKING77 (Casanueva et al., 2020), and HUW64 (Liu et al., 2019b). In addition, we create few-shot learning settings from these datasets, to better match real world low-resource scenarios. Furthermore, we measure the "in the wild" robustness of the systems via creating difficult test subsets from existing test sets. Finally, we evaluate the classification accuracy and training time of these models because it directly affects the usability and development lifecycle of an conversational AI solution.

We build upon the existing study in Arora et al. (2020) which benchmarked commercial solutions aside from IBM Watson Assistant (i.e., Dialogflow, LUIS, and RASA). We extend this study by adding Watson Assistant and recent large-scale pretrained LMs. We also explore few-shot and robustness settings, and compare the resource efficiency and training times of different commercial solutions as well as pretrained LMs. Among these solutions, Watson Assistant's new intent detection algorithm performs better than other commercial solutions (Figure 1), and achieves comparable accuracy when compared to large-scale pretrained LMs (Figure 2) while being much more efficient.

[2]Inference time is usually dependent on service-level agreements between the provider and the user which determine the response time upper bounds of the APIs. This is hard to measure and compare across services in a reliable way for the purpose of this study.

2 Related Work

Several datasets have been released to test the performance of intent detection for task-oriented dialog systems such as Web Apps, Ask Ubuntu and Chatbot corpus from Braun et al. (2017); ATIS dataset (Price, 1990) and SNIPS (Coucke et al., 2018). The ATIS and SNIPS datasets have been created with focus on voice interactive chatbots. Voice modality has some specific characters, i.e., it does not contain typos and it is less noisy than text-based communication. Thus, these datasets are oversimplified version of the text-based intent detection task "in the wild" due to well-constructed dataset and limited number of classes.

Recently, CLINC150 (Larson et al., 2019), BANKING77 (Casanueva et al., 2020), and HWU64 (Liu et al., 2019b) have been used to benchmark the performance of intent detection systems. These datasets cover a large number of intents across a wider range of domains, which captures more real-world complexity of doing fine-grained classification. Arora et al. (2020) proposed a new collection of datasets called HINT3, containing a noisy and diverse set of intents and examples across three domains sourced from domain experts and real users.

Prior work from Arora et al. (2020), Braun et al. (2017), and Liu et al. (2019a) study the performance of different conversational AI services using the datasets mentioned above. Casanueva et al. (2020), Larson et al. (2019), Arora et al. (2020), Bunk et al. (2020) and others have benchmarked several state-of-the-art (SOTA) pretrained LMs such as BERT (Devlin et al., 2019) on the aforementioned datasets.

We aim to standardize the benchmarking tests that need to be run while developing an industry scale intent detection system. The tests should cover a variety of real-world datasets, settings such as few-shot scenarios and testing on semantically dissimilar test examples. Additionally, the tests should also cover resource efficiency and training time - since they affect the overall deployment costs of a virtual assistant cloud service. A carefully chosen trade-off between accuracy and efficiency is the decision making factor in choosing the algorithm for the real-world intent detection system.

3 Evaluation Settings

3.1 Datasets

We create our proposed evaluation settings based on the following public intent detection datasets:

CLINC150 consists of $22,500$ in-scope examples that cover 150 intents in 10 domains, such as banking, work, travel, etc. The dataset also comes with $1,200$ out-of-scope examples. In this work, we only focus on the in-scope examples.

HWU64 contains $25,716$ examples, covering 64 intents in 21 domains. The data creation process aims to reflect human-home robot interaction. We are using one fold train-test split with $9,960$ training examples and $1,076$ testing examples.

BANKING77 is a single domain dataset created for fine-grained intent detection. It focuses on the banking domain, and has $13,083$ examples covering 77 intents.

3.2 Practice-Driven Benchmark Settings

Full-set setting This corresponds to the standard evaluation setting that uses the full training and testing sets.

Few-shot setting In the real-world setting, users may not provide a large number of labelled examples to train a conversational AI system. Labeling data is extremely time consuming and difficult, so we need to make our intent detection systems robust enough to handle the few-shot scenarios and improve time to value for the user. We create a few shot setup for all the datasets by sampling 5 examples per intent and 30 examples per intent on CLINC150, HWU64 and BANKING77 datasets.

Difficult test setting Most of the current SOTA classification models can achieve 90%+ test accuracy on the aforementioned public datasets. However this is due to the presence of a large number of similar and standard queries in the training and test set. To reflect the performance in realistic settings, where users can input non-standard paraphrases of the queries, we propose to create more difficult subsets of the provided test sets to mimic the real-world setting.

Following Arora et al. (2020), we create a subset of each test set with semantically dissimilar sentences from the training set. Instead of using ELMo (Peters et al., 2018) and entailment scores, we use TF/IDF cosine distance to pick the most difficult examples from the original test sets. Each intent is treated separately during the selection process. First, all training utterances in a specific intent are tokenized (using simple white-space based tokenizer, ignoring punctuation). These tokenized training utterances are concatenated and transformed to TF/IDF vector space. Then, each testing example of the intent is transformed using the initialized TF/IDF transformer and cosine similarities with the transformed training set are calculated. Finally, 5 least similar examples per intent are selected for inclusion to the difficult test set. For example, the CLINC150 dataset has 150 intents, so our algorithm creates a test set of 750 examples. Analogous process is used for the other two datasets. [3]

4 Experiment I: Comparison with Pretrained LMs

Pretrained LMs finetuned for intent detection have been shown to perform very well in recent literature, such as (Casanueva et al., 2020). Users can modify and adapt pretrained LMs to serve them as part of a scalable solution. However, this often requires a complex solution design, an example of which can be found in Yu et al. (2020). In this work we evaluate and compare the commercial services with the following pretrained LMs: $\textbf{USE}_{\textbf{base}}$, i.e., Universal Sentence Encoder (Cer et al., 2018); $\textbf{Distilbert}_{\textbf{base}}$ (Sanh et al., 2020); $\textbf{BERT}_{\textbf{base}}$, $\textbf{BERT}_{\textbf{large}}$ (Devlin et al., 2019); and $\textbf{RoBERTa}_{\textbf{base}}$ (Liu et al., 2019b).

We compare Watson Assistant, RASA, and the aforementioned pretrained-LMs on the datasets and settings described in Section 3, and measure the training time as well as accuracy.

Watson Assistant We evaluate both the *classic* version of IBM Watson Assistant (WA) [4] and the *enhanced* version with improved intent detection algorithm. Public API is used to train and evaluate the model. For training time, we measure the round-trip latency from sending the training request until we receive the status that the model is trained and available for serving. [5]

[3]We release the difficult subsets at `https://github.com/haodeqi/BenchmarkingIntentDetection` to facilitate repeatability and future research.

[4]`https://www.ibm.com/cloud/watson-assistant`

[5]Note that the training times may vary depending on the load on the web API.

	CLINC150	HWU64	BANKING77	Average
WA classic	93.9	88.8	90.6	91.1
WA enhanced	95.7	90.5	92.6	92.9
RASA	89.4	84.9	89.9	88.1
Distilbert-base	96.3	91.7	92.1	93.4
BERT-base	96.8	91.6	93.3	93.9
BERT-large	**97.1**	91.9	93.7	94.2
USE-base	94.7	88.9	89.9	91.2
RoBERTa-base	97.0	**92.1**	**94.1**	**94.4**

Table 1: **Accuracy on CLINC150, HWU64 and BANKING77 for Watson Assistant (WA), RASA and pretrained LMs**. Training is performed on the full train sets and evaluation on full test sets.

RASA[6] The tool offers the flexibility to incorporate other open-source models such as Transformer-based (Vaswani et al., 2017) models into the pipeline. For our experiments, we use the default training setting that trains a count-based feature ensemble with the DIETClassifier (Bunk et al., 2020).

Pretrained LMs For BERT-based models, we add a softmax classifier on top of the [CLS] token and finetune all layers. We use AdamW (Loshchilov and Hutter, 2018) with 0.01 weight decay and a linear learning rate scheduler. We choose a batch size of 32, max sequence length 128 and learning rate warmup for the first 10% of the total iterations, peaking at 0.00004. For training set variants of $5/30/all$ examples per intent, we train for $50/18/5$ epochs, respectively. For USE_{base} model, we train a softmax layer on top of the sentence representation and finetune all layers for 100 epochs. A learning rate of 0.05 and batch size of 32 are used for all training set variants. All models are trained with a single CPU core and a single K80 GPU.

4.1 Results and Analysis

Results in the full-set setting Table 1 shows results of Watson Assistant, RASA and pretrained LMs on CLINC150, HWU64, and BANKING77. We train on the full training sets and report result on the full test sets, measured by accuracy. The overall best finetuned LM $RoBERTa_{base}$ achieves 1.5% higher accuracy than Watson Assistant *enhanced*. However, the improvement from finetuning large pretrained LMs requires more computational resources.

Results in the few-shot setting Table 2 shows results on few-shot setting for 5/30/all examples per intent on CLINC150, HWU64 and BANKING77 datasets on the full test sets. For experimental settings and dataset details, refer to Section 4.

CLINC150						
	5 ex/class		30 ex/class		full	
	Training time	Accuracy	Training time	Accuracy	Training time	Accuracy
WA classic	0.58	78.1	0.78	90.3	1.04	93.9
WA enhanced	0.66	83.6	0.63	92.5	1.81	95.7
RASA	1.25	53.2	5.6	79.4	13.93	89.4
Distilbert-base	15.23	82.2	31.65	93.2	35.98	96.3
BERT-base	29.67	83.8	61.43	94.7	71.08	96.8
BERT-large	125	87	280	95.8	270	97.1
USE-base	1.63	83.9	6.5	92.9	14.73	94.7
RoBERTa-base	33	86.3	85	95.4	90	97.0
HWU64						
	5 ex/class		30 ex/class		full	
	Training time	Accuracy	Training time	Accuracy	Training time	Accuracy
WA classic	0.39	64.1	0.59	81.4	0.85	88.8
WA enhanced	0.75	71.0	0.54	86.2	0.82	90.5
RASA	0.67	43.7	2.17	72.4	9.43	84.9
Distilbert-base	6.32	71.1	13.92	86.3	20.35	91.7
BERT-base	12.73	70.1	27.18	87.5	39.48	91.6
BERT-large	52	77.3	120	89.3	175	91.9
USE-base	1.2	72.5	2.46	86.3	8.92	88.9
RoBERTa-base	13	71.7	40	88.8	60	92.1
BANKING77						
	5 ex/class		30 ex/class		full	
	Training time	Accuracy	Training time	Accuracy	Training time	Accuracy
WA classic	0.38	64.2	0.49	84.7	0.64	90.6
WA enhanced	0.65	69.9	0.52	87.0	1.22	92.6
RASA	0.89	45.1	3.67	81.6	15.45	89.9
Distilbert-base	7.87	69.8	16.83	87.8	20.35	92.1
BERT-base	15.23	68.3	32.72	88.9	38.75	93.3
BERT-large	92	71.2	210	89.9	175	93.7
USE-base	1.33	65.3	2.95	86.8	9.47	89.9
RoBERTa-base	17	75.9	42	90.4	57	94.1

Table 2: **Accuracy and training time (in minutes) comparing Watson Assistant (WA) with RASA and pretrained LMs**. We use $5/30/all$ examples per intent on CLINC150, HWU64 and BANKING77 datasets. Results are the on the respective full test sets.

	CLINC150	HWU64	BANKING77
WA classic	79.3	83.4	75.2
WA enhanced	86.0	85.8	80.6
RASA	68.3	78.9	76.9
Distilbert-base	85.7	87.4	79.2
BERT-base	87.6	87.6	81.7
BERT-large	**89.5**	**89.2**	**83.9**
USE-base	81.6	83.4	74.5
RoBERTa-base	88.4	88.5	83.8

Table 3: **Accuracy on CLINC150, HWU64 and BANKING77 for Watson Assistant (WA), RASA and pretrained LMs**. Models are trained on full train sets and evaluated on Tfidf-difficult test sets.

Results in the difficult test setting Table 3 shows results on our difficult test sets. We observe that there is a significant drop in accuracy compared to the full test set, going from 90%+ to 80%s. This shows that these test sets are indeed more difficult for all algorithms, and they provide a better testbed for identifying the robustness of a

[6] https://rasa.com

	CLINC150					
	5 ex/class		**30 ex/class**		full	
	Training time	Accuracy	Training time	Accuracy	Training time	Accuracy
WA classic	0.58	54.0	0.78	69.9	1.04	79.3
WA enhanced	0.66	65.1	0.63	76.7	1.81	86.0
RASA	1.25	29.6	5.6	52.5	13.93	68.3
Distilbert-base	15.23	63.4	31.65	76.8	35.98	85.7
BERT-base	29.67	64.6	61.43	81.1	71.08	87.6
BERT-large	125	72.0	280	85.6	270	89.5
USE-base	1.63	66.6	6.5	77.5	14.73	81.6
RoBERTa-base	33	70.8	85	83.7	90	88.4
	HWU64					
	5 ex/class		**30 ex/class**		full	
	Training time	Accuracy	Training time	Accuracy	Training time	Accuracy
WA classic	0.39	53.9	0.59	72.3	0.85	83.4
WA enhanced	0.75	62.7	0.54	80.0	0.82	85.8
RASA	0.67	34.5	2.17	63.5	9.43	78.9
Distilbert-base	6.32	63.4	13.92	79.7	20.35	87.4
BERT-base	12.73	61.6	27.18	82.1	39.48	87.6
BERT-large	52	71.1	120	85.3	175	89.2
USE-base	1.2	66.3	2.46	79.8	8.92	83.4
RoBERTa-base	13	64.5	40	83.9	60	88.5
	BANKING77					
	5 ex/class		**30 ex/class**		full	
	Training time	Accuracy	Training time	Accuracy	Training time	Accuracy
WA classic	0.38	43.2	0.49	64.5	0.64	75.2
WA enhanced	0.65	49.1	0.52	69.7	1.22	80.6
RASA	0.89	26.9	3.67	57.9	15.45	76.9
Distilbert-base	7.87	50.0	16.83	69.0	20.35	79.2
BERT-base	15.23	48.3	32.72	73.4	38.75	81.7
BERT-large	92	52.6	210	75.8	175	83.9
USE-base	1.33	44.5	2.95	68.6	9.47	74.5
RoBERTa-base	17	57.1	42	75.7	57	83.8

Table 4: **Accuracy and training time (in minutes) comparing Watson Assistant (WA) with RASA and pretrained LMs.** We use 5/30/all examples per intent on CLINC150, HWU64 and BANKING77 datasets. Results are the on the respective Tfidf-difficult test sets.

intent detection system. In addition, we conduct the comparison in few-shot settings, where we use 5 examples per intent for training, and increase to 30 and full training sets. The complete set of results of few-shot setting on the difficult test sets can be found in Table 4. Results show that $\text{BERT}_{\text{large}}$ performs the best in terms of accuracy. However, Watson Assistant still stands on top considering the trade-off between training time and accuracy.

Training time vs accuracy trade-off We report the training times and resources used for all models across the three datasets in Table 5. We observe that the pretrained LMs require significantly more training time compared to Watson Assistant. For example, $\text{RoBERTa}_{\text{base}}$ achieves comparable performance to Watson Assistant but requires 90 minutes training time on CLINC150. Figure 2 shows a visualization of accuracy and training time for each model. Watson Assistant offers the best trade-off in terms of accuracy vs. training time.

We report results on HINT3 datasets for completeness and are discussed in Section 5 Table 8.

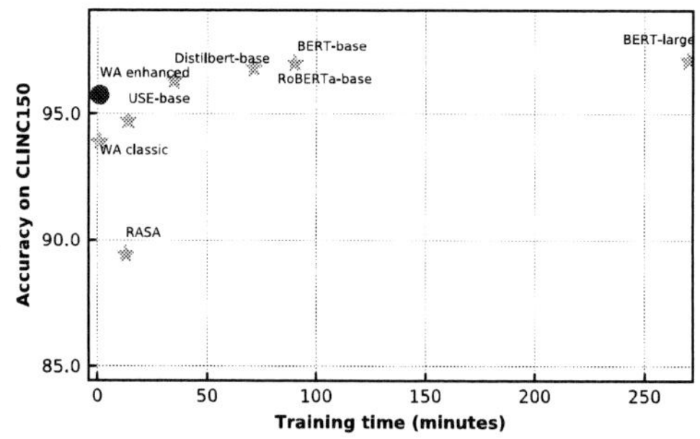

Figure 2: **Training time vs. accuracy on CLINC150** for Watson Assistant (WA), RASA and pretrained LMs. Full training set and test set are used. All methods except Watson Assistant are trained using GPU. Watson Assistant offers the best trade-off between training time and accuracy.

Algorithm	Resources	CLINC150 Training time	HWU Training time	BANKING77 Training time
WA classic	-	**1.04**	0.85	**0.64**
WA enhanced	-	1.81	**0.82**	1.22
RASA	GPU	13.93	9.43	15.45
Distilbert-base	GPU	35.98	20.35	20.35
BERT-base	GPU	71.08	39.48	38.75
BERT-large	GPU	270	175	175
USE-base	GPU	14.73	8.92	9.47
RoBERTa-base	GPU	90	60	57

Table 5: **Training time (in minutes) and resource requirements** for Watson Assistant (WA), RASA and pretrained LMs. Training is performed on full training sets. All methods except for Watson Assistant are trained using a single NVIDIA K80 GPU.

5 Experimental II: Comparison among Commercial Solutions

Finally, we conduct comparison studies among commercial services. Commercial solutions are more suitable for enterprise customers and are designed for users who have limited knowledge of machine learning and natural language processing. One of the challenges in comparing the performance of commercial services and designing experiments lies in the fact that most service providers have terms of use prohibiting any type of benchmarking on their services. To overcome this challenge, we use the prior benchmarking study from Arora et al. (2020) to obtain the performance of existing commercial solutions. In this benchmark, HINT3 dataset collection is used which contains three tasks with small amounts of training data. We extended the study by including the results on the Watson Assistant service.

In this section, we evaluate the perfor-

	SOFMattress		**Curekart**		**Powerplay11**	
	Train	Test (in-scope / out-of-scope)	Train	Test (in-scope / out-of-scope)	Train	Test (in-scope / out-of-scope)
Full	328	231/166	600	452/539	471	275/708
Subset	180	231/166	413	452/539	261	275/708

Table 6: **HINT3 training and test set statistics**. HINT3 consists of three datasets - SOFMattress, Curekart and Powerplay11. Each training set contains two versions - *Full* and *Subset*. The test set is also broken down into in-scope queries and out-of-scope queries.

mance of the following commercial solutions: **IBM Watson Assistant**[7], **Google Dialogflow**[8], **Microsoft LUIS**[9], and the open-source solution **RASA**[10]. We use the prior benchmarking study from Arora et al. (2020) to obtain the performance of these commercial solutions, except for Watson Assistant.

5.1 Datasets

HINT3 is a collection of three datasets: SOFMattress, Curekart, and Powerplay11. The statistics of the datasets are shown in Table 6. Each dataset has two training set variants referred to as *full* and *subset*. The subset variant was created by discarding semantically similar sentences using ELMo (Peters et al., 2018) and entailment score > 0.6 (Arora et al., 2020). We used both variants of the training data in our experiments. The test sets contain both in-scope and out-of-scope examples.

5.2 Experimental Setup

We use the same experimental setup as described in Arora et al. (2020). Following their methodology, we use a confidence threshold of 0.1. For the BERT model reported in their paper, they used $\text{BERT}_{\text{base}}$ and finetuned all layers upto 50 epochs, learning rate of 4×10^{-5} with warmup period of 0.1 and early stopping.

5.3 Results

Table 7 shows full results on the in-scope test examples of each dataset measured by accuracy using a confidence threshold of 0.1.

On average across the datasets (Table 8), Watson Assistant *enhanced* achieves 73.8% accuracy when trained on the full training sets and evaluated on the in-scope examples, outperforming DialogFlow by 4.57%, and LUIS by 13.87%. Training on the subset variant of the datasets, Watson Assistant also consistently outperforms the other commercial solutions. It is worth noting that Watson Assistant also does better than BERT by 4.4% on average.

	SOFMattress		**Curekart**		**Powerplay11**	
	full	subset	full	subset	full	subset
WA classic	73.6	66.2	83.2	79.9	63.3	57.1
WA enhanced	**74.0**	**68.4**	**86.7**	**85.4**	60.7	57.8
Dialogflow	73.1	65.3	75.0	71.2	59.6	55.6
RASA	69.2	56.2	84.0	80.5	49.0	38.5
LUIS	59.3	49.3	72.5	71.6	48.0	44.0
Haptik	72.2	64.0	80.3	79.8	**66.5**	**59.2**
BERT	73.5	57.1	83.6	82.3	58.5	53.0

Table 7: **In-scope Accuracy on HINT3 using commercial solutions.** We report the in-scope accuracy with a threshold of 0.1 for various intent detection methods. Results for all methods except Watson Assistant (WA) are obtained from (Arora et al., 2020).

	Full	**Subset**	**Average**
WA classic	73.4	67.7	70.6
WA enhanced	**73.8**	**70.5**	**72.2**
Dialogflow	69.2	64.0	66.6
RASA	67.4	58.4	62.9
LUIS	59.9	54.6	57.5
Haptik	73.0	67.6	70.3
BERT	71.9	64.1	68.0

Table 8: **Average In-scope Accuracy on HINT3 using commercial solutions.** We report the average in-scope accuracy across the three datasets with a threshold of 0.1 on Full and Subset versions of the HINT3 collection. Results for all methods except Watson Assistant (WA) are obtained from (Arora et al., 2020).

6 Conclusion

We proposed a new methodology to assess the performance of intent detection "in the wild" in task-oriented dialog systems. In practice, the platforms developed for building and deploying virtual assistants have to consider several scenarios and trade-offs. These systems have to train the best performing models in few-shot settings, strike a compromise between training time and accuracy, and adapt seamlessly to a wide range of domains.

We compare the performance of leading commercial services which are designed to develop task-oriented dialog systems on the publicly available datasets and also compared their performance against popular pretrained LMs. Our results demonstrate that Watson Assistant outperforms mar-

[7] https://www.ibm.com/cloud/watson-assistant

[8] https://cloud.google.com/dialogflow

[9] https://www.luis.ai

[10] https://rasa.com

ket competitors on the HINT3 dataset collection, which comprises real-world queries. Our results also show that Watson Assistant is competitive with pretrained LMs across a wide range of datasets and settings but trains much faster - which is a key factor in usability of a commercial conversational AI solution.

References

Gaurav Arora, Chirag Jain, Manas Chaturvedi, and Krupal Modi. 2020. HINT3: Raising the bar for intent detection in the wild. In *Proceedings of the First Workshop on Insights from Negative Results in NLP*, Online. Association for Computational Linguistics.

Daniel Braun, Adrian Hernandez Mendez, Florian Matthes, and Manfred Langen. 2017. Evaluating natural language understanding services for conversational question answering systems. In *Proceedings of the 18th Annual SIGdial Meeting on Discourse and Dialogue*, pages 174–185, Saarbrücken, Germany. Association for Computational Linguistics.

Tanja Bunk, Daksh Varshneya, Vladimir Vlasov, and Alan Nichol. 2020. Diet: Lightweight language understanding for dialogue systems.

Iñigo Casanueva, Tadas Temcinas, Daniela Gerz, Matthew Henderson, and Ivan Vulic. 2020. Efficient intent detection with dual sentence encoders. In *Proceedings of the 2nd Workshop on Natural Language Processing for Conversational AI*, pages 38–45, Seattle.

Daniel Cer, Yinfei Yang, Sheng yi Kong, Nan Hua, Nicole Limtiaco, Rhomni St. John, Noah Constant, Mario Guajardo-Cespedes, Steve Yuan, Chris Tar, Yun-Hsuan Sung, Brian Strope, and Ray Kurzweil. 2018. Universal sentence encoder.

Alice Coucke, Alaa Saade, Adrien Ball, Théodore Bluche, Alexandre Caulier, David Leroy, Clément Doumouro, Thibault Gisselbrecht, Francesco Caltagirone, Thibaut Lavril, et al. 2018. Snips voice platform: an embedded spoken language understanding system for private-by-design voice interfaces. *arXiv preprint arXiv:1805.10190*.

Jacob Devlin, Ming-Wei Chang, Kenton Lee, and Kristina Toutanova. 2019. BERT: Pre-training of deep bidirectional transformers for language understanding. In *Proceedings of the 20th Annual Conference of the North American Chapter of the Association for Computational Linguistics: Human Language Technologies (NAACL-HLT)*, pages 4171–4186, Minneapolis. The Association for Computational Linguistics.

Stefan Larson, Anish Mahendran, Joseph Peper, Christopher Clarke, Andrew Lee, P. Hill, Jonathan K. Kummerfeld, Kevin Leach, M. Laurenzano, L. Tang, and J. Mars. 2019. An evaluation dataset for intent classification and out-of-scope prediction. In *EMNLP/IJCNLP*.

X. Liu, A. Eshghi, P. Swietojanski, and Verena Rieser. 2019a. Benchmarking natural language understanding services for building conversational agents. *ArXiv*, abs/1903.05566.

Yinhan Liu, Myle Ott, Naman Goyal, Jingfei Du, Mandar Joshi, Danqi Chen, Omer Levy, Mike Lewis, Luke Zettlemoyer, and Veselin Stoyanov. 2019b. RoBERTa: A robustly optimized BERT pretraining approach. *arXiv preprint arXiv:1907.11692*, pages 1–13.

Ilya Loshchilov and Frank Hutter. 2018. Decoupled weight decay regularization. In *International Conference on Learning Representations*.

Matthew Peters, Mark Neumann, Mohit Iyyer, Matt Gardner, Christopher Clark, Kenton Lee, and Luke Zettlemoyer. 2018. Deep contextualized word representations. In *Proceedings of the 19th Annual Conference of the North American Chapter of the Association for Computational Linguistics: Human Language Technologies (HLT-NAACL)*, pages 2227–2237, New Orleans. The Association for Computational Linguistics.

Patti Price. 1990. Evaluation of spoken language systems: The atis domain. In *Speech and Natural Language: Proceedings of a Workshop Held at Hidden Valley, Pennsylvania, June 24-27, 1990*.

Victor Sanh, Lysandre Debut, Julien Chaumond, and Thomas Wolf. 2020. Distilbert, a distilled version of bert: smaller, faster, cheaper and lighter.

Ashish Vaswani, Noam Shazeer, Niki Parmar, Jakob Uszkoreit, Llion Jones, Aidan N. Gomez, Łukasz Kaiser, and Illia Polosukhin. 2017. Attention is all you need. In *Advances in Neural Information Processing Systems (NIPS)*, pages 5998–6008, Long Beach, CA.

Shi Yu, Yuxin Chen, and Hussain Zaidi. 2020. A financial service chatbot based on deep bidirectional transformers.

Industry Scale Semi-Supervised Learning for Natural Language Understanding

Luoxin Chen[*] Alexa AI luoxchen@amazon.com

Francisco Garcia[*] Alexa AI fgmz@amazon.com

Varun Kumar[*] Alexa AI kuvrun@amazon.com

He Xie[*] Alexa AI hexie@amazon.com

Jianhua Lu Alexa AI jianhual@amazon.com

Abstract

This paper presents a production Semi-Supervised Learning (SSL) pipeline based on the student-teacher framework, which leverages millions of unlabeled examples to improve Natural Language Understanding (NLU) tasks. We investigate two questions related to the use of unlabeled data in the production SSL context: 1) how to select samples from a huge unlabeled data pool that are beneficial for SSL training, and 2) how do the selected data affect the performance of different state-of-the-art SSL techniques. We compare four widely used SSL techniques, Pseudo-Label (PL), Knowledge Distillation (KD), Virtual Adversarial Training (VAT), and Cross-View Training (CVT) in conjunction with two data selection methods including committee-based selection and submodular optimization-based selection. We further examine the benefits and drawbacks of these techniques when applied to intent classification (IC) and named entity recognition (NER) tasks in the English language using a public dataset (SNIPS) and real-world data from Amazon Alexa. To conclude we provide guidelines specifying when each of these methods might be beneficial to improve large-scale NLU systems.

1 Introduction

Voice-assistants with speech and natural language understanding (NLU) are becoming increasingly prevalent in every day life. These systems, such as Google Now, Alexa, or Siri, are able to respond to queries pertaining multiple domains (e.g., music, weather). An NLU system commonly consists of an intent classifier (IC) and named entity recognizer (NER). It takes text input from an automatic speech recognizer and predicts intent and entities. For example, if a user asks "play lady gaga", the IC classifies the query to intent of PlayMusic, and the NER classifies "lady gaga" as Artist. An important requirement for voice-assistants is the ability to continuously add support for new functionalities, i.e., new intents, or new entity types, while improving recognition accuracy for the existing ones. Having high quality labeled data is the key to achieve this goal. However, obtaining human annotation is an expensive and time-consuming process.

Semi-Supervised Learning (SSL) provides a framework for utilizing large amount of unlabeled data when obtaining labels is expensive (Chapelle et al., 2006; Blum and Mitchell, 1998; Zhou and Li, 2005). SSL techniques have been shown to improve deep models performance across different machine learning tasks, including text classification, sequence labeling, machine translation and image classification (Clark et al., 2018; Miyato et al., 2019, 2017; Yalniz et al., 2019; Berthelot et al., 2019; Chen et al., 2020). A common practice to evaluate SSL algorithms is to take an existing labeled dataset and only use a small fraction of training data as labeled data, while treating the rest of the data as unlabeled dataset. Such evaluation, often constrained to the cases when labeled data is scarce, raises questions about the usefulness of different SSL algorithms in a real-world setting (Oliver et al., 2018).

In voice assistants, we face additional challenges while applying SSL techniques at scale including (1) how much unlabeled data should we use for SSL and how to select unlabeled data from a large pool of unlabeled data? (2) Most SSL benchmarks make the assumption that unlabeled datasets come from the same distribution as the labeled datasets. This assumption is often violated as, by design, the labeled training datasets also contain synthetic data, crowd-sourced data to represent anticipated usages of a functionality, and unlabeled data often contain a lot of out of domain data. (3) Unlike widely used NLU datasets such as SNIPS (Coucke et al., 2018), ATIS (Price, 1990), real-world voice assistant datasets are much larger and have a lot

[*]Equal contribution

Proceedings of NAACL HLT 2021: IndustryTrack Papers, pages 311–318
June 6–11, 2021. ©2021 Association for Computational Linguistics

of redundancy because some queries such as "turn on lights" might be much more frequent than others. Due to such evaluation concerns, performance of different SSL techniques in "real-world" NLU applications is still in question.

To address these issues, we study three data selection methods to select unlabeled data and evaluate how the selected data affect the performance of different SSL methods on a real-world NLU dataset in the English language. This paper provides three contributions: (1) Design of a production SSL pipeline which can be used to intelligently select unlabeled data to train SSL models (2) Experimental comparison of four SSL techniques including, Pseudo-Label, Knowledge Distillation, Cross-View Training, and Virtual Adversarial Training in a real-world setting using data from Amazon Alexa (3) Operational recommendations for NLP practitioners who would like to employ SSL in production setting.

2 Background

Semi-Supervised Learning techniques are capable of providing large improvements in model performance with little effort, which could play a crucial role in large scale systems in industry. In supervised learning, given a labeled dataset $\mathcal{D}_l$ composed of input-label pairs (x, y), the goal is to learn a prediction model $f_\theta(x)$, with parameters θ, that is able to predict the correct label y' corresponding to a new unseen input instance x'. SSL techniques aim to leverage an unlabeled dataset, $\mathcal{D}_u$, to create better performing models than those that could be obtained by only using $\mathcal{D}_l$.

The two widely used SSL methods are: Pseudo-Label (PL), and Knowledge Distillation (KD). In PL, a teacher model trained on labeled data is used to produce pseudo-labels for the unlabeled data set. A student model trained on the union of the labeled and pseudo-labeled data sets, often outperforms the teacher model. (Yarowsky, 1995; McClosky et al., 2006). On the other hand, KD SSL methods do not assign a particular label to an unlabeled instance, but instead consider the whole distribution over the label space (Parthasarathi and Strom, 2019; Liu et al., 2019b; Aguilar et al., 2020). In KD, it is hypothesized that leveraging the probability distribution over all labels provides more information than assuming a definitive label belonging to one particular class (Hinton et al., 2015).

In addition to PL and KD, Virtual Adversarial Training (VAT) and Cross-View Training (CVT) have achieved state-of-the-art SSL performance on various tasks including text classification, named entity recognition, and dependency parsing (Miyato et al., 2019; Clark et al., 2018; Miyato et al., 2017; Chen et al., 2020). In this paper, we conduct comprehensive experiments and analysis related to these commonly used SSL techniques, and discuss their pros and cons in the industry setting.

Data selection for SSL has been explored for different tasks including image classification (Ding et al., 2018), NER (Ji and Grishman, 2006; Ruder and Plank, 2018). Model confidence based data selection is a widely used technique for SSL data selection where unlabeled data is selected on the basis of a classifier's confidence. Due to the abundance of unlabeled data in production voice-assistants, model confidence based filtering leads to a very large data pool. To overcome this issue, we study different data selection algorithm which can further reduce the size of unlabeled data.

3 Methods

We are interested in studying two different questions relevant to the use of unlabeled data in production environments: 1) *how to effectively select SSL data from a large pool of unlabeled data*, and 2) *how do SSL techniques perform in realistic scenarios?* To do so, we focus on the tasks of intent classification (IC) and named entity recognition (NER), two important components in NLU systems.

The model architecture we study is an LSTM-based multi-task model for IC and NER tasks, where we use 300-dimension fastText word embeddings (Bojanowski et al., 2016), trained on a large voice assistant corpus.[1] A shared 256-dimension Bi-LSTM encoder and two separate task-specific Bi-LSTM encoders (256-dimension) are applied to encode the sentences. A softmax layer and a conditional random field (CRF) layer are used to produce predictions for IC and NER, respectively.

Below we describe our implementation of the SSL techniques and the data selection methods studied.

3.1 Data Selection Approaches

In the industry setting, we often encounter the situation where we have extremely large pool of un-

[1] The text corpus contains data transcribed by an automatic speech recognition system.

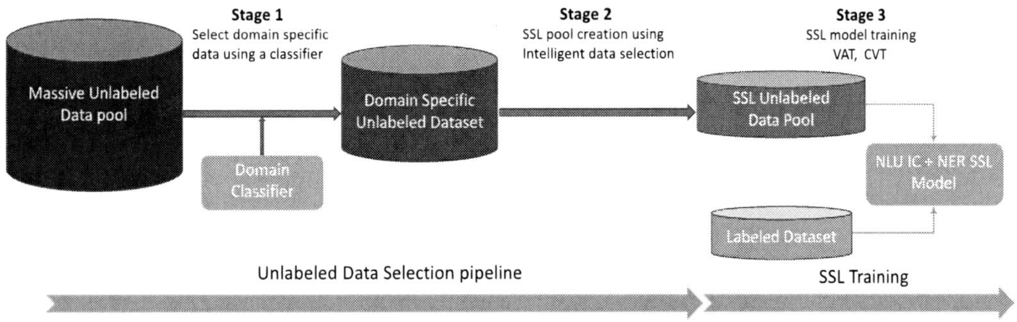

Figure 1: SSL pipeline. Domain specific unlabeled data are first selected using a domain classifer. We then select a subset of the unlabeled data using submodular optimization or committee based selection. Finally we train different SSL models using selected data combined with the labeled data.

labeled data, intractable to have SSL methods run on the entire dataset. Given this challenge, we propose a two stage data selection pipeline to create an unlabeled SSL pool, $\mathcal{D}_u$, of a practical size, from the much larger pool of available data.

Data selection pipeline, shown in Figure 1, first uses a classifier's confidence score to filter domain specific unlabeled data from a very large pool of unlabeled data, which might contain data from multiple domains. For a production system, first stage filtering might result in millions of examples, so we further filter data using different selection algorithms to find an SSL data pool, which facilitates effective SSL training. While the first stage filtering tries to find domain specific examples from a large pool, the goal of the second stage filtering is to find a subset of data which could result in better performance in SSL training.

For first stage filtering, we train a binary classifier on the labelled data, and use it to select the in-domain unlabelled data. In our experiments, switching between different binary classifiers (linear, CNN, LSTM, etc) does not significantly change the selected data. Consequently, in this study, we simply use a single-layer 256-dimension Bi-LSTM for the first stage of filtering. Based on our initial experiments, we use confidence score 0.5 as the threshold for data selection[2]. For second stage filtering, we explore data selection using a committee of models and using submodular optimization. While this paper explores only two data selection methods, it's worth mentioning that any data selection algorithm can be used in the second stage filtering to further optimize the size of SSL pool.

[2]We tried confidence larger than 0.5 but found that a high confidence score degrades the performance. Our hypothesis is that a high confidence score leads to selecting data similar to labeled data hence a less diverse SSL pool.

Selection by Submodular Optimization: Submodular data selection is used to select a diverse representative subset of samples from given dataset. This method has been applied in speech recognition (Wei et al., 2015), machine translation (Kirchhoff and Bilmes, 2014) and natural language understanding tasks (Cho et al., 2019). For SSL data selection, we use feature-based submodular selection (Kirchhoff and Bilmes, 2014), where submodular functions are given by weighted sums of non-decreasing concave functions applied to modular functions. For SSL data selection, we use 1-4 n-gram as features and logarithm as the concave function. We filter out any n-gram features which appear less than 30 times in $\mathcal{D}_l \cup \mathcal{D}_u$. The lazy greedy algorithm is used to optimize submodular functions. The algorithm starts with $\mathcal{D}_l$ as the selected data and chooses the utterance from the candidate pool $\mathcal{D}_u$ which provides maximum marginal gain.

Selection by Committee: SSL techniques work well when the model is able to provide an accurate prediction on unlabeled data. However, when this is not the case, SSL can have a detrimental effect to the overall system, since the model could be creating SSL data that is annotated incorrectly. Ideally, we would like to have a way of detecting when this might be the case. Typically, for a given input x, neural networks provide a point estimate that is interpreted as a probability distribution over labels. If the point x is easy to learn, neural networks trained from different initial conditions will learn a similar probability distribution for x. On the other hand, if x is difficult to learn, their predictions are likely to disagree or converge to low confidence predictions. This phenomenon has been observed in several works addressing uncertainty estimation (Liu et al., 2019a; Ashukha et al., 2020). As a consequence, data points with high uncertainty are more likely to be incorrectly predicted than those with low uncertainty.

To detect data points on which the model is not reliable, we train a committee of n teacher models (we use $n = 4$ in this paper), and compute the average entropy of the probability distribution for every data point. Specifically, let $P(y; x, \theta_i)$ denote the probability of label y for input x according to the ith teacher, we compute the average entropy of the predicted label distribution of x as: $H(x) = -\frac{1}{n}\sum_{y\in\mathcal{Y}}\sum_{i=1}^{n} P(y; x, \theta_i)\log P(y; x, \theta_i)$. We then identify an entropy threshold with an acceptable error rate for mis-annotations (e.g., 20%) based on a held-out dataset. Any committee annotated data whose entropy level is higher than the identified threshold, is deemed "not trustworthy" and filtered out.

3.2 Semi-Supervised Learning Approaches

We explore the following four Semi-Supervised Learning techniques:

PL based self-training is a simple and straightforward method of SSL (Yarowsky, 1995; McClosky et al., 2006). Using a labeled data set $\mathcal{D}_l$, we first train a "teacher" model, f_θ. We then generate a dataset of pseudo-labeled data from $\mathcal{D}_u$, by assigning for each input instance x_u, the label $\hat{y}$, predicted by the teacher. A new model, to which we refer as a "student", is then trained on the union of both pseudo-labeled and labeled datasets.

In **KD**, for a given input, a teacher model produces a probability distribution over all possible labels. The predicted probability distribution is often referred to as "soft label". The student model is then trained alternating between two objectives: minimizing the loss on the labeled data, defined respectively for different tasks, and minimizing the cross-entropy loss between the student and teacher predicted "soft label" on the unlabeled data (Hinton et al., 2015). The soft labels on intents are generated by the IC's softmax layer, while the soft labels on label sequences are generated per token, by running softmax on the logits for each token before the CRF layer.

VAT is an efficient SSL approach based on adversarial learning. It has been shown to be highly effective in both image (Miyato et al., 2019) and text classification (Miyato et al., 2017) tasks. Given an unlabeled instance, VAT generates a small perturbation that would lead to the largest shift on the label distribution predicted by the model. After getting the adversarial perturbation, the objective is to minimize the KL divergence between the label distribution on the original instance and the instance with perturbation.

CVT is another SSL approach proved to be efficient on text classification, sequence labeling and machine translation (Clark et al., 2018). Using an Bi-LSTM, CVT uses the the bi-directional output from current state as an auxiliary prediction, takes the single-directional output from current and neighboring LSTM neurons, and forces them to predict the same label as the auxiliary prediction.

4 Data Sets

The main motivation of our study is to evaluate different data selection and SSL techniques in a production scale setting where we have a large amount of unlabeled data. To understand impact of data selection, we create two benchmark datasets for our experiments. In both experiments, using the pipeline shown in Figure 1, we first select M utterances from a very large pool of unlabeled data, and then apply intelligent data selection to further select N unlabeled utterances.

Commercial Dataset: Our commercial dataset provides an experimental setup to compare SSL techniques where *labeled training data and unlabeled data come from a similar distribution*. We choose four representative domains (i.e., categories for which the user can make requests) from a commercially available voice-assistant system for English language. The four selected categories are 1) Communication: queries related to call, messages, 2) Music: queries related to playing music, 3) Notifications: queries related to alarms, timers, and 4) ToDos: queries related to task organization. For each domain, NLU task is to identify the intent (IC), and the entities (NER) in the utterance.
For each domain, our dataset contains 50k unique training, 50k unique testing utterances, and hundreds of millions of utterances of unlabeled data. Since, we do not know in advance to which domain each unlabeled utterance belongs, we first select 500K unlabeled utterance per domain to form their respective unlabeled data pool, using a domain classifier, as shown in Figure 1. The choice of 500K

Table 1: Relative error rate reduction using KD, over baseline trained with only labeled data, for Music domain. Unlabeled data SSL pool size varies from 50K to 1M utterances. 50K labeled examples are used for all experiments. The metric for IC is classification error rate, and for NER is entity recognition F1 error rate.

Task	50K	100K	300K	500K	1M
IC	-3.81%	-3.37%	-4.40%	**-4.49%**	-4.09%
NER	-6.05%	-7.49%	-6.96%	**-8.07%**	-7.20%

size is based on a series of KD based SSL experiments in Music domain, with the SSL data pool size varying from 50K to 1M. It is observed that increasing SSL pool size beyond 500k starts to reduce the performance gain from SSL (Table 1). To evaluate the effect of intelligent data selection, out of 500k, we further select 300k utterances via different data selection approaches and use them as unlabeled data in SSL experiments.

SNIPS Dataset: We also create a benchmark setup where *labeled and unlabeled data come from different distributions*. We use SNIPS (Coucke et al., 2018) dataset as labeled data, and use unlabeled data from our commercial dataset as SSL pool data. Similar to our commercial dataset, we train a binary classifier for each intent on SNIPS and use it to select $300,000$ utterances as the unlabeled data pool for each intent. Then, we apply data selection approaches to filter for $20,000$ utterances per intent for SSL experiments.

5 Results

This section presents evaluations of different SSL techniques using different data selection regimes. For all experiments, hyperparameters are optimized on development set. The SSL techniques evaluated are: PL, KD, VAT, CVT. The data selection methods evaluated are: random selection (Random), submodular optimization based selection (Submodular), and committee-based selection (Committee).

5.1 Results on Commercial Dataset

Due to confidentiality, we could not disclose absolute performance numbers on the commercial dataset. Only relative changes over baseline are reported. A summary of the results for the various data selection and SSL techniques is given in Table 2. "Baseline" refers to model trained with only labeled data. The metric for IC task is intent classification error rate. The metric for NER task is entity recognition F1 error rate. The table shows the relative error reduction compared to baseline. The bold font shows the best performing SSL method for each data selection approach.

Comparison of Data Selection Methods: We observe that both Submodular and Committee based selection outperforms random selection across all domains and SSL techniques. This shows the effectiveness of Stage 2 data filtering. While on Notifications and ToDos domain, submodular selection performs better than other methods, on Communication and Music domain, committee based selection performs the best.

Comparison of SSL Techniques: Table 2 shows that KD improves performances over PL in virtually all scenarios (except for NER in ToDos). This supports the hypothesis that using the full distribution predicted by the teacher model, instead of using solely the predicted label, allows for the transfer of extra information when training a student model. In addition, though both VAT and CVT consistently outperform KD and PL, their benefits are task dependent. VAT shows stronger benefits on all NER experiments, while CVT performs better in most IC experiments. From an accuracy perspective, VAT is more beneficial in NER tasks while CVT is more beneficial in classification tasks.

SSL Techniques Computation Comparison: We time each SSL technique on the data selected for Music domain. While PL and KD took approximately 30 minutes to train each epoch on a Tesla V100 GPU, VAT and CVT took 62 minutes and 75 minutes, respectively. Given that PL and KD have similar compute requirement and KD consistently outperforms PL, KD should be preferred over PL for SSL. The decision between CVT and VAT relies on the trade-off between accuracy and cost.

5.2 Results on SNIPS Dataset

Test results on SNIPS dataset are summarized in Table 3. The test results on SNIPS aligns with our observations on commercial dataset in that VAT and CVT are the superior SSL techniques; except for the IC task with submodular data selection, these techniques outperformed PL and KD in every other situation. Moreover, the results show that VAT and CVT provide good generalization even when the labeled and unlabeled data are from different sources and of different distributions. In contrast to the commercial dataset where intelligent data selection leads to better performance, on SNIPS dataset, we found that submodular optimization or committee

Table 2: Error reduction of SSL methods, relative to baseline. **Bold** represents the best SSL method for a given data selection technique. **Bold**† represents the best performance across all SSL methods and data selection techniques.

SSL Algorithm	Selection Approach	Communication IC	Communication NER	Music IC	Music NER	Notifications IC	Notifications NER	ToDos IC	ToDos NER
Baseline	Random	0	0	0	0	0	0	0	0
PL	Random	-3.61%	-2.86%	-4.86%	-3.70%	-2.79%	-4.06%	-2.94%	-3.33%
KD	Random	-6.35%	-2.97%	-6.96%	-4.40%	-3.48%	-4.84%	-4.18%	-1.59%
VAT	Random	-8.14%	**-8.18%**	**-11.15%**	**-9.26%**	-6.90%	**-8.55%**	-4.07%	**-4.59%**
CVT	Random	**-9.61%**	-5.26%	-7.21%	-8.13%	**-7.39%**	-7.19%	**-4.75%**	-2.38%
Baseline	Submodular	0	0	0	0	0	0	0	0
PL	Submodular	-4.90%	-3.11%	-4.61%	-3.35%	-1.48%	-4.62%	-1.70%	-4.32%
KD	Submodular	-6.69%	-3.40%	-8.19%	-3.63%	-2.91%	-4.32%	-5.01%	-2.59%
VAT	Submodular	-11.56%	**-8.39%**	**-14.72%**†	**-11.03%**†	-8.70%	**-11.86%**†	-6.24%	**-5.77%**
CVT	Submodular	**-14.72%**	-5.91%	-9.84%	-9.94%	**-8.72%**†	-10.61%	**-6.30%**	-3.13%
Baseline	Committee	0	0	0	0	0	0	0	0
PL	Committee	-10.54%	-3.91%	-9.02%	-3.93%	-6.90%	-4.47%	-4.55%	-3.67%
KD	Committee	-11.13%	-4.46%	-11.98%	-4.09%	-7.76%	-5.06%	-6.10%	-2.61%
VAT	Committee	-13.16%	**-9.40%**†	**-13.63%**	**-10.10%**	-8.50%	**-11.82%**	-5.75%	**-5.99%**†
CVT	Committee	**-15.25%**†	-6.53%	-8.72%	-8.27%	**-8.72%**†	-10.40%	**-7.34%**†	-3.58%

Table 3: Model performance by different SSL methods and data selection methods, for SNIPS data set. The metric for IC task is classification error rate, and for NER task is entity recognition F1 error rate.

SSL Algorithm	Selection Approach	SNIPS IC	SNIPS NER
Baseline	Random	0.9744	0.9367
PL	Random	0.9743	0.9326
KD	Random	0.9743	0.9424
VAT	Random	0.9814	**0.9604**
CVT	Random	**0.9871**	0.9565
Baseline	Submodular	0.9744	0.9367
PL	Submodular	0.9743	0.9342
KD	Submodular	**0.9786**	0.9403
VAT	Submodular	0.9728	**0.9579**
CVT	Submodular	0.9785	0.9524
Baseline	Committee	0.9744	0.9367
PL	Committee	0.9700	0.9272
KD	Committee	0.9729	0.9353
VAT	Committee	0.9772	0.9501
CVT	Committee	**0.9780**	**0.9518**

based selection do not provide any gain over random selection. This difference in performance is likely a result of the difference in data distribution between our commercial dataset and SNIPS. The unlabeled data from SNIPS differs significantly from the training data, which makes the data selection algorithms susceptible to noisy unlabeled data selection. For example, submodular optimization primarily optimizes for data diversity which makes it more likely to select diverse, out of domain examples than random selection. In contrast, the unlabeled data from our commercial dataset is highly related to the training data, containing many paraphrases or similar entities. Following the previous example, the inherent diversity of submodular selection is likely to capture diverse paraphrases of known intents, which in turn expands the space of possible utterances that the underlying IC models can correctly classify.

5.3 Diversity of Selected Data

In supervised machine learning, a diverse training set often correlates with good generalizability. To understand the correlation between the diversity of SSL training data set and model performance, we measure the diversity of the selected data by computing the unique n-gram ratio present in $\mathcal{D}_l \cup \mathcal{D}_u$ and $\mathcal{D}_l$ data. This provides a sense of how different the selected data is from the data used for training. The higher the ratio, the more diverse the n-grams of unlabeled data are compared to the labeled data. Table 4 shows the unigram and 1-4 gram ratios for the different selection algorithms. A unigram ratio of 2 means that a selection algorithm has expanded the vocabulary size by two. Similarly, 1-4 gram ratio represents the ratio by which n-gram vocabulary has expanded. We observe that a diverse SSL pool does not necessarily lead to better performance. For example, in the Todos domain, while randomly selected data is more diverse, committee-based selection consistently outperforms random on both IC and NER tasks. This result highlights that simply optimizing for token diversity is not enough for improving SSL performance.

Table 4: Unique unigram and 1-4 grams ratio present in $\mathcal{D}_l \cup \mathcal{D}_u$ and $\mathcal{D}_l$

Domains	Random		Committee		Submod	
	Unigram	1-4 gram	Unigram	1-4 gram	Unigram	1-4 gram
Communication	3.21	9.29	**3.29**	**10.21**	1.41	6.17
Todos	**2.88**	**6.04**	1.4	3.51	1.51	3.19
Music	3.19	6.42	3.24	6.39	**3.43**	**7.18**
Notifications	3.04	**6.01**	**3.08**	5.9	1.77	3.97

6 Recommendations

Based on our empirical results, we make the following recommendations for industry scale NLU SSL systems.

Prefer VAT and CVT SSL techniques over PL and KL: When selecting SSL techniques, CVT usually performs better for classification task while VAT is preferable for NER task. In general, we would recommend VAT since its performance in classification task is comparable to CVT and also because VAT excels in NER task which is usually harder to achieve performance gain.

Use data selection to select a subset of unlabeled data: For industry setting where the volume of unlabeled data is impractically large, we introduce a data filtering pipeline to first reduce the size of unlabeled data pool to a manageable size. Our experiments show that both submodular as well as committee based data selection could further improve SSL performance. We recommend Submodular Optimization based data selection in light of its lower cost and similar performance to committee based method.

From experiments on SNIPS data sets, we observe that further data selection does not bring extra improvement comparing to random selection. Optimizing data selection, when unlabeled data pool is of a drastically different distribution from the labeled data, remains a challenge and could benefit from further research.

7 Conclusion

In this paper, we conduct extensive experiments and in-depth analysis of different SSL techniques applied to industry scale NLU tasks. Industrial settings come with some unique challenges such as massive unlabeled data with a mixture of in domain and out of domain data. In order to overcome these challenges, we also investigate different data selection approaches including submodular optimization and committee based filtering.

Our paper provides insights on how to build an efficient and accurate NLU system, utilizing SSL, from different perspectives (e.g. model accuracy, amount of data, training time and cost, etc). By sharing these insights with larger NLP community, we hope that these guideline will be useful for researchers and practitioner who aim to improve NLU systems while minimizing human annotation effort.

8 Ethical Considerations

Our paper proposes a two stage data selection pipeline to efficiently utilize large amount of unlabeled data. While the focus of this work is to improve NLU models, selected unlabeled data might introduce biases in the trained models. We suggest carefully examining the potential bias exhibited due to the selected data before deploying SSL models in any real-world applications.

References

Gustavo Aguilar, Yuan Ling, Yu Zhang, Benjamin Yao, Xing Fan, and Chenlei Guo. 2020. Knowledge distillation from internal representations. In *AAAI*, pages 7350–7357.

Arsenii Ashukha, Alexander Lyzhov, Dmitry Molchanov, and Dmitry Vetrov. 2020. Pitfalls of in-domain uncertainty estimation and ensembling in deep learning.

David Berthelot, Nicholas Carlini, Ian Goodfellow, Nicolas Papernot, Avital Oliver, and Colin A Raffel. 2019. Mixmatch: A holistic approach to semi-supervised learning. In *Advances in Neural Information Processing Systems*, pages 5049–5059.

Avrim Blum and Tom Mitchell. 1998. Combining labeled and unlabeled data with co-training. In *Proceedings of the eleventh annual conference on Computational learning theory*, pages 92–100.

Piotr Bojanowski, Edouard Grave, Armand Joulin, and Tomas Mikolov. 2016. Enriching word vectors with subword information.

Olivier Chapelle, Bernhard Schölkopf, and Alexander Zien. 2006. Introduction to semi-supervised learning. In *Semi-Supervised Learning*.

Luoxin Chen, Weitong Ruan, Xinyue Liu, and Jianhua Lu. 2020. SeqVAT: Virtual adversarial training for semi-supervised sequence labeling. In *Proceedings of the 58th Annual Meeting of the Association for Computational Linguistics*, pages 8801–8811, Online. Association for Computational Linguistics.

Eunah Cho, He Xie, John P. Lalor, Varun Kumar, and William M. Campbell. 2019. Efficient semi-supervised learning for natural language understanding by optimizing diversity. *2019 IEEE Automatic Speech Recognition and Understanding Workshop (ASRU)*.

Kevin Clark, Minh-Thang Luong, Christopher D. Manning, and Quoc V. Le. 2018. Semi-supervised sequence modeling with cross-view training. In *Proceedings of the 2018 Conference on Empirical Methods in Natural Language Processing, Brussels, Belgium, October 31 - November 4, 2018*, pages 1914–1925. Association for Computational Linguistics.

Alice Coucke, Alaa Saade, Adrien Ball, Théodore Bluche, Alexandre Caulier, David Leroy, Clément Doumouro, Thibault Gisselbrecht, Francesco Caltagirone, Thibaut Lavril, Maël Primet, and Joseph Dureau. 2018. Snips voice platform: an embedded spoken language understanding system for private-by-design voice interfaces. *ArXiv*, abs/1805.10190.

Yifan Ding, Liqiang Wang, Deliang Fan, and Boqing Gong. 2018. A semi-supervised two-stage approach to learning from noisy labels. *2018 IEEE Winter Conference on Applications of Computer Vision (WACV)*.

Geoffrey Hinton, Oriol Vinyals, and Jeff Dean. 2015. Distilling the knowledge in a neural network. *arXiv preprint arXiv:1503.02531*.

Heng Ji and Ralph Grishman. 2006. Data selection in semi-supervised learning for name tagging. In *Proceedings of the Workshop on Information Extraction Beyond The Document*, pages 48–55, Sydney, Australia. Association for Computational Linguistics.

Katrin Kirchhoff and Jeff Bilmes. 2014. Submodularity for data selection in machine translation. In *Proceedings of the 2014 Conference on Empirical Methods in Natural Language Processing (EMNLP)*, pages 131–141.

Jeremiah Liu, John W. Paisley, M. Kioumourtzoglou, and B. Coull. 2019a. Accurate uncertainty estimation and decomposition in ensemble learning. In *NeurIPS*.

Xiaodong Liu, Pengcheng He, Weizhu Chen, and Jianfeng Gao. 2019b. Improving multi-task deep neural networks via knowledge distillation for natural language understanding. *arXiv preprint arXiv:1904.09482*.

David McClosky, Eugene Charniak, and Mark Johnson. 2006. Effective self-training for parsing. In *Proceedings of the main conference on human language technology conference of the North American Chapter of the Association of Computational Linguistics*, pages 152–159. Association for Computational Linguistics.

Takeru Miyato, Andrew M. Dai, and Ian J. Goodfellow. 2017. Adversarial training methods for semi-supervised text classification. In *5th International Conference on Learning Representations, ICLR 2017, Toulon, France, April 24-26, 2017, Conference Track Proceedings*. OpenReview.net.

Takeru Miyato, Shin-ichi Maeda, Masanori Koyama, and Shin Ishii. 2019. Virtual adversarial training: A regularization method for supervised and semi-supervised learning. *IEEE Trans. Pattern Anal. Mach. Intell.*, 41(8):1979–1993.

Avital Oliver, Augustus Odena, Colin Raffel, Ekin D. Cubuk, and Ian J. Goodfellow. 2018. Realistic evaluation of deep semi-supervised learning algorithms.

Sree Hari Krishnan Parthasarathi and Nikko Strom. 2019. Lessons from building acoustic models with a million hours of speech. In *ICASSP 2019-2019 IEEE International Conference on Acoustics, Speech and Signal Processing (ICASSP)*, pages 6670–6674. IEEE.

P. J. Price. 1990. Evaluation of spoken language systems: the atis domain. In *HLT*.

Sebastian Ruder and Barbara Plank. 2018. Strong baselines for neural semi-supervised learning under domain shift. *Proceedings of the 56th Annual Meeting of the Association for Computational Linguistics (Volume 1: Long Papers)*.

Kai Wei, Rishabh Iyer, and Jeff Bilmes. 2015. Submodularity in data subset selection and active learning. In *International Conference on Machine Learning*, pages 1954–1963.

I Zeki Yalniz, Hervé Jégou, Kan Chen, Manohar Paluri, and Dhruv Mahajan. 2019. Billion-scale semi-supervised learning for image classification. *arXiv preprint arXiv:1905.00546*.

David Yarowsky. 1995. Unsupervised word sense disambiguation rivaling supervised methods. In *33rd annual meeting of the association for computational linguistics*, pages 189–196.

Zhi-Hua Zhou and Ming Li. 2005. Tri-training: Exploiting unlabeled data using three classifiers. *IEEE Transactions on knowledge and Data Engineering*, 17(11):1529–1541.

Association for Computational Linguistics
209 N. Eighth Street
Stroudsburg, Pennsylvania 18360

ISBN 978-1-7138-3010-8

CURRAN ASSOCIATES INC.
proceedings.com